Encyclopedia of Literature and Politics

○○○ *ENCYCLOPEDIA OF* ○○○
Literature and Politics

Censorship, Revolution, and Writing
VOLUME I: A–G

○ ○ ○

Edited by M. Keith Booker

GREENWOOD PRESS
Westport, Connecticut • London

Library of Congress Cataloging-in-Publication Data

Encyclopedia of literature and politics : censorship, revolution, and writing / edited by M.
 Keith Booker.
      p.   cm.
     Includes bibliographical references and index.
     ISBN 0–313–32928–1 ((set) : alk. paper)—ISBN 0–313–32939–7 ((vol. 1) : alk. paper)—
     ISBN 0–313–32940–0 ((vol. 2) : alk. paper)—ISBN 0–313–33568–0 ((vol. 3) : alk. paper)
     1. Politics and literature—Encyclopedias.   I. Booker, M. Keith.
  PN51.E63   2005
   809'.93358'03—dc22   2005008522

British Library Cataloguing in Publication Data is available.

Library of Congress Catalog Card Number: 2005008522
ISBN 0–313–32928–1 (set)
       0–313–32939–7 (Vol. I)
       0–313–32940–0 (Vol. II)
       0–313–33568–0 (Vol. III)

First published in 2005

Greenwood Press, 88 Post Road West, Westport, CT 06881
An imprint of Greenwood Publishing Group, Inc.
www.greenwood.com

Printed in the United States of America

The paper used in this book complies with the
Permanent Paper Standard issued by the National
Information Standards Organization (Z39.48–1984).

10 9 8 7 6 5 4 3 2 1

For Amy, Adam, Marcus, Dakota, Skylor, and Benjamin

○○○ *Contents* ○○○

○○○ *Preface* ○○○

During the past few decades, literary studies have come to be dominated by approaches that emphasize the social, historical, and political significance of literary works. This development (after the cold-war decades, in which political approaches to literature were out of favor) reemphasizes the close connection that has existed between literature and politics throughout Western history. This three-volume encyclopedia brings together a wide variety of information on the relationship between literature and politics in a conveniently accessible encyclopedia format.

The encyclopedia is international in scope, covering relevant information from the ancient Greeks forward, though with a necessary emphasis on the modern era (after 1900). Indeed, because the topic of the encyclopedia is so broad, it has been necessary to make a number of choices in emphasis. For example, because the encyclopedia is written in English and because English is expected to be the principal language of most readers, the various entries concentrate especially on American and British literature, with the expectation that this literature will be most relevant to the majority of readers. Secondary emphasis has been given to other Anglophone literatures (from Canada, Australia, the Caribbean, and Africa), while it has been possible only to touch on the highlights of other world literatures (from Latin America, Russia and the Soviet Union, China, Europe, and the Middle East).

The more than five hundred entries in the encyclopedia are of a number of basic types. The most numerous entries are biographical ones, which summarize the careers of important authors, critics, and literary theorists, as well as historical figures who have had an impact on the evolving relationship between literature and politics. There are also a number of entries describing important works of literature, as well as crucial critical nonfiction works and literary journals. A number of broader entries survey national literatures or important literary movements (such as Soviet socialist realism, American proletarian fiction, or postcolonial literature), while others cover broad critical categories, such as Marxist criticism, feminist criticism, or postcolonial studies. Finally, additional entries provide coverage of specific themes, concepts, and genres toward the goal of providing a single reference point for a general approach to the relationship between literature and politics. The various entries are cross-referenced using a system of boldfacing; in any entry, the first mention of an item that is also covered in an entry of its own will be given in boldface.

The entries in the encyclopedia have been written by expert scholars who work in the field to which the entries are relevant. In that sense, the information provided is the best that could be obtained. However, the length restrictions inherent in a work such as this one require that the information included here is merely a starting point and should not be taken as complete and comprehensive. In this sense, readers interested in more complete and detailed information should pay serious attention to the suggestions for further reading that are included at the ends of the entries and should consult the suggested sources for further information.

✣✣ *Alphabetical List of Entries* ✣✣

○○○ *Categorical List of Entries* ○○○

CRITICS AND THEORISTS

Lefebvre, Henri
Lukács, Georg

Macherey, Pierre
Mariátegui, José Carlos
Marx, Karl
McLuhan, Herbert Marshall
Mohanty, Chandra Talpade
Mulvey, Laura

Negri, Antonio

Ohmann, Richard

Reed, John
Robinson, Lillian S.

Said, Edward
San Juan, Epifanio, Jr.
Sartre, Jean-Paul
Sedgwick, Eve Kosofsky
Spivak, Gayatri Chakravorty

Weber, Max
Williams, Raymond
Wollstonecraft, Mary

Zizek, Slavoj

HISTORICAL EVENTS, GROUPS, AND MOVEMENTS

Académie Française
Anticommunism
Apartheid

Black Nationalism
Brecht-Lukács Debate

Chinese Writers' Association
Cold War, The
Comintern. *See* Third International
Communist Party
Cuban Revolution

Easter Rising

Federal Writers' Project
French Revolution

Gastonia Mill Strike
General Strike

Haitian Revolution
Harlem Renaissance

Indigenismo
Industrial Workers of the World (IWW)

John Reed Clubs

McCarthyism. *See* Anticommunism

Nigerian Civil War

Popular Front

Russian Revolution

Soviet Writers' Congress (1934)
Spanish Civil War

Third International

World War I
World War II

HISTORICAL FIGURES

Goldman, Emma

Lenin, Vladimir Ilyich

Mao Zedong

Nkrumah, Kwame

Padmore, George

Stalin, Joseph Vissarionovich

The Threepenny Opera

U.S.A. Trilogy

We

NATIONAL AND REGIONAL LITERATURES

African American Literature
African Literature (Anglophone)
African Literature (Francophone)
American Literature (after 1900)
American Literature (before 1900)
Anglophone African Literature. *See* African
　　Literature (Anglophone)
Anglophone Caribbean Literature. *See*
　　Caribbean Literature (Anglophone)
Asian American Literature
Australian Literature

Brazilian Literature
British Immigrant Literature
British Literature (after 1900)
British Literature (Nineteenth Century). *See*
　　British Novel (Nineteenth Century);
　　Romanticism
British Novel (Nineteenth Century)
British Working-Class and Socialist Literature

Canadian Literature (Anglophone)
Canadian Literature (Francophone)
Caribbean Literature (Anglophone)
Caribbean Literature (Francophone)
Chinese Literature
Cuban Literature

Eastern and Central European Literature
English Literature (Medieval)
English Literature (Renaissance)
English Literature (Restoration and Eighteenth
　　Century)
English Studies and Politics

Francophone African Literature. *See* African
　　Literature (Francophone)

Francophone Caribbean Literature. *See*
　　Caribbean Literature (Francophone)
French Literature

German Literature

Indian Literature. *See* South Asian Literature
Irish Literature
Italian Literature

Jewish American Literature

Latin American Literature
Latina/o Literature

Native American Literature

Postcolonial Literature

Russian Literature (Nineteenth Century)

Scandinavian Literature
Scottish Literature
Socialist Realism (Soviet)
South African Literature
South Asian Literature
Spanish Literature (Twentieth Century)

Yugoslav Literature

PERIODS, GENRES, AND LITERARY MOVEMENTS

Beat Movement
Bildungsroman
Black Arts Movement

Chartism

Detective and Crime Fiction
Dystopian Literature

Epic Theater

Gothic Literature

° A °

ABRAHAMS, PETER (1919–). Born in Vrededorp, in the South African city of Johannesburg, the son of an Ethiopian émigré miner and a Cape Colored mother, Abrahams was cast into desperate poverty following the death of his father. He then lived the life of a street urchin on the wrong side of the color bar, but his fortunes changed dramatically when he discovered the Bantu Men's Social Centre in Johannesburg, whose library exposed him to the African American **Harlem Renaissance** writers, from whom he took a fervent black nationalist ideology, and from where he obtained scholarships to two leading Anglican mission schools. There he was drawn to the liberal Christian humanism of the staff, whose vision of a nonracial democracy provided a critical and redemptive perspective on South Africa.

The "new liberalism" of the period was developed by whites in the industrializing Witwatersrand as a response to the threat of black proletarian militancy, and it tried to convince the black leadership to abandon militancy and rely on education, moderation, and patience. This depended for its success on the gradual reform of the racist state apparatus, and was thrown into crisis as white domination rooted itself more firmly through the 1930s. Thus, while at school, Abrahams was converted to Marxism, which he described as a "miraculous revelation" that, unlike liberalism, offered a radical opposition through organized mass militancy to colonial capitalism.

The three discourses of Christian liberalism, black nationalism, and Marxism (or socialism) would weave their way through Abrahams' writing career. His second novel, *Mine Boy* (1946), merges all three to articulate a radical liberalism relevant to the militant ambitions of the black working class. Abrahams went into exile in 1939, arriving in London in 1941, where he moved in bohemian left-wing circles. He was briefly a subeditor at the British **Communist Party** newspaper, the *Daily Worker*, but was increasingly disillusioned with communists, complaining of their political intransigence and racism. He was instead drawn to the Independent Labour Party and what he called its "pre-Marxist" socialism, which was "Christian, humane, caring." In 1948 he married Daphne Miller; they have three children.

The family moved to Jamaica in 1956, where as a supporter of the social democratic People's National Party he achieved success as a journalist and daily commentator on Radio Jamaica, from which he retired at the age of eighty. Abrahams has published youthful collections of short stories and poetry; eight novels, five of which are set in South Africa; two powerful autobiographies; and two travelogues. Of his novels, *The Path of Thunder* (1948) shows the impossibility of cross-racial reconciliation in the face of Afrikaner intransigence. *A Wreath for Udomo* (1956) controversially identifies the greatest obstacle to African development as a backward "tribalism." *This Island Now* (1966) is a critique of neocolonialism in an island nation modeled on Haiti and Jamaica, while *The View from Coyoba* (1985) employs a Jamaican setting to fulfill Abrahams' lifelong interest in the "color question"; it advocates a strategic retreat for blacks around the world from the West in order to build a confident and independent identity. Some of Abrahams' best writing is contained in his autobiographies, *Tell Freedom* (1954) and *The Coyoba Chronicles: Reflections on the Black Experience in the 20th Century* (2000).

Selected Bibliography: Ensor, Robert. *The Novels of Peter Abrahams and the Rise of Nationalism in Africa.* Essen: Verlag Die Blaue Eule, 1992; Harris, Michael T. *Outsiders and Insiders: Perspectives of Third World Culture in British and Post-colonial Fiction.* New York: Peter Lang, 1992; Wade, Jean-Philippe. "Song of the City and Mine Boy: The 'Marxist' Novels of Peter Abrahams." *Research in African Literatures* 21.3 (1990): 89–101; Wade, Michael. *Peter Abrahams.* London: Evans, 1972.

Jean-Philippe Wade

ACADÉMIE FRANÇAISE. On February 22, 1635, Louis XIII approved the formation of the Académie française (modeled on the Italian Accademia Della Crusca), which brought together forty "lettrés"—among them writers, poets, playwrights, philosophers, prelates, and scholars—chosen by their peers and elected for life. The new Académie française had a precise mandate: to compose a rhetoric (never completed); a grammar (published only in 1935, it was very poorly received and withdrawn from the market); a poetic (never published); and a dictionary of the French language (nine editions to date: 1694, 1718, 1740, 1762, 1798, 1835, 1878, 1935, and 1989). The Parliament of Paris granted the organization its "lettres patentes" on July 10, 1637—more than two years after Louis XIII's approval, fearing the Académie would claim the role of literary censor (held by the Parliament). On August 8, 1789, one of the first measures adopted by the new revolutionary government was the suppression of the Académie as a relic of the Old Regime. In October 1795, however, the Académie was "re-created" with new members, under the name Institut (held until 1815). In 1798, the Institut published a new edition of the dictionary, which incorporated a large appendix featuring "the words that the Revolution and the Republic had added to the French language" (e.g., *club, idéologue, tyrannicide*).

From its inception, the Académie has been accused of being a "language police," moreover an incompetent and reactionary one. It was said to be both too slow in incorporating neologisms in its dictionary and too eager to dispose of archaisms. In fact, since its first edition in 1694, the *Dictionnaire de l'Académie française* has recorded "contemporary proper usage," discarding words that were no longer in use as well as those that were deemed not yet commonly used. For two centuries, the *Dictionnaire de l'Académie française* remained the ultimate reference, even in printing shops. It was dethroned by Émile Littré's *Dictionnaire historique de la langue française* (1863–1872), and then again by *Le Robert* since 1960. It has been modernized in the 1980s but no longer enjoys its former prestige. However, a "fauteuil" in the Académie française still remains a coveted honor.

Selected Bibliography: Merlin-Kajman, Hélène. *L'Excentricité académique: Littérature, institution, société.* Paris: Les Belles Lettres, 2001; Oster, Daniel. *Histoire de l'Académie française.* Paris: Vialetay, 1970; Quémada, Bernard, ed. *Les Préfaces du Dictionnaire de l'Académie française.* Paris: Honoré Champion, 1997; Seguin, Jean-Pierre. "La langue française aux XVIIe et XVIII siècles." *Nouvelle Histoire de la langue française.* Ed. Jacques Chaurand. Paris: Seuil, 1999.

Yannick Portebois

ACHEBE, CHINUA (1930–). One of the most prominent and influential African novelists and essayists, Chinua Achebe's international recognition grew from acclaim for his first novel, *Things Fall Apart* (1958). Read and studied around the world either in the original English or in one of many translations, the novel dramatizes in an accessible and incisive manner the integrity of traditional African culture and the divisive, destabilizing impact European colonialism and Christian evangelism had on it. Achebe's reputation has flourished due to the dignity and insight that characterize not only *Things Fall Apart* but also his four other novels; his short stories, poems, essays, and children's books; the many interviews he has granted; and his work as a broadcaster, speaker, editor, and teacher. In addition, his essay "An Image of Africa" (1976), which describes what he sees as the racist aspects of **Joseph Conrad**'s *Heart of Darkness*, has become one of the most controversial and widely read works of literary criticism in the past several decades.

During his career, Achebe has been a stern critic of colonial and postcolonial Western domination and exploitation of Africa, and the cultural, racial, and economic arrogance on which such domination rests. Nevertheless, he has been periodically, criticized for being too mild in his strictures against the West and for writing mainly in English. Certainly Achebe's varied oeuvre attests to a humane vision that honors the arts and progressive contributions of many cultures—including those of the West—and that resists narrow political categorization. All the same, Achebe has presented a clear-eyed view of the cultural, political, and economic ravages imposed on the non-Western world by Western systems of power and influence since the colonial era, while casting a withering eye on the injustices and failures of leadership in Africa, particularly those in his native Nigeria.

Achebe was christened Albert Chinualumogu Achebe on November 16, 1930, in Nneobi, in the southeastern part of colonial Nigeria. The son of Christian missionaries, Chinua was nevertheless highly attentive to the vestiges of traditional Igbo culture around him. He showed exceptional academic talent from an early age and read avidly. His formal education followed the British colonial and church curricula available to promising students, and included study of African cultures and languages. He attended St. Philip's Central School, Ogidi, and Nekede Central School, and later won prestigious scholarships to the Government College Umuahia and University College, Ibadan, from which he graduated in 1953 with specialties in English, religious studies, and history.

In 1954, Achebe was hired as a producer for the Nigerian Broadcasting Service, which became the Nigerian Broadcasting Corporation (NBC) in 1961. In that year,

NBC appointed him director of external broadcasting, and the same year saw his marriage to Christiana Chinwe Okoli, with whom he has raised two daughters and two sons (and who presently teaches, like her husband, at Bard College in New York). Achebe's work at NBC came to end in 1966 when persecution of the Igbo forced him to leave Lagos. He returned to southeastern Nigeria, the homeland of—among others—the Igbo people, and in 1967 this part of the nation declared itself the independent Republic of Biafra.

Achebe supported, and served as a spokesman for, Biafra during the **Nigerian Civil War** (1967–1970), but the cause was doomed. Biafra suffered catastrophic losses to the federal government with its vastly superior resources, and among the civilian population alone, more than one million may have died from malnutrition and disease. Although the Achebe family survived the war, barely managing to stay out of harm's way, they endured devastation of various kinds. Achebe lost, for example, his longtime friend and associate Christopher Okigbo, an important Nigerian poet of Igbo ancestry, who was killed while serving in the Biafran army. The war itself became a focus of Achebe's creative attention in both poetry and short stories. One volume of poetry, *Beware, Soul-Brother and Other Poems*, appeared in 1971 (and was later published in the United States, in a revised and expanded edition, as *Christmas in Biafra and Other Poems*), while Achebe's volume of short fiction, *Girls at War and Other Stories*, was published in 1972 and includes not only works directly related to the war but also stories that he had written well before it.

Achebe's novels have become one of the best-known bodies of work in modern world literature. *Things Fall Apart* portrays the British and Christian missionary forces arrayed against coherent cultural survival in the Igbolands, and *Arrow of God* (1964), Achebe's third novel, treats the attempts by a traditional head priest, Ezeulu, and other members of a recently colonized Nigerian village to accommodate the new colonial regime and religion while maintaining aspects of their own cultural heritage. Achebe's second novel, *No Longer at Ease* (1960), takes up the story of the Okonkwo family two generations after the demise of Okonkwo, the protagonist of *Things Fall Apart*. Set in the late 1950s, *No Longer at Ease* depicts Obi Okonkwo's embrace of British education, Western modernity, and a concept of Nigeria that in essential ways has already been defined by the soon-to-depart colonizer. His ultimate disgrace prophesies the danger that lies ahead for the postcolonial African nation.

A Man of the People (1966) is a political satire detailing the corruption of postcolonial politics, leading to a military takeover of a newly independent, democratic, but corrupt African nation, obviously based on Nigeria. In fact, the events so closely anticipated those that unfolded in Nigeria immediately after the novel's publication that Achebe was actually accused of involvement in the coup. In the much later *Anthills of the Savannah* (1987), Achebe further elaborates on some of the same dilemmas he raised in *A Man of the People*: the ruthless drive for political power in an African nation, the processes that corrupt that power, and the heavy impact of Western influences on those processes. Still, one source of hope that may be discerned in the volatile context that Achebe portrays in both novels is the goodness and decency of some exceptional and ordinary people. Yet individual goodwill is clearly insufficient, and while Achebe offers in this novel no elaborate model for African political success, he does make clear that the bane of so many struggling

African nations is the recurring consolidation of power by autocratic rulers or ruling elites.

Selected Bibliography: Achebe, Chinua. *Home and Exile.* New York: Oxford UP, 2000; Achebe, Chinua. *Hopes and Impediments: Selected Essays.* New York: Doubleday, 1989; Achebe, Chinua. *Morning Yet on Creation Day: Essays.* New York: Doubleday, 1975. Achebe, Chinua. *The Trouble with Nigeria.* Oxford: Heinemann, 1984; Booker, M. Keith, ed. *The Chinua Achebe Encyclopedia.* Westport, CT: Greenwood, 2003; Carroll, David. *Chinua Achebe: Novelist, Poet, Critic.* 2nd ed. Houndmills, UK: Macmillan, 1990; Ezenwa-Ohaeto. *Chinua Achebe: A Biography.* Bloomington: Indiana UP, 1997; Gikandi, Simon. *Reading Chinua Achebe: Language and Ideology in Fiction.* Portsmouth, NH: Heinemann, 1991; Innes, C. L. *Chinua Achebe.* New York: Cambridge UP, 1990; Killam, G. D. *The Writings of Chinua Achebe.* London: Heinemann, 1977; Ogede, Ode. *Achebe and the Politics of Representation.* Trenton, NJ: Africa World P, 2001; Wren, Robert M. *Achebe's World: The Historical and Cultural Context of the Novels of Chinua Achebe.* Washington, DC: Three Continents P, 1980.

Thomas J. Lynn

ADORNO, THEODOR WIESENGRUND (1903–1969), German philosopher, social theorist, musicologist, and literary critic associated with the **Frankfurt School.** After the Nazis closed the institute in 1933, Adorno fled the country, eventually arriving in the United States. He was deeply marked by the failure of the German workers' movement to resist Nazism (which disillusioned him with orthodox socialism), by the experience of exile during the war, and by the horrors of the war itself—particularly Auschwitz, with which he remained preoccupied (along with repetitions like the **Vietnam War**) for the rest of his life. *Dialectic of Enlightenment: Philosophical Fragments* (1944) and *Minima Moralia: Reflections from Damaged Life* (1951) date from the period of exile, after which Adorno returned to the institute in Frankfurt, acting as one of its directors from 1956 until his death, and wrote many books and essays, including *Notes to Literature* (1958, 1961, 1965); *Mahler* (1960); *Three Studies on Hegel* (1963); *The Jargon of Authenticity* (1964); and his two late masterpieces, *Negative Dialectics* (1966) and *Aesthetic Theory* (1970).

Dialectic of Enlightenment, coauthored with his friend Max Horkheimer, is Adorno's best-known work in the United States. The Enlightenment promised to free human beings from the struggle for survival by giving them the power to dominate nature; in this work Adorno and Horkheimer set out to explain "why humanity, instead of entering a truly human state, is sinking into a new kind of barbarism" (xiv), to explain why the project of dominating nature resulted in the domination and exploitation of human beings. Their point is not to repudiate the Enlightenment in favor of a return to some pre-capitalist "golden age"; the first long chapter shows how the system of myth in the *Odyssey* already carries the seeds of Enlightenment rationality. But Enlightenment's disenchantment of the world turns into another mythology to the extent that Enlightenment rationality fails to recognize its irrational underpinnings. Their main target is "instrumental reason," reason as a tool, unable to criticize itself. Fascism was not, in their view, an irrational deviation from Enlightenment, but a manifestation of Enlightenment's underlying instrumental tendencies.

The same totalitarian logic structures the U.S. "culture industry" (and its democratic European counterparts); they argue that its products are not innocent "entertainment," and that it does not give people what they want but trains them to desire what is offered. "The appearance of competition and choice," in their view, conceals actual uniformity (97). All of the culture industry's products are designed to discourage thought, not least by providing spurious means of escape: "Amusement always means putting things out of mind, forgetting suffering, even when it is on display. At its root is powerlessness. It is indeed escape, but not, as it claims, escape from bad reality but from the last thought of resisting that reality" (116). The culture industry falsifies both "high" and "low" art, so this analysis is not a traditionalist attack on popular culture.

In this country, Adorno's cultural criticism is far better known than his strictly philosophical work, of which his crowning achievement is *Negative Dialectics*, an attempt to formulate a materialist dialectic that would not fall prey either to false concretion or to unreflective metaphysics. Dialectic logic tries to overcome the separation between things and concepts, and between subject and object, by finally equating them in the higher unity of unity and difference; according to Adorno, this process always leaves something out, hence his project is to think this nonidentical remainder without subordinating it to a false reconciliation. His method is what he calls "constellation": maintaining a tense configuration of concepts that will not collapse into a homogeneous absolute, insisting upon a negativity that does not dissolve into affirmation. These apparently abstruse metaphysical concerns are deeply related, in Adorno's view, to the possibility of political change; "the need to let suffering become eloquent is the condition of all truth" (17–18, my translation). The culture industry ensures that suffering remains mute and always promises guiltless happiness while concealing the fact that no happiness is truly happy if it is purchased at the cost of someone else's misery.

The more philosophy tries to break out of being merely discursive and abstract (the curse of Enlightenment), the more it aspires to approximate the concretion of art. But high art is now compromised by the culture industry; Adorno's final work, *Aesthetic Theory*, thus sets out to do philosophical aesthetics in an age that has made autonomous art simultaneously impossible and necessary. By "autonomous" he does not mean that the work escapes social reality but that it stands in opposition to the social, an opposition that makes it into a negative image of the social order it resists. Part of the gap between artwork and discursive thought is a result of what Adorno calls the artwork's "enigma-character," its tendency to simultaneously invite and prevent interpretation; this makes it possible for art to open a rift in the tightly woven fabric of social reality and point to a different order of things. But also because of their enigma-character, artworks cannot positively present any vision of utopia and cannot make consoling or liberating political statements. What Adorno calls "truth-content" dwells in art's negativity: artworks are mirror-images of a bad social order, which fracture the facturedness of that order, suggesting only negatively a world better than the present one. Despite the best efforts of various interpreters, Adorno has regularly been accused of elitism, pessimism, or outright quietism ever since his unsympathetic reaction to the student movement of the 1960s, whose tendencies toward mass action and anti-intellectualism struck him as dangerously reminiscent of fascist enthusiasm. The second-generation critical theorists, most prominently **Jürgen Habermas**, have grown wary of Adorno's tendency to present the situation of thought as an impossible one, and have accordingly drifted toward pragmatism. But the stringency of Adorno's thought is the result of the demand practice makes on it: the demand that suffering come to an end. Adorno's strategy is very much Hegel's "way of despair": a hope that is not just an apology for infinite atrocity but one that will only be visible by the dark light of relentless negativity.

Selected Bibliography: Adorno, Theodor W. *Aesthetic Theory.* Trans. Robert Hullot-Kentor. Minneapolis: U of Minnesota P, 1997; Adorno, Theodor W. *Minima Moralia.* Trans. Edmund Jephcott. London: Verso, 1974; Adorno, Theodor W. *Negative Dialectics.* Trans. E. B. Ashton. New York: Seabury P, 1973; Horkheimer, Max, and Adorno, Theodor W. *Dialectic of Enlightenment: Philosophical Fragments.* Trans. Edmund Jephcott. Stanford, CA: Stanford UP, 2002; Jameson, Fredric. *Late Marxism: Adorno, or, The Persistence of the Dialectic.* London: Verso, 1990; Jarvis, Simon. *Adorno: A Critical Introduction.* New York: Routledge, 1998.

Robin J. Sowards

AFRICAN AMERICAN LITERATURE. African American literature expresses three hundred years of resistance, reformation, and revolutionary response to U.S. racism, gender inequality, and capitalism. It has been most politically efficacious when leading or conjoined to widespread social justice movements, such as abolitionism, communism and socialism, civil rights, and feminism. Black literature has often served a vanguard function in eras of progressive political change. Likewise, aggressively political African American writing has suffered from backlash; the post-Reconstruction era, the cold war purges of the postwar period, and the post–civil rights era of the 1980s and 1990s saw a loss of political significance in African American literature. Formally, African American literature often relies on repetition, revision, and reconstruction of earlier themes, techniques, and ideas, many of them also political in nature. African American poet and critic **Amiri Baraka** has referred to this strategy as the "changing same," a creative dialectical tension between tradition and improvisation. In recent years, African American literature has developed an international audience and a sizable commercial market. It has developed its own canon, critical schools of thought, and benchmarks; it has been especially central to the establishment of liberal multiculturalism in the university.

In "We raise de wheat," an undated secular rhyme from the nineteenth century, slaves improvised a work song patterned on the rhythms of their own exploitation:

> We raise de wheat,
> Dey gib us de corn:
> We bake de bread,
> Dey gib us de crust;
> We sif de meal,
> Dey gib us de buss;
> We peel de meat,
> Dey gib us de skin;
> And dat's de way

Dey take us in;
We skim de pot,
Dey gib us de liquor,
And say dat's good enough for nigger.

Dialectical critique of racism and capitalism here finds form in call and response, the counterpoint of singer and chorus. The rhyme articulates group consciousness and cultural expression as the vehicle for describing and surviving what the spirituals call "the troubles I've seen" and the blues, "the dirty low down." Early African American poetry, much influenced by eighteenth-century British verse, revealed the constraints and limits of articulating a similar message in standard English under the master's watchful eye. Phyllis Wheatley, captured in West Africa at age seven or eight and named for the slave ship that carried her, published "On Being Brought from Africa to America" in the first book of poems published by a black American, *Poems on Various Subjects, Religious and Moral* (1773): "Twas mercy brought me from my Pagan land; / Taught my benighted soul to understand / That there's a God, that there's a Saviour too: Once I redemption neither sought nor knew. / Some view our sable race with scornful eye; 'Their colour is a diabolic dye.' / Remember Christians, Negros, black as Cain, May be refind's, and join th' angelic train." Wheatley's couplets, Anglicized diction, and missionary rhetoric joust with Christian racism and the prescriptions of slavery; the poem enacts what **W.E.B. Du Bois** would famously describe as "double consciousness," the feeling of being "an American, a Negro," or literally African American. Other early black literature reveals the inevitable absorption by slaves of republican ideology. Lucy Terry's "Bars Fight," the earliest known work of literature by a black writer, sympathetically renders the death of whites after a 1746 Indian ambush. Like Wheatley, Terry was born in Africa and converted to Christianity after being captured into slavery.

Indeed, the institution of slavery was the dominant occasion, subject, and even marketing strategy for nearly all of the first one hundred years of literature produced by African Americans. African American prose narrative tradition begins with **slave narratives**, an autobiographical genre of laying witness to the institution and describing the survival and making of the self within it. In 1789, Olaudah Equiano, who grew up among Nigerian Igbo, published *The Interesting Narrative of the Life of Olaudah Equiano, or Gustavus Vassa, the African, Written by Himself.* The book describes Equiano's travels in captivity between Africa, England, and the Americas. It charts his own spiritual enlightenment and economic success while documenting the horrors of the Middle Passage. Typical of eighteenth- and nineteenth-century African American literature, the book enacts black participation in the Enlightenment as both its benighted Other and its aspirant citizen. Significantly, Equiano wrote the book himself and helped establish to an always skeptical American and European readership the capacity of Africans to write and master English.

The next major published slave narrative was **Frederick Douglass**'s *The Narrative of the Life of Frederick Douglass, an American Slave, Written by Himself* (1845). Douglass was born Frederick Bailey in Tuckahoe, Maryland. His book offered a masterly account of his life written with ethnographic objectivity, occasionally graphic melodrama, and strategic restraint calculated to win rather than alienate white readers.

The book was published with prefatory attestations of authorship by William Lloyd Garrison and Wendell Phillips—white abolitionists who encouraged Douglass to write and facilitated the book's publication by the Anti-Slavery Office in Boston. In his preface, Garrison compared Douglass to Patrick Henry as a way of demonstrating the abolitionist view that the American Revolution would not be complete until all slaves were emancipated. Douglass's book outsold **Thoreau**'s *Walden* in its time, made Douglass a public figure on the abolitionist circuit, and enabled him to publish two more autobiographies before his death in 1895. Douglass was a fervent critic of British colonialism after visiting Ireland in the 1850s, and a regular speaker at women's rights conventions in the United States, where he linked the emancipation of women to the freedom of slaves.

The next major slave narrative publication—significant, too, because it was written by a woman—was Harriet Jacobs's *Incidents in the Life of a Slave Girl (1860)*. Jacobs was born in Edenton, South Carolina, around 1815. James Norcom, her own master, pursued her sexually from adolescence onward. To avoid him, she bore two children by a white lawyer, fled the plantation, and hid for seven years in a crawl space, hoping to be reunited with her children. Jacobs masked the sensational, graphic, and humiliating details of her story by publishing the book pseudonymously as "Linda Brent." Jacobs deployed sentimental narrative technique, picaresque structure, and a canny understanding of the "cult of true womanhood"—ideals about chastity and femininity for her white female readers, which she references and exploits to create sympathy for herself. Jacobs's account came with attestations by Lydia Maria Child and Amy Post—white Quaker abolitionists and feminists who encouraged her to write and facilitated her book's publication. Because of its characteristic mediation, the slave narrative has been described as a "black message in a white envelope." The commercial and critical success of the slave narrative in fostering abolitionist sympathy, however, cannot be underestimated. Jacobs's life story drew the attention of **Harriet Beecher Stowe**, and her book sold widely upon its publication. Like Douglass, Jacobs became a public spokesperson for both abolitionist and women's rights struggles.

Somewhat ironically, the prominence of the slave narrative overshadowed the development and publication of other African American literary forms during the nineteenth century. Proliferating slave songs, spirituals, gospels, and folktales spun from the belly of slavery had to wait until the turn of the century for literary transcription, publication, and commentary. For most of the nineteenth century, African American "literary" productivity in vernacular form remained primarily oral. Du Bois's call for attention to "sorrow songs" (spirituals) in *The Souls of Black Folk* in 1903 was part of an aesthetic and political reconsideration of earlier literary subgenres, and coincided with other retrospective gestures by black authors: Paul Laurence Dunbar's "dialect" poems, often written in idioms reminiscent of white authorial renderings of black voices during slavery; Charles Chesnutt's *Conjure Woman* (1899), stories drawn from slavery's oral traditions; and James Weldon Johnson's recasting of early black sermons and creation tales. Significantly, later blues musicians would also return to and codify in musical form slave legends and tall tales—for example, the Ballad of John Henry, the Signifying Monkey, Stagolee—and a variety of work songs and field hollers. Gospel music would both inspire and repel the secular themes of the so-called "devil's music." Robert Johnson's blues classic "Hellhound on My Trail," recorded in 1936, would invoke—indirectly and directly—fugitive slave rhymes like "Run, Nigger, Run." More direct literary adaptation of nineteenth-century orature also came in the form of twentieth-century black poetry. Sterling Brown's "Strong Men" recuperated the rhythms and protest intent of work songs; Zora Neale Hurston's anthropological studies, such as *Mules and Men* (1935), recuperated legends like High John the Conquerer; and during the 1930s, the Works Progress Administration oral history project and producer Alan Lomax's field recordings of work songs, shouts, and hollers signaled a Depression-era populism's reclamations of folk tradition. **Ralph Ellison**'s *Invisible Man* (1952) is a compendium of allusions to tricksters and liars, as well as allusions to vernacular black culture in general. During the **black arts movement** of the 1960s, Baraka, Larry Neal, and a generation of poets would use nineteenth-century orature as a touchstone for a new protest vernacular, captured in poetry and prose and social histories like Baraka's *Blues People*.

Nineteenth-century African American fiction also developed slowly, due to the absence of both a readership and a market. The first black novel, *Clotel; or, The President's Daughter*, by William Wells Brown, was not published until 1853, eight years after Douglass's slave narrative. Brown also published the first drama by an African American—*The Escape; or, A Leap for Freedom*—in 1858. In 1859, Harriet Wilson published *Our Nig*, a novel. In the same year, Frances Ellen Watkins Harper published the first short story by an African American writer, "The Two Offers." Generally, this fiction served an abolitionist purpose and mimicked nineteenth-century conventions of social realism and melodrama. This limited publishing activity in other genres, however, created the foundation for publication of other literary work by black writers. In 1872, Harper published her own first novel, *Iola Leroy*, a more sophisticated work than Brown's or Wilson's. More impactful than the novel, however, was African American nonfiction—including the essay and the article—as black entrepreneurs started newspapers, magazines, and journals often tied to the cause of abolition or civil rights. Abolitionist and protonationalists like David Walker, Martin R. Delany, and Henry Highland Garnet wrote essays, speeches, and articles for the black press. Walker and Delany both voiced cultural nationalist positions documenting African and black contributions to world cultures. The ex-slave Sojourner Truth's 1851 address to a women's rights convention in Akron, Ohio—recorded in the press as "Ar'n't I a Woman?"—was widely circulated after publication of her ghostwritten autobiography. The essay called for the unification of the nascent women's rights movement with abolitionism. The aforementioned Harper was likewise a prominent black swing figure between literary and journalistic culture, women's rights, and abolition; she wrote for Garrison's abolitionist paper *The Liberator* yet also published *Poems on Miscellaneous Subjects* in 1854, a book which included the powerful and moving "The Slave Mother."

Harper's career as writer, publisher, journalist, and social activist predicts the expanded shape of late-seventeenth- and early-twentieth-century black literary production. Women writers, especially those of an emerging middle class, gained a strong footing between 1890 and 1910. Often their writing was dedicated to liberal or reformist themes. Alice Moore Dunbar-Nelson, one-time wife to Paul Laurence Dunbar, published *Violets and Other Tales*, a mixed-genre collection about Louisiana creoles in 1895; Anna Julia Cooper's groundbreaking treatise *A Voice from the South by a Black Woman from the South* (1892) pled the case for women's higher education; and Ida B. Wells-Barnett vocalized black women's response to the national lynching epidemic in her pamphlet "Southern Horrors: Lynch Law in All Its Phases" (1892). Black women likewise became cultural entrepreneurs during this period, as African American cultural institutions struggled for autonomy in the wake of Plessy vs. Ferguson, "separate but equal," the rise of Jim Crow, and the prevalence of anti-black violence. Pauline Hopkins's novel *Contending Forces* (1900) was published by the Colored Cooperative Publishing Company, which also published the important magazine *Colored American*, founded by Hopkins in 1900. *Crisis*, the publishing arm of the NAACP, founded in 1910, dedicated many of its early articles to the antilynching campaign that had given impetus to the organization. *Crisis* itself became a vanguard vehicle for publication of black poetry and short fiction. Much more than *The Souls of Black Folk*, his seminal 1903 book, Du Bois's stewardship of *Crisis* was responsible for the public shaping of black intellectual and artistic discourse.

The **Harlem Renaissance**, or New Negro Movement, synthesized and absorbed many of the intellectual currents preceding it, while producing a polyphony of new political ideas catalyzed by world events. As scholars like William Maxwell have shown, the Renaissance arguably begins with the publication of the Jamaican poet **Claude McKay**'s "If We Must Die" in the radical African Blood Brotherhood newspaper *The Liberator*. The poem was written to commemorate the "Red Summer" of 1919 in which black workers in northern industries were slaughtered "like hogs / Hunted and penn'd in an inglorious spot." McKay's sonnets—informed by his native anticolonialism, Bolshevist sympathies, and daring experiments with literary form—foreshadowed the numerous "roots and routes," as Paul Gilroy calls them, of twentieth-century black cultural politics. Post-1919 African American literature was utterly changed by the globalization of black intellectual experience, earth-shattering events like **World War I** and the **Russian Revolution**, and the concomitant world interest in the question of race in the United States. Alain Locke's 1925 *New Negro* anthology, for example, argued for Harlem as the political and cultural equal to Ireland's Dublin; Locke's own contribution to the volume contradictorily argued for both a nationalist and an internationalist understanding of black culture. Marcus Garvey's *Negro World* newspaper, popular in Harlem in the 1920s, was a forum for his ethnocentric Pan-Africanism and its allure to working-class blacks in particular. Du Bois's undervalued 1928 novel *Dark Princess* described an imaginary coalition between a black train porter and an Indian socialist revolutionary with ties to the Comintern. **Jean Toomer**'s *Cane* (1923), though produced outside of Harlem (four months as a superintendent at a black school in Sparta, Georgia, inspired the book), included lynching and post–World War I racist hysteria in its purview.

Likewise, black women writers were central to Harlem's renaissance and offered the beginnings of a black protofeminism. This took two forms: female participation as leaders in pioneering black cultural projects, and coded if unmistakably feminist writing. Jesse Fauset—author of the novel *Plum Bun: A Novel Without a Moral* (1929)—gained cultural prominence as fiction editor for *Crisis* in 1919; Gwendolyn Bennett's poems were included in James Weldon Johnson's 1922 *Book of American*

Negro Poetry, and her artwork appeared on the covers of both *Crisis* and *Opportunity*, the journal of the Urban League. Nella Larsen, of mixed Scandinavian and black ancestry, wrote two of the best "passing" novels of the century: *Quicksand* (1928) and *Passing* (1929). Especially in *Passing*, Larsen also used the passing theme to connote black women's bisexuality or lesbianism. A young Zora Neale Hurston, meanwhile, collaborated with **Langston Hughes**, Wallace Thurman, and Bruce Nugent to produce *Fire!!*, a single issue magazine that included short stories by both Hurston and Gwendolyn Bennett. The Hughes-Hurston collaboration took other forms, which emblematized their mutual interest in African American folk culture, including blues and jazz. Hughes's first book of poems, *The Weary Blues*, was a companion to his seminal 1926 essay "The Negro Artist and the Racial Mountain," in which he invoked the "tom-tom"—a black vernacular musical expression—as the sounding board for his own poetic ideas. In the late 1920s, Hughes and Hurston co-authored *Mule Bone*, a play based on African American folk style and stories. Their collaboration ended angrily, but of the Harlem Renaissance writers, Hurston and Hughes went on to earn the most lasting reputations. Hurston's 1937 novel *Their Eyes Were Watching God*, a small and unappreciated book in her time, was much later "discovered" by Alice Walker, who quickly made Hurston an ancestral muse for contemporary black feminists. *Their Eyes* is a tour de force **bildungsroman** of intense lyricism. It is especially ahead of its time regarding the representation of female sexual development and domestic violence. On the other hand, on many political questions Hurston was a conservative. She was strongly anticommunist and often mocked black nationalist aspirations. Hazel Carby has noted that the restoration of Hurston's literary reputation in the 1980s and 1990s may reveal her usefulness to an American culture in search of conservative black icons.

Many African American writers, like their white counterparts, moved left during the 1930s. Langston Hughes, who was a fellow traveler to the Communist Party, wrote poems like "Christ in Alabama," using lynching as the occasion for musings on the role of revolution and communism in black American struggle. Other writers who were veterans of the 1920s likewise cast their work in both nationalist and internationalist, or at least proletarian, directions. Sterling Brown's first book, *Southern Road* (1932), includes paeans to black work songs, prisoners, and blues; and Countee Cullen, best known for his romantic poems on cultural heritage, wrote "Scottsboro, Too, Is Worth Its Song" in the wake of the notorious arrest and trial of nine black boys accused of raping two white women on an Alabama train. Meanwhile, the "Great African American Migration," the persistent racial terror of Jim Crow, the Depression, and the leftward swing of American labor politics helped to reconstitute African American literary expression. Emblematic of all of these swings was the work of **Richard Wright**. His first book, *Uncle Tom's Children* (1938), documented the horrors of Jim Crow in taut, dense, symbolic stories undergirded by his belief in communism's ability to combat racism. Written while a member of the Chicago Communist Party's **John Reed Clubs**, the stories anticipated *Native Son*, Wright's 1940 blockbuster. That book deepened, and moved north, Wright's examination of racism, poverty, and modernity. Protagonist Bigger Thomas is sentenced to death for a murder he accidentally commits and a rape he does not. *Native Son* made Chicago, and the northern city, the new crucible for examining the making of the black proletariat and underclass after migration. It also tested the limits of the "proletarian novel," failing to produce a revolutionary resolution to Bigger's tragic circumstances.

Unquestionably, Wright influenced a generation of African American authors committed either to an explicit leftist analysis of race or to social protest literature and artistic experiment, especially in prose narration. Willard Motley, in *Knock on Any Door* (1946), recasts the naturalism of *Native Son* in the story of an Italian American, Nick Romano; Ann Petry's 1946 novel *The Street* rewrites the social violence of *Native Son* as racial and sexual violence against black women, replacing Bigger with Lutie Johnson, an upwardly mobile single mother beset by dire isolation and false consciousness. **William Attaway**'s underrated proletarian classic *Blood on the Forge* documents the recruitment of three southern black migrants to work as strikebreakers for Pennsylvania steel. Ralph Ellison's *Invisible Man* (1952) adopts the existential motifs of *Native Son* and Wright's story "The Man Who Lived Underground." It also expands the modernist vocabulary of *Native Son*, dense with allusions to **Dostoevsky**, Gothic fiction, existential philosophy, and surrealism. **James Baldwin**, meanwhile, established his critical voice and emerging presence with "Everybody's Protest Novel," a 1952 essay criticizing Wright for producing a reductive and, in Baldwin's view, reactionary representation of black-white relationships tied to melodramatic and sentimental paradigms. Wright's own later work, like his 1945 memoir *Black Boy*, disavowed his own Communist past. Collectively, *Native Son* and its descendants—and the debates surrounding them—illuminated the complex relationship of African American literature to Communism and radicalism during and after the **cold war**. For committed leftist writers like Frank Marshall Davis, Lloyd Brown, Alice Childress, Paul Robeson, and W.E.B. Du Bois, Communism, anti-imperialism and anti-colonialism represented a necessary continuity with "old Left" traditions like 1920s Garveyism and 1930s Communism. For cold warriors like Ellison, and to a lesser extent Baldwin, black radicalism's public past became a dangerous vulnerability. Indeed, Barbara Foley's recent scholarship demonstrating Ellison's deliberate anticommunist revisions of *Invisible Man* are perhaps the best textual evidence available of how McCarthyism, the Red Scare, and a general zeitgeist of **anticommunism** left fingerprints on African American literature's most important texts during the 1940s and 1950s.

During what has been dubbed "the black arts era," black nationalism, black cultural nationalism, and vestigial reconfigurations of earlier political and aesthetic battles confronted the new dynamisms of civil rights protest and second-wave feminism, producing a variety of brilliant and diverse new literary voices. The most influential books of the era—both politically and culturally—were black male protest books like Malcolm X's *Autobiography* (1965) and Eldridge Cleaver's *Soul on Ice* (1968), which offered rites of passage from poverty to prison to education and political empowerment as means of combating white supremacy. The cultural companion to the black power and black nationalist themes of these books was the black arts movement, which called for a synthesis of "ethics and aesthetics," or social protest and artistic innovation. Its seminal manifestoes were Amiri Baraka and Larry Neal's anthology *Black Fire* (1968), Maulana Karenga's "Black Art: Mute Matter Given Force and Function," and Addison Gayle Jr.'s 1971 book *The Black Aesthetic*. Yet the most compelling literary innovations, and the most ardent statements of Black Arts' newness, came in black women's expressions of feminist, lesbian, and internationalist themes. **Audre Lorde**'s poems, essays, and autobiographies—beginning with her first collection, *The First Cities* (1968)—explore the relationships among domestic racism, sexism, and homophobia, and U.S. imperialism. Lorde, like Wright in the 1940s, was a singular catalyst for formal and thematic experimentation with revolutionary themes. After 1968, Sonia Sanchez, June Jordan, Lucille Clifton, Jayne Cortez, and Nikki Giovanni each produced books of poetry, often in an orally inflected vernacular, speaking to black women's position in relationship not only to black power and black nationalist struggles but to the nascent—and predominantly white—national women's movement. Alice Walker, whose second book of poems, *Revolutionary Petunias* (1972), preceded such fame-making novels as *The Color Purple* (1982), coined the term "womanism" to describe a feminism inclusive of women of color, and representative of the sexual, social, and spiritual lives of black women.

Walker's womanism was also a response to second-wave feminism's dominance by white middle-class women. Walker was in fact codifying feminist themes in the work of black women novelists and prose writers like Paule Marshall (*Browngirl, Brownstones*, 1959), Sherley Anne Williams (*Dessa Rose*, 1986), and Maya Angelou (*I Know Why the Caged Bird Sings*, 1970). Collectively, these works by black women form a bridge between black arts experimentation and a feminist literature that has arguably had the most long-standing impact on African American literature of the contemporary period. Indeed **Toni Morrison**'s first novel, *The Bluest Eye* (1970), an examination of sexual violence, incest, and white beauty standards foisted upon working-class black girls in a pre-feminist era, bespeaks the historical roots and reverberations of these themes across generational lines. Morrison was not affiliated with either the black arts movement or second-wave feminism, but her work gathered up and historicized their themes, interwoven with a dense, mythic imagination; a resolute interest in folklore and music; and a historical novelist's attention to period and generational detail. Each of Morrison's novels explores a moment from the African American past, dialectically perceiving its relationship to the present without succumbing to racial or cultural nostalgia. Of these, *Song of Solomon* (1974) and ***Beloved*** (1987) are likely to be remembered as most outstanding. The latter, a fictional retelling of the infanticide of Margaret Garner, an escaping Kentucky slave, was primarily responsible for Morrison winning the Nobel Prize for Literature in 1992, the first African American so honored.

Morrison's critical and commercial success is emblematic of African American literature's comfortable place within the mainstream of post–civil rights, post-integrationist U.S. society. Contemporary African American literature both keeps alive its own major traditions and intersects with dominant and emergent cultural forms within the United States—and external to it. Its wide-ranging subjects include black middle-class life, immigration and repatriation, postmodernity, genre fiction, hip-hop culture, queerness, transnational identity, as well as traditional themes like slavery, colonialism, and racism. The most astonishing commercial and critical lightning rod for the broad success of contemporary black writing is August Wilson, whose work is now performed in more theaters in the United States than any other living dramatist. Wilson, born and raised in Pittsburgh, the setting of several of his plays, has structured his career around a cycle of plays examining individual decades in African American history. The best-known of these—*The Piano Lesson* (1987), *Fences* (1985), *Ma Rainey's Black Bottom* (1984), and *Joe Turner's Come and Gone* (1986)—use music (especially blues), sports, labor, and family as organizing motifs, and convey a blend of traditional naturalism, indebted to Tennessee Williams and Eugene O'Neill, and to black cultural expression. Wilson has argued for a nationalist aesthetic in black theater, continuing a commitment forged during the black arts and black power movements, out of which Wilson formed his own cultural and political consciousness.

Contemporary African American literature also reflects what critic Paul Gilroy calls a "diaspora consciousness," reflective of contemporary U.S. migration patterns and the widening sphere of black intellectual discourse. This is reflected both in the preeminence of writers born outside the United States now residing here, and the continuing reflection on the spatial, geographic, and temporal experience of race. The Barbadian American author Paule Marshall, the Antiguan Jamaica Kincaid, the Jamaican-born Michelle Cliff, and the British national Caryl Phillips have each established the triangular, or transversal, relationship among African, Caribbean, and U.S. black experience as their literary domain. They have likewise blurred genres—short story, novel, memoir, autobiography—to elucidate the permeable borders of identity particular to what **Gloria Anzaldúa** calls *mestizaje* consciousness. Like hip-hop, jazz, or reggae, literature produced by these writers carries the cultural accent marks of transatlantic black experience. Collectively, these authors have pushed the national and thematic boundaries of African American literature, complicated essentialist or nation-bound understandings of race, and forced American readers to more complex analyses of the role of the United States—and the Western world—in processes of colonialism, imperialism, slavery, and migration. In a different vein and genre, namely **science fiction**, writers like Octavia Butler, **Samuel Delany**, and Walter Mosley (best known for his **detective and crime fiction**) have used time travel, utopia, and transmigration to explore the shifting ground of racial identity and "race" in a contemporary climate increasingly skeptical of the biological, scientific, or otherwise epistemological complex of its understanding. Placelessness and the science-fiction imaginary, in the work of these writers, allows the allegorization of diasporic themes via **utopian fiction**, **dystopian literature**, or otherwise unreal settings. Still others, such as Gayl Jones, write in a more realistic vein, but move their stories easily from the United States to other worlds. Jones's novel *Corregidora* (1975), for example, shifts between Kentucky and Brazil while remaining focused on the legacy of slavery.

Still other contemporary authors continue exploration of familiar historical problematics beholden to more conventional principles of psychological and social realism, yet inflected by dominant cultural tendencies like **postmodernism**, new historicism, and metafiction. Charles Johnson's *The Oxherding Tale* (1974) and *Middle Passage* (1990) use slavery and the slave-narrative genre to interrogate and implicate multiple Western philosophical ideas in the establishment of slavery. Likewise David Bradley's *The Chaneysville Incident* (1981) is a fictional retelling of a historical study of thirteen runaway slaves who chose death over recapture. John Edgar Wideman's fiction—much of it centered in Pennsylvania, where he grew up and attended college—is a continuous and contiguous meditation on race and time and uses metafictional technique to complicate the relationship between narrative and history. His story "Fever" fictionalizes historical accounts of a yellow-fever epidemic in Philadelphia in 1793, while *Philadelphia Fire* (1990) attacks black bourgeoisie politics under the Wilson Goode administration and fictionalizes the 1985 bombings of the MOVE headquarters in Philadelphia. Wideman is also an accomplished memoirist whose fiction contains heavy doses of autobiography. *Brothers and Keepers* (1984) is a searing indictment of the U.S. justice system spun out of his brother Robbie's arrest and incarceration. The common reworking of African American history in these books represents the idea of "re-memory," as described by Toni Morrison in *Beloved*—namely the importance of actively reimagining and learning from the African American past in order to frame and move beyond it.

The political register of contemporary African American literature is difficult to gauge. Few contemporary black authors articulate a specific political agenda or framework from which to read their writing. Fewer still, outside of the academy, identify as public intellectuals on topical issues. Important exceptions might be Alice Walker's outspoken criticism of genital mutilation in Africa; Toni Morrison's critical writings on the Clarence Thomas–Anita Hill trial; Walter Mosley's book-length meditation on race and capitalism, *Workin' on the Chain Gang* (2000); and Amiri Baraka's attempt at political commentary, "Someone Blew Up America," in the wake of 9/11. But the widespread public call for censure of Baraka for what was perceived as his anti-Semitism and knee-jerk anti-imperialism also underscores African American literary and political culture's uneasy relationship to the broad contemporary moment of U.S. multiculturalism. The latter has advanced the purchase and purchasing power of black writers while normalizing the rules of its production. Black romance, confessional, self-help, and genre literature, like the detective novel, now constitute a growing portion of the black U.S. book market. Film adaptations of black best-sellers, from *Beloved* to Terri McMillan's 1992 *Waiting to Exhale*, and the commercial success of young black playwrights like Suzan Lori-Parks have likewise forced traditionally political themes into new packages and venues, and created multicultural audiences whose own politics are difficult to discern easily. For the moment, African American literature occupies a modestly oppositional space within American culture. Its critical and commercial fortunes seem assured if not its political direction.

Selected Bibliography: Baraka, Amiri. *Blues People: Negro Music in White America*. New York: William Morrow, 1963; Carby, Hazel. "The Politics of Fiction, Anthropology and the Folk: Zora Neale Hurston." *Zora Neale Hurston's "Their Eyes Were Watching God": A Casebook*. New York: Oxford UP, 2000; Du Bois, W.E.B. *The Souls of Black Folk: Essays and Sketches*. 1903. London: Penguin, 1996; Foley, Barbara. "From Communism to Brotherhood: The Drafts of *Invisible Man*." *Left of the Color Line: Race, Radicalism, and Twentieth-Century Literature of the United States*. Ed. Bill Mullen and James Smethurst. Chapel Hill: U of North Carolina P, 2003. 163–182; Gates, Henry Louis, Jr., and Nellie McKay, eds. *The Norton Anthology of African American Literature*. New York: Norton, 2004; Gayle, Addison, Jr., ed. *The Black Aesthetic*. New York: Doubleday, 1971; Gilroy, Paul. *The Black Atlantic: Double Consciousness and Modernity*. Cambridge, MA: Harvard UP, 1993; Hill, Patricia Liggins, ed. *Call and Response: The Riverside Anthology of the African American Literary Tradition*. Boston: Houghton Mifflin, 1998; Maxwell, William J. *New Negro, Old Left*. New York: Columbia UP, 1999; Walker, Alice. *In Search of Our Mother's Gardens: Womanist Prose*. New York: Harcourt, 1983.

Bill V. Mullen

AFRICAN LITERATURE (ANGLOPHONE). One of the most important phenomena of world culture in the second half of the twentieth century was the rise to global prominence of African literature. This is particularly true of the African novel, though many important works of political drama have also been produced by such African playwrights as Nigeria's **Wole Soyinka** and South Africa's Athol Fugard, while poets such as Nigeria's Christopher Okigbo and Uganda's Okot p'Bitek have produced powerful political statements as well. The intense political engagement (often from radical perspectives) of much African literature injected vital energies into global culture at a time when the political climate was decidedly inimical to the production of radical literature in the West. In particular, African novelists have engaged with the colonialist traditions of Western historiography in an attempt to contribute to the development of viable postcolonial identities of their new nations.

African writers from former British colonies have generally produced their works in English. Among Anglophone novelists, writers such as Kenya's **Ngũgĩ wa Thiong'o** Nigeria's **Festus Iyayi**, and South Africa's **Alex La Guma** have written from radical perspectives heavily influenced by Marxism. Meanwhile, writers such as Nigeria's **Chinua Achebe** and Ghana's **Ayi Kwei Armah** have critiqued both the Western colonial domination of Africa and the corruption of postcolonial societies from perspectives that might be considered Left liberal. Women writers have also been prominent in African literature, with novelists such as Buchi Emecheta, Bessie Head, and Tsitsi Dangarembga producing politically engaged works that have been particularly strong in their treatment of gender and the plight of African women. Finally, the works of writers such as Fugard, La Guma, Peter Abrahams, André Brink, and **Nadine Gordimer** have occupied a special position in the development of politically engaged African literature because of their opposition to **apartheid**, an opposition that ultimately contributed to the downfall of that baleful phenomenon.

Achebe led the way in the development of the Anglophone African novel with *Things Fall Apart* (1958), a searching exploration of the destruction of traditional Igbo society due to the British colonial invasion of what is now Nigeria. *Arrow of God* (1964) continues this critique of colonialism, while novels such as *No Longer at Ease* (1960), *A Man of the People* (1966), and *Anthills of the Savannah* (1987) explore the chaos and corruption of postcolonial Nigeria. Armah's *The Beautyful Ones Are Not Yet Born* (1969) is another crucial exploration of postcolonial corruption in West Africa, as is Iyayi's *Violence* (1979), while Iyayi's *Heroes* (1986) focuses on the political context of the bloody civil war that wracked Nigeria from 1967 to 1970.

Ngũgĩ is the leading figure in the development of the East African novel, while joining Achebe as an important essayist whose nonfiction works have helped to elaborate the politics of postcolonial African literature. Ngũgĩ's work began from a liberal humanist critique of colonialism, but has gradually moved toward a Marxist critique (heavily influenced by the work of **Frantz Fanon**) of postcolonial Kenyan society. He has produced such Anglophone novels as *Weep Not, Child* (1964), *The River Between* (1965), *A Grain of Wheat* (1967), and *Petals of Blood* (1977). Ngũgĩ is also an important playwright, and the 1977 production of his satirical play *Ngaahika Ndeenda* (written in Gikuyu with Ngũgĩ wa Mirii, English translation *I Will Marry When I Want*) marked a crucial turning point in his career. In response to the play he was arrested, and during detention he became committed to the idea of writing his future novels in Gikuyu, feeling that the production of African literature in European languages might contribute to the ongoing cultural domination of Africa by its former colonial rulers. In prison, Ngũgĩ covertly authored a novel in Gikuyu, *Caitaani Mutharaba-ini*, published after his release to brisk sales in 1980, followed in 1982 with the publication of his own English translation, *Devil on the Cross*. His Gikuyu novel *Matigari* (1986, English translation by the same title in 1987) draws heavily on traditions of Gikuyu oral narrative to link the ongoing need for revolutionary change in Kenya to the legacy of the anticolonial Mau Mau rebellion of the 1950s.

South African Anglophone literature got off to an early start with Peter Abrahams' *Song of the City* (1945) and *Mine Boy* (1946), which show the influence of his political commitment with their overtly Marxist themes of opposition to class-based oppression under industrial capitalism (which, in South Africa as in the United States, is inseparable from racial oppression). Later novels, such as *The Path of Thunder* (1948), *Wild Conquest* (1950), *A Wreath for Udomo* (1956), and *This Island Now* (1966), explored other dimensions of this issue within the context of colonialism and neocolonialism. Abrahams' *Tell Freedom* (1954) was the first published autobiography by a black South African. Alex La Guma—like Abrahams, a Communist Party activist—is the most important radical South African novelist to date, producing a series of searing critiques of apartheid within the context of a larger critique of the class-based inequities of capitalism, all of which were published abroad because they were banned in South Africa. His early novels include *A Walk in the Night* (1962), *And a Threefold Cord* (1964), and *The Stone Country* (1967). *In the Fog of the Seasons' End* (1973), perhaps La Guma's most notable work, explores the possibilities for armed resistance to apartheid, representing a step toward a Fanonian advocacy of violent revolution that can be seen as a significant turning point in La Guma's career. La Guma's brief final novel, *Time of the Butcherbird* (1981), is his most symbolic, employing intensely suggestive images in a further elaboration of his support for armed rebellion against apartheid.

Gordimer is perhaps South Africa's best-known novelist on an international scale, partly because of her 1991 Nobel Prize for Literature. In novels such as *The Late Bourgeois World* (1966), *A Guest of Honour* (1970), and *The Conservationist* (1974), Gordimer criticizes social conditions in South Africa in increasingly strong terms, though she continues to concentrate on the damaging effects of apartheid on South Africa's white population. The later *July's People* (1981) is an imaginative study of a future South African society in which a black revolution has toppled white rule. Novels such as *Burger's Daughter* (1979) and *A Sport of Nature* (1987) are particularly strong as political novels because their sweeping scope (which encompasses both whites and nonwhites) so effectively places South African society as a whole within its historical context, the latter envisioning the end of apartheid only a few years before it actually occurred. In novels such as *The Pickup* (2001), Gordimer has extended her examination of South African society into the postapartheid era.

Selected Bibliography: Booker, M. Keith. *The African Novel in English*. Portsmouth, NH: Heinemann, 1998; Booker, M. Keith. "Writing for the Wretched of the Earth: Frantz Fanon and the Radical African Novel." *Rereading Global Socialist Cultures After the Cold War: The Reassessment of a Tradition.* Ed. Dubravka Juraga and M. Keith Booker. Westport, CT: Praeger, 2002. 27–54; Booker, M. Keith, and Dubravka Juraga. "The Reds and the Blacks: The Historical Novel in the Soviet Union and Postcolonial Africa." *Socialist Cultures East and West: A Post–Cold War Reassessment.* Ed. Dubravka Juraga and M. Keith Booker. Westport, CT: Praeger, 2002. 11–30; Gugelberger, Georg M., ed. *Marxism and African Literature.* London: James Currey, 1985; Ngara, Emmanuel. *Art and Ideology in the African Novel: A Study of the Influence of Marxism on African Writing.* London: Heinemann, 1985; Udenta, Udenta O. *Revolutionary Aesthetics and the African Literary Process.* Enugu, Nigeria: Fourth Dimension, 1993.

M. Keith Booker

AFRICAN LITERATURE (FRANCOPHONE). The term "Francophone African literature" is widely used to designate sub-Saharan African literature written in French by authors living in Africa or abroad. It derives from *Francophonie,* the nineteenth-century neologism coined by the French geographer Onésine Reclus (1837–1916). In the African context, the concept gained relevance in the 1960s under the aegis of **Léopold Senghor** and Habib Bourguiba, two African presidents who advocated the creation of an organization linking all the nations sharing the French language and culture. In a way, their idea was a response to the creation of the British Commonwealth (1965), an organization gathering former British colonies. Thereafter, a series of Francophone institutions were created: ACCT (Agence de Coopération Culturelle et Technique) in 1970, CIRTEF (Conseil International des Radios-Télévisions d'-Expression Française) in 1977, AIMF (Association Internationale des Maires Francophones) in 1979. With the emergence and consolidation of literary writings in Francophone countries, it was worth classifying and studying these new authors and their work. At various stages, critics started speaking of Quebecois literature, Belgian Francophone literature, Maghrebian literature, French Caribbean literature, and Francophone African literature. Although some critics have expressed their uneasiness in defining African literature along the Anglophone-Francophone linguistic divide reminiscent of colonial history, Francophone African literature is widely used as a descriptive category.

During the colonial era, Francophone African literature was dominated by the **negritude** movement, although some critics trace its beginnings to René Maran's publication of *Batouala* (1921). In the 1930s, black students from the Caribbean and African French colonies rebelled against the assimilation policies of their education and vied to revalorize their common African cultural roots, which colonization had systematically devalued. **Aimé Césaire**, Léon-Gontran Damas, and Senghor led this movement, which not only galvanized black students but appealed to prominent members of the French literary establishment, such as **Jean-Paul Sartre**, **Simone de Beauvoir**, André Gide, Marcel Griaule, Michel Leiris, and André Breton. From this revolt rose a whole body of writings (especially poetry) that celebrated the African roots of black cultures long considered manifestations of barbarism. Sartre's "Black Orpheus," the preface to Senghor's *Anthologie de la nouvelle poésie nègre et malgache d'expression française* (1948), highlighted the main ideas of this literary movement. The review *Présence africaine,* published in both French and English, was created to serve as one of the main means of transmission (1947). This collectivization of suffering in the name of the race fostered highly visible cultural activities, including two meetings of the Congress of Black African Writers in Paris (1956) and in Rome (1959); it nevertheless showed weaknesses in accounting for the wide range of black experience with the traumas of colonialism. Negritude literature focused on extolling blackness while denouncing derogatory colonial policies; Anglophone writers concentrated their attention on the main differences between Western and local cultures. This difference in perception is often illustrated by **Wole Soyinka**'s terse reply to the narcissistic tendency of negritude: "the tiger doesn't proclaim its tigerness; it jumps on its prey." In the 1950s, novels by Francophone writers were published, including those by Camara Laye, Mongo Beti, **Ousmane Sembène**, and Ferdinand Oyono.

Decolonization was a triumph for negritude writers who, in many instances, played important roles in the struggle for freedom. In the earlier days of independence, the need to denounce the forced assimilation of African masses and the positive reassessment of the so-called primitive cultures gave way to close scrutiny of the elite's performance. When euphoria subsided, issues forced a redirection of energy on pressing problems besieging new nations in need of consolidation. Hamidou Kane, Ahmadou Kourouma, and Yambo Ouologuem were among the prominent figures in this new literary phenomenon.

In the postindependence era, the urgency of problems facing the new nations created the need to scrutinize one's specific location. Therefore, Caribbean writers and critics gradually realized the importance of focusing on their "Caribbeanness" (such as **Edouard Glissant** in *Le Discours antillais*, 1981), resulting from a sedimentation of elements drawn from African, European, and Asian cultures. Going even further than Glissant, the Caribbean tandem of Bernabé, Chamoiseau, and Confiant (*Eloge de la créolité*, 1989) claimed the era of *créolité*, whereby attachment to their creole culture took precedence over a far-removed romantic Africa. Likewise, African writers went beyond racial issues to deal with problems specific to their communities. In their case, the use of European languages has raised questions on the essence of African literature and on being African. Some critics, such as the Kenyan writer **Ngũgĩ wa Thiong'o**, saw the Africans' experiences as unique to all and suggested their subsequent writings as falling into two categories, namely Europhone and African literatures.

Since independence, Francophone African literature has evolved along a trajectory similar to its English counterpart. In the 1960s, many writers dealt with the clash of cultures, disillusionment with the native elites, and the latter's gross mismanagement of public affairs. This trend culminated into what is known as "Afropessimism." The 1980s saw the rise of women writers, pioneered by the Senegalese novelist Mariama Bâ, whose *Une Si Longue Lettre* (1981) marked the watershed moment when women found and used their own voices. Award-winning authors such as Aminata Sow Fall, Werewere Liking, Calixthe Beyala, Ken Bugul, and Véronique Tadjo have become familiar names in literary circles. In the 1990s and 2000s, reflecting the multidimensional crisis rocking the continent, Francophone writers such as Kourouma, Dongala, Bugul, Tadjo, and Monenembo have focused on the fate of the child, not as perceived in Laye's *L'Enfant noir* but as victimized by a deceitful adult world bent on exploring his innocence. Francophone literature has grown in scope with seasoned writers and refined works in drama, poetry, novels, essays, and folktales. However, as in earlier years, society remains its main focus.

Selected Bibliography: Cornevin, Robert. *Littératures d'Afrique noire de langue française*. Paris: PU de France, 1976; Irele, Abiola. *The African Experience in Literature and Ideology*. London: Heinemann,

1981; Kesteloot, Lilyan. *Anthologie négro-africaine: Panorama critique des prosateurs poètes et dramaturges noirs du XXe siècle*. Vanve, France: EDICEF, 1993; Miller, Christopher. *Theories of Africans: Francophone Literature and Anthropology in Africa*. Chicago: U of Chicago P, 1990; Ngandu Nkashama, Pius. *Littératures africaines (de 1930 à nos jours)*. Paris: Silex, 1984.

Kasongo M. Kapanga

AKHMATOVA, ANNA (1889–1966). Among the greatest of all Russian poets, Akhmatova composed subtly nuanced explorations of personal experience. Her poems of the 1910s and early 1920s grew out of the Russian realist novels of the nineteenth century. Restrained miniatures composed by a young woman of privileged background, these lyrics contain precise imagery, controlled rhythms, and an ironic depiction of love. Along with Nikolai Gumilev (Akhmatova's first husband, executed in 1921) and **Osip Mandel'shtam**, Akhmatova was associated with acmeism, a poetic movement that opposed the otherworldliness of symbolism. Mandel'shtam's description of acmeism as a "longing for world culture" applies especially to Akhmatova's later poetry. The poetic cycles *Requiem* (*Rekviem*) and *Poem Without a Hero* (*Poema bez geroya*) are epic in scope, saturated with European literary allusions. Both works were composed over a period of many years—the former primarily between 1935 and 1940, the latter from 1940 until 1962. These cycles of historical and personal tragedy highlight the role of the poet as prophet and truthful witness. In one poem from *Requiem*, Akhmatova writes that "one hundred million people scream" through her "tortured mouth." Famously, and unlike many contemporary intellectuals of similar sensibility, Akhmatova chose not to emigrate.

By the 1940s, much of the Soviet public lionized Akhmatova, considering her poetic voice to be the true voice of Russia. Histories of the Stalinist era routinely refer to her poems about the Great Terror of the 1930s (*Requiem*); prisoners of the gulags would secretly keep handwritten copies of her poems. Akhmatova's early volumes of lyrical poetry gained acclaim in the 1910s. After the Russian Revolution, the Soviet authorities quickly came to see her poetry as counter to the new political and social order. Between 1925 and 1940, Akhmatova was not allowed to publish her poems. During **World War II** it was useful to the state for such a publicly revered figure to be allowed some visibility, but in 1946 Akhmatova was expelled from the Union of Soviet Writers. Politburo member Andrei Zhdanov officially denounced her work as "individualistic . . . the poetry of an overwrought upper-class lady . . . half nun, half harlot." Akhmatova's son was arrested several times in the 1930s and 1940s and spent years in prison camps and exile. (His principal crime: he was the son of Akhmatova and Gumilev.) Circumstances improved for Akhmatova after "the Thaw" in the 1950s, and her son was released in 1956. She was allowed to publish in the following decade, and was even able to travel to Italy and England to receive honors. Generally regarded as the greatest living Russian poet, she became a mentor to young writers such as Joseph Brodsky. From Modigliani's 1911 sketch (drawn when they met in Paris) to written depictions in memoirs of numerous authors, Akhmatova appears as a regal figure. Because of her dignity and moral courage throughout many years of hardship, Akhmatova is beloved in Russia not only as a great poet but also as a hero.

Selected Bibliography: Amert, Susan. *In a Shattered Mirror: The Later Poetry of Anna Akhmatova*. Stanford: Stanford UP, 1992; Haight, Amanda. *Anna Akhmatova: A Poetic Pilgrimage*. New York: Oxford UP, 1976; Reeder, Roberta. *Anna Akhmatova: Poet and Prophet*. New York: St. Martin's, 1994.

Joy Dworkin

ALBIAC, GABRIEL (1950–). A Spanish author who began his political life with the anti-Francoist student movement of the late 1960s and the Paris student demonstrations of May 1968 (*Mayo del 68. Una educación sentimental* [May 68: A Sentimental Education], 1993), Albiac was one of the young European philosophers who worked with **Louis Althusser** (re)reading the classics of Marxism. He has practiced numerous genres—always with a distinctively high, though very sober, degree of literary elaboration—in a risky personal style, in between the tragic and the lyrical. In 1979, Albiac published the book that marked both a threshold and a limit to his philosophical positioning and political thinking; *De la añoranza del poder o consolación de la filosofía* (On the Longing for Power or the Consolation of Philosophy) is a Platonist-oriented approach to the nature of politics and philosophy and to the effects of their distorted relationship in twentieth-century history in general and in the struggles of the 1960s and 1970s in particular, a critical essay done under the influence of **Michel Foucault**'s theories on knowledge and power and within the anti-Stalinist Communist tradition. **Antonio Negri**, one of the major European intellectuals of that tradition, wrote the prologue to *Todos los héroes han muerto* (All Heroes Have Died), 1986, Albiac's first collection of articles originally published in the daily press, political magazines, and philosophical journals. As part of his ongoing critique of the mystification behind the use of the left/right division in contemporary politics, and his reassessment of the failure/death of communism and the ideological foundations of fascism, Albiac's analysis of the fascist tendencies informing post-transitional politics in Spain—particularly during the Spanish Socialist Party's (PSOE) administrations in the 1980s and 1990s—formed the political core of *Desde la incertidumbre. Pasado lo político (pensar contra la izquierda y la derecha)* (From Uncertainty: When Politics Is Over [Thinking Against Left and Right], 2000), and of his second and third collections of press articles, *Adversus Socialistas* (Facing Socialists), 1989, and *Otros mundos* (Other Worlds), 2002—an anthology of his collaborations in the opinion pages of the Madrid daily newspaper *El Mundo*, where Albiac is a member of the editorial board. Albiac has also published a twice-a-week column in *El Mundo* on current issues, philosophy, aesthetics, history, and politics since the foundation of the paper in 1989, and has served as a special international correspondent for the paper in a number of occasions. Albiac (lecturer since 1974 and professor of philosophy since 1988 at the University Complutense in Madrid) has gained international reputation as a scholar for his work on Baruch Spinoza (*La sinagoga vacía. Un estudio de las fuentes marranas del espinosismo* [The Empty Synagogue: A Study of the Marrano Sources of Spinozism], 1987, winner of the Spanish National Prize for Literature in the modality of nonfiction, 1988). Together with his studies of Blaise Pascal's work and his rearticulation of the Freudo-Lacanian theories on death (*La muerte: metáforas, mitologías, símbolos* [Death: Metaphors, Mythologies, Symbols], 1996), love, and the uncanny (*Caja de muñecas* [Doll's Box], 1995), his

Spinozist stance informs most of his writing, favoring an approach to nonfiction that attempts a balance between the pamphlet and the erudite treatise. Albiac's literary work comprises three novels and one poetry volume (*R & R*, 1993), all linked by the challenging instability of a precarious subjective configuration. *Ahora Rachel ha muerto* (Now Rachel Is Dead), 1994, is a multivoiced narrative in which, through the political and religious persecutions of seventeenth-century Europe, a consciously anachronistic, at times, gallery of mirrors reflects the impossible formulation of any fixed identity. In the thrillers *Últimas voluntades* (Last Will), 1998, and *Palacios de invierno* (Winter Palaces), 2003, Albiac gives two articulations—not multivoiced but polyhedral—to the memory and experiences of the 1968 Spanish generation, trapped inside the epic of their double-folded political defeat and the lyricism of their sentimental conformation, with rock and roll and cinema as their own major ethical and aesthetic references.

Selected Bibliography: Albiac, Gabriel. *Otros mundos.* Edición de J. Marchante, A. Mira, and J. Sánchez Tortosa. Madrid: Páginas de Espuma, 2002; Fernández Liria, Carlos. *Sin vigilancia y sin castigo. Una discusión con Michel Foucault.* Madrid: Libertarias/Prodhufi, 1992.

Álvaro J. Vidal-Bouzon

ALGREN, NELSON (1909–1981). A novelist and essayist of Swedish and German-Jewish ancestry, Algren achieved international fame for his realistic fiction. Literary and popular acclaim came with *The Man with the Golden Arm* (1949), which won the first National Book Award. *A Walk on the Wild Side* (1956) was equally successful, and both novels were made into films.

Earlier, Algren had been associated with the radical literary movement of the 1930s and had worked with Jack Conroy to start *Anvil*, a magazine devoted to proletarian writing. During the New Deal, he wrote scripts featuring working-class characters for the Works Progress Administration and published numerous poems and short stories. His first two novels were *Somebody in Boots* (1935) and *Never Come Morning* (1942). The latter eventually sold more than a million copies and had a French translation by **Jean-Paul Sartre**. Algren's stories were collected in *The Neon Wilderness* (1956).

Algren's writing focused on America's have-nots, those whom academics often term the working poor. Rather than the triumphalist social realism of some leftist contemporaries, Algren's work has a sense of foreboding and pessimism marked by dark, if sometimes outlandish, manic humor. Algren's battered guys and troubled dolls were constantly betrayed or compromised by friends and relatives as they went for desperate long-shot solutions to their many woes. Algren's often poetic prose usually gave his failed characters dignity but rarely victory.

The great love of Algren's life was **Simone de Beauvoir**, whom he met in 1947. Although his feelings were reciprocated and he spent considerable time with her in Paris, ultimately de Beauvoir's complex relationship with Sartre proved an impossible negotiation. De Beauvoir wrote of their romance in *The Mandarins* (1954) and was buried wearing the ring Algren had given her to confirm his love.

Algren staunchly defended blacklisted writers during the 1950s and served as chairman of a Chicago committee seeking to prevent the execution of the Rosenbergs. Although close to the Communist Party, there is no evidence Algren was ever a member, and he was often criticized by Communists for lacking ideological discipline. Moreover, he remained close to writers—such as **Richard Wright**—who had fallen out of favor with the party, and greatly admired **Ernest Hemingway**, who returned the sentiment, telling legendary editor Max Perkins that Algren was the best young writer in postwar America. Algren was closest in spirit to Studs Terkel, with whom he often caroused in Chicago throughout the 1960s. His later essays on American life are marked by antiauthoritarian sentiments of the kind associated with anarchists. His posthumously published *The Devil's Stocking* (1983) retained his trademark sensibilities but was not as innovative as his earlier work. Just days before his death, Algren was named a Fellow of the American Academy and Institute of Arts and Literature.

Selected Bibliography: Algren, Nelson. *Nonconformity: Writing on Writing.* New York: Seven Stories P, 1998; Donohue, H. E. *Conversations with Nelson Algren.* New York: Hill and Wang, 1964; Drew, Bettina. *Nelson Algren.* Austin: U of Texas P, 1989.

Dan Georgakas

ALIENATION. Term used to describe the breakdown of relations between people and the world in which they live; also estrangement from one's essential nature, a nature that may be thought of as inherent but corruptible—thus Rousseau's famous dictum: "Man is born free but is everywhere in chains." Unlike Rousseau, Hegel saw alienation as part of an inevitable historical process. According to Hegel, people create a culture that then confronts them as an alien force. For Hegel, human activity is an expression of spirit (zeitgeist), which acts through people. He believed history is dialectical, operating by thesis, antithesis, synthesis, and we will one day be united with absolute spirit, no longer alienated. **Karl Marx**, ultimately the most important theorist of alienation, agreed that history is dialectical but rejected the idea of spirit, insisting that we collectively create a material history, and that only we can collectively wrest control from history and end alienation.

For Marxist theorists, alienation from world, others, and self occurs when people sell their labor power—that is, become commodities—in order to earn a living. The capitalist owns the labor process and the product of the worker's labor. When the product enters the market, the relations involved in the making of the product are obscured. The worker does not see herself in what she makes, and feels alienated from self and from others involved in the production process. Furthermore, capitalism fragments society into isolated, competitive individuals who pursue their own limited aims. All relations become antagonistic and thus alienated.

For modernist writers, the horror of alienation became a major trope. However, with the advent of consumer-monopoly capitalism, postmodernist writers suggest we have become too fragmented to have a self from which to be alienated. They tend to celebrate fragmentation, asserting we can playfully, or ludically, perform whatever roles we choose. Marxist theorists argue that ludic postmodernists—who live in relative economic comfort—perpetuate capitalist brutality by ignoring the way capitalism creates an exploited class. Imaginary ludicism for the upper class is made possible on the backs of the poor, and only by ignoring history. Marxism offers an alternative to the injustices of capitalism, claiming that exploitation, the commodification of people, and alienation can be overcome only by people working collectively, in a classless society, to meet their mutual needs, and working as an exploration and expression of their own nature (once they are no longer subjected by capitalism)—not just to earn a living or make a profit.

Selected Bibliography: Marx, Karl. *Economic and Philosophical Manuscripts of 1844.* Trans. Martin Milligan. Amherst, NY: Prometheus Books, 1988; Ollman, Bertell. *Alienation: Marx's Conception of Man in a Capitalist Society.* 2nd ed. Cambridge: Cambridge UP, 1977; Williams, Raymond. *Keywords: A Vocabulary of Culture and Society.* Rev. ed. New York: Oxford UP, 1983.

Sandy Rankin

ALLENDE, ISABEL (1942–). The best-known female author from Latin America, Allende's work examines the roles of women in the nineteenth and twentieth centuries, beginning with her native Chile but expanding to include much of South America and, in her later books, North America. Her work takes the feminist adage "the personal is political, the political is personal" and gives a view of history and society that does not ignore the public events of the past, but makes them subordinate yet connected to the private events and mores of her characters. However, some feminist critics have argued that Allende's women are too dependent on men for their self-image, protection, sustenance, and authorization to control their own language and destiny. Later criticism has been about Allende's "authenticity," since she married an American, moved to the United States, and began writing novels set there: *The Infinite Plan* (*El plan infinito*), 1991, and *Daughter of Fortune* (*Hija de la fortuna*), 1998.

Allende's first novel, *The House of the Spirits* (*La casa de los espíritus*), 1982, is her paean to Chile—from an imagined past of the nineteenth century filled with **magical realism** to her protagonist's imprisonment, rape, and torture at the hands of the military (in the person of a bastard member of her family), following the coup that overthrew Salvador Allende (the author's uncle) in 1973. Much has been made of the connections and similarities between this text and **Gabriel García Márquez's** *One Hundred Years of Solitude* (1967), with the harshest (and most often male) critics denigrating Allende's novel as a mere copy of García Márquez's work. This does not do the novel the justice it deserves, however, because the two works, while sharing notable characteristics, also have striking differences. Both books are multigenerational family sagas that employ a conceit (first used by **Miguel de Cervantes** in *Don Quijote*) of a protagonist who encounters a text that turns out to be the same one being read by the reader. Differences begin with this handling of the text, however, for García Márquez's character is reading the work of another, while Allende's is writing the text that we read as a family history, based on the notebooks of her beloved grandmother. The change in Latin American literature from the boom of the 1960s to the postboom after 1975 is evident here. Earlier authors tried to re-create the world, making the reader a participant with the characters, calling into question the nature of reality while ignoring more human concerns. Allende and her fellow writers tell stories that are more intimate, that do not attempt to rewrite the world but rather focus on Latin American reality and express it, ugly though it may be, rather than mythifying it. For this reason, the magical realism in Allende's text only appear in the first half of the book; as the story approaches 1950, the magic begins to disappear.

Selected Bibliography: Bloom, Harold, ed. *Isabel Allende.* Philadelphia: Chelsea House, 2003; Feal, Rosemary Geisdorfer, and Yvette E. Miller, eds. *Isabel Allende Today: An Anthology of Essays.* Pittsburgh, PA: Latin American Literary Review P, 2002; Levine, Linda Gould. *Isabel Allende.* New York: Twayne, 2002; Ramblada-Minero, María de la Cinta. *Isabel Allende's Writing of the Self: Trespassing the Boundaries of Fiction and Autobiography.* Lewiston, NY: E. Mellen P, 2003; Riquelme Rojas, Sonia, and Edna Aguirre Rehbein, eds. *Critical Approaches to Isabel Allende.* New York: Peter Lang, 1991; Swanson, Philip. "California Dreaming: Mixture, Muddle and Meaning in Isabel Allende's North American Narratives." *Journal of Iberian and Latin American Studies* 9.1 (2003): 57–67.

Jason G. Summers

ALTHUSSER, LOUIS (1918–1990) was, especially during the 1960s and 1970s, one of the most influential Marxist philosophers in Europe. His work has also been highly regarded in Latin America and in other parts of the world. Just as Jacques Lacan set out to recover the trajectory of Freud's thinking from institutions (such as the International Psychoanalytic Association) that distorted it while attempting to preserve it, so did Althusser set out to do the same for the ideas of **Karl Marx**. Althusser believed that within Marx's texts (especially those concerning **ideology**), Marxism never stopped struggling to be born and that it was left to him to give Marx's thought its theoretical form, which it had not yet assumed at the time of Marx's death.

The complex textual history of *Capital* alone justifies Althusser's sense that Marx required the sort of critical reading that he supplied in *Reading Capital,* a collection of papers he wrote for his seminar on that text at the École Normale Supérieure in 1965. In its intimidating three volumes, *Capital* runs to approximately three thousand pages. From 1863 to 1883, Marx worked on various portions of his great text, but he insisted on composing its three volumes simultaneously, moving back and forth, writing and rewriting. Only the first volume was complete and published before his death in 1883. Volumes two and three were edited by his devoted colleague Frederick Engels, who explains his painstaking efforts as editor and interpreter in his various prefaces. Before Engels died in 1885, his huge task was still incomplete, but he appointed Karl Kautsky to deal with what would have been volume four. In 1905 it was published as a separate work under the title *Theories of Surplus Value.* Although he deals mainly with the French translation of the first volume, Althusser (in *Reading Capital*) does an exemplary job of carrying out his project of giving Marx's thought a new theoretical form.

In the preface to *A Contribution to the Critique of Political Economy*, Marx summarizes with rare clarity what he called "the guiding principle of my studies":

> In the social production of their life, men enter into definite relations that are indispensible and independent of their will, relations of production which correspond to a definite stage of development of their material productive forces. The sum total of these relations of production constitutes the economic structure of society, the real founda-

tion, on which rises a legal and political superstructure and to which correspond defi-
nite forms of social consciousness. The mode of production of material life conditions
social, political and intellectual life process in general. It is not the consciousness of
men that determines their being, but, on the contrary, their social being that determines their consciousness. (4)

The relationship between the "real," economic foundation of social relations and
the ideological structure that is built on it (the two are sometimes referred to as the
"base and superstructure" of society) is the central subject of Althusser's most influential text, "Ideology and Ideological State Apparatuses." In this long essay (included in the volume *Lenin and Philosophy and Other Essays*), Althusser succeeds in
giving Marx's thought what he called its "theoretical form" by clarifying what Marx
meant by ideology. In one of the best-known formulations of this essay, Althusser
describes the process of "interpellation," through which institutions such as the
school, church, and family operate within bourgeois ideology to construct the individual subject. He does this by carefully reading Marx's conceptual metaphors and
by critically examining and complicating them. In particular, Althusser argues both
the relative autonomy of the superstructure and the "reciprocal action of the superstructure on the base" (136).

Althusser was one of the most controversial figures in Western Marxism. For many,
Althusser's use of the structuralist methodology then dominant in French intellectual
circles gave his work a particular theoretical clarity; for others, it stripped Marxism
of its crucial historical dimension. The Marxist historian E. P. Thompson, for example, in *The Poverty of Theory*, dismisses Althusser's work as "unhistorical shit," while
Terry Eagleton, in *Against the Grain*, praises Althusserianism for "its theoretical richness and intricacy, and its trenchant defence of the centrality of theoretical enquiry
as such." Certainly two of the most controversial things about him concerned the
essence of his work and the tragic ending of his life. Just as Lacan had placed great
emphasis on Freud the writer (what he called "Freudian poetics"), Althusser concentrated much of his attention on Marx the writer. Both Freud and Marx, of course,
had another side to their work; in Marx's case, that has come to be called "the scientific Marx," which refers to his determined effort to lay the foundation for a new
science of political economy. Nevertheless, Marx was often a great writer, and his theoretical constructions were certainly built on a network of metaphor, which Althusser
emphasized.

The tragic ending of Althusser's life, however, has nothing to do with the substance of his thought. In November 1980, in a state of madness, he killed his wife,
to whom he had been devoted for thirty-five years. At the time of his death, following a long period of confinement in an asylum, his autobiographical writings, which
included an agonizingly frank reflection on his guilt and manic depression, were
handed over by his nephew and executor to two excellent editors, who promptly issued the French edition of *The Future Lasts Forever*.

Selected Bibliography: Althusser, Louis. *The Future Lasts Forever: A Memoir.* Trans. Richard Veasey.
New York: New P, 1993; Althusser, Louis. *Lenin and Philosophy and Other Essays.* Trans. Ben Brewster.
London: Monthly Review P, 1971; Eagleton, Terry. *Against the Grain: Selected Essays.* London: Verso,
1986; Jameson, Fredric. *The Political Unconscious: Narrative as a Socially Symbolic Act.* Ithaca, NY: Cor-

nell UP, 1981; Marx, Karl, and Frederick Engels. *The Marx-Engels Reader.* 2nd ed. Ed. Robert Tucker. New York: W. W. Norton, 1978; Payne, Michael. *Reading Knowledge: An Introduction to Barthes, Foucault and Althusser.* Oxford: Blackwell, 1997.

Michael Payne

AMADO, JORGE (1912–2001). Born and reared on a cacao plantation in the state of Bahia in northeastern Brazil, Amado went on to become Brazil's most internationally renowned novelist and one of the most important writers in the history of Lusophone literature. His career saw not only the production of numerous socially engaged novels but also active participation in Brazilian politics. In 1946, Amado was elected to the Constituent Assembly, after more than a decade in which his radical political activism (including membership in the Communist Party) had led him to both imprisonment and exile, leading to periods of residence in Paris and Prague. In fact, it was only in 1952 that he permanently returned from exile. Many of his early books were banned in both Brazil and Portugal because of their radical political vision, though he remained highly productive throughout the twentieth century, writing a series of colorful novels that draw on the folk energies of the common people of Brazil, dramatizing not only their suffering but their vitality and exuberance in the face of difficulty.

Amado's early work was dominated by a series of novels dealing with social conditions in his native Bahia, including *Captains of the Sands* (*Capitães da areia*), 1937, the title characters of which are a gang of abandoned children who live in a waterfront warehouse and survive by stealing from the rich, while most in their society remain oblivious to their plight. This highly successful novel established Amado as an author to be reckoned with. *The Violent Land* (*Terras do sem fim*), 1942, which concerns the plight of exploited workers who pick the cacao beans on the plantations of Bahia, is perhaps the best known of Amado's early period. Such works indicate a sympathy with the working classes and an antipathy toward their exploiters, which would inform the rest of his career.

Amado's later writing, after his return to Brazil, tends to be lighter and is often highly entertaining, while still containing a great deal of social satire. These works often celebrate sexuality and sensuality, as in *Gabriela, Clove and Cinnamon* (*Gabriela, cravo e canela*), 1958, and *Dona Flor and Her Two Husbands* (*Dona Flor e seus dois maridos*), 1966. Both of these novels were adapted to film in Brazil by Bruno Barreto (in 1983 and 1976, respectively), and many of Amado's novels were adapted for Brazilian television, contributing to his reputation as a national treasure. Other late works, including *Tent of Miracles* (*Tenda los milagres*), 1969; *Tieta, the Goat Girl* (*Tieto do agreste*), 1977; *Show Down* (*Tocaia grande*), 1984; and *The War of the Saints* (*Sumico da santa*), 1993, maintained Amado's leftist political vision as well. Amado's works have been translated into forty-eight languages and have sold more than twenty million copies worldwide. Beginning with his first nomination in 1966, he was long considered a prime candidate for the Nobel Prize in Literature, though he never won.

Selected Bibliography: Brower, Keith H., Earl E. Fitz, and Enrique E. Martinez-Vidal, eds. *Jorge Amado: Critical Essays.* New York: Routledge, 2001; Chamberlain, Bobby J. *Jorge Amado.* Boston: Twayne, 1990; Ellison, Fred P. *Brazil's New Novel: Four Northeastern Masters; José Lins do Rego, Jorge*

Amado, Graciliano Ramos, Rachel de Queiroz. Berkeley: U of California P, 1954; Vieira, Nelson H. "Testimonial Fiction and Historical Allegory: Racial and Political Repression in Jorge Amado's Brazil." *Latin American Literary Review* 17.34 (July–Dec. 1989): 6–23.

M. Keith Booker

***AMERICA IS IN THE HEART* (1946).** Often lauded as the classic Filipino ethnobiography in which author **Carlos Bulosan** used his life and family as a paradigm for a collective history, *America Is in the Heart (AIH)* has been abused to legitimate the myth of the Asian "model minority" success story. This is hardly the case for both this quasi-autobiography and the Filipino community's position in the United States. Now three million strong, the economic and social status of Filipino immigrants (mostly professionals after 1965) still rank below those of their Japanese, Indian, and Chinese counterparts, due chiefly to the dependent, neocolonial character of the national formation with which they are still identified. Under the tight hegemony of U.S. corporate power, the Philippines languishes in backwardness and sends thousands of migrant workers to the United States and other countries in a global diaspora without parallel, sustaining elite power by remittances and heroic sacrifices.

AIH may be more justly appraised as a speculative instrument for understanding this paradox of "success" in failure. It presents a massive documentation of the varieties of racism, exploitation, alienation, and inhumanity suffered by Filipino workers on the U.S. West Coast and in Alaska in the decade beginning with the Depression and ending with the outbreak of **World War II**. Scenes of abuse, insult, neglect, brutalization, and outright murder of these colonial "wards"—the term used for the United States only direct colony in Asia from 1898 to 1946—are rendered with naturalistic candor. Naturalism, however, is tempered by typifying, allegorical depictions of characters performing their craft of survival and resistance, thus repudiating any kind of economic or biological determinism inherent in the commonsensical prejudices and policies of white society.

The key to the whole narrative unfolding—a compulsive repetition of bootstrap individualism wrecked by social circumstance—may be found in the first twelve chapters of the book. In this first part, feudal exploitation and U.S. colonial oppression of the peasantry explain the endurance, shrewd patience, and stoic cunning of natives like the narrator and his compatriots. This generation of peasants uprooted from their villages and exiled to cities had undergone the revolutionary experience of fighting the Spaniards and the American invaders together with their local allies (landlords and compradors), a schooling in insurrectionary politics never to be forgotten. This goes a long way toward understanding why the narrator never loses hope, always dreaming of emancipation amid horrific suffering; but he remains to the end a colonized subaltern mixing among American left-wing intellectuals, unable to shed his peasant and proletarian roots, affirming internationalist solidarity with all "the wretched of the earth."

Bulosan casts himself in *AIH* as alternatively the detached narrator, protagonist, and witness of events in a polyphonic orchestration of a multitude of characters and picaresque episodes. The last three parts (from chapters 13 to 49) chart the passage of the youthful narrator in a land of privation, terror, and violence. This passage begins with his victimization by corrupt labor contractors upon his arrival in Seattle, his anguished flight from lynch mobs and beating by policemen, his desperate flirtation with petit bourgeois intellectuals—vicissitudes punctuated in the middle of the book by his testicles being crushed by white vigilantes, a castration incident that emblematizes the emasculation of the Asian/colonial "Other" in a segregated polity. A hundred pages after this ordeal, the fictional representative of about thirty thousand Filipinos in California concludes by protesting loudly his faith in "America." In this context, the "America" invoked in the title easily becomes a metaphoric space "sprung from all our hopes and aspirations," a mythical projection or libidinal sublimation.

The ironical weave of the narrative confronts readers with the unavoidable question, How do we reconcile the stark discrepancy between thought and reality, between fact (the social wasteland of racist violence) and fantasy ("America" as a land of equality, freedom, brotherhood)? Is this simply an astute strategy to syncopate naive narrator with subversive author, thus multiplying polyvalent readings and intensifying the pleasure of the indeterminate text? In his provocative study *The Cultural Front*, Michael Denning suggests that Bulosan's work is the "sentimental education of a writer" becoming part of the Popular Front culture of his epoch in the struggle against worldwide fascist barbarism.

However, in addition to Denning's insight, the utopian thrust of *AIH* needs to be underscored as antithetical to naive romanticism. From this derives an interpretive framework that necessarily structures all possible "horizons of expectation," a framework centered on what the bulk of the narrative wants to forget but cannot, what is in fact the noticeable absence, or lacuna, whose manifold traces everywhere constitute the text of *AIH*—namely, U.S. genocidal violence, the Filipino-American War of 1899–1902, the killing of over a million natives, and its aftermath in the neocolonial system that persists to this day. It is this erased episode that actually subjugated the natives and drove Bulosan and his family into permanent exile. Its other name is "fascism," whose genealogy includes Spanish *falangists* and Filipino sympathizers, American racist vigilantes and police, and Japanese aggression—this last event (which concludes the book) evoking what the text dare not name: U.S. invasion of the islands and its violent suppression of the Filipino revolutionary army and government. The text's archaeology of repetition seeks to capture the time of self-determination and national sovereignty won from the Spanish colonizers; the time of the mother and all women who have been victimized by patriarchal law; and a dream time whose excess value is measured and then dispersed into the derelict space called "America," where Filipino men found themselves "castrated" under its regime of capital accumulation premised on white supremacy, the logic of commodity-reification, and imperial globalization.

Selected Bibliography: Denning, Michael. *The Cultural Front: The Laboring of American Culture in the Twentieth Century.* New York: Verso, 1996; San Juan, E., Jr. *Carlos Bulosan and the Imagination of the Class Struggle.* Quezon City, Philippines: U of the Philippines P, 1972; San Juan, E., Jr. *From Exile to Diaspora: Versions of the Filipino Experience in the United States.* Boulder, CO: Westview P, 1998; San Juan, E., Jr. *The Philippine Temptation.* Philadelphia, PA: Temple UP, 1996.

Epifanio San Juan Jr.

AMERICAN LITERATURE (AFTER 1900). At the turn of the twentieth century, American literary expressions of political themes generally focused on the repercussions of the large-scale industrialization and urbanization that marked the second half of the nineteenth century. **Naturalism** and **realism** were the predominant modes of American political literature, as evidenced by the journalistic prose of Lincoln Steffens and Ida Tarbell, the autobiographical narratives of Booker T. Washington and Henry Adams, or the profusion of socially conscious fiction written in the manner of Émile Zola. From 1900 to 1914, writers such as **Theodore Dreiser**, **Jack London**, Frank Norris, and **Upton Sinclair** produced fiction that used naturalistic techniques—informed, with the exception of Norris, by Socialist leanings—to critique aspects of post–Gilded Age America. Although late in their respective careers, Mark Twain and **Henry James** were still writing politically polemical works during this time. Twain vociferously opposed imperialism and satirized American politics for much of the last decade of his life. James examined American culture from a more genteel but no less disapproving stance. All of these writers in some measure helped to lay the political and aesthetic foundations for the modernists that followed in the wake of **World War I**.

Much like its British and European counterparts, American **modernism** was a fractious entity. As a result, the politics of its various branches varied widely in terms of intensity, salient issues, and the degree to which aesthetics was privileged over **ideology**. Although there is little in American literature from this period that is comparable to **Soviet Socialist realism** in terms of being "pure" political art—work by writers of **proletarian fiction** in the1930s comes close—American literature between the world wars was nevertheless heavily politicized.

Composed of Communists, Socialists, and other ideological fellow travelers, the diverse group that might be considered writers of proletarian fiction had existed since the early 1900s and was bolstered by the **Russian Revolution** in 1917. These writers became most prominent, however, after the onset of the Great Depression. Authors such as **John Steinbeck**, Sinclair Lewis, Eugene O'Neill, and Thornton Wilder are the most critically recognized members of this group, having all won the Nobel and/or Pulitzer prize. Other proletarian writers including **John Dos Passos**, Dreiser, **James T. Farrell**, **Josephine Herbst**, **Meridel LeSueur**, and **Tillie Olsen** were widely read during the 1920s and 1930s. In addition, a noteworthy group of critics and editors, including **Jack Conroy**, **Michael Gold**, and **Granville Hicks**—many of whom were also novelists and poets—helped to promote the work of leftist writers through their work with such publications as *Anvil*, *New Masses*, and *Partisan Review*. The group of writers/critics known as the Agrarians—many of whom helped formulate **New Criticism**—were also vigorously opposed to industrial capitalism, though from the Right.

The concerns of the proletarian writers often intersected with those of the **Harlem Renaissance** and other writers of **African American literature**, especially **W.E.B. Du Bois**, **Langston Hughes**, **Claude McKay**, and **Richard Wright**, all of whom were at some point affiliated with the **Communist Party**. Although not all Harlem Renaissance writers were overtly politicized, the goal of cultural "uplift" for African Americans melded together issues arising from race, class, and gender politics, especially among the more outspokenly leftist authors and those affiliated with **black nation-**

alism. Although the Harlem Renaissance only partly succeeded in creating a self-sustaining African American literature—in part because of political infighting among its principals—it paved the way for later politically incisive African American writers such as **James Baldwin**, **Amiri Baraka**, **Ralph Ellison**, **Chester Himes**, **Audre Lorde**, and **Toni Morrison**, as well as such systematic efforts as the **black arts movement**.

By comparison with the preceding groups, the so-called "high modernists"—such as **Willa Cather**, **T. S. Eliot**, **William Faulkner**, **Ernest Hemingway**, **Ezra Pound**, and Gertrude Stein—were more aloof from politics. During the 1920s, their treatment of political themes tended to emphasize the psychological and sociological aftereffects of World War I. This changed somewhat by the mid-1930s, when, for example, Hemingway started writing about the **Spanish Civil War** and Pound infamously wrote pieces sympathetic to Mussolini and the Italian Fascists.

After **World War II**, significant political themes for American writers were found in both the domestic and international realms. The development of nuclear weapons and the concurrent onset of the **cold war** spurred a variety of literary expressions of political dissent. **Howard Fast**, **Dashiell Hammett**, **Lillian Hellman**, and Arthur Miller were among those writers persecuted by the forces of **McCarthyism** and **anti-communism** in the early 1950s, and each responded in their subsequent work. **Science fiction** experienced a golden age during the 1950s and 1960s, with writers such as Isaac Asimov, Ray Bradbury, Arthur C. Clarke, **Philip K. Dick**, **Robert Heinlein**, **Ursula K. Le Guin**, and Kurt Vonnegut Jr. writing politically themed works in that genre. **Dystopian** works, especially those with nuclear themes, were also common during this period, especially within the **popular culture** forms of the B movie and pulp paperback.

Many prominent modernist writers and even some former proletarian writers remained active and highly visible in the first two decades after World War II, though in many cases their politics had been tempered somewhat by a political climate intolerant of leftist dissent. The new political voice belonged primarily to a younger group of novelists including Robert Coover, E. L. Doctorow, William Gaddis, Joseph Heller, **Norman Mailer**, and Thomas Pynchon, all of whom produced works of **postmodernism** that examined aspects of the American political landscape in a cold-war context.

The civil rights movement and the growing counterculture—partly inspired by the work of **Allen Ginsberg** and other members of the **beat movement**—of the 1960s served to expand the scope of politics in literature over the final third of the century. At the same time, the women's movement brought new attention to gender issues and helped propel women writers such as Toni Morrison to the forefront of American literature. Discontent over the **Vietnam War** helped to solidify this dissent against the political and literary establishment. As works by members of previously underrepresented groups became more common in American literature, issues of race, class, ethnicity, sexuality, and gender entered the literary mainstream as never before, thereby openly challenging the notions of literary **canon and canonicity**. Furthermore, **feminist criticism**, **Marxist criticism**, **new historicism**, and **cultural studies** all radically transformed the discourse of American literature by helping establish the intellectual validity of previously marginalized perspectives.

Selected Bibliography: Booker, M. Keith. *The Modern American Novel of the Left: A Research Guide.*

Westport, CT: Greenwood, 1999; Foley, Barbara. *Radical Representations: Politics and Form in U.S. Proletarian Fiction, 1929–1941*. Durham, NC: Duke UP, 1993; Gilbert, James. *Writers and Partisans: A History of Literary Radicalism in America*. 1968. New York: Columbia UP, 1992; Mullen, Bill, and Sherry Lee Linkon, eds. *Radical Revisions: Rereadings of 1930s Culture*. Urbana: U of Illinois P, 1996; Pizer, Donald. *Twentieth-Century American Literary Naturalism: An Interpretation*. Carbondale: Southern Illinois UP, 1992; Rideout, Walter B. *The Radical Novel in the United States, 1900–1954*. Cambridge: Harvard UP, 1956; Wald, Alan M. *Exiles from a Future Time: The Forging of the Mid-Twentieth-Century Literary Left*. Chapel Hill: U of North Carolina P, 2002; Washington, Robert E. *The Ideologies of African American Literature: From the Harlem Renaissance to the Black Nationalist Revolt*. Lanham, MD: Rowman and Littlefield, 2001; Weisenburger, Steven. *Fables of Subversion: Satire and the American Novel, 1930–1980*. Athens: U of Georgia P, 1995.

Derek C. Maus

AMERICAN LITERATURE (BEFORE 1900). Its larger millennialist project aside, John Winthrop's "A Model of Christian Charity" addressed social anxieties in a new world far from the governing structures of the old. Speaking aboard the Arbella, bound for Massachusetts in 1629, Winthrop cited self-interest, mutual identification, group surveillance, and God's wrath as compelling reasons for colonists to put differences aside and behave as a unified polity. Roger Williams took a more radical view of this polity (which got him in trouble with Winthrop) when he advocated what would become cornerstones of American constitutional democracy: religious freedom, separation of church and state, and right to property. Charles I, he argued, could not give the colonists land that already belonged to the Indians. This regard for Indians finds its antithesis in John Smith's writing on Virginia, which scarcely bothers to hide its aim to reassure investors that natives in that colony were few in number, militarily weak, and open to exploitation.

Operating between Smith's opportunism and the idealism of Williams, Winthrop was pragmatic in the problems he sought to resolve and the tactics he used, which relied as much on emotional as on reasoned argument. "A Model of Christian Charity" serves also, then, as a model of politics in early American literature. If ideals and opportunities changed over time, no writer could afford to be more weighted in one than the other. In the nineteenth century, John Ross and William Apess invoked republican principles to argue, like Williams, that Indians be treated as equal to whites before the law. More telling were fictional Indians, however, who sent a different political message. In novels by James Fenimore Cooper, Lydia Maria Child, and Catherine Sedgwick (whose *Hope Leslie* casts Winthrop in a deciding role), Indians act with dignity and honor. Yet all are finally killed, banished, or otherwise eliminated from narratives (and worlds) in which they no longer have a place—albeit sadly. Supposed pity for the Indians in such reading laid the affective basis for policies like the 1830 Indian Removal Act, which forced thousands of Cherokee Indians (including John Ross) from tribal lands in Georgia coveted by white settlers.

Expediency and feeling were no less characteristic of more manifestly political writing. Jefferson balanced legalistic principles in the first part of the Declaration of Independence with material danger and outrage in the second. True to its title, Paine's *Common Sense* was most convincing when it exposed the obvious wrongs of monarchy and inherited privilege. "Join or Die," Franklin put it, practically and terrifyingly. In drama, Mercy Otis Warren used mockery and indignation to advance the cause of liberty. After independence, Federalists succeeded in constitutional debates by leveraging fear of local (state) tyranny (Madison's letter #10, for example). Anti-Federalists forced inclusion of a bill of rights by creating like suspicions of centralized government.

Reflecting the need for Americans to imagine themselves in positive ways too, Michel de Crevecoeur's "What Is an American?" (1782) described the impending nation as socially and materially utopian. Optimism persisted in the nineteenth century, notably in the transcendentalist writings of Emerson and Whitman, fiction like Horatio Alger's rags-to-riches novels, and rhetoric of American nationalism generally. But skepticism grew, from the lighthearted, such as Irving's conceit of personal liberty in "Rip Van Winkle" or Cooper's ridicule of Jacksonian democracy, to the dystopianism of Poe, Melville, and Ambrose Bierce. Doubt stemmed from changes that left little room for Crevecoeur's vision of pastoral egalitarianism: urbanization, industrialization, sectional strife, class conflict, the failure of Reconstruction. It also resulted from the marriage of political partisanship to an emerging print-culture industry. A host of reform movements sprang from this union in decades preceding the Civil War, ranging from temperance and abolitionism to diet reform and the water cure. Rhetorically, writers like William Alcott and Henry Ward Beecher followed an evangelical tradition characterized by a highly emotionalized disciplinary idiom. Others, like T. S. Arthur and writers associated with Christian tract societies, operated at a lower pitch in poetry and didactic fiction that evolved out of eighteenth-century sentimentalism.

From this period emerged a wide range of writing that would form the basis of modern criticism in the United States. Some treated American failures and aspirations in general terms: Ralph Waldo Emerson, Nathaniel Hawthorne, **Henry David Thoreau**, William Dean Howells, **Henry James**, Edward Bellamy, and Thorstein Veblen. Others were more focused, especially in areas of identity politics. Early figures like Judith Sargent Murray, Hannah Foster, and Charles Brockden Brown paved the way for those who later sought to advance women's interests: Margaret Fuller, **Harriet Beecher Stowe**, Fanny Fern, Kate Chopin, and Charlotte Perkins Gilman. Many joined the cause of women with that of slaves; Stowe's *Uncle Tom's Cabin* (1851) championed both in one of the most politically influential novels in history. Other abolitionist writers included Lydia Maria Child, David Walker, and William Lloyd Garrison. Slave narratives were effective in chronicling the lives of those who suffered under chattel slavery (**Frederick Douglass**, Harriet Jacobs). Among writers who represented African American concerns after emancipation were Francis Harper, Charles Chesnutt, **W.E.B. Du Bois**, and Booker T. Washington. Class inequity was also addressed, especially after early unionizing efforts and the rise of a cheap popular press in the 1830s. **George Lippard**'s *The Quaker City* (1845) was the best-selling American novel before *Uncle Tom's Cabin*. Pamphlet novelist George Thompson mixed republican critique with pornographic ridicule of the middle class. Other authors who included significant class criticism in their work include Herman Melville, Rebecca Harding Davis, and Hamlin Garland. The rise of American naturalism in the work of Stephen Crane, Frank Norris, and **Theodore Dreiser** closed the nineteenth century with a new level of detail in exploring social issues, often directly related to the effects of an emergent American capitalism.

Selected Bibliography: Bercovitch, Sacvan. "The Problem of Ideology in American Literary History." *Critical Inquiry* 12.4 (Summer 1986): 651–53; Bercovitch, Sacvan, and Myra Jehlen, eds. *Ideology and Classic American Literature.* New York: Cambridge UP, 1986; Douglas, Ann. *The Feminization of American Culture.* New York: Knopf, 1977; Kaplan, Amy, and Donald Pease, eds. *Cultures of American Imperialism.* Durham, NC: Duke UP, 1993; Reynolds, David S. *Beneath the American Renaissance: The Subversive Imagination in the Age of Emerson and Melville.* Cambridge, MA: Harvard UP, 1988; Slotkin, Richard. *The Fatal Environment: The Myth of the Frontier in the Age of Industrialization, 1800–1890.* Norman: U of Oklahoma P, 1998; Tompkins, Jane. *Sensational Designs: The Cultural Work of American Fiction.* New York: Oxford UP, 1985; Walters, Ronald. *American Reformers, 1815–1860.* New York: Hill and Wang, 1978.

David M. Stewart

ANAND, MULK RAJ (1905–). Born in Peshawar in what is now Pakistan, the son of a Hindu coppersmith, Anand studied at the University of Punjab, then traveled to England, where he studied at Cambridge University and the University of London, from which he received his doctorate in philosophy in 1927. Anand lived largely in England from 1924 to 1945 (when he returned permanently to India) and was much influenced by the cultural and (leftist) political milieu there. In the late 1930s, he fought in the International Brigade in the **Spanish Civil War**. Still, his work is very much rooted in Indian culture, as can be seen from his first (and probably still best-known) novel, *Untouchable* (1935)—a searing critique of the Indian caste system. At the same time, the book's description of the humiliations suffered by Bakha— a young Indian "Untouchable," fated by his low birth to work as a latrine sweeper, can also be read as a broader socialist critique of class-based inequality.

Anand's second novel, *Coolie* (1936), is reminiscent of the **British working-class and socialist literature** that reached a high point during the 1930s. It traces the experiences of Munoo as he undergoes a variety of forms of exploitation. The child of impoverished parents in a rural village, he is orphaned early on and forced to go, at age fourteen, to the town of Shampur to work as a much-abused household servant in order to support himself. As the book proceeds, he moves on to the small city of Daulatpur, where he works in a pickle factory and then as a coolie seeking odd jobs in the city's market. Eventually he comes to Bombay, where he works in a large British-owned textile mill, in the end moving to Simla to become the servant of Mrs. Mainwaring, a somewhat disreputable, though socially ambitious, Anglo-Indian woman.

Along with R. K. Narayan and Raja Rao, Mulk Raj Anand is usually identified as one of the three leading Indian novelists writing in English prior to the 1980s, when **Salman Rushdie** brought new international prominence to English-language novels by Indian writers. Anand is also often identified as India's most politically committed writer. Saros Cowasjee argues that "no Indian writer of fiction in English comes anywhere near Mulk Raj Anand in providing a social and political portrait of India from the time of the Delhi Durbar of 1911 to the demise of the Indian princes following Indian Independence in 1947" (96).

Other novels written in Britain include *The Village* (1939), *Across the Black Wa-*

ters (1940), and *The Sword and the Sickle* (1942). Anand remained productive and extremely active in various literary and cultural organizations after his return to India. His later work also includes poetry and essays, while his later novels take a more introspective and autobiographical turn. The best-known of these is probably the *The Private Life of an Indian Prince* (1953).

 Selected Bibliography: Cowasjee, Saros. *Studies in Indian and Anglo-Indian Fiction.* New Delhi: HarperCollins, 1993; Dhawan, R. K., ed. *The Novels of Mulk Raj Anand.* New Delhi: Prestige, 1992; Rajan, P. K. *Mulk Raj Anand: A Revaluation.* New Delhi: Arnold, 1994; Sharma, E. K., ed. *Perspectives on Mulk Raj Anand.* Atlantic Highlands, NJ: Humanities P, 1982; Sinha, Krishna Nandan. *Mulk Raj Anand.* New York: Twayne, 1972.

M. Keith Booker

LES ANCIENS CANADIENS (1863; Translated as *Canadians of Old*, 1974), by Philippe Aubert de Gaspé, is a classic nineteenth-century-Quebec historical novel. While its main action is centred around the Seven Years' War between England and France, it is full of digressions that foreground legends, songs, presages, and other folkloric elements. Thus, at one and the same time, it adhered to and violated the precepts of literary ideologues who, fearing realism, urged writers to draw heavily from traditional folklore while eschewing "political" subjects. An immediate success, it has been republished at regular intervals ever since.

 Les Anciens Canadiens is a retrospective novel that was inspired by François-Xavier Garneau's monumental *Histoire du Canada* (1845–1848), which countered British diplomat Lord Durham's denunciation of the French Canadians as "a people without a history and without a literature." The action begins in 1757, in New France, just three years before the defeat of the French armies on the Plains of Abraham in Quebec City. The first chapters give an idealized portrait of the French regime from the point of view of the author's seigneurial class. The two young male protagonists, Jules d'Haberville and his schoolmate of Scottish origin, Archibald (Arché) de Locheill, both belong to the nobility. The d'Haberville manor, on the south shore of the St. Lawrence River, is presented as a utopia of social harmony and generosity, as between the landowners and the landless, masters and servants. But this tranquility ends with the British invasion, in which Arché participates in the sacking of the d'Haberville estate. However, when the hostilities end, he helps his erstwhile friend's family and chooses to live nearby.

 The oscillation between the reconciliation theme and the conflictual one continues to the end. Even Aubert de Gaspé himself, addressing his readers directly, alternates between welcoming the British victory for "saving" the Francophones from the effects of the **French Revolution**, and weeping over their defeat at the hands of the new masters. He predicts another hundred years of struggle for his people's rights after the first hundred years between the Treaty of Paris (1763) and his book's appearance (1863).

 Near the book's end, Arché and Jules's sister, Blanche d'Haberville, although strongly attracted to one another, are separated by the chasm of history, remaining unmarried neighbors. Jules, however, marries an Anglophone woman, and his father makes peace with the new British governor. The compensatory nature of Arché's remorse at his imposed military deeds, and the symbolic ethnic fusion in Jules's marriage are exemplary of a trend in French-Canadian historical fiction whereby authors "resolve" in their imaginary universes intractable problems of social reality (Maurice Lemire). But one of the last scenes of the novel has Arché and Blanche, now old, playing chess—that game of imaginary war and conquest.

Selected Bibliography: Hayne, David M. *"Les Anciens Canadiens." The Oxford Companion to Canadian Literature.* Ed. Eugene Benson and William Toye. 2nd ed. Toronto: Oxford UP, 1997. 33–34; Lemire, Maurice. *"Les Anciens Canadiens." Dictionnaire des oeuvres littéraires du Québec.* Vol 1. Montreal: Fides, 1978. 16–24; Shek, Ben-Z. *French-Canadian and Québécois Novels.* Toronto: Oxford UP, 1991; Tassie, James S. "Philippe Aubert de Gaspé." *Our Living Tradition: Second and Third Series.* Ed. Robert L. MacDougall. Toronto: U of Toronto P, 1959. 55–72.

Ben-Z. Shek

ANGLOPHONE AFRICAN LITERATURE. *See* AFRICAN LITERATURE (ANGLOPHONE).

ANGLOPHONE CARIBBEAN LITERATURE. *See* CARIBBEAN LITERATURE (ANGLOPHONE).

ANTICOMMUNISM, or the systematic application of hatred to the signifier of the "communist," is a potent ideological factor in every society where capitalist production rules. It is part of the turning of that specter that haunts capital as nemesis— the image of an aroused and class-conscious proletariat—into an instrument by means of which alternatives to bourgeois rule can be suppressed. This much is true throughout the whole range of capitalist societies, because they are grounded in exploitation, produce poverty along with wealth, and hence become permanently subject to threats from below, which have to be manipulated through the demonization of the ideologies that bid to supersede the reign of capital.

These general principles are subjected to a great range of variations according to national pattern and historical conjuncture. Each country has its own demonic culture; each has a particular configuration of threat from below, shaped by concretely unfolding events. By all odds, however, the most impressive national variant of anticommunism is that found in the United States.

American anticommunism is by no means the bloodiest specimen of the genus. Its record of domestic mayhem scarcely compares, for example, to the case of Indonesia, where half a million Communists and alleged Communists were slaughtered in the space of a few months in 1965, during the (CIA-aided) coup that brought Suharto to power; or to Nazi Germany, for that matter, the initial goal of which was to wipe out "Judeaocommunism," for the purpose of which the concentration camps that were to become the setting of the Holocaust were first packed with leftists of all stripes. But in no nation has the fear-and-loathing complex plunged so deeply or held so powerful a grip on national culture for so long as in the United States. There are no parallels, for example, to an inquisitorial body like the House Committee on Un-American Activities, precisely because in no other country did being a Communist come to signify a loss of identity as a member of the nation.

This fact, which placed a potent instrument of repression in the hands of architects of anticommunist repression like J. Edgar Hoover, is rooted in the American culture of nativism, which in turn stems from a complex of sources. These include the polyglot origins of the nation, its Puritan heritage, its religiosity, its history of chattel slavery and ensuing racism, its hectic pace of immigration, its equally hectic pace of modernization (which lent an aura of anomie to American capitalism), and, with special significance for anticommunism, its extermination of indigenous people. The shadow of "wild Indians" hovering outside the scattered settlements of developing America became readily transferable to the "alien" movements that threatened to radicalize the turbulent working classes; thus "redskins" and "red politics" became linked.

The connection hardened with the triumph of Bolshevism in the **Russian Revolution** of 1917, which led to the violent Red Scare of 1919–1920; it was reinforced again in the wake of the Great Depression, when threatened collapse forced capital to accommodate labor. In the United States, this led to an unprecedented degree of social democracy under Roosevelt's New Deal, thereby setting the stage for a major rollback of left gains once the system regained its potency. This took place under the accession of the United States to global, nuclear superpower status after 1945. The era was defined by binary opposition with the other superpower, the USSR. The actual defects of Soviet Stalinism provided a rich culture medium for the proliferation of anticommunism, and enabled the real conflicts of the era, which centered about the management of the postcolonial world system, to be mystified.

These factors provided the matrix for the Joseph McCarthy era, within which the infamous junior senator from Wisconsin played a spectacular but ultimately secondary and opportunistic role. Indeed, the actual inquisition began in 1947, two years before McCarthy burst into national awareness, with the Democrat Truman's initiation of loyalty oaths for federal employees. Fundamentally, the era was about welding together state and civil society to lead resurgent American capitalism into an era of global hegemony and permanent war economy. The great stakes determined the ferocity of the reaction, its depth, and its extension into every sphere of national life. In the process, domestic Communist movements took a beating from which they never recovered. More significant still, organized labor (having made significant advances in the 1930s) was tamed, and went into a decline that is still under way.

Fostered by state intervention, the cultural implications of anticommunism were immense and varied. The newly formed CIA manipulated scholarly journals and international congresses, as academia turned increasingly away from radical thought and Marxism. The prosecution and execution of Julius and Ethel Rosenberg cemented allegiance to the nuclear state; it also became a show trial of Jewish loyalty, and drove Jewish Americans to the political right. Extensive inquisition into the entertainment industry turned cinema away from exploration of social issues and into celebrations of patriarchal domesticity and fantasies about alien—or Communist— invasion (for example, 1956's *Invasion of the Body Snatchers*). Abstract expressionism became promoted as the quintessential American school of painting over social realism. Left-leaning novelists like **John Steinbeck** and **Ernest Hemingway** were supplanted in the public eye by authors like the rabidly anticommunist Ayn Rand. As a result of the inquisition, some six hundred suspect college professors were fired under Truman and Eisenhower, the FBI set up shop in elite universities, and an immense pall settled in over intellectual life.

The "Great Purge" began winding down when its work was done. By the 1960s, its central assumptions had come under challenge within a milieu defined by antiracist struggle, countercultural upsurge, and the delegitimation brought about by the **Vietnam War**. One turning point in its cultural demise was Stanley Kubrick's 1964 film *Doctor Strangelove, or How I Learned to Stop Worrying and Love the Bomb*, a black comedy that, by holding anticommunist fanaticism up to withering derision, emboldened the critical spirit.

Needless to add, the histories, both of anticommunism and of state repression of dissidents and radicals, continued past this point, although with the demise of Communism as a political alternative, new diabolic signifiers have had to be pressed into service: the predatory sex offender, the drug addict, even Greens. It is clear, however, that with the figure of the terrorist, the ideology has found a new haven. But as long as the basic contradictions of capitalism are in place, anticommunism, whether directly or through some displacement, will continue to function as a master narrative of repression.

Selected Bibliography: Belfrage, Cedric. *American Inquisition 1945–1960.* 1973. New York: Thunder's Mouth P, 1989; Ceplair, Larry, and Steven Englund. *The Inquisition in Hollywood.* Berkeley: U of California P, 1983; Kovel, Joel. *Red-Hunting in the Promised Land.* New York: Basic Books, 1994; Saunders, Frances Stonor. *The Cultural Cold War: The CIA and the World of Arts and Letters.* New York: New P, 1999; Schrecker, Ellen. *No Ivory Tower.* New York: Oxford UP, 1986; Wald, Alan M. *The New York Intellectuals: The Rise and Decline of the Anti-Stalinist Left from the 1930s to the 1980s.* Chapel Hill: U of North Carolina P, 1987.

Joel Kovel

ANTONI, ROBERT (1958–) was born in the United States but grew up in the Bahamas and Trinidad. He earned a master's degree from Johns Hopkins University and a doctorate from the Writers' Workshop at the University of Iowa. Drawing on his family's two-century history in Trinidad and Tobago, Antoni's three novels are each set on the island nation of Corpus Christi, a fictionalized Trinidad. Antoni's first novel, *Divina Trace* (1991, winner of the Commonwealth Writers Prize), explores cultural and national identity among the island's ethnically diverse populations through a mythological reconstruction of the history of La Divina Pastora, the black Madonna of Trinidad, from the contradictory perspectives of seven different narrators. Ninety-year-old Johnny Domingo's search for the "truth" of a miraculously hybrid *crapochild* (the half-man, half-frog progeny of Magdalena Divina) serves as an analogue of the search for authentic Trinidadian identity. *Divina Trace* achieves intercultural polyvocality by providing a discursive space for *all* the cultures of Trinidad. For example, by decentering Carnival (an Afrocentric cultural icon) and constructing his tale of slippery Caribbean identity over the embedded narrative of the Hindu Ramayana, Antoni dispenses with the familiar notion that the East Indian must be "allowed into" an already existent Trinidadian national culture, although, paradoxically, no East Indian characters figure prominently in the book. Thus, the Afro-

Trinidadian and Creole characters of *Divina Trace* are depicted as both participating in and produced by a culture that is already, among many other things, "Indianized."

Blessed Is the Fruit (1997) revisits the familiar tropes of Afro-Trinidadian culture (Carnival, mas, calypso) and interrogates African and Creole identity and their intertwining histories alongside equally vexed considerations of gender in the story of a white Creole mistress living in a dilapidated colonial mansion with her black servant. The two women's histories are told in a braided twin narrative (one of Antoni's characteristically experimental narrative strategies) that reveals crucial points of racial, cultural, and sexual similarity and difference. *My Grandmother's Erotic Folktales* (2001) is a comically bawdy and politically subtle commentary on the continued American neocolonial presence in Trinidadian culture since the establishment of a U.S. military base on the island during World War II. As in his previous two novels, Antoni utilizes the bodily grotesque, this time to enact cunning literary revenge on Western cultural luminaries from Sir Walter Raleigh, Dwight D. Eisenhower, and **Ernest Hemingway** to Colonel Sanders. Invoking the Scheherazade motif common in postcolonial fiction, *Folktales* features the Granny Myna character from *Divina Trace*, who must nightly distract the U.S. servicemen from the island's brothels by inventing tales strategically designed to appeal to the appropriate sense of consumable Caribbean excess and exoticism while simultaneously protesting the United State's continued cultural hegemony.

Selected Bibliography: Patteson, Richard F. "Robert Antoni: The Voyage In." *Caribbean Passages: Critical Perspectives on New Fiction from the West Indies.* Boulder: Lynne Rienner, 1998. 143–73; Smith, Eric D. "Johnny Domingo's Epic Nightmare of History." *Ariel* 31 (2000): 103–15.

Eric D. Smith

ANVIL (1932–1935)/*NEW ANVIL* (1939–1940).

ANVIL (1932–1935)/NEW ANVIL (1939–1940). The two *Anvils* belong in the American tradition of poets and fiction writers publishing their own work rather than seeking acceptance from the existing literary journals. In the 1930s, a number of such magazines devoted themselves to defining proletarian writing in America. Among these were *Left Front* (Chicago), *Left Review* (Philadelphia), *Leftward* (Boston), *New Force* (Detroit), *Blast* (New York) and *Rebel Poet* (northern Minnesota). The *Anvils* differed from their counterparts in that they did not publish any criticism, only fiction and poetry.

The chief figure in the first *Anvil* was **Jack Conroy**, who had just published a proletarian novel, *The Disinherited*. Conroy later wrote that his magazines were "rough-hewn and awkward, but bitter and alive from the furnace of experience." Conroy knew good writing when he saw it. Among the writers he published were three unknowns soon to become best-selling novelists: **Richard Wright**, Frank Yerby, and **Nelson Algren**. He became particularly close to Algren, with whom he would maintain a lifelong friendship. Although hailed by leftist writers, the initial print run of one thousand did not grow, and Conroy decided to merge *Anvil* with **Partisan Review**. The results proved so unsatisfactory that *Anvil* contributors asked Conroy to start a new *Anvil*. Most fervent about a resurrection of *Anvil* was Algren, with whom Conroy would share an apartment for more than half a year when he moved from Missouri to Chicago.

Funds to publish *New Anvil* were raised by staging plays and public readings. Donations also came from writers now working at the Works Progress Administration. Poet-publisher Ben Haggland, who had produced *Rebel Poet*, served as one of the editors and hand-printed the new *Anvil* as he had the original. *New Anvil* would have six issues of approximately twenty-five hundred copies each. Again, among those published were numerous writers who would be prominent in various literary genres for decades. In addition to Algren, Conroy, Wright, and Yerby, they included Erskine Caldwell, August Derleth, Stuart Engstrand, **James T. Farrell**, **Michael Gold**, **Meridel LeSueur**, **William Carlos Williams**, John Malcolm Brinnin, Tom McGrath, Kenneth Patchen, **Langston Hughes**, and **Margaret Walker**. Moreover, Tom Tracey's "Homecoming" won an O. Henry award (1940) after appearing in *New Anvil*. The young J. D. Salinger had the dubious honor of having a story rejected, but he stated that the rejection note sent by Conroy was instructive.

New Anvil ceased publication with the advent of **World War II**, as public interest waned and various contributors pursued their careers. What remains remarkable about the two *Anvil*s is how well they mixed artistic and political passion. The contributors, some of the best American writers of their time, had explored the potential of proletarian writing. Rather than battling abstractly on theoretical lines, the contributors had expressed themselves creatively in poetry and fiction.

Selected Bibliography: Conroy, Jack. *The Disinherited*. 1933. Columbia: U of Missouri P, 1991; Conroy, Jack, and Curt Johnson, eds. *Writers in Revolt: The Anvil Anthology*. Westport, CT: Lawrence Hill, 1973; Drew, Bettina. *Nelson Algren*. Austin: U of Texas P, 1989.

Dan Georgakas

ANZALDÚA, GLORIA E. (1942–). Born in the Rio Grande Valley (south Texas) to sixth-generation Mexican Americans, Gloria Anzaldúa is a leading cultural theorist and a highly innovative writer. Her work has challenged and expanded previous views on queer theory, **cultural studies**, ethnic identities, feminism, composition, lesbian studies, and U.S. American literature. As one of the first openly queer Chicana authors, Anzaldúa has played a major role in redefining lesbian and Chicano/a identities. And as coeditor of two groundbreaking multicultural feminist anthologies, *This Bridge Called My Back: Writings by Radical Women of Color* (1981) and *This Bridge We Call Home: Radical Visions for Transformation* (2002), she has played an equally vital role in developing inclusionary multicultural feminist movements.

Anzaldúa explores a diverse set of issues in her writings. Through prose, poetry, and fiction, she exposes the destructive effects of externally imposed labels and critiques the interlocking systems of oppression that marginalize people who—because of their class, color, gender, language, physical (dis)abilities, religion, and/or sexuality—do not belong to dominant cultural groups. Other key issues include Chicana/o identities, queer and lesbian sexualities, butch/femme roles, bisexuality, altered states of reality, transformational identity politics, and homophobia and sexism within both the dominant U.S. culture and Mexican American communities.

Anzaldúa's *Borderlands/La Frontera: The New Mestiza* (1987) is her most widely acclaimed book and was named one of the 100 best books of the century by both *Hungry Mind Review* and *Utne Reader*. In the book, Anzaldúa blends personal experience with history, and social protest with poetry and myth, creating what she calls "autohistoria-teoría." Interweaving accounts of the racism, sexism, and classism she experienced growing up in South Texas with historical and mythic analyses of the successive Aztec and Spanish conquests of indigenous gynecentric peoples, Anzaldúa simultaneously reclaims her political, cultural, and spiritual Mexican/Nahuatl roots and invents a mestizaje identity, a new concept of personhood that synergistically combines apparently contradictory Euro-American and indigenous traditions. *Borderlands/La Frontera* has significantly influenced how contemporary scholars think about border issues, ethnic/gender/sexual identities, and conventional literary forms.

In her more recent writings, such as *Interviews/Entrevistas* (2000) and *This Bridge We Call Home*, Anzaldúa develops these ideas further, creating what she calls "spiritual activism"—a synthesis of traditional spiritual practices and political acts. She draws on indigenous Mexican belief systems to create theories of "nos/otras," "nepantla," "conocimiento," and "new tribalism." Anzaldúa's publications also include *Making Face, Making Soul/Haciendo Caras: Creative and Critical Perspectives by Feminists-of-Color*, a multigenre edited volume used in many university classrooms throughout the country, and two bilingual children's books—*Friends from the Other Side/Amigos del otro lado* and *Prietita and the Ghost Woman/Prietita y la Llorona* (1996).

Selected Bibliography: Alarcón, Norma. "Chicana Feminism: In the Tracks of 'The' Native Woman." *Living Chicana Theory.* Ed. Carla Trujillo. Berkeley: Third Woman P, 1998. 371–82; Barnard, Ian. "Gloria Anzaldúa Queer Mestisaje." *MELUS* 22 (1997): 35–53; Keating, AnaLouise. *Women Reading Women Writing: Self-Invention in Paula Gunn Allen, Gloria Anzaldúa, and Audre Lorde.* Philadelphia: Temple UP, 1996; Yarbro-Bejarano, Yvonne. "Gloria Anzaldúa's *Borderlands/La Frontera*: Cultural Studies, 'Difference,' and the Non-Unitary Subject." *Cultural Critique* 28 (1994): 5–28; Zita, Jacquelyn N. "Anzaldúan Body." *Body Talk: Philosophical Reflections on Sex and Gender.* New York: Columbia UP, 1998. 165–83.

AnaLouise Keating

APARTHEID (the Afrikaans word for "separation") was the invention of the white nationalist government in South Africa, which enshrined racist discrimination in a legal and social system that endured from 1948 to 1990. Apartheid had its roots in the segregationist legislation of previous decades, which had consistently privileged the white minority—including the Land Acts of 1913 and 1936, which limited the land that black South Africans could own. The National Party was elected in 1948 on a platform specifically set against the equality of the races, and by the 1960s, the philosophy of apartheid permeated every aspect of society to embrace employment, public transport, education, and even marriage; the Mixed Marriage Act and the Immorality Act outlawed interracial sex.

A series of related acts were passed, including the Population Registration Act (1950), instituting social division strictly by racial classification—the ideology which lay at the heart of the nationalist project. South Africans were designated as white, colored, Indian, or black (African), with those of mixed heritage included within the colored category. While systems of segregation existed in colonial territories and in the U.S. South, apartheid was the most extreme symbol of racist oppression. The

Group Areas Act (1950) carved out "Bantustans" for blacks to ensure the "separate development" of the races, and involved the forced removal of around three million people as suburbs were racially polarized. The Public Safety Act and the Criminal Law Amendment Act (1953) allowed the government to call a "state of emergency" whenever the system was challenged.

The history of apartheid was marked by resistance despite the fact that many protesters were imprisoned for life, including Nelson Mandela; thousands died in custody during the regime, as in the case of Steve Biko; and many political protesters were placed under house arrest, such as writer and activist **Alex La Guma**. The African National Congress (ANC) had committed itself to resistance within the law, but even peaceful protests were dealt with severely, such as the 1956 ratification of the Freedom Charter, during which 156 leaders and protesters were arrested and later paraded before the court at the spurious Treason Trial of 1956–1961. The Pan-Africanist Congress (PAC) formed in 1959, and in March 1960 it organized demonstrations against laws requiring the carrying of pass books—without which travel about the country was not allowed—which led to the Sharpeville Massacre, the event generally understood as inaugurating the end of peaceful resistance.

The Bantu Education Act (1953) had authorized that black children be schooled in inferiority, taught not to aspire to equal status with whites and trained as service workers to labor for whites. The African Students Movement was created in 1968, a year of revolution and rebellion around the world, and evolved as a political organization. In 1976, schoolchildren in Soweto, south of Johannesburg, demonstrated against Afrikaans being the official language of education and were gunned down in the streets, images of which were beamed into homes around the world. Despite world disapproval, the apartheid regime held fast to its tenets. However, under the "moderate" leadership of F. W. de Klerk, the government finally conceded that apartheid should be dismantled. The release of Mandela in 1990 signaled the effective end of a racist ideology that had maintained a stranglehold on the majority population of South Africa for over fifty years, leading to 1994 national elections in which all races were allowed full participation for the first time, and in which the ANC emerged as the nation's ruling party.

Selected Bibliography: Beinart, William. *Twentieth-Century South Africa.* Oxford: Oxford UP, 1994; Bunting, Basil. *The Rise of the South African Reich.* Harmondsworth: Penguin, 1963; Lodge, Tom. *Black Politics in South Africa.* London: Longman, 1983; Norval, Aletta J. *Deconstructing Apartheid Discourse.* London: Verso, 1996; Posel, Deborah. *The Making of Apartheid.* Oxford: Oxford UP, 1991.

Nahem Yousaf

ARAGON, LOUIS (1897–1982). Poet, novelist, essayist, and political activist, born Louis Andrieux in Paris. Early in his career, Aragon showed a strong interest in dadaism, **surrealism**, and other avant-garde movements, founding in 1919, along with André Breton, the important surrealist review *Littérature*. He published his first collection of poetry, the surrealist-inspired *Feu de joie* (Bonfire); his first novel, *Paris Peasant* (*Le Paysan de Paris*), 1926, also reflected his interest in surrealism. In 1927, Aragon joined the French Communist Party, for which he became an important public spokesman in subsequent years. In 1928, he met the Russian-born Elsa Triolet, sister-in-law of **Vladimir Mayakovsky** and herself a productive novelist. Triolet would eventually become Aragon's wife, as well as an important support and inspiration for him in the following decades.

Aragon's Communist commitment led him to visit the Soviet Union in 1930; when he returned, he published a poem influenced by Mayakovsky, *The Red Front* (*Le Front rouge*), 1930, which advocated revolution in France. In turn, Aragon was arrested and given a five-year suspended sentence. His growing political commitment caused him to break with the surrealists in 1933 and travel to Spain to fight for the Republican cause during the **Spanish Civil War**. Aragon's important four-volume novel sequence *Le Monde réel* (The Real World), 1934–1945—all volumes have been translated into English—was a historical saga that covered the period from 1880 to the end of the 1920s, envisioning the decline of the bourgeoisie and the historical movement toward proletarian revolution from a Marxist perspective, much in the mode of **socialist realism**. Subsequent novels, including the six-volume sequence *Les Communistes* (1949–1951) and *Holy Week* (*La Semaine sainte*), 1958, were vaguely autobiographical, while maintaining strong support for the Communist Party.

Aragon's collections of poetry, including *Le Crève-coeur* (The Heartbreak), 1941, and *La Diane française* (The French Diana), 1945, expressed the same political perspective, while showing a strong patriotic support for a France then under German occupation, which Aragon opposed as a leader of the French Resistance. Other collections, including *Les Yeux d'Elsa* (Elsa's Eyes), 1942, and *Le Fou d'Elsa* (Elsa's Madman), 1963, focused on love poetry devoted to his wife, though maintaining a political dimension as well. Aragon remained a strong proponet of the French Communist Party during the decades following World War II, editing *Les Lettres françaises*, the party's weekly journal of arts and literature, from 1953 to 1972. He served on the central committee of the French Communist Party from 1950 to 1960 and was awarded the Lenin Peace Prize in 1957.

Selected Bibliography: Adereth, M. *Aragon, the Resistance Poems: "Le Crève-coeur," "Les Yeux d'Elsa" and "La Diane française."* London: Grant and Cutler, 1985; Adereth, M. *Elsa Triolet and Louis Aragon: An Introduction to Their Interwoven Lives and Works.* Lewiston, NY: Mellen, 1994; Kimyongür, Angela. *Socialist Realism in Louis Aragon's "Le Monde réel."* Hull, UK: U of Hull P, 1995.

M. Keith Booker

ARENDT, HANNAH (1906–1975). Political philosopher and New York intellectual Hannah Arendt was a German Jew who studied with Martin Heidegger and Karl Jaspers before fleeing Nazi Germany in 1933. After arriving in New York in 1940, she learned English and wrote all her mature work in her adopted tongue. Her first major book, *The Origins of Totalitarianism* (1951), links Stalinist Russia and Nazi Germany to nineteenth-century racism and imperialism, while highlighting the totalitarian urge to "remake reality" and to "destroy the political." Her subsequent work during the 1950s, especially her best-selling *The Human Condition* (1957), develops her distinctive notion of the political as a public space of interaction in which freedom is possible because issues of economic and biological necessity are banished. In *On Revolution* (1962), Arendt illustrates her classical republican ideal of the "political happiness" that results from virtuosic deeds performed publicly in front of one's peers. Arendt's view of the political, like Kant's view of the aesthetic, stresses a disinterested pleasure in noninstrumental action and originality. But even those who criticize her divorce of politics from interest-group conflict recognize that she sharpens for us the question of what the political encompasses and how it contrasts with the nonpolitical.

Arendt's career took a dramatic turn when she covered the trial of the Nazi war criminal Adolf Eichmann for the *New Yorker* magazine. The resulting book, *Eichmann in Jerusalem* (1963), with its famous phrase, "the banality of evil," caused a firestorm. Arendt had been shocked by the normality of Eichmann, the sense that he was just doing his job like any good public employee. Readers were shocked by Arendt's seeming to claim that the Jews, lulled by that same normality, had docilely sleepwalked to their deaths. Arendt's unfinished and posthumously published *The Life of the Mind* (1978) is her attempt to develop a full moral philosophy around her claim that Eichmann was "thoughtless," unable to step outside of himself enough to criticize his own views or, crucially, see anything from another's viewpoint.

Arendt's work was somewhat neglected in the fifteen years following her death, but the last fifteen years have seen an outpouring of secondary literature (much of it superb) that engages with her lifelong themes of plurality, equality, freedom, and participatory political action, while also considering her account of the wrong turns taken by modernity.

Selected Bibliography: Benhabib, Seyla. *The Reluctant Modernism of Hannah Arendt.* Thousand Oaks, CA: Sage, 1996; Canovan, Margaret. *Hannah Arendt: A Reinterpretation of Her Political Thought.* New York: Cambridge UP, 1992; Hinchman, Lewis P., and Sandra K. Hinchman. *Hannah Arendt: Critical Essays.* Albany: SUNY P, 1994; Kristeva, Julia. *Hannah Arendt.* New York: Columbia UP, 2001; McGowan, John. *Hannah Arendt: An Introduction.* Minneapolis: U of Minnesota P, 1998; Villa, Dana, ed. *Cambridge Companion to Hannah Arendt.* New York: Cambridge UP, 2002; Young-Bruehl, Elizabeth. *Hannah Arendt: For Love of the World.* New Haven: Yale UP, 1982.

John McGowan

ARMAH, AYI KWEI (1939–), important Ghanaian novelist and essayist. Born to Fante-speaking parents in Takoradi in the British colony of the Gold Coast, he received secondary education just outside of Accra at Achimota College, by then widely respected as one of the finest secondary schools in Africa. In 1959, Armah traveled to the United States, where he entered Harvard University in the fall of 1960, intending to major in literature but eventually shifting his focus to the social sciences. By 1963, Armah had decided not to complete his degree at Harvard, returning to Ghana to participate in the process of revolutionary change he hoped to be underway there.

The Beautyful Ones Are Not Yet Born, Armah's first novel, was published in 1968, and it is clear that by this time, Armah's early enthusiasm over the prospects of postcolonial Ghana had been colored by an extreme skepticism toward the conditions he observed around him. The book is bitterly critical of the corruption of postcolonial Ghanaian society, at the same time attributing much of this corruption to the impact of the seductive "gleam" of Western capitalism on the new nation. Armah's next novel, *Fragments* (1970), continues this theme, focusing on the experiences of a young

Ghanaian intellectual who returns from education in America only to find a society rife with corruption and enthralled by the lure of Western commodity culture. *Why Are We So Blest?* (1972) is informed by an even more pessimistic vision, suggesting that the corruption associated in Armah's earlier books with postcolonial African societies has infected even supposedly revolutionary African anticolonialist movements.

Armah's political vision during the period of these early novels is clearly expressed in essays such as "African Socialism: Utopian or Scientific?" (1967), in which he makes clear his disappointment with the failure of postcolonial African societies to fulfill the utopian expectations created by the rhetoric of the anticolonial movements that led to independence. He is particularly critical of one-time heroes of anticolonialism such as Ghana's recently deposed **Kwame Nkrumah** and the Senegalese poet and politician **Léopold Senghor**. Armah also makes clear in this essay his basic sympathy with the kinds of socialist ideals originally espoused by **Karl Marx** and Friedrich Engels, though **Frantz Fanon** emerges here as the most important direct influence on Armah's thought.

Armah's next novel, *Two Thousand Seasons* (1973), employs a narrative voice reminiscent of traditional Akan oral narratives to tell the story of Ghana from the original migration of the Ashanti to the area, through the intrusions of Arab slave traders and European colonizers, and on into the contemporary postcolonial era. The book acknowledges the failures of the past, but suggests great hope for a utopian future that would take its inspiration from the traditions of the past. *The Healers* (1979) is a historical novel (employing techniques from oral storytelling) based on events leading to the fall of the Ashanti Empire in the 1860s and 1870s, focusing especially on the second Anglo-Ashanti War of 1873–1874. *Osiris Rising*, published in Africa in 1995, uses the Isis-Osiris myth as a sort of structural scaffolding to address many of the concerns of Armah's earlier work, including African history, the possibility of a better African future, and the relationship between Africa and African Americans.

Selected Bibliography: Fraser, Robert. *The Novels of Ayi Kwei Armah: A Study in Polemical Fiction.* London: Heinemann, 1980; Lazarus, Neil. *Resistance in Postcolonial African Fiction.* New Haven: Yale UP, 1990; Ogede, Ode. *Ayi Kwei Armah, Radical Iconoclast: Pitting Imaginary Worlds Against the Actual.* Athens: Ohio UP, 2000; Wright, Derek. *Ayi Kwei Armah's Africa: The Sources of His Fiction.* London: Hans Zell, 1989; Wright, Derek, ed. *Critical Perspectives on Ayi Kwei Armah.* Washington, DC: Three Continents P, 1992.

M. Keith Booker

AL-ASHQAR, YUSUF HABSHI (1922–1992). Lebanese novelist, born in Beit Shabab, Lebanon. Al-Ashqar passed away four years after completing *al-Zill wa al-Sada* (The Shadow and the Echo), 1989, the third novel in his epic trilogy that spans a period of thirty years, highlighting the life of the main character, Iskandar al-Hammani—his numerous relationships, his nostalgic revisiting of the history of previous Lebanese generations, and culminating in the tragic Lebanese civil war.

When al-Ashqar's first novel and the beginning of the trilogy, *Arba'at Fursan Humr* (Four Red Horsemen) appeared in 1964, the literary community saw the birth of a new genre in Arabic fiction termed "the psychological novel." In this novel, al-Ashqar demonstrates his exceptional ability to afford his readers the chance to live his characters' joys and sorrows and identify with their concerns, masterfully employing such Western techniques as flashbacks and multiple points of view. The events in *Arba'at Fursan Humr* foreshadow the cataclysmic events and the sense of loss and fear that will plague his characters as they head into the destructive Lebanese civil war (1975–1990), which begins between the second part of the second book in the trilogy, *La Tanbut Judhur fi al-Samaa'* (Roots Don't Grow in the Skies), 1971, and *al-Zill wa al-Sada*.

The trilogy, which consists of 1,395 pages, is a compendium of all the factors that led to the Lebanese civil war—or any civil war for that matter. When it finally happens, the civil war had been seen against the background of a hundred years of slow descent into chaos and the dissolution of the moral fabric of Lebanon's society, a descent from faith, cultural mores, and community into hatred, selfishness, and despair. *Al-Zill wa al-Sada*, in particular, depicts the slow death of the Lebanese "self," as it vacillates between the echo (*al-Sada*) of benevolent indigenous culture and the shadow (*al-Zill*) of the "others" who are intent on bringing about chaos.

Al-Ashqar's style is also characterized by a new language that stays close to everyday diction yet remains capable of sustaining sophisticated philosophical musings and queries. This language was a far cry from the classical diction of most of the early Arab novelists, and was also the inspiration for a large number of young Lebanese novelists. The trilogy has been the main inspiration for the war novels of Elias Khoury, Huda Barakat, and Rashid al-Daif, to mention only three of the most prominent Lebanese novelists.

Al-Ashqar has also published the highly acclaimed short-story collection *al-Mizalla wa al-Malik wa Hajis al-Mawt* (The Umbrella, the King, and the Fear of Death), perhaps the best Lebanese short-story collection to date. He has also written a long play, *Mubarak* (Blessed One), which deals with the same events and concerns that figure in his novels, with the added power of a drama enacted on stage and adapted for television. Al-Ashqar is considered by many critics as one of the greatest modern Arab writers, though very little has been written about him, except for short articles and commentaries in Lebanese newspapers and literary magazines.

Selected Bibliography: Campbell, Robert. *A'laam al-Adab al-Arabi al-Muaasir; Siyar wa Siyar Dhatiyya*. Beirut: Goethe Institute for Oriental Research, 1996; Haydar, P., and A. Haydar. "Yusef Habshi al-Ashqar: *The Shadow and the Echo*." *Banipal* 4 (Spring 1999): 30–36; Saydaawi, Rafif. *Al-Nadhra al-Riwaaiyya Ila al-Harb al-Lubnaaniyya, 1975–1995*. Beirut: Dar al-Farabi, 2003.

Adnan Haydar

ASIAN AMERICAN LITERATURE. Although Asian American authors have been producing works in English for over a century, dating back to the Chinese Canadian writer Sui Sin Far, the term "Asian American literature" is a relatively recent one that reflects the impact of the Asian American civil rights movement of the 1960s and 1970s. A brief overview of the field might mark three phases in its development: the activist period of the 1970s, in which texts and authors from earlier in the century were recovered; the mainstreaming period of the 1980s, in which contemporary Asian

American literature found a popular audience; and the expansion of the genre's boundaries from the 1990s to the present.

In 1974, a group of writer-activists produced the groundbreaking anthology *Aiiieeeee!* which constituted the first attempt to collect literary works by Asian Americans and to define a new genre. In their preface, the editors discuss the exclusion of Asian American writers from participation in American literary history, and they passionately exclaim, "AIIIEEEEE!!!! It is more than a whine, shout, or scream. It is fifty years of our whole voice" (viii). Several of the works excerpted in *Aiiieeeee!* were later republished in their entirety—for example, John Okada's *No-No Boy* (1979) and Hisaye Yamamoto's *Seventeen Syllables and Other Stories* (1988). By recovering authors like Okada, who portrays the upheaval in the Japanese American community following **World War II**, and **Carlos Bulosan**, who depicts the struggles of Filipino migrant workers in the 1930s, the editors reveal the contours of an Asian American literary tradition. They also define Asian American authorship in terms of a "sensibility" that is distinct from that of Asia or mainstream America (viii). Frank Chin, one of the editors of the anthology, is significant on two other counts—as one of the first Asian American playwrights, and for his heated debates with Maxine Hong Kingston over the proper representation of Chinese American culture (for the latter, see his introductory essay to *The Big Aiiieeeee!*). With the publication of *The Woman Warrior* (1975), Kingston became the best known Asian American writer to date, garnering a diverse readership far larger than that of the more politically confrontational *Aiiieeeee!* Kingston's story of growing up both Chinese American and female, and her intermingling of fact and fiction, proved extremely significant to a body of literature that was actively seeking to define its concerns.

Throughout the 1980s and into the 1990s, Asian American literature both gained a wider commercial audience and established its presence in the academy. Key events in the growing popularity of Asian American literature include the enormous success of Amy Tan's novel *The Joy Luck Club* (1989) and David Henry Hwang's *M. Butterfly* (1988), the first play by an Asian American to reach the Broadway stage and the winner of that year's Tony Award for best play. In poetry, Cathy Song won the Yale Younger Poets award for *Picture Bride* (1983), while Jessica Hagedorn edited *Charlie Chan Is Dead* (1993), an extensive collection of short fiction by contemporary Asian American writers. *The Big Aiiieeeee!* an expanded anthology of Chinese American and Japanese American literature, came out in 1991. On the academic front, Asian American studies programs began spreading to institutions across the United States, and Elaine Kim published the first full-length study of Asian American literature in 1982. With the increased commercial success and academic legitimacy of the field, scholars began to explore in depth the intricate relationships between politics and aesthetics in Asian American literature.

As Asian American literature has proliferated and begun to command a wider readership, questions of how to define that literature have grown increasingly complex. Chinese American, Japanese American, and Filipino American authors were the first to be considered in early discussions of the genre; more recently, writers of South Asian and Southeast Asian descent have expanded the boundaries of the field. Works like Bharati Mukherjee's *The Middleman and Other Stories* (1988) as well as the pieces collected in *Watermark: Vietnamese American Poetry and Prose* (1998) have been important contributions in this regard. Meanwhile, other authors have explored questions of sexuality and queer identity, and still others have broadened the geopolitical borders of Asian American literature. Jessica Hagedorn's *Dogeaters* (1990), for example, is a novel that represents Filipino experience in a transnational frame. Recent Asian American authors, in contrast to their predecessors, have sought to represent a wide range of experiences and identities in their works and have been less concerned with the idea of shattering stereotypes (see, for instance, the novels of Korean American author Chang-rae Lee). In academic circles, the most significant discussion of Asian American diversity has been Lisa Lowe's essay, "Heterogeneity, Hybridity, Multiplicity: Marking Asian American Differences" (first published in *Diaspora* in 1991 and republished in a slightly revised version in Lowe's *Immigrant Acts*). Lowe embraces the term "Asian American" but insists that we also see how differences of class, national origin, and gender inform that identity. The wealth of scholarship on Asian American literature over the past decade reflects ongoing attempts to understand the complexities of this ever-evolving genre.

Selected Bibliography: Chin, Frank. "Come All Ye Asian American Writers of the Real and Fake." *The Big Aiiieeeee! An Anthology of Chinese American and Japanese American Literature.* Ed. Frank Chin et al. New York: Penguin, 1991; Chin, Frank, Jeffery Paul Chan, Lawson Fusao Inada, and Shawn Hsu Wong, eds. *Aiiieeeee! An Anthology of Asian-American Writers.* Washington, DC: Howard UP, 1974; Hagedorn, Jessica, ed. *Charlie Chan Is Dead: An Anthology of Contemporary Asian American Fiction.* New York: Penguin, 1993; Kim, Elaine. *Asian-American Literature: An Introduction to the Writings and Their Social Context.* Philadelphia: Temple UP, 1982; Li, David Leiwei. *Imagining the Nation: Asian American Literature and Cultural Consent.* Stanford, CA: Stanford UP, 1998; Lowe, Lisa. *Immigrant Acts.* Durham, NC: Duke UP, 1996; Wong, Sau-ling Cynthia. *Reading Asian American Literature: From Necessity to Extravagance.* Princeton, NJ: Princeton UP, 1993.

Nancy Cho

ASTURIAS, MIGUEL ANGEL (1899–1974). Asturias, born in Guatemala to middle-class parents, was the first Latin American novelist to be awarded the Nobel Prize. He spent the years 1924–1933 in Paris, participating in the experiences and discoveries of the international avant-garde. There he wrote his first major works, *Leyendas de Guatemala* (Legends of Guatemala), 1930, and *El Señor Presidente* (The President), 1946. The latter, a portrait of the era of Manuel Estrada Cabrera (Guatemalan president, 1898–1920), was the first and most influential of the Latin American "dictator novels," even though, because Asturias spent the period 1933–1944 back in Guatemala under the rule of another notorious dictator, Jorge Ubico, this great novel—a rare combination of political content and avant-garde form—could not be published until 1946. Meanwhile, Asturias had been secretly writing perhaps his greatest work of all, *Hombres de maíz* (Men of Maize), 1949, an extraordinary poetic narrative that explores the world of Guatemala's Indian majority from Maya times to the moment when the novel—Latin America's first great work of **magical realism**—was written.

In the late 1940s, Asturias was a diplomat representing the Guatemalan Revolution (1944–1954), first in Mexico City and then in Buenos Aires. In 1949 he wrote *Viento fuerte* (Strong Wind), the first volume of what he would call his Banana Trilogy—a literary history of banana production in Guatemala since the end of the nineteenth century involving an attack on United States imperialism in the shape of the United Fruit Company. Later volumes were *El Papa Verde* (The Green Pope), 1954, and *Los ojos de los enterrados* (The Eyes of the Interred), 1960. The three novels account for more than a thousand pages and, despite a lukewarm reaction from critics, represented one of the most determined efforts at "committed literature" hitherto written in Latin America. When the Guatemalan Revolution was overthrown in 1954 by a military insurrection backed by the United States, Asturias, then in El Salvador, went into exile and wrote a collection of stories about the events of the counterrevolution (*Weekend en Guatemala*, 1956).

Asturias's later novels—*Mulata de tal* (Mulata), 1963; *Maladrón* (The Bad Thief), 1969; *Tres de Cuatro Soles* (Three of Four Suns), 1971; and *Viernes de Dolores* (Black Friday), 1972—were less overtly political. In 1966 he was awarded the Lenin Peace Prize and in 1967 the Nobel Prize. By that time, he was ambassador in Paris for Guatemala's Méndez Montenegro government (1966–1970) at a time when Cuban-inspired guerrillas (including Asturias's own son Rodrigo) were active in the country, and the United States had sent in the first Green Berets to suppress them. Asturias, however, had been urged to take the ambassadorship by colleagues from the former revolutionary regime, including ex-president Jacobo Arbenz. Unaware of this secret advice, most of the younger writers of the era, that of the so-called Latin American boom of the 1960s, criticized the older writer for his decision; he spent his last years under an undeserved political shadow.

Selected Bibliography: Brotherston, Gordon. *The Emergence of the Latin American Novel.* Cambridge: Cambridge UP, 1977; Callan, Richard J. *Miguel Angel Asturias.* Boston: Twayne, 1970; Harss, Luis, and Barbara Dohmann. *Into the Mainstream: Conversations with Latin American Writers.* New York: Harper and Row, 1968; Henighan, Stephen. *Assuming the Light: The Parisian Literary Apprenticeship of Miguel Angel Asturias.* Oxford: Legenda, 1999; Martin, Gerald. *Journeys through the Labyrinth: Latin American Fiction in the Twentieth Century.* London: Verso, 1989; Prieto, René. *Miguel Angel Asturias's Archeology of Return.* Cambridge: Cambridge UP, 1993.

Gerald Martin

ATTAWAY, WILLIAM (1911–1986). The full story of William Attaway is yet to be told and needs to be reconstructed as part of the broader project of articulating the matrix of the African American and leftist literary traditions. However, while Attaway might seem to be a marginal figure in African American and leftist literary history, such was not always the case. His novels were reviewed for the most part positively, particularly *Blood on the Forge* (1941), and he was heralded by the *New York Times Book Review* as "an authentic young artist not to be watched tomorrow but now" after the publication of *Let Me Breathe Thunder* (1939).

While *Let Me Breathe Thunder* has been described as an "assimilationist proletarian novel" or a "run-of-the-mill" work of **proletarian fiction**, perhaps because its main characters are white, this view overlooks Attaway's creative encoding of racial and nationalist issues in the proletarian form in ways that deepen and complicate the conceptual representation of class and class struggle in racial terms. The novel narrates the wanderings of two white migrant workers, Ed and Step, along with Hi Boy, a young Mexican orphan who attaches himself to them as he flees New Mexico on a freight train. Hi Boy is effectively silenced in the novel as he does not speak English, but his very silence comments on the racist persecution of both documented and un-documented Mexicans in the southwest during the Great Depression. His character also calls attention to the Mexican Revolution and its cultural and political legacies of resistance, as well as the continuation of U.S. imperialist practice abroad and in-ternal colonialism at home.

In *Blood on the Forge*, Attaway more directly addresses the racial and cultural con-flicts that undermine working-class unity that were left muted in his first novel, per-haps influenced by the **Communist Party**'s **Popular Front** politics, which stressed American unity against Fascism and downplayed internal differences. *Blood on the Forge* treats the migration of three African American brothers from rural Kentucky to the Pittsburgh steel factories during the Great Migration of 1919, representing the cultural disorientation and dissolution they undergo and also the racism they endure at the hands of white European workers. The novel does not resolve these racial di-visions but points to the need for African Americans to restore their historical and cultural consciousness as a precursor to dealing with racism and to achieving class solidarity.

While best known for these novels, after their publication, Attaway began writing for film and television. As a member of the Harlem Writers Club in the late 1940s and early 1950s, he was intensely interested in the emergence of the new phenome-non of television. While not acknowledged in the credits, he wrote the film *The Hus-tler* (and was even flown to Paris to talk Paul Newman into taking the lead role) in addition to the 1980 televison miniseries *Skag*, which featured Karl Malden as an aging Pittsburgh steelworker, and the miniseries *The Atlanta Child Murders* (1985), about the actual murders of African American youths in Atlanta. In the mid-1950s, he wrote for the Colgate Hour anthology show, for which he wrote some Calypso music for his friend Harry Belafonte, including the famous "Banana Boat Loader's Song."

Selected Bibliography: Bell, Bernard. *The Afro-American Novel and Its Tradition*. Amherst: U of Mas-sachusetts P, 1987; Foley, Barbara. "Race and Class in Radical African-American Fiction of the De-pression Years." *Nature, Society, and Thought* 3.3 (1990): 305–24; Yarborough, Richard. Afterword. *Blood on the Forge* by William Attaway. New York: Monthly Review P, 1987. 295–315.

Tim Libretti

ATWOOD, MARGARET (1939–). Poet, fiction writer, and essayist, Atwood is the most renowned English-Canadian writer of the last quarter century. Her celebrity began in the 1960s when her sharp-edged poetry and satirical fiction wittily reflected the anti-patriarchal grievances and liberatory aspirations of second-wave feminism. Born in Ontario to Nova Scotian parents, Atwood read widely in modern and Cana-dian poetry; fantastic literature; and classical, folk, and Aboriginal legends, which re-main the bones of her allusive and often parodic texts. At the University of Toronto, she was influenced by the myth criticism of Northrop Frye, which sought out the fundamental patterns of plot and character beneath a variety of individual texts. At-wood described a national typology of such patterns in *Survival: A Thematic Guide* *to Canadian Literature* (1972), which argues that Canadian literature expresses victimization and survival rather than heroism and triumph. This complemented a widespread liberal-left nationalism that saw Canada itself as a victim of (earlier) British and (latterly) American cultural and economic imperialisms. Although Atwood's typology has been judged too homogenizing, a widespread tendency to view Canadian literature as anti-imperialist has endured.

The critical representations of patterns of relationships between men and women in Atwood's poetry—as in the collections *Power Politics* (1971) and *You Are Happy* (1974)—and in her novels—beginning with *The Edible Woman* (1969)—have been considered feminist in their explicit critique of patriarchal values and institutions. This critique is exemplified in her dystopian novel *The Handmaid's Tale* (1985), which portrays a future society ruled by a religiously fundamentalist, politically totalitarian, and sexually misogynist patriarchy. Atwood has been active in political organizations such as PEN Canada. Her website is www.owtoad.com.

Selected Bibliography: Ingersoll, Earl, ed. *Margaret Atwood: Conversations.* Willowdale, ON: Firefly, 1990; Wilson, Sharon Rose. *Margaret Atwood's Fairy-Tale Sexual Politics.* Jackson: U of Mississippi P, 1993.

Glenn Willmott

AUDEN, W(YSTAN) H(UGH) (1907–1973). The political phase of Auden's work is usually ascribed to the 1930s, when he was prominent among British intellectuals who took up leftist causes like the **Spanish Civil War** and felt the urgency of choosing between Fascism and democratic Socialism as potential European futures. Indeed, Samuel Hynes has famously dubbed the politically engaged British writers of this period the "Auden generation." Yet such periodization is misleading, both in passing over Auden's sometimes hesitant and contradictory feelings regarding the political role of the bourgeois poet or artist, and in overlooking strong continuities between Auden's early political sentiments and the centrality of moral and ethical issues in his later work.

Among Auden's political activities in the 1930s are his work with Rupert Doone's Group Theatre and with John Grierson and the GPO Film Unit—both utilizing art for the purposes of advocating social change—and two months in Spain aiding the Valencia government by writing and broadcasting anti-Franco propaganda. For other intellectuals of his generation, he served as a beacon and incited their own political activism. Auden's political concerns, his hope for a socialist future and for international democracy, are reflected in many of his essays during the 1930s, such as "Psychology and Art To-day"; "The Good Life," published in a volume titled *Christianity and the Social Revolution*; and "Democracy's Reply to the Challenge of Dictators." In the latter two, he refers to politics and social democracy, respectively, as necessitating a change in the environment rather than in the organism inhabiting it. His poems during this period were part of an effort to bridge the divide between private life and political, global realities. In the poem "Out on the lawn I lie in bed" (1933), he notes the disjunction between dire political developments abroad and the complacent comforts of British middle-class life. Yet even "Spain," his most emblematically political poem, reveals—and this despite its large-scale rhetorical shape and forward-propelling rhythm—the ambiguous nature of the revolutionary "To-morrow" and the problematic aspects of the struggle's "To-day."

Auden's later writings and interviews reveal that he was conflicted about the nature of revolutionary practices and his role in them. His poems in the late 1930s explore the nagging question of the role of the poet in public life and as a historical force, as in the well known "In Memory of W. B. Yeats" or "September 1, 1939," written on the occasion of Hitler's invasion of Poland. In a 1955 essay, he concluded that he and his fellow leftists in the 1930s had been interested in Marx for more psychological than political reasons, seeing Marx, like Freud, as a tool for the unmasking of middle-class ideologies.

While the political aspect of Auden's activities and writings appear to fade with his move to the United States and his conversion in 1939–1940, his poetic work demonstrates a continuity of interests. Earlier concerns for the "just city" ("Spain"), indifference to suffering ("Musée des Beaux Arts"), the fate of modern man ("The Unknown Citizen"), and democracy and universal love ("Sept. 1, 1939") are echoed in later poems that possess the same politico-ethical strain: a critique of authoritarian officialdom ("Under Which Lyre"), of violence ("The Shield of Achilles"), of the potential misuse of science ("After Reading a Child's Guide to Modern Physics" and "Moon Landing").

The question of Auden's politics is therefore not easily settled, for while he may no longer have participated directly in political causes after the 1930s, his political perspective is present in his moral tone and his continued concern with the problems of contemporary life—its alienations, its potential pleasures, and the role of the artist expressing them.

Selected Bibliography: Brodsky, Joseph. "On 'September 1, 1939.'" *Less than Zero.* New York: Farrar, Straus and Giroux, 1986. 304–56; Hynes, Samuel. *The Auden Generation: Literature and Politics in England in the 1930s.* New York: Viking, 1977; Mendelson, Edward. *Early Auden.* New York: Farrar, Straus and Giroux, 1981; Mendelson, Edward. *Late Auden.* New York: Farrar, Straus and Giroux, 1999.

Yaël R. Schlick

AUSTRALIAN LITERATURE. While the cultures of the indigenous peoples of Australia are among the oldest in the world, a written Australian literature dates only from the establishment of a British penal colony at Sydney in 1788. This event was in part the result of political actions elsewhere; the American Revolution meant that Britain could no longer transport her convicts to America. The political implications of the British occupation of Australia under the legal fiction that it was "terra nullius," or land that belonged to no one, have, however, only been fully realized in the last decade, after a prolonged and continuing struggle by indigenous Australians for civil rights and recognition of their prior ownership of the land. These struggles have been reflected in much recent writing by both Aboriginal and non-Aboriginal Australians.

During the nineteenth century, while a few writers, especially those familiar with similar struggles in Ireland, protested against Aboriginal dispossession, most shared the general belief that the indigenous peoples would die out with the coming of civilization. Issues of greater concern were abolition of convict transportation, achievement of self-government, extension of the electoral franchise, and, at the end of the century, federation of the colonies into the Commonwealth of Australia. After a rapidly suppressed rebellion by Irish convicts near Sydney in 1804, the only major civil uprising occurred at Ballarat in Victoria in 1854 during the gold rushes. In protest at the undemocratic and corrupt system of miner's licenses, a group of miners armed themselves and set up a stockade, but were also soon overwhelmed by government forces. The leader of the rebellion escaped and later became a Victorian parliamentarian, but the Eureka Stockade and its associated rebel flag of the Southern Cross have been extensively mythologized in much later poetry, fiction, drama, and film.

Nineteenth-century Australian newspapers and magazines published much satirical prose and verse about local political affairs, but most of this has been forgotten today. Influenced by **Dickens** and Hugo, Marcus Clarke wrote an epic novel denouncing the horrors of the convict system, *His Natural Life* (1874), though the system was by then long in the past. A later writer, Price Warung, wrote darkly ironic tales set in convict times for the radical Sydney magazine, the *Bulletin* (1880–), published during the 1890s with a nationalist, heavily anti-British and republican agenda. Henry Lawson, best known now for his short stories of bush life, also contributed much revolutionary verse to the *Bulletin* and other radical papers—among these "Faces in the Street," on the plight of city workers. The 1890s, marked by a major drought and economic depression, saw the growth of the trade union movement and the foundation of the Australian Labor Party as well as the achievement of female suffrage. Louisa Lawson, Henry's mother, established a radical women's newspaper, *The Dawn* (1888–1905), to further feminist causes, while other women writers, including Rosa Praed, "Tasma," Ada Cambridge, Barbara Baynton, and Miles Franklin, cast quizzical eyes over women's lives in bush and city. William Lane published a polemical novel set in Sydney, *The Workingman's Paradise* (1892), arguing that Australia was now anything but this, and later led a band of followers to establish a short-lived communist settlement called New Australia in Paraguay.

One of those who spent time in Paraguay was the poet Mary Gilmore. After returning to Australia, she spent twenty-three years as editor of the women's page of the *Worker* newspaper, publishing many collections of poems on political and other topics, including Aboriginal dispossession. Many of the same causes were later taken up with even more vigor by the poet Judith Wright. A member of a leading pioneering pastoral family, she later repudiated her heritage and worked tirelessly for Aboriginal causes as well as for conservation of Australia's natural resources. Patrick White, the only Australian to have been awarded the Nobel Prize for Literature, came from a similar background to Wright. While his novels are not as overtly political, White was continually aware of his marginalization within Australian society as a homosexual and wrote with sympathy of similarly marginalized groups, including workers, indigenous Australians and new migrants. Another leading novelist, **Christina Stead**, lived and wrote mainly overseas, where she was closely associated with Marxist circles.

In the period between the two world wars, many other Australian writers became involved in left-wing political groups of one kind or another, whether working for world peace and against Fascism, or more directly as members of the Australian Communist Party (ACP). Novelist **Katharine Susannah Prichard** was a founding member of the ACP and, unlike many others, did not leave the party during the 1950s. Others writers heavily involved with the ACP include Frank Hardy, Judah Waten, John Morrison, Jean Devanny, and Dorothy Hewett. A number of new theater groups were set up, producing socialist plays and work by local dramatists like Dymphna Cusack and Betty Roland. Groups of realist writers were established, together with literary magazines such as *Overland* (1954–). Another Melbourne magazine, *Meanjin*, founded by C. B. Christesen in 1940, advocated the broadly leftist sympathies associated with the group of radical nationalist critics, novelists, and historians who were to publish seminal works in the 1950s: Vance Palmer, A. A. Phillips, Manning Clark, and Russell Ward. A rival right-wing magazine, *Quadrant,* was established in 1956 by the poet and critic James McAuley.

The various liberation movements of the late 1960s—associated with protests against the **Vietnam War** and with increased political action by Aboriginals, women, and homosexuals—had a strong impact on the Australian literary scene. A group of young, university-educated, and mostly male writers, often called "the generation of '68," established new outlets for fiction and poetry, and theater collectives were set up to produce local plays. Leading figures were the poets John Tranter and Robert Adamson, fiction writers Frank Moorhouse and Michael Wilding, and playwrights Jack Hibberd and John Romeril. The 1960s also saw the beginning of contemporary Aboriginal writing, with the publication of works by **Oodgeroo**, **Kevin Gilbert**, and **Jack Davis**. Germaine Greer's *The Female Eunuch* appeared in 1970, followed in 1975 by Kate Jennings' anthology of women's poetry, *Mother I'm Rooted*. During the 1970s and 1980s, a series of significant feminist novels were published by writers such as Helen Garner, Kate Grenville, and Sara Dowse, while dramatists Louis Nowra and Stephen Sewell examined the interplay between personal and political power.

Since the 1990s, two main political issues have confronted Australians: the continuing struggle for justice by indigenous Australians (with an associated debate about interpretations of Australia's past) and border protection, related to the ongoing war against terrorism and the influx of illegal refugees. So far the former issue has been attracting most attention from writers, mainly in the form of novels and plays reassessing Australian history, though a leading novelist, Tom Keneally, has published *The Tyrant's Novel* (2003), about an Iraqi writer in detention in Australia, and many nonfictional works have appeared, together with plays and poems.

Selected Bibliography: Bennett, Bruce, and Jennifer Strauss, eds. *The Oxford Literary History of Australia.* Melbourne: Oxford UP, 1998; Ferrier, Carole, ed. *Gender, Politics and Fiction: Twentieth Century Australian Women's Novels.* St. Lucia: U of Queensland P, 1986; Hodge, Bob, and Vijay Mishra. *Dark Side of the Dream: Australian Literature and the Postcolonial Mind.* Sydney: Allen & Unwin, 1991; McLaren, John. *Writing in Hope and Fear: Literature as Politics in Postwar Australia.* Cambridge: Cambridge UP, 1996; Webby, Elizabeth, ed. *The Cambridge Companion to Australian Literature.* Cambridge: Cambridge UP, 2000.

Elizabeth Webby

◦B◦

BAKHTIN, MIKHAIL MIKHAILOVICH (1895–1975). The Russian philosopher and polymath Mikhail Bakhtin, whose works have been generally known in the West only since the 1970s, was once described by the critic Tzvetan Todorov as "the most important Soviet thinker in the human sciences and the greatest theoretician of literature in the twentieth century." A stunningly original thinker, Bakhtin's work has had implications not only for literary criticism but for ethics, philology, semiotics, psychology, and cultural anthropology. His relative obscurity was in great part an effect of the tumultuous history of Russia and the Soviet Union during the twentieth century.

Born in Orel, south of Moscow, Bakhtin followed a course in classics at Petersburg University from 1913 to 1917. When he and his family moved to Nevel to avoid some of the chaos caused by the civil war in Petersburg, the first "Bakhtin circle" formed around him, including the linguist and musicologist Vološinov, the literary scholar Pumpiansky, and the philosopher Kagan. After a move to Vitebsk, the group was joined by Pavel Medvedev, an established critic who at that time had official connections and a good reputation with the government. The nature of the group's intellectual enterprise was extremely collaborative. Indeed, to this day books originally published under the names of Medvedev and Vološinov are claimed by some to have been substantially written by Bakhtin, and are sometimes attributed to Bakhtin/Medvedev or Bakhtin/Vološinov. Certainly Bakhtin was unpopular with the government authorities for most of his career, and might well have been prevented from publishing under his own name. On the other hand, the books purportedly written by Medvedev and Vološinov are much closer to traditional Marxism than are the books originally published under Bakhtin's name. It is ironic but appropriate, given the thrust of Bakhtin's thought about language and authorship, that such a fundamental question about him as to what he wrote should be radically uncertain.

During the mid-1920s, Bakhtin worked on a series of papers in moral philosophy and aesthetics (some of which have recently been translated and published under the title *Art and Answerability*). These were rooted in Ernst Cassirer and Hermann Cohen's neo-Kantianism, but gradually moved in his own direction, which would center increasingly on a new conception of language. By 1929 Bakhtin, now living in Leningrad as a semi-invalid, was arrested and sent into exile, apparently on account of the active Christian involvement of his friends. But his first book, *Problems of Dostoevsky's Poetics*, had appeared and been hailed as promising, and other friends of his managed to get his sentence softened to internal exile in Kazakhstan. By 1936, Medvedev had found him a teaching job in Saransk. Bakhtin worked on a book on the European **bildungsroman** but its publication was held up by the war, and only fragments of it have survived. He became a doctoral student at the Gorky Institute—**Maxim Gorky** had been an early supporter of his—and attempted a dissertation on "Rabelais in the History of Realism," but his defense was postponed; when he finally held it, in 1952, he was awarded only a candidate's degree. This work, however, was the original version of the book *Rabelais and His World*, which later appeared to considerable acclaim.

By the late 1950s, the Russian formalists, who were beginning to be recognized as substantial critics in the West—their full influence would not be felt until the arrival of structuralism—had begun to mention Bakhtin as an important thinker. Shklovsky and Jakobson were the most notable of these. Some younger Russian scholars were attempting to republish the Dostoevsky book when they discovered, to everyone's surprise, that Bakhtin was still alive. During his last years, which were spent in an atmosphere of far greater physical comfort and intellectual acclaim than he had been accustomed to, Bakhtin revised that book and developed the Rabelais manuscript. He also worked on notebook entries and essays, some of which were later published in English as *Speech Genres and Other Essays*. He died in 1975, having neither conclusively affirmed nor denied the rumors that he was responsible for the Medvedev and Vološinov books.

Among Bakhtin's earliest public quarrels was that with the formalists, but for all its vigor this was a family argument—both he and they affirmed that language was key to analyzing and evaluating both experience and art, although his own vision of language was, unlike theirs, always ideological. Although Bakhtin certainly is not, strictly speaking, a Marxist, he does center his thought on humanity as social beings who are created in dialogue with others and exist in a perpetual state of conversation, whether literal or metaphorical. His idea of the self is one radically dependent on the other, as the self is a gift of the other, something like an act of grace. Each human consciousness negotiates with other selves by way of their individual "languages," so that selfhood is supremely social.

A surprising consequence of his idea of the importance of language in selfhood is that for him, we might call consciousness, which is greatly made up of language, an extraterritorial part of the human organism, one that includes strong elements of otherness. We might say that for Bakhtin, subjectivity is only formed by way of intersubjectivity. As he says, language "lies on the border between oneself and the other." Bakhtin is always at pains to deny the idea of human belongs as finalizable; they are always more than any single vision of them can encompass. Like good and fully developed characters in novels, they "do not coincide with themselves," as Bakhtin puts it, in a somewhat existential formulation. For Bakhtin, Freud's idea of the unconscious is mistaken; the consciousness itself contains most of the contradictions, irrationalities, and alien drives that psychoanalysts ascribe to the unconscious mind. But then, Freud's idea of the ego is far too unitary and rational a place for the perpetual dynamic interchange that Bakhtin calls consciousness.

In formalist terms, Bakhtin's interest is always in *parole*—an individual instance of speech, with its accompanying context—rather than in *langue*—the abstract system that orders speech. His quarrel with conventional linguistics, and with the formalists who embraced it, was that abstract rules of language could never reflect the way in which speech is always embedded in living, material situations, which give to speech acts much of the meaning they hold. An utterance is always unique and cannot be repeated, while the sentence is an objective fact and can be reiterated at will—even if these two are, to a formalist, the same. Each remark carries the aura of the system of ideas, more or less explicitly political as it may be, that the speaker carries with him or her. Further, utterances are always made *toward* someone and bear the mark of that "addressivity." Bakhtin uses the term "heteroglossia" to refer to the fact that speech is always multiple, a combination of different languages, each of which claims privilege. Finally, what Bakhtin envisioned was a "translinguistics" or "metalinguistics" that could investigate the material situation-types out of which speech springs, rather than merely the forms of speech stripped of their material roots.

For Bakhtin, language is always "double-voiced," including forms of both the language of the speaker—which is itself composed of the multiple voices of family, friends, intellectual influences, lovers, and so on—and the anticipated addressee, toward whom the speaker may feel any combination of a variety of attitudes and adopt a host of different postures. Throughout his thought, it is the confrontation with fundamental difference, with *alterity*, that is constitutive of the richness of human experience and expression. In *The Dialogical Imagination*—the most influential collection of his writings in the English-speaking world—Bakhtin celebrates the dialogism he finds in the most fully realized novels. He opposes the novel and its early Greek forms, such as the dialogue, the Menippean satire, and the symposium; epic and lyric poetry; and even drama, all of which in his view are hypertrophies of a monologic authoritative language, recalling the official language of the church in the Middle Ages. Thus Bakhtin inverts the classical hierarchy of the literary arts, elevating the "popular" upstart form of the novel at the expense of poetry's supposed higher status. In his Dostoevsky book, Bakhtin argues that it is that author who best embodies dialogical qualities in his novels, and in fact it is the capacity to assimilate other genres and forms that is responsible for the artistic triumph of the novel genre. Indeed, it can hardly be called a genre, liable as it is to engulf competing and subsidiary forms like the newspaper story, melodrama, the prose essay, the confession, satire, and even poetry itself; it is a super genre, and encompasses the highest possibilities of literature.

Another influential Bakhtinian concept, and one easily susceptible to misunderstanding and abuse, is carnival. Based on the medieval ritual celebration in which ordinary hierarchies and values are temporarily overthrown, carnival embodies a folk wisdom that opposes all forms of traditional authority even as it celebrates the body in its materiality. Bakhtin terms it "a pageant without footlights and without a division into performers and spectators." Here Bakhtin's sympathy and identification with the underdog—not to mention the underclass—comes to the fore. Bakhtin celebrates the "licensed misrule" of carnival, the ridicule of the mighty and crowning of a fool. He praises the characteristic forms of carnival expression, such as blasphemy and profanation, mockery, parody, and the affirmation of the "bodily lower stratum" in images of birth, ingestion, copulation, death, defecation, and urination—virtually any image that emphasizes the spaces where inside and outside meet. The mode of carnival is "grotesque realism." Rabelais, for him, is the carnival author par excellence, but Bakhtin traces an entire alternative line of the novel—not the one stressed by traditional criticism that culminates in the social realism of Stendhal, Austen, Trollope, Balzac, Tolstoy, and James, but one with its roots in the dialogues and in Menippean satire and in the works of Apuleis and Petronius. This line runs through the uncategorizable fictions of Rabelais, **Cervantes**, Sterne, **Goethe**, and **Dostoevsky**. As a number of contemporary critics have suggested, the carnival line may well continue through the Joyce of *Ulysses* as well as through works by John Barth and Thomas Pynchon—unless Bakhtin would see these as a degenerate form of carnival, without the true spirit of "unofficial culture."

It has been frequently suggested that Bakhtin, no friend to the Stalinist state that rather halfheartedly persecuted him, was writing in a kind of Aesopian language in his attacks on the official language of the church; in any case, he is a philosopher who values the free expression of a polyphony of voices and admires "the people" in their desire to level artificial social distinctions. Probably one of the reasons for his popularity in the United States is the way in which his thought in popularizations is often reduced to a weak liberal pluralism, although it is in fact far more complex than that. Critics of a wide variety of persuasions, from **Julia Kristeva** to Wayne Booth, have learned from him, and even feminists, who have found much to object to in his praise for Rabelais, have also noticed that the concept of an embattled woman's voice can be useful. A few Christian critics have adapted some of his thought to their purposes, relying on his closeness at points to Buber. And Marxists of various persuasions find him useful in offering a materially grounded, politically sophisticated group of ideas that allows for considerable analysis of the play of language in the deployment of ideas in literature.

Selected Bibliography: Bakhtin, Mikhail M. *Art and Answerability: Early Philosophical Essays by M. M. Bakhtin.* Ed. Michael Holquist and Vadim Liapunov. Trans. Vadim Liapunov. Austin: U of Texas P, 1990; Bakhtin, Mikhail M. *The Dialogic Imagination: Four Essays by M. M. Bakhtin.* Ed. Michael Holquist. Trans. Caryl Emerson and Michael Holquist. Austin: U of Texas P, 1981; Bakhtin, Mikhail M. *Problems of Dostoevsky's Poetics.* Ed. and Trans. Caryl Emerson. Minneapolis: U of Minnesota P, 1984; Bakhtin, Mikhail M. *Rabelais and His World.* Trans. Hélène Iswolsky. Cambridge, MA: MIT P, 1984; Bakhtin, Mikhail M. *Speech Genres and Other Late Essays.* Ed. Caryl Emerson and Michael Holquist. Trans. Vern W. McGee. Austin: U of Texas P, 1986; Bakhtin, M. M. / Medvedev, P. N. *The Formal Method in Literary Scholarship: A Critical Introduction to Sociological Poetics.* Trans. Albert J. Wehrle. Cambridge, MA: Harvard UP, 1985; Clark, Katerina, and Michael Holquist. *Mikhail Bakhtin.* Cambridge, MA: Harvard UP, 1984; Todorov, Tzvetan. *Mikhail Bakhtin: The Dialogical Principle.* Trans. Wlad Godzich. Minneapolis: U of Minnesota P, 1984; Vološinov, V. N. *Freudianism: A Critical Sketch.* Ed. I. R. Titunik and Neil R. Bruss. Trans. I. R. Titunik. Bloomington: Indiana UP, 1987; Vološinov, V. N. *Marxism and the Philosophy of Language.* Trans. Ladislav Matejka and I. R. Titunik. Cambridge, MA: Harvard UP, 1986.

R. Brandon Kershner

BALDWIN, JAMES (1924–1987). One of the most influential voices of the civil rights era, Baldwin devoted his forty-year writing career to exposing American dishonesty about race. Baldwin was born in Harlem and grew up there in a poor and religiously confining household that was a world apart from the intellectual ferment of the **Harlem Renaissance**. He escaped first to Greenwich Village, and then to Paris in 1948, following the example of **Richard Wright** and other black artists. Although he never returned permanently to the United States, Baldwin remained an outspoken critic of American society until he died.

Among Baldwin's six novels, the most critically acclaimed are the earliest: *Go Tell It on the Mountain* (1953), *Giovanni's Room* (1956), and *Another Country* (1962). Yet it is as an essayist, especially as author of the pieces collected in *Notes of a Native Son* (1955), that Baldwin proved most successful at bringing together a stinging indictment of injustice and remarkable prose. With the publication of *The Fire Next Time* (1963), Baldwin was widely recognized as a prophetic voice of the civil rights movement and was credited with raising white consciousness about racism to an unprecedented degree. In the view of some critics, Baldwin's later work—including *The Fire Next Time*—suffered, as it became more overtly political. But to divide his career into literary and political periods is to neglect both the ferocious critique of the essays of the 1940s and 1950s and the artistic achievement of works like the essay *No Name in the Street* (1972) and his last novel, *Just above My Head* (1979).

During the 1960s, Baldwin traveled widely in the United States, participating in marches and speaking for the Congress of Racial Equality, the Student Nonviolent Coordinating Committee, and other organizations. Although he was not active in the gay rights movement, Baldwin argued that homophobia was rooted in the same fears that produced racism and was just as destructive. His honesty about his own attachments to other men and his frank exploration of homosexuality in his writing still inspire queer activists and scholars.

Baldwin's fortunes as a public figure and as an artist waned in the last two decades of his life. On the one hand, his relentless attention to the gap between democratic ideals and American practices after the achievements of the 1960s alienated Baldwin from white Americans who had earlier sought his opinion. On the other hand, his insistence on the dangers of all forms of racial nationalism and his open homosexuality made him an object of scorn by younger black militants. What both groups refused to confront was the radicalism that defined Baldwin's career. Americans, in his view, would need to "dare everything" if they wanted to achieve more than superficial social change, and his writings remain a revolutionary call to consciousness for Americans of all races.

Selected Bibliography: Balfour, Lawrie. *The Evidence of Things Not Said: James Baldwin and the Promise of American Democracy.* Ithaca: Cornell UP, 2001; Campbell, James. *Talking at the Gates: A Life of James Baldwin.* New York: Penguin, 1991; Leeming, David. *James Baldwin.* New York: Knopf, 1994; Ross, Marlon B. "White Fantasies of Desire: Baldwin and the Racial Identities of Sexuality." *James Baldwin Now.* Ed. Dwight A. McBride. New York: New York UP, 1999. 13–55; Troupe, Quincy, ed. *James Baldwin: The Legacy.* New York: Simon and Schuster, 1989.

Lawrie Balfour

BALZAC, HONORÉ DE (1799–1850). Born during the troubled times that marked the transition between the First Republic and the Napoleonic Empire, Balzac was—like many of his peers—a political hybrid. During the Restoration period, Balzac was predominantly attached to the liberal ideals of the **French Revolution**, to which his own class owed its existence. Later on, especially after the July revolution of 1830, Balzac became attracted to the legitimist cause, to the point of declaring, in the *avant-propos* to the first edition of his collected works (1842), that his writing was inspired by "two eternal Truths: Religion, and Monarchy, two necessities proclaimed by recent events." In spite of this political bias, it would be difficult to find a more lucid critic than Balzac of the French society of the first half of the nineteenth century. His remarkable understanding of social and economic mechanisms explains why **Karl Marx** viewed Balzac's fiction as a documentary source, and recommended his novels to Friedrich Engels. Even more to the point, Balzac knew very well how many "respectable" bourgeois fortunes were made during the revolutionary wars, and many of the characters of his vast novel sequence *La Comédie humaine* reflect the irony of history, which made the new bourgeoisie rise to social prominence on the spoils of the Old Regime.

Balzac's father, Bernard-François Balssa, came from a modest family of farm holders. After a brief career as a clerk during the Old Regime, he entered the political fray that followed the fall of the Bastille, a turbulent period that Balzac later evoked in several of his works. These range from the reconstructed "Memoirs" of Henry Sanson, the public executioner (1829) (republished in part as *Un Épisode sous la terreur*, in *La Comédie humaine*) to *Les Paysans*, a novel "without a hero," which appeared posthumously in 1855, in which Balzac analyzed the decay of the aristocracy and its replacement by the bourgeois "dynasties" that consecrate the rule of *mediocracy* initiated by the French Revolution. Notwithstanding his plebeian origins, Balzac had aristocratic aspirations that his father had encouraged when he replaced the rustic name of Balssa with Balzac (Honoré later added the "de" to make the name sound more aristocratic). Moreover, the harsh critique of the bourgeois class, apparent throughout *La Comédie humaine*, did not prevent Balzac from entertaining financial ambitions, which he could only fulfill vicariously through the destiny of his characters and, at a symbolic level, in the literary "capital" he accumulated in writing more than ninety novels in addition to other works.

Balzac studied law (in accordance with his father's wishes), but although he obtained his *licence* and served in the offices of a notary and a solicitor, he seemed little inclined to dedicate his life to the legal profession, and chose against the wishes of his family to become a man of letters. From 1820 to 1822, Balzac took refuge in reading and writing, living from hand to mouth in a Parisian garret. During this period, he produced the tragedy *Cromwell*, which reveals already the writer's ambivalence toward the French Revolution, whose effects were deeply felt by the romantic generation as a whole. His early novelistic production—assembled in *Oeuvres de jeunesse*—plays into the popular taste for gothic excitement dominant during the Restoration. Since Balzac's ventures into the world of publishing and printing ended in failure, writing became his main source of financial support and a means of escaping the pressure of his growing debts.

In seeking refuge from his creditors in Britanny, Balzac found the inspiration for his historical novel, *Le Dernier Chouan* (1829), the first work he signed Honoré Balzac. The novel follows Walter Scott in its treatment of history, and earned the praise of **Georg Lukács** in *The Historical Novel*, as did Balzac's work as a whole, which for Lukács epitomized the best realistic fiction in its ability to present society as an interconnected totality and individual characters as the products of larger historical forces. More importantly, in writing about the period of the French Revolution, Balzac discovered his vocation as social historian, and created a method of description and analysis that he later used in his works devoted to contemporary history. While honing his novelistic skills, Balzac was also active as a contributor to journals. His energy seemed to know no bounds. In 1830 alone, he published more than a hundred articles. Some of the articles published in journals, such as *Physiologie du marriage* and *Traité de la vie élégante*, were later included in *La Comédie humaine*. It is also in these articles that Balzac formulated philosophical and political ideas that were later developed in his novels.

During the period of intense work that followed, Balzac found support in the correspondence he entertained with his sister Laure, as well as with a number of older aristocratic ladies: Madame de Berny, the model for Mme de Mortsauf in *Le Lys dans la vallée* (1835); the Marquise de Castries; and finally the Polish-Russian countess Evelina Hanska, whom he married a couple of months before his premature death from overwork and excessive coffee consumption. While living an active social life, Balzac was also building, with a zeal and persistence rarely matched by other writers, the edifice of *La Comédie humaine*. This vast social fresco constitutes, in many ways, a work in progress. Until the end of his life, Balzac continued to add pieces to it and modify others, creating new connections among the parts. The deliberate coherence of the whole, including the title itself, as the result of a "retrospective illumination," as Marcel Proust famously put it.

Starting in 1834, Balzac introduced recurrent characters whose lives were echoed in the new novels he wrote. It is a memorable, seemingly infinite gallery, in which social types come to life with their individual quirks. According to one estimate, there are about four thousand fictional characters that populate this vast work, not mentioning the historical characters that also appear on the stage. Moreover, *La Comédie humaine* is a vast museum or a huge collection of contemporary details and objects, which reconstruct with ethnographic precision the first half of the nineteenth century in France. The total effect of Balzac's work, as gauged by critics like Eric Auerbach or Lukács, is one of intense reality, although Balzac's realism is often colored by strong romantic tones. As Victor Hugo stated in his funeral oration on Balzac's death, it is the combination of "intelligence and imagination" that gives the key to Balzac's creation.

Indeed, Balzac combined, as few writers have ever done, lucid, clinical observation with insight and imaginative verve. In this respect, Balzac was also a product of his times. Like many other writers of his generation, he was influenced by the emerging sciences of biology, physics, and chemistry, as well as by various mystic currents—such as theosophy and illuminism—at a time when the difference between the scientific and nonscientific disciplines was not clearly defined. Balzac's totalizing ambitions made him embrace not only all forms of experience in his novels but also all possible perspectives. Like many of his characters, Balzac was endowed with a tremendous appetite for knowledge fueled by an indomitable will, which often translates into an insatiable desire for power.

In philosophy, Balzac was influenced by the materialist doctrine of La Mettrie, Buffon, and Geoffroy Saint-Hilaire, as much as he was by the spiritualist thought of Leibniz and Malebranche. Although Balzac never produced more than philosophical sketches, philosophical ideas permeate his work well beyond the *Philosophical Studies* included in *La Comédie humaine*. Throughout, he tried to combine a synthetic, organic view of nature with an analytical one. Although the social world described in Balzac's novels is viewed on a naturalist model, which explains the writer's propensity for classifications and "physiologies" inspired by the studies of Gall and Lavater, this fictional world does not lack in complexity and psychological depth.

Politically, Balzac followed the ideological trajectory of his generation, from the liberal tendencies prevalent during the Restoration, to the conservative mindset that dominated the July monarchy. These were, succinctly put, the tendencies of the new bourgeoisie, caught between an attachment for the liberal values put in circulation by the French Revolution and to which it owed its very existence, and a desire for stability in the face of the chaotic forces of change. No one more than Balzac was able to give a comprehensive, objective, as well as sympathetic view of these contradictions.

Selected Bibliography: Auerbach, Eric. *Mimesis: The Representation of Reality in Western Literature.* Trans. Willard R. Trask. Princeton, NJ: Princeton UP, 1953; Guyon, Bernard. *La Pensée politique et sociale de Balzac.* Paris: Armand Colin, 1967; Lukács, Georg. *The Historical Novel.* Trans. Hannah Mitchell and Stanley Mitchell. Lincoln: U of Nebraska P, 1983; Lukács, Georg. *Studies in European Realism: A Sociological Survey of the Writings of Balzac, Stendahl, Tolstoy, Gorky, and Others.* Trans. Edith Bone. New York: Fertig Howard Inc., 2002; Rancière, Jacques. *The Flesh of Words: The Politics of Writing.* Stanford, CA: Stanford UP, 2004; Robb, Graham. *Balzac: A Life.* New York: Norton, 1994.

Alina Clej

BARAKA, AMIRI (1934–).

Born in Newark, New Jersey, to a lower-middle-class family and baptized Everett Leroy Jones, Amiri Baraka first published under the name LeRoi Jones but changed his name in 1968, following his conversion to Islam. An accomplished poet, playwright, essayist, and critic, Baraka is perhaps best known as one of the principle architects of the **black arts movement**. In 1964, he won an Obie award for his play *Dutchman,* and in 2001, he was named the poet laureate of New Jersey. In addition to his literary achievements, Baraka has taught at Yale, Columbia, and the State University of New York at Stony Brook, and he has consistently worked to effect political change at the grassroots level.

Baraka's early career was marked by abrupt shifts in his attitudes and beliefs. He attended Howard University but left without completing a degree. He then served a three-year stint in the U.S. Air Force but was dishonorably discharged for being found in possession of allegedly communist writings. After his discharge in 1957, Baraka settled in Greenwich Village, New York, and established relationships with members of the **beat movement**, writing extensively and cofounding the influential beat literary journal *Yugen*. Interestingly, very little of the work Baraka produced during this period reflected his later interest in black arts.

Baraka's views on African American writing changed radically following a trip to Cuba in 1960. His writing was greatly influenced by the artists of that postrevolutionary country, as well as by the civil rights and black nationalist movements in the United States. At the same time, Baraka immersed himself in the work of jazz musicians who demonstrated ways that black artists could produce avant-garde art rooted in African American cultural traditions. While Baraka became increasingly involved with militant political organizations during the 1960s, it was the assassination of Malcolm X in 1965 that led to his final break with the predominantly white bohemian world. Shortly thereafter, Baraka moved to Harlem, where he founded the Black Arts Repertory Theatre/School (BART/S). Instrumental in the rise of the black arts movement, the BART/S was designed to promote a well-defined black aesthetic, and to provide a blueprint for similar theaters across the country. During that period, Baraka espoused an Afrocentric doctrine of separatism, self-determination, and communal African American cultural and economic self-development. However, in the early 1970s, he began to identify weaknesses in black nationalism, adopting a Marxist ideology, which he felt better addressed the interrelated problems of racism, national oppression, colonialism, and neocolonialism. Though currently retired, Baraka remains controversial as a writer and political activist; most recently, he has come under attack for making allegedly anti-Semitic comments in his post 9/11 poem, "Somebody Blew Up America."

Selected Bibliography: Baraka, Amiri. *The Autobiography of LeRoi Jones/Amiri Baraka*. New York: Freundlich Books, 1984; Baraka, Amiri. *The LeRoi Jones/Amiri Baraka Reader*. Ed. William J. Harris. New York: Thunder's Mouth P, 1991; Sollors, Werner. *Amiri Baraka/LeRoi Jones: The Quest for a "Populist Modernism."* New York: Columbia UP, 1978.

Jeff Solomon

BARKER, PAT (1943–). Pat Barker was born in Thornaby-on-Tees, in the northeast of England. Her father was an officer in the Royal Air Force, but her parents were not married, and Barker was raised by her maternal grandparents. Bright and energetic, Barker went to grammar school and on to the London School of Economics, where she earned a B.S. in 1965. While teaching vocational classes, Barker tried her hand at fiction writing, but she succeeded only in producing some unpublished manuscripts described as "middle class novels of manners." She married David Barker, a professor of zoology, and had two children. Her writing career really took off after she attended a fiction course taught by **Angela Carter**, who encouraged her to explore the working-class milieu of her youth. The result was *Union Street* (1982), a caustic novel of social realism that examined the lives and loves of a group of urban working women mired in the postindustrialism of Thatcherite Britain. Barker showed an immense talent for keenly rendered dialogue and a kind of community consciousness that was both feminist and working class in its political aspirations.

A group of women also feature in Barker's second novel, *Blow Your House Down* (1984), a community this time connected by prostitution and the shadow of a serial killer (the story is loosely based on that of the Yorkshire Ripper from the 1970s).

Harrowing in detail yet deeply evocative of resilience and the power of memory, the novel confirmed Barker's cogent understanding of the minutiae and scarcities of the everyday existence of working-class women. Yet Barker has also proved herself to be a social realist and critic in the broadest sense; her career includes novels that are not especially feminist or working class in their outlook or affiliation. Indeed, if there is a centerpiece to her fiction, it would be the Regeneration trilogy (*Regeneration* [1991], *Eye in the Door* [1993], and *The Ghost Road* [1995], the latter of which won the Booker Prize for fiction that year), which focuses primarily on the psychological effects of trench warfare in **World War I**. While it can certainly be argued that working-class and women's themes animate the trilogy, Barker's main concern is to examine the war as a commentary on the present, in which the violence of recent history renders problematic or unspoken a history of violence. As if to underline the persistence of this theme, Barker's next novel, *Another World* (1998), also tracks the effects of war on the present, although in a comparatively circumspect manner, while *Border Crossing* (2001) considers the psychic edge of violence in the relationship of Danny, previously accused of murdering an old woman, and Tom, a psychologist whose testimony was instrumental in Danny's release. In her tenth novel, *Double Vision* (2003), the effects of violence again lurk tangibly, this time in the tale of a sculptor whose husband, a photographer, is killed in the war in Afghanistan. Indeed, it is clear that exploring the political, psychological, and social effects of violence lies at the heart of Barker's impressive achievements.

Selected Bibliography: Harris, Greg. "Compulsory Masculinity, Britain, and the Great War: The Literary-Historical Work of Pat Barker." *Critique* 39 (Summer 1998): 290–305; Hitchcock, Peter. *Dialogics of the Oppressed.* Minneapolis: U of Minnesota P, 1993; Hitchcock, Peter. "What Is Prior? Working-Class Masculinity in Pat Barker's Trilogy." *Genders* (Online Publisher: www.genders.org). Volume 35 (2002); Kirk, John. "Recovered Perspectives: Gender, Class, and Memory in Pat Barker's Writing." *Contemporary Literature* 40 (Winter 1999): 603–26; Whitehead, Anne. "Open to Suggestion: Hypnosis and History in Pat Barker's *Regeneration*." *Modern Fiction Studies* 44 (Fall 1998): 674–95.

Peter Hitchcock

BARTHES, ROLAND (1915–1980). The most influential literary and cultural critic of his generation, Barthes was also a supreme stylist who crossed freely and prolifically from literature to theater, painting, music, film, and photography. Educated at the Sorbonne (1935–1941), he was troubled throughout his life by illness, including tuberculosis, which initially ended his hopes of a university career, although he ultimately succeeded in attaining the highest academic position in France, a chair at the Collège de France. His critical adventure began with **Marx** and **Brecht**, notably in his theater reviews of the 1950s; and his first major work, *Degree Zero of Writing* (1953), diverged from **Jean-Paul Sartre** to propose a notion of writing (*écriture*) aligned between language and style, which asserted a morality of form over literary genres, as in the case of the nouveau Roman. Barthes's interest in the semiology of Saussure produced his most famous work, *Mythologies* (1957), the first serious (structuralist) analysis of popular culture in France. Here Barthes examines more than fifty instances of contemporary, apparently natural bourgeois myths, notably from advertising, which he demystified with elegance and wit. *On Racine* (1963) was a highly contestatory, psychobiographical study of Racine; *Michelet* (1954) detailed the obsessions of Michelet's historical writing; while *The Fashion System* (1967) extended Barthes's groundbreaking work on the structural analysis of narrative to the study of social phenomena. May 1968 effectively passed him by, and when members of the Tel Quel group—such as Philippe Sollers, whom Barthes championed—went to China to encounter Mao firsthand, Barthes took a detour to Japan to immerse himself in marvelous alien signs (*Empire of Signs* [1970]).

S/Z (1970) marked a watershed in Barthes's critical practice. With the aid of Lacanian psychoanalysis, he broke down a **Balzac** short story into 561 units of meaning in order to make explicit the narrative codes at work in a realist text. This dense, almost musical weave of textual fragments revealed as much about the reader and reading process as it did about the story "Sarrasine." *The Pleasure of the Text* (1973), a series of aphorisms in alphabetical order, promoted important new binaries such as pleasure (*plaisir*) versus bliss (*jouissance*) and both undermined and joyously celebrated the textual. This more personalized and intuitive poststructuralist mode continued with *Roland Barthes* (1975)—an unstable mix of essay, autobiography, and fiction—and *A Lover's Discourse* (1977), which explored directly the critical self or subject and again mixed conventions of genres. Barthes's last published text was a moving study of photography, *Camera Lucida* (1980), which privileged pathos and affect and was essentially a Proustian work of mourning for his recently deceased mother. The critic who had once declared "the death of the Author" had became a true writer, blurring the very distinction between criticism and poetic writing. The posthumously published *Incidents* (1987), which disclosed aspects of his personal gay life, merely confirmed Barthes's long-standing wish to write a novel.

Selected Bibliography: Knight, Diana. *Barthes and Utopia: Space, Travel, Writing.* Oxford: Clarendon P, 1997; Lavers, Annette. *Roland Barthes: Structuralism and After.* Cambridge, MA: Harvard UP, 1982; Moriarty, Michael. *Roland Barthes.* Cambridge: Polity, 1991; Ungar, Steven. *Roland Barthes: The Professor of Desire.* Lincoln: U of Nebraska P, 1983.

James S. Williams

BASE AND SUPERSTRUCTURE. A key Marxist distinction that holds that the economic system is the most fundamental aspect, or "base," of any society, while all other aspects of society (culture, politics, religion, and so on) are parts of an ideological "superstructure," whose properties are to some extent dependent on the nature of the base. However, Marxist analysis of the relationship between the base and the superstructure is generally complex, and Marxist thinkers such as **Fredric Jameson** have even held that in the postmodernist era of late capitalism, so many traditional distinctions break down that the distinction between base and superstructure no longer has meaning. Meanwhile, the field of **post-Marxism** can be virtually defined in terms of its attempts to deconstruct the base-superstructure opposition.

Post-Marxist deconstruction will often focus on the meaning of determination, especially when determination is defined simplistically as reflection or correspondence, as in the political superstructure reflecting or corresponding to the base. Sometimes these metaphors of reflection are interpreted so as to suggest that the base automatically determines the superstructure. Following this line of argument, it might be inferred that once you know the economic base, you can predict the superstructure. But this is clearly false if it is meant to suggest that capitalism—the base here defined as "capitalism in the abstract"—everywhere will produce an identical culture (as one component of superstructure).

These criticisms have been effective in showing how the base is itself contaminated by the superstructure, that the economy is always already political. They have also been good at pointing out the frequent noncorrespondence between working-class interests—defined objectively by one's position in the base—and working-class politics. Marxists have had varying responses. The first—employed by such thinkers as Friedrich Engels and **Louis Althusser**—is to loosen the relation between base and superstructure, invoke concepts like mediation and relative autonomy, and acknowledge mutual determination, or overdetermination, that the superstructure can react back on the base even if the latter is "ultimately determinant."

Another approach is to reject economic determinism and metaphors of simple correspondence, as well as affiliated architectural metaphors of "levels," as if the economy were the basement and the superstructure the upper floors (first you build the foundation, then the rest). This approach acknowledges that mental and material, politics and economics are entangled, codetermining the socioeconomic and political command structure of capital (Meszaros), thus enabling class analysis to explain both structural inequality and the forces that help reproduce it. This version of historical materialism is then at odds with both technological or economic determinism and Althusserian structuralist Marxism, which—via its mode of production/ social-formation distinction—ironically undermines a coherent concept of class structure and opens the door to the view that the ultimate determination of the base, defined as the economy, is in the last instance a metaphysical abstraction.

Such an understanding of class structure, class rule, and class struggle rejects any kind of pluralist analysis of power or reformist analysis of the state. Reproduction of relations functional enough to the ruling classes always takes place in the context of class struggle. Reproduction is *not* guaranteed, which is one reason why reproducing dominant ideology is hard work. Class struggle can render the class structure dysfunctional and threaten its basis, but its basis is the structural domination of capital over labor—not the same as base determining superstructure.

Selected Bibliography: Althusser, Louis, and Etienne Balibar. *Reading Capital.* London: Verso, 1970; Jameson, Fredric. *Postmodernism; or, The Cultural Logic of Late Capitalism.* Durham, NC: Duke UP, 1991; Meszaros, Istvan. *Beyond Capital.* New York: Monthly Review P, 1995; Williams, Raymond. *Marxism and Literature.* Oxford: Oxford UP, 1977; Wood, Ellen Meiksins. *Democracy against Capitalism.* Cambridge: Cambridge UP, 1995.

Gregory Meyerson

BATES, RALPH (1899–2000). Born in Swindon, a railway town in England, Bates was one of a small number of working-class writers active on the literary Left during the 1930s. An indentured fitter, turner, and erector at the Great Western Railway factory, he began writing when attending a reading group run by the archdeacon of North Wiltshire. He first went to Spain in 1923. Haunted by E. H. Spender's *Through the High Pyrenees* (1898), he became a mountain climber in the Pyrenees, and celebrated his experiences in the short stories in *Sierra* (1933). In the late 1920s, he worked as a traveling mechanic and electrician in Spain and became fluent in Castilian and Catalan. Later he worked as a fisherman and in the Barcelona docks. By the early 1930s, he was in London taking part in a literary club with Edward and David Garnett, Stephen Spender, and Storm Jameson. The novel *Lean Men* appeared in 1934, dramatizing the Spanish political activity of an English Communist, Frances Charing, in and after 1930. **Wyndham Lewis** drew on this novel, and on Bates's tough political personality, in his *Revenge for Love* (1937).

Bates was not a Communist Party member, but when the **Spanish Civil War** began in June 1936, he went to Barcelona and became a political commissar with the International Brigades. He made propaganda tours in the United States in 1936–1937 and again in October–November 1937, encouraging many Americans to fight in Spain. In Madrid, he edited and largely wrote the first eight numbers of *The Volunteer for Liberty* (May–July 1937). Throughout, he vigorously supported the Comintern line on the unified people's army, and criticized anarchists and Trotskyists. Lengthy propaganda tours to Mexico followed in 1938, and there are suggestions that Bates was kept away because he knew too much about the political realities of republican Spain. His literary achievement is *The Olive Field* (1936, rev. 1966), which dramatizes Catalan politics, rural life, and the Asturias rising of 1934. The many Spanish stories were collected in *Sirocco* in 1939.

In 1939, the Soviet invasion of Finland put an end to Bates's support for the Communist parties, and his renunciation, "Disaster in Finland," appeared in *New Republic*. Henceforth he worked as a journalist in the United States, notably as staff editorial writer for *The Nation*; from 1947 to 1966, he taught at New York University. After 1966, Bates divided each year between the Greek island of Naxos and New York, where he died at age 100.

Selected Bibliography: Bates, Ralph. "Disaster in Finland." *New Republic*, 13 December 1939: 221–25; Munton, Alan. "Ralph Bates." Obituary. *Independent*, 7 December 2000, sec. 2: 6; Munton, Alan. "Ralph Bates." *Seven Writers of the English Left: A Bibliography of Literature and Politics, 1916–1980*. Ed. Alan Munton and Alan Young. New York: Garland, 1981. 83–115.

Alan Munton

BAUDRILLARD, JEAN (1929–). The son of civil servants and the grandson of peasant farmers, Baudrillard has gone on to become a leading French intellectual of his era. Though he was trained as a Germanist and translated German literary works, including ones by **Bertolt Brecht** and **Peter Weiss**, he has not really engaged in literary criticism or theorized literature as a specific cultural form. Baudrillard became renowned for his theorizations of developments in contemporary society—including development of the consumer society, media and technology, cyberspace and the information society, and biotechnology—that he claimed had produced a postmodern rupture with modern culture and society. While modern societies for Baudrillard were organized around production and political economy, postmodern societies were organized around technology and generated new forms of culture, experience, and subjectivities. He is perhaps best known for his vision of the "hyperreality" of the postmodern world, in which all is simulation, and reality in the conventional sense no longer exists.

Baudrillard's own work is highly literary and, especially since the 1980s, he has produced an increasingly literary mode of thought and writing. He frequently cites his favorite writers, and in his earlier works, Georges Bataille was a privileged source (though Baudrillard appeared to be more influenced by Bataille's theoretical writings than his literary ones). During his postmodern period, there were frequent references to Jorge Luis Borges, J. G. Ballard, **Philip K. Dick**, and **science fiction** as a genre. For Baudrillard, the world was becoming increasingly fictionalized and the great science-fiction writers anticipated the radical changes brought about by science and technology. Borges developed a genre of creating alternative literary worlds that Baudrillard adapted to present the alterability and novelty of the contemporary world.

In *Fatal Strategies* and succeeding writings, Baudrillard seems to be taking theory into the realm of metaphysics, but it is a specific type of metaphysics, deeply inspired by the pataphysics developed by Alfred Jarry, as "the science of the realm beyond metaphysics. . . . It will study the laws which govern exceptions and will explain the universe supplementary to this one; or, less ambitiously, it will describe a universe which one can see—must see perhaps—instead of the traditional one" (Jarry 131).

Like the universe in Jarry's *Ubu Roi, The Gestures and Opinions of Doctor Faustroll*, and other literary texts—as well as in Jarry's more theoretical explications of pataphysics—Baudrillard's is a totally absurd universe where objects rule in mysterious ways, and people and events are governed by absurd and ultimately unknowable interconnections and predestination. (The French playwright Eugene Ionesco is another good source of entry to this universe.) Like Jarry's pataphysics, Baudrillard's universe is ruled by surprise, reversal, hallucination, blasphemy, obscenity, and a desire to shock and outrage.

In his increasingly literary and philosophical writings from the 1980s to the present, Baudrillard develops what he terms "theory fiction," or what he also calls "simulation theory" and "anticipatory theory." Such theory intends to simulate, grasp, and anticipate historical events that he believes are continually outstripping all contemporary theory. The current situation, he claims, is more fantastic than the most fanciful science fiction or theoretical projections of a futurist society. Thus, theory can only attempt to grasp the present on the run and try to anticipate the future.

While in his earlier work, Baudrillard identified with the revolutionary left and supported the May 1968 student movement in France, he became increasingly nihilistic and apolitical in his later work. This post-1980s work arguably exaggerates the break between the modern and the postmodern, takes future possibilities as existing realities, and provides a futuristic perspective on the present, much like the tradition of dystopic science fiction, ranging from **Aldous Huxley** to cyberpunk. Baudrillard's later work can thus be read as science fiction that anticipates the future by exaggerating present tendencies, and provides early warnings about what might happen if present trends continue.

Selected Bibliography: Baudrillard, Jean. *America*. Trans. Chris Turner. London: Verso, 1988; Baudrillard, Jean. *Cool Memories*. Trans. Chris Turner. London: Verso, 1987; Baudrillard, Jean. *Fatal Strategies*. Trans. Philip Beitchman and W.G.J. Niesluchowski. Ed. Jim Fleming. New York: Semiotext(e), 1990; Baudrillard, Jean. *In the Shadow of the Silent Majorities; or, The End of the Social, and Other Es-*

says. Trans. Paul Foss, John Johnston, and Paul Patton. New York: Semiotext(e), 1983; Baudrillard, Jean. *Simulations.* Trans. Paul Foss, Paul Patton, and Philip Beitchman. New York: Semiotext(e), 1983; Kellner, Douglas. *Jean Baudrillard: From Marxism to Postmodernism and Beyond.* Stanford, CA: Stanford UP, 1989; Kellner, Douglas, ed. *Baudrillard: A Critical Reader.* Oxford: Blackwell, 1994.

Douglas Kellner

BEAT MOVEMENT (1944–1960). In "This is the Beat Generation," John Clellon Holmes describes, a generation of young people emerging from the Depression and **World War II** into a duck-and-cover, **cold war** world, becoming thoroughly routinized and ordered according to corporate interests. Holmes finds this generation all too willing to either lose themselves in giant corporations or drop out of organized society altogether. They were "beat," which Holmes defines as "more than mere weariness . . . the feeling of having been used, of being raw . . . a feeling of being reduced to the bedrock of consciousness" (SM10). Many of the writers and artists of this generation found established culture—its aesthetics, politics, spirituality, and general consciousness—profoundly stifling and sought escape from the modern world, from prefabricated futures and state-sanctioned cultural production.

Yet while many may have felt "beat," the "beat generation," as a label, is usually reserved for **Allen Ginsberg**, William Burroughs (*Junky* [1953], *Naked Lunch* [1959]), Jack Kerouac, Gregory Corso (*Gasoline* [1958], *The Happy Birthday of Death* [1960]), and their 1940s and early 1950s network of inspirational friends and traveling companions. Ginsberg's October 1955 reading of the poem "Howl" at San Francisco's Six Gallery and the obscenity trial following the poem's publication connected the writers and artists with "beat" young people worldwide, and for a few, brief years, the Beats and the writers and artists of the San Francisco Renaissance (e.g., Kenneth Rexroth, Michael McClure, and Robert Duncan) were national news.

The beats advocated spontaneity, and an honest and open connection, in both form and content, between everyday experience and art (often becoming confessional), which clashed with 1950s paranoia, especially when the everyday experience involved homosexuality. Libertarian might best describe their politics. Although most beat generation–associated writers had read their Marx and recognized the "Moloch" in laissez-faire capitalism, **Stalin** gave reason to doubt Socialism as the path to a new consciousness. Kerouac and others espoused rugged individualism and reclusiveness, while others (Gary Snyder, Philip Whalen, Ginsberg) embraced or experimented with various forms of Buddhism. For many, drug use was a necessary part of the creative process and the search for an enlightened consciousness. While the beat generation was predominantly a white male phenomenon, connections to the female experience (**Denise Levertov**, Ruth Weiss) and black experience (**LeRoi Jones**, Bob Kaufman) existed.

Ginsberg's homoerotic poetry, Burroughs' chronicles of drug experimentation, and Kerouac's tales of surviving outside wage slavery sent a shock wave through the middle class and helped to establish the West Coast as a liberal, antiestablishment sanctuary, but by the end of 1957, what started as mutual recognition of a shared condition and a sharing of ideas had become a competition of ideas, and the movement began to dissolve. By the late 1950s, conservatives had written the movement off as a refuge for slothful and ungrateful Americans or a phase for rebellious youth. Yet the beats were instrumental in the sea change of U.S. culture's self-regard, from 1950s optimism to 1960s skepticism, though the mechanism is indirect and complex, and owes much to the civil rights movement. Despite its clash with conservatism, the beat lifestyle was perhaps the first national youth movement to be co-opted by the interests of business—a move that set the stage for the culture industry's dominance in subsequent U.S. cultural production. Perhaps most importantly, the liberal shock of the beat generation was foundational to 1960s counterculture and the antiwar movement.

Selected Bibliography: Foster, Edward Halsey. *Understanding the Beats.* Columbia, SC: U of South Carolina P, 1992; George, Paul S. "Beat Politics: New Left and Hippie Beginnings in the Postwar Counterculture." *Cultural Politics: Radical Movements in Modern History.* Ed. Jerold M. Starr. New York: Praeger, 1985; Holmes, John Clellon. "This Is the Beat Generation." *New York Times Magazine*, 16 November 1952: SM 10–13; O'Neil, Paul. "The Only Rebellion Around." *Life* 47 (November 1959): 115–30; Podhoretz, Norman. "The Know-Nothing Bohemians." *Partisan Review* 25 (Spring 1958): 305–18; Watson, Steven. *The Birth of the Beat Generation.* New York: Pantheon, 1995.

David Leaton

DE BEAUVOIR, SIMONE ERNESTINE LUCIE MARIE BERTRAND (1908–1986).

French author, philosopher, and political activist Simone de Beauvoir was born in Montparnasse to a bourgeois family. Although Simone's early childhood could be said to be typical of her milieu, the relative impoverishment of her family would later force them to allow her to pursue her education in preparation for a teaching career. While studying at the Sorbonne, Beauvoir met **Jean-Paul Sartre**, with whom she was to enjoy the most important relationship of her adult life. Neither partner wished this relationship to be an exclusive one, but it was a strong and enduring bond that influenced the thinking and writing of each in fundamental ways. After teaching philosophy in Marseilles, Rouen, and Paris, Beauvoir published her first novel, *She Came to Stay* (*L'Invitée*, 1943). This work was heavily influenced by existentialist thought, of which she and Sartre were to remain leading exponents, and also constituted a fictionalized version of the sexual dynamics of the trio formed by Beauvoir, Sartre, and one of her ex-students Olga Kosakievicz. Beauvoir's second novel, *The Blood of Others* (*Le Sang des autres*, 1945) is concerned with the political issues raised by the occupation of France during **World War II**. Beauvoir then joined *Les Temps modernes*, an influential journal founded in 1945 by Sartre, Maurice Merleau-Ponty, and their circle of friends; she would remain on the journal's editorial board throughout the rest of her life. The following year her third novel, *All Men Are Mortal* (*Tous les hommes sont mortels*, 1946), was published. In this work, Beauvoir continues to explore existentialist issues through the character of Fosca, an immortal who gives an account of his life from the thirteenth century on. Although this work is often bleak in tone, it emphasizes the familiar existentialist values of individual freedom and responsibility while eschewing moral absolutes.

The year 1946 marked a new stage in Beauvoir's life as she began working on *The Second Sex* (*Le Deuxième Sexe,* 1949); soon afterward, she embarked on a lecture tour of the United States, where she met the American author **Nelson Algren**, with whom she began a passionate affair. Like Sartre, Algren would help feed Beauvoir's intellectual curiosity; this influence is manifested in *America Day by Day* (*L'Amérique au jour le jour,* 1948), an account of her first encounter with the United States. On its publication, *The Second Sex,* a trenchant analysis of patriarchy, invited women to achieve self-determination by resisting the molding of family, church, and society; its success made Beauvoir the subject of criticism and adulation on both sides of the Atlantic. Her fame was further enhanced by the publication of the critically acclaimed *The Mandarins* (*Les Mandarins,* 1954). This roman à clef explores the growing conflict between Communism and capitalism as experienced by Western intellectuals. This work was awarded the Prix Goncourt, which contributed greatly to her reputation as an author in her own right in spite of her close association with Sartre. Its success also gave Beauvoir financial security for the first time, and so she was able to buy the small apartment in Montparnasse in which she would live for the rest of her life. In the 1950s, Beauvoir and Sartre were invited to visit the People's Republic of China as the guests of the government. This led to her writing *The Long March* (*La Longue Marche,* 1957), in which she returns to the social and political themes of *The Mandarins,* but with a more pronounced communist inflection to her writing; as a result, she was accused of political naivete. On the other hand, her stand against colonialism and more specifically against the war in Algeria would remain relevant for years to come.

After the success of *The Second Sex* and *The Mandarins,* Beauvoir's writing becomes more markedly introspective, as she begins to shape an image of herself intended for posterity. The first volume of her autobiography, *Memoirs of a Dutiful Daughter* (*Mémoires d'une jeune fille rangée,* 1958), imaginatively retraces her childhood and adolescence in order to present herself as the future author of *The Second Sex* from the earliest age. *The Prime of Life* (*La Force de l'âge,* 1960), *The Force of Circumstance* (*La Force des choses,* 1963), and *All Said and Done* (*Tout compte fait,* 1972) continue her life story from early adulthood; given the fact that political commitment was part of this life story, these texts also provide a compelling portrayal of the French nation in the twentieth century. In response to the death of her mother in 1963, Beauvoir wrote the short, poignant text *A Very Easy Death* (*Une Mort très douce,* 1963), in which the mother's life and her relationship to Beauvoir are reevaluated in a relatively sympathetic way; this creates a marked contrast with the portrait provided by *Memoirs of a Dutiful Daughter.* Subsequently, Beauvoir returns to works of fiction, publishing *Les Belles Images,* 1966, and *The Woman Destroyed* (*La Femme rompue,* 1968). Here she revisits topics dear to her as she denounces the French bourgeoisie and depicts the plight of women in patriarchal society and specifically within the family unit.

During the political and social upheaval of May 1968 and its aftermath, Beauvoir became further involved in feminist issues as she campaigned with the Mouvement de Libération des Femmes for the right to abortion. She then turned her attention to the plight of the elderly in *Old Age* (*La Vieillesse,* 1970). Her political activities and her work with Sartre continued until he died in 1980; on account of his deteriorating health, he was increasingly dependent on Beauvoir during this period, for both the comfort of his everyday existence and the continuation of his writing. Shortly after his death, she published *Adieux: A Farewell to Sartre* (*La Cérémonie des adieux suivie d'entretiens avec Jean-Paul Sartre*, 1981) to deal with the vacuum his death had left; at the same time, the work represents a continuation of her concern with the problems afflicting the elderly in the West. De Beauvoir died on April 14, 1986, and was buried with Sartre in the Montparnasse cemetery not far from her home.

Selected Bibliography: Bair, Deirdre. *Simone de Beauvoir: A Biography.* New York: Simon and Schuster, 1990; Fallaize, Elizabeth, ed. *Simone de Beauvoir: A Critical Reader.* New York: Routledge, 1998; Moi, Toril. *Simone de Beauvoir: The Making of an Intellectual Woman.* Oxford: Blackwell, 1994; Simons, Margaret. *Beauvoir and "The Second Sex": Feminism, Race, and the Origins of Existentialism.* Lanham, MD: Rowman and Littlefield, 1999.

Ana de Medeiros

BECKETT, SAMUEL (1906–1989). Beckett, best known for his plays *Waiting for Godot* (1953), *Endgame* (1957), *Happy Days* (1961), and *Krapp's Last Tape* (1958), and highly regarded for his French trilogy of experimental novels, *Molloy* (1951), *Malone Dies* (1951), and *The Unnamable* (1953), has by and large been understood as a philosophical playwright whose characters and situations are divorced from the mundane political concerns of the real world. This view, evolving largely from Martin Esslin's categorization of Beckett among the absurdists, argues that Beckett's writing in general, and his plays in particular, attempt to revise liberal humanist notions of identity and agency along lines similar to the investigations of such existentialist philosophers as Albert Camus and **Jean-Paul Sartre.** As a result, the standard view of Beckett's work is that it concerns itself primarily with the philosophy of individual identity, which it explores in a vacuum. Indeed, the barren landscapes and confined spaces in which Beckett's character's frequently find themselves invite comparison to Sartre's plays of self-recognition, *The Flies* (1943) and *No Exit* (1944). However, as early as **Theodor W. Adorno**'s essay "Trying to Understand *Endgame*" (1961) and in line with the negative dialectics propounded in Adorno's many works of political, social, and aesthetic criticism, Beckett's works began to be understood—though not yet widely recognized—as confrontational in their political implications. Both in his early, full-length plays and in his later, short plays—including *Catastrophe* (1983; dedicated to then-political prisoner **Vaclav Havel**), *Rockaby* (1981), and *What Where* (1983)—the notion of the individual as a legible political unit comes under sustained attack. *Endgame* and *Godot*, for instance, in putting on display various individuals' failed searches for unproblematically unified identities, seem to posit a profoundly communitarian, and hence politicized, mode of identity construction. *Krapp*, *Rockaby*, and Beckett's film *Film* (1963), focusing as they do on characters alone in their quest for self-understanding, nevertheless implicate literal and metaphorical mechanisms of domination as essential to, and yet preventive of, that understanding. Frequently, as in *Rockaby* and *Play* (1963), the very mechanism of theatrical production—including rehearsal strategies, lighting, and sound cues—becomes the object of inquiry, implying as it often does the wider social mechanisms to which characters' self-identification must conform. As a result, Beckett's drama lays bare the structures of late-capitalist self-fashioning and, thereby, demystifies the myth of autonomous individual agency and the social and political ideologies of guilt and personal responsibility that rely on such a myth.

Selected Bibliography: Birkett, Jennifer, ed. *Samuel Beckett.* New York: Longman, 1999; Brater, Enoch, ed. *Around the Absurd.* Ann Arbor: U of Michigan P, 1990; Burkman, Katherine H., ed. *Myth and Ritual in the Plays of Samuel Beckett.* Madison: Fairleigh Dickinson UP, 1987; Esslin, Martin. *The Theatre of the Absurd.* 3rd ed. New York: Vintage-Random House, 2004; Knowlson, James. *Damned to Fame: The Life of Samuel Beckett.* New York: Simon and Schuster, 1996.

Craig N. Owens

THE BEGGAR'S OPERA (1728), a ballad opera by John Gay that set the standard for a new kind of drama on the English stage. *The Beggar's Opera* engages in politics on two distinct fronts. Insistently English, it challenges the snobbishly fashionable taste for Italian opera fostered by the German Handel and the equally German royal family. In addition, it engages in party politics by its allegorical linking of Robert Walpole's Whig government with London's underworld of organized crime. Gay (1685–1732) was probably the least disaffected, and certainly the most affable, member of the Tory Scriblerus Club, whose satirical impulse was more fully expressed by **Jonathan Swift** and Alexander Pope. *The Beggar's Opera* had its likely origin in Swift's suggestion to Pope that Gay should write "a Newgate pastoral among the whores and thieves there." The central political joke of the piece is in the association of greatness with criminality. Walpole, the great man who had rescued the British economy after the disastrous bursting of the South Sea Bubble (1720), is doubly represented by the back-room criminal mastermind Peachum and the highwayman Macheath, who carries Peachum's boldest schemes into action. The systematized corruption through which Walpole maintained his power base was a regular theme in the work of Tory writers in the years following the runaway success of *The Beggar's Opera*, which was performed an unprecedented sixty-two times (nine performances signaled a theatrical hit) in its first season at the playhouse in Lincoln's Inn Fields.

Scholars have disputed Gay's political commitment in *The Beggar's Opera*, arguing that his greater concern was with the invention of a popular form of musical comedy; it is true that through his fitting of new words to sixty-nine variously familiar and popular tunes, Gay ensured that good humor would be the pervading tone of his unoperatic opera. Walpole was shrewd enough to laugh with the rest of the audience, knowing that he would look silly if he seemed to take it seriously. However, his hand is almost certainly present in the subsequent banning of Gay's sequel, *Polly*, which would otherwise have been performed at the same playhouse in 1729. By then, political commentators had intervened to point up the satirical import of *The Beggar's Opera*, and the London stage was exhibiting a dangerous taste for imitative ballad operas. Exactly two centuries later, **Bertolt Brecht**, Elisabeth Hauptmann, and Kurt Weill would combine to update Gay's seminal work, applying it directly to the dog-eat-dog capitalism of the German Weimar Republic. *The Threepenny Opera* (1928) reincarnated *The Beggar's Opera*, with its political fangs exposed—and was applauded by the very audiences whose values it satirized.

Selected Bibliography: McIntosh, William A. "Handel, Walpole and Gay: The Aims of *The Beggar's Opera*." *Eighteenth Century Studies* 7 (1974): 415–33; Noble, Yvonne, ed. *Twentieth-Century Interpretations of "The Beggar's Opera."* Englewood Cliffs, NJ: Prentice-Hall, 1975; Nokes, David. *John Gay: A Profession of Friendship.* New York: Oxford UP, 1995; Salmon, Richard J. "Two Operas for Beggars: A Political Reading." *Theoria* 57 (1981): 63–81; Winton, Calhoun. *John Gay and the London Theatre.* Lexington: UP of Kentucky, 1993.

Peter Thomson

BEI DAO (1949–). In China, the relationship between literature and politics has been of central significance from the earliest written records to the present day. Traditionally, literary subject matter ranges far and wide, but the concept of literature is fundamentally situated in a sociopolitical framework. Early in the twentieth century, advocates of modernization mobilized literature to effect social change, and the politicization of literature grew ever more acute, following domestic and international conflict. After the People's Republic of China (PRC) was founded in 1949, the **Mao**ist view of literature as explicitly subordinate to politics shaped the face of the first three decades, when the literary field was entirely controlled by the state.

During the Cultural Revolution (1966–1976), official literature became sheer propaganda. Simultaneously, young poets created an underground circuit of poetry characterized by obscure imagery and flaunting the rules of **socialist realism**. Foremost among them was Bei Dao, editor-in-chief of the privately published journal *Today (Jintian)*, which took underground poetry aboveground in 1978, when the political climate became less oppressive. *Today* was closed down by the police in 1980, but it had been a watershed, auguring emancipation and pluriformity in PRC literature. Bei Dao's poetry became hugely popular, notwithstanding a publication ban in 1983–1984, during the government campaign to eradicate spiritual pollution. His work appeared in official journals, collective anthologies, and his own collection *Poetry by Bei Dao (Bei Dao shixuan,* 1986), with English translations in *Notes from the City of the Sun* (1983) and *The August Sleepwalker* (1988). In the late 1980s, his poetry was invoked by students demonstrating against government corruption and for democracy. While some of his work carries clear ideological overtones, he never aspired to be a dissident poet in the political sense. Chinese student demonstrators are one example of the forces portraying him as such; Western media are another.

Bei Dao is the best-known modern Chinese poet. His foreign audiences gained in importance when the suppression of the 1989 Tiananmen Square protest movement made it impossible for him to return home from a trip abroad. He lived in several European countries and revived *Today* in exile before settling in the United States. When he attempted to reenter China in 1994, the authorities at Beijing Airport summarily deported him. Banned in his native land since 1989, his work continued to appear in Hong Kong and Taiwan. Translations include the bilingual collections *Old Snow* (1991), *Forms of Distance* (1994), *Landscape over Zero* (1996), and *Unlock* (2000). In China, 2003 finally saw the publication of *Bei Dao's Poetry (Bei Dao shige ji)*, a slightly censored but representative survey of his oeuvre, and of new scholarship on his work.

The poetic voice in Bei Dao's earliest work is influenced by the politico-literary establishment he resists. A subsequent personal turn has been variously interpreted as de-politicization and indirect re-politicization, the latter reading claiming that under totalitarianism, to turn away from politics is a political act. Even if in his later work politics feature in occasional, concrete traces—images of the nation, tanks, books burned, exile, borderlines, speaking Chinese to the mirror—it would be inaccurate to call him a political poet *per se*. Rather, themes such as exile and the experience of repression naturally find a place in his original, individual art. The politicization of Bei Dao and his writings ultimately stems from the power Chinese governments have ascribed to literature through the ages.

Selected Bibliography: Li, David Leiwei. *Imagining the Nation: Asian American Literature and Cultural Consent.* Stanford, CA: Stanford UP, 1998; McDougall, Bonnie S. "Bei Dao's Poetry: Revelation and Communication." *Modern Chinese Literature* 1.2 (1985): 225–52; van Crevel, Maghiel. "Underground Poetry in the 1960s and 1970s." *Modern Chinese Literature* 9.2 (1996): 169–219.

Maghiel van Crevel

BELOVED (1987), Toni Morrison's fifth novel, won the Pulitzer Prize in 1988. The novel is set in Cincinnati during Reconstruction. However, flashbacks during the complex nonlinear narrative are set during the past at Sweet Home, a slaveholding plantation in Kentucky. Via the flashbacks, we learn of the character Sethe's flight from slavery for Ohio, where her three young, recently escaped children await. During the trek, Sethe gives birth to a fourth child, Denver, and the crux of the narrative occurs a month after their arrival: with slave hunters on their way to send mother and children back to slavery, Sethe attempts to kill her children rather than see them enslaved. She succeeds in killing only the two-year-old girl before she is apprehended.

This past literally haunts Sethe in the form of the dead girl's ghost. When Paul D, who was also a Sweet Home slave, unexpectedly arrives at Sethe's home, he drives away the ghost, allowing Paul D and Sethe to embrace the prospect of a future together, along with Denver. However, freedom from the past proves temporary. An eighteen-year-old woman appears at their door, apparently the grown-up reincarnation of the dead daughter. The newcomer, called Beloved, drives away Paul D.

Beloved is based on the real-life story of slave Margaret Garner. In 1856, Garner escaped a Kentucky farm and began a life of freedom in Cincinnati. She was captured but not before she cut her daughter's throat to free her from the horrors of slavery. The slave-narrative tradition also fits into a discussion of *Beloved*'s relationship to history. In addition to dedicating the novel to those Africans who died during the passage to slavery in America, who never had the opportunity to tell their stories, Morrison says her fiction writing can be described as an attempt to "fill in the blanks that the slave narratives left" (113).

In filling in those blanks, particularly regarding the experiences of black women during and after slavery, the novel explores how memory operates in a community's and an individual's relationships to the past. Just as Sethe needs to both remember and forget her murderous act of love, the community needs to address its responsibility. The community failed to warn Sethe of the approaching slave hunters, and it is the community that Sethe now needs to exorcize the ghost, whose presence is killing her. It is in confronting a flesh-and-blood reminder of the past, Beloved, that the community unites. Paul D returns, fittingly telling Sethe, "we got more yesterday than anybody. We need some kind of tomorrow" (273).

Selected Bibliography: Gates, Henry Louis, Jr., and K. A. Appiah, eds. *Toni Morrison: Critical Perspectives Past and Present.* New York: Amistad, 1993; Henderson, Mae G. "Toni Morrison's *Beloved*: Re-Membering the Body as Historical Text." *Comparative American Identities: Race, Sex, and Nationality in the Modern Text.* Ed. Hortense J. Spillers. New York: Routledge, 1991. 62–86; Morrison, Toni. "Site of Memory." *Inventing the Truth: The Art and Craft of Memoir.* Rev. ed. Ed. William Zinsser. Boston: Houghton Mifflin, 1998. 183–200; Rushdy, Ashraf. "Daughters Signifyin(g) History: The Example of Toni Morrison's *Beloved.*" *American Literature* 64.3 (1992): 567–97.

Lori Bailey

BELY, ANDREI (1880–1934). The son of a prominent Russian mathematician, Bely emerged at the beginning of the twentieth century as one of Russia's most innovative writers, celebrated for his symbolist prose and poetry written in the tumultuous years surrounding the 1917 **Russian Revolution.** Born Boris Bugaev, he adopted the pseudonym Andrei Bely in 1902 so as not to jeopardize his father's academic and social standing with his "decadent" verse, and its overt challenge to more traditional, established Russian culture. Bely graduated from Moscow University in 1903 with a degree in the natural sciences, but literature constituted his primary interest, as he quickly developed his distinctive artistic voice in the chaotic environment of *fin de siècle* Tsarist Russia.

Belonging to a generation of Russian symbolist poets who perceived revolution as a salutary, transformative force, Bely introduced avant-garde images and themes of apocalyptic change in both his verse and his prose. Yet doubts about symbolism's mystical and revolutionary potential increasingly plagued Bely, as shown, for example, in his *Second Symphony* (*Vtoraia simfoniia*, 1902), an experimental prose work in which characters routinely mistake mundane occurrences for momentous events. This skepticism intensified in the ensuing years; *The Silver Dove* (*Serebriannyi golub'*, 1910), Bely's most overtly political novel, parodies the ideals of Russian intellectuals traveling to the countryside to improve the plight of the peasantry. An ambiguous perspective on Russian idealistic fervor also characterizes Bely's masterpiece *Petersburg* (*Peterburg*, 1916–1921), labeled one of the twentieth century's four greatest novels by **Vladimir Nabokov.** A modernist synthesis of earlier Russian literary visions of this famous northern city, *Petersburg* highlights the rebellious, nationalistic turmoil of 1905 in the former Russian capital through a fragmented plot line in which the protagonist Nikolai Ableukhov, a young revolutionary, is pressured to assassinate his father Apollon, a high-ranking government official. Informed by Bely's interest in anthroposophy (the theory of cosmic evolution), *Petersburg* both celebrates and scorns the possibility of a social and political revolution within the phantasmagoric sphere of the Russian city.

When the Russian Revolution occurred in 1917, Bely discerned apocalyptic signs in the violent, sweeping events. In his 1918 essay "Christ Has Risen" (*Khristos voskres*), Bely expressed his hopes for spiritual apotheosis in Russia, yet by 1921 he had grown disillusioned with the new government, leaving soon afterwards for Western Europe. In 1923, Bely returned to Soviet Russia, yet henceforth he generally avoided close involvement in politics, devoting most of his energies to literature, including the novel cycle *Moscow* (*Moskva*, 1926–1932). Although Bely's legacy was to be more stylistic than ideological, his works encapsulated the ambivalence of modern Russian writers toward the era's chaotic political developments.

Selected Bibliography: Alexandrov, Vladimir E. *Andrei Bely: The Major Symbolist Fiction*. Cambridge, MA: Harvard UP, 1985; Cioran, Samuel. *The Apocalyptic Symbolism of Andrej Belyj*. The Hague: Mouton, 1973; Keys, Roger. *The Reluctant Modernist: Andrei Bely and the Development of Russian Fiction, 1902–1914*. New York: Oxford UP, 1996; Malmstad, John E., ed. *Andrey Bely: The Spirit of Symbolism*. Ithaca, NY: Cornell UP, 1987.

Timothy Harte

A BEND IN THE RIVER **(1979).** V. S. Naipaul's *A Bend in the River* is set in Africa, but the country remains unnamed. As events unfold, however, it becomes unmistakably clear that the novel is set in Zaire—renamed the Democratic Republic of Congo a few years ago—under the rule of Mobutu Sese Seko in the late sixties and early seventies. Ruled by a power-mad dictator, Zaire/Congo experienced great political strife at that time.

While it is customary to view Naipaul's characters as unhinged individuals struggling to survive in a fragmented world, few other of his novels depict characters as rootless as those in *Bend*. Salim, the novel's protagonist of Indo-Arab origin, relocates in a central African country from the continent's east coast in search of business prospects. Initially he does well, but tribal upheavals often leading to violence soon erupt in the quiet town. He loses his business to a nationalist drive aimed at stripping non-Africans like him to reward Africans with political connections. He is put in jail when his family servant, Metty, informs the authorities of his illegal ivory smuggling, a dealing Salim got involved in out of desperation. He is then rescued by another African, Ferdinand, whose education he has financed. Ferdinand helps Salim escape from the country under the grip of feverish jingoism. As Salim departs on a steamboat, a barge it has been carrying breaks loose when young soldiers try to force the vessel to return to the dock. The attempt fails, leaving the barge adrift in the dark night; pathetically, it remains unaware of its lost state. This is Naipaul's symbol to convey Africa's failure to comprehend and accommodate modernity.

Curiously, Naipaul links the issue with what seems to be Africa's potential for some variety of social Darwinism. "The world is what it is; men who are nothing, who allow themselves to become nothing, have no place in it." These are the novel's opening words. Toward its close, when Metty, who turned in Salim out of a feeling of neglect rather than malice, wants to accompany him on his final departure, he tells Metty, "You have to take your chance. That's what we've always done. Everybody has done that here." Salim gives him his car and condo, but Metty remains unsure of his future. He is, in fact, frightened of his own safety because he is not native to that region of Africa. Besides, he can read and write and has worn jackets, abilities the new political movement treats with deep suspicion.

A Bend in the River is powerfully written, but its tone is one of unrelieved gloom. The novel is heavily stamped with the author's monologic point of view. Both the nation and the individuals fare extremely poorly in this treatment of a decolonized third-world country. There are many references to the despotism of the Big Man (Mobutu); clearly, Naipaul attributes the country's failure of nationalism to the failed political system put in place by the Big Man. However, nowhere does Naipaul refer to the outside forces behind the Big Man. Naipaul's representation of Africans is equally troublesome. Chinua Achebe sums up the work best. Referring to *Bend*, he observes, "Although he [Naipaul] was writing about Africa, he was not writing about Africans."

Selected Bibliography: Cudjoe, Selwyn. *V. S. Naipaul: A Materialist Reading.* Amherst: U of Massachusetts P, 1988; Feder, Lillian. *Naipaul's Truth: The Making of a Writer.* New York: Rowman and Littlefield, 2001; Prescott, Lynda. "Past and Present Darkness: Sources for V. S. Naipaul's *A Bend in the River.*" *Modern Fiction Studies* 30.3 (1984): 547–59; Weiss, Timothy. *On the Margins: The Art of Exile in V. S. Naipaul.* Amherst: U of Massachusetts P, 1992; Wise, Christopher. "The Garden Trampled: The Liquidation of African Culture in V. S. Naipaul's *A Bend in the River.*" *College Literature* 23 (October 1996): 58–72.

Farhad B. Idris

BENJAMIN, WALTER (1892–1940). From his doctoral thesis, "The Origin of German Tragic Drama" (1925), to his last major essay, "On the Concept of History," written in the spring of 1940 as the German army was sweeping across Europe, Benjamin's thought exudes a deep sense of melancholy. His brief but successful career as a literary critic in Weimar Germany was cut abruptly by the rise to power of the Third Reich. Like many other Jewish-German intellectuals and left-wing thinkers, Benjamin was forced into exile. He settled in Paris, where he led a reclusive and precarious existence, spending most of his time in the Bibliothèque nationale, collecting and classifying materials for his magnum opus, the *Arcades Project* (*Das Passagen-Werk*). Trying to flee occupied France by crossing the Franco-Spanish border on foot, Benjamin was overcome by fatigue and despair, and took his own life during the night of September 25, 1940. The papers that he left behind were burned so that the Gestapo would not get hold of them. Nobody knows for sure what manuscripts, if any, were lost in the process.

Benjamin was a unique thinker, never entirely committed to either Marxism or Zionism as he wove the singular conception of culture and history that comes across in his essays. Benjamin never developed his thought into a coherent system, nor did he firmly belong to a literary group or circle, although he had strong affinities with **surrealism** and intellectual ties with the **Frankfurt School**. He clearly preferred **Bertolt Brecht**'s "crude thinking" to **Theodor Adorno**'s or Gershom Scholem's philosophical rigor. Briefly put, Benjamin defined a style of thought much more than a philosophical method. His writings continue to attract critics and theorists around the world, perhaps because the aphoristic, paradoxical, and unsystematic quality of his thought appeals to a postmodern age that has seen the "end of ideologies."

Benjamin's political reticence and ideological wavering may be easier to understand by taking into account the social and historical context of Central Europe before

World War II. Like so many other intellectuals coming from assimilated Jewish families, Benjamin was torn between the social and cultural advantages of integration and the spiritual appeal of the Jewish tradition. He had to continue to write in German to achieve recognition as a literary critic, but he could not forego the rich sources of his Jewish heritage, which contributed to the originality of his thinking. To understand modernity, Benjamin had to come to Paris, "Capital of the Nineteenth Century" and world center of the surrealist movement. As Benjamin argued in his essay entitled "Surrealism: The Last Snapshot of the European Intelligentsia" (1929), surrealism presented the last opportunity to effect the intellectual change that would pull the world back from the brink.

Benjamin felt that surrealism contained energies that might help destroy the stultifying power of bourgeois ideology and revolutionize humdrum modes of perception and behavior. Meanwhile, for a brief period Benjamin also set his hopes for social renewal on the promise offered by the Soviet Union, which led him to undertake a trip to Moscow in December 1926. Benjamin chose to write his later famous essay, "The Work of Art in the Age of Mechanical Reproduction" (1936, included in the volume *Illuminations*), for the German edition of the Moscow Journal *International Literature*, only to find it rejected. Benjamin's subtle arguments about the impact of technology and its potential for creating a new form of social culture could not be heard in a period dominated by strong political passions and partisan polemics on both sides of the ideological divide. The essay remained without a publisher, a work in progress.

In trying to answer, like Heidegger, the "question regarding technology," Benjamin saw both the "loss of aura" caused by the "reproducibility" of the work of art, and the potential of new technologies. Photography and cinema had revealed new forms of perception ("the optical unconscious") and new means of social communication and involvement. But technology had also found its "unnatural use" in war and the "aesthetic of modern warfare," whereby humankind, in an act of extreme "self-alienation," can "experience its own annihilation as a supreme aesthetic pleasure" (epilogue to "The Work of Art"). These dire thoughts, however, did not deter Benjamin from his messianic enterprise, which he pursued in the quiet haven of the Bibliothèque nationale in Paris, and among the pages of dusty books.

In his essays devoted to Baudelaire, whose *Tableaux parisiens* he translated, Benjamin offers an interpretation of modernity, which is part of the larger *Arcades* project. The mood is somber, as Benjamin explores, through Baudelaire's persona, the imminent demise of the bourgeois intellectual, which is also the demise of Benjamin's own class. In this original form of cultural history, the perspective is more often geological than sociological. Benjamin was evidently more at ease when speaking of fossils and petrified forms of culture, or of sleeping shapes that one day might be awakened to a new life, than he was when addressing immediate social issues. For Benjamin, the collective dreams of nineteenth-century history found themselves materialized in the visible shapes of architectural forms and artifacts, which could reveal their utopian promise to the attentive eye of the critical reader.

In Benjamin's "magical" imaginary, the *Arcades* project takes the labyrinthine structure of the modern city, where inside and outside, private and public spaces are confused. The hieroglyphic nature of urban life evoked in the *Arcades* project is reminiscent of **Karl Marx**'s metaphorical references to the exchange market in *Capital*, where the inanimate commodity appears endowed with a spectral life, whereas live beings are turned into objects. Benjamin replicates this structure in the formal design of his project, divided into folios and "convolutes," where quotes are juxtaposed in meaningful "constellations" aimed at making sense of nineteenth-century capitalist modernity.

Benjamin's final answer to the dilemmas of history is conveyed, in enigmatic form, in his essay "On the Concept of History" (1940), his last major writing. Here, the allegorical figure of the "angel of history," caught in a storm "blowing from paradise" that paralyzes his wings, is that of humankind caught in the storm of progress that leaves behind a wreckage of debris. The angel turned with its back to the future is none other than the hunchback, the "prototype of distortion" and forgetting. To be able to face the future, and in a different sense the light of truth, the angel has to fight against the storm of oblivion. Benjamin's image of liberation from the nightmare of history takes on a violent form, presenting the historian with the formidable task of "blast[ing] out the continuum of history."

This radical tactic is reminiscent of other similar "explosive" moments in Benjamin's writings, especially the concept of "gesture" inspired by Brecht's "epic theater," where, in Benjamin's words, it connotes "the interrupting of the action," the scenic element that breaks the illusion of "the naturalistic stage." The gesture, thus conceived, is in fact a condensed event, and can have the fulguration of an unexpected attack or the surprise effect of a surrealist metaphor; it annihilates and brings to life what was previously latent, in what Benjamin called "dialectics at a standstill." Contradictions are suddenly brought together and simultaneously illuminated.

Selected Bibliography: Benjamin, Walter. *The Arcades Project.* Trans. Howard Eiland and Kevin McLaughlin. Cambridge, MA: Belknap P, 1999; Benjamin, Walter. *Illuminations.* New York: Harcourt, Brace & World, 1968; Benjamin, Walter. *Selected Writings.* Ed. Marcus Bullock and Michael W. Jennings. 4 vols. Cambridge, MA: Belknap P, 1996–2003; Buck-Morss, Susan. *The Dialectics of Seeing: Walter Benjamin and the Arcades Project.* Cambridge, MA: MIT P, 1989; Eagleton, Terry. *Walter Benjamin; or, Towards a Revolutionary Criticism.* London: Verso, 1981; Wismann, Heinz, ed. *Walter Benjamin et Paris.* Paris: Cerf, 1986; Witte, Bernd. *Walter Benjamin: An Intellectual Biography.* Detroit: Wayne State UP, 1991; Wolin, Richard. *Walter Benjamin: An Aesthetics of Redemption.* New York: Columbia UP, 1982.

Alina Clej

BERGER, JOHN (1926–). John Berger was born in London, England. At sixteen, he ran away from boarding school in Oxford and instead studied art in London. Berger served in the infantry in **World War II**. After the war, Berger went back to art school and soon began teaching as well as painting. A lifelong Marxist humanist, Berger is a creative polymath whose political and aesthetic purview is registered in essays, short stories, novels, criticism, poetry, plays, film scripts, and one of the most famous television series on art, *Ways of Seeing* (1972). Eloquently iconoclastic, Berger had a significant impact on art criticism almost from the beginning of his career, when he wrote a regular column for the *New Statesman* in the 1950s. His fiction has caused just as much a critical stir. His first novel, *A Painter in Our Time*

(1958), was recalled by the publisher amid a controversy over its protagonist, Janos Lavin, a Hungarian émigré and artist whose commitment to politics and art is built around a unified theory of ethical engagement with the world. Lavin disappears, but it turns out he has chosen to join Janos Kadar and the Hungarian Communists, a radical alignment at odds with the aura of conservatism and cold-war rhetoric in England at the time.

Berger himself was appalled by the intermingling of art and property relations that was exacerbated by consumer culture in the postwar period. Like *A Painter in Our Time*, his next two novels, *The Foot of Clive* (1962) and *Corker's Freedom* (1964), were bold criticisms of English quietude and cultural blandness, while Berger's broadsides against the art establishment and purveyors of art history were continued in *The Success and Failure of Picasso* (1965) and *Art and Revolution* (1969). With the triumph of *Ways of Seeing*, quickly followed by a succession of prizes (including the Booker) for his experimental novel *G* (1972), Berger had become famous; then, however, in a move some deemed romantic and others politically consistent, he decided to flee the spotlight and move with his family to a peasant village, Quincy, in the Giffre River valley of the French Haute-Savoie, where he has largely remained. Not only has this not stopped his critical output but it has facilitated what many believe is his finest work of fiction, the trilogy *Into Their Labors* (*Pig Earth* [1979], *Once in Europa* [1987], and *Lilac and Flag* [1990]). Using a variety of narrative styles and points of view, Berger brilliantly evokes the time and space of peasant life with phrasing that simultaneously conjures an oral tradition and the emergence of a mechanical age that somehow deracinates it and the community to which it belongs. As in his art criticism, Berger is true to his Benjaminian beliefs about aesthetic aura and what can be lost to the "advances" of capitalism. In some respects, this makes Berger a child of modernist innovation but only as it distances and questions the saturated commodification of the present.

Selected Bibliography: Dyer, Geoff. *Ways of Telling: The Work of John Berger*. London: Pluto, 1986; Hitchcock, Peter. "'Work Has the Smell of Vinegar': Sensing Class in John Berger's Trilogy." *Modern Fiction Studies* 47.1 (Spring 2001): 12–42; Papastergiadis, Nikos. *Modernity as Exile: The Stranger in John Berger's Writing*. Manchester: Manchester UP, 1993; Robbins, Bruce. "Feeling Global: John Berger and Experience." *Postmodernism and Politics*. Ed. Jonathan Arac. Minneapolis: U of Minnesota P, 1986. 145–61.

Peter Hitchcock

BILDUNGSROMAN, literally, the "novel of formation," though alternately defined as the novel of apprenticeship, education, maturation, or development. Used generically, this term encompasses several similar genres: the *Entwicklungsroman*, or novel of psychological development; the *Erziehungsroman*, or novel of formal education; and the *Künstlerroman*, or novel of artistic development. Typically, the protagonist of the bildungsroman suffers from some form of social **alienation** or oppression in his youth; the bulk of the novel is designed to resolve this alienation, portraying the social, romantic, and professional maturation of the protagonist along the way, usually culminating in the protagonist's marriage. While many novels following this classic model of the genre have been produced, it is important to recognize that there is an equally significant body of literature that critiques this proposed social integration by altering established conventions to address the concerns of subaltern subjects and to pose alternate resolutions to the conflict of social alienation. Indeed, the modern bildungsroman is more likely to portray the unsuccessful social integration of a culturally marginalized protagonist than to follow the pattern set by the prototypical example, **Goethe**'s *Wilhelm Meister* (1795).

The term "bildungsroman" was coined by critic Karl von Morgenstern in the 1820s, though philosopher Wilhelm Dilthey is more commonly credited with its popularization in literary criticism. In his definition of the genre, Morgenstern outlines the formal characteristics that mark the bildungsroman, explaining that a work will be identified as such "first . . . because it depicts the hero's *Bildung* [development] as it begins and proceeds to a certain level of perfection, but also secondarily because, precisely by means of this depiction, it promotes the *Bildung* of the reader to a greater extent than any other type of novel" (Emmel 78). This pedagogical function has been increasingly explored by critics in recent years. M. M. Bakhtin was among the first to point out that the bildungsroman privileges a very specific worldview, positing social conformity over individuality as the ideal goal in life. In a complementary exploration of this social function, Franco Moretti points out that the bildungsroman rose to popularity in Europe on the heels of the **French Revolution**, in accordance with the rise of the bourgeois class. During the eighteenth century, Moretti writes, "Europe plunges into Modernity, but without possessing a *culture* of modernity" (5). The bildungsroman offers a model of behavior for the new bourgeoisie who possess no previous model on which to base their behavior. Not surprisingly, the popularity of this genre declined in Europe during the early decades of the twentieth century, after the European bourgeoisie had achieved cultural hegemony.

While the classic European model of the genre was influential, it existed in its ideal form for a very brief period, beginning in the late eighteenth century and ending by the mid-nineteenth century. In contrast to the successful social integration portrayed in this first incarnation of the genre, later nineteenth-century examples such as Hardy's *Jude the Obscure* (1896) explored the limitations of social integration, depicting a protagonist forced into an unhappy accommodation with his society. Typically, postrevolutionary French examples such as Stendhal's *The Red and the Black* (1830) portray even more dire circumstances for the individual, ending with the protagonist's absolute refusal to accept the limitations imposed on his/her freedom by society, choosing suicide or exile in favor of an accommodation to the requirements of capitalist society. In this regard, the twentieth-century examples emerging from postcolonial nations or those that depict the development of female or otherwise subaltern subjects in Europe or America tend to resemble the French model of the genre much more closely than the earlier German or English versions.

While the genre has decreased in popularity in the developed world, it is currently enjoying a resurgence of popularity in the developing world. In an insightful reading of **Salman Rushdie**'s postcolonial bildungsroman *Midnight's Children* (1980), Dubravka Juraga suggests that the popularity of the bildungsroman in the developing world is due to a correspondence between the developing bourgeois societies of eighteenth- and nineteenth-century Europe and the development of bourgeois postcolonial societies. Conceding that the story of individual incorporation into society is common around the world, she correctly points out that many twentieth-century writers have attempted to use the genre "either for aesthetic or political reasons . . . to undermine the tradition of bourgeois fiction" (172). Indeed, throughout the world, overtly leftist writers who attempt to overcome the split between public and private life common under capitalist societies have been increasingly drawn to the bildungsroman. As a genre that allows for the development of a protagonist opposed to the dominant order of a given society, the bildungsroman has become increasingly popular among writers who come from marginalized groups, and there is a growing body of criticism dedicated to these emerging trends, including explorations of the female bildungsroman, the African American bildungsroman, and the postcolonial bildungsroman of many different types.

Selected Bibliography: Bakhtin, Mikhail M. "The Bildungsroman and Its Significance in the History of Realism." *Speech Genres and Other Late Essays.* Ed. C. Emerson and M. Holquist. Austin: U of Texas P, 1986. 10–59; Emmel, Hildegard. *History of the German Novel.* Trans. Ellen Summerfield. Detroit: Wayne State UP, 1984; Fraiman, Susan. *Unbecoming Women: British Women Writers and the Novel of Development.* New York: Columbia UP, 1993; Juraga, Dubravka. " 'The Mirror of Us All': *Midnight's Children* and the Twentieth-Century Bildungsroman." *Critical Essays on Salman Rushdie.* Ed. M. Keith Booker. New York: G. K. Hall, 1999. 169–87; LeSeur, Geta. *Ten Is the Age of Darkness: The Black Bildungsroman.* Columbia: U of Missouri P, 1995; Moretti, Franco. " 'A Useless Longing for Myself': The Crisis of the European Bildungsroman, 1898–1914." *Studies in Historical Change.* Ed. Ralph Cohen. Charlottesville: U of Virginia P, 1992: 43–59; Moretti, Franco. *The Way of the World: The Bildungsroman in European Culture.* London: Verso, 1987.

Jeff Solomon

BLACK ARTS MOVEMENT. In "The Black Arts Movement," the movement's manifesto, Larry Neal labeled the black arts movement (1960–1975) "the aesthetic and spiritual sister of the Black Power concept" (Gayle 257). The primary focus of the movement became converting the political action of urban unrest and the rhetoric of black power into a workable cultural aesthetic. The black arts movement struggled to make sense of the changing political landscape of a post-segregation America while integrating the perspective of "the brother on the block" into a workable cultural aesthetic, which was called "the black aesthetic." In 1968, the same year that Neal published his manifesto, the Congress of Racial Equality (CORE) and the Student Nonviolent Coordinating Committee (SNCC), two of the leading organizations of the civil-rights era, ceased to be multiracial and pro-integrationist. In its quest to define itself as a "black organization," CORE, under the leadership of Roy Innis, expelled its white organizers and supporters. As CORE, SNCC, and other political organizations struggled to redefine their mission in a post–civil rights era, the ideological and intellectual battle to create "Black Studies" raged on university and college campuses, even turning occasionally violent.

The black arts movement's critics and practitioners responded to the question of "black art" and the post-segregation problematic of African American artists and intellectuals by calling for an art that would, as Neal writes, "speak directly to the needs and aspirations of Black America. . . . The Black Arts Movement is radically opposed to any concept of the artist that separates him from his community" (Gayle 257).

This notion of community was constituted around oppositional struggle and became the basis for the form and function that was designated the black aesthetic. As Ron Karenga writes in *The Black Aesthetic*, a key text of the movement, "[A]ll African art has at least three characteristics: that is, it is functional, collective and committing or committed," and "Black art, like everything else, must respond positively to the reality of revolution" (32, 31). The call for the creation of a black arts movement was answered not only by individuals but through the formation of artistic collectives and publishing houses, including Third World Press and the Organization of Black American Culture in Chicago, Spirit House in Newark, Broadside Press and Boone House in Detroit, and the Black Arts Repertory Theater in New York City. Many of these cultural venues were created by the key artists/intellectuals of the movement, including Dudley Randall, Margaret Danner, Don L. Lee, LeRoi Jones/**Amiri Baraka**, Hoyt Fuller, Gwendolyn Brooks, Larry Neal, Carolyn Rodgers, and Mari Evans. Together with Baraka, Neal anthologized much of the work of the movement in *Black Fire: An Anthology of Afro-American Writing*.

Selected Bibliography: Baker, Houston A., Jr. *Afro-American Poetics: Revisions of Harlem and the Black Aesthetic*. Madison: U of Wisconsin P, 1988; Brooks, Gwendolyn, ed. *A Broadside Treasury*. Detroit: Broadside P, 1971; Gayle, Addison, Jr., ed. *The Black Aesthetic*. New York: Doubleday, 1971; Neal, Larry. *Visions of a Liberated Future: Black Arts Movement Writings*. Ed. Michael Schwartz. New York: Thunder's Mouth P, 1989; Neal, Larry, and LeRoi Jones. *Black Fire: An Anthology of Afro-American Writing*. New York: William Morrow, 1968; Randall, Dudley. *Black Poetry: A Supplement to Anthologies Which Exclude Black Poets*. Broadside Press, 1969.

Amy Abugo Ongiri

BLACK NATIONALISM is a political theory that asserts the need for a black state to ensure the interests of black African peoples or people of black African descent. Like other nationalisms, black nationalism is based on a racialized notion of the "national" subject. It claims that African or African-descended people share a distinct identity that subsumes class, gender, geographical, political, or other differences between black people. Generally, black nationalist discourses posit that the black subject's national identity is determined biologically; however, some black nationalist discourses maintain that the unifying black identity is historically produced. In either case, the shared black identity is said to determine the black subject's loyalty to his race and nation, whether real or imagined. Black nationalism's philosophy of racial uplift endeavors to make the black subject proud of his or her race.

Black nationalism arose during the nineteenth century in the American slave colonies. Initially, it had taken the form of various colonization and immigration schemes; American blacks, it was argued, would fare better by creating a colony of their own in Africa or Latin America than by residing in the United States. In its more liberatory articulation, nineteenth-century black nationalism was clearly a defensive strategy against the systematic oppression and exploitation of black Americans by Southern slavery and the abject economic and political condition of "free" blacks. For major black nationalists such as Alexander Crummell and Martin Delany, the project of creating a free black state was often tied to teleological notions of an African or black destiny indissoluble from the Christian missionary aims of its believers: Africa could be "redeemed" and therefore become great through the actions of black colonists.

The key premise of all black nationalism, especially after **World War I**, was the so-called right of national self-determination for subject peoples. The Wilsonian nationalist Marcus Garvey, founder of the Universal Negro Improvement Association, recruited millions of people worldwide to his Back-to-Africa program in the 1920s, claiming that Africans possessed the same rights as other "national" peoples to establish a country of their own. Marxist black nationalists—also known as "revolutionary nationalists"—such as the African Blood Brotherhood or those in the **Communist Party**, viewed the right of national self-determination as inherently anti-imperialist and anticolonialist. Twentieth-century black nationalism generally viewed itself as upholding the principles and practices of the bourgeois revolutionary tradition that claims to guarantee the rights of freedom and democracy to all peoples.

While black nationalism continues to have its adherents, it is also subject to criticism within political and scholarly circles for many reasons. Some critics argue that black nationalism problematically appropriates mystical and pseudo-scientific notions of racial identity originally developed and still employed by ruling classes to divide and dominate working-class people of all colors. Other critics dispute the black nationalists' belief that black workers can "self-determine" their existence without abolishing the inegalitarian wage labor-capital relation inherent to capitalism. "Racial" or "national" loyalty is itself an ideological tool employed by ruling classes to discipline workers into accepting structural inequalities.

Selected Bibliography: Carlisle, Rodney. *The Roots of Black Nationalism.* Port Washington, NY: Kennikat, 1975; Dawahare, Anthony. *Nationalism, Marxism, and African American Literature between the Wars: A New Pandora's Box.* Jackson: UP of Mississippi, 2003; Foley, Barbara. *Spectres of 1919: Class and Nation in the Making of the New Negro.* Urbana: U of Illinois P, 2003; Moses, Wilson. *The Golden Age of Black Nationalism: 1850–1925.* Oxford: Oxford UP, 1988.

Anthony Dawahare

BLOCH, ERNST (1885–1977),

BLOCH, ERNST (1885–1977), German Marxist philosopher and cultural critic, initially dismissed by many Marxists (who were intent on a negative hermeneutic of ideological critique) as a mystic and subjectivist for his emphasis on the utopian dimension of both culture and cultural critique. Now recognized as a philosopher and cultural critic of the greatest importance, perhaps the greatest utopian thinker of the twentieth century, Bloch influenced the New Left of the 1960s and 1970s and continues to influence utopian thinkers and contemporary Marxist cultural critics, such as **Fredric Jameson**. Jameson's practice of identifying a **political unconscious** in cultural productions derives from Bloch's directive to use positive hermeneutic in which one discerns "emancipatory moments which project visions of a better life that put in question the organization and structure of life under capitalism" (Kellner 81). Bloch calls these moments "cultural surplus," or "red arrows," which he identifies as moving through history, anticipating and pointing toward a socialist society.

In his most influential work—the massive and encyclopedic three volume *The Principle of Hope* (*Das Prinzip Hoffnung*, 1959)—Bloch provides a "systematic examination of the ways that daydreams, fairy tales and myths, popular culture, literature, theater, and all forms of art, political and social utopias, philosophy, and religion" contain these emancipatory moments (Kellner 81). For Bloch, hope is the "imperceptible tending of all things towards Utopia, for the future which stirs at its convulsive but microscopic work within the smallest cells of the vast universe itself, make themselves known as *Spuren* in the world both within and without: traces, spoor, marks, and signs" (Jameson, *Marxism and Form* 121). Bloch distinguishes, however, between hope that manifests itself in "soap bubble dreams" versus "hope with a will," which reaches into a future; hope that is anticipatory rather than compensatory. Bloch's conception of utopia is largely a practical and scientific one. By definition, Bloch's version of utopia is never reached, but it can be worked toward. Utopian thought is always thought that reaches beyond the real, but for Bloch, genuine utopian thought is shot through with concrete possibility, its goal being the transformation of reality, not an escape from it. Moreover, Bloch's vision, however poetic it may sometimes appear, is resolutely historical. Among other things, his vision of thinking beyond the present is always oriented toward the future, not the past. Utopian thought, for Bloch, must reach toward the "Not-Yet-Conscious . . . towards the side of something new that is dawning up, that has never been conscious before, not, for example, something forgotten, something rememberable that has been" (Bloch, *Principle* 1: 11). It is therefore the task of the cultural and literary critic "to discern and unfold this progressive potential and to relate it to the struggles and possibilities of the present" (Kellner 94).

Selected Bibliography: Bloch, Ernst. *The Principle of Hope.* 3 vols. Trans. Neville Plaice, Stephen Plaice, and Paul Knight. Cambridge, MA: MIT P, 1995; Bloch, Ernst. *Spuren.* Berlin: Suhrkamp, 1959; Daniel, Jamie Owen, and Tom Moylan, eds. *Not Yet: Reconsidering Ernst Bloch.* London: Verso, 1997; Geogeghan, Vincent. *Ernst Bloch.* New York: Routledge, 1996; Hudson, Wayne. *The Marxist Philosophy of Ernst Bloch.* New York: St. Martin's, 1982; Jameson, Fredric. *Marxism and Form: Twentieth-Century Dialectical Theories of Literature.* Princeton, NJ: Princeton UP, 1971; Jameson, Fredric. *The Political Unconscious: Narrative as a Socially Symbolic Act.* Ithaca, NY: Cornell UP, 1981. Kellner, Douglas. "Ernst Bloch, Utopia, and Ideology Critique." *Not Yet: Reconsidering Ernst Bloch.* Ed. Jamie Owen Daniel and Tom Moylan. London: Verso, 1997. 80–95.

Sandy Rankin

BOND, EDWARD (1935–). Among the most prolific and politically engaged playwrights in the world, Bond has produced works whose immediate topical significance has not tempered their longevity in Britain. Bond first came to widespread public notice when his play *Saved*, produced by the English Stage Company, opened at the Royal Court Theatre in 1965. Made up of short scenes representing episodes in the lives of the English urban underclass, the play raised critics' and spectators' hackles by depicting the savage and senseless stoning of an infant. The outrage over that scene in the British press echoed the early critical disgust at the plays of **Henrik Ibsen** and remained the example of theatrical controversy par excellence until **Sarah Kane's** *Blasted* debuted thirty years later. Bond's *Early Morning* (1968)—a fanciful depiction of the English Empire's afterlife, in which Queen Victoria, Prince Albert, and Florence Nightingale, among other prominent figures of the colonial period, engage in cannibalism, sexual promiscuity, and genocide—would eventually lead to the decommissioning of Lord Chamberlain's censorship of the stage. Bond, however, does not confine his staged politics to social comment on historical or contemporary realities. His War Plays (1985)—*Red Black and Ignorant, The Tin Can People*, and *Great Peace*—represent the potentially dire future consequences of nuclear proliferation and the increasing concentration of wealth, while *Lear* (1971)—his rewriting of **Shakespeare**'s tragedy—investigates the corruptibility of political power. Though Bond is widely understood as working in the combined lineage of **Bertolt Brecht** and Antonin Artaud, some of his more recent works, including *Coffee* (1997) and *At the Island Sea* (1995), have narrowed the epic scope and the stark depictions of violence that mark his earlier plays. Instead, these works, though fundamentally political in their concerns, question the possibility of theatrically representing the horrors of history, and emphasize their own self-conscious awareness of the way theater specifically and artistic work more generally must always mediate, distort, dismember, and reconstruct its own particular version of truth, morality, ethics, and politics. Indeed, the lengthy commentary with which Bond accompanies almost all of his plays, in the tradition of **George Bernard Shaw**'s prefaces, have always implicitly acknowledged the limitations of the staged event to depict a coherent, unproblematic worldview or reality. Almost certainly, his relative obscurity in the United States testifies to the unwavering political commitment of his work. Produced with intentional and studied crudity, explicitly examining world politics from a British perspective, and retaining the alienating texture of **epic theater**, these plays make no concession to big-budget, highly produced, aggressively marketed mass-cultural aesthetics.

Selected Bibliography: Eagleton, Terry. "Nature and Violence: The Prefaces of Edward Bond." *Critical Quarterly* 26.1–2 (1984): 127–35; Hay, Malcolm, and Philip Roberts. *Bond: A Study of His Plays.* London, 1980; Innes, Christopher. "The Political Spectrum of Edward Bond: From Rationalism to Rhapsody." *Modern Drama* 25.2 (1982): 189–206; Spencer, Jenny S. *Dramatic Strategies in the Plays of Edward Bond.* Cambridge: Cambridge UP, 1992; Worth, Katharine J. "Edward Bond." *Essays on Contemporary British Drama.* Ed. Hedwig Bock and Albert Wertheim. Munich: Hueber, 1981. 205–22.

Craig N. Owens

BONHEUR D'OCCASION (1945; TRANSLATED AS *THE TIN FLUTE*) by

Gabrielle Roy is, together with Roger Lemelin's *Au pied de la pente douce* (*The Town Below*, 1944) and Ringuet's *Trente arpents* (*Thirty Acres*, 1938), a pioneering work of urban social realism. A classic of French-Canadian literature, it won the prestigious French Femina prize in 1947, was translated into numerous languages, and was made (under the same title) into a tear-jerking film (1983) by Claude Fournier, which weakened much of its potent critique of capitalism.

The original title means "secondhand or occasional happiness." This is the lot of the heroine, the waitress Florentine, and most of the characters who struggle to keep body and soul together in the spring of 1940 in Montreal's poor quarter of Saint-Henri. The devastating Depression—particularly hard on Florentine's alienated ex-carpenter father, the dreamer Azarius—gives way to the ironic "salvation" of **World War II** for him and some of the younger "lost generation," who leave for overseas in uniform. His wife, Rose-Anna, bravely tries to feed her large family but is unable to stop its disintegration, having been "brought up on pious religious tracts."

Florentine desperately tries to escape the crushing ambient poverty by attaching herself romantically to the ambitious apprentice engineer Jean Lévesque. But after she becomes pregnant, he disappears from Saint-Henri, cynically seeking big wages in war production. His middle-class friend, Emmanuel, becomes the indirect (and not always convincing) spokesman for the author's social-democratic vision of a more just world. In love with Florentine, he marries her without knowing she is carrying Jean's child. He, too, will march off to war, convinced that the veterans will not be satisfied with tin medals when they return.

In spite of cuts to the second and subsequent editions of *Bonheur d'occasion*, which somewhat weakened the impact of the work's critique of the dominant socioeconomic system, Roy's first novel is a powerful condemnation of capitalism and its reliance on war. Similarly, but without the same social sweep, her third work of fiction, *Alexandre Chenevert* (*The Cashier*, 1954), flayed lay and clerical powers-that-be in a combination of social realism, existentialism, and theater of the absurd.

Bonheur d'occasion has been praised for its consummate characterization, skillful combination of narration/action and flashbacks, rhythmic devices reminiscent of **Zola** and **Steinbeck**, and deft use of symbolic description. Some ultra-leftist critics, however, have scored it for alleged "reactionary" ideas (see Shek, "La critique").

Selected Bibliography: Shek, Ben-Z. "*Bonheur d'occasion.*" *The Oxford Companion to Canadian Literature.* Ed. Eugene Benson and William Toye. 2nd ed. Toronto: Oxford UP, 1997. 130–31; Shek, Ben-Z. "La critique gauchiste (et gauche?) de *Bonheur d'occasion.*" *Colloque international "Gabrielle Roy."* Ed. André Fauchon. Saint-Boniface: Presses universitaires de Saint-Boniface, 1996. 55–68; Shek, Ben-Z. *Social Realism in the French-Canadian Novel.* Montreal: Harvest House, 1977.

Ben-Z. Shek

BOURDIEU, PIERRE (1930–2002). Bourdieu's work provides a useful companion to the understanding of twentieth-century consumer societies, specifically European ones, though his "reflexive" sociology was ultimately unable to transcend the ethnocentric perspective it was meant to correct. Bourdieu remains a quintessentially French thinker, whose contributions to sociology can be best understood in the context of the intellectual debates that took place in France in the late 1950s and 1960s, when the philosophical establishment was represented by **Jean-Paul Sartre**. This may explain why young thinkers like **Gilles Deleuze**, **Jacques Derrida**, **Michel Foucault**, Michel Serres, and Bourdieu himself were looking beyond phenomenology, a domain that Sartre had monopolized. They found other venues both in structuralism and in the dispassionate approach to knowledge exemplified by the philosophers of science, Gaston Bachelard, Georges Canguilhem, and Jean Cavaillès.

Like many of his peers, Bourdieu studied at the École normale supérieure, where he completed an *agrégation* in philosophy. But it is **Louis Althusser**'s Marxism and Claude Lévi-Strauss's structural anthropology that defined Bourdieu's future career as a sociologist. His concept of a reflexive sociology was the result of his early ethnographic experience in Algeria, where he taught as part of his military duties. After his return to France, Bourdieu taught philosophy at the Sorbonne, and then at the École des hautes études. In 1982, Bourdieu was elected chair of sociology at the

Collège de France, where he played an important, although controversial, role in forming a new generation of sociologists in France. Bourdieu's numerous works, which according to some critics suffer from repetition and obscurity, have only in recent years acquired a larger currency in the Anglo-Saxon academic world, due to increased translation and the concurrent fading of poststructuralist theories.

In spite of Bourdieu's critique of **Karl Marx** and Althusser, his sociology remains indebted to a Marxist analysis of social relations in terms of production and exchange. Bourdieu's interest in practices, not to be confused with Foucault's "discursive practices," is similarly in line with Marx's emphasis on human activity and its material determinations. Bourdieu's innovation was to extend Marx's economic analysis to the sphere of symbolic relations and representations—including symbolic violence—in areas such as culture, religion, and education. In this respect, Bourdieu is indebted to Émile Durkheim's social functionalism, Marcel Mauss's theory of magic, and **Max Weber**'s study of religion, where Bourdieu found the "symbolic" dimension missing in Marx's theory of ideology.

As Bourdieu states in the introduction to *Distinction*, his object of study is the "economy of cultural goods," which has its own "specific logic." The purpose of the sociologist's investigation is to demystify the hierarchy of cultural values by showing how it corresponds to "a social hierarchy of consumers" defined by status ("symbolic capital") and "cultural competence" ("cultural capital"). Borrowing from Althusser the idea that domination perpetuates itself through the reproduction of repressive structures ("ideological state apparatuses") and from Lévi-Strauss the concept of culture as a network of relations, Bourdieu demonstrates how access to certain forms of education privileged by the dominant system can secure a position in a field, in which individuals jostle for power; social institutions and practices legitimate the winners. While associated with the economic advantages given by class, "cultural capital" can be gained through other means as well; in republican France, these are provided by the *grandes écoles*—the elitist institutions that form both the haves and the have-nots, provided the latter are seen as future assets to the system. Bourdieu, who was born in a modest provincial family and made a brilliant career by studying at the École normale supérieure in Paris, is himself a case in point.

Although Bourdieu reintroduced "reflexivity" into scientific analysis and stressed the importance of agency, his notion of "*habitus*" (and later concept of "masculine *habitus*") allows for little choice in terms of identity building or self-determination. It is here that the difference between his theory and those of poststructuralists, especially feminists, is most striking. For example, Bourdieu's notion of performativity differs substantially from that in **Judith Butler**'s *Gender Trouble* (1990) because for Bourdieu, individual performance has no force outside an institutionalized framework that legitimates it.

In his final years, Bourdieu spoke out against globalization and the increased commercialism of the media; he stressed the need for intellectuals to reengage in political struggle on the side of the disenfranchised. He did not shy away, however, from using the media and the press in the name of a just cause. In 1996 he founded *Liber/Raisons d'agir* for the publication of pamphlets mainly directed against neoliberalism and other social evils, and also took part in creating the Parliament of Intellectuals. In the end, in personality at least, Bourdieu came to embody the Sartrean intellectual—the "*monstre sacré*" that his generation tried to avoid, and which among his peers he was best suited to impersonate.

Selected Bibliography: Bourdieu, Pierre. *Distinction: A Social Critique of the Judgment of Taste.* London: Routledge, 1984; Bourdieu, Pierre. *La Domination masculine.* Paris: Seuil, 1998; Bourdieu, Pierre. *Language and Symbolic Power.* Cambridge, MA: Harvard UP, 1991; Bourdieu, Pierre. *The Logic of Practice.* Cambridge: Polity, 1990; Bourdieu, Pierre. *The Rules of Art.* Stanford, CA: Stanford UP, 1995; Bourdieu, Pierre. *Sociologie de l'Algérie.* Paris: PUF, 1962; Bourdieu P., and Loic Wacquant. *An Invitation to Reflexive Sociology.* Cambridge: Polity, 1992.

Alina Clej

BRATHWAITE, EDWARD KAMAU (1930–). Born Lawson Edward Brathwaite in Bridgetown, Barbados, Brathwaite went on to study at Cambridge University and the University of Sussex, where he received his Ph.D. in history for a study of Creole society in Jamaica. He taught for a number of years in Ghana and then at the University of the West Indies, Jamaica. He resigned from his position in Jamaica in 1991 to become professor of comparative literature at New York University.

Brathwaite began publishing poetry in the 1950s, but his major phase as a poet began with the publication of the volumes *Rights of Passage* (1967), *Masks* (1968), and *Islands* (1969), published together as *The Arrivants* in 1973. These volumes show an attempt to invigorate Caribbean cultural identity by drawing on the energies of African cultural traditions, which would mark much of Brathwaite's poetry with its sense of the redemptive power of poetry to heal the spiritual wounds of Caribbean history. A later trilogy, comprising *Mother Poem* (1977), *Sun Poem* (1982), and *X/Self* (1987), also focuses on cultural identity, but more specifically in Barbados.

Later volumes of poetry include *The Visibility Trigger* (1986), *Jah Music* (1986), *Shar* (1990), and *The Zea/Mexican Diary* (1993). In addition to his poetry, Brathwaite has made important contributions as a critic and historian, including such studies as *Folk Culture of the Slaves in Jamaica* (1970) and *The Development of Creole Society in Jamaica, 1770–1820* (1971).

Selected Bibliography: Bobb, June. *Beating a Restless Drum: The Poetics of Kamau Brathwaite and Derek Walcott.* Trenton, NJ: Africa World P, 1998; Brown, Stewart. *The Art of Kamau Brathwaite.* Bridgend, Mid Glamorgen, Wales: Seren, 1995; Naylor, Paul. *Poetic Investigations: Singing the Holes in History.* Evanston, IL: Northwestern UP, 1999; Reiss, Timothy J., ed. *For the Geography of a Soul: Emerging Perspectives on Kamau Brathwaite.* Trenton, NJ: Africa World P, 2001.

M. Keith Booker

***BRAVE NEW WORLD* (1932).** *Brave New World* was **Aldous Huxley**'s nearest approach to popular fiction. His impetus for the book was to have a bit of fun by pulling the leg of his friend **H. G. Wells.** Wells at the time was devoting himself to formulating utopian visions of the future based on advanced technologies, including eugenics. So Huxley decided to craft a visionary tale based on Wells's own technologies but countering Wells's **utopian literature** with a dystopian vision of technological hell rather than heaven. He finished the novel in only four months, but it has gone on to become one of the most influential and widely read works in the entire history of **dystopian fiction**.

Huxley's future society, his "World State," is based on absolute centralization of political and economic power within the context of runaway consumer capitalism. Citizens, grown in glass decanters and genetically designed to play specific roles in society, form a social hierarchy deeply conditioned for performance and obedience. There is no personal freedom, no intimate relationships, and no art. People are trained to pleasure themselves incessantly (with multiple sex partners and a deeply comforting drug called "soma") and never to ask questions. Those who disobey are severely punished, but the World Controllers offer so many pleasures and distractions that the populace is too comfortable either to reflect or to complain. When Bernard Marx, one of the main characters, tells his friend Lenina that he doesn't want to play Electro-magnetic golf because he finds it a waste of time, she asks, in astonishment, "Then what's time for?"

Brave New World is not one of Huxley's most literary novels but it contains several brilliant moments. The third chapter ends with a ten-page tour de force in which Huxley overlaps several simultaneous conversations (often shifting back and forth between them after only a single line) in a way that creates an affective dissonance and layer upon layer of irony. At the climax, the main character—John the Savage, a visitor from outside the World State—argues against the World Controller in a dialogue clearly, and cleverly, paralleling the Grand Inquisitor's conversation with Jesus in **Dostoevsky**'s *Brothers Karamozov*.

Brave New World is often compared to **George Orwell**'s later *Nineteen Eighty-four*, but Huxley's novel, written sixteen years earlier, may ring more true. Huxley once suggested the reason for this in a letter he wrote to Orwell himself, arguing that totalitarianism can grow much more effectively in society (and with less threat of revolution) through pleasure addiction than pogroms of "boot-on-the-face" repression. He believed that governments and dictators would come to realize there is less waste of human life and other usable resources when people are seduced—rather than bludgeoned—into giving up their freedoms.

After reading *Brave New World*, Wells accused Huxley of a "defeatist pessimism," but today we see Huxley's tale as more chillingly prophetic than defeatist. It is a warning against materialism and cultural decadence, and against the erosion of personal freedom from consolidated control, over-stimulation, over-medication, and the seductions of comfort.

Selected Bibliography: Baker, Robert S. *Brave New World: History, Science, and Dystopia*. Boston: Twayne, 1990; Deery, Jane. *Aldous Huxley and the Mysticism of Science*. New York: St. Martin's, 1996; Firchow, Peter Edgerly. *The End of Utopia: A Study of Aldous Huxley's* Brave New World. Lewisburg, PA: Bucknell UP, 1984; Huxley, Aldous. *Brave New World Revisited*. 1958. *"Brave New World" and "Brave New World Revisited."* New York: Harper and Row, 1965; Watt, Donald. *Aldous Huxley, the Critical Heritage*. London: Routledge & Kegan Paul, 1975.

Dana Sawyer

BRAZILIAN LITERATURE. If we choose to divide Brazilian literature according to its political context, it is impossible not to take into consideration the differences between the colonial (1500–1822) and the postcolonial (1822–) periods. In the early days of the Portuguese colony, the most spoken language in Brazil was the *língua geral*, a mixture of native Brazilian Tupinambá languages, systematized by the Jesuit priests. Until 1750, when it became mandatory to speak Portuguese, it was not a general practice to speak it, even for the sons of European settlers. Nevertheless, the collection of written material that is today known as Brazilian literature is exclusively in Portuguese.

In the seventeenth century, Father Antonio Vieira (1608–1697) and Gregório de Matos (1623–1696) were the most distinguished writers. Although their style followed the main trend of the period, which had Quintilianus, Baltasar Gracián, and Emanuele Tesauro as rhetorical masters, both developed their own forms of political dissent toward the local authorities, which cost them imprisonment or exile.

In the eighteenth century, there was a gold rush in the Brazilian backlands, and the city of Vila Rica became the economic center of the Portuguese Empire. The gold from Brazil not only provided funds for the metropolis but was also an important source of resources for England at the time. Nevertheless, the locals were not disposed to continue paying taxes on the gold—especially at the end of the century, when the gold was not as abundant as before. So when the local authorities began planning an extensive compulsory tax-collection program that included mandatory searches and confiscation of private goods, they were met with the beginnings of an anticolonial movement. The two main writers of that century—Tomás Antônio Gonzaga (1729–1789) and Cláudio Manuel da Costa (1744–1810?)—were involved with others (Inácio José de Alvarenga Peixoto [1744–1792], Manuel Inácio da Silva Alvarenga [1749–1814]) in an anticolonial conspiracy. In the end, Gonzaga was exiled and da Costa was murdered in prison. Both had been poets, and followed the neoclassical style, making use of the repertoire of genres, leitmotifs, topoi, and ways of writing that were then seen as classical (that is, worth imitating). Together with the revival of Renaissance pastoralism, they introduced some local themes, paving the way for the romantic poets.

The Brazilian postcolonial period started in 1822, after which an entire generation of romantic writers were responsible for creating a national literature. Gonçalves Dias (1823–1864) Joaquim Manuel de Macedo (1820–1882), Bernardo Guimarães (1825–1884), and José de Alencar (1829–1877) belonged to this generation. Their first goal was to enhance the difference between the culture of their former Portuguese rulers and that of the newborn nation. That is why they chose to focus on Brazilian themes (its nature, natives, way of doing things) and gave so much attention to the differences between Portuguese and Brazilian ways of writing and speaking Portuguese.

After independence, it was necessary to consolidate a national identity; that was the task of intellectuals, writers, and institutions throughout the century. Such an institutionalization process was in many ways sponsored by the new state and was crucial to the support and dissemination of specific modes of knowing and talking about Brazil, modes that paved the way for the creation of a collective memory based on some of the most cherished values of the European descendant elite. From the nineteenth century on, with the ensuing standardization of the school system, an array of textbooks and compendiums for the study of the national language, literature, and history would reproduce these early patterns of thought.

Nevertheless, from the second half of the nineteenth century on, there were also writers who were critical of the norms associated with the use of language, the most praised literary styles of the day, and the romantic version of collective memory. Machado de Assis (1839–1908) was the most important of these writers. Instead of feeling obliged to produce "national heroes" or to praise his people and his land, he thought that "What must be demanded from the writer is a certain intimate feeling that makes him a man of his time and his country, even when he is dealing with remote (in space or time) subjects."

With the coming of the twentieth century, there was an increasing complexity in the Brazilian literary scene. In the 1920s, a whole generation of modernist authors was starting to make itself know for a wider audience. Mário de Andrade (1893–1945), Oswald de Andrade (1890–1954), and Manuel Bandeira (1886–1968) were the most famous of them. From then on, there were at least three important trends. The first one was the production of texts that intended to depict the country "such as it is," criticizing its social structures. The most popular writer from this group was **Jorge Amado** (1912–2001), but the best was Graciliano Ramos (1892–1953).

The second trend was the production of texts that focused on the aesthetic trends their authors believed in, which resulted in reflexive works strongly concentrated on their own making. The fictionist Osman Lins (1924–1978) and the poet Haroldo de Campos (1929–2003) are the most famous writers from this group. The third trend was the production of texts about persons or characters who, looking for answers to fundamental existential questions of human life, pose questions about their own existence: their sexuality, their family, their life in big cities or in rural communities, and so on. Writers from this group include Clarice Lispector (1920–1977), Adélia Prado (1935–), Cyro dos Anjos (1906–1994), and Carlos Drummond de Andrade (1902–1987).

Of course, this classification oversimplifies the works of these writers, which were certainly more complex than this scheme suggests. And there were at least two other internationally acclaimed contemporary writers whose works were a combination of the three trends: João Cabral de Melo Neto (1920–1999) and João Guimarães Rosa (1908–1967).

Selected Bibliography: Bosi, Alfredo. *História concisa da literatura brasileira.* São Paulo: Cultrix, 2002; Candido, Antonio. *Formação da literatura brasileira.* 2 vols. São Paulo: Martins, 1959; Coutinho, Afranio. *A literatura no Brasil.* 2nd ed. 6 vols. Rio de Janeiro: Editorial Sul Americana, 1968–1971; Rocha, João Cezar de Castro, ed. "Brazil 2001—A Revisionary History of Brazilian Literature and Culture." Special number of *Portuguese Literary and Cultural Studies* 4–5 (Spring/Fall 2000).

José Luís Jobim

BRECHT, BERTOLT (1898–1956). Although his preference would have been for a proletarian birthright, Eugen Berthold Brecht was born in the industrial city of Augsburg, where his father was employed in a paper mill of which, in 1914, he became managing director. Brecht's childhood and early youth, then, belonged to the

last years of the German Empire, and like many of his generation, he owed his political awakening to the carnage of **World War I.** A cardiac irregularity delayed his
military service (as a medical orderly) until October 1918, when the war was almost
over, and he was demobilized in January 1919. By then, Brecht was forging a literary career for himself (as Bertolt, or plain Bert, Brecht) in Munich, the capital city
of Bavaria, and beginning to distance himself from Augsburg. Bavaria, until the abdication of Ludwig III in the aftermath of World War I, was a sovereign state within
the German Empire, and Munich was the central site of a dizzying sequence of postwar political events. In the wake of Ludwig III's abdication, a new government under
the socialist intellectual Kurt Eisner was established, but Eisner was assassinated in
February 1919 to be succeeded by a hastily organized socialist soviet, itself soon to
be swept aside by a better programmed communist faction. The prospect of a communist Bavaria rang alarm bells for the government of the newly established republic of Germany, and the army marched on Munich. By the end of May 1919, the
Bavarian political adventure was effectively over. Brecht's response to these events, of
which he was necessarily a witness, is surprisingly difficult to determine. There is
some evidence of his early sympathy with Eisner's socialist program, but the mood
of his early plays (first produced in 1922 and 1923)—*Baal, Drums in the Night*, and
In the Jungle—is angrily anarchic.

The deep divisions within the Weimar Republic were exacerbated by the hyper-
inflation of the 1920s. Brecht's first visit to Berlin ended on March 13, 1920, the
very day on which the Prussian landowner Wolfgang Kapp captured the city in an
attempt to overthrow the government and restore the monarchy. Brecht was working in Leipzig in November 1923 when Hitler joined other right-wing leaders in a
similar, though even more theatrical, assault on Munich. Between the Kapp Putsch
and Hitler's "Beer-Hall Putsch," there was a communist-inspired revolution in central Germany. Sooner or later, the anarchic Brecht would have to abandon his political fence sitting. The catalyst was his move to Berlin, as assistant dramaturg in the
Deutsches Theater in September 1924. Under the influence there of informed Marxists—the actress Helene Weigel (whom he married in 1928) and his literary collab-
orator Elisabeth Hauptmann among them—he undertook a systematic study of Marx
at the Marxist Workers School. The significant shift in his dramatic priorities was
first evident, however elusively, in *Man Is Man* (1926), and subsequently in such collaborative (with Kurt Weill and others) deconstructions of capitalism as *The Threepenny Opera* (1928), *The Rise and Fall of the City of Mahagonny* (1930), and *Saint
Joan of the Stockyards* (1932). He had in mind a dramatic method that would introduce to the theater some of the qualities of epic poetry, above all its emphasis on
events rather than character, and was initially content to align himself with the innovative director Erwin Piscator as an exponent of "**epic theater.**" But it was in the
formal innovation of the group of plays he called *Lehrstück* ("learning plays") that
he most openly sought for a specifically communist dramaturgy. It was one of this
group, *The Measures Taken* (1930), that provided a focus for hostile questions from
the House Un-American Activities Committee (HUAC) in 1947.

After the quelling of the Beer-Hall Putsch, Brecht was among those who found
the posturing Hitler funny, but the joke turned sour in the 1930s. Brecht's last attempt at political intervention in Berlin was the severely censored and quickly banned

film, *Kuhle Wampe*. Knowing he figured on Hitler's hit list, Brecht fled the city the day after the Reichstag fire in February 1933, thus beginning fifteen years of exile. Domiciled successively in Denmark, Sweden, and Finland, and thus denied access to a German-speaking theater, Brecht developed his politically interrogative style in poems, plays, letters, journals, dramaturgical treatises, and everyday discourse. In occasional essays and in the deceptively random jottings to which he was restlessly committed, he constantly refined his own dramatic theory, always with the intention of investing audiences with a responsibility for interactive political thinking. From ideas promulgated by the Soviet critic Viktor Shklovsky, Brecht elaborated his influential notion of the *Verfremdungseffekt* (often misleadingly translated as "alienation effect"), the conscious aim of which was to expose to audiences the strangeness of political and social conditions that they took for granted. Temperamentally disinclined to the adoption of a party line, and always confident that dissidence was a valuable element in the dialectical progress toward a Marxist revolution, he worked, with various companions in exile, on manuscripts that would later be recognized as masterpieces of the left-wing theater—*The Good Person of Szechwan* and **Mother Courage** among them. These manuscripts were with him when the advance of Hitler's army into Scandinavia drove him to the United States in the summer of 1941. They included early drafts of sections of his *Short Organum for the Theater*, completed in 1948, which offers the clearest account of what is best called "dialectical theater"—Brecht's innovative amalgam of modernism and Marxism.

Brecht's American years, most of them spent among fellow exiles in California, were uneasy. His own abrasiveness did nothing to ease his passage into Hollywood, which he came to characterize as "a branch of the narcotics trade," and he struggled, mostly unsuccessfully, to bring his dramatic projects to fruition. But it was in California that he completed the first draft of **The Caucasian Chalk Circle**, began his eventually abandoned versification of *The Communist Manifesto*, and worked with Charles Laughton toward the world premiere of *Life of Galileo* in Los Angeles on July 31, 1947. The play was still running when Brecht was interrogated by HUAC. An arch-interrogator himself, he subtly eluded the committee with a mixture of equivocation and truth (he had, after all, never joined the Communist Party), then promised to remain in the country and flew to Paris the next day.

The fledgling government of the new East Germany, in search of cultural authentication, offered Brecht a theatrical home in Berlin (he had been refused a visa for the American zone), and with disguised reluctance, he accepted the offer. The last years of his life (1949–1956) are inseparably linked with the creation and operation of the Berliner Ensemble. Given the disparity between an inflexible government and a playwright who thrived on dialectic, these last years were inevitably ones of political compromise, which came to a head with the workers' uprising of June 1953. Looked to for a gesture on behalf of the workers, Brecht remained silent (his published work proclaims his antagonism to heroes and martyrs). Only later did he write a sardonic epigram proposing to the East German government that they "dissolve the people and elect a new one."

Selected Bibliography: Benjamin, Walter. *Understanding Brecht*. Trans. Anna Bostock. London: NLB, 1973; Brooker, Peter. *Bertolt Brecht: Dialectics, Poetry, Politics*. London: Croom Helm, 1988; Dickson, Keith A. *Towards Utopia: A Study of Brecht*. Oxford: Clarendon P, 1978; Jameson, Fredric. *Brecht and*

Method. London: Verso, 1998; Lyon, James K. *Bertolt Brecht in America*. Princeton, NJ: Princeton UP, 1980; Thomson, Peter, and Glendyr Sacks, eds. *The Cambridge Companion to Brecht*. Cambridge: Cambridge UP, 1994.

Peter Thomson

BRECHT-LUKÁCS DEBATE. One of the central Marxist cultural debates of the twentieth century, the disagreement between **Bertolt Brecht** and **Georg Lukács** concerned the cultural and political relevance of literary movements in furthering social change. It centered on the relative values of **modernism** and **realism**, and also included questions regarding the role of modernism (especially expressionism) within the rise of fascism. *Das Wort*, a journal published by and for German artists and intellectuals in exile in Moscow, became the medium for much of the discussion, although Brecht himself did not publish his essays there. The Brecht-Lukács debate was not a controversy between two diametrically opposed camps; both shared negative views of the more abstract sides of modernist aesthetics as well as of naturalism and some authors associated with realism.

As a critic of capitalism from a humanistic, aesthetic perspective, Lukács was criticized by Brecht for his lack of interest in using literature as a direct means of change. Where Lukács insisted on the need for literature as an expression of the totality of human experience as both individual and part of history, Brecht wanted a more direct link between literature and sociopolitical change. Lukács called for the use of the nineteenth-century realist novel as a model for true social realism that could provide a realistic construction of the human experience—and of the sweep of history leading to Socialism. On the other hand, Brecht's concept of the **epic theater**, with devices such as distancing and loss of the fourth wall, and his interest in new media (such as radio and film) were aimed at avoiding illusion and identification in order to motivate audiences into taking action. His definition of realism required the uncovering of no-longer-questioned social constructions. Lukács praised bourgeois realist writers such as **Honoré de Balzac** and **Leo Tolstoy** for showing the struggle of the individual within larger social and historical contexts more plausibly and effectively than socialist realists. Brecht tended to dismiss those traditionalists because their writings held little value for contemporary social struggles. To Brecht, Lukács was taking a formalist approach by suggesting imitation would lead to innovation; Lukács rejected this criticism by emphasizing the lasting literary quality of some realist novels and dramas, which could inspire twentieth-century writers and provide a sense of cultural continuity. Instead, he dismissed avant-garde art as decadent and expressionism as irrational. A proponent (and practitioner) of modernism, Brecht considered Lukács' position on realism utopian and idealistic, and criticized what he saw as a Marxist tendency to categorize and eliminate aesthetic movements alongside political ones.

Selected Bibliography: Bronner, Stephen Eric. *Of Critical Theory and Its Theorists*. Cambridge, MA: Blackwell, 1994; Lukács, Georg. *Essays on Realism*. Ed. Rodney Livingstone. Cambridge, MA: MIT P, 1981; Lunn, Eugene. *Marxism and Modernism: An Historical Study of Lukács, Brecht, Benjamin, and Adorno*. Berkeley: U of California P, 1982; Schmitt, Hans-Jürgen. *Die Expressionismusdebatte*. Frankfurt am Main: Suhrkamp, 1973; Taylor, Ronald, ed. *Aesthetics and Politics*. London: NLB, 1977.

Sabine Schmidt

BRITISH IMMIGRANT LITERATURE. Unsurprisingly, given its historical status as a world power and cultural center, Britain has a long and rich tradition of immigrant literature. For example, several of the great modernists, notably **Henry James**, **Joseph Conrad**, and **T. S. Eliot**, were born overseas. Britain's imperial history also generated a long line of immigrant writers from the colonies beginning in the late eighteenth century, when figures like Sake Dean Mohammed and Olaudah Equiano inaugurated a black British literary tradition.

With the progressive decolonization of the British empire from 1947 on, this tradition has developed exponentially. Many new writers arrived in the wave of migration to Britain in the 1950s, including Attia Hosain, Nirad Chaudhuri, **George Lamming**, and **V. S. Naipaul**, and their numbers swelled in subsequent decades. The predominant focus of such figures was initially on describing their countries and cultures of origin (for both a metropolitan and "home" audience), as in Chaudhuri's *Autobiography of an Unknown Indian* (1951), Lamming's *In the Castle of My Skin* (1953), and Hosain's *Sunlight on a Broken Column* (1961). However, texts addressing the realities of diasporic life in the metropolis soon emerged. Notable early instances include Sam Selvon's *The Lonely Londoners* (1954), Naipaul's *The Mimic Men* (1967), Buchi Emecheta's *In the Ditch* (1972), and Kamala Markandaya's *The Nowhere Man* (1973).

From around 1980, there has been something of a boom in immigrant literature. The breakthrough was provided by **Salman Rushdie**'s *Midnight's Children* (1981), which won the most prestigious national book award, the Booker Prize. In its wake came an avalanche of new writing from every conceivable immigrant group in Britain. Some of the most interesting is by British-born members of such communities, including a good proportion of women writers—for example, Meera Syal, Zadie Smith, and Monica Ali—and writers of mixed race, such as Ben Okri and Caryl Phillips. Such writers are strategically preoccupied with reconceptualizing traditional notions of British identity with a view to making them more responsive to, and inclusive of, diasporic histories and experience. Their more hybrid conception of national belonging is often accompanied by narrative modes that partly draw on the resources of their sometimes already distant cultures of family origin.

While British immigrant writing is in a state of rude health, in recent years, many such writers have increasingly disavowed what Kobena Mercer describes as "the burden of representation," the duty to act as representative or spokesperson of their putative cultures of origin or the diasporic communities from which they have emerged. For example, Hanif Kureishi's recent writing does not engage with ethnic issues to the extent of the earlier work that made his name. This demonstrates that British immigrant literature has varied modalities, thematic concerns, and cultural politics and that it resists easy homogenization. It may even write itself out of existence as a category, as the communities from which it has emerged become more fully admitted to, and established within, British society.

Selected Bibliography: Buford, Bill. "Introduction." *Granta* 3 (1980): 7–16; Innes, C. L. *A History of Black and Asian Writing in Britain 1700–2000*. Cambridge: Cambridge UP, 2002; Mercer, Kobena. "Black Art and the Burden of Representation." *Third Text* 10 (Spring 1990): 61–78; Nasta, Susheila. *Home Truths: Fictions of the South Asian Diaspora in Britain*. Basingstoke: Palgrave, 2002; Phillips, Michael, and Trevor Phillips, eds. *Windrush: The Irresistible Rise of Multi-racial Britain*. London: HarperCollins, 1998; Proctor, James. *Dwelling Places: Postwar Black British Writing*. Manchester: Manchester

UP, 2003; Proctor, James, ed. *Writing Black Britain, 1948–1998: An Interdisciplinary Anthology.* Manchester: Manchester UP, 2000; Rushdie, Salman. *Imaginary Homelands: Essays and Criticism 1981–1991.* London: Granta, 1991.

Bart Moore-Gilbert

BRITISH LITERATURE (AFTER 1900). Aesthetic judgments that promote restrictive definitions of the literary have often resulted in equally narrow definitions of the political, leading to the (generally dismissive) characterization of only certain decades of modern British literature—notably the 1930s—or certain kinds of literature—such as **British working-class and socialist literature**—as politically informed. But in actual fact, the literature of the entire period after 1900 engages with or reflects every significant contemporary issue, from turn-of-the-century explorations of the place of the new woman to recent investigations of the tensions of a multicultural Britain.

While reactions against straw-man versions of Victorian verities were later to mark much of the literature of **modernism**, the 1890s had already seen the burgeoning of works that interrogated notions of sexual morality, most notably in relation to the figure of the new woman. As Ann Ardis has pointed out, Edwardian novelists such as Arnold Bennett continued to mobilize this trope, even as the women's suffrage movement gathered steam, producing powerful propaganda works like Elizabeth Robins's *The Convert* (1907). Writers such as Havelock Ellis and Edward Carpenter continued to popularize the discourse of sexual reform, directly influencing such works as **James Joyce**'s play *Exiles* (1918). Meanwhile, Olive Schreiner's *Women and Labour* (1911) linked feminist and anti-imperial concerns; concern with the ethics of empire, too, marked not only **Joseph Conrad**'s *Heart of Darkness* (1899) but also his more densely realist *Nostromo* (1904).

H. G. Wells and **George Bernard Shaw**—both at one time members of the loosely aggregated, paradoxically elitist Fabian society, with Shaw its best-known member and Wells its most disruptive—became the paradigmatic chroniclers of Edwardian controversies. Wells, himself parodied as the scientific "new man" in Shaw's *Man and Superman* (1903), took on in *Tono-Bungay* (1909) commodity capitalism, new money, and the suffocating gentility of the upwardly mobile classes. Shaw's didactic plays, such as *Major Barbara* (1905) and *Pygmalion* (1914), disrupted received ideas about class, gender, and virtue; his *Heartbreak House* (1910), like E. M. Forster's *Howards End* (1910), seemed uncannily to anticipate the coming conflict of **World War I** even as it reflected the contemporary crisis of liberalism expressed in such works as C. F. Masterman's *The Condition of England* (1909). Among the prewar avant-garde, the vorticist violence of Wyndham Lewis's *Blast* echoed the sense that society was already—perhaps happily—in mid-explosion.

While World War I, then, exacerbated rather than caused the societal fractures for which it is blamed in much of the literature about the conflict, it nevertheless served as a nexus for the reevaluation of national self-image. Writers as diverse as **Siegfried Sassoon**, **Rebecca West**, Vera Brittain, and (once again) Wells all focused on the war's production of a disjunction between reality and self-justificatory rhetoric—the lies a nation tells itself. In the mood of postwar disillusion, the modern city celebrated in

Virginia Woolf's *Mrs. Dalloway* (1926), for example, was just as often seen as the exemplar of modern decay and "the inevitability of British contraction" (Esty 36). Once imperial center, now **T. S. Eliot**'s "Waste Land," London was characterized as the site of unproductive commerce and unproductive sex—the kind of directionless, joyless circuits that mark novels such as **Aldous Huxley**'s *Antic Hay* (1923) and the early works of Evelyn Waugh.

The **General Strike** of 1926 and the interwar slump as a whole served as catalysts, in many cases, for the political radicalization of younger bourgeois writers like **C. Day Lewis** and Edward Upward, with explicit political commitment often tied, as the 1930s wore on, to a rejection of modernist experiment and the valorization of socialist realism (as outlined at the 1934 **Soviet Writers Congress**). The embrace of plain language and of action over introspection was in Upward's work carried to a paradoxical extreme, with his own earlier surrealist-tinged writing now configured thematically as the neurotic outcome of political denial. In an influential essay, Storm Jameson called for documentarianism—as in the writing of **George Orwell** and the sociological work of the group Mass Observation—as the most responsible mode of socialist expression; activists also sought out and promoted proletarian literature, like Walter Greenwood's ***Love on the Dole*** (1933) and **Lewis Jones**'s *Cwmardy* (1937), which followed in the footsteps of Robert Tressell's great proletarian classic, *The Ragged Trousered Philanthropists* (1914; full version 1955).

Political concerns found their expression, too, in generic experimentation—not only in what **W. H. Auden** termed "parable-art" but also in the growing use of popular genres, including **detective fiction**. Even as writers publicly took sides on the **Spanish Civil War** (with several—including **Christopher Caudwell** and **Ralph Fox**, who both died there—enlisting in the International Brigades), novelists such Naomi Mitchison, **Sylvia Townsend Warner**, Stevie Smith, and Katherine Burdekin dramatized their concerns about the rise of fascism in **dystopian literature** and **historical novels**.

In the years after **World War II**, a sense of postimperial diminishment and a kind of national squaldness led to the iconoclastic cynicism of the so-called "angry young men"—a term that described novelists John Wain, Kingsley Amis, John Braine, and **Alan Sillitoe**, and, with perhaps more accuracy, playwrights John Osborne (*Look Back in Anger*) and Arnold Wesker (*Chicken Soup with Rice*). Social commentary took experimental form in the works of **Harold Pinter**, Tom Stoppard, and Joe Orton, who made use of discontinuities and grotesquerie of plot and various forms of linguistic play to revealing the realities beneath convention. The continuing political engagement of the British theater—as in the work of **Edward Bond**, John Arden, David Hare, and **Caryl Churchill**—made it an important area for the emergence of black British writers. So too was poetry, with such writers as Louise Bennett, **Edward Kamau Brathwaite**, Linton Kwesi Johnson, and—more recently—Benjamin Zephaniah making use of oral traditions that foreground poetry as a site of social critique.

The postimperial influx of immigrants into Britain, with its attendant cultural tensions and transformations, was chronicled both in **British immigrant literature**, such as Sam Selvon's *The Lonely Londoners* (1956), and by sympathetic observers, such as Colin MacInnes in his *City of Spades* (1957) and *Absolute Beginners* (1959). Recent years have seen a burgeoning in the number and importance of works—such as those of Hanif Kureishi and Zadie Smith—that foreground Britain's multiculturalism as the occasion for exploring evolving ideas of "Englishness." The most provocative of these, such as **Salman Rushdie**'s *The Satanic Verses* (1988), Bernardine Evaristo's *The Emperor's Babe* (2001), and Hari Kunzru's *The Impressionist* (2002), make use of the techniques and theories of **postmodernism** to challenge traditional models of citizenship.

Selected Bibliography: Ardis, Ann. *New Women, New Novels: Feminism and Early Modernism.* New Brunswick: Rutgers UP, 1990; Benson, Frederick R. *Writers in Arms: The Literary Impact of the Spanish Civil War.* New York: NYU P, 1967; Booker, M. Keith. *The Modern British Novel of the Left: A Research Guide.* Westport, CT: Greenwood, 1998; Bradbury, Malcolm. *The Social Content of Modern English Literature.* New York: Schocken, 1971; Buitenhuis, Peter. *The Great War of Words: Literature as Propaganda 1914–18 and After.* 1987. London: Batsford, 1989; Croft, Andy. *Red Letter Days: British Fiction in the 1930s.* London: Lawrence and Wishart, 1990; Esty, Jed. *A Shrinking Island: Modernism and National Culture in England.* Princeton, NJ: Princeton UP, 2004; Hewison, Robert. *In Anger: British Writing in the Cold War 1945–60.* New York: Oxford UP, 1981; Hewison, Robert. *Too Much: Art and Society in the Sixties 1960–75.* New York: Oxford UP, 1987; Hewison, Robert. *Under Siege: Literary Life in London 1939–45.* New York: Oxford UP, 1977; Horsley, Lee. *Fictions of Power in English Literature: 1900–1950.* London: Longman, 1995; Hynes, Samuel. *The Edwardian Turn of Mind.* Princeton, NJ: Princeton UP, 1968; Hynes, Samuel. *A War Imagined: The First World War and English Culture.* New York: Collier, 1990; Lassner, Phyllis. *British Women Writers of World War II: Battlegrounds of Their Own.* New York: St. Martin's, 1998; Light, Alison. *Forever England: Femininity, Literature and Conservatism Between the Wars.* London: Routledge, 1991; Montefiore, Janet. *Men and Women Writers of the 1930s: The Dangerous Flood of History.* London and New York: Routledge, 1996; Nasta, Susheila. *Home Truths: Fictions of the South Asian Diaspora in Britain.* Basingstoke: Palgrave, 2002; Procter, James. *Dwelling Places: Postwar Black British Writing.* Manchester: Manchester UP, 2003; Sinfield, Alan. *Literature, Politics and Culture in Postwar Britain.* Berkeley: U of California P, 1989; Watson, George. *Politics and Literature in Modern Britain.* Totowa, NJ: Rowman and Littlefield, 1977.

Debra Rae Cohen

BRITISH LITERATURE (NINETEENTH CENTURY). *See* BRITISH NOVEL (NINETEENTH CENTURY); ROMANTICISM.

BRITISH NOVEL (NINETEENTH CENTURY). The political context of nineteenth-century British literature is given its most immediate expression in what are conventionally referred to as "social problem novels," including such works as **Charles Dickens**'s *Hard Times* (1854), **Elizabeth Gaskell**'s *Mary Barton* (1848) and *North and South* (1855), Charles Kingsley's *Alton Locke* (1850), Benjamin Disraeli's *Coningsby* (1844) and *Sybil* (1845), and **George Eliot**'s *Felix Holt* (1866). What distinguishes these novels in critical retrospect is their interest in representations of, and the relations among, class, labor, and gender.

If there is a keyword for understanding what takes place in such novels, that word is *transition*. The language of class is itself vital in producing the novels, and novelists such as Kingsley, Gaskell, and Dickens attempt to allow different class positions to speak through the agency of particular characters. However, this can be overdetermined, tense, or contradictory. Kingsley's Alton Locke speaks from a clearly Christian position, while Stephen Blackpool, the working-class hero of *Hard Times*, is used by Dickens to position an individual, humanist voice against a perceived threat of the masses. Thus, in privileging individual voices, political novels in the nineteenth century may be said to fall into middle-class liberal positions concerning class debate, thereby militating against a more radical class-based position.

The language of class in the Victorian period is dependent on a perception of the relation between economic and social status. This language therefore transforms Victorian self-awareness at social and cultural levels, even as it comes to replace, throughout the century, the more static, hierarchically fixed and organic language of rank and station, which one sees at work in more rurally focused novels such as Eliot's *Middlemarch* (1871–1872).

The issue of class is intertwined with a number of key transformations in the Victorian period. The First Reform Act (1832) was one of a number of highly significant transitional political events during the first third of the nineteenth century. In the years following 1832 until the coronation of Victoria (1837), other equally significant acts were passed, including the 1834 Poor Law Amendment Act. This decreed that no able-bodied person was eligible for poor relief unless he or she entered the workhouse. The fear of the workhouse and debate about it was so strong and long lasting that if we take the works of just one novelist, Dickens, we find ambivalent reference from *Oliver Twist* (1838) through *A Christmas Carol* (1843), *Bleak House* (1853), and *Little Dorrit* (1857), to *Our Mutual Friend* (1865).

1835 witnessed the Factory Act, which sought to guarantee inspection of working conditions in factories. In the same year, legislation was passed abolishing slavery in all colonies of the British Empire. In 1836, the People's Charter, or **Chartism**, was established, while in 1838, the Anti-Corn Law League was founded. Thus, in a six-year period, there were a number of determining hegemonic and counter-hegemonic political events that governed the shape of both national identity and the literature of the century in its responses to and fictionalizations of that identity. Understanding this, it would be a mistake to see as available in nineteenth-century British literature some simple univocal position that is not marked by contradiction and strife.

Disraeli's *Coningsby* (1844), like Eliot's *Felix Holt* (1866), is set during the time of the 1832 Reform Act, by which the franchise in Great Britain was extended. Thus, each novel steps back in time to develop a narrative that situates a beginning for a Victorian concept of modern political identity, and this is, itself, a political gesture. The Victorian novel can be read as placing itself in a period that it reads as distinctly political, and this is its identifying trait. That novelists such as Disraeli and Eliot make such a gesture indicates that the novel is understood as a device for political discourse. The status of the novel is itself political then, and that status changes as the discourses comprising literary and fictional prose take on actively political language and historical events. In this, there is an acknowledgement by such novelists that the world and its aesthetic representations are actively textual. With *Sybil* and *Tancred* (1847), Disraeli's *Coningsby* is not only about political events; it is a political attempt to influence and contain paradoxical political views within the illusion of an organic whole in the guise of a novel.

Like *Coningsby*, Dickens's *Little Dorrit* constructs a historical narrative that provides a mediated view of mid-Victorian political life by focusing on the 1820s. In this it offers a reading of two distinct political moments in the formation of Victorian self-awareness. On the one hand, it allows access to the transitional moments of the reign of William IV, those cultural instances underway that make possible Victorian identity. On the other hand, the period of the novel's setting allows Dickens a political gesture of critical satire in his representation of the Office of Circumlocution as a figure for the practice, institution, and discourse of British politics and, more specifically, as a means of issuing a critique of governmental failure to provide supplies during the Crimean War. There is, thus, a sense of great political ambivalence regarding the politics of mid-Victorian Britain in *Little Dorrit*, and this is extended beyond government and civil service to include entrepreneurial sharp practice in a free-market capitalist economy, which critique is also to be found, though with differing emphases, in Anthony Trollope's *The Way We Live Now* (1875)—a novel in which nothing is quite what it seems. If politics is the subject of the novel, then politics is revealed as a series of untrustworthy simulacra, and the ideological import of this is given full attention in Trollope's problematization of the status of the "gentleman," a figure supposedly synonymous with Englishness. In this novel, the means by which a gentleman is identified is radically destabilized through the narrative of Melmotte, the European-Jewish entrepreneur of undecidable origin; this destabilization in turn reflects back on uncertainties at the heart of Victorian political and cultural life.

The Victorian political novel provides fictions of the political, but at the heart of such fictions is a self-aware understanding that one can no longer separate text from context. Inasmuch as the Victorian era was modern, self-aware, and actively concerned in the production of necessary fictions and narratives concerning itself, then the novel—and, by extension, the literary—remarks itself as always profoundly political.

Selected Bibliography: Ermath, Elizabeth Deeds. *The English Novel in History, 1840–1895*. London: Routledge, 1997; Gallagher, Catherine. *The Industrial Reform of English Fiction: Social Discourse and Narrative Form, 1832–1867*. Chicago: U of Chicago P, 1985; Guy, Josephine M. *The Victorian Social-Problem Novel: The Market, the Individual, and Communal Life*. London: Macmillan, 1996; Hall, Catherine, Keith McClelland, and Jane Rendall. *Defining the Victorian Nation: Class, Race, Gender and the Reform Act of 1867*. Cambridge: Cambridge UP, 2000.

Julian Wolfreys

BRITISH WORKING-CLASS AND SOCIALIST LITERATURE. The categories of "working-class" and "socialist" literature are not necessarily synonymous—particularly now, when the politics and culture of such literature are less conjoined by the active engagement of historical circumstance. However, there is a long and rich history of British working-class culture that has tended to be strongly informed by socialist ideas. This is not to condemn the notion of a working-class socialist culture to the past, but it is to recognize that its living texture cannot be assumed by dint of its rich and provocative past.

The working class is not a club; it has no membership list or executive committee. Its composition is a product of both economic relations (for which **Karl Marx**'s *Capital* remains a key touchstone) and a kind of shared ethos in which people construct viable communities of mutual interest because of and despite the fact of the general exploitation of their labor power by capitalists. Thus, the working class itself has a complex and historically variable definition, which makes the definition of working-class culture all the more difficult. Nevertheless, there have been moments in that history when "British working-class and socialist literature" had a somewhat less problematic aura. In the nineteenth century, for instance, novelists such as **Charles Dickens** and **Elizabeth Gaskell** sometimes sought to represent the working class in their novels, but were able to do so only in superficial ways that lacked psychological and sociological depth. What was clearly needed was an alternative body of writing in which workers themselves could represent the lived conditions of their class from within its day-to-day experience and day-to-day textures. Indeed, there had already been isolated examples of such expression, as in the work of the plebeian poets of the eighteenth century (including Stephen Duck, Mary Collier, and Robert Tatersal), supporting the argument that the trajectory of British working-class literature, while varying in intensities, is not simply an effect of class consciousness but contributes to its substance and articulation.

This constitutive effect may not be evident in a survey approach to the literature (even in the otherwise laudable research of Phyllis Mary Ashraf), but it is certainly discernible in those interpretations that take seriously the attempt, from the eighteenth century on, to transcribe and narrate worker experience as a catalyst of consciousness in class discourse (see, for instance, Gustav Klaus, *The Literature of Labor*). True, the emergence of this writing was tied not just to an increase in the number of workers associated with the industrial age but also to a bourgeois fascination with the lives of its providers, so that publishing houses actively sought out working-class expression for its shock or entertainment value. The latter reflex is highly symptomatic of the culture of slumming, and continues as a facet of class discourse and negotiation into the present day (often applied to postcolonial and migrant subcultures or subsets of a newly minted world literature).

An alternative approach emphasizes that the production of working-class literature is most evident during periods of social crisis so that rather than attempt to construct a continuous lineage, one looks for literature that is, in a sense, entangled in the volatile elements of social contradiction at its most acute moments. The literature of **Chartism**, for example, may not always have been produced by working-class writers themselves, but it lent to the study of British working-class literature a platform from which to analyze in more detail the logic of social formation and its links to the cultural and political spheres. In *The Working Classes in Victorian Fiction*, P. J. Keating productively engages "the literature of social crisis" thesis although, because of the centrality of Chartist literature to it, he tends to occlude the possibility that worker-writers, as distinct from social activists, had a significant role to play within it. Of course, activists and workers are not exactly mutually exclusive categories but the Chartist moment, a political crisis in which working people and sympathizers rallied to the cause of a social charter that affirmed and protected their rights, provides several conceptual and categorical lessons. One is that working-class writing is often closely allied with socialist literature when class warfare intensifies. In *The Industrial Muse*, Martha Vicinus shows that while one must hold to the notion that the working class produces its own writers, socialist literature is of the working class in the sense that it is formed in the crucible of its political and cultural interests. It does not exclude workers from the possibility of its production but neither does it believe that advocacy from beyond the working class must be expunged at all costs to preserve an image of authenticity or genuine class character.

Gareth Stedman Jones, in his then controversial book *Languages of Class*, places form at the center of his polemic, but he does not mean it in the more narrow, literary sense. His argument is about the difficulties in assigning an appropriate language to the Chartist movement, a vocabulary of protest actually experienced by its participants rather than superimposed by the dictates of an already formed class consciousness. A discursive approach (but not necessarily in the sense of Michel Foucault), Jones's strategy is to call into question E. P. Thompson's confidence, in *The Making of the English Working Class,* that the English working class was present at and responsible for its own making by drawing attention to the function of ideology in the space between the experience of the Chartist movement and the more declarative characterizations provided by Friedrich Engels in *The Condition of the Working Class in England* (1844). This is another enduring lesson of Chartism for the study of British working-class and socialist literature: To what extent is it permissible to allow language to rewrite the concept of class? Does this signal simply the eclipse of consciousness and agency as usually construed, or does it creatively permit a level of discontinuity between those who make history and the range of expression in which that class discourse is precipitate?

If the nature of class and crisis trumps in advance the solidity of tradition, literary form often stymies British working-class expression. One reason for the enormous impact of cultural studies on our sense of class is not just that class was present at cultural studies' making (Thompson, Richard Hoggart, **Raymond Williams**, **Stuart Hall**) but that it had to look beyond the literary to gauge the experience of class as a "whole way of life" (as Williams puts it). Indeed, it sometimes had to move beyond experience itself as the guarantee of class negotiation or effects.

Chartism provided an early test of whether a perceived maturity in class formation might interweave the working class and socialist determinants in its purview, yet it was not until the crises and upheavals of the early twentieth century that together they formed a critical mass, beginning in the 1920s. In the interim period, literary output of a distinctly working class or socialist kind diminished somewhat. True, there was the afterlife of the social-problem novel from a middle-class perspective—as in George Gissing's *The Nether World* (1889)—and the work of important writers like Margaret Harkness—as in *A City Girl* (1887) and *Out of Work* (1888)—who was a good deal closer to the social problems described, but even with the impress of socialism in a famous writer like **George Bernard Shaw**, the earlier momentum could not be sustained. Again, this puts a particular onus on the critical vocabulary of class that may not share the continuities afforded by literature as a cultural category, it also places a stress on the force of history itself in how social class is articulated.

The catalysts spurring a resurgence were many, including the political fallout from the decimation of the working class during **World War I**; the formalizing of a political opposition in the Labour Party; reflections on the momentous rise to power of the Bolsheviks in the **Russian Revolution**; numerous networks of anticapitalists, including a renewed and expanded international; and the fulcrum provided by the General Strike of 1926. Much of what constitutes the pinnacle of British working-class and socialist literature resides in the complex fabric of those years. It has to be said, however, that the most influential text was written before those events: Robert Tressell's *The Ragged Trousered Philanthropists*.

Tressell died in 1911, and his novel was published in abridged form three years later. Tressell's narrative of working-class life in Hastings ("Mugsborough") certainly stretches the definition of the novel in challenging ways, and indeed might be said to answer the problems of form encountered by his Chartist forebears. Frank Owen, the hero of the tale, faces a significant problem: how to persuade working-class folks that their misery is not simply the product of their failings, drinking, laziness, big families, and the like. From the very beginning of the book, Tressell through Owen aims to trip up the conventions of storytelling with some fairly bold-faced ideological struggle. If there is tension, it is often dispensed quickly for lessons in political economy and activist strategy. In part, this comes out of the formal genesis of the work, which was precisely in political pamphleteering and the art of persuasion. It also emerges from Tressell's decision not to coddle or romanticize working-class life, but to stir a passion for change by satirizing the weaknesses in its diversions. The combination of these aspects contributed to the extraordinary life of this novel after publication and Tressell's untimely death from tuberculosis. Even though the unexpurgated version of *The Ragged Trousered Philanthropists* did not appear until 1955, it was the hidden classic of the British working class for forty years. Copies were regularly passed from person to person just like pamphlets, with no thought for ownership but only for the pleasure of reading the novel's lessons and humor. Legends abound about its circulation among soldiers and workers, and it was also adapted for the stage on more than one occasion. If Marxists like **Terry Eagleton** and Williams balked at its literary quality, it was more than literary enough to pique the imagination and participation of thousands. As Peter Miles has underlined, Tressell's book shows that the working class need not feel encumbered by literary conventions that issue from beyond its purview but that the writer can adapt and create by any means possible in the articulation of its real foundations. Again, while we emphasize the literature of crisis here, it does not exhaust the possibilities of a counter-literature that, like so much else of working-class substance, remains largely hidden from history.

H. Gustav Klaus (1982) deftly brings to light some less influential but significant works of the 1920s by writers partly inspired by the Russian Revolution of 1917 to imagine Socialism and Communism in the British grain. For instance, *The Underworld* (1920) by James C. Welsh, a Lanarkshire miner, tracks the vicissitudes in love and labor of protagonist Robert Sinclair against a carefully drawn backdrop of Scottish pit culture. Although Klaus faults Welsh for verging on melodrama (Sinclair dies during a pit rescue), the novel emphasizes that however much solidarity may triumph, struggle has its victims, and that this might actually unpin the sentimentality so often ascribed to working-class portrayals. Ethel Carnie's *This Slavery* (1925) mixes convention and didacticism more freely while providing a provocative formal division in her novel. In the first half, she focuses on a life of poverty shared by two sisters, Rachel and Hester. Where the former hones herself for Socialism by, for instance, reading *Das Kapital*, Hester decides that only marrying above her will improve her station. In the novel's second half, the sisters come to occupy the positions of labor and capital themselves, and the narrative examines this opposition in terms of the cotton industry. Eventually Hester reveals her true colors and stands by labor, but she is "accidentally" killed in the process—a warning perhaps for class traitors but more positively an indication of the actual violence that occurs in the struggle of labor and capital.

One of the most interesting novels of labor of the 1920s was neither working class nor socialist in the conventional sense: *Living* (1929), by Henry Green. Resisting realism and the desire for working-class heroes, Green succeeds in evoking the timber of British working-class existence by submitting the sentence to modernist experimentation. Ironically, for this piece of imaginative engagement, Green—of aristocratic stock despite a spell on the floor of one of his father's factories—has been described by the likes of **Harold Heslop** and **Christopher Isherwood** as the finest proletarian writer of the period. Hitchcock ("Passing") has examined this phenomenon in some detail, but the point here is to indicate that the topic of British working-class and socialist literature can embrace all kinds of unlikely allies. Green himself was once termed a "closet socialist," and there remains a significant amount of outing to be done in order to understand more fully the affective embrace of the political on the imagination. During the General Strike, he said he could not look a laborer in the eye, but the topic of desire and the gaze has been undertheorized in relation to class, and so a discovery of the precise nature of Green's achievement lies before us.

As Andy Croft outlines in *Red Letter Days*, numerous other writers with working-class or socialist orientations responded to the cultural and political crises of British society, especially with the advent of the Depression decade of the 1930s. Heslop himself wrote some searing fiction of socialist import, and his *Last Cage Down* (1935) is like Welsh's *The Underground*, **Lewis Jones**'s *Cwmardy* (1937), and Gwyn Jones's *Times Like These* (1936), a cogent exploration of the miner's life and community. Coal mining in Britain, of course, was a key engine of the Industrial Revolution and often laid bare the economic contradictions between labor and capital as well as the unequal relations between the great urban centers and the black seams that served them. When Margaret Thatcher launched a full-scale political and ideological war on the miners in the 1980s, it was not just to break their union but to sever a community from a discursive attachment to the taxonomies of class and class antagonism. The mines may be all but gone, but the question of class cannot be resolved institutionally or by government fiat.

As well as impressive literature of mining, the 1930s featured working-class and socialist expression throughout the culture of work. Walter Brierley, a miner, showed in his novel *Means Test Man* (1935) that his perspective on the industry could provide an understanding of society in general, albeit through the means of naturalism and realism. In the end, although comparisons with **Émile Zola**'s *Germinal* can only produce frustration, Brierley's novel does succeed in conveying the minutia of everyday existence in a form that always pushes beyond the descriptive narrowness of individual passages. Because of its trenchant focus on the difference between work and unemployment, particularly for its main protagonist, Jack Cook, not only was Brierley's novel in touch with a major proletarian concern of the time, but it can also be usefully compared to the often crushing effects of deindustrialization in Britain in the contemporary period. Indeed, in a world where generational and systemic unemployment are not simply anomalies, Brierley's novel provides its own means test of today's social fabric in which far too many out-of-work workers are statistically excluded in order to buttress the claims of a classless New Britain. Another searing social document, Walter Greenwood's *Love on the Dole* (1933) also addresses the effects of unemployment on its main character, Harry Hardcastle, although much critical ink has been spent arguing whether the novel is compromised by the bourgeois individualism associated with the form, certainly a relevant concern but not one that is Greenwood's monopoly. Roger Webster suggests that the narrative actually cuts against the grain of the form's prescriptions by questioning the status of its literary language itself (it is replete with sophisticated literary allusions and an often jarring high-style vocabulary). It is an important point but, to the extent that many of the descriptive passages are out of joint with the characters in their communities, Greenwood seems to resist the lesson provided by Tressell, that working-class literature is in part defined by its readership and not simply its putative subject.

This is not an iron law of the literature, yet some sense of projected readership lends credence to the social dimension of class discourse. Certain class markers— topoi associated with the representation of social relations—may well be translatable across a range of languages, but often the reader has to work hard to understand another form of literacy, the idiosyncracies of regional dialects and intra-language difference. For instance, **Lewis Grassic Gibbon**'s trilogy *A Scots Quair*, comprising *Sunset Song* (1932), *Cloud Howe* (1933), and *Grey Granite* (1934), is justly revered for its tenacious **modernism** and social perspicacity, yet its Scottish intonations make clear that its innovation is also linguistic in a way that the umbrella term "British" does not always do justice. Ramon Lopez Ortega has noted the efficacy of Gibbon's approach, which underlines that resistance to the reader has a specific class inflection in Gibbon's epic cycle, especially as it distances and defamiliarizes English—the language of landowners and occupiers from the south. It also, of course, measures the distance between the dissolution of the lowland peasantry and the urban and sometimes urbane locutions of the industrial working class. Ortega sees in both Gibbon and Lewis Jones an appreciable revolutionary technique: "a mastery of the spoken word and the endowment of old literary forms with the most modern devices of radical expression," and it is through the canny deployment of Scottish and Welsh respectively that summary notions of the working class are both problematized and made new. While there are other socialist novels that critically reflect on the turmoil of the time (for instance, James Lansdale Hodson's *Harvest in the North* [1934] and James Barke's *Major Operation* [1936]), *A Scots Quair* is the most ambitious and, with *The Ragged Trousered Philanthropists*, represents a peak in working-class and socialist literature in the first half of the twentieth century.

It is a commonplace to note that the protest literature of class in the 1930s contributed directly to social reform and the creation of the welfare state. Equally important, the outbreak of **World War II** often smothered dissent through nationalism and the full employment delivered by the war machine. Another factor that affected literary production was the intensification of the cold war from the 1940s on, creating an ideological climate in which honest working-class expression was often equated with trumped-up communist brainwashing. In such an atmosphere, it is not surprising to see working-class writers turn to reflection on the past rather than take sides in the present. For instance, Jack Common's autobiographical novels, *Kiddar's Luck* (1951) and *The Ampersand* (1954), both focus on his upbringing and life before the war, yet nevertheless convey—sometimes through humor and sometimes simply through the brute realities of existence—that the past haunts the present, and that Common is not just doomed personally by his birth into the working class ("I at once came under the minus-sign which society had already placed upon my parents") but that society is doomed in general should its class divisions subsist. By the middle of the 1950s, the ghost of class returned in a surprising way; while the Oxbridge literati set about satirizing the degree to which they were functionally effete, the working class was reminded that despite their growing interpellation as loyal consumers, the catchphrase of the day was not cultural quietism. Just as the Soviet invasion of Hungary in 1956 caused a rash of realignments by British Socialists and Communists, the relative retreat of scarcity precipitated a rethinking of what counted for working-class identity and culture. For some, the major catalyst was John Osborne's play *Look Back in Anger* (1956), which mixed socialist cynicism and sagacity in equal measure. It is true that Osborne's work had an immense impact and helped to project the image of the "angry young man" into the cultural consciousness of the late 1950s and early 1960s. It should also be noted, however, that the class coordinates of the "angries" were complicated by competing narratives: those of the working-class scholarship boy who makes good (as in John Wain's earlier *Hurry on Down* [1953]) and those that favored the representation of less exceptional circumstances. The latter would include Shelagh Delaney's *A Taste of Honey* (1958), David Storey's *This Sporting Life* (1960), Keith Waterhouse's *Billy Liar* (1959), and Stan Barstow's *A Kind of Loving* (1960).

However, the major and distinctive voice among the working-class writers of the time was **Alan Sillitoe**. Sillitoe's first novel, *Saturday Night and Sunday Morning* (1958), brings to a head some of the competing claims on working-class identity but does so in a way that appears neither forced nor as a simple reaction to the maelstrom created by *Look Back in Anger*. The "hero," Arthur Seaton, righteously rejects propaganda from all directions. Not only is he suspicious of the claims of actually existing Socialists, but he refuses the government's ideology of affluence as a ruse to keep people buying rather than barricading. Weak and often self-centered in his personal relations, Seaton is flawed but resilient, a thorn in the side of his everyday working-class community in Nottingham and the platitudes and proclamations of officialdom. One of the enduring achievements of Sillitoe's novel is not just its impressive integration of everyday dialogue into its artistic vision (a trait often discernible in many of the works listed above) but its deft representation of work itself as not simply outside the identities built in the narrative. Perhaps one of the differences between working-class and socialist literature is this: the former is less interested in the sociological facts of work and more focused on its active and affective insinuation in the very texture of existence. Sillitoe is also justly revered for his early short story "The Loneliness of the Long-Distance Runner," (1959) a tale whose first-person narrator, Smith, raises his rebellious exploits as a Borstal boy to the level of existential drama. True, Sillitoe's subsequent literary career (over fifty works of poetry, fiction, and children's books) has rarely struck the chord of this bright beginning, but this owes as much to shifts in cultural expression more generally construed as it does to a failure of imagination.

The "angry" period in British culture (1956–1963) announced a significant disaffection with the tendencies of modern society while also showing that working-class consumers had more than purchasing power over their representation; they actively sought out culture that gave substance to their lives. It is not coincidental that many of the literary works of this period were made into films with varying degrees of success, a kind of British new wave that solidified the impact of this cultural formation. Indeed, working-class cinema has continued to occupy an important place in British society right up to the films of Ken Loach and Mike Leigh in the present day. And television (e.g., the series *Coronation Street* and *Eastenders*) and pop music of various kinds has augmented or surpassed its literary correlatives in the working-class imagination.

From the so-called "kitchen sink" drama of Arnold Wesker to the more cerebral socialism and feminism of **Caryl Churchill**, theater has also been a credible venue for class expression. Indeed, while regional and community theater has generally suffered from bouts of severe state underfunding, the performance arts have offered a continuing commentary on British working-class relations. As suggested at the outset, however, it is difficult to characterize the contemporary period not because of a paucity of literature or because of the availability of viable alternatives on the topic but because the terms of the category are being rethought and redefined. There is no doubt that socialist writing has been produced (one thinks of Raymond Williams's trilogy *Border Country* [1960], *Second Generation* [1964], and *The Fight for Manod* [1979]; and the equally impressive "Into Their Labors" trilogy of **John Berger**: *Pig Earth* [1979], *Once in Europa* [1987], and *Lilac and Flag* [1990]). Similarly, working-class fiction is well represented by the likes of Sid Chaplin (e.g., *The Day of the Sardine* [1961] and *The Mines of Alabaster* [1971]) and **Pat Barker** (*Union Street* [1982] and *The Century's Daughter* [1986]), who has also challenged the inherent masculinism in the tradition if not in class itself. Yet in addition to the impact of a renewed and interrogative gender politics, race has also reconfigured the claims of class, particularly since, from the end of World War II on, immigration and devolution have had to decolonize the assumptions that gird what counts for British. Thus, alongside a poet like Tony Harrison, who has sometimes eloquently and sometimes controversially conveyed a certain embeddedness to the experience of class in Britain, one must take seriously the intervention of the dub poet Linton Kwesi Johnson, who has explored how, for instance, systemic racism fractures working-class alliances. And, while Sillitoe may have captured much of the nuance of working-class Nottingham, the Trinidadian novelist Sam Selvon has done as much for the experience of the West Indian working class in London in such works as *The Lonely Londoners* (1956) and *The Housing Lark* (1965).

British immigrant literature in the contemporary period has often shattered the platitudes and inherent elitism of Britain's literary establishment, although it is true that figures like **Salman Rushdie** and **V. S. Naipaul** have identified with that very stratum. Sukhdev Sandhu has eloquently explored this complex tension between tradition and countertradition in *London Calling* (2003), in which he not only identifies the main currents of immigrant experience in the capital but also explores its provocative subcultures. Selvon has also contributed to this unsentimental representation of the criminal borders of the black working class in *Moses Ascending* (1975), but it is Victor Headley's somewhat infamous "Yardie" trilogy—*Yardie* (1992), *Excess* (1993), and *Yush!* (1994)—that has given full vent to this aspect. In Jamaica, the inhabitants of urban "yards" comprised a criminal underworld that thrived on social deprivation and state disorder. In London, from the 1980s on, these "Yardies" quickly established themselves as some of the toughest gang members in town. The language and plots of Headley's novels eschew any kind of sentimentalizing portrait of the Yardies' often seedy activities but in the process have become classics of black working-class expression. If their literary finesse falls short of the technical expertise of Zadie Smith's brilliant London extravaganza *White Teeth* (2000), or the interclass frisson of South Asians in Hanif Kureishi's *The Buddha of Suburbia* (1990), their populism refuses the studied inclusionism of the new cosmopolitans and the stylish pretensions of "Cool Britannia." Just as Irvine Welsh has foregrounded the inner city anomie of the Scottish working class in *Trainspotting* (1993), so Headley underlines the fact that the unemployment and systemic racism that scar the new economy reveal a working class in flux and often anonymity. If this change rarely finds recognizable political forms (in the 1970s and 1980s, rioting sometimes served this purpose), it is partly because the languages of class are much more difficult to define. Just as literature itself must now compete in a crowded visual and media culture, so working class and socialist jostle with competing terms of political constituency. Indeed, it is precisely that struggle that makes British working-class and socialist literature so necessary of careful study today.

Selected Bibliography: Ashraf, Phyllis Mary. *Introduction to Working-Class Literature in Great Britain. Part II: Prose.* Berlin: VEB Kongres und Werbedruck Oberlungwitz, 1979; Booker, M. Keith. *The Modern British Novel of the Left: A Research Guide.* Westport, CT: Greenwood, 1998; Croft, Andy. *Red Letter Days: British Fiction in the 1930s.* London: Lawrence and Wishart, 1990; Hawthorn, Jeremy, ed. *The British Working-Class Novel in the Twentieth Century.* London: Edward Arnold, 1984; Hitchcock, Peter. "Passing: Henry Green and Working-Class Identity." *Modern Fiction Studies* 40.1 (Spring 1994): 1–31; Hitchcock, Peter. *Working-Class Fiction in Theory and Practice: A Reading of Alan Sillitoe.* Ann Arbor, MI: UMI, 1989; Jones, Gareth Stedman. *Languages of Class.* Cambridge, UK: Cambridge UP, 1983; Keating, P. J. *The Working Classes in Victorian Fiction.* London: Allen and Unwin, 1971; Klaus, H. Gustav, ed. *The Literature of Labour: Two Hundred Years of Working-Class Writing.* New York: St. Martin's, 1985; Klaus, H. Gustav, ed. *The Socialist Novel in Britain: Towards the Recovery of a Tradition.* London: Harvester, 1982; Miles, Peter. "The Painter's Bible and the British Workman: Robert Tressell's Literary Activism." *The British Working-Class Novel in the Twentieth Century.* Ed. Jeremy Hawthorn. London: Edward Arnold, 1984. 1–18; Ortega, Ramon Lopez. "The Language of the Working-Class Novel of the 1930s." *The Socialist Novel in Britain.* Ed. H. Gustav Klaus. London: Harvester, 1982. 122–43; Sandhu, Sukhdev. *London Calling: How Black and Asian Writers Imagined a City.* New York: HarperCollins, 2003; Thompson, E. P. *The Making of the English Working Class.* New York: Vintage-Random House, 1966; Vicinus, Martha. *The Industrial Muse: A Study of Nineteenth-Century British Working-Class Literature.* London: Croom Helm, 1974; Webster, Roger. "*Love on the Dole* and the Aesthetic of Contradiction." *The British Working-Class Novel in the Twentieth Century*. Ed. Jeremy Hawthorn. London: Edward Arnold, 1984. 49–62.

Peter Hitchcock

BROWN, LLOYD L. (1913–2003), labor organizer, journalist, and novelist, for years an editor of *New Masses* and its successor, *Masses and Mainstream*. Born to an African American father—Ralph L. Dight—and a German American mother—Magdalen Paul—Brown (the surname he assumed in tribute to abolitionist John Brown when he became an organizer and joined the Communist Party) was primarily raised in Catholic orphanages after his mother's death when he was four years old. His mother's family rejected the Dight children after her death, and it became apparent that his father, a railroad man, could not care for them all. As a consequence, Brown's early vision of the world was a product of the curricula of Catholic grade schools and his own innate curiosity about a world outside the confines of the Index. He considered himself largely self-educated about things that mattered (human rights, economics, history), but he drew heavily on his school reading of the Western European classics of fiction and poetry for his own writing.

In the 1930s, Brown traveled as a journalist to the Soviet Union, and in 1934, while attending the **Soviet Writers Congress** in Moscow, met Lily Kashin, a young dental assistant on holiday with her brother. Their courtship continued back in the United States and they were married, despite initial opposition from her family because of his race. Later, Lily's father apologized to Brown for having tried to intervene. The Browns moved to Pittsburgh where, in 1940, he was arrested, convicted, and sentenced to prison for his organizing activities. While he was incarcerated, Brown and several party colleagues, who had been convicted on the same charges, got involved in the case of Willie Jones, a young man sentenced to death and held in the same facility. The (unsuccessful) efforts of Brown and his group to turn their prison time to good use and to free Jones became the basic material for Brown's 1951 novel, *Iron City*.

After his release from prison and subsequent military service during **World War II**, the Browns moved to New York City, where he took up a succession of editorial positions in progressive and party publications. He also worked as a copyeditor for the *New York Times*. In the late 1940s, he began his association with Paul Robeson, coauthoring Robeson's 1958 autobiography, *Here I Stand*, and years later writing a short biography of the young Robeson. Brown's editing career continued through the McCarthy era, during which time he was under surveillance by the FBI. On his retirement from active journalism, he and Lily became stalwarts of the upper Manhattan community in which they lived. She was an active community organizer, and after her death in 1996, a park in the Washington Heights section of the city was named for her. Lloyd Brown died of complications from a fall and pulmonary fibrosis.

Beyond his years of editorial and journalistic service, *Iron City* was Brown's most important contribution to the left/progressive movement in America. A superbly crafted and cleanly written example of a kind of "revolutionary romanticism" rarely attempted by American proletarian writers, the novel is perhaps the best explication in fiction we have of the reasons why communism was attractive to Americans of color in the first half of the twentieth century.

Selected Bibliography: Brown, Lloyd L. *The Young Paul Robeson: "On My Journey Now."* Boulder: Westview, 1997; Robeson, Paul. *Here I Stand.* 1958. Preface by Lloyd L. Brown. "Introduction" by Sterling Stuckey. Boston: Beacon, 1988; Suggs, Jon-Christian. *"Iron City*: Race and Revolutionary Romanticism Behind Bars." *Legal Studies Forum* 25 (2001): 449–59.

Jon-Christian Suggs

BULGAKOV, MIKHAIL (1891–1940). Born in Kiev, the capital of today's Ukraine, Bulgakov found himself squarely in the middle of political debates in the Soviet Union in the 1920s and 1930s. As a prominent literary figure during the repressive years of Stalinism, Bulgakov fostered an ironic yet highly moral voice that only posthumously received its full due. The son of a professor of theology, Bulgakov studied medicine in the years preceding the 1917 **Russian Revolution**, practicing briefly as a doctor in the Ukrainian countryside. With the onset of the Russian Civil War, Bulgakov enlisted in the anti-Bolshevik Volunteer Army, acquiring a firsthand look at the protracted conflict between the Reds and the Whites. This war experience served as the basis for Bulgakov's novel *The White Guard* (*Belaia gvardiia*, 1924), which portrays the plight of Russian intellectuals caught up in the civil strife.

In 1921, Bulgakov moved to Moscow, where he began writing humorous newspapers sketches—short works that presented a sarcastic, somewhat guarded perspective on the rapid rise of the new Soviet society and the Bolsheviks' brief new economic policy. Bulgakov's sketches led to a series of feuilletons and other lengthier works, such as the novella *Heart of a Dog* (*Sobach'e serdtse*, 1925)—a satire of both modern (social) science and the utopian Soviet dream to transform the working class. Given its ideological tone, *Heart of a Dog* was deemed unsuitable for publication in Soviet Russia, a taste of censorship to come under **Joseph Stalin**. In the increasingly regulated environment of the 1920s, Bulgakov resorted to writing plays, such as the historical *Day of the Turbins* (*Dni Turbinykh*, 1926) and his 1932 dramatization of **Nikolai Gogol**'s famous nineteenth-century novel *Dead Souls* (*Mertvye dushi*).

By 1929, with Stalin firmly in power and **socialist realism** emerging as the country's predominant literary mode, Bulgakov's plays were banned, a decree that prompted the author's unsuccessful appeal to the government for permission to emigrate. At this time, Bulgakov began writing what was to become his most celebrated work, *The Master and Margarita* (*Master i Margarita*, 1928–1940), a novel that merges satire of life in corrupt Soviet Moscow, grotesque surrealism, and a fictionalized version of the biblical story of Jesus and Pontius Pilate to highlight the ongoing battle between forces of good and evil, a veiled condemnation of Stalinist repression. Due to the novel's religiosity and conspicuous political undercurrent, it was not until the 1960s that *The Master and Margarita* was finally published, albeit posthumously and in censored form. Since the appearance of this controversial yet renowned novel, Bulgakov's reputation has increased tenfold, with his fantastical prose continuing the subversive tradition of Gogolian satire in the Stalinist period.

Selected Bibliography: Curtis, J.A.E. *Bulgakov's Last Decade: The Writer as Hero.* New York: Cambridge UP, 1987; Milne, Lesley. *The Master and Margarita: A Comedy of Victory.* Birmingham, UK: Birmingham Slavonic Monographs, 1977; Proffer, Ellendea. *Bulgakov: Life and Work*. Ann Arbor, MI: Ardis, 1984; Wright, A. Colin. *Mikhail Bulgakov: Life and Interpretations*. Toronto: U of Toronto P, 1978.

Timothy Harte

BULOSAN, CARLOS (1911–1956). Almost a decade after brutal U.S. colonization of the Southeast Asian archipelago (Spanish American War, 1898; Filipino American War, 1899–1902), Carlos Bulosan was born of the peasantry in Mangusmana, Binalonan, of the Pangasinan Province. Uprooted from the semi-feudal Philippine countryside, Bulosan joined thousands of Filipino migrant workers on U.S. plantations (100,000 in Hawaii and 30,000 in California) and in fish canneries along the West Coast during the Depression. Arriving in 1930 without finishing high school, Bulosan forged an alternative education as an organic intellectual, through his involvement in the labor movement.

Bulosan participated in the United Cannery, Agricultural, Packing and Allied Workers of America, and developed a lasting friendship with Filipino labor organizer Chris Mensalvas. In 1934, he edited the worker's magazine *The New Tide*, which connected him to Sanora Babb, **Richard Wright**, **William Carlos Williams**, and others. Hospitalized in Los Angeles for serious health issues (including tuberculosis) from 1936 to 1938, Bulosan received encouragement from his brother Aurelio, friend Dorothy Babb (Sanora's sister), and *Poetry* editor Harriet Monroe to nurture his craft. He enthusiastically studied a wide variety of authors including **Gorky**, **Neruda**, **Tolstoy**, Rizal, Bonifacio, and various Marxist literary critics. According to friend Dolores Feria, Bulosan sharpened his political analysis with issues of *New Masses*, the *New Republic*, and the *Nation*.

Bulosan was a prolific writer of essays, poems, and fiction from the early 1930s until his death in 1956. Through **World War II**, Bulosan produced some of his most widely recognized works: *Laughter of My Father*, a satirical indictment of Philippine class society (1944); and *America Is in the Heart*, his classic "ethnobiographical" testament to the resourcefulness and militancy of the Philippine peasantry and Filipino workers (1946). Bulosan occupied a prominent position on the U.S. cultural Left as well as in the popular imagination of the American public. He was listed in *Who's Who* and commissioned by President Roosevelt in 1943 to write "Freedom from Want," which was displayed at the San Francisco federal building and published in the *Saturday Evening Post* with a Norman Rockwell illustration. Despite celebrity, Bulosan remained committed to advancing the struggles of working and exploited people in the United States and the Philippines.

Blacklisted in America and by CIA-supported Philippine President Magsaysay, Bulosan reaffirmed his political/artistic visions during the postwar period. In 1949, he defended the rights of leading figures of the Local 7, FTA–CIO—Ernesto Mangaoang, Chris Mensalvas, Ponce Torres, Casimiro Bueno Absolor, and Joe Prudencio—charged for membership in the **Communist Party**, USA. In 1952, Mensalvas invited Bulosan to edit the International Longshoreman's and Warehousemen's Union, Local 37, Yearbook (Seattle), which includes a passionate call to release imprisoned Philippine-based poet/labor-union leader **Amado V. Hernandez**. Around

1955, inspired by Luis Taruc's *Born of the People* (1953), Bulosan wrote *The Cry and the Dedication*, a complexly layered dramatization of the anti-imperialist Huk peasant insurgency in the Philippines. It was posthumously edited and published in 1977 by U.S.-based Filipino scholar-activist, cultural theorist, and artist **E. San Juan Jr.** (republished, 1995).

Scholars and activists continue to reclaim Bulosan's imagination, which fuses U.S. proletarian literary aesthetics and third-world subaltern resistance. In the late 1980s, revered Philippine-based playwright Bienvenido Lumbera created an opera in Filipino, the national language, based on *America Is in the Heart*. During the 1990s, Bulosan was a prominent subject of dissertations (Timothy Libretti), and landmark publications in American studies (Michael Denning) and U.S. ethnic/cultural studies (E. San Juan Jr.).

Selected Bibliography: Campomanes, Oscar V. "Carlos Bulosan." *Encyclopedia of the American Left.* Ed. Mary Jo Buhle et al. Urbana: U of Illinois P, 1992; Denning, Michael. *The Cultural Front: The Laboring of American Culture in the Twentieth Century.* New York: Verso, 1996; De Vera, Arleen. "Without Parallel: The Local 7 Deportation Cases, 1949–1955." *Amerasia Journal* 20.2 (1994): 1–25; Evangelista, Susan. *Carlos Bulosan and His Poetry: A Biography and Anthology.* Quezon City, Philippines: Ateneo de Manila UP, 1985; Libretti, Tim. "First and Third Worlds in U.S. Literature: Rethinking Carlos Bulosan." *MELUS* 23.4 (Winter 1998): 135–55; Patrick, Josephine. "Remembering Carlos: Interview with Josephine Patrick." By Odette Taverna. *Katipunan* (April 1989): 13–14; San Juan, E., Jr. *Carlos Bulosan and the Imagination of the Class Struggle.* Quezon City, Philippines: U of the Philippines P, 1972; San Juan, E., Jr. *From Exile to Diaspora: Versions of the Filipino Experience in the United States.* Boulder, CO: Westview P, 1998; Schirmer, Daniel B., and Stephen Rosskamm Shalom, eds. *The Philippines Reader: A History of Colonialism, Neocolonialism, Dictatorship, and Resistance.* Boston, MA: South End P, 1987.

Jeffrey Arellano Cabusao

BURGER'S DAUGHTER (1979), by **Nadine Gordimer**, is probably the most profound political novel to have come from South Africa, and one of the major political novels of the twentieth century. Emerging from the depths of the apartheid era, it tells the story of Rosa Burger, daughter of Lionel Burger, inspirational South African communist revolutionary, whose legacy Rosa comes to question. In the character of Lionel Burger in particular, the novel indicates its documentary proximities—in this case to the figure of Bram Fischer, the Afrikaner Communist and lawyer, on whose life Burger's is loosely based. The novel's other major encounter with its wider setting relates to the Soweto Revolt of 1976, an event that had a significant impact on Gordimer. The revolt was for the most part led and sustained by schoolchildren who, inspired by the ideology of black consciousness, rejected both what they saw as the quiescence of their parents' generation and the duplicities of white liberalism and radicalism. Together these two focal areas comprise the thematic arena of the novel, for the revolt of children against parents and the development of an alternative ethic of engagement in harsh times is exactly what Rosa's story is about.

This is where the particular genius of the novel lies, for all of this is worked through Rosa's internal life, as these forces fuse and break within her. Growing up, her whole world had been defined by her parents' version of politics; now, after her father's death in prison, she feels the need for a private life, realizing too the limits of her father's "litany" of beliefs when it comes to questions of existential reality. At the same time, the black consciousness ethos, marginalizing any space for white involvement in the liberation movement in South Africa, has effectively displaced her. For Rosa, the net effects are climactic; after witnessing an act that seems to summarize the depth of human suffering and cruelty, and realizing that she does not know how to live in her father's country, Rosa leaves for the south of France to seek out a surrogate mother figure, her father's first wife, Katya. There she falls in love in a fairly sybaritic world where freedom is always personal and heroism safely in the past. But on a visit to London she encounters again the black man who as a young boy had been like a brother to her, living in the Burger household; a midnight telephone conversation with him, filled with all the intense recrimination and tortured love of a familial conflict, is partly what prompts her to return to South Africa, where she takes up work as a physiotherapist dealing with the wounded and damaged children of the Soweto Revolt. This is not a function of Lionel's ideology, but in some sense Rosa has found her legacy and her "place"; our last vision of her is in prison, awaiting trial for undisclosed activities.

This is a **bildungsroman** with a difference, therefore, and other aspects of the novel's form are equally crucial. At stake are the fragments and composition of Rosa's identity. Her narrative is also fractured, ranging from first-person recitation; to Rosa's second-person dialogue with various absent figures, including her father; to a range of third-person narratives; to an actual historical document released by the Soweto Students Representative Council. *Burger's Daughter* is an epic novel with a wide historical and intellectual sweep; it is at the same time extraordinarily nuanced in its understanding of the intricacies of personal and political life. It is a novel that, like the watermark of sunlight Rosa sees in prison, offers a reduced though translucent sense of endurance and hope.

Selected Bibliography: Gordimer, Nadine, et al. *What Happened to Burger's Daughter, or How South African Censorship Works*. Johannesburg: Taurus, 1980; Newman, Judie, ed. *Nadine Gordimer's* Burger's Daughter: *A Casebook*. Oxford: Oxford UP, 2003; Yelin, Louise. "Problems of Gordimer's Poetics: Dialogue in *Burger's Daughter*." *Feminism, Bakhtin and the Dialogic*. Ed. Dale M. Bauer and Susan Jaret McKinstry. Albany: SUNY P, 1991. 219–38.

Stephen Clingman

BURKE, FIELDING (1869–1968). Pseudonym of Olive Tilford Dargan, writer of poetry, novels, and nonfiction focusing on the southern Appalachian area. Olive Tilford was born on a farm in Grayson County, Kentucky, to abolitionist parents. When she was ten, her parents moved to the southern Ozarks and started a school, where Olive was teaching by the age of fourteen. She attended Peabody Teacher's College in Nashville and later Radcliffe. While at Radcliffe she met her future husband, Pegram Dargan, a poet. They married in 1898, and in 1906 they bought a farm in Almond, North Carolina, which was operated by tenant farmers. Olive Dargan began publishing poetry and verse drama in 1904. She traveled extensively, living in England from 1911 to 1914, where she published *The Mortal Gods*, a drama about the oppression of the working class. Her husband drowned in 1915, and she lived from then until 1923 at the farm, publishing a book of sonnets dedicated to her husband, *The Cycle's Rim* (1916), and poetry focusing on the region, *Lute and Furrow* (1922). In 1925 she moved to Asheville and published her highly acclaimed collection of short stories, *Highland Annals*, republished in 1941 as *My Highest Hill* (with photographs by Bayard Wootten).

Dargan considered herself a Marxist and a feminist. In the 1930s she reinvented herself as a writer of **proletarian fiction**, writing under the Fielding Burke pseudonym. *Call Home the Heart* (1932) and *A Stone Came Rolling* (1935) focus on the 1929 **Gastonia Mill strike**. These revolutionary novels are also feminist in content, focusing on a female protagonist struggling for independence. *Sons of the Stranger* (1947), also a proletarian novel, is set during a miner's strike in Colorado. After these three novels, Burke returned to poetry; one of these collections, *The Spotted Hawk* (1958), won several awards. She published her last work, *Innocent Bigamy and Other Stories*, in 1962.

Selected Bibliography: Cook, Sylvia Jenkins. *From Tobacco Road to Route 66: The Southern Poor White in Fiction.* Chapel Hill: U North Carolina P, 1976; Foley, Barbara. *Radical Representations: Politics and Form in U.S. Proletarian Fiction, 1929–1941.* Durham, NC: Duke UP, 1993; Hapke, Laura. *Daughters of the Great Depression: Women, Work, and Fiction in the American 1930s.* Athens: U of Georgia P, 1995; Mullen, Bill, and Sherry Lee Linkon, eds. *Radical Revisions: Rereadings of 1930s Culture.* Urbana: U of Illinois P, 1996; Rideout, Walter B. *The Radical Novel in the United States, 1900–1954.* Cambridge: Harvard UP, 1956.

Renny Christopher

BUTLER, JUDITH (1956–). Currently the Maxine Elliot Professor in the Departments of Rhetoric and Comparative Literature at the University of California, Berkeley, Butler is one of the most influential theorists in the United States, especially in the fields of gender studies and queer theory. She received her Ph.D. in Philosophy from Yale University in 1984. A prolific author (often criticized for her opaque and unnecessarily complex writing style), she has published a number of works on philosophy, politics, and gender, all marked by a radical feminist perspective inflected through poststructuralism. Her numerous books include *Subjects of Desire: Hegelian Reflections in Twentieth-Century France* (1987), *Gender Trouble: Feminism and the Subversion of Identity* (1990), *Bodies That Matter: On the Discursive Limits of "Sex"* (1993), *The Psychic Life of Power: Theories of Subjection* (1997), *Excitable Speech* (1997), *Antigone's Claim: Kinship Between Life and Death* (2000), and *Contingency, Hegemony, Universality,* with Ernesto Laclau and **Slavoj Zizek** (2000). She has also published numerous essays on philosophy and feminist and queer theory.

Gender Trouble and *Bodies That Matter* are clearly Butler's most important works, elaborating her most influential ideas about the performativity of gender, in which the categories "male" and "female" are understood as a repetition of culturally embedded actions instead of natural or inevitable absolutes. Adopting a particularly radical, poststructuralist notion of the social construction of gender, Butler argues that even our perceptions of the physical body are conditioned by assumptions about gender, and that feminists have all too easily accepted these perceptions as absolutes. For her, feminists have made a crucial mistake by attempting to define a single "woman's" perspective. Butler notes that feminists rejected the idea that biology is destiny, but then developed an account of patriarchal culture that assumed that masculine and feminine genders would inevitably be built, by culture, on "male" and "female" bodies, making the same destiny just as inescapable. That argument allows no room for choice or difference and no basis for resistance. For Butler, gender is not a fixed attribute but a fluid variable that shifts and changes in different contexts and at different times. Further, she argues that current, repressive notions of gender identity can be challenged through a recognition of the performativity of gender. In particular, she urges the performance of transgressive gender identities as a way to destabilize rigid assumptions about the nature of gender.

The *Judith Butler Reader*, coedited by Butler and Sara Salih, appeared in 2002. Butler's recent publications include *Precarious Life: Powers of Violence and Mourning* (2004)—a collection of writings on the impact of war on language and thought—and *Undoing Gender* (2004)—a collection of essays on gender and sexuality.

Selected Bibliography: Butler, Judith. *Bodies That Matter: On the Discursive Limits of "Sex."* New York: Routledge, 1993; Butler, Judith. *Excitable Speech: A Politics of the Performative.* New York: Routledge, 1997; Butler, Judith. *Gender Trouble: Feminism and the Subversion of Identity.* New York: Routledge, 1990; Butler, Judith. *Subjects of Desire: Hegelian Reflections in Twentieth-Century France.* New York: Columbia UP, 1987; Butler, Judith, Slavoj Zizek, and Ernesto Laclau. *Contingency, Hegemony, Universality: Contemporary Dialogues on the Left.* London: Verso, 2000; Salih, Sara. *Judith Butler.* London: Routledge, 2002; Salih, Sara, and Judith Butler, eds. *The Judith Butler Reader.* Oxford: Blackwell, 2002.

M. Keith Booker

C

CALVINO, ITALO (1923–1985) won celebrity across the English-speaking world in the 1970s after shedding his commitment to Marxism and politically oriented realist narrative, climaxing with his ultra-postmodern metanovel *Se una giornata d'inverno un viaggiatore* (*If on a Winter's Night a Traveler*, 1979). His educational background was as scientific as it was literary. Anti-Fascism drew him first into the Resistance and then into the **Communist Party**, in which he was active until 1956. His neorealist fictional narratives on the Resistance and postwar living in the Italy of the economic miracle showed a "magic" element, which took over in the playful moral and political allegory of the historical fantasy trilogy *I nostri antenati* (*Our Ancestors*) of the 1950s. Having contributed significantly to the left-wing intellectual debates of the early 1950s, Calvino joined Elio Vittorini in editing the journal *Il Menabò di letteratura* (The Printer's Dummy, 1959–1967), which theorized the relation between literature and industry not in terms of realist subject matter but in terms of revolutionizing the literary medium itself, largely in parallel with information technology. This led Calvino's fiction writing into increasingly postmodern directions, including pseudoscientific reflective fantasies and *giochi combinatori*—that is, permutations on either preexistent sign systems, such as tarot cards, or imaginary ones, as in *Le cittá invisibili* (*Invisible Cities*, 1972). What all of Calvino's narrative fiction has in common, linking his early Marxism with his abiding scientism and his waxing postmodernism, is the deletion of individualism. Some of his essays on literature and politics are available in English in *The Uses of Literature*.

Selected Bibliography: Calvino, Italo. *The Uses of Literature: Essays*. Trans. by P. Creagh. New York: Harcourt, 1986; Gatt-Rutter, John. "Calvino Ludens: Literary Play and Its Political Implications." *Journal of European Studies* 5 (1975); McLaughlin, M. L. *Italo Calvino*. Edinburgh: Edinburgh UP, 1997; Re, Lucia. *Calvino and the Age of Neo-realism: Fables of Estrangement*. Stanford, CA: Stanford UP, 1990.

John Gatt-Rutter

CANADIAN LITERATURE (ANGLOPHONE). The distinction of Canada as a political and cultural territory has its taproot in the latter decades of the eighteenth century—in the churning years of commercial and military contest between France and Britain for North American domination, followed by the upheavals of the American Revolution. Spurred by the search for settlement or by the strategies of commerce or war, the period saw vast movements of Aboriginal, French, and British groups, all of whose changing and local circumstances required spontaneously close collaborations, and whose feelings for and formal allegiances with each other were often ambivalent or volatile. Thus, an imaginary stage was set for an anxious triangle of "Canadian" types—Québécois, British, and Indian—whose mutual contradictions must repeatedly be explored and imaginatively resolved in the literature of the coming century. Often a fourth type, the new American, produced a fretful square. This political allegory plays itself out in personal dramas at the center of novels such as John Richardson's *Wacousta* (1832) and its sequel *The Canadian Brothers* (1840), Rosanna Leprohon's *Antoinette de Mirecourt* (1864), and William Kirby's *The Golden Dog* (1877); of poetry by Charles Mair, Isabella Valancy Crawford, and Duncan Campbell Scott; and of settler memoirs such as Susanna Moodie's *Roughing It in the Bush* (1852). At the start of the twentieth century, the first important Canadian political novel, Sara Jeannette Duncan's *The Imperialist* (1904), began to turn away from this triangle in order to confront the contradiction between an internalized American social formation and a residual British culture. Meanwhile, Mohawk poet **Pauline Johnson** emerged influentially to write political poetry and criticism that radically revised the nineteenth-century Indian type employed as a catalyst in the imaginary synthesis of French and English elements. However, this triangular political allegory never disappears, returning in such later texts as Leonard Cohen's novel *Beautiful Losers* (1966).

Near the end of the nineteenth century, the influence of maternal and new woman feminisms produced complex, ambivalent critiques of patriarchal power and social norms that broke away from the constraints of domestic realism, in novels such as Joanna Wood's *The Untempered Wind* (1894) and Duncan's *A Daughter of Today* (1895). An important focus was the trials of the professional woman, as in Madge Macbeth's *Shackles* (1926). In the period between the world wars, the critical representation of oppressive patriarchy was an important element in fiction by Mazo de la Roche and Martha Ostenso, as well as by male writers such as Frederick Philip Grove and Sinclair Ross. In the latter half of the twentieth century, many influential female writers emerged alongside second-wave feminism, such as Margaret Laurence, Phyllis Webb, Alice Munro, **Margaret Atwood**, and Daphne Marlatt. Struggling additionally to illuminate racial oppression were writers such as Caribbean Canadian poet Dionne Brand and Japanese Canadian fiction writer Joy Kogawa. Such feminist influences have also powerfully intertwined with Aboriginal experience in a rapidly growing body of Inuit and First Nations literature, as in poetry by Louise Bernice Halfe and fiction by Jeannette Armstrong.

Literature between the Great War and the 1950s reflected new concerns arising from the substantial immigration of groups neither French nor British, such as the Scandinavian and German communities in the fiction of Grove and Martha Ostenso. It also explicitly registered and explored new class conflicts and class consciousness, which arose from bank foreclosures of land in rural economies, widespread industrialization, and urban growth, all capped by the Depression. The rise of leftist labor, political, and artists' organizations and the currency of Marxist discourse is central to the development of canonical modernism in Canada—foremost the poets F. R. Scott and Dorothy Livesay, along with other poets active on the left, such as A. M. Klein, Phyllis Webb, and Earle Birney. Novelists such as J. G. Sime, in *Our Little Life* (1921), and Morley Callaghan explored the walls between working and bourgeois classes via urban realism. A landmark novel by Irene Baird, *Waste Heritage* (1939), creates a vision of modern society based on the organized mass protest of unemployed workers in Vancouver and Victoria in 1938. The class exploitation political concerns of these decades are inherited by activist poets Milton Acorn and Bronwen Wallace, the **Neruda**-influenced poet Pat Lowther, and the covert-operations scholar and poet Peter Dale Scott, author of *Coming to Jakarta* (1988). Such concerns are also found in fiction—for example, in Armstrong's novel of aboriginal oppression, *Whispering in Shadows* (2000); Margaret Sweatman's novel of the 1919 Winnipeg General Strike, *Fox* (1991); and Brian Fawcett's *Cambodia* (1986). Influenced by such sources as McLuhanism (see **Marshall McLuhan**), language writing, and *écriture feminine*, a left-ist politics has also been explored as a formal possibility in language media by writers such as Steve McCaffery in *North of Intention* (1986).

Finally, it may be observed that antipatriarchal, antiracist, antihomophobic, and class-based social critiques are typical of contemporary Canadian fiction writing in English by writers such as Atwood, Laurence, and Marlatt, already mentioned, and most notably by **Michael Ondaatje**, Timothy Findley, Rudy Wiebe, Robert Kroetsch, Jane Urquhart, Susan Swan, and Tomson Highway. These and others have turned to poetic or fictional forms that use historical records and documents to explore political and social conflicts, or find alternative historical communities, in the past. A powerful example of the latter is George Elliott Clarke's evocation of an African Canadian community in *Whylah Falls* (1991); and, of the former, Wayne Johnston's historiographic metafiction of Newfoundland, *The Colony of Unrequited Dreams* (1998).

Selected Bibliography: Brydon, Diana, ed. *Testing the Limits: Postcolonial Theories and Canadian Literature.* Special issue of *Essays on Canadian Writing* 56 (Fall 1995); Craig, Terrence. *Racial Attitudes in English-Canadian Fiction, 1905–1980.* Waterloo, ON: Wilfrid Laurier UP, 1987; Creelman, David. *Setting in the East: Maritime Realist Fiction.* Montréal: McGill-Queen's UP, 2003; Davey, Frank. *Canadian Literary Power.* Edmonton: NeWest P, 1994; Dean, Misao. *Practising Femininity: Domestic Realism and the Performance of Gender in Early Canadian Fiction.* Toronto: U Toronto P, 1998; Heble, Ajay, Donna Palmateer Pennee, and J. R. (Tim) Struthers, eds. *New Contexts of Canadian Criticism.* Peterborough, ON: Broadview P, 1997; Kertzer, Jonathan. *Worrying the Nation: Imagining a National Literature in English Canada.* Toronto: U Toronto P, 1998; Neuman, Shirley, and Smaro Kamboureli, eds. *A Mazing Space: Writing Canadian, Women Writing.* Edmonton: Longspoon/NeWest P, 1986; Willmott, Glenn. *Unreal Country: Modernity in the Canadian Novel in English.* Montréal: McGill-Queen's UP, 2002.

Glenn Willmott

CANADIAN LITERATURE (FRANCOPHONE). The first French Canadian novel appeared only in 1837, because of the condemnation of this genre by powerful clerical and lay leaders. The imitative gothic mode was the main trend until the mid-1840s when there emerged the *roman de la terre* (novel of the land). After the defeat of the 1837–1838 uprisings for independence from Britain, ideologues imposed a defensive, mythic nationalism that held that French Canadian survival lay in a traditional Catholic, farm-based society and culture. Realism and naturalism were taboo. Thus, the novel of the land would dominate novel production well into the 1950s even though an urban, industrialized society was already pronounced on the eve of **World War I**.

Cracks in the armor of the generally otherworldly *roman de la terre* (also called the *roman de la fidélité*, "novel of faithfulness") appeared as early as 1863 with Philippe Aubert de Gaspé's **historical novel**, *Les Anciens Canadiens*. At the beginning of the twentieth century, Rodolphe Girard's *Marie Calumet* (1904), in a mode of Rabelaisian anticlerical satire, and Albert Laberge's *Bitter Bread* (*La Scouine*, 1918), in a mode of stark naturalism, attacked the idealization of the land. On the other hand, the celebrated *Maria Chapdelaine* (1916), by the gifted Brittany-born Louis Hémon, rekindled the traditional novel with its mystical tones combined with realistic touches. In 1937, Philippe Panneton (writing as "Ringuet") produced his classic work *Thirty Acres* (*Trente Arpents*), which basically sealed the fate of the idealized rural novel with its fatalist picture of the fragility of farm life in the face of war, market instability, rural exodus to city factories, and resulting linguistic and social alienation. Similarly, though with more warmth, Germaine Guèvremont's *The Outlanders* (*Le Survenant*, 1945) flayed rural isolationism and stressed collective "giving" over individualistic "taking." The last major novel of *fidélité* was F.-A. Savard's *Master of the River* (*Menaud maître-draveur*, 1938), which treated French Canadian dispossession with mythic and ethnocentric essentialism.

With the massive movement of rural folk to the cities from the eve of **World War II** to 1950, the novel inevitably set its preferred milieu in the crowded working-class areas of large urban centers. Roger Lemelin's satirical *The Town Below* (*Au pied de la pente douce*, 1944) and Gabrielle Roy's emblematic work of social realism, *The Tin Flute* (**Bonheur d'occasion**, 1945) irrevocably affected this fundamental change. The Depression, the conscription crisis, and the weakening influence of the church on people's lives emerged in these and subsequent works by the two authors, especially in Roy's *The Cashier* (*Alexandre Chenevert*, 1954), with its pointed critique of capitalism and religion's role in its maintenance. The early postwar era also witnessed the publication of the automatiste artists' manifesto, *Refus global* (Total Rejection, 1948), by Paul-Emile Borduas, which also scored capitalism and religion, as well as Stalinism, and has had a pronounced influence on artistic and literary experimentation until the present time.

Industrial conflict appeared episodically in the works of the pioneers of urban social realism. In the 1950s, writers of lesser talent, like Jean-Jules Richard and Pierre Gélinas, gave greater play to this phenomenon. The former's *Le Feu dans l'amiante* (Fire in Asbestos, 1956) treats the pivotal miners' strike of 1949, while the latter's *Les Vivants, les morts et les autres* (The Living, the Dead, the Others, 1959) includes chapters on lumber and retail walkouts, as well as the iconic hockey riot of 1955 and the crisis in the radical Left following Khrushchev's condemnation of **Stalin** before the Soviet Communist Congress of 1956. Yet neither work succeeds in creating full-blooded characters. André Langevin's existentialist *Dust over the City* (*Poussière sur la ville*, 1953) is also set in the asbestos region of eastern Quebec, but only as background for a tragedy of failed love between a petty bourgeois doctor and his wife of humbler origin. It underlines the cultural and economic alienation of French-speaking workers in the employ of U.S.-owned mines.

It would be some two decades before there would be another ambitious attempt to create a saga of working-class life against the background of economic and political strife. Paul Villeneuve's long novel *Johnny Bungalow* (1974) covers the late Depression period to the first violent acts in 1963 by the Front de Libération du Québec (FLQ). It was particularly successful in its portrayal of the courageous matriarch, Marguerite, but criticized for structural flaws.

With the death of the repressive Quebec premier, Maurice Duplessis, in 1959, the floodgates opened to rapid modernization and secularization throughout Quebec. Novels by major writers helped usher in the subsequent so-called Quiet Revolution, which, as noted, also saw turbulent events staged by the minuscule but influential FLQ (1963–1970). The term "Québécois" replaced the vaguer "Canadien français" to designate a majority within the limits of Quebec, which a substantial number of citizens wanted to make an independent nation-state. First-person narration became a hallmark of the novel, as did outbursts of eroticism, anger, and verbal violence, some of it paralleling real events.

Gérard Bessette's *Not for Every Eye* (*Le Libraire*, 1960)—a self-reflexive journal-novel in which a jaded antihero outsmarts his boss and clerical censors by selling books on the Index—marked an important turning point by creating the first Québécois protagonist. The latter's *Knife on the Table* (*Le Couteau sur la table*, 1965), Claude Jasmin's *Ethel and the Terrorist* (*Ethel et le terroriste*, 1964), and especially Hubert Aquin's *Next Episode* (**Prochain épisode**, 1965) presented heroes engaged in, or contemplating, political violence. Godbout coined the term "texte national" for these and other works that reflected rising national consciousness. His positively self-assertive *Hail Galarneau* (*Salut Galarneau*, 1967) was followed by the pessimistically nationalist *Les Têtes à Papineau* (Papineau's Heads, 1981), a fantasy about a bicephalic (and bilingual) "character" who loses his French nature following surgery. This work, and Yves Beauchemin's xenophobic best-seller *The Alley Cat* (*Le Matou*, 1981), can be seen as varied fictional reactions to the defeat of the sovereignty-association referendum of 1980. Godbout's most recent novel, *The Golden Galarneaus* (*Le Temps des Galarneau*, 1993), like *Le Matou*, reflects animosity toward immigrants.

The young writers grouped around the journal *Parti pris* (Our Stand Is Taken, 1963–1968)—which promoted a secular, socialist, and independent Quebec—chose *joual*, the highly anglicized, truncated jargon of poor French-speaking workers of Montreal, as a literary tool meant to hold up a mirror to their alienation in order to overcome it. The most characteristic work in this mold was Jacques Renaud's lower-depths novella *Broke City* (*Le Cassé*, 1964).

Jacques Ferron, a brilliant writer of tales, also produced novels that reflected the preoccupations of the *Parti pris* group. But unlike their naturalistic/realistic approach, he chose the mode of **magic realism** for his *Dr. Cotnoir* (*Cotnoir*, 1962) and *The Juneberry Tree* (*L'Amélanchier*, 1970), both treating "deviant" mental behavior caused by social dysfunction.

Two premier novelists who made their mark in the 1960s are Marie-Claire Blais and Réjean Ducharme. The first used the long-repressed carnivalesque mode and surrealism in her satire of the pre–World War II idealized rural family and the church in *A Season in the Life of Emmanuel* (*Une Saison dans la vie d'Emmanuel,* 1965). The second, through verbal fireworks and bizarre characters, showed nationalist tendencies in *Le Nez qui voque* (an untranslatable word play, 1967) and *Wild to Mild* (*L'Hiver de force,* 1973), particularly concerning the central language issue. But in the latter, he distanced himself from the pretentiousness of the new elites of the pro-independence Parti Québécois, his heroes' employers.

One of Quebec's finest writers is Anne Hébert, author of the striking short story "Le Torrent" (1950), which symbolically thrashed the toll caused by guilt-ridden Catholic *rigorisme.* First a major poet, she turned to the novel form in *The Silent Rooms* (*Les Chambres de bois,* 1958). Although set in northern France, it may be an allegory for Quebec's shift from traditionalism to modernism. In it, the metal worker's daughter, Catherine, escapes from the demented ambiance of the Parisian apartment she shares with her wealthy husband to find freedom and love with a manual worker/potter in the sunny Midi. Hébert reached a summit in her formidable protofeminist *Kamouraska* (1970), with its echoes of the risings of 1837–1838 and cultural alienation. Hébert continued her feminist quest in *In the Shadow of the Wind* (*Les Fous de Bassan,* 1982), a violent tale of rape and murder in an Anglophone sectarian community strongly resembling the inbred French-speaking parishes of yore.

Another protofeminist writer, Claire Martin, produced an outstanding two-volume autobiography that reads like a novel: *In an Iron Glove* and *The Right Cheek* (*Dans un gant de fer,* 1965, 1966). Covering her first quarter century, the books center on the sadistic father and brutalized mother and their daughters, all trapped in a web of church-inspired sexual dualism. Martin denounces, too, the anti-Semitism of her convent education.

Gabrielle Roy, a pioneer in sympathetically treating Canada's mosaic of races and cultures, published *Windflower* (*La Rivière sans repos,* 1970), set in subarctic Ungava. The heroine is an Inuit woman who is raped by a southern-born U.S. soldier during World War II. Her son becomes a bomber pilot in Vietnam, the brutalized people of which remind her of her own dark-skinned folk. Yves Thériault is a prolific novelist, many of whose characters also belong to ethnic or racial minorities. Self-taught, he, like Martin, flayed "Christian" anti-Semitism in his *Aaron* (1954, 1957), and presented strong Amerindian figures in *Ashini* (1960) and *N'tsuk* (1968). But his breathtaking best-seller *Agaguk* (1958) and the rest of his "Eskimo" trilogy is stamped with neocolonialism. His Inuit characters resemble Amerindians in their social organization, and repressed Québécois in their sexual mores.

It is generally accepted that the most important trend in Quebec novel writing in the 1970s was the appearance of a cohort of feminist writers who revolutionized the form and content of the genre. Nicole Brossard's *These Our Mothers; or, The Disintegrating Chapter* (*L'Amer; ou le chapitre effrité,* 1977) attacks Quebec's long-lasting stress on women's reproductive function. Louky Bersianik's *L'Euguélionne* (The Euguelionne, 1976), meaning "she who brings the good news," is a multigeneric compendium of fiction, essay, manifesto, feminist dictionary, and sex manual. It mixes satire (of Freud, Lacan, the Old and New Testaments) with a denunciation of war and colonialism. France Theoret's *Nous parlerons comme on écrit* (We'll Talk the Way One Writes, 1982), in a more autobiographical vein, treats imposed female silence in striking surrealistic images. While dealing positively with Quebec's ideological evolution in the 1960s and 1970s, the narrator's persona criticizes the leftist dogmatism of colleagues in her teachers' union and elsewhere.

Strong women characters also appear in Antonine Maillet's novels set in French-speaking New Brunswick. Author of the brilliant *La Sagouine* (1971)—the dramatic monologues in the Acadian dialect of her slattern-washerwoman, with their dialectical, biting commentaries on the haves and have-nots—she followed it with *Maria, Daughter of Gélas* (*Mariaagélas*, 1973), about a resourceful rum smuggler of the prohibition era who sets fire to a fish-packing plant in protest of its grim work environment. Her best-known work is *Pélagie, the Return to a Homeland* (*Pélagie-la-charrette*, 1979)—a text replete with legends and folktales that recount the 1755 expulsion of the Acadians, their scattering in the American colonies, and their epic trek back to their land (1770–1780) through the eyes of generations of chroniclers.

A critique of U.S. politics and culture has appeared in a number of Quebec novels of the last thirty years. André Langevin's *L'Elan d'Amérique* (1972) used nouveau roman techniques to paint a depressing picture of the assault on traditional life in the North by American technology. Jacques Godbout's *L'Ile au dragon* (Dragon Island, 1976) and *An American Story* (*Une Histoire américaine*, 1986) use wit and fantasy to attack, respectively, a financier who wants to dump atomic waste on a Quebec island, and the military laboratories of California that are preparing "the end of the world . . . inexorably." Marie-Claire Blais's much deeper, richly crafted *These Festive Nights* (*Soifs*, 1995), set in Key West, presents characters haunted by the memory of Nazi atrocities, the resurgence of the Ku Klux Klan, the electrocution of black prisoners, and the bombing of Baghdad during the first Gulf War. Also outstanding is Jacques Poulin's *Volkswagen Blues* (1984), which probes *Américanité* (Americanness) through the eyes of its two protagonists—the Quebec City writer, Jack, and his traveling companion, the Métis car mechanic, Pitsémine. They crisscross the United States from northeast to southwest, each reading American history from their respective Francophone and Amerindian heritages. While he is excited by the traces of French colonialism, she is appalled by the killings and dispossession of Native peoples. Jack finds his estranged brother, Théo, in San Francisco, but the latter understands no French, thus symbolizing the loss of culture in the melting pot.

The gay colony of Key West figures prominently in celebrated dramatist Michel Tremblay's novels *The Heart Laid Bare* (*Le Coeur découvert. Roman d'amours*, 1986) and *Heartburst* (*Le Coeur éclaté*, 1993). These largely autobiographical works are set against the AIDS crisis, and treat the end of a decades-long homosexual relationship. Artificially sprinkled with *joual*, they lack the social dimensions and magic of the earlier cycle of novels drawn from his childhood in Montreal's poor East End, especially *The Fat Woman Next Door Is Pregnant* (*La Grosse Femme d'à côté est enceinte*, 1978) and *Thérèse and Pierrette and the Hanging Angel* (*Thérèse et Pierrette à l'école des Saints-Pères*, 1980).

A much-commented phenomenon in Québécois letters is the significant presence over the past three decades of writers born abroad. They come from many corners of the world: the Far and Middle East, the Carribean (particularly Haiti), Latin America, and several European countries. A parallel phenomenon is the presence of figures from Quebec's ethnic and racial minorities in novels by writers of the majority culture (and not exclusively negative portraits, as in the examples above). Many of these writers highlight political and social concerns in their works at a time when native novelists adopted more psychological and autobiographical modes. Among the above writers are the Haitian natives; the late Emile Ollivier (*Passages*, 1990) and Dany Laferrière (The Taste for Young Girls [*Le Goût des jeunes filles*, 1991]), who invoke the horrors of the Duvalier years and the Tontons-Macoute; and Gloria Escomel (Traps [*Pièges*, 1991]), who treats with sympathy the struggle for social justice in her birthplace, Uruguay, while posing pertinent questions about the ends and means of politics, and the tensions between political engagement and co-optation.

There are also important works by the Parisian native Régine Robin and the prolific Brazilian-born Sergio Kokis (*Le Pavillon des miroirs* [*The Pavilion of Mirrors*, 1994]), who portrays the lumpen-proletarian ambiance of his birthplace, Rio de Janeiro, with stunning naturalistic and somewhat misogynic portraits and, like most of the foreign-born novelists, is obsessed by problems of identity. Robin penned *Le Cheval blanc de Lénine* (Lenin's White Horse, 1979), the much more artistic *The Wanderer* (*La Québécoite*, 1983), and striking essays like *Socialist Realism, an Impossible Aesthetic* (1995). Of Polish-Jewish origin, an academic with a militant radical past, and a miraculous survivor of the Nazi occupation of France, haunted by the deaths of scores of relatives in the Holocaust, she is torn between her birthplace and Montreal. Her deftly structured *La Québécoite* (a neologism, meaning "the silent Quebec woman") sounds the narrator's/author's search for identity, expressing fear of xenophobia in France and narrow Francophone nationalism in Quebec, but also revulsion over the Montreal Jewish establishment's right-wing views, especially its condoning of Israeli repression of the Palestinians.

As for the growing consciousness by Quebec old-stock writers of the new face of multilingual, multiethnic Montreal, a significant case in point is Francine Noël's *Nous avons tous découvert l'Amérique* (We All Discovered America, 1990). Set in the upper-middle class, largely Francophone area of Outremont in Montreal, it deals sensitively with tensions between the dominant group and Hassidic newcomers, ending on gestures of mutual respect and understanding, as implied by the title. Monique La Rue's booklet *L'Arpenteur et le navigateur* (The Surveyor and the Navigator, 1995) created a broad debate on like issues by exposing xenophobic attitudes of some native writers toward foreign-born colleagues.

The last decades, as noted, were dominated by introspective novels, though politically engaged works have continued to appear, including satires on the formerly dominant Catholic culture, such as François Barcelo's *Je vous ai vue, Marie* (I Saw You, Saint Mary, 1990) and Pierre Léon's *Un Huron en Alsace* (A Huron in Alsace, 2002); depictions of Nazism and the Holocaust, such as Monique Bosco's *Confiteor* (1996) and F. Carniccioni's *La Juive* (The Jewish Woman, 2002); and critiques of colonialism, such as Louis Lefebvre's *Guanahanni* (1991). Moreover, with Quebec doubling, proportionately, the number of novels appearing yearly in France, and the surge of the socially progressive Bloc Québécois in the 2004 federal elections, perhaps there will be a significant reappearance of the fiction of *engagement*.

Selected Bibliography: Gould, Karen. *Writing in the Feminine: Feminism and Experimental Writing in Quebec.* Carbondale: Southern Illinois UP, 1990; Major, Robert. *The American Dream in Nineteenth-Century Quebec: Ideologies and Utopia in Antoine Gérin-Lajoie's "Jean Rivard."* Toronto: U of Toronto P,

1996; Purdy, Anthony. *A Certain Difficulty of Being: Essays on the Quebec Novel.* Montreal: McGill UP, 1990; Shek, Ben-Z. *French-Canadian and Québécois Novels.* Toronto, Oxford UP, 1991; Shek, Ben-Z. *Social Realism in the French-Canadian Novel.* Montreal: Harvest House, 1977; Smart, Patricia. *Writing in the Father's House: The Emergence of the Feminine in the Quebec Literary Tradition.* Toronto: U of Toronto P, 1991; Toye, William E., ed. *The Oxford Companion to Canadian Literature.* New York: Oxford UP, 1997; Warwick, Jack. *The Long Journey: Literary Themes of French Canada.* Toronto: U of Toronto P, 1968; *Yale French Studies* 65 (1983). Special issue entitled "The Language of Difference: Writing in Québéc(ois)."

Ben-Z. Shek

CANONS AND CANONICITY. The word *canon* and its cognates (*canonical, canonicity,* etc.) has various, related meanings, all of which imply a sense of authority. In literary contexts, a canon is a list of works that are regarded as classics of their kind. A canonical text is one that is regarded as among the great works of literature, and canonicity is the status of being canonical, or a part of the canon. More narrowly, it can also mean the works of a single author that are considered to be authentic—for example, the **Shakespeare** canon comprises thirty-eight plays, the sonnets, two long narrative poems, and a handful of short poems. In religion, a canon is a church decree or law, and to canonize is to sanctify or to be sanctioned by church authority, as when the Catholic church canonizes a new saint.

The idea of a canon derives from the ancient Greek word for a rule or standard by which things could be measured. Over time, it came to signify ideal models or benchmarks that were most worthy of study and imitation. Although originally applied to works of architecture and sculpture, the concept eventually included philosophical and literary texts as well. In the ancient Roman era, poets and playwrights often based their works on Greek models, just as artists and sculptors copied or adapted what they considered exemplary works of Greek art. Virgil's use of Homer's *Iliad* and *Odyssey* for his own work, *The Aeneid,* is but one famous example. By the fourth century c.e., the canon was understood to be a comprehensive list of books, such as those of Christian literature, from which moral principles and ethical truths could be gleaned. However, secular canonical texts were more often than not synonymous with the classics of antiquity, which were taken as authoritative sources of scientific knowledge and philosophical wisdom. In schools, they also served as grammatical models for the study of Latin, the language of the educated elite in Europe throughout the Middle Ages. It was not until the fourteenth century c.e., with Boccaccio and Dante, that the first canon of works in a vernacular language—Italian—was established.

In the modern era, literary canons began to have nationalistic as well as linguistic connotations, generally reflecting the rise of modern nation-states. For instance, the early French and English literary canons were shaped in the seventeenth and eighteenth centuries, respectively, when the nascent national identities of France and England were beginning to form. The canon of German literature followed in the nineteenth century. By the early twentieth century, in both Europe and the United States, schools and universities were providing courses for the study of national literature, a practice that was accelerated with the outbreak of the two world wars. Although there have been several periods in history when the inclusion of specific canonical texts has been controversial, it was not until the 1970s and 1980s, when a new generation of literary critics became skeptical of traditional literary values, that the authority of canonical texts, indeed the very notion of a literary canon, came into question.

In the aftermath of the civil rights movement and with the impact of feminism in the United States, along with the radicalization of literary theory in Europe in the 1960s and 1970s, academics and critics began to challenge the prevailing devotion to "Shakespeare and company," as the literary canon has been described. Some wanted simply to expand the list of great books that are studied in schools, to make it more representative of modern, culturally pluralistic societies. By including more works of literature written by women, homosexuals, and ethnic minorities—alongside the traditionally accepted classics—it was believed that a more sympathetic understanding of cultural diversity would be fostered in schools and universities. The recent trend of recovering lost works and reevaluating forgotten authors, sometimes in an explicit attempt to remake the canon, is a result of this approach. Others have demanded more radical change, making the point that as the great works of Western literature have generally been written and celebrated by white men, they have been used as tools of white, male hegemony, excluding the voices of writers who do not fit that description. By this line of reasoning, the canon of "dead, white, European males" should be discarded in favor of more diverse, and less ethnocentric, approaches to works of literature and literary history. **Postcolonial** and **feminist criticism and theory**, for example, have done much to expose the ideological content of canonical works. Still others have questioned the academic favoritism accorded literary texts in general, arguing that the category of "literature" as such already presupposes a superior kind of writing at the expense of alternative, less venerated forms of cultural expression such as film and popular fiction. The discipline of **cultural studies** is, in part, a product of this argument.

The backlash against these skeptical readings of the literary canon has been fierce, particularly in the United States, and it reached a peak in the **culture wars** of the 1990s. Rising in defense of what they perceive as the monuments of Western literature, conservative writers and academics have assailed the critics of the canon as left-wing ideologues who are using their arguments against the great books only to espouse their own political beliefs. By contrast, conservative humanists maintain that canonical texts deserve the closest scrutiny because they enshrine the core values of Western culture and tradition. They argue that to cast aside the works that have formed the basis of our intellectual heritage would be to open a Pandora's box of competing values and even relativism, ultimately undermining our very ability to distinguish between good and bad, to judge right from wrong, or to appreciate writing of the highest quality as opposed to mere doggerel. In fact, these commentators insist that the works of Plato and Aristotle, Shakespeare and Molière, **Milton** and **Goethe**, and all of the most canonical books have fostered our sense of critical reading to begin with. Such texts are open to an infinite variety of interpretations, which explains their longevity and continuing fascination for us today. Other proponents of the Western canon have made more pragmatic arguments in its favor. A canon of great works, like the concepts of literary genres and movements, is a necessary tool with which to organize and understand the past. Without it, literary history would be incomprehensible. Moreover, due to the finite nature of the scholastic calendar, a list of great books is not only useful but inevitable. Because not everything can be included on the syllabus, selectivity is unavoidable.

Each of these arguments, whether for or against the literary canon, raises a number of questions and problems that are not always addressed, even by those who are making them. In many cases, certain political and theoretical assumptions are made without adequate examination. For instance, the claim that literary texts, based on the race and gender of their authors, necessarily represent certain sociological groups is more often asserted than demonstrated. But it is unclear that Toni Morrison's novels, for instance, speak for African American women in particular, any more than Ernest Hemingway's represent the interests of Caucasian-American men in any simple way. If their works had such narrow purpose, then what interest would they have for other readers? Another argument proposes that the literary canon can and should be remade by changing the classroom syllabus. But this claim, like the related fear that the canon has already been undermined by radical intellectuals, is based on unhistorical assumptions about literary history and a poor understanding of how literary canons are formed. The aesthetic and, indeed, political judgments of generations of writers, scholars, and critics—however strongly they are resisted—are not likely to be overturned in the course of a semester. In fact, the role of schools and universities in the formation of canons is often exaggerated at the expense of a deeper understanding of the broad cultural impact of canonical works, apart from their effect in the classroom or appearance in textbooks. That Dante's *Inferno* is perhaps the archetypal vision of hell in Western cultural discourse, or that **Orwell's** *Nineteen Eighty-Four* has become the standard portrait of totalitarian society, is owing more to their cultural familiarity than to whether or not they have been formally taught in schools. In other words, if the symbolic impact of canonical works goes far beyond the schools, then the struggle to modify the syllabus may be irrelevant.

Finally, the polarized rhetoric of the debate that pits left-wing critics of the canon against right-wing reactionaries is somewhat misleading. In fact, both sides share several assumptions about the nature and function of literary canons that are not without problems. For instance, there is general agreement that a specific body of texts has been used to exemplify Western literature and even cultural values, whether to the detriment or to the benefit of its readers. But this presupposes a rather static account of literary history and a limited understanding of the function of literature in society. First, it is doubtful whether a singular canon of texts has ever existed unchallenged or remained unchanged for very long. The history of Western canon formation attests to its variability. Second, the degree to which cultural values are transmitted via works of literature is open to question. That a particular novel or poem would instill a sense of diversity on the one hand or respect for tradition on the other—or that these values are mutually exclusive—is a simplistic interpretation of the act of reading. In any case, the social effects of canonical literature are probably not so transparent or easily defined, in spite of the apparent certainty and sometimes heated rhetoric of those making such claims. The fact that liberal pluralists who would open the canon to greater cultural diversity and conservative humanists who resist canonical change both maintain that literature has a primarily pedagogical function also indicates their shared belief in the instrumental value of literature. Instead of seeing literature as an end in itself, critics across the political spectrum typically evaluate it in terms of its social relevance and ideological orientation. There is no question that works of literature are informed by specific ideological inclinations; however, literature (like the aesthetic in general) seems to have a remarkable potential to escape the bounds of those inclinations and to mean different things to different readers. Perhaps that is why canonical works sometimes retain their interest over long periods of history, beyond their original readership and apart from whatever political intentions their authors, or their critics, may have had.

Selected Bibliography: Bloom, Harold. *The Western Canon: The Books and School of the Ages.* New York: Harcourt, Brace, 1994; Guillory, John. *Cultural Capital: The Problem of Literary Canon Formation.* Chicago: U of Chicago P, 1993; Jay, Gregory S. *American Literature and the Culture Wars.* Ithaca, NY: Cornell UP, 1997; Kermode, Frank. *Forms of Attention.* Chicago: U of Chicago P, 1985; Kolbas, E. Dean. *Critical Theory and the Literary Canon.* Boulder, CO: Westview P, 2001; Lauter, Paul. *Canons and Contexts.* Oxford: Oxford UP, 1991.

E. Dean Kolbas

THE CANTOS (1925–1968). **Ezra Pound**'s sprawling, fragmented, and intensely imagistic epic poem was written over six decades; it includes 116 individual cantos and runs to approximately 24,000 lines. A classic of modern literature, the masterpiece is known for its encyclopedic referentiality, its aesthetic play of detail and structure, and its ceaseless blurring of the line between aesthetic form and social commentary. Pound intended his long "poem including history" to be urgent and didactic, showing the ways in which politics, economics, and art work together to reflect and reinforce social values.

Taken as a whole, *The Cantos* functions as a record of the poet's intellectual and spiritual journey through history. Pound works through "luminous details," patterning cultural fragments (such as legal documents, poems, and speeches) to resurrect specific moments of an increasingly distant past. His crisp, lapidary style serves to convey the relative degree of aesthetic clarity and political perfection that each society attains, contrasting, for example, the virtues and vices of Renaissance Venice, Confucian China, and Jeffersonian America. Thematic concerns include the Neoplatonic force of creation and its various worldly manifestations, men of genius and their efforts to achieve aesthetic perfection in the mortal realm, the excesses of capitalism, the persistent threat of usury, and the inevitability of war. As a modernist political document, *The Cantos* is best defined by its antimodernism. Pound everywhere rails against the fall from pagan grace and the increasing commercialism, alienation, and violence of the modern period. The beauty of *The Cantos* is increasingly marred by its shrillness, anti-Semitism and homophophia. Pound's aesthetic commitments lead to absurd rhetorical violence, culminating in two Italian cantos (72–73), one in which he praises a young Fascist girl for leading a troop of Canadians into a minefield.

Pound's interest in Italian Fascism, which shapes a large portion of *The Cantos*, is perhaps one of the most bizarre and unfortunate episodes of Anglo-American modernism. The poet believed that Mussolini was a modern incarnation of the "factive personality," a man born to reunite a fragmented Italy and to restore the Western world to glory. In 1933, in fact, Pound obtained an interview with Mussolini and read to him several sections of *The Cantos* (Mussolini found the work *divertente*). During **World War II**, Pound broadcasted sections of *The Cantos* on Rome Radio, accompanied by explicitly anti-American, pro-Fascist statements.

In May 1945, Pound was arrested by occupying American forces and confined to an outdoor cage in Pisa, where he wrote what some believe are his most beautiful cantos, "The Pisan Cantos." Contemplating his past and the political failure of Fascism, the poet expresses intense despair, impotent rage, genuine remorse, and absolute confusion.

Selected Bibliography: Carpenter, Humphrey. *A Serious Character: The Life of Ezra Pound.* Boston: Houghton Mifflin, 1988; Casillo, Robert. *The Genealogy of Demons: Anti-Semitism, Fascism, and the Myths of Ezra Pound.* Evanston, IL: Northwestern UP, 1988; Casillo, Robert. "Fascists of the Final Hour: Pound's Italian Cantos." *Fascism, Aesthetics, and Culture.* Ed. Richard J. Golsan. Hanover: UP of New England, 1992. 98–127; Kenner, Hugh. *The Pound Era.* Berkeley: U of California P, 1971; Nicholls, Peter. *Politics, Economics and Writing: A Study of Ezra Pound's "Cantos."* London: Macmillan, 1984; North, Michael. *The Political Aesthetic of Yeats, Eliot, and Pound.* Cambridge: Cambridge UP, 1991.

Ed Comentale

ČAPEK, KAREL (1890–1938). Novelist, playwright, poet, translator, philosopher, and journalist, he was one of the great figures of modern Czech literature. He is widely known as the author of *R.U.R.* (*Rossum's Universal Robots,* 1920), the play that introduced the word *robot* (from the Czech word for "worker" or "serf") to the global lexicon. His novel *War with the Newts* (1936)—a complex satire of Fascism and fascist ideology—is regarded today as a classic of science fiction.

Čapek was born in Malé Svatonovice, Bohemia (then a province of Austria-Hungary). His intellectual development was nurtured in a middle-class household, where both Karel and his older brother Josef (1887–1945)—who became a successful painter, novelist, and dramatist—were encouraged to pursue their artistic and intellectual interests. Čapek began writing poetry and short stories in high school. In 1909, he entered the Charles University of Prague to study philosophy. His enthusiasm for poetry and the short story evolved into a deeper subject of inquiry through his discovery of William James, Ortega y Gasset, and Henri Bergson.

Čapek was influenced by **H. G. Wells** and **George Bernard Shaw**. His most important work explores social and philosophical problems, especially the future of industrial society. Čapek demonstrates that the exploitation of labor through technology and eugenics leads to disaster. In *R.U.R.*, scientists build robots that learn how to reproduce themselves without their human masters, against whom they rebel and destroy. In *War with the Newts*, a sea captain discovers a race of intelligent talking newts that are bred by speculators in large numbers to work in factories. The Newts develop a totalitarian philosophy, then succeed in flooding the dry land to destroy the human race. Čapek's large philosophical themes are matched by the boldness of his stylistic experimentation. His use of elaborate parody, self-reference, and multiple authorial voices represent classic expressions of **Menippean satire** (and **postmodernism**). However, Čapek wrote in many different styles and genres, from fairy tales, to starkly realistic stories of Czech life, to panegyrical farces (for example, on how society could be improved if people had wheels instead of legs), to short commentaries on aesthetics, Nazism, racism, and the decline of democracy in Europe.

Čapek's career was rooted in the causes of democracy, liberal politics, and Czech nationalism. He worked through the Society of Nations and the worldwide PEN Club to alert European consciousness to the true character of the Nazi movement. When H. G. Wells nominated Čapek for standing chairmanship of the PEN Club, Čapek immediately resigned to protest the European situation. Citing his antiwar message, the Norwegian press nominated Čapek for the Nobel Prize for Literature in 1936. The nomination was vetoed by the Swedish Academy, who feared reprisals from Hitler. In September 1938, the settlement of Munich canceled any remaining guarantees of Czechoslovakia's integrity. Exhausted by his efforts and disillusioned by Europe's capitulation, Čapek died of pneumonia on Christmas Day 1938, three months before the German invasion. He had been the third man on the Gestapo's arrest list of dangerous Czech nationals. Josef Čapek was arrested after the annexation and died in a concentration camp in 1945.

Selected Bibliography: Bradbrook, Bohuslava R. *Karel Čapek: In Pursuit of Truth, Tolerance and Trust.* Brighton: Sussex Academic P, 1997; Klima, Ivan. *Karel Čapek: Life and Works.* Trans. by Norma Comrada. North Haven: Catbird P, 2002.

Carter Kaplan

CARDENAL, ERNESTO (1925–). Poet, Catholic priest, and Marxist revolutionary, Cardenal easily ranks as the most important literary figure to have emerged from Nicaragua since the luminary of *modernista* poetry, **Rubén Darío**, at the turn of the century. His life and work are closely bound to the often turbulent modern history of his small Central American homeland. Widely known as the rebel priest and standard-bearer of Latin American liberation theology, who served as minister of culture for the triumphant Sandinista Revolution between 1979 and 1988, Cardenal has also been a prolific and original poet, comparable in stature in twentieth-century Latin America to Octavio Paz and **Pablo Neruda**, whose mystic idealism and earthliness, respectively, to some degree he synthesizes. Alongside the "anti-poetry" of Chile's Nicanor Parra, Cardenal's work established a new style of "concrete" social and political poetry in Latin America. Heavily influenced by **Ezra Pound**, Cardenal called his style *exteriorismo* and defined it as an "objective" poetry employing narrative elements, everyday diction, nonmetaphorical language, and a dense array of historical references.

Cardenal's life falls into three major phases, all chronicled in his recent trilogy of memoirs. The first phase begins with his precocious adolescence as a poet of amorous obsession and bohemian dissipation under the spell of Darío, moves through growing political awareness during his student days in Mexico and New York City, and culminates in his participation in a failed attempt to overthrow Nicaraguan dictator Anastasio Somoza García in the April rebellion of 1954. The poems in *Epigrams* (*Epigramas*, 1961) and *Zero Hour* (*Hora 0*, 1959) were products of this first phase.

Cardenal's second phase began when he experienced religious revelation in 1956 and entered the Trappist monastery in Gethsemani, Kentucky, to apprentice under the novice master Thomas Merton from 1957 to 1959. This second phase is highlighted by the utopian community Cardenal established in 1966 on an island in the Great Lake of Nicaragua's archipelago of Solentiname; it was destroyed in 1977 by Somoza's government troops. Cardenal's prolific poetic output from this period includes *Gethsemani, Ky.* (1960), *Psalms* (*Salmos*, 1964), *Marilyn Monroe and Other Poems* (*Oración por Marilyn Monroe y otros poemas*, 1965), *Homage to the American Indians* (*Homenaje a los indios americanos*, 1969), and the long historical poem *The Doubtful Strait* (*El estrecho dudoso*, 1966).

In his third phase, Cardenal relinquished strict nonviolence and took an active leadership role in the Sandinista Liberation Front (FSLN) and its overthrow of the Somoza Debayle dictatorship in 1979. As minister of culture, Cardenal launched an ambitious program to democratize the means of cultural production in Nicaragua, including most famously a series of poetry workshops established across the country for workers and former FSLN combatants. Soon after the closure of the Ministry of Culture in 1988, two major volumes of Cardenal poetry appeared; both *Golden UFOs: The Indian Poems* (*Los ovnis de oro: poemas indios*, 1991) and the massive *Cosmic Canticle* (*Cántico cósmico*, 1989) incorporate many previously published poems alongside new ones, and serve as summa and reformulations of his poetic career. Cardenal severed his affiliation with the Sandinistas when corruption among the FSLN leadership was exposed following their electoral defeat in 1990.

Selected Bibliography: Borgeson, Paul W., Jr., *Hacia el hombre nuevo: poesía y pensamiento de Ernesto Cardenal.* London: Tamesis, 1984; Dawes, Greg. *Aesthetics and Revolution: Nicaraguan Poetry, 1979–90.* Minneapolis: U of Minnesota P, 1993; Johnson, Kent, ed. *A Nation of Poets: Writings from the Poetry Workshops of Nicaragua.* Los Angeles: West End P, 1985; Whisnant, David E. *Rascally Signs in Sacred Places: The Politics of Culture in Nicaragua.* Chapel Hill: U of North Carolina P, 1995.

Steven M. Bell

CARIBBEAN LITERATURE (ANGLOPHONE). The cluster of English-speaking islands, once damned as uncreative and culturally sterile by British colonial travelers, has emerged as a dynamic area of literary and cultural production. While it is true that the Caribbean literary legacy continues to be marked by exile, it is still a formidable one given its relative youth. With only little more than a century of established writing behind it, Anglophone Caribbean literature already has several identifiable traits despite its variety. While Jamaica, Trinidad, and to some extent Guyana and Barbados are the most productive areas of literary output, smaller islands like Antigua and St. Lucia have contributed famous writers such as Jamaica Kincaid and the 1992 Nobel laureate Derek Walcott. The latter's epic *Omeros* immortalizes his native island while depicting a shared Caribbean history of genocide, colonization, slavery, plantation labor, and continued diasporic migration. Walcott's plays and poetry emphasize survival, redemption, and renewal despite the violence and brutality of the past, an ethical stance repeated in the work of Dennis Scott (Jamaica), Samuel Selvon (Trinidad), and Earl Lovelace (Trinidad).

One of the most striking characteristics of Anglophone writing in general, however, is the often stark contrast to the lighthearted, tourist stereotypes of the region. Unlike the sunny celebrations and ceaseless smiles of travel advertisements, modern

Anglophone writing, with **George Lamming** (Barbados), Andrew Salkey (Jamaica), Michael Thelwell (Jamaica), and Orlando Patterson (Jamaica) as examples, is serious, dark, and burdened by the sins of the past, the failure of the present, and the fears of the future. Even comic renditions such as Selvon's include portrayals of violence and poverty. More contemporary writers such as Caryl Phillips (St. Kitts) echo this portentous mood as they explore the continuing legacy of slavery and racism. As critic and novelist Sylvia Wynter (Jamaica) has insisted, the failures catalogued in the pre- and postindependence period of writing accurately captured the malaise of (post)colonial societies. Wynter, Erna Brodber (Jamaica), and **Kamau Brathwaite** (Barbados) demonstrate another postcolonial characteristic, which is that creative writers in the Anglophone Caribbean wear many hats, using their scholarly backgrounds for critical purposes, and combining sociological analysis with art and performance.

Although Caribbean writing began earlier than the twentieth century, critics tend to identify a more canonical, distinctly local tradition only later. Even modern writers of the 1950s struggled to articulate an original rather than an epigonous legacy, a shift from the British West Indies or Commonwealth nomenclature to the independent Caribbean. Therefore, much of the earlier writing, particularly the poetry, imitated English forms, which—considering that most of the writing was by white Creoles with conflicted ties to their "mother country," England—was not surprising. Poems by Mary Adella Wolcott and Tom Redcam express sentimental attachments to the Caribbean islands but in poems that seem more tied to English traditions, with an infusion of local landscape and lifestyle. Not until **Claude McKay**—the Jamaican poet and later novelist who migrated to the United States and went on to influence the **Harlem Renaissance** there and the **negritude** writers in France—was poetry that spoke directly to the lives of poor black Jamaicans, the majority population, given much attention. McKay's so-called dialect verse, which unabashedly used black Jamaican Creole, ultimately revolutionized later Anglophone writing, especially the performance poetry of Louise Bennett, the dub poetry of Linton Kwesi Johnson, Michael Smith, Jean Binta Breeze, and the Sistren Theater Collective, all from Jamaica. Despite McKay's bold innovations, however, succeeding writers such as Lamming, Wilson Harris (Guyana), and **V. S. Naipaul** (Trinidad) were largely colonial descendants of Victorian or high modernist prose traditions. Even as late as 1979, Brathwaite's lecture, "History of the Voice," demanded a "nation language" and orality more suitable to Caribbean rhythms, arguing famously that the "hurricane does not roar in pentameter." Brathwaite's own poetry and criticism seek to rehabilitate African connections as well, since the legacy of slavery had distorted black identity and pride. The controversial Nobel laureate Naipaul is the most prominent Indo-Caribbean writer; David Dabydeen (Guyana), now in the United Kingdom, Cyril Dabydeen, and Naipaul's nephew, Neil Bissoondath (Trinidad), based in Canada, are promising younger Indo-Caribbean writers.

The writers who made their reputation following the 1950s may have left the most distinct imprint on modern Anglophone writing, but they owe much to an earlier generation of intellectuals who struggled to initiate a distinct Caribbean tradition. The nationalist fervor of the 1930s and 1940s, the working-class movements, the peasant rebellions, the anticolonial rhetoric, and the early winds of independence revolutions that were sweeping much of the British colonial territories influenced a group of writers from different races and backgrounds. Given the paucity of indigenous publication industries, their pioneering efforts were published in local literary journals such as *The Beacon* (Trinidad), *Bim* (Barbados), *Focus* (Jamaica), and *Kyk-over-al* (Guyana). Alfred Mendes and **C.L.R. James** (Trinidad), Edgar Mittelholzer and A. J. Seymour (Guyana), Roger Mais and Vic Reid (Jamaica), and Frank Collymore (Barbados) were the names most associated with this "awakening," as Reinhard Sander's book on Trinidadian literature of this period puts it. The leftist novelist **Ralph de Boissière** (Trinidad) also began writing within this context. But despite the gradual rise of indigenous publishing outlets such as Ian Randle and the University of West Indies Press, the literary scene, once established in England and even on the islands by the BBC radio program, *Caribbean Voices*, is still dominated by the United Kingdom and the United States, and now, with recent Caribbean migration there, Canada.

The contemporary scene bodes well for women writers, once an invisible species and now increasingly ascendant. The poetry of Grace Nichols (Guyana), Lorna Goodison (Jamaica), Marlene Nourbese Philip (Tobago), Mahadai Das (Guyana), and Meiling Jin (Guyana); the novels of Phyllis Allfrey (Dominica), Beryl Gilroy (Guyana), Merle Hodge (Trinidad), Rosa Guy (Trinidad), Paule Marshall (Barbados), Zee Edgell (Belize), Michelle Cliff (Jamaica), and Jamaica Kincaid (Antigua); the short stories of Opal Palmer Adisa (Jamaica), Olive Senior (Jamaica), and Ramabai Espinet (Trinidad) are now part of the Caribbean literary tradition. While more attention needs to be paid to the local scene, there is no doubt that Edwidge Danticat (Haiti) and Zadie Smith (Jamaica), the former based in the United States and the latter in the United Kingdom, are among the most spectacular talents in contemporary world literature.

Selected Bibliography: Birbalsingh, Frank. *Passion and Exile: Essays on Caribbean Literature*. London: Hansib, 1988; Booker, M. Keith, and Dubravka Juraga. *The Caribbean Novel in English: An Introduction*. Portsmouth, NH: Heinemann, 2001; Dabydeen, David, and Nan Wilson-Tagoe. *A Reader's Guide to West Indian and Black British Literature*. Rev. ed. London: Hansib, 1997; Dash, J. Michael. *The Other America: Caribbean Literature in a New World*. Charlottesville: UP of Virginia, 1998; Davies, Carole Boyce, and Elaine Savory Fido. *Out of the Kumbla: Caribbean Women and Literature*. Trenton, NJ: Africa World P, 1990; Gikandi, Simon. *Writing in Limbo: Modernism and Caribbean Literature*. Ithaca, NY: Cornell UP, 1992; King, Bruce, ed. *West Indian Literature*. 2nd ed. Carbondale: Southern Illinois UP, 1995; Sander, Reinhard W. *The Trinidad Awakening: West Indian Literature of the Nineteen-Thirties*. Westport, CT: Greenwood, 1988.

Supriya Nair

CARIBBEAN LITERATURE (FRANCOPHONE), or Antillean literature, is the literature in French from Guadeloupe, Martinique, French Guiana, and Haiti. Except in the case of Haiti, this literature developed along three major concepts: **negritude**, Caribbeanness, and **Creoleness**. Critics trace its origins to the rise of the negritude movement (in the 1930s), when black students, intellectuals, and artists revolted against France's assimilation policies to adopt an ideology aimed at restoring black and African values embedded in popular culture. The literary landmark was undoubtedly **Aimé Césaire**'s *Notebook of a Return to My Native Land* (*Cahier d'un retour au pays natal*, 1939).

Four centuries of slavery and colonization had a debilitating effect on the Antilleans' psyche, fostering the belief that rescue from savagery was possible only through Western culture. For **Frantz Fanon** (*Black Skin, White Masks*), this existential crisis created in the slave a pathological self-hate that undermined his social equilibrium in a race-conscious community. When, after the **Haitian Revolution** and Haiti's independence (1804) and the abolition of slavery (1848), the mostly French-educated middle class took to writing, their main goal was to conceal the barbaric side of Africa and uphold the virtues of Western culture. Writers, ashamed of black culture, imitated French masters (Hugo, Baudelaire, Rimbaud) to enlist full acceptance into the mainstream. However, some writers, such as Oruno-Lara and Suzanne Cascade, recognized their roots. Precursors of the black pride rationale included the *indigenist* movement, ideas from Cuba, and the **Harlem Renaissance** in the United States. In Haiti, the U.S. occupation (1915–1934) rekindled interests in indigenous culture as a patriotic reaction to outside domination. Jean Price-Mars's *Ainsi Parla l'Oncle* and the journal *La Revue Indigène* played a pivotal role in the revival. The Cuban poet **Nicolás Guillén** had celebrated the African heritage that shaped Cuban popular culture. In the United States, the experience of the Harlem Renaissance writers (**Claude McKay**, **Langston Hughes**, James W. Johnson, Sterling Brown) and musicians already articulated the main tenets of black pride, as Alain Locke's anthology *The New Negro* illustrated.

In the 1930s, new ways of thinking that informed movements such as **surrealism**, dadaism, and cubism created an atmosphere of doubt that challenged assumptions of universal values embodied in Western proclamations. Negritude joined in by denouncing derogatory ontological claims and by revalorizing the African foundation of the Caribbean culture. This newly found source of pride initiated a rich crop of literary writings on the islands. Leading figures included Césaire, Léon-G. Damas, René Ménil, Etienne Léro, **Jacques Roumain**, Stephen Aléxis, Guy Tirolien, Joseph Zobel, and Carl Brouard. The recurrent themes were the suffering during slavery, colonization, exploitation, and nostalgia for Africa. Poetry was the most dynamic literary field in which Césaire was the dominant voice. Following in the footsteps of René Maran, novelists explored the past of the islands and their connections to Africa. In Haiti, the "roman paysan" depicted with realism the cornerstone elements (storytelling, voodoo, customs) of the popular culture. In drama, Césaire was also the main playwright with *La Tragédie du roi Christophe*, *Une Saison au Congo*, and *Une Tempête*. The journal *Présence Africaine* and the two international congresses of black writers and artists (Paris, 1956; and Rome, 1959) enlisted an important participation by Caribbean writers.

Negritude as an umbrella concept could not account for the complexity of Caribbean experience. Different political choices (departmentalization for the French West Indies and independence for African colonies) set Africa and the Caribbean on different paths. **Maryse Condé** illustrates the failure to reconnect with the motherland, whereas Myriam Warner-Vieyra's experience came out differently. The specificity of the French Caribbean islands required new conceptualizations of identity quest and addressed vital issues; Caribbeanness and Creoleness were the responses.

The emphasis on Caribbeanness also made important contributions to the growth of Francophone Caribbean literature. In *The Caribbean Discourse,* Glissant situates the identity quest within the context defined by the constant creative flux of uprooting and transformation. The desire to valorize the very conditions Caribbeans were facing urged writers to focus on pressing issues (poverty, alienation, economic dependence) relevant to their survival. Such writers rejected the trap of the negritude dichotomy based on the dualistic oppositions Africa versus Europe and black versus white. Rather than advocating a return to a pristine Africa that no one could actually recapture, Glissant recognizes the duty of the artist to restore the disrupted history by unearthing and linking the cultural past overshadowed by the traumatic lives under slavery to a meaningful future. He believes that the foundation of his world is the cross-cultural experience resulting from a network of rhizomic relations in need of recognition and validation.

During this time, women writers emerged and gained in scope and substance. Leading figures include Simone Schwarz-Bart, Michèle Lacrosil, Condé, Myriam Warner-Vieyra, Gisèle Pineau, Jacqueline Manicon, and Ina Césaire. Schwarz-Bart's novel *The Bridge of Beyond* (*Pluie et vent sur Télumée Miracle,* 1972) is the prototype of a new wave of Francophone Caribbean writing by women.

As developed in a seminal work entitled *In Praise of Creoleness* (*Eloge de la Créolité,* 1989) by Jean Bernabé, Patrick Chamoiseau, and Raphaël Confiant, the concept of Creoleness has exerted an important influence on recent Francophone writing from the Caribbean. This concept insists on the Creole language and culture as the cornerstone of society. It recognizes the specificity of the Caribbean Islands and their racial diversity, popular culture, language, and multiethnic history, and valorizes literature that contributes to the ongoing establishment of a viable Creole cultural identity in the Caribbean.

Meanwhile in Haiti, economic and political hardships stretching from the Duvaliers to Aristide forced out many writers and intellectuals, thus creating diasporic sites where they debate issues relevant to Haiti. Writers working from North America include Gérard Étienne, Joël Lerosier, Emile Ollivier, Dany Laferrière, Anthony Phelps, and Edwige Danticat; from France, Jean Métellus, René Depestre, and Jean-Claude Charles; from Africa, Jean-François Brierre, Roger Dorsainville, and Félix Morisseau-Leroy. Meanwhile, writing in Creole reached a peak with Frankétienne (*Dézafi,* a novel) and gained in prestige in Martinique (Confiant's *Jik deye do Bondye* and *Bitako-A*) and Guadeloupe.

Recent directions in Francophone Caribbean literature reflect its peculiar geographical position and the complex nature of its cultural and political mix. If Martinicans write from their country, dislocation—forced or voluntary—remains a determining factor in the career of other French Caribbean writers. Many Francophone works and writers have received recognition through two most prestigious French literary prizes. Maran's *Batouala* (1921) and Chamoiseau's *Texaco* (1992) received the Prix Goncourt; Glissant's *La Lézarde* (1958) and *Hadriana dans tous mes rêves* (1988) received the Renaudot.

Selected Bibliography: Antoine, Régis. *La Littérature franco-antillaise.* Paris: Karthala, 1992; Arthur, Charles, and Dash, J. Michael. *Libète: A Haitian Anthology.* New Jersey: Markus Wiener, 1999; Dash, J. Michael. *Edouard Glissant.* New York: Cambridge UP, 1995; Dash, J. Michael. *Literature and Ideology* *in Haiti 1915–61.* London: Macmillan, 1981; Fanon, Frantz. *Black Skin, White Masks.* New York: Grove, 1982; Fonkoua, Romuald Blaise. *Essai sur une mesure du monde au XXe siècle: Edouard Glissant.* Paris: Honoré Champion, 2002; Glissant, Edouard. *Caribbean Discourse: Selected Essays.* Trans. J. Michael Dash. Charlottesville: UP of Virginia, 1989; Glissant, Edouard. *Poetics of Relation.* Trans. Betsy Wing. Ann Arbor: U of Michigan P, 1997; Hoffmann, Léon-François. *Le roman haïtien.* Sherbrooke: Naaman, 1982; Kesteloot, Lilyan. *Black Writers in French: A Literary History of Negritude.* Philadelphia: Temple UP, 1974.

Kasongo M. Kapanga

CARNIE, ETHEL. *See* HOLDSWORTH, ETHEL CARNIE.

CARPENTIER, ALEJO (1904–1980). Son of a French father and Russian mother, Alejo Carpentier was a novelist, short-story writer, essayist, musicologist, and critic. According to his birth registry, he was actually born in Lausanne, Switzerland, on December 26, 1904, although he consistently claimed to have been born in Havana on that same date. He studied music at an early age with his mother, and briefly began a career in architecture at the University of Havana in 1921. In that same year, he became known as a writer of criticism in several Havana periodicals. Due to his opposition to the dictatorship of Gerardo Machado, he was imprisoned in 1927; the following year he left for Paris, where he resided until 1939. While there, he carried out extraordinary work as an ambassador of Cuban culture and came into contact with the most outstanding representatives of the avant-garde movement—especially the members of the surrealist movement, who exerted an important influence, though Carpentier ultimately rejected surrealism. His definitively anti-Fascist position led him to declare himself in favor of the republican cause during the **Spanish Civil War** and to take part as Cuban representative at the Second Congress for the Defense of Culture, held in Madrid and Valencia in 1937. Upon returning to Cuba, he stayed on the island until 1945, and then moved to Caracas, where he produced a significant part of his literary work.

He returned to Cuba as a result of the 1959 **Cuban Revolution**, after which he held relevant positions in the cultural sphere of his country. From 1966 until his death, he held the position of minister adviser at the Embassy of Cuba in Paris. Among other international recognitions, he was awarded the Cino del Duca World Award (1975), the Alfonso Reyes International Award (1975), the Foreign Medicis Award (1979), and the Miguel de Cervantes Saavedra Award (1979), the highest prize awarded to Spanish-speaking writers. His works have been translated into many languages and have been adapted to the cinema on more than one occasion.

Carpentier's numerous novels reveal his deep humanism and his devotion to promoting Latin American culture as an important component of world culture. Important novels include *The Kingdom of This World* (*El reino de este mundo,* 1949), *Manhunt* (*El Acoso,* 1956), *Explosion in a Cathedral* (*El siglo de las luces,* 1962), *Reasons of State* (*El recurso del método,* 1974), *Baroque Concierto* (*Concierto Barroco,* 1974), *The Consecration of Spring* (*La consagración de la primavera,* 1978), and *The Harp and the Shadow* (*El arpa y la sombra,* 1979). Perhaps his greatest masterpiece was *The Lost Steps* (*Los pasos perdidos,* 1953), a crucial forerunner of both the Latin American boom and the entire phenomenon of magic realism.

Selected Bibliography: Chaple, Sergio. *Estudios de narrative cubana.* Havana: Ediciones Unión, 1996; González Echeverría, Roberto. *Alejo Carpentier: The Pilgrim at Home.* Ithaca, NY: Cornell UP, 1977; González Echeverría, Roberto, and Klaus Muller-Bergh. *Alejo Carpentier: Bibliographical Guide.* Westport, CT: Greenwood, 1983; Padura Fuentes, Leonardo. *Un camino de medio siglo; Carpentier y la narrative de lo real maravilloso.* Havana: Editorial Letras Cubanas, 1994; Shaw, Donald Leslie. *Alejo Carpentier.* Boston: Twayne, 1985.

Sergio Chaple (trans. David H. Uzzell Jr.)

CARTER, ANGELA (1940–1992). Born to middle-class parents in Eastbourne, England, and educated at the University of Bristol, Carter was an influential novelist, short-story writer, scriptwriter, and journalist whose work explored the cultural politics of gender and sexuality. Influenced by the revolutionary spirit of the 1960s, Carter saw herself as a committed Socialist-feminist. In her work, she typically draws on and often crosses many genres and literary modes, including gothic fiction, fantasy, new wave **science fiction**, magic realism, folktales, and fairy tales.

In her essay "Notes from the Front Line" (1983), Carter declares that as a writer she is in "the demythologizing business" (38) because she is mainly concerned with critiquing the myths or social fictions that attempt to universalize sexual relations, gender, and the body. Much like **Roland Barthes** in *Mythologies* (1957), Carter views myths as ideologies, and in her work she intends to expose the reactionary political agendas behind them and to liberate the mind from these "extraordinary lies designed to make people unfree" (38). Carter approaches her subjects from a provocative materialist standpoint, viewing the body and human relationships as products of history and socioeconomic relations. Her basic assumption, as she explains in *The Sadeian Woman* (1978), is that "our flesh arrives to us out of history, like everything else does. We may believe we fuck stripped of social artifice; in bed, we even feel we touch the bedrock of human nature itself. But we are deceived. Flesh is not an irreducible human universal" (9). Carter agues that to accept traditional myths about the body and sexual relations is to lose sense of the real material conditions of life and the basis for political change.

Carter's demythologizing is on display in such well-known novels as *The Infernal Desire Machines of Doctor Hoffman* (1972), *The Passion of New Eve* (1977), and *Nights at the Circus* (1984), but perhaps the best-known example is *The Bloody Chamber* (1979), a collection of short stories that rewrites traditional fairy tales and legends to reveal and subvert their patriarchal perspectives on gender, sexuality, and marriage. Carter's attempt to critique traditional forms of fiction from a materialist-feminist standpoint is typical of her overall work, which critically engages many images, stories, and genres from the history of Western European literature. In this regard, as Carter herself has noted, she may be compared to "certain Third World writers, both female and male, who are transforming actual fiction forms to both reflect and to precipitate changes in the way people feel about themselves . . . [u]sing fictional forms inherited from the colonial period to create a critique of that period's consequences" (Notes 42).

Selected Bibliography: Carter, Angela. "Notes from the Front Line." *Shaking a Leg: Collected Writings.* New York: Penguin, 1998. 36–43; Carter, Angela. *The Sadeian Woman and the Ideology of Pornog-*

raphy. New York: Harper Colophon Books, 1978; Gamble, Sarah. *The Fiction of Angela Carter*. New York: Palgrave Macmillan, 2002; Harron, Mary. "I'm a Socialist, Damn It! How Can You Expect Me to Be Interested in Fairies?" *The Guardian*, 25 September 1984, 10; Katsavos, Anna. "Angela Carter." *Modern British Women Writers: An A-to-Z Guide*. Ed. Vicki K. Janik and Del Ivan Janik. Westport, CT: Greenwood, 2002. 63–71.

Mitchell R. Lewis

CARTER, MARTIN WYLDE (1927–1997). Born in Georgetown, British Guiana, Martin Carter came from a family of mixed African, Indian, and European ancestry that was part of the colored middle class. He attended the prestigious Queen's College between 1939 and 1945, when he got a job in the civil service, first in the post office, then as secretary to the superintendent of prisons. By 1945, it seems likely that he had come into contact with the Marxist ideas of Guianan radicals such as Cheddi Jagan, and he soon became involved in the Guianese independence movement.

Carter's first poems began to appear in *Thunder* in 1950 and in *Kyk-over-Al* in the following year. He was also writing political pieces in *Thunder* under the pseudonym of M. Black (to protect his civil service post). In 1951, he published his first short collection, *The Hill of Fire Glows Red*, followed by *The Kind Eagle (Poems of Prison)* in 1952, early poems that established his distinctive revolutionary voice of protest. In 1953, Carter was imprisoned by the British colonial government as it moved (with support from the United States) to prevent a popularly elected government headed by Jagan and his People's Progressive Party (PPP) from moving toward independence; while in prison he wrote the poems that would be published in 1954 as the collection that established Carter's international reputation, *Poems of Resistance from British Guiana*. After his release from prison, Carter worked as a schoolteacher from 1954 to 1959, during which time he broke with the PPP after Jagan criticized him as an ultra leftist.

Carter continued his anticolonial activism, however, and in 1965 he was part of Guiana's delegation to the Constitutional Conference in London to negotiate the terms of Guyanese independence. After independence, he served the new Guyanese government in various capacities, including delegate to the United Nations (1966–1967) and minister of information and culture (1967–1970). Through it all, however, he continued to write poetry, especially after leaving government service in 1971, discouraged with the growing corruption, authoritarianism, and racism of the People's National Congress (PNC) government, which had supplanted the PPP as the leading political party of Guyana in 1966.

Carter's poems of the 1970s became more personal and meditative, leading to the publication of the volume *Poems of Succession* in 1978. Carter remained politically active, however, joining Walter Rodney's Working Peoples Alliance (WPA) in its endeavor to resist the attempts of the PNC to solidify their power. Subsequent political violence led to the killing of several WPA leaders, including Rodney. Carter's poetic response to this violence came in the eloquent, courageous poems of *Poems of Affinity 1978–80* (1980).

Though long seen largely as a poet of protest, of relevance primarily in a Caribbean context, Carter has gained a growing international critical reputation in recent years.

The publication of his *Selected Poems* in 1989 (revised edition 1997) aided this reputation by calling attention to his considerable body of work, while *Poesias Escogidas* (1999), which presents selected poems in a dual English/Spanish translation, helped to place Carter in the company of the great Latin American political poets, such as **Pablo Neruda**, **Nicolás Guillén**, and **César Vallejo**. Unfortunately, much of the recent critical attention to Carter's work has come after his death in 1997.

Selected Bibliography: Brown, Stewart, ed. *All Are Involved: The Art of Martin Carter.* Leeds: Peepal Tree, 2000; Rohlehr, Gordon. *Cultural Resistance and the Guyana State.* Havana: Casa de las Americas, 1984; Roopnaraine, Rupert. *Web of October: Rereading Martin Carter.* Leeds: Peepal Tree, 1987.

M. Keith Booker

CATHER, WILLA (1873–1947). Born in Virginia, Willa Cather grew up in Nebraska, the setting for much of her fiction, including her novel *O Pioneers!* (1913). After graduating from the University of Nebraska, she moved first to Pittsburgh and then to New York City. Her writings include twelve novels and four collections of short stories. None of Cather's works focus on politics, but her underlying conservatism is clear enough. Three of her novels narrate episodes in the European settlement of North America from the viewpoint of the settlers. *O Pioneers!* tells the story of Alexandra Bergson, who becomes a successful farmer on the Nebraska Divide; *Shadows on the Rock* (1931) takes place in French Quebec in the era of Frontenac; and *Death Comes to the Archbishop* (1927) describes the Catholic Church's mission in the American Southwest in the nineteenth century. In direct contrast to the stance taken by contemporary postcolonial studies, the novels all affirm the fundamental rightness of the settlement project. Although *Shadows on the Rock* tells little about military expeditions, the novel encourages the reader to admire the tenacity of Frenchwomen like Madame Auclair in preserving their way of life in the new world. *O Pioneers!* celebrates Alexandra Bergson's farm as a work of art that signifies her harmony with the land. *Death Comes to the Archbishop* acknowledges the mistreatment of the original inhabitants of the land, but the archbishop of the title reflects at the end of his life that he has lived long enough to see justice done through the abolition of slavery and, equally important to him, the return of the Navajos to their own territory.

Cather's fiction condemns those who gain wealth through semilegal swindling of the poor and unwary. In *A Lost Lady* (1923), old Judge Pommeroy warns the young narrator against becoming a lawyer, since it is no longer a career for an honorable man. Jim Laird in "The Sculptor's Funeral" (1905) confesses that he has become a shyster lawyer rather than a great man because the businessmen of Sand City, Kansas, demanded a shyster. The crooked moneylender Wick Cutter is the most unscrupulous figure in *My Ántonia* (1918). On the other hand, the political radicalism of characters like Alexandra's brother Lou in *O Pioneers!* seems based on little more than envy and misguided self-importance. Lou's political ally, Frank Shabata, certain that life has not treated him as well as he deserves, blames both his wife, Marie, and the rich for his discontent. His pent-up anger results in tragedy when he finds Marie and Alexandra's brother Emil lying together in the grass and kills them without waiting for second thoughts. In "Two Friends" (1932), the narrator recalls with regret how the emotions aroused by William Jennings Bryan's free-silver crusade precipitated the breakup of the friendship of the town's two most successful businessmen, the two men the narrator most admired. Taken as a whole, Cather's writings affirm a deep conservatism that renders current attempts to enlist her work on behalf of radical feminism or any other radicalism quixotic at best.

Selected Bibliography: Acocella, Joan Ross. *Willa Cather and the Politics of Criticism.* Lincoln: U of Nebraska P, 2000; Lindemann, Marilee. *Willa Cather: Queering America.* New York: Columbia UP, 1999; O'Brien, Sharon. *Willa Cather: The Emerging Voice.* New York: Oxford UP, 1987; Seaton, James. "On Politics and Literature: The Case of *O Pioneers!*" *Perspectives in Political Science* 28.3 (1999): 142–46.

James Seaton

THE CAUCASIAN CHALK CIRCLE (1944), by **Bertolt Brecht**, is a classic example of **epic theater** and Brecht's *Verfremdung*, or estrangement effect. The play's opening scene is set in a valley in the Caucasus, which has been recently liberated from the Nazis by Soviet forces. Two agricultural collectives, Galinsk and Rosa Luxemburg, dispute the right to cultivate the valley, and the resolution of the dispute is marked by the Rosa Luxemburg collective performing a play—*The Chalk Circle*—for the Galinsk collective. This play within a play is presented throughout by a singer-narrator, who comments on the action and even voices the private thoughts of the characters. The actors from the Luxemburg collective wear masks, thereby frustrating identification with the characters by both the on-stage audience—the Galinsk collective—and the theater audience, who are constantly made aware that they are witnessing theater as opposed to an illusionist slice of life.

The *Chalk Circle* play within a play is set in an archetypal feudal society and has two parallel plotlines, which in temporal terms take place simultaneously, but in theatrical terms are presented consecutively until they intertwine in the final scene. These two plotlines focus on the figures of Grusche and Azdak, whose situations are used by Brecht to explore themes of maternity, justice, revolution, and historical change. Grusche had taken into her care the abandoned child of Governor Abashvili when he was deposed and executed, but when the political situation returns to "normal," the child's birth mother takes legal action to reclaim him. At the same time, these chaotic political circumstances also lead to Azdak, the village clerk, being made a judge. Azdak is used to expose the venality and class bias of the legal system, and he ultimately awards the child to Grusche, the implication being that maternity is not grounded in blood relationships or innate dispositions, but is a function of mutual care and social dependence.

The Caucasian Chalk Circle's own engagement with history and politics is more complex and contentious. The play within a play indicates that under feudal social relations, radical political change typically involves transfer of power from one ruling elite to another, while popular uprisings are brutally suppressed. There is a temporal and historical linkage between the opening scene set in 1944 and the feudal society of the *Chalk Circle*, implied by references to the liberation of the serfs in nineteenth-century Tsarist Russia. But Brecht glosses over the actualities of twentieth-century Russian revolutionary politics, and presents a self-consciously idealized yet ambivalent image of Soviet society encapsulated in the poet Mayakovsky's exhortation, "The home of the Soviet people *shall also be* [my italics] the home of Reason." It is also not clear that the maternal dispute contained in the play within a play is an adequate parable for the land dispute between the collectives, as the singer suggests in his final words, and while some of Azdak's judgments justify the claim that he acts in the interests of the poor, others are arbitrary, willful, and sexist. Crucially, the singer describes Azdak's time as a judge as "a brief / Golden Age that was almost just"; the question which Brecht poses to the theater audience concerns the precise nature of justice and the measures to be taken to inaugurate a social and political utopia.

Selected Bibliography: Fuegi, John. *Bertolt Brecht: Chaos, According to Plan.* Cambridge: Cambridge UP, 1987; Speirs, Ronald. *Bertolt Brecht.* London: Macmillan, 1987; Suvin, Darko. *To Brecht and Beyond.* New York: Barnes and Noble, 1984.

Steve Giles

CAUDWELL, CHRISTOPHER (1907–1937) produced the first systematic Marxist literary theory in English. *Illusion and Reality* (1937), his central work, remained widely influential for a popular Left audience in Britain and the United States for many years, and it was never out of print until the last years of the twentieth century. Admired for the heroic scope of its vision but often scorned by scholars for its lack of precision, Caudwell's work became a focus of controversy in 1950–1951 when the quality of his Marxism was debated in the British Communist Party journal *Modern Quarterly.* Caudwell himself achieved a rather romantic Left image. He had been practically unknown to the Left intelligentsia when he joined the British Battalion of the International Brigades in the **Spanish Civil War.** At the age of twenty-nine, he was killed in action, covering the retreat of his machine-gun company; *Illusion and Reality* was still in proof. A long, probing, and welcoming review article in *Left Review* quickly helped to establish a reputation for the book.

Caudwell did not move in artistic or literary circles. Born Christopher St. John Sprigg, he left school at fifteen, worked as a journalist in trade publishing, wrote several books on aviation and flying, and became a successful crime novelist, publishing in that genre under his birth name. By 1935, he was engaged in an explicitly Marxist work that eventually became *Illusion and Reality,* and he joined the Communist Party. His interests, scientific as well as literary, gave his theoretical work a practical orientation, as he produced a theory of the function of literature. As Alick West, another Marxist critic of the period, succinctly put it, "He showed poetry to be part of the theory and practice by which men learn and decide what can and shall exist, and change dream into reality."

The subtitle of *Illusion and Reality,* "a study of the sources of poetry," characterizes Caudwell's approach. He regarded literature as a social product, and therefore its origins had to be sought in the workings of society. In contrast to the academic tendency to examine literature largely within the context of literary history, Caudwell started from a social perspective, drawing on **Karl Marx**'s classic statement in *A Contribution to the Critique of Political Economy* of the relation between base and superstructure: "It is not the consciousness of men that determines their existence, but, on the contrary, it is their social existence that determines their consciousness."

Whereas some of his contemporaries used Marx's statement in a depressingly mechanical fashion to connect a society's productive relations directly to the culture it produced, Caudwell understood "social existence" to be complex and requiring detailed analysis not only of the relationships figured in literary products but also of the linguistic and psychological mechanisms used by poetry.

The notion of social being determining consciousness was already well established but was frequently regarded as reflective; that is, historical differences in the arts appeared as the patterns of social organization changed because culture reflects the economic base. Caudwell, perhaps because he was a more thoroughgoing Marxist and not associated with any official party positions on culture, had a more dialectical approach; he assumed that the relationship between culture and social organization had a character of mutual determination, and thus he explored the question of how culture affects social existence.

Caudwell opens the argument by contrasting the "instinctive" with the "economic" in "primitive society" (a conventional source of example for many Marxists ever since Engels's *Origin of the Family, Private Property and the State*). Caudwell writes:

> Unlike the life of beasts, the life of the simplest tribe requires a series of efforts which are not instinctive, but which are demanded by the necessities of a non-biological economic aim—for example a harvest. Hence the instincts must be harnessed to the needs of the harvest by a social mechanism.

Such a mechanism is the harvest festival, which can generate and organize the emotional energy necessary to sustain the labor that will produce the harvest. Thus culture is a functional, productive element of social life:

> Ants and bees store instinctively; but man does not. Beavers construct instinctively; not man. It is necessary to harness man's instincts to the mill of labour, to collect his emotions and direct them into the useful, the economic channel.

Caudwell is not a vulgar materialist who reduces everything to economics—he says poetry is economic "in origin"; otherwise, economics is mediated or the term used metaphorically. His point is to stress poetry's social rather than private nature and therefore its actual functionality. "The poem," said Caudwell, "is what happens when it is read."

This functionality for Caudwell depends on the illusion of the book's title. He is not designating by "illusion" a false picture of the world; rather it is the transformation of a reality on the basis of feelings about it. The art thus generates and organizes emotion in relation to a potential reality. It makes a feeling judgment of the reality that affects action; that is, it creates an illusion that can help bring into being a new reality. In our own society, obviously, the process has many more elements and is more diffuse, but nevertheless, the illusion created in whatever medium conditions attitudes that have an effect in the outside world. It is in that sense that Caudwell calls poetry a guide to action, as a device that encourages an emotional orientation that affects behavior. Anticipating **Gramsci**, Caudwell shows how art can exercise a hegemonic function.

Caudwell's lack of university training was both advantage and disadvantage. In regard to the arts, he was never conditioned to reproduce the dominant ideology but neither did he acquire the forms of disciplined argument that could have made him acceptable to academics. *Illusion and Reality* is disorganized and often unclear; it is frequently self-indulgent and idiosyncratic. But it moves from a vision of art as static, as something consumed, to an active process of engaging with the world. Caudwell's vision of poetry, literature, and art resonates with Marx's exhortation (in the *Theses on Feuerbach*) that the point is not to interpret the world but to change it.

Selected Bibliography: Caudwell, Christopher. *Scenes and Actions: Unpublished Manuscripts.* Ed. and introduction, Jean Duparc and David Margolies. New York: Routledge & Kegan Paul, 1986; Clark, Jon, et al. *Culture and Crisis in Britain in the Thirties.* London: Lawrence and Wishart, 1979; Margolies, David. *The Function of Literature: A Study of Christopher Caudwell's Aesthetics.* New York: International Publishers, 1969; Pawling, Christopher. *Christopher Caudwell: Towards a Dialectical Theory of Literature.* Basingstoke: Macmillan, 1989; Sullivan, Robert. *Christopher Caudwell.* London: Croom Helm, 1987.

David Margolies

CERTEAU, MICHEL DE (1925–1986). Certeau was an extremely wide-ranging thinker whose ideas have exerted substantial influence in fields as diverse as historiography, anthropology, sociology, theology, cultural studies, philosophy, and psychoanalysis. He joined the Jesuits in 1950, and his early work developed in close association with this order. The years 1968–1971 represent a transitional period that brought him to engage more directly with a wider range of intellectual and political domains.

Certeau's first explicitly political book was *The Capture of Speech* (*La Prise de parole*, 1968), which explained the French political crisis of that year in terms of a divorce between people's effective beliefs and practices and the conceptual models and political institutions that "represented" them. Certeau was subsequently drawn into various political-cultural circles and think tanks (notably around university reform and cultural policy formation). Writings issuing from such circumstances can be found in *Culture in the Plural* (*La Culture au pluriel*, 1974), which considers how political and institutional resources can be redeployed in favor of the disseminated and unrepresented creativity of ordinary people and user groups. In *The Practice of Everyday Life* (*L'Invention du quotidien*, vol. 1, *Arts de faire*, 1980), Certeau presents a number of models designed to allow such anonymous creativity to be grasped more clearly. He sets the strategies of institutions that can map and control their terrain against the tactics of users who must make do with the resources they have on hand. He draws on Emile Benveniste's linguistics of utterance: as speakers appropriate a preexisting linguistic system for their own ends, so inhabitants creatively appropriate an imposed urban system, and readers "poach" across texts they have not written. These analyses have been massively influential in Anglophone cultural studies, as well as in sociological and ethnographic approaches to contemporary society.

His explicitly political writings constitute only one facet of Certeau's oeuvre, though his many historical studies also deploy incisive modes of properly political analysis. *The Possession of Loudun* (*La Possession de Loudun*, 1970) traces how royal authority appropriated and staged a case of diabolic possession in seventeenth-century

France. *The Writing of History* (*L'Ecriture de l'histoire*, 1975) analyzes the politics of historiography, as well as the transition in Europe over the early modern period from religiously to explicitly politically ordered societies. *Une Politique de la langue: La Révolution française et les patois* (1975) analyzes the linguistic policies of the **French Revolution**, while *The Mystic Fable* (*La Fable mystique*, 1982) traces the institutional "politics" that developed around early modern mystics. Across all his writings, Certeau probes key political categories, such as the relations between representations and practices, the production of belief, and socially constructed figures of alterity.

Selected Bibliography: Ahearne, Jeremy. *Between Cultural Theory and Policy: The Cultural Policy Thinking of Pierre Bourdieu, Michel de Certeau and Régis Debray*. Warwick, England: Centre for Cultural Policy Studies, U of Warwick, 2004; Ahearne, Jeremy. *Michel de Certeau: Interpretation and Its Other*. Stanford, CA: Stanford UP, 1996; Buchanan, Ian. *Michel de Certeau: Cultural Theorist*. London: Sage, 2000; Dosse, François. *Michel de Certeau: le marcheur blessé*. Paris: La Découverte, 2002; Giard, Luce, ed. *Michel de Certeau*. Paris: Centre Georges Pompidou, 1987; Giard, Luce, Hervé Martin, and Jacques Revel. *Histoire, mystique et politique: Michel de Certeau*. Grenoble: Jérome Millon, 1991.

Jeremy Ahearne

CERVANTES SAAVEDRA, MIGUEL DE (1547–1616).

Born into a family of modest means in the university town of Alcalá de Henares, Cervantes is considered a key figure not just in Spanish literature but also in world literature. Little is known about Cervantes's youth, but in 1569 he went to Italy in order to serve Cardinal Acquaviva. In the following year, he enlisted in the army, and in 1571 fought against the Turks in the Battle of Lepanto, where he lost the use of his left hand. On his return to Spain in 1575, Cervantes was taken prisoner by Turkish pirates and was held in Algiers until 1580, when Trinitarian friars secured his ransom. Shortly after his return to Spain, Cervantes married Catalina de Salazar, and he held minor government positions, including a stint as a requisitioner and purchaser for the Spanish Armada of 1588. Also during these years, Cervantes began writing and publishing his most significant works, though without much public acclaim. In the 1590s, Cervantes faced a few personal setbacks, as he was denied permission to immigrate to America, and imprisoned due to accounting irregularities while working as a tax collector. In addition, Cervantes separated for some time from his wife, and he remained impoverished throughout much of the rest of his life.

Cervantes cultivated prose, drama, and poetry. Many literary scholars consider Cervantes the first modern novelist and his *Don Quijote* (part 1, 1605; part 2, 1615) the first modern novel. Cervantes' other major literary achievements include a pastoral romance (*La galatea*, 1585), a collection of Italianate short stories (*Novelas ejemplares*, 1613), a narrative poem (*Viaje del Parnaso*, 1614), and a posthumously published Byzantine romance (*Los trabajos de Persiles y Sigismunda*, 1617). Cervantes' literary works occasionally reflect personal life experiences, yet consistently illustrate the universal experience of life as shared by all humans. His writings draw from a vast repertoire of literary genres such as chivalric, epic, pastoral, and picaresque. Though none of Cervantes' works are political propaganda, much of his drama and prose explores themes of political importance, such as power relations, poverty, empire, identity, and good government.

Selected Bibliography: Cascardi, Anthony J., ed. *The Cambridge Companion to Cervantes*. Cambridge: Cambridge UP, 2002; Cruz, Anne J., and Carroll B. Johnson, eds. *Cervantes and His Postmodern Constituencies*. Hispanic Issues, vol. 17. New York: Garland, 1999; Finello, Dominick L. *Cervantes: Essays on Social and Literary Polemics*. Rochester, NY: Tamesis, 1998; Forcione, Alban K. *Cervantes and the Humanist Vision: A Study of Four Exemplary Novels*. Princeton, NJ: Princeton UP, 1982; Fuchs, Barbara. *Passing for Spain: Cervantes and the Fictions of Identity*. Urbana: U of Illinois P, 2003; Johnson, Carroll B. *Cervantes and the Material World*. Urbana: U of Illinois P, 2000; Wilson, Diana de Armas. *Cervantes, the Novel, and the New World*. Oxford and New York: Oxford UP, 2000.

R. John McCaw

CÉSAIRE, AIMÉ (1913–). The Martinican poet and statesman Aimé Césaire is undoubtedly the seminal figure of the twentieth-century movement of decolonization in the French-speaking world. Other political figures such as Sékou Touré (Guinea) and **Kwame Nkrumah** (Ghana) played a more direct role in the political process of decolonization, and writers such as **Frantz Fanon** and **Edouard Glissant** also contributed to the cultural critique of colonialism. With the possible exception of **Léopold Senghor**, however, only Césaire combined the enormous cultural influence of a literary and critical attack on colonialism with an active political engagement, both as deputy in the French Constituent Assembly and mayor of Fort-de-France, Martinique. Césaire's poem *Notebook of a Return to my Native Land* (*Cahier d'un retour au pays natal*, 1939) constitutes the superlative poetic critique of Western imperialism. Combining elements of surrealism and the influence of radical French poets such as Rimbaud, Lautréamont, and Mallarmé with a violent condemnation of the alienation of the colonized in French-controlled Martinique, Césaire's modernist poem served as a primary element in the drive to overthrow French colonialism by the 1960s. Following discussions with fellow colonial students in Paris in the 1930s, Césaire's *Cahier* also invented the term "**negritude**," thus launching the movement that would spearhead the drive to decolonization on the cultural plane.

After 1945, Césaire continued to publish his own distinctive form of surrealist-inspired poetry in volumes such as *Les armes miraculeuses* (1946) and *Soleil cou coupé* (1948), while his polemical text *Discourse on Colonialism* (1956) condemned the process of colonialism in the harshest terms, explicitly linking Western imperialism with the Nazi genocide. In the 1950s, Césaire increasingly and explicitly strove to make his writing accessible to a wider public. While his poetry thus came to address the political problems of imperialism and decolonization (*Ferrements,* 1960), Césaire simultaneously turned to theater as a vehicle to achieve a broader impact for his writing. *The Tragedy of King Christopher* (1963) described the attempt of Henri Christophe to lead Haiti from its independence from France in 1804 to full autonomy by totalitarian means. The play thus served, in its contemporary context, as an allegorical and prescient warning for newly independent African states tempted by authoritarian rule. *A Season in the Congo* (1966) confirmed this orientation in its explicit critique of the assassination of Patrice Lumumba. Césaire's historical study *Toussaint Louverture* (1959) traced the history of the Haitian Revolution (1791–1804), underlining its implications as the founding historical act of the decolonization movement. Césaire's work is marked by a fundamental and critical sense of the ambiguity of history and human action, an ambiguity that extends into his political legacy. Though he participated actively in the critique of imperialism, Césaire simultaneously oversaw the integration of Martinique, Guadeloupe, French Guyana into the French state as "overseas departments," in effect intensifying their dependency on the French metropolis. Nonetheless, in contrast to Frantz Fanon's defense of anticolonial violence, Césaire's refusal to support unequivocally the goal of a free society achieved by any means available gives his texts a critical valence that allows them to speak beyond the mere historical moment of decolonization to illuminate the fundamental and enduring search for human freedom.

Selected Bibliography: Arnold, A. James. *Modernism and Negritude.* Cambridge, MA: Harvard UP, 1981; Césaire, Aimé. *Discourse on Colonialism.* Trans. Joan Pinkham. New York: Monthly Review P, 1972; Depestre, René. *Bonjour et adieu à la Négritude.* Paris: Seghers, 1980; Irele, Abiola, ed. *Aimé Césaire: Cahier d'un retour au pays natal.* Ibadan: New Horn Press Limited, 1994.

Nick Nesbitt

CHARTISM. A militant working-class movement that emerged in England, Scotland, and Wales between the 1830s and the early 1850s, named for its six-point charter. Although it lasted no more than twenty years, the political effects of the struggle carried on by industrial and agrarian workers were long lasting in Great Britain. The charter was drafted by William Lovett and first published in London on May 8, 1838, based on the following demands: redistribution of the franchise to include workers; abolition of the monarchy and the House of Lords; the election of sheriffs and justices of the peace; law reform; abolition of tithes and thereby the end of a state church; and the abolition of conscription, excise tax, and the privileges of peers, corporations, and trading companies. The six demands of the charter were equal electoral districts, abolition of property qualifications for members of Parliament, universal suffrage for men, annual parliaments, vote by secret ballot, and payment for members of Parliament.

By the twentieth century, the Chartist demands had been realized, but when the charter was delivered to Parliament on April 10, 1848, it was openly ridiculed, and by May, rioting had broken out in London and in other cities. Thereafter the Chartists were under continual attack by the British government, and through police action, mass arrests, transportation to the colonies, and the infiltration of police spies, the Chartists began to give way.

The Chartists were part of a tradition of political radicalism in England that went back at least to the 1640s—to the English Revolution—at least two hundred years before the term *Chartism* was coined in 1837. Such political movements as the Levellers, the Diggers, and the Ranters played much the same political and ideological role as the Chartists assumed. Though the Chartist movement was largely ignored in the United States and often savagely suppressed in England itself, several influential Victorian writers who popularly championed the working poor—Benjamin Disraeli, **Charles Dickens**, Charles Kingsley, **Elizabeth Gaskell**, and **George Eliot**— loosely based much of their subject matter on the Chartist movement. However, they did so with great ambivalence and sometimes unconcealed hostility. The ideology of the Chartists stood in contrast to the prevailing middle-class values appearing in the mainstream prose fiction of the first half of the nineteenth century in England, and even such populists as Dickens could not countenance inviting workers into Parliament.

During their brief lifetime, the Chartists managed to produce a unique body of working-class literature, in particular poetry and a radical press including magazines, journals, and newspapers. However, important fiction was produced as well, including such works as Thomas Martin Wheeler's *Sunshine and Shadow* (1849–1850) and Ernest Jones's *De Brassier: A Democratic Romance* (1850–1851). As Martha Vicinus notes, "Culturally Chartist writers sought to create a class-based literature, expressive of the hopes and fears of the people. The years of the movement saw an outpouring of speeches, essays, prison letters, dialogues, short stories, novels, songs, lyrical poems, epics and, later in the century, autobiographies" (7).

For an intense moment in nineteenth-century English literature, the gap between politics and culture virtually disappeared, since the Chartists saw little contradiction between the aims of art and the demands of politics; literature, particularly poetry, became another political weapon. Chartist verse was primarily written by artisans and industrial workers, the great majority of whom were self-educated, and their works were published in Chartist magazines, journals, and newspapers. Perhaps the most enduring aspect of Chartist poetry then and now is that it represented an alternative, working-class culture, a culture in sharp contrast to an English culture dominated by the Anglican Church—a fading aristocracy—and by an emerging middle class. In general, Chartist poetry extolled the same values as did Chartist rallies: democracy, the right of nations to self-rule, the emancipation of workers from an oppressive social system, and the elevation of the working man and woman to full human status.

Selected Bibliography: Charlton, John. *The Chartists: The First National Workers' Movement.* London: Pluto, 1997; Scheckner, Peter, ed. *An Anthology of Chartist Poetry: Poetry of the British Working Class, 1830s–1850s.* Rutherford, NJ: Fairleigh Dickinson UP, 1989; Thompson, E. P. *The Making of the English Working Class.* New York: Vintage-Random House, 1966; Vicinus, Martha. "Chartist Fiction and the Development of a Class-Based Literature." *The Socialist Novel in Britain.* Ed. H. Gustav Klaus. London: Harvester, 1982. 7–25.

Peter Scheckner

CHERNYSHEVSKY, NIKOLAI (1828–1889). Chernyshevsky was born the son of an Orthodox priest in the Russian provincial town of Saratov. Originally, it was intended that he should follow in his father's footsteps, so he was enrolled in a seminary. However, his parents later made the decision to send him to St. Petersburg for a university education that led to his becoming the leading radical figure in nineteenth-century Russia. By the mid-1850s, Chernyshevsky had already established himself in the so-called thick journals and was in position to take advantage of the thaw that ensued in Russia after its defeat in the Crimean War. In the span of less than a decade, Chernyshevsky authored work after work that would have enormous influence on the Russian left. Indeed, the Tsarist government came to see him as a dangerous man and decided to deal with him. In 1862, Chernyshevsky was arrested and detained in the infamous Peter and Paul Fortress. He was kept there for over a year before the Russian government brought him to trial. As a result of his trial, acknowledged as a sham even by his detractors, Chernyshevsky was sentenced to hard labor in Siberia to be followed by lifelong exile.

In his brief career, Chernyshevsky published several works that can be considered milestones. In particular, Chernyshevsky's *The Aesthetic Relation of Art to Reality* not only is credited with announcing a new, realist aesthetics in Russian culture but, together with his "The Anthropological Principle in Philosophy," was crucial in the overthrow of idealist philosophy among the Russian left. In his literary criticism, Chernyshevsky is credited with the first use of the term "interior monologue." However much Chernyshevsky may have contributed to Russian culture with his political articles, his fame (or infamy) assuredly rests on his novel *What Is to Be Done?* (1863), which became the gospel of Russian radicalism. The novel focuses on the progressive circles of the younger generation in mid-nineteenth-century Russia. It has been regarded by many as an extremely subversive work, with some seeing it as an attack on marriage and the family, while others have viewed it as a call to violent revolution. Although legally published while the author was in prison awaiting trial, it was quickly outlawed by the Russian government. *What Is to Be Done?* has been denounced by many as devoid of any artistic merit, but the novel became enormously influential in Russia. Russian radicals of all trends looked to Chernyshevsky as a forefather and his novel as a major development in the revolutionary movement. Lenin declared *What Is to Be Done?* a great work of art, and it later became part of the official canon of the Soviet Union.

Selected Bibliography: Chernyshevsky, N. G. *Selected Philosophical Essays.* Moscow: Foreign Languages Publishing House, 1953; Drozd, Andrew M. *Chernyshevskii's What Is to Be Done? A Reevaluation.* Evanston, IL: Northwestern UP, 2001; Paperno, Irina. *Chernyshevsky and the Age of Realism.* Stanford, CA: Stanford UP, 1988; Pereira, N.G.O. *The Thought and Teachings of N. G. Černyševskij.* The Hague: Mouton, 1975; Randall, Francis B. *Chernyshevskii.* New York: Twayne, 1967; Woehrlin, William F. *Chernyshevskii: The Man and the Journalist.* Cambridge, MA: Harvard UP, 1971.

Andrew M. Drozd

CHINESE LITERATURE. The Chinese concept of literature (*wenxue*) traditionally included ancient works of philosophy, history, and divination, as well as poetry, prose, and fiction. The first of what were referred to as the "five classics" is *Classic of Changes*, a series of ancient commentaries on sixty-four hexagrams (six-line binary diagrams), determined through casting milfoil stalks. Long thought in both East and West to be a text with magical powers, it contains stark and hauntingly beautiful images, such as "fire in the lake," which became part of Chinese literature. The German philosopher Leibniz was influenced by study of the hexagrams when he devised his system of binary mathematics, which led in turn to the invention of the modern computer.

The *Classic of Odes* (known in the West in Arthur Waley's rendering as the *Book of Poetry* or as Bernhard Karlgren's *Book of Odes*) is of greatest importance from a literary standpoint in that it contains the texts of over three hundred folk songs, poems, dynastic hymns, and religious odes, typically written in four-character lines with end rhymes of varying schemes. The folk songs were traditionally viewed as a gauge of public opinion or read as containing prescriptions for morality and good governance. Confucius is said to have commented that they contained "no heterodox thoughts," though a number are racy in content, describing trysting lovers; extramarital liaisons; and rebellious sentiments against cruel government, tax collectors, landlords, and exploiters of the peasantry. Some also display protodemocratic sentiments. Most of these anonymous poems date from the eleventh through the sixth centuries B.C.E. (the early Zhou era) and are thought to represent a northern tradition. Remarkably, many of the end rhymes can still be detected in modern Mandarin pronunciation.

Another anthology, the *Elegies of Chu*, has been identified by some scholars with a southern tradition, and was thus translated by David Hawkes under the title *Songs of the South*, although recent scholarship has questioned the extent of the validity of this north/south distinction. Lines are of irregular length, and the length of the poems varies, but they employ rhyme. Its authorship, or at least compilation, has been ascribed to one poet, the wronged statesman Qu Yuan (ca. 340–ca. 278 B.C.E.), who was slandered by rivals at the court of Chu—a large kingdom lying in present-day Hubei and Hunan provinces (central China)—and wandered in exile, estranged from his king. The elegies have rich mythological and shamanistic features, often detailing quests by a male shaman for a meeting with a river or mountain goddess. Some describe rituals or mourn the fallen dead in warfare. The centerpiece of the anthology, a long poem "Encountering Sorrow," is rich in flower and plant imagery. It has traditionally been interpreted allegorically as venting the speaker's sorrow at having had his counsel rejected by his king. Other recent rereadings focus on the surrealistic journey described in the poem as having been inspired by shamanic dream flight, and again suggest the questing-after-beauty theme.

Literary historians see the *sao*-style as the direct ancestor of the descriptive prose poem, or "rhapsody" (*fu*). Sima Xiangru (179–117 B.C.E.), the most esteemed practitioner of the Han *fu*, penned "A Description of the Shanglin Park," delineating the wondrous fish and creatures with which this imperial hunting ground had been stocked; he then goes on to describe the wonders of the hunt, thereby criticizing the extravagance of the imperial lifestyle. The *fu* were normally lengthy compositions, but lyric short *fu* also exist.

The *yue fu* (music bureau), another genre, contains both ritual hymns and popular ballads, the latter reflecting the hardships of the common people and expressing criticism of the government. The name was derived from a bureau established by Emperor Wu of the Han dynasty to collect folk songs as a means of sampling popular opinion, so as to determine whether the conduct of his officialdom was good or not. The longest of the *yue fu*, "Southeast Fly the Peacocks" tells the tragic story of a couple in love who are forced by the young man's mother to separate and eventually take their own lives. As such, it makes the case for freedom to choose one's partner over arranged marriages. Perhaps under the influence of the *yue fu*, the second century C.E. saw the rise of a new verse form, the five-character line *shi*, replacing the four-character shi meter prevailing since the *Classic of Odes*. The earliest extant poems in this form, which reflect on death and separation, are known collectively as the "Nineteen Old Poems." The *yue fu* also had an influence on what Marxist literary historians call the first representatives of the "feudal" literature, the aristocratic poets Cao Cao (155–220), his brother Cao Zhi (192–232) and Wang Can (177–

217), whose works reflect the depravations of war, famine, and pestilence. The works of poets known as the Seven Sages of the Bamboo Grove—learned men, including Ruan Ji (210–263) and Ji Kang (223–262), who withdrew from court politics and indulged in "pure talk," drugs, and alcohol—reflect antidespotic sentiments. Tao Yuanming (aka Tao Qian, 365–427), who came from a declining gentry family, served in government for twelve years before renouncing official life, after which he retired to the countryside as a farmer, composing poems idealizing rural life, rejecting court life, and implicitly criticizing the political order. He is considered one of the greatest writers in Chinese history.

At this point poetry became more formalistic, as Xie Lingyun (385–433) began to write nature poetry using an ornate style entailing elaborate parallelism and a descriptive realism characterized by the critical notion of verisimilitude. Shen Yue (441–513) is credited with developing a four-tone system of prosody calling for the correlation of level (*ping*) and oblique (*ze*) tones within individual lines, which would prove highly influential on later poetry. By the Tang dynasty (618–907), the quatrain gave way to the regulated verse form—poems of eight lines (five or seven characters in length) which used the four-tone system along with rhyme and parallelism or antithesis between two lines as the ideal verse form.

The high Tang poet Wang Wei (701–761) looked back to Tao Yuanming as a model in his verse, which seeks to blend the self into nature. Li Bai (alt. Li Po or Li Bo, 701–762), nicknamed the "Immortal of Wine," was an eccentric romantic figure in the manner of the old Daoists or Ruan Ji, who favored the freer "ancient style" verse over regulated verse. Du Fu (alt. Tu Fu, 712–770), more the sedulous craftsman, favored regulated verse. Li Bai was a dissident with a cultivated flair, a principled hedonist who held "kings and marquises in contempt." The mature Du Fu was a Confucian humanist who took as his overriding concern the plight of his country and people. Bai Juyi (772–846) declared he would attempt to write in language simple enough to be read to the common people. He penned poems denouncing injustice and social inequity, as well as ballads telling the tragic stories of mistreated women and the consequences of the An Lushan rebellion, in which Yang Guifei, the emperor's beloved consort, was hanged in his own encampment by rebellious troops, the emperor powerless to save her.

Poetry in these and other classical-style forms such as the "lyric" (*ci*) was composed during Song (960–1279), Yuan (1279–1368), Ming (1368–1644), and Qing (1644–1911) times. It continued through the early years of the Republic and arguably until the present day, though by the May Fourth Movement (1919), a call had gone out among intellectuals to create a new style of poetry in the vernacular to address a different era, and a few poets, such as Wen Yiduo (1899–1946), were able to distinguish themselves in the new freer forms. Notable progressive literati such as Chen Sanli (1852–1937) and the essayist and short-story writer **Lu Xun** (1881–1936), often referred to as the "Father of Modern Chinese Literature," continued to compose poetry in the old forms.

Prose writing in the classical language was greatly influenced by the style of the philosophers: Confucius (ca. 551–479 B.C.E.), who took benevolence and humanity as his starting point; Mencius (ca. 372–289 B.C.E.), who put the people before the monarch and affirmed their right to overthrow a tyrant; Xunzi (ca. 313–238 B.C.E.), who argued that human nature was inherently bad, but advocated rules and teaching to transform the people; Han Fei (ca. 280–233 B.C.E.), a Machiavellian "legalist" who counseled the emperor to enact a system of strict laws and punishments; Mozi, who advocated universal love, and the Daoists Laozi (ca. 570–ca. 490 B.C.E.) and Zhuangzi (ca. 369–ca. 286 B.C.E.), who questioned man's artificiality and separation from nature. The book of *Zhuangzi* challenges conventional ways of seeing and mocks the Confucians' attempts at categorizing the world as petty and limiting. It also coined the term that later came to mean "fiction": *xiao shuo*. *Zhuangzi* contains brilliant flights of fancy, which are in fact protofiction.

Prose was also shaped and influenced by Sima Qian (145–90 B.C.E.), who compiled the *Records of the Grand Historian* (*Shiji*), a history of China and the known world from the beginning to the early Han (his own day). The *Shiji* uses re-created dialogues, dramatic episodes, and a swift narrative style, techniques that make it partially akin to fiction. It also develops the character known as the *xia* (swordsman, or "knight errant"), later featured in *wuxia*, or "kung-fu" fiction. Sima Qian's style became a model not only for subsequent dynastic histories but also for classical Chinese prose written in China, Korea, and Japan. The work posits existential questions without recourse to pat answers and assigns both agency and responsibility to major figures in history.

Fiction first appeared in the short tales of the supernatural stories of Han, Wei, and Six Dynasties periods, in part inspired by the insecurities of years of war and rebellion at the end of the Han (220) and in the periods of North-South division and civil war that followed. An early example is the *Records in Search of Spirits* compiled by Gan Bao (ca. 285–360). These were followed by longer tales of the marvelous, which flourished during the Tang. The Ming saw full-length novels such as *Romance of the Three Kingdoms*, a stirring tale of an ill-fated attempt overthrow tyranny and restore the Han; *The Water Margin*, a novel which lionizes a rebel band during the Song for their defiance of the corrupt officialdom and their aid to just causes; *Journey to the West*—translated by Arthur Waley as *Monkey*—the story of the Tang-era monk Xuanzang's pilgrimage to India to obtain Buddhist sutras, guarded by comic supernatural beings, including the famed monkey Sun Wukong and a part-human pig, Zhu Bajie.

The greatest novel of the Qing era, *Dream of the Red Chamber*—probably written by Cao Xueqin (ca. 1715–1763) and Gao E, translated by Hawkes and John Minford as *The Story of the Stone* and by the Yangs as *Dream of Red Mansions*—highlights the tragedy of its young protagonists Jia Baoyu and Lin Daiyu, who fall in love as they grow up in a great and wealthy household. The novel indicts the patriarchy and a materialistic society. As such, it is a direct ancestor of *The Family* (1931), a modern novel set in the 1920s by the anarchist writer Ba Jin (1904–). Similarly, *The Scholars*, by Wu Jingzi (1701–1754), makes witty use of over ten interconnected stories to satirize the empty standards of literati, the civil-service exams, and widespread corruption. It provided a classic model for the novels of the castigatory genre in the late nineteenth century, which are more scathing in their attacks but lack their precursor's subtlety and literary refinement.

Many writers of the twentieth century responded to the call put forth by Chen Duxiu (1879–1942) and Hu Shi (1891–1962) in the journal *The New Youth* circa

1918–1919 for a new literature written in the vernacular, aiming at social and political abuses to awaken the nation in the face of warlord, gentry, and compradore misrule as well as the continuing Western and Japanese imperialist incursions in China. Lu Xun was the most prominent writer to respond with a series of short stories and the satiric novella *The True Story of Ah Q.*

During the nationalist decade (1927–1937), censorship was increasingly tightened, and after the victory of the Communists in the civil war in 1949, literary control became institutionalized. Still, some limited dissent was possible (Liu Binyan, 1925– ; Wang Meng, 1934–). Socialist realism was promoted in the early 1950s: already prominent woman writer **Ding Ling** (1904–1986) won the Stalin Prize in 1951 but was later officially criticized. Revolutionary romanticism came to the fore during the Cultural Revolution (1966–1976) with the novelist Hao Ran (1932–), a time that was also demarcated by the revolutionary model operas, extolling heroism (often by women or volunteeristic male leaders), anti-imperialism, and class consciousness. These were usually set prior to the communist era, during the civil war against the nationalists (1927–1949) or the War to Resist Japan (1937–1945).

After the death of Chairman **Mao Zedong**, and the fall from power of the "Gang of Four" and Hua Guofeng, a group of stories criticizing the excesses of the Cultural Revolution appeared in 1978, later referred to collectively as "the literature of the wounded" or "scar literature." Women writers such as Zhang Jie (1937–) and Wang Anyi (1954–) began to revive feminist issues. By the early 1980s, Western literature was again being translated in quantity; magical realism and postmodernism made a notable impact (Yu Hua, 1960– ; Can Xue, 1953–). The 1980s became a decade of experimentation: the "Misty" poets (**Bei Dao**, 1949– ; Mang Ke, 1950– ; Shu Ting, 1952– ; Gu Cheng, 1956–1993; Yang Lian, 1955– ; Duo Duo, 1951–) with their obscure references defied the censors and riled the critics; the theater of the absurd made its debut with **Gao Xingjian**; a search for Chinese roots (*xungen*) independent of the communist metanarrative of the revolution, or at least the calling for a reexamination of the history of the revolution (**Mo Yan**, 1956– ; Su Tong, 1963– ; Ah Cheng, 1949– ; Han Shaogong, 1953– ; Jia Pingwa, 1953–); and the so-called cultural fervor, which was sparked by popular journals for intellectuals, such as *Reading*.

With the suppression of the prodemocracy demonstrations in Tiananmen Square in June 1989, a genre sometimes referred to as "hooligan" literature by **Wang Shuo** (1958–), which also had its beginnings in the 1980s, took on greater prominence. It gives a cynical, alternately bleak and humored depiction of jaded, alienated characters inhabiting a crass society, whose values they deride, constantly in search of a quick fix. The racy novel *Shanghai Baby* by Wei Hui, a young woman writer, features debauched urban youth broaching topics like interracial sex and sadomasochism. The cynicism of these works offers a marked contrast to the enthusiasm for all things cultural of the 1980s and may be symbolic of resistance toward the post-1989 order, which combined political repression with crass materialism, the disassembly of state-owned enterprises, and greater disparities between wealth and poverty, urban seaboard and rural hinterland, against the backdrop of hegemonic global forces.

Selected Bibliography: Gibbs, Donald A. *A Bibliography of Studies and Translations of Modern Chinese Literature, 1918–1942.* Cambridge, MA: East Asian Research Center, Harvard University, 1975;

Hsia, C. T. *A History of Modern Chinese Fiction*. New Haven, CT: Yale UP, 1961; Kowallis, Jon Eugene von. *The Lyrical Lu Xun: A Study of His Classical Style Verse*. Honolulu: U of Hawaii P, 1996; Kowallis, Jon Eugene von. *The Subtle Revolution: Poets of the "Old Schools" in Late-Qing and Early Republican China*. Berkeley: Institute of East Asian Studies, University of California, 2004; Lee, Leo Ou-fan. *The Romantic Generation of Modern Chinese Writers*. Cambridge, MA: Harvard UP, 1973; Liu, James J. Y. *Chinese Theories of Literature*. Chicago: U of Chicago P, 1975; Liu, Wu-chi. *An Introduction to Chinese Literature*. Bloomington: Indiana UP, 1966; Liu, Wu-chi, and Irving Lo, eds. *Sunflower Splendor: Three Thousand Years of Chinese Poetry*. Bloomington: Indiana UP, 1975; Lynn, Richard John. *Chinese Literature: A Draft Bibliography in Western European Languages*. Canberra: Australian National UP, 1979; McDougall, Bonnie S., and Kam Louie. *The Literature of China in the Twentieth Century*. New York: Columbia UP, 1997; Nienhauser, William H. *The Indiana Companion to Traditional Chinese Literature*. 2 vols. Bloomington: Indiana UP, 1986; Wang, David Der-wei. *Fin-de-Siècle Splendor: Repressed Modernities of Late Qing Fiction, 1849–1911*. Stanford, CA: Stanford UP, 1997; Watson, Burton. *Early Chinese Literature*. New York: Columbia UP, 1962.

Jon Eugene von Kowallis

CHINESE WRITERS' ASSOCIATION (CWA) is a professional organization for writers, critics, and editors in the People's Republic of China. It was established in 1949 (known as the Chinese Literary Workers' Association until 1953) after the model of the Union of Soviet Writers. Like its Soviet model, the CWA organizes writers and directs their creativity according to the guidelines set by the Chinese **Communist Party** (CCP). It plays a duel role of facilitator and censor through the administration of literary prizes, literary magazines, and membership scanning. The CWA has branches in every province and municipality. Up to the late 1980s, it dominated every phase of literary production, making it practically impossible for anyone outside the network to survive as a full-time writer. Until the 1990s, a majority of its members were salaried writers or critics employed by cultural institutions or bureaus. Following the economic reform (known as the dual-track system of market economy and communist ideology) initiated by Deng Xiaoping, the CWA's monopoly on literary production has been modified by market mechanisms. A growing number of nonestablishment writers and freelance writers have emerged.

The CWA accepted **socialist realism** as its recommended aesthetic, which in the Chinese context has been reworded many times in accordance with the shifts and turns that have reshaped Chinese cultural and social scenes since 1949. At its first national congress held in 1949, the CWA endorsed "proletarian realism," avoiding the too obvious Soviet connection of socialist realism. Socialist realism was officially accepted and used to replace proletarian realism at the second CWA congress in 1953, during the peak hours of Sino-Soviet fraternity. In 1958, following the CCP's increasing estrangement from the Soviets, socialist realism was replaced by Mao's "revolutionary realism and romanticism."

The CWA suffered a devastating setback during the Cultural Revolution (1966–1976). The administrative body was abolished. With a few exceptions, CWA members were dispatched to reform farms. Their ideological reeducation was superintended by representatives from the military and factories. In 1979, CWA held its third national congress. It nonetheless took another five years for the CWA to resume its institutional functions, such as recruiting new members. While socialist realism was dropped from the vocabulary of the CWA charter after the Cultural Revolution, efforts were made to reclaim the works CWA members had published in the years prior to the Cultural Revolution, which were actually products of socialist realism. At its fourth national congress held in 1984, the CWA substituted realism in the sense of truth seeking for socialist realism, though the realism so promoted was tempered by emphasis on political agendas such as that of economic reform. A more recent rhetorical shift took place at the fifth congress held in 1996, in which main melody literature was prioritized. "Main melody" with regard to Chinese literature means anything ranging from communist history to topic themes of broad sociohistorical interest.

Selected Bibliography: Chung, Hilary, et al., eds. *In the Party Spirit: Socialist Realism and Literary Practice in the Soviet Union, East Germany and China.* Atlanta: Rodopi, 1996; Goldblatt, Howard, ed. *Chinese Literature for the 1980s: The Fourth Congress of Writers and Artists.* Armonk, NY: M. E. Sharpe, 1982.

Donghui He

CHURCHILL, CARYL (1938–). Born in London, Churchill grew up in England and Canada. In 1960, she received a B.A. in English from Oxford University, by which time she had already begun writing plays. After graduation, she honed her craft as a playwright by writing radio plays for the BBC. Churchill served as resident dramatist at the Royal Court Theatre in 1974–1975, where *Owners*, her first professional stage production, had premiered in 1972. Taking inspiration from the collective effort of working with such groups, during the 1970s and 1980s she worked with other theater companies as well, including Joint Stock and Monstrous Regiment, both of which used highly collaborative techniques such as extended workshop periods in their development of new plays. While working with Joint Stock and Monstrous Regiment, Churchill wrote a number of her most successful plays, including *Light Shining on Buckinghamshire* (1976), *Vinegar Tom* (1976), *Cloud Nine* (1979), and *A Mouthful of Birds* (1986).

Churchill's plays include strong utopian dimensions, but also address the sometimes severe obstacles that society places in the path of utopian desires. *Cloud Nine*, perhaps her best-known play, is typical of the way many of her plays challenge conventional assumptions about gender and identity while maintaining a simultaneously socialist and feminist perspective. In it, characters constantly change their sexual identities and alliances. Meanwhile, the play makes sudden leaps in time, moving between colonial Africa in the Victorian age to contemporary Britain, establishing a dialogue between the attitudes of 1879 and 1979. Thus, though in a more absurdist vein, Churchill employs techniques of estrangement similar to those found in the work of **Bertolt Brecht** to ask audiences to reexamine their inherited assumptions and to imagine possible alternatives to our current conceptions of individual identity and the relationships among individuals.

Even after striking out on her own, Churchill continued to use many techniques learned in working with theater companies, including improvisational workshops. Her plays also maintained an intense engagement with contemporary reality, as in *Mad Forest: A Play from Romania* (1990), written after Churchill, the play's director, and a group of student actors from London's Central School traveled to Romania in the wake of the fall of the Ceausescu regime to assess for themselves the social and political conditions there. The play itself summarized their findings, revealing the damage done to people's lives by years of repression, followed by chaotic and violent change. The later *Far Away* (2000) similarly protests recent violent events in various parts of the world.

In her later plays, Churchill has seemed to feel less and less bound by realism, as her plays have become more experimental, sometimes tending toward the spareseness of a **Samuel Beckett** or the absurdity of a **Harold Pinter**. For example, *The Skriker* (1994) employs the logic of a dream to explore the experience of modern urban life as it follows the protean title character, a sort of genie-like demon, as it pursues two young women to London, assuming a variety of shapes along the way. Other Churchill plays include *Top Girls* (1982), *Softcops* (1984), *Serious Money* (1987), and *A Number* (2002), which addresses the subject of human cloning. Churchill married David Harter in 1961 and has three sons. *Cloud Nine, Top Girls,* and *Serious Money* all won Obie Awards, and Churchill was given an Obie for Sustained Achievement in 2001.

Selected Bibliography: Aston, Elaine. *Caryl Churchill.* Plymouth, UK: Northcote House, 1997; Cousin, Geraldine. *Churchill: The Playwright.* London: Methuen, 1989; Kritzer, Amelia Howe. *The Plays of Caryl Churchill: Theatre of Empowerment.* London, Basingstoke: Macmillan, 1991; Rabillard, Sheila, ed. *Essays on Caryl Churchill: Contemporary Representations.* Winnipeg: Blizzard, 1997.

M. Keith Booker

COLD WAR. After **World War II** the United States and the Soviet Union squared off in a struggle for world dominance that would continue until the latter's collapse in 1991. This struggle was called the cold war because the two main combatants—China emerged as a third force with the Communist takeover in 1949—engaged each other through ideology, diplomacy, and covert operations rather than through actual military conflict. This was undoubtedly a good thing given the nuclear weapons that both sides possessed, which they came closest to deploying against each other during the 1962 Cuban missile crisis. Yet the name cold war must have seemed like a bitter misnomer to those involved in the protracted, bloody struggles that the major powers fought or financed in such places as Korea, Vietnam, Angola, and Afghanistan. The hot warfare waged in these and other countries serves as a reminder that the cold war unfolded amid the collapse of the Western European empires and was a struggle over which system—capitalism or Communism—would succeed these empires by guiding the process of modernization in the developing world. But the struggle for "hearts and minds" (in Lyndon Johnson's phrase) was not restricted to the so-called third world. Some of the most important effects of the cold war were felt within the United States and the Soviet Union themselves, as both combatants sought to create support for their positions among their own citizens.

Much of the important work on the relationship between the cold war and literature has focused on the effects of such domestic indoctrination in the United States during the crucial decade of the 1950s. This was, of course, the high point of U.S. **anticommunism** as expressed in such phenomena as the HUAC trials, the Rosenberg executions, and McCarthyism, which set a standard for political witch hunting and the infringement of civil liberties that had not been equaled until the current USA PATRIOT Act era. But anticommunist ideology also found a covert (and for that reason so much the more effective) home in literature and literary criticism, where its presence illustrates the proposition that the denial of politics (in critical approaches such as the **new criticism**) is itself a form of politics. Intellectuals dedicated themselves to asserting art's necessary commitment to the individual rather than the group, the psychological rather than the political, the broadly human rather than the historically contingent. Such assertions—made in the name of artistic discriminations but in fact congruent with developments in film and mass media—had the effect of denigrating the left-leaning art of the 1930s. Thus **Ralph Ellison**'s supposedly more universal account of African American alienation in *Invisible Man* (1952) was understood (by Ellison as well as by others) as an advance over **Richard Wright**'s supposedly dogmatic (and not coincidentally communist-sympathetic) portrayal of Bigger Thomas in *Native Son* (1940). The cold war continues to shape American literature, for instance in the concern with privacy central to postconfessional poetry.

Evidence that the CIA did in fact support cold war intellectual projects like the London-based journal *Encounter* suggests that the cold war understanding of literature also served a purpose abroad. Partisans of U.S. culture promoted American literature and other art forms such as abstract expressionist painting and jazz as salutary alternatives to the stifling orthodoxy associated with Soviet culture and its official aesthetic doctrine of socialist realism. In fact the Soviet state—especially under **Stalin** and his culture czar A. A. Zhdanov—did exert far greater direct influence over literary production than the U.S. government did, although this should not blind us to the fact that American aesthetics themselves constituted a different sort of orthodoxy. Throughout the Soviet period, Russian literature (including the work of dissidents like Alexander Solzhenitsyn) remained committed to the idea, anathema to American cold-war aesthetics, that literature not only could but indeed must be political.

Outside the United States and the Soviet Union, the national literature most shaped by the cold war was probably the **literature of Germany**, which was of course two countries prior to reunification, and whose literature continues to wrestle with the questions raised by its cold-war division into East and West. Elsewhere the postwar French novel was shaped by the discourse of capitalist modernization by means of which the country navigated its declining imperial power and its new subordination to U.S. interests. A similar situation in the United Kingdom, meanwhile, contributed to the flourishing of the most important popular genre of the cold-war era, the spy thriller as practiced by **Graham Greene**, Ian Fleming, and John LeCarré.

Postcolonial literature also dealt with the cold war as it impinged materially and ideologically on national liberation struggles. One of the great ironies of this period, however, is the way in which the cold war also provided a conduit for events in the third world to influence the struggles of subordinated groups within the United States. Insofar as the United States sought to position itself as the superior model for third-world nations struggling to free themselves from European domination, it participated in a discourse of rebellion that would return to trouble cold-war imperatives in the era of black power and Vietnam.

Selected Bibliography: Brennan, Timothy. "The Cuts of Language: The East/West of North/South." *Public Culture* 13.1 (Winter 2001): 39–63; Clark, Katerina. *The Soviet Novel: History as Ritual.* Chicago: U of Chicago P, 1985; Hoberek, Andrew. "Cold War Culture to Fifties Culture." *Minnesota Review* 55–57 (2002): 143–52; Hobsbawm, Eric. *The Age of Extremes: A History of the World, 1914–1991.* New York: Pantheon, 1994; Medovoi, Leerom. "Cold War American Culture as the Age of Three Worlds." *Minnesota Review* 55–57 (2002): 167–86; Nelson, Deborah. *Pursuing Privacy in Cold War America.* New York: Columbia UP, 2002; Ross, Kristin. *Fast Cars, Clean Bodies: Decolonization and the Reordering of French Culture.* Cambridge, MA: MIT P, 1995; Saunders, Frances Stonor. *The Cultural Cold War: The CIA and the World of Arts and Letters.* New York: New P, 1999; Schaub, Thomas Hill. *American Fiction in the Cold War.* Madison: U of Wisconsin P, 1991.

Andrew Hoberek

COLERIDGE, SAMUEL TAYLOR (1772–1834). Though much of his training and family background seemed to point him toward a religious vocation, Coleridge pursued instead an independent literary career, which soon brought him into contact with William Wordsworth and his sister, Dorothy, and later took him to Germany, where he studied the philosophy of Kant, Schiller, and Schelling, who were instrumental in the elaboration of the doctrine of **romanticism**. Although he could not bring himself to embrace the ministry, Coleridge remained concerned with religious matters in all his later pursuits as a poet, philosopher, literary critic, and political writer.

Coleridge's intellectual and political development was heavily marked by the **French Revolution**, which made him embrace some of its radical ideas in the early part of his life. This influence is evident in the public speeches on politics and religion he gave in Bristol, where he met Robert Southey. The speeches were published in 1795 under the title *Conciones ad Populum.* During the same period, Coleridge collaborated with Southey on a play, *The Fall of Robespierre,* which appeared in 1794. Coleridge also dedicated a series of sonnets to well-known radical thinkers such as **William Godwin** and Joseph Priestley, which were published in the *Morning Chronicle,* a Whig journal owned at the time by James Perry. In Bristol, Coleridge made the acquaintance of Joseph Cottle, the bookseller who became his patron and trustworthy friend, and who published Coleridge's first volume of poetry, *Poems,* in 1796.

Coleridge made many acquaintances in the literary world, but the most enduring was his friendship with Wordsworth. Although their relationship soured over time, it still offers the example of a remarkable artistic collaboration. Its best-known outcome is the volume *Lyrical Ballads,* first published by Cottle in 1798. The poems assembled in the volume defined a new aesthetic sensibility—announcing English romanticism, and characterized by a desire to look for poetic inspiration in both the commonplace, exemplified by Wordsworth, and the supernatural, as illustrated by Coleridge and his long poem *The Rime of the Ancient Mariner.*

Although Coleridge never relinquished his interest in politics, his opinions became increasingly conservative as he grew older. Even his religious thinking, originally favorable to Unitarianism, and even pantheism, gradually swayed in the direction of Christian orthodoxy. Coleridge's thought continued to fluctuate, however, at least with respect to religion. Schelling's philosophy of nature and theosophical movement functioned at times as a substitute religion, and Coleridge would often lean in its direction. Coleridge also found in Schelling (from whom he often borrowed without acknowledging his debt, as was his habit) an important source for his aesthetic thought. Such seminal critical distinctions as the difference between fancy and imagination, symbol and allegory, mechanical and organic form, culture and civilization were popularized, developed in the lectures that Coleridge gave at the Royal Institute in London, and then published in *Biographia Literaria* (1817).

Coleridge's late writings (*Lay Sermons*, 1816 and 1817, and *Aids to Reflection*, 1825) were almost entirely devoted to social and religious issues, and exerted an important influence on the Christian Socialists in England. Coleridge's monograph, *Church and State* (1830), was influential in defining the concept of a "national culture," which found a responsive critical reception with writers like Matthew Arnold and John Henry Newman. Coleridge's brilliance as a conversationalist was captured in the posthumous volumes of *Table Talk* (1836). Although uneven in his inspiration and writing, Coleridge's mental energy remains contagious. He was, in spite of his addictive habits and spiritual vacillations, "an archangel slightly damaged," as Lamb memorably put it, and the haunting figure of the ancient mariner is still with us.

Selected Bibliography: Colmer, John. *Coleridge: Critic of Society.* Oxford: Clarendon P, 1959; Haney, David P. *The Challenge of Coleridge: Ethics and Interpretation in Romanticism and Modern Philosophy.* University Park: Pennsylvania State UP, 2001; Whale, John C. *Imagination under Pressure 1789–1832: Aesthetics, Politics, Utility.* Cambridge: Cambridge UP, 2000; Woodring, Carl R. *Politics in the Poetry of Coleridge.* Madison: U of Wisconsin P, 1961.

Alina Clej

COMINTERN. *See* THIRD INTERNATIONAL.

COMMODIFICATION. One of the central concepts used in **Marxist criticism**, commodification is the process through which not only goods and services, but also ideas, activities, relationships, and even human beings are reduced to the status of commodities (goods that are valued only for the price they can command on the open market) in a capitalist society. Commodities, though they may be physical articles like shoes, hats, or candlesticks, have a decidedly abstract quality: they are valued not for their own genuine characteristics but for their ability to participate in a money economy, the workings of which are inscrutable to most individuals. The commodity thus represents the embodiment of powerful and mysterious hidden forces, which in some cases endows the commodity with an almost mystical quality, in which individuals become enthralled to the lure of the commodity as fetish. The gradual shift to a commodity economy under capitalism thus contributes to the progressive estrangement from material reality that for **Karl Marx** is a central effect of capitalism. Further, the nature of a capitalist economy, which treats the labor of individuals as a source of commodities, eventually leads to the treatment of human beings as abstract economic quantities, again valued not for their own individual characteristics but for their economic function. In short, it leads to the commodification of human beings, a phenomenon closely associated with their alienation and most directly represented in the treatment of factory workers as mere pieces of manufacturing machinery.

When applied to the criticism of literature, the concept of commodification is used in two principal ways. First, it can provide insights into texts in which commodification of one sort or another is a theme. Second, it can provide a useful framework within which to read the importance of the fact that literary texts are not produced as pure art but as part of a publishing industry in which such texts are themselves quite literally and overtly regarded as commodities.

Commodification occurs as a theme in literary texts in a variety of ways. For example, one of the most striking aspects of **James Joyce**'s *Ulysses*, a complex canonical text of **modernism**, is the way in which commercial relations penetrate every aspect of the lives of the characters. Money is constantly changing hands in the text, and we are frequently informed of the amount and nature of these transactions. Meanwhile, the text is densely populated with commodities of various kinds, some of which are invested with special fetish-like qualities.

Commodification can also be enacted in literary texts in more subtle ways. One might again consider *Ulysses*, in which Joyce shows an intense awareness of typography and thus of the physical status of his book as a commodity to be manufactured and sold. One might also consider the famous "junk" style of **Theodore Dreiser**, which **Fredric Jameson** in *The Political Unconscious* has seen as a reflection of the larger phenomenon of commodification through the use of language that is itself overtly commodified. Finally, a special case of the thematization of commodification occurs in literary texts—such as **Honoré de Balzac**'s *Lost Illusions* (1837–1843) or George Gissing's *New Grub Street* (1891)—that directly address the business of literature and the pressures this business places on authors.

In a broader sense, the concept of commodification provides useful insights into the ways in which market forces determine the conditions under which literature is produced. One might cite, for example, Ian Watt's classic study of the rise to prominence of the genre of the novel in the eighteenth century, a rise that he sees as part of the larger phenomenon of the rise of capitalism. In particular, he details the ways in which the rise of a free-market economy caused many of the basic conventions of the novel as a genre to be determined primarily by economic rather than aesthetic considerations. Similarly, Richard Ohmann's *Selling Culture* describes the impact on American **popular culture** of the rise of American consumer capitalism at the beginning of the twentieth century.

Selected Bibliography: Jameson, Fredric. *The Political Unconscious: Narrative as a Socially Symbolic Act.* Ithaca, NY: Cornell UP, 1981; Marx, Karl. *Capital: A Critique of Political Economy.* Vol. 1. Trans. Samuel Moore and Edward Aveling. Ed. Frederick Engels. New York: International Publishers, 1967; Ohmann, Richard. *Selling Culture: Magazines, Markets, and Class at the Turn of the Century.* London: Verso, 1996; Watt, Ian. *The Rise of the Novel: Studies in Defoe, Richardson, and Fielding.* Berkeley: U of California P, 1957.

M. Keith Booker

COMMUNIST PARTY—one of any number of modern political parties worldwide, generally espousing Marxist-Leninist ideas. The roots of the Communist Party go back at least as far as 1848, when, in the midst of a wave of revolutions sweeping Europe, **Karl Marx** and Friedrich Engels wrote *The Communist Manifesto* to explain and promote the program of a German group known as the Communist League. Modern Communist parties have their roots in the Russian Social Democratic Labor

Party, especially in the more radical Bolshevik wing of that party, which came into power in the **Russian Revolution** of 1917. With the subsequent founding of the Soviet Union, the Communist Party of the Soviet Union (the CPSU) became the bulwark of all Communist parties, especially under the auspices of the **Third International**, or Comintern, which worked (in the spirit of internationalism already present in *The Communist Manifesto*) to coordinate the activities of Communist parties around the world. The Comintern was officially dissolved in 1943, but the CPSU remained the ruling party in the Soviet Union (and the most important Communist party worldwide) until the collapse of the Soviet Union in 1991, after which the party was banned by the new government of Boris Yeltsin.

After the demise of Soviet Communism, the Chinese Communist Party (CCP), which remains in power in China at this writing, became the world's most important Communist party, though Communist parties continued to function in a variety of locations, such as the Republic of South Africa, where the Communist Party of South Africa (CPSA) continued to enjoy an unusual prominence and prestige, largely because of the proud legacy of the party's opposition to **apartheid**. Communist parties continued to participate in the electoral process in many European democracies, though a variety of Socialist parties (which tended to espouse a combination of Marxist and liberal ideas) were the principal bearers of leftist political ideas in Europe.

In Great Britain, for example, the nominally socialist Labour Party (whose policies were increasingly indistinguishable from those of liberal parties such as the U.S. Democratic Party) took power in the elections of 1997 and remained in power at the end of 2004. The Communist Party of Great Britain (CPGB), which had been a potent force in British politics in the 1930s, was reduced to a marginal role after **World War II**, when the pressures of the **cold war** made it increasingly difficult for the party to gain mainstream support. This was even more the case in the United States, where the Communist Party of the United States (CPUSA) was effectively crippled as a political organization by the wave of **anticommunism** that swept through the United States in the cold-war years.

Among other things, the decline of the CPUSA did much to efface the historical memory of the active role played by the party in former decades, especially the 1930s. The roots of the CPUSA can be found in the Socialist Party, whose more radical wing, encouraged by the Russian Revolution of 1917, ultimately split to form a separate party by 1919. The history of the party in the 1920s was complicated by factional disputes and by the desire to coordinate its activities with those of international Communism, under the leadership of the Third International. Popular doubts about capitalism due to the onset of the Great Depression greatly energized the party, though party leader William Z. Foster's 1932 presidential bid garnered little popular support. In the next few years, the CPUSA was active on a number of fronts, making particularly notable efforts in the fight against racism in the United States Communist organizers became prominent in a number of labor unions, including John L. Lewis's new Congress of Industrial Organizations (CIO). CPUSA priorities changed substantially in 1936 with the coming of the **Popular Front** and a reorientation of party activities into a fight against the spread of Fascism rather than opposition to the capitalist system as a whole. The party gained additional membership and prestige from its efforts to ally itself with various other antifascist organizations during this period, though it was also forced to compromise many of its positions.

The CPUSA devoted much attention to cultural affairs, believing that procommunist literature and culture could do much to help the party gain support in the United States. This project also reached its peak in the 1930s, particularly with the efforts of communist journals such as *New Masses* to promote the development of **proletarian literature** in the United States, including the organization of **John Reed Clubs** designed to teach young writers to write from the point of view of the working class. Writers such as **Mike Gold**, **Jack Conroy**, and **Agnes Smedley** produced notable contributions to proletarian literature, though the most successful works influenced by this effort involved more politically ambiguous products of the Popular Front period, such as **John Steinbeck's** *The Grapes of Wrath* (1939) and **Richard Wright's** *Native Son* (1940). In addition, the leftist literature of the 1930s has had far-ranging, if subtle, effects on subsequent American culture, just as the political influence of the CPUSA goes well beyond its own specific activities. Meanwhile, in the early twenty-first century, the CPUSA continues to function, a remarkable survivor of the cold war and one whose history may be just beginning.

Selected Bibliography: Bart, Philip, Theodore Bassett, William W. Weinstone, and Arthur Zipser, eds. *Highlights of a Fighting History: Sixty Years of the Communist Party, USA.* New York: International Publishers, 1979; Buhle, Paul. *Marxism in the USA: Remapping the American Left.* London: Verso, 1987; Croft, Andy, ed. *A Weapon in the Struggle: The Cultural History of the Communist Party in Britain.* London: Pluto, 1998; Denning, Michael. *The Cultural Front: The Laboring of American Culture in the Twentieth Century.* New York: Verso, 1996; Draper, Theodore. *American Communism and Soviet Russia.* New York: Viking, 1960; Draper, Theodore. *Roots of American Communism.* New York: Viking, 1957; Foley, Barbara. *Radical Representations: Politics and Form in U.S. Proletarian Fiction, 1929–1941.* Durham, NC: Duke UP, 1993; Hutchinson, Earl Ofari. *Blacks and Reds: Race and Class in Conflict: 1919–1990.* East Lansing: Michigan State UP, 1994; Isserman, Maurice. *If I Had a Hammer: The Death of the Old Left and the Birth of the New Left.* Middletown, CT: Wesleyan UP, 1982; Isserman, Maurice. *Which Side Were You On? The American Communist Party during the Second World War.* Middletown, CT: Wesleyan UP, 1982; Maxwell, William J. *New Negro, Old Left.* New York: Columbia UP, 1999; Meissner, Boris. *The Communist Party of the Soviet Union: Party Leadership, Organization, and Ideology.* Westport, CT: Greenwood, 1976; Ottaneli, Fraser M. *The Communist Party of the United States: From the Depression to World War.* New Brunswick, NJ: Rutgers UP, 1991.

M. Keith Booker

COMPOSITION STUDIES AND LITERATURE. At the beginning of the twenty-first century, English studies is divided between the seemingly antithetical fields of literary studies and composition studies. The first has historically been associated with the freedom to produce texts with theory and research; the latter with pedagogy, and the practical need to teach large numbers of undergraduates. Historically, literary studies has been male, composition female; literary studies relatively well-off, composition impoverished. Literature has defined the field of English for insiders within the profession, but composition has defined the field for most of the public, for if they attend college, they are almost certainly required to encounter a course in rhetoric and composition.

Almost from their inception, English departments in the United States have been structured by the hierarchical binary between literature and composition. In the nineteenth-century U.S. college, rhetoric (predominantly public speaking) had an important place in the curriculum. Literary studies was a comparative latecomer, and its early development in women's colleges is an indicator of its low status. However, as **Richard Ohmann** and others have argued, with the development of the modern university under industrial capitalism, it was necessary to train students to write for the growing bureaucracies of American business. By the turn of the century, courses in rhetoric were becoming unmanageable, as a feasible class size for oral rhetoric became much too large for writing classes. As Robert Connors points out, Harvard professor Barrett Wendell read over 24,000 student papers in 1892. It is not surprising that professors soon fled from composition to literature. One result was that graduate research, as Connors notes, became defined by literature, and research in rhetoric and composition floundered until composition became—to paraphrase the late James Berlin—a nonfield, the only field in the American university where the instructor's knowledge of the discipline was often encompassed by the textbook she used. And yet it was—and is—the perceived need for composition that made English departments so large.

Although some of the inequality between literature and composition has diminished with the development of feminism, affirmative action, and various kinds of cultural studies within the English profession, the unequal status of literature and composition has continued. As Eileen Schell argues in *Gypsy Academics and Mother-Teachers*, composition is still a field that is defined by female contingent labor. By the end of the twentieth century, new Ph.D.s in composition were receiving more job offers than those in literature, and many composition scholars became tenured. Yet composition specialists in many universities rarely (if ever) teach first-year composition; instead, they supervise an army of underpaid graduate students and part-time teachers (predominantly female) who teach composition. Substantially improving working conditions for this group of teachers appears to be the only meaningful way that the division between literature and composition can be overcome, but that appears to be a long way off, despite increased awareness, efforts at unionization, and increased public protest (see **English studies**).

Selected Bibliography: Berlin, James. *Rhetorics, Poetics, and Culture: Refiguring College English Studies*. Urbana, IL: NCTE, 1996; Connors, Robert. "Rhetoric in the Modern University: The Creation of an Underclass." *The Politics of Writing Instruction: Postsecondary*. Ed. Richard Bullock and John Trimbur. Portsmouth, NH: Boynton/Cook, 1991. 55–84; Ohmann, Richard. *Politics and Letters*. Middletown, CT: Wesleyan UP, 1988; Schell, Eileen. *Gypsy Academics and Mother-Teachers: Gender, Contingent Labor, and Writing Instruction*. Portsmouth, NH: Boynton/Cook, 1998.

Raymond A. Mazurek

CONDÉ, MARYSE (1937–). Born Maryse Boucolon in Pointe-à-Pitre, Guadeloupe, Condé is the daughter of a self-made teacher-turned-banker father, who was awarded the Legion of Honor, and a mother who was among the first black women teachers in Guadeloupe. After what she describes as a dull childhood in a non-Creole-speaking family proud of being both black and middle class, she has gone on to become one of Guadeloupe's best-known, and certainly most prolific, writers.

In 1953, Condé left Guadeloupe for Paris, where she studied comparative literature at the Sorbonne. In 1958, she married the African actor Mamadou Condé, who was a member of the black theater troupe *Les Griots*. Together they traveled to Guinea, and from 1960 to 1964 she taught at the École Normale Supérieure, Conakry, before leaving her husband and taking up teaching jobs first in Ghana and then in Senegal. In 1968, Condé moved to London, where she worked for the BBC and met her second husband, Richard Philcox, who is now her translator. During the 1970s and 1980s, Condé held teaching positions at various divisions of the University of Paris and also began writing for publication. In 1986, she returned to Guadeloupe and has lived there for at least part of the year ever since, spending the rest of her time in the United States, where she has held teaching positions at several universities. She now teaches Caribbean and French literature at Columbia University.

Condé's first two works, *Dieu nous l'a donné* (God Given, 1972) and *La Mort d'Oluwémi d'Ajumako* (Death of a King, 1973), were plays and did not receive a huge amount of attention. Her first novel, *Hérémakhonon*, was published in 1976 to a largely negative reception. In part a critique of **negritude**, the novel is set in Africa (as is her second novel, *A Season in Rihata* [*Une Saison à Rihata*, 1981]), and recounts the experiences of a visiting Guadeloupean lecturer, Véronica, whose sexual promiscuity, distanced narrative style, and indifference to the political situation of the country in which she finds herself shocked and alienated readers. It was not until the publication of *Segu* (*Ségou,* 1984–1985)—a historical saga also set in Africa that became the first best-seller in France by a writer of Caribbean origin—that Condé's work began to gain wide recognition. Since then, she has written several works of literary criticism, collections of short stories, children's books, plays, and over ten more novels, as well as republishing her first novel to far greater critical acclaim. Her preoccupation with Africa came to an end after *Segu*. *Tree of Life* (*La Vie scélérate*, 1987) and *Crossing the Mangrove* (*Traversée de la mangrove*, 1989) marked a literary return to Guadeloupe. Since then, her novels have concerned themselves with issues of identity, exile, and migration throughout the black diaspora. While she has resolutely resisted the label of "feminist," her work remains preoccupied with the experiences of women. She has received numerous literary prizes; her 1986 novel *I, Tituba, Black Witch of Salem* (*Moi, Tituba, sorciére noire de Salem*) won the *Grand Prix Littéraire de la Femme,* and she won the highly coveted *Prix de l'Académie française* (bronze medal) in 1988 for *La Vie scélérate*. In 1993, she was the first woman to receive the Putterbaugh prize, awarded in the United States to writers in French. Most recently she was given France's most prestigious award for literature and the arts, becoming *commandeur dans l'Ordre des Arts et des Lettres.*

Selected Bibliography: Callaloo 18.3 (1995). Special Issue on Maryse Condé; Condé, Maryse. "*Créolité* without Creole Language?" *Caribbean Creolization: Reflections on the Cultural Dynamics of Language, Literature and Identity.* Ed. Kathleen Balutansky and Marie-Agnès Sourieau. Gainesville: UP of Florida, 1998; Haigh, Sam. *Mapping a Tradition: Francophone Women's Writing from Guadeloupe.* Leeds: Maney, 2000; Pfaff, Françoise. *Conversations with Maryse Condé.* Lincoln: U of Nebraska P, 1997.

Sam Haigh

CONRAD, JOSEPH (1857–1924). Born in Russian-occupied Polish Ukraine as Josef Teodor Konrad Korzeniowski, Conrad was the only son of Apollo and Ewelina (*née* Bobrowski), who, as patriotic members of the Polish gentry, sought the overthrow of Russian rule. When they were sentenced to exile in Siberia for helping to plot a revolution, Conrad went with them. In 1865, Conrad's mother died of tuberculosis; in 1868, he and his father were released and returned to Cracow, but in 1869 his father, too, was overcome by tuberculosis. Conrad was eleven years old and an orphan, having spent most of his life in a Russian penal camp. The resulting antipathy toward all things Russian, articulated in essays such as "The Crime of Partition," "Note on the Polish Problem," "Poland Revisited," and "Autocracy and War," stayed with him his entire life.

At age sixteen, Conrad left Poland for Marseilles, where he joined the French merchant marine. While there, Conrad made voyages to the West Indies, smuggled guns to the Carlist rebels in Spain, and attempted suicide. At the age of twenty, Conrad left France for London, where he joined the British merchant marine. He served there for the next eighteen years, eventually earning the rank of captain. His experiences during these years formed the basis of many of his novels and short stories, including *Almayer's Folly* (1895), *An Outcast of the Islands* (1896), *The Nigger of the "Narcissus"* (1897), *Lord Jim* (1900), and *Victory* (1915). Chief among these experiences is Conrad's fateful trip to the Belgian Congo in 1890, which provided the basis for his most famous and controversial work, ***Heart of Darkness*** (1899 serial; 1902 book).

For many years, Conrad's works were primarily taken as exemplars of the modern psychological novel, but since the late 1960s, more and more critics have begun paying attention to their political dimensions. *Heart of Darkness* and *Lord Jim* in particular have been reevaluated in these terms, often provoking fiery debate over their representations of indigenous peoples, imperialist practices, and European values. With *Nostromo* (1904), Conrad's works begin to take on explicitly political themes. Set in South America at around the time of the Panama crisis and Theodore Roosevelt's extension of the Monroe Doctrine, *Nostromo* continues Conrad's interest in imperialism, but also considers capitalism, the motivations for revolution and counterrevolution, and the complex politics of long-colonized lands. Many of these same issues, with the significant addition of domestic anarchism, are taken up in the ensuing works *The Secret Agent* (1907), *Under Western Eyes* (1911), and *The Rover* (1923), all of which bring the problems of autocracy, political organization, and violent revolution home to Europe. Building friendships and picking fights with anarchist sympathizers and conservatives alike, Conrad was perpetually dissatisfied with the world as it was and with the available means of changing it. His work consistently undertakes precisely the kind of "ruthless criticism of the existing order" that Marx called for shortly before Conrad's birth.

Selected Bibliography: Baines, Jocelyn. *Joseph Conrad: A Critical Biography.* 1960. London: Weidenfield, 1993; Fleishman, Avrom. *Conrad's Politics: Community and Anarchy in the Fiction of Joseph Conrad.* Baltimore, MD: Johns Hopkins UP, 1967; Meyers, Jeffrey. *Joseph Conrad: A Biography.* 1991. New York: Cooper Square P, 2001; Stape, J. H., ed. *The Cambridge Companion to Joseph Conrad.* New York: Cambridge UP, 1996.

Stephen Ross

CONROY, JOHN WESLEY (JACK).

Jack Conroy was born in 1899 in Monkey Nest, a mining camp in Missouri. His father died when he was ten, and Conroy began working at age fourteen in the Wabash railroad yards. He spent most of the rest of his life struggling to balance his work and family commitments with his literary ambitions. Conroy's 1933 novel, *The Disinherited*, was heralded at the time as a breakthrough in American **proletarian literature** because of its authenticity, its immediacy, and its representation of working-class vernacular language. Yet in the late 1920s and 1930s, Conroy was just as important to the flourishing literary left for his editorial work. Keeping a low profile in the McCarthy era, Conroy essentially terminated his literary career and worked as a staff writer for an encyclopedia company in Chicago. He continued to collect the industrial and labor folklore, tales, stories, and songs that he had begun recording for the New Deal's **Federal Writers' Project**. In the 1970s, a resurgent interest in proletarian literature lifted Conroy back into view; *The Disinherited* was reissued, and several collections of his shorter writings were published.

Conroy's editorial work began with the *Spider*, a small local magazine he published and edited in 1927 while working at the Willys-Overland plant in Toledo, Ohio. Soon, he had joined the Rebel Poets, an organization for radical and working-class writers that anticipated the **Communist Party**'s **John Reed Clubs**. He helped to edit several Rebel Poet anthologies before starting up ***Anvil*** in 1933. This magazine quickly became a premiere venue for radical fiction in the United States, publishing celebrities like **Maxim Gorky** and **Langston Hughes**, and then-unknowns like **Tillie Olsen** and **Richard Wright**. In 1939, Conroy and **Nelson Algren** launched *New Anvil*, an effort that lasted about a year.

In *The Disinherited*, hard-hitting portraits of work, workers, and working-class life from the "prosperity" of the 1920s through the onset of the Depression are arranged around protagonist Larry Donovan's quest to find a way of reconciling his cultural ambitions with his working-class loyalties. Like so many other narratives by working-class writers, *The Disinherited* is a fractured and wildly polyvocal text, one in which multiple languages compete for authority and in which multiple genres—autobiography, folk tale, popular fiction—are stitched together. This fragmented form may reflect the novel's origins; many chapters were first published as short stories and sketches in places like H. L. Mencken's *American Mercury*, *International Literature*, and radical American magazines. Conroy's second and last novel, *A World to Win* (1935), recognizes the conflict between his role as writer and his role as worker by dividing its narrative between two protagonists who are brothers—one who quests to become a writer and the other who is a down-and-out worker during the Depression. This cumbersome splitting, like the messy textuality of *The Disinherited*, may be Conroy's most profound testament to the difficult lived realities of the worker-writer who must traverse conflicting cultural and social worlds.

Selected Bibliography: Elistratova, Anne. "Jack Conroy: American Worker-Writer." *International Literature* 1 (May 1934): 112–18; Fabre, Michel. "Jack Conroy as Editor." *New Letters* 39.2 (Winter 1972): 115–37; Wixon, Douglas. Introduction to *The Disinherited* by Jack Conroy. Columbia, MO: U of Missouri P, 1991. ii–xxvi; Wixon, Douglas. *Worker-Writer in America: Jack Conroy and the Tradition of Midwestern Literary Radicalism, 1898–1990*. Urbana: U of Illinois P, 1994.

Larry Hanley

CREOLENESS (CRÉOLITÉ) is a concept developed in a seminal work entitled *In Praise of Creoleness* (*Eloge de la Créolité*, 1989) by the Martinican writers Jean Bernabé,

Patrick Chamoiseau, and Raphaël Confiant. This Caribbean-centered conceptualization is a cultural, historical, and literary manifesto establishing the Creole language and culture as the cornerstones of society, and has exercised a powerful influence on recent **Francophone Caribbean literature**. It recognizes the specificity of the Caribbean Islands themselves and particularly their racial diversity, popular culture, language, and multiethnic history. Grasped within the Caribbean stream of thought, it is a refinement of the concepts of negritude and Caribbeanness. It marks an acceptance by Caribbeans of their "Creole identity," resulting from the crossing of African, native Caribbean, European, and Asian elements over four hundred years.

Creoleness recognizes the valuable contributions of the negritude movement in its validation of the African dimension of Caribbean culture as a means to help restore the dignity of people in the Caribbean. However, the proponents of Creoleness feel that the emphasis on Africa in negritude represents an imposition of elements from outside the Caribbean society. They long to scrutinize and consolidate their identity from within their own culture and space rather than seeking solace from outside. Likewise, Creoleness is a step further from the concept of Caribbeanness, as elaborated by **Edouard Glissant** and Antonio Bénitez-Rojo. It dissociates itself from the overarching attempts to represent an all-encompassing black and/or geographical experience, and stresses instead the originality and validity of the long process of creolization.

Extending their concept outwardly, they praised the mixing of cultures by highlighting the process of sedimentation of various elements. Their reevaluation of the cross-cultural experience allows an extension of this concept to other societies that went through similar historical experiences of conquest, survival (the maroon is a key actor), struggle, and coexistence. They find more affinity with other French islands such as La Réunion, Mauritius, and other islands in the Pacific Ocean than with other Caribbean neighbors. Despite a warm acclaim by various quarters, Creoleness has its critics, including James Arnold, Willy Alante-Lima, and **Maryse Condé**.

In Condé's judgment, the exclusive focus on low social strata as the bedrock of Creoleness is reminiscent of the limitations of any essentialist assumption. She further argues for a Creoleness without recourse to the Creole language, insisting instead on the urgency to look beyond the specificity of each island in order to find a changing Caribbean identity. A culture, being a phenomenon in flux submitted to a crossing of many variables (such as languages, peoples, ethnic groups, and trends), cannot remain constant throughout. Likewise, Richard E. D. Burton believes that the concept may be altogether retrospective and regressive. Such a reality is diametrically opposed to the idea of Creoleness, as it bases itself on the coexistence of partners engaged in identity subscription in a given framework. Despite these objections, Creoleness as a movement is a validating testimony to the dynamism of the Francophone and human diversity.

Selected Bibliography: Balutansky, Kathleen M., and Marie-Agnès Sourieau, eds. *Caribbean Creolization: Reflections on the Cultural Dynamics of Language, Literature, and Identity.* Gainesville: U of Florida P, 1998; Bernabé, Jean, Patrick Chamoiseau, and Raphael Confiant. *Eloge de la Créolité* and *In Praise of Creoleness.* Bilingual edition. Paris: Gallimard, 1993; Burton, Richard E. D., and Fred Reno, eds. *French and West Indian: Martinique, Guadeloupe, and French Guiana Today.* Charlottesville: U of Virginia P, 1995. 137–66; Condé, Maryse, and Madeleine Cottenet-Hage, eds. *Penser la créolité.* Paris:

Karthala, 1995; Glissant, Edouard. *Poetics of Relation.* Trans. Betsy Wing. Ann Arbor: U of Michigan P, 1997.

Kasongo M. Kapanga

CUBAN LITERATURE. The development of Cuban literature can be divided into four periods: a background period from the origins to 1790; a second period during the formation and crystallization of the national consciousness (1790–1898); a third period between 1899 and 1958, divided into two main stages, 1899–1923 and 1923–1958; and a fourth period, from the 1959 revolution to the present.

In the first period, the early centuries of colonial domination were reflected in the works of outsiders, such as the diary of Christopher Columbus. However, by the middle of the eighteenth century, literary representations began to produce an incipient notion of "cubanía" (Cuban nature) that would not crystallize until the second period. In the period between 1790 and 1829, Cuban literature made a significant leap forward with the creation of institutions such as the Economic Society of Friends of the Country (1793) and the Board for Promotion (1795), and the founding of the newspaper *Papel Periódico de la Havana* (sic) (Havana Newspaper, 1790), all of which represented an emerging creole leadership whose interests began to conflict with those of the island's Spanish colonial government. A budding prose literature began to express the political and philosophical nonconformism of figures such as Francisco Arango y Parreño, José Agustín Caballero, and (especially) Félix Varela, the foremost thinker and essayist of his time. Poets such as Manuel de Zequeira and Manuel Justo Rubalcava, both of neoclassical affiliation, produced poetry that showed a growing awareness of the need to articulate the elements of an emerging Cuban cultural identity.

Cuban literature particularly blossomed during the period from 1820 to 1868, when **romanticism** exerted a strong influence on the lyric poetry of such writers as José María Heredia. Much of the poetry of this period was strongly informed by an anticolonial spirit of liberation. One leading romantic poet, Gabriel de la Concepción Valdes (*Plácido*), was shot by the Spanish government. Other leading figures included José Jacinto Milanés and Gertrudis Gomez de Avellaneda, both of whom extended the movement into drama. A second stage of development during this period consisted of a "good taste reaction" against the aesthetic excesses of the first stage of lyrical romanticism. The most representative figures of this period are Juan Clemente Zenea (also shot by the Spanish government), Rafael María de Mendive, Joaquin Lorenzo Luaces, and Luisa Pérez de Zambrana. As a whole, the romantic lyrics of this period were of a high aesthetical quality and are considered among the best work produced in the Spanish language in this genre.

Drama and fiction did not, in general, reach the same level of achievement in the nineteenth century. The most important novelist was Cirilo Villaverde, who produced the first version of what would eventually become one of the most important Latin American novels of the century, *Cecilia Valdés*, whose definitive version was published in 1882. This novel participated in an important trend toward representation in fiction of the experience of slavery, of which the most striking example might have been *Apuntes autobiográficos* (Autobiographical Notes) by the slave Juan

Francisco Manzano, an exceptional statement of the horrors of slavery written prior to *Uncle Tom's Cabin* by **Harriet Beecher Stowe**.

The Cuban War of Independence from Spain took place between 1868 and 1898, and the literature produced during this time reflected quite accurately the convulsions of the times. Lyrics drifted from romanticism to **modernism**, a movement pioneered by **José Martí** with *Ismaelillo* (1892), *Versos sencillos* (Simple Verses, 1891), and *Versos libres* (Free Verses, written between 1878 and 1882 but not published until 1913). Martí is also one of the great figures in Cuban history, a leader of the fight for independence and an iconic figure of that struggle. Another important figure in the Latin American modernist movement was Julián del Casal, author of numerous notable poems—the collection *Nieve* (Snow, 1891) containing many of the finest.

Perhaps most important among the novelists to emerge during this period was Ramón Meza, author of *Mi tío el empleado* (My Uncle the Clerk, 1887), significant particularly for its abundance of futurism. Also important was Martín Morúa Delgado, who, in novels such as *Sofía* (1891) and *La familia Unzúazu* (The Unzúazu family, 1901), initiated the Cuban naturalist novel. Nonfiction prose was especially prominent during this period, including the genre of "campaign literature," devoted to the War of Independence. The modern genre of the *testimonio* also became important during this period.

The comic opera also rose to prominence at the end of the nineteenth century, contributing to the expression of significant elements of Cuban cultural identity, especially the crystallization of the types of the negrito, mulata, and gallego (small negro boy, mulatto woman, and Galician), traditional characters of a popular theater whose period of greatest splendor was reached during the initial decades of the republican period. The first stage of this period (1899–1923) began within a social framework in which a feeling of republican frustration prevailed due to the continuing neocolonial domination of Cuba by the United States. Naturalism was a suitable vehicle for the expression of this feeling in fiction, as can be seen in the works of such writers as Carlos Loveira (*Generales y Doctores* [Generals and Doctors, 1920] and *Juan Criollo* [1927]); Miguel de Carrión (*Las honradas* [The Honest Ones, 1918] and *Las impuras* [The Impure Ones, 1919]); and Jesus Castellanos (*La conjura* [The Conspiracy, 1909]). Alfonso Hernández Catá produced a large body of works that placed him among the greatest storytellers of his time in the Spanish language. Important poets who emerged at this time included Regino Boti (*Arabescos mentales* [Mental Arabesque, 1913], and *El mar y la montaña* [The Sea and the Mountain, 1921]) and José Manuel Poveda (*Versos precursors* [Precursor Verses, 1917]). Such poets, in what was perhaps an understandable reaction to the prevailing social situation, opted for nonpolitical poetry of high aesthetic quality. Achievement in theater remained slight, although comic opera continued to satirize the prevailing sociopolitical situation.

A decisive turn occurred during the second stage of this period (1923–1958), when, due to the influence of significant historical developments such as **World War I** and the **Russian Revolution**, Cuban political and literary life entered a revolutionary stage. This stage produced a full identification between the political and aesthetic avant-garde. The most significant political figures were also of significance in the literary field, including Rubén Martínez Villena, Juan Marinello, **Nicolás Guillén**, and Raúl Roa. The search of the literary-political avant-garde for a new expression of Cuban national identity led in 1923 to the formation of the *Grupo Minorista* (Minority Group), which used the magazine *Revista de Avance* (1927–1930) as its main organ of expression until the repression of the dictatorial government of Gerardo Machado caused the cessation of its publication as well as the activities of the group.

Poets such as Guillén, José Lezama Lima, and Dulce María Loynaz produced important work during this period, while significant writers of fiction included Jorge Mañach, José Zacarías Tallet, Enrique Serpa, José Antonio Fernández de Castro, **Alejo Carpentier**, Enrique Labrador Ruiz, and Lino Novás Salvo. The latter three in particular contributed to a renewal in Cuban narrative, incorporating the influences of important American writers such as **Ernest Hemingway**, **John Dos Passos**, **William Faulkner**, Taylor Caldwell, and F. Scott Fitzgerald.

The 1959 revolution transformed Cuban literature as well as Cuban society. For example, the national literacy campaign carried out in 1961 set the foundation for the formation of a greatly enlarged reading audience, and to this campaign were added numerous institutions that promoted the production and consumption of literature, including el Consejo Nacional de Cultura (the National Culture Council, currently the Ministry of Culture), la Casa de las Américas (the House of the Americas), la Unión Nacional de Escritores de Cuba (the National Union of Writers of Cuba), el Instituto del Libro (the Institute of the Book), and el Centro Nacional de Derechos de Autor (the National Center for Copyright). In just over four decades, these institutions have completely transformed the situation of writers, who for the most part had previously had to finance the publication of their own books. Furthermore, they have now ensured that thousands of copies and editions will be printed for national and international promotion.

In these four decades, numerous writers have left an indelible imprint on Cuban culture. In poetry, great authors such as Guillén, Lezama Lima, Regino Pedroso, Manuel Navarro Luna, Mirta Aguirre, Samuel Feijóo, Eliseo Diego, Cintio Vitier, Fina Garcia Marrúz, Jesús Orta Ruiz, and Carilda Oliver Labra continued to produce new works that were now for the first time widely distributed both nationally and internationally. They were joined by younger authors who became known in the 1950s. This group consolidated their work in the 1960s to form the first generation of poets of the revolution. Among these authors were Roberto Fernández Retamar (also a remarkable essayist), Fayad Jamis, Pablo Armando Fernández, Heberto Padilla, Rolando Escardó, and Jose A. Baragaño.

In fiction, well-known authors such as Carpentier, Félix Pita Rodríguez, Onelio Jorge Cardoso, Dora Alonso, and Virgilio Piñera reached their full maturity—as well as international prominence—in the decades after the revolution. The poet Lezama Lima attained fame as a novelist with *Paradiso* (1966), while the notable poet and essayist Vitier also became known as a novelist. Other writers of fiction who attained prominence included Guillermo Cabrera Infante, José Soler Puig, Severo Sarduy, Reinaldo Arenas, Lisandro Otero, Miguel Barnet, Jesús Díaz, Manuel Cofiño, Eduardo Heras, Julio Travieso, Antonio Benítez, Leonardo Padura Fuentes, and Senel Paz, whose tale "El lobo, el bosque y el hombre nuevo" (The Wolf, the Forest and the New Man)—internationally honored with the Juan Rulfo Award—served as the basis for the successful film by Tomás Gutiérrez Alea, *Fresa y Chocolate* (Strawberry and Chocolate, 1993).

With the triumph of the revolution, Cuban theater reached new heights of development. Theater halls multiplied, and—in the case of the Escambray theater—plays were staged in the mountains with the active participation of peasants. Previous works that had been banned or heavily censored were now widely produced. The initial work of Piñera, Rolando Ferrer, and Carlos Felipe was continued by playwrights such as Abelardo Estorino, perhaps the most remarkable author to come out of this period, as well as José R. Brene, Héctor Quintero, José Triana, Eugenio Hernández Espinosa, Nicolás Dorr, Abilio Estévez, Alberto Pedro, and Freddy Artiles.

For the most part, the postrevolutionary period has been generous in producing essayists and literary critics that continue the Cuban tradition in such genres. Important among these are such figures as Vitier, Retamar, Marrúz, Graziella Pogolotti, Angel Augier, Manuel Moreno Fraginals, Salvador Bueno, Ambrosio Fornet, and Rine Leal. A number of other genres rose to new prominence in the postrevolutionary period, including literature for children and young readers (represented in the works of Alonso, Nersys Felipe, and Julia Calzadilla); police literature (produced by Daniel Chavarría, a Uruguayan novelist living in Cuba; Luis Rogelio Nogueras; and the aforementioned Padura); science fiction; and testimonial literature (whose highest expressions are due to Barnet, and where can be mentioned, among others, Enrique Cirules and Victor Casaus). On the other hand, the fact must be stressed that literary creation has ceased being a basically urban activity in Cuba; it has become a national fact visible in each province of the country with a wide variety of authors. Furthermore, the considerable female presence is quantitatively and qualitatively without precedent in Cuban history.

The literature produced throughout the postrevolutionary period in Cuba is characterized by its ethics, its reaffirmation of the continuity with the central line of national literature, its link with the cause of social progress, and its independence with regard to the cultural policies of the bygone socialist countries, a fact that prevented **socialist realism** from becoming an important mode in Cuba. It is important to point out that outside Cuba, important literature has been produced by writers such as Cabrera Infante and Arenas, who have disavowed the revolution, but who were formed as artists in the bosom of the revolution. Such writers are still regarded in Cuba as participants in Cuban literature, and numerous works continue to be published by Cuban editorial houses by well-known national writers who emigrated from Cuba after 1959. On the other hand, the emergence of new generations of authors of Cuban origin born outside the island who in many cases do not express themselves in the Spanish language presents an interesting complication to historians of the Cuban literary process.

Taking into consideration the relative youth of the Cuban literary process—really only two hundred years, in spite of five hundred years of national history—its great richness and maturity are extremely impressive. Writers such as Martí, Carpentier, Guillén, Lezama Lima, and Loynaz have earned important places in the history of world literature, and Cuban literature as a whole—notwithstanding conditions especially adverse for its development—occupies an important place in global culture.

Selected Bibliography: Instituto de Literatura y Lingüística. *Diccionario de la literatura cubana.* Havana: Editorial Letras Cubanas. Vol. 1, 1980. Vol. 2, 1984; Lazo, Raimundo. *La Literatura Cubana, esquema histórico (desde sus orígenes hasta 1966).* Havana: Editora Universitaria, 1967; Portuondo, José Antonio. *Bosquejo histórico de las letras cubanas.* Havana: Editora del Ministerio de Educación, 1962.

Sergio Chaple (trans. David H. Uzzell Jr.)

CUBAN REVOLUTION. Fidel Castro and a small group of revolutionaries attacked the Moncada barracks on July 26, 1953, in a failed attempt to topple the military government of Fulgencio Batista. However, in 1956, Castro and other conspirators began a successful revolution from the mountains of the Sierra Maestra in eastern Cuba, slowly gaining popular support. After decades of overt political corruption under the Batista dictatorship (combined with concern over U.S. economic domination of Cuba), change was welcome; many Cubans thus cheered when Batista suddenly fled the island on January 1, 1959, as the "bearded" revolutionaries advanced toward Havana.

As the new revolutionary government centralized the Cuban economy and dealt violently with its opposition, a mass exile of mainly upper- and middle-class Cubans fled the island. With such leaders as Ché Guevara at its ideological center, the new regime sought to implement a Marxist-Leninist political and economic system that would end Cuba's neocolonial relationship with Washington. In the midst of the **cold war**, the Cuban revolutionary government proclaimed Cuban sovereignty and U.S. anti-imperialism as its driving force. The new Cuban government formed an economic alliance with the Soviet Union and came increasingly into conflict with the United States, punctuated by such events as a U.S.-imposed trade embargo in 1960, the Bay of Pigs invasion in 1961, and the missile crisis of 1962. At a domestic level, the revolutionary government instituted numerous reforms that bettered the lives of its citizens, including a nationwide literacy campaign; a redistribution of income, goods, and services; and access to basic education and free health care for all Cubans. Because of these advances, numerous intellectuals worldwide supported the new revolutionary government, but after the Padilla affair of 1971 (which involved official sanctions against the poet Heberto Padilla for his "counterrevolutionary" poetry), the regime's international popularity declined.

In the midst of a growing economic crisis (caused partly by the ongoing U.S. economic boycott), Castro proclaimed in 1980 that any Cubans who wished to leave the island were free to do so. Over the six-month period of the "Mariel boatlift," more than 125,000 refugees came to the United States. The collapse of the Soviet Union and the loss of Soviet subsidies thereafter furthered worsened the economic situation in Cuba. In the 1990s, the Cuban government worked with various countries to develop tourism. The influx of foreigners visiting the island led to the establishment of dollar stores; the loosening of government control over small, private enterprises; and the expansion of an already existent black market for goods not available under Cuba's rationing system. Events such as the Pope's visit to Cuba in 1998 have kept Cuba in the international news, its future contingent on the well-being of the now aging Castro and those who will replace him once he is gone.

Selected Bibliography: Azicri, Max. *Cuba Today and Tomorrow: Reinventing Socialism.* Gainesville, FL: UP of Florida, 2000; Bethell, Leslie, ed. *Cuba: A Short History.* New York: Cambridge UP, 1993; Brenner, Phillip, et al. *The Cuba Reader: The Making of a Revolutionary Society*. New York: Grove, 1989; Domínguez, Jorge. *Cuba: Order and Revolution*. Cambridge, MA: Belknap P, 1978; Horowitz, Irving Louis, and Jaime Suchlicki, eds. *Cuban Communism, 1959–2003*. 11th ed. New Brunswick, NJ: Transaction P, 2003; Pérez, Luis A., Jr. *Cuba: Between Reform and Revolution*. 2nd ed. New York: Oxford UP, 1995.

Carmen Lamas

CULTURAL STUDIES. In the past half century, the field of cultural studies has challenged the traditional elitism of literary studies by moving beyond a focus on canonical literature to include a variety of forms of popular culture (including fiction, music, film, television, radio, magazines, and even sports). The development of cultural studies has a clear origin that can be traced back to post–**World War II** Britain when pioneering practitioners Richard Hoggart, **Raymond Williams**, and E. P. Thompson initially outlined a critical approach to the elitist and antidemocratic traditions and methodologies characterizing the study of cultural expression. They challenged the definition of culture as arts and letters, or customs and manners, and overhauled such foundational assumptions of the humanities that the study of art and literature is separate from the study of society, and that the object of study in the humanities is a canon of timeless classic works that provide universal reflections and insights on the human. Williams, for example, stressed understanding culture as a whole way of life that included the forces and relations of production, family structure, governing institutions, and forms of communication. These initial formulations shifted focus to study how culture is made and practiced with the objective of grasping and exposing how social classes and groups struggle for cultural domination.

Understanding cultural struggle as a fight for legitimacy and cultural status and asserting that the ruling classes established and upheld power by legitimizing their cultural forms and practices as *culture itself*, working-class intellectuals like Hoggart, Williams, and Thompson endorsed working-class culture against the "high culture" of the bourgeoisie and upper classes as well as against the onslaught of mass culture. Thompson's *The Making of the English Working-Class* (1963) altered conventional understandings of British history in his focus on the concerns and experiences of the working classes, their differing comprehensions of British culture, and their own cultural formulations of class consciousness. He highlighted, for example, how different class cultures might in fact share sources, such as John Bunyan's *Pilgrim's Progress*, yet make radically opposed meanings of those works in arriving at a consciousness of one's relational position in society. Influenced by the literary studies of F. R. Leavis, both Hoggart and Williams adopted similar perspectives on working-class agency in the cultural production of meaning and forms that exist independently of the dominant culture. In his inaugural cultural studies text *The Uses of Literacy* (1957), describing changes in working-class life in postwar Britain in a deeply autobiographical way, Hoggart centered culture as an important category to emphasize that a life practice such as reading, among others, cannot be understood independently from the context of other practices—from the "whole way of life," such as working, family life, and sexuality. While agreeing with Leavis's view that the value of culture lies in its ability to widen and deepen experience and that, in the face of mass culture's onslaught, reading the works of the great tradition in British literature was important not just as entertainment but to mature individuals into fully rounded citizens, both Williams and Hoggart also understood that "Leavisism," in its exclusive focus on the "great tradition," ignored the rich working-class communal forms in which they were socialized. Williams in particular worried over and argued that such conceptions of aesthetic or literary value underwrite the ideological structures of the dominant culture and foster contempt for and dismissal of both the common efforts and cultural productions of the working classes—the ordinary people. Thus, the work of these three intellectuals articulates the basic approach of cultural studies, which is always to study culture as a set of practices in relation to power—that is, to expose power relationships, and to explore how cultural practices influence and are influenced by power relationships. However, exactly how "power" is understood—and exactly how cultural studies differs from the ideological analysis of Marxism—becomes a matter of controversy in cultural studies' evolution.

The work of key practitioners at the Birmingham Centre for Contemporary Cultural Studies (CCCS), founded by Hoggart in 1963, such as **Stuart Hall**, the first director of the center, reflects the evolution in methodological focus and in the conceptualization of culture itself proceeding, in **Epifanio San Juan Jr.**'s analysis, from "the empiricism of its initiators to a structuralist phase, then to an Althusserian/Lacanian one, followed by a Gramscian moment, up to its dissolution in the deconstructive poststructuralism of Ernesto Laclau and Chantal Mouffe" (San Juan 207). Operating on the premise that working-class communal forms were becoming increasingly fragmented, cultural studies practice underwent a shift in focus from experiential, locally produced cultures to larger cultural structures that produced consciousness from afar, what **Theodor Adorno** and Max Horkheimer termed "the culture industry." As the study of the relationship between consciousness and society, between subject and object, evolved in cultural studies, a **Louis Althusser**-inspired structuralism that asserted ideology as the cultural mediation whereby subjects are produced, or individuals interpellated into subject positions, paved the way for the displacement of experience as a key category—as it was for Williams, Hoggart, and Thompson—in favor of centering discursive practice, textuality, and representation through ideological state apparatuses, mass media, and other information technologies as the site of subject formation.

Thus, from its theorization as a "whole way of life" by Williams, culture came to be understood within cultural studies practice as a set of discursive and representational practices where subjects and meanings are produced. Political struggles, then, were conceived primarily as struggles over representation. Certainly, the influence of the thought of the Italian Communist **Antonio Gramsci**, particularly his crucial concept of hegemony to describe relations of domination as secured through the consent of the dominated, led cultural studies to a more nuanced conceptualization of the subject as an actively experiencing subject. Nonetheless, the narrow focus on discourse and representation has left cultural studies vulnerable to the critique that it had abandoned any sense of political struggle understood in terms of transformation of the material structures of the socioeconomic system of capitalism.

Thus, the emergence and even popular ascendancy of something called cultural studies in contemporary academic practice, institutionally legitimated by the support of university budgets, however, has a more ambiguous history in terms of its relationship to the Marxist left and to the original cultural studies project developed by Williams, Hoggart, and Thompson. While Cary Nelson, Paula Treichler, and Lawrence Grossberg celebrate cultural studies as holding "special intellectual promise" for "the fragmented institutional configuration of the academic left" because it cuts across "diverse social and political interests and address[es] many of the struggles within the current scene" (Nelson et al. 1), Michael Denning observes that "the suspicion of cultural studies is widely shared on the left these days" (Denning 147). These dual and opposed assessments of the Left's attitude toward and political alignment with cultural studies reflect conflicting positions on Marxism's utility to the original cultural studies project and its survival in and relevance to contemporary cultural studies practice. Some critics, such as **Fredric Jameson**, stress that the cultural studies, or "cultural materialism," of Williams constituted not just a fervently committed political project but a deeply Marxist one that contemporary cultural studies practice often overlooks in its gross caricatures of Marxist theory. Williams's landmark essay "Marxism and Culture," for example, from his foundational and classic cultural studies text *Culture and Society* (1958), rigorously addresses the classic Marxist problematic of the relation between the economic base and superstructure, not to dismiss Marxism but to refine it. Certainly, Williams and Thompson reacted to a rigidly economistic and determinist Marxism that posited thought and action as the direct effect of economic forces, but their project refocused Marxist inquiry on everyday life experiences as crucial actions of social groups in making history.

Other tendencies of cultural studies, however, either reject Marxism outright or engage it tactically as one possible methodology among many to be drawn on strategically but not wholly endorsed. Often, the roots of cultural studies in its deep engagement with and indebtedness to Marxism are forgotten as Marxism is sloppily and uniformly equated with a vulgar economism and hence demonized. In some of the dominant tendencies of cultural studies, "economism" and "Marxism" have been established as the new theoretical taboos. Proclaiming that he generally works within "shouting distance of Marxism," Stuart Hall, for example, who has alternated in his sympathy with and distancing from Marxism, has condemned Marxism for "a certain reductionism and economism, which . . . is not extrinsic but intrinsic to Marxism" and for a "profound Eurocentrism." He sees Marxism as outdated, writing, "The radical character of Gramsci's 'displacement' of Marxism has not yet been understood and probably won't ever be reckoned with, now we are entering the era of post-Marxism." While in an essay such as "The Problem of Ideology: Marxism without Guarantees" Hall takes a more subtle and sympathetic approach to Marxism in the spirit of Williams's "Marxism and Culture," the statements here echo a typical caricature of Marxism as economistic and deterministic found in contemporary cultural studies practice. Moreover, in such statements, Hall also ignores both the rich tradition of Marxist humanism and that of third-world Marxists such as Amilcar Cabral, **Frantz Fanon**, and **C.L.R. James**, who all theorized third-world cultural resistance from a non-Eurocentric Marxist perspective. If cultural studies was initially energized by a profound critical engagement with Marxism, contemporary cultural studies practice seems to sidestep any serious confrontation with Marxism, as typified by Angela McRobbie proudly announcing cultural studies' evasion of Marxism, writing, "The debate about the future of Marxism in cultural studies has not yet taken place. Instead, the great debate around modernity and postmodernity has quite conveniently leapt in and filled that space."

Indeed, while critics such as Denning see cultural studies as a potential replacement for Marxism, and others, such as McRobbie and at times Hall, see it as a transcendence of Marxism, often these gestures of substitution and transcendence are premised on an amnesia of many elements of the Marxist tradition of literary and cultural analysis. For example, when Lawrence Grossberg attributes the rise of cultural studies to the emergence of a New Left that responded in part "to the failure of the traditional marxist left to confront, in both theoretical and political terms, the beginnings of late capitalism, the new forms of economic and political colonialism and imperialism, the existence of racism within the so-called democractic world, the place of culture and ideology in relations of power, and the effects of consumer capitalism on the working classes and their cultures" (Grossberg 25), he ignores, just as Hall ignores third-world non-Eurocentric Marxists, many elements of the Marxist intellectual tradition that cannot be characterized as economistic. Indeed, in terms of the study of culture and its relation to economic development, Williams's classic study *The Country and the City* (1973), in which he analyzes English pastoral poetry in relation to the growth of a highly developed agrarian capitalism as it evolved into the Industrial Revolution, stands as an excellent example. It is such blindness to the nonvulgar Marxist tradition that prompts San Juan to write, "All commentators agree that a version of Marxist reductionism, otherwise known as *economism*, triggered the revolt against the left." But, he asks, "What happened in reaction to a caricatured 'actually existing' Marxism?" (San Juan 221).

For San Juan, what happened was cultural studies developed into method focused so narrowly on formalist analysis of textuality that it ceased to be a meaningful agent for emancipation from the material structures of capital exploitation and oppression. Nonetheless, the very nature of cultural studies raises difficulty for assessing its politics in any unified way. Denning, for example, characterizes cultural studies as less a discipline in itself than a critique of disciplinarity itself. Patrick Brantlinger similarly suggests that cultural studies emerged "not as a tightly coherent, unified movement with a fixed agenda, but as a loosely coherent group of tendencies, issues, and questions" that does not espouse or constitute a methodology in itself but makes use of a range of methods. Frequently, cultural studies practice encompasses thematics and theory of both third-worldist anticolonial theory and postcolonial theory, of Marxism and post-Marxism, which seems to take us beyond defining cultural studies as a Left dialogue but rather as a kind of liberal pluralism that doesn't attempt to resolve or work through these political and methodological contradictions as much as to celebrate their plurality.

Selected Bibliography: Brantlinger, Patrick. *Crusoe's Footprints: Cultural Studies in Britain and America.* New York: Routledge, 1990; Denning, Michael. *Culture in the Age of Three Worlds.* London: Verso, 2004; During, Simon, ed. *The Cultural Studies Reader.* London: Routledge, 1993; Grossberg, Lawrence. "The Formations of Cultural Studies: An American in Birmingham." *Relocating Cultural Studies: Developments in Theory and Research.* Ed. Valda Blundell et al. New York: Routledge, 1993. 21–66; Grossberg, Lawrence, Cary Nelson, and Paula Treichler, eds. *Cultural Studies.* New York: Routledge, 1992; Hall, Stuart. "Cultural Studies and Its Theoretical Legacies." *Cultural Studies.* Ed. Lawrence Grossberg, Cary Nelson, and Paula Treichler. New York: Routledge, 1992. 277–85; Hall, Stuart. "The Problem of Ideology:

Marxism without Guarantees." *Stuart Hall: Critical Dialogues in Cultural Studies.* Ed. David Morley and Kuan-Hsing Chen. New York: Routledge, 1996. 25–46; Hoggart, Richard. *The Uses of Literacy.* Harmondsworth: Penguin, 1957; Jameson, Fredric. "On Cultural Studies." *The Identity in Question.* Ed. John Rajchman. New York: Routledge, 1995. 251–95; McRobbie, Angela. "Post-Marxism and Cultural Studies: A Post-Script." *Cultural Studies.* Ed. Lawrence Grossberg, Cary Nelson, and Paula Treichler. New York: Routledge, 1992. 719–30; Morley, David, and Kuan-Hsing Chen, eds. *Stuart Hall: Critical Dialogues in Cultural Studies.* New York: Routledge, 1996; San Juan, E., Jr. *Racism and Cultural Studies: Critiques of Multiculturalist Ideology and the Politics of Difference.* Durham, NC: Duke UP, 2002; Thompson, E. P. *The Making of the English Working Class.* New York: Vintage-Random House, 1966; Williams, Raymond. *The Country and the City.* New York: Oxford UP, 1971; Williams, Raymond. *Culture and Society: 1780–1950.* New York: Columbia UP, 1958.

Tim Libretti

CULTURE WARS. Term used to refer to the sometimes heated debates regarding literary studies in American universities. These debates have centered on the literary canon and the ways literature is taught and studied in the university. The current culture wars are the result of the social changes that began taking place in the 1960s. Social and political activists in this decade generated awareness in the academy of the cultural implications of issues such as race, gender, and class. Since then, many literary scholars have sought to expand the literary canon to include more works by marginalized groups. These scholars have also been concerned with more political approaches to literature. For instance, race critics have come to understand **Joseph Conrad**'s *Heart of Darkness* as a fundamentally racist text, a characteristic that was overlooked before the onset of political criticism. Likewise, feminist critic Mary Ellmann published her *Thinking about Women* in 1968, a work that outlines eleven major stereotypes of women found in the literature of male authors. Both the attempt to expand the canon and the desire to approach literature from social and political perspectives have been major sources of contention between academic liberals and cultural conservatives. While academic liberals support the goals that grew out of the 1960s, cultural conservatives believe these goals to be the demise of American education.

Since the 1980s, cultural conservatives have relentlessly attacked the university and the professoriate for what they see as an abandonment of truth and an acceptance of cultural relativism. At the forefront of this conservative movement are several writers who have taken antagonistic positions toward efforts in the academy to develop a more inclusive canon and to promote politically motivated approaches to literature. For these cultural conservatives—who include writers such as Allan Bloom, William J. Bennett, Lynne Cheney, Dinesh D'Souza, and Roger Kimball—the university has reached a moment of severe crisis. In *Illiberal Education* (1991), Dinesh D'Souza bemoans what he sees as an absence of the "Great Books" on required reading lists. For D'Souza, this exclusion reflects a politically motivated bias against white male authors that has resulted in the marginalization of the greatest works of Western literature. Similarly, Allan Bloom, in *The Closing of the American Mind* (1987), suggests that the "morally degraded" condition of students today is due to the fact that they are no longer taught the "Great Classics" of Western literature and philosophy. For Bloom, the alleged cultural relativism of the 1960s marks the beginning of the decline of education in America. Since the cultural conservatives believe that the "Great Classics" derive their status from the universal truths and timeless values they contain, these conservatives decry liberals who emphasize the social and political significance of literary works.

As a result of the cultural conservatives' attacks on the goals of liberal scholarship, the 1990s witnessed a preponderance of books by scholars on the Left. Foremost among these scholars are Gerald Graff, Henry Louis Gates, Jr., Paul Lauter, and Lawrence Levine. In *Beyond the Culture Wars* (1992), Graff argues that many of the disagreements in the culture wars are the result of the conservatives' misunderstanding of the literary canon's formation. As Graff maintains, the canon has always evolved according to the needs of the present cultural milieu. Similarly, in *Canons and Contexts* (1991), Lauter documents the development of the American literary canon in the early twentieth century, finding that many historical factors were at play when the canon was formed. For instance, Lauter suggests that since the majority of academic professionals in early twentieth-century America were white and male, it is not difficult to imagine these academics choosing works by white males like themselves for inclusion in the canon. Both Graff and Lauter devote chapters to Allan Bloom's *The Closing of the American Mind*, criticizing it for not having a bibliography and for propagating the "myth of the vanishing classics." Indeed, the attempt to expose the exaggerated nature of the cultural conservatives' arguments is at the center of all the aforementioned academic liberals' writings. Additionally, these liberals have attempted to demonstrate the highly political nature of the conservative position, which many conservatives claim is nonpolitical.

Over the last decade, scholars have proposed various solutions to the conflicts that comprise the culture wars. In *The Opening of the American Mind* (1996), Lawrence Levine suggests that scholars must reenvision America in such a way that the consideration of race, gender, and class will no longer be seen as "political correctness" but rather as "historiographical necessity." Levine asserts that giving attention to a wide variety of distinct groups in America is the best way for students to learn about the whole society. In a more detailed solution, Graff argues that literature professors should "teach the conflicts." For Graff, the most effective way to handle the conflicts of the culture wars is to educate students about them. With regard to diversity in the American literary canon, Lauter calls for a "comparative model" approach in which various American *literatures* would be contrasted. More radical solutions that have been suggested include disposing of canons altogether.

Selected Bibliography: Bloom, Allan. *The Closing of the American Mind: How Higher Education Has Failed Democracy and Impoverished the Souls of Today's Students.* New York: Simon and Schuster, 1987; D'Souza, Dinesh. *Illiberal Education: The Politics of Race and Sex on Campus.* New York: Free P, 1991; Gates, Henry Louis, Jr. *Loose Canons: Notes on the Culture Wars.* New York: Oxford UP, 1992; Graff, Gerald. *Beyond the Culture Wars: How Teaching the Conflicts Can Revitalize American Education.* New York: Norton, 1992; Jay, Gregory S. *American Literature and the Culture Wars.* Ithaca, NY: Cornell UP, 1997; Lauter, Paul. *Cannons and Contexts.* Oxford: Oxford UP, 1991; Levine, Lawrence W. *The Opening of the American Mind: Canons, Culture, and History.* Boston: Beacon P, 1996.

M. Elizabeth "Betsy" Wood

CUNARD, NANCY (1896–1965). Nancy Clara Cunard was the only child of the middle-aged English baronet Sir Bache Cunard and his young American wife, Maud Alice Burke. Her privileged upbringing included exposure to the numerous prominent writers, artists, musicians, and politicians entertained by her mother. Educated at private schools in London, Germany, and Paris, Cunard as a teenager had already become friends with such figures as **Ezra Pound**, in whose circle she discussed politics and poetry in Parisian cafés. She also began to publish her own poetry in magazines by 1916.

After a return to London and a brief, ill-fated marriage, Cunard moved to Paris in 1920, where she continued to write poetry, influenced by Dadaism and **modernism**. She also became interested in Communist politics, though she never formally joined the **Communist Party**. She published several volumes of poetry, including *Outlaws* (1921), *Sublunary* (1923), and *Parallax* (1925). In 1927, she founded the Hours Press in an old farmhouse in Reanville, outside Paris. Here she printed works by new and established (mostly modernist) writers, including Pound, Norman Douglas, Laura Riding, and **Samuel Beckett.**

In 1928, Cunard met and became involved with Henry Crowder, a black American jazz musician playing in a local nightclub. This relationship was a considerable scandal at the time, causing Cunard to break with her family; it also caused her to become conscious of the African American struggle for civil rights, which led to a years-long project in which she worked to compile a record of black American history and culture. The volume, entitled *Negro*, was finally published in 1934 and included contributions from both black and white artists in America and Europe. Controversial at the time, the volume remains in print and is still studied today as a landmark in African American cultural history.

Cunard maintained a strong interest in other civil-rights issues for the rest of her life. During the **Spanish Civil War**, she served as a freelance correspondent in Spain, publishing reports primarily in the *Manchester Guardian*. Subsequently, she produced a substantial amount of politically informed travel writing, based on her own journeys through South America, the Caribbean, and Tunisia. Her work of this period often focused on colonialism and on the issue of race in her home country of England. After **World War II**, Cunard continued her travels, abandoning the farmhouse in Reanville after it had been looted and vandalized during the occupation. Deteriorating health, both physical and mental, added to the isolation of her later years; she died alone in a Parisian charity hospital in 1965.

Selected Bibliography: Chisholm, Anne. *Nancy Cunard: A Biography*. New York: Alfred Knopf, 1979; Cunard, Nancy, ed. *Negro: An Anthology*. 1934. New York: Continuum, 1996; Marcus, Jane. *Hearts of Darkness: White Women Write Race*. New Brunswick, NJ: Rutgers UP, 2004.

M. Keith Booker

◦D◦

AL-DAIF, RASHID (1945–). Lebanese novelist and critic, born in Zgharta, Lebanon, and first educated in north Lebanon, where he learned French and Arabic and began an ambitious program in Arabic and French literature. His undergraduate education was at the Lebanese University, where he earned a *License* (1970) and a *Diplome d'Etudes Approfondie D.E.A.* (1971) in Arabic language and literature. In 1974, he received a *Doctorat* in modern literature (*lettres modernes*) from Paris III University. He then earned a D.E.A. in linguistics from Paris V University in 1978.

To date, al-Daif has published eleven novels. In 1999, the first of his novels to be translated into English appeared as *Dear Mr. Kawabata* (*Azizi al-Sayyed Kawabata*, 1995), also translated into seven other languages: French, Italian, German, Spanish, Swedish, Polish, and Dutch. The enthusiastic response to *Dear Mr. Kawabata* produced great international interest in al-Daif's other novels as well.

Other novels by al-Daif translated into English include *Passage to Dusk* (originally published in French as *Passage au crepuscule*, 1992) and *This Side of Innocence* (*Nahiyat al-Baraa'a*, 1997). Other novels in Arabic include the straight-faced, ironically titled *Unsi Yalhu Ma' Rita, li al-balighin* (Unsi Dallies with Rita, for Mature Readers, 1982); *Al-Mustabidd* (The Despot, 1985); *Fusha Mustahdafa Bayn al-Nu'as wa al-Nawm* (A Targeted Space between Sleepiness and Sleep, 1986); *Ahl al-Zill* (The Dwellers of the Shade, 1987); *Taqaniyyat al-Bu's* (The Techniques of Misery, 1989); *Ghaflat al-Turab* (When the Earth Dozes Off, 1991); *Lernin' Inglish* (Learning English, 1998); *Tistifil Meryl Streep* (To Hell with Meryl Streep, 2001); and *Insay al-Sayyara* (Forget about the Car, 2002). Two of al-Daif's novels have been made into films: *Passage au crepuscule*, based on the novel by the same name, directed by Simon Edelstein and released in Germany in 2000, and *Zannar al-Nar* (Belt of Fire), based on *Al-Mustabidd*, directed by Bahij Hojeij and released in Beirut in 2002.

In all his novels, al-Daif has devised an aesthetic system that values the unsaid and the unseen. It is an art of absences and negative spaces and shapes, something totally new to much of Arabic fiction. His interests are not in the forms readers are used to; he constantly pursues what we might call the psychological, the philosophical, and the idiosyncratic. There is always a mismatch between his interior world and the social world around his characters. He only offers glimpses and fragments of his stories, never allowing his readers to visualize his world. But there is always a suspense-filled plot that readers are invited to construct for themselves, and yet when we accept the invitation, we realize that the events that hold the plot together evade our grasp and leave us disoriented and wanting to know more.

The enthusiastic reception of al-Daif's work in both the Arab world and the West is testimony to the high regard critics hold for his writing and for the exciting developments in the novel in Lebanon in the past forty to fifty years.

Selected Bibliography: Aghacy, Samira. "The Use of Autobiography in Rashid Al-Daif's *Dear Mr. Kawabata.*" *Writing the Self.* Ed. Robin Ostle, Ed DeMoor, and Stefan Wild. London: Saqi Books, 1998. 217–28; Seigneurie, Ken. "The Importance of Being Kawabata: The Narratee in Today's Literature of Commitment." *Journal of Narrative Theory* 31.1 (Winter 2004): 111–30; Starkey, Paul. "Crisis and Memory in Rashid Al-Daif's *Dear Mr. Kawabata*: An Essay in Narrative Disorder." *Crisis and Memory: The Representation of Space in Modern Levantine Narrative.* Ed. Ken Seigneurie. Wiesbaden: Reichert, 2003. 115–30; Weber, Edgard. *L'Univers Romanesque de Rachid el-Daif et la Guerre du Liban.* Paris: L'Haumattan, 2001.

Adnan Haydar

THE DAILY WORKER (1924–1958). The first Communist English-language daily among many foreign-language papers, the *Daily Worker* originated in 1924 to communicate the perspectives and activities of the **Communist Party** of the United States (CPUSA) to a broad audience. Accordingly, in its early years, the paper rather laboriously documented the party's preoccupations until 1935 when, under the skilled editorship of Clarence Hathaway, the paper increasingly reflected the Popular Front's expansiveness. The theoretical and factional tone was replaced by notable coverage of both domestic and global news; a commitment to antiracism; and features such as the sports column, cartoons, and theater, film, and literature reviews. The newspaper also featured an impressive variety of contributors, from author **Mike Gold**'s regular "Change the World" column to items by folksinger Woody Guthrie and novelist **John Dos Passos**.

In particular, the newspaper's attention to race distinguished it from other dailies. Through its antilynching campaign (most prominently with the Scottsboro Nine); its Harlem Section (edited by **Richard Wright**), which addressed community issues; and Lester Rodney's very popular sports column, which consistently and sensitively addressed racism within sports, the *Daily Worker* effectively employed high-quality journalism to augment the party's antiracism work. Indeed, the newspaper was indispensable in mobilizing the election of *Daily Worker* editor and CPUSA leader Benjamin Davis to the New York City Council in 1943 (Horne 217).

After reaching a peak circulation of over thirty thousand readers in 1940, the paper's popularity began to decline. In the 1950s, the substantiation of **Stalin**'s excesses disillusioned many readers; in addition, the effects of **anticommunism** forced many remaining Communists underground and made other progressive, less dangerous newspapers appealing, thus significantly reducing the *Daily Worker*'s audience. While it was always significantly subsidized, decreased subscriptions made the cost of maintaining the paper untenable, and it closed in 1958.

Appropriately, the achievements and shortcomings of the *Daily Worker* mirror trends within the CPUSA itself. In the uneven capabilities of its editors (with some, like Hathaway and John Gates, bringing journalistic experience to the paper and others selected for their political positions), the contrast between its often prescient and comparatively extraordinary assessment of world affairs like the **Spanish Civil War** and its uncritical veneration of the Soviet Union, its vivid and compelling columns and occasionally formulaic pieces, its desire for a broader popularity and the cost of its political commitments during the early years of the **cold war**, and above all its commitment to expressing the concerns of the working class while occasionally trying to define them, the *Daily Worker* encapsulates some of the most contentious aspects in historical assessments of the Left.

Selected Bibliography: Horne, Gerald. "The Red and the Black: The Communist Party and African Americans in Historical Perspective." *New Studies in the Politics and Culture of U.S. Communism.* Ed. Michael E. Brown et al. New York: Monthly Review P, 1993. 199–238; Isserman, Maurice. *If I Had a Hammer: The Death of the Old Left and the Birth of the New Left.* Middletown, CT: Wesleyan UP, 1982; Levenstain, Harvey A. "*The Worker:* Cleveland, Chicago, and New York, 1922–1924; *Daily Worker:* Chicago and New York, 1924–1958." *The American Radical Press 1880–1960.* Volume 1. Ed. Joseph R. Conlin. Westport, CT: Greenwood, 1974. 224–43; Ottaneli, Fraser M. *The Communist Party of the United States: From the Depression to World War.* New Brunswick, NJ: Rutgers UP, 1991.

Rachel Peterson

DALTON, ROQUE (1935–1975). In the 1980s, this Salvadoran writer was principally known as a revolutionary poet. Most literary criticism of the period characterized him as a Marxist-Leninist who wrote from the armed, leftist front. Dalton was assassinated by some leaders of the former Salvadoran guerilla movement, the Farabundo Martí Front for National Liberation (FMLN), and his poetic legacy has not been completely evaluated or translated to English. *In the Dampness of the Secret: A Poetic Anthology of Roque Dalton* (*En la humedad del secreto: Antología poética de Roque Dalton*) by Rafael Lara Martínez (1994) and *Other Roques: The Polypoetics of Roque Dalton* (*Otros Roques: La poética múltiple de Roque Dalton*), edited by Lara Martínez and Dennis Seager (1999), perhaps do more than any other extant critical sources to elaborate the complexities of Dalton's work.

Dalton's work was long suppressed in his own country, so until the early 1990s, it was easier to read the works of Dalton abroad than in El Salvador. Then, in 1994–1995, the Publications Office of the Salvadoran Ministry of Education published a rather exhaustive anthology of his work. In 1997, one of his first collections of poems, *The Window in the Face* (*La ventana en el rostro*) became part of the Basic Library of Salvadoran Literature and was widely distributed throughout the country. Perhaps his most important work, *Taverns and Other Places* (*Tabernas y otros lugares*, 1966–1967), earned Dalton the prestigious Casa de las Américas prize of 1969. "Tavern," the title poem of this collection, exemplifies Dalton's insistence on speaking *from* and not *to* the people. This feature has prompted some critics to observe that Dalton's work can be compared to the "conversational poetry" of **Nicolás Guillen** and **Roberto Fernández Retamar**. González and Treece relate this aspect of Dalton's work to the "exteriorist poetry" of **Ernesto Cardenal**. Articulating a public voice that sometimes gives rise to a revolutionary ideology while renouncing any lyrical dimension to his work seems to define much of Dalton's poetry. His short poem "Poetry" expresses this notion: "Poetry, Pardon me for having helped you to understand / that you aren't made exclusively of words" ("Poesía, Perdóname por haberte ayudado a comprender / que no estás hecha sólo de palabras").

In addition to poetry, Dalton published numerous essays, the testimonial novel *Miguel Mármol* (1974), *The Banned Histories of the Little Thumb* (*Las historias prohibidas del Pulgarcito*, 1975), and the posthumous novel *Poor Little Poet That I Was* (*Pobrecito poeta que era yo . . .*, 1976).

Selected Bibliography: Beverley, John. "Poetry in the Central American Revolution: Ernesto Cardenal and Roque Dalton." *Journal of the Society of Contemporary Hispanic and Lusophone Revolutionary Literatures* 1 (1984–1985): 295–312; Beverley, John, and Marc Zimmerman. *Literature and Politics in the Central American Revolutions*. Austin: U Texas P, 1990; González, Mike, and David Treece. "Roque Dalton: Speaking Aloud." *The Gathering of Voices: The Twentieth-Century Poetry of Latin America*. London: Verso, 1992. 298–305; Lara Martínez, Rafael. *En la humedad del secreto: Antología poética de Roque Dalton*. San Salvador: Concultura, 1994; Lara Martínez, Rafael, and Dennis L. Seager. *Otros Roques: La poética múltiple de Roque Dalton*. New Orleans: UP of the South, 1999.

Dennis L. Seager

DARÍO, RUBÉN (1867–1916). Rubén Darío was born in the village of Metapa (subsequently renamed Ciudad Darío), Nicaragua, into a humble family. From his early youth, he showed a prodigious poetic talent and the determination to become a great poet. In his pursuit of this goal and given his weak financial situation, he confidently sought the patronage of the politically powerful, first in El Salvador at age fifteen, then in Chile and Argentina, his fame as a poet preceding him in all cases. In 1883, while in El Salvador, he wrote two poems that were to extend his fame throughout Spanish America: "Al libertador Bolívar" (To the Liberator, Bolivar) and "Unión Centroamericana" (Central American Union). In the first of these poems, he extols the decisive anticolonialism of Simón Bolívar, and in the second, he champions the idea of unifying the five Central American republics, a theme to which he often returned in his writings.

Darío left Nicaragua for Chile in 1886. There he produced the book—*Azul Blue*, 1888—that would bring him fame throughout the Hispanic world. A review of the book by Spanish author and diplomat Juan Valera contributed substantially to that fame. Valera facilitated the general viewing of Darío's contribution of a new sensuousness, splendor, and opulence to Hispanic poetry, but in his jealous attribution of this novelty primarily to French sources, he undervalued the eclectic basis of the richness of Darío's imagery and the range of his technical skills. Darío was a keen observer of the strategies and effects of the Greco-Roman writers as well as of the stalwarts in the Spanish tradition. He had also looked, not without some disdain, at his Spanish American precursors.

The strangeness and arrogance of his renovating effort did not endear him to the leading Spanish American literary critics of the nineteenth century. While Darío called his writing modernism, they called it decadence, not detecting in it the constructive Spanish American sentiment that had been obvious in the work of his predecessors. Only in his 1898 essay on Darío's second book of poetry, *Prosas profanas* (1896, *Profane Prose*), did the most prominent of these critics, José Enrique Rodó, declare: "Yo soy un modernista también" (I am a modernist too). Rodó noted the allegorical character of the exoticism present in *Prosas profanas* and the Spanish American rootedness of Darío's most esoteric work. In his subsequent major books, *Cantos de vida y esperanza* (1905) and *El canto errante* (1907), Darío, while always attentive to his lofty expressive goals, contributes poems of enduring political content.

While many studies of Darío's poetry have given inordinate weight to form, there is a strong sociopolitical bent to his poetry. He was Nicaraguan when Nicaragua was under threat from a colonial or imperialist power such as Great Britain; Central American in his zeal for the political unity of those republics; Spanish American when actions of North American imperialism aggressively wounded Spanish American spirits; and universally humanist when human progress was hindered in the last years of his life by a devastating war. When Darío wrote about democracy, he clearly meant popular democracy—not free market democracy. His political relevance sparkled in the time of the Sandinista revolution in his homeland.

Selected Bibliography: Ellis, Keith. *Critical Approaches to Rubén Darío.* Toronto: U of Toronto P, 1974; Jrade, Cathy Login. *Rubén Darío and the Romantic Search for Unity: The Modernist Recourse to Esoteric Tradition.* Austin: U of Texas P, 1983.

Keith Ellis

DAVIS, JACK (1917–2000). Despite a limited formal education typical of mixed-race children born in Australia in the first half of the twentieth century, Jack Davis went on to become a leading Indigenous Australian writer, administrator, and educator. While he published several volumes of poetry, Davis is especially known for his political plays dealing with the impact of European culture on the indigenous Nyoongah people of the southwest of Western Australia. Born in Perth, Western Australia, he grew up in the countryside, where his father's early death cut short his education. He held a succession of jobs ranging from stockman and horse breeder to truck driver and boxer. During these years, however, Davis continued his self-education, learning about Nyoongah culture and language as well as that of the new comers to his land.

In 1967, he became the director of the Aboriginal Centre in Perth and subsequently first chair of the Aboriginal Lands Trust in Western Australia. His first play, *Kullark (Home)*, written in 1979 for the 150th anniversary of European settlement in Western Australia, provides a counter-narrative to celebration of the achievements of the white pioneers, tracing the accompanying dispossession and destruction of indigenous peoples and their cultures. He subsequently drew more directly on the history of his own family for his trilogy, *The First-Born*, which traces the history of Aboriginal dispossession through the generations. In *The Dreamers* (1983), the Wallitch family is shown living in suburban Perth; the death of old Uncle Worru (originally played by Davis himself) removes their last links with tribal culture. *No Sugar* (1985) goes back in time, depicting Worru's family's forced removal from their traditional land to the notorious Moore River Native Settlement, while *Barungin* (1988) records the continued impact of cultural loss through the many Aboriginal men who have committed suicide while in prison.

Selected Bibliography: Davis, Jack. *A Boy's Life*. Broome, Western Australia: Magabala Books, 1991; Gilbert, Helen. *Sightlines: Race, Gender and Nation in Contemporary Australian Theatre*. Ann Arbor: U of Michigan P, 1998; Mudrooroo. *Writing from the Fringe: A Study of Modern Aboriginal Literature*. Melbourne, Victoria: Hyland House, 1990; Van Toorn, Penny. "Indigenous Texts and Narratives." *The Cambridge Companion to Australian Literature*. Ed. Elizabeth Webby. Cambridge: Cambridge UP, 2000. 19–49.

Elizabeth Webby

DAVIS, REBECCA HARDING (1831–1910). Born in Washington, Pennsylvania, Rebecca Harding spent her first five years in Florence, Alabama, but subsequently grew up in Wheeling, West Virginia, which would provide the setting for her most enduring work, the long story "Life in the Iron Mills" (1861). The wife of important newspaper editor and abolitionist Clarke Davis and the mother of Richard Harding Davis, who became famous as a novelist, playwright, and war correspondent, Davis was a member of one of America's most prominent literary families. A pioneer in the development of American realist fiction and an important forerunner of American **proletarian fiction**, she herself became nationally known as a writer and journalist during her lifetime, but was subsequently largely forgotten until the republication of "Iron Mills" in 1972.

It was this same story that ultimately helped catapult Davis to fame, though it was initially published anonymously in *Atlantic Monthly*. The story breaks new ground in American fiction both with its naturalistic style and in its focus on working-class characters, detailing the horrific conditions suffered by two workers—the deformed and pathetic Deborah and her cousin Hugh Wolfe, a would-be artist whom Laura Hapke compares to Thomas Hardy's Jude the Obscure as a figure of brutally frustrated ambitions (77). Meanwhile, Deborah's obsessive devotion to Wolfe only worsens her own suffering, and the story is important today as much for its exploration of gender as for its exposé of industrial working conditions. Particularly important is Davis's suggestion that selfless devotion and hard work brutalize, rather than ennoble, the working-class female.

Davis followed in 1862 with the novel *Margret Howth* (1862), which also details the sufferings of mill women, though its protagonist is a relatively privileged bookkeeper who eventually rises in class by marrying her employer. Davis continued to produce socially engaged fiction and nonfiction throughout her career, exploring the operations of race, gender, and class in American society, with special attention to such issues as the situation of the woman artist. At the same time, Davis is unable to envision collective action by workers to improve their lives as a positive good. The best her characters can hope for is to escape altogether from the working class, which she tends to envision as inherently brutish and debased. Like British novelists such as **Charles Dickens** and **Elizabeth Gaskell**, Davis wrote of but not for the working classes. Her intended audience were middle- and upper-class readers, whom she hoped would initiate reforms to improve the conditions she described. Davis's autobiography, *Bits of Gossip*, was published in 1904.

Selected Bibliography: Hapke, Laura. *Labor's Text: The Worker in American Fiction.* Rutgers UP, 2001; Harris, Sharon M. *Rebecca Harding Davis and American Realism.* Philadelphia: U of Pennsylvania P, 1991; Pfaelzer, Jean. *Parlor Radical: Rebecca Harding Davis and the Origins of American Social Realism.* Pittsburgh: U of Pittsburgh P, 1996; Rose, Jane Atterbridge. *Rebecca Harding Davis.* New York: Twayne, 1993; Schocket, Eric. "'Discovering Some New Race': Rebecca Harding Davis's 'Life in the Iron Mills' and the Literary Emergence of Working-Class Whiteness." *PMLA* 115.1 (January 2000): 46–59.

M. Keith Booker

DAY LEWIS, C(ECIL) (1904–1972). Day Lewis was born at Ballintubber, Queen's County, Ireland. In 1905, his father, a Church of Ireland minister, moved the family to England, where his mother died in 1908. Day Lewis published his first collection of poetry, *Beechen Vigil*, in 1925. His early poetry was very much indebted to the pastoral tradition and reflected a personal individual experience. He went to Oxford, where he met Rex Warner and Maurice Bowra. While at Oxford (sometime in 1926–1927), Day Lewis also met **W. H. Auden**, with whom he edited *Oxford Poetry, 1927. Transitional Poem* (1929) was Day Lewis's first attempt to leave behind his early style, which he characterized as "adolescent," and reflect a more mature, socially aware, outward-looking poetry. He left Oxford in 1927 with a degree in classics and taught school until 1935. Day Lewis joined the Communist Party of Great Britain in 1936, leaving the party in 1938. While in the party, he drew on his teaching experience to bridge Communist ideology and culture, explaining the ideas behind Communism in essays like "Letter to a Young Revolutionary," published in *New Country* (1933), and *A Hope for Poetry* (1934). Day Lewis also edited *The Mind in Chains* (1937), a collection of essays that examined the links between Socialism and culture, which included contributions from Warner and Edward Upward, among others. His autobiography, *The Buried Day* (1960), charts his gradual acceptance (and eventual rejection) of Communism. He published four collections of poetry in the 1930s: *From Feathers to Iron* (1931), *The Magnetic Mountain* (1933), *A Time to Dance* (1935), and *Overtures to Death* (1938), as well as a verse play, *Noah and the Waters* (1936). Day Lewis also published three novels in the 1930s: *The Friendly Tree* (1936), *Starting Point* (1937), and *Child of Misfortune* (1939). During **World War II**, he worked for the Ministry of Information. Under the pseudonym Nicholas Blake, Day Lewis published a series of detective novels beginning with *A Question of Proof* (1936). He also translated the works of Virgil—*The Georgics of Virgil* (1940) and *The Aeneid of Virgil* (1952)—and was professor of poetry at Oxford between 1951 and 1956. In his later life, he moved away from his more radical past, increasingly becoming an establishment figure, and was named poet laureate in 1967, a post he held until his death. *The Whispering Roots* (1970) was his final collection of poetry. Throughout his career, his work reflected a constant struggle between his public and private selves, a "divided self." His early work envisioned that struggle as a conflict on the public stage, a struggle between the new and the old, but his later work turned inward, concentrating on the poet's personal world.

Selected Bibliography: Day Lewis, Sean. *C. Day Lewis: An English Literary Life.* London: Weidenfeld and Nicolson, 1980; Dyment, Clifford. *C. Day Lewis.* London: Longmans, Green, 1955; Gelpi, Albert.

Living in Time: The Poetry of C. Day Lewis. New York: Oxford UP, 1998; Riddel, Joseph N. *C. Day Lewis.* New York: Twayne, 1971.

Steve Cloutier

DE BOISSIÈRE, RALPH (1907–). Born in Trinidad, de Boissiére began his career as a key participant, along with **C.L.R. James** and Alfred Mendes, in the so-called Trinidad Renaissance, involving the collective efforts of the group of leftist Trinidadian intellectuals associated with the *Beacon* journal, which was published in twenty-eight issues in Port of Spain from March 1931 to November 1933. De Boissière published stories in *Beacon*, but devoted much of his time and energy to the mundane task of trying to make a living. Between 1935 and 1938, he struggled to write his first novel, focusing on the decadence of the middle class in colonial Trinidad. By that time, Depression-era labor unrest in Trinidad had led to the 1937 oilfield uprising and subsequent police riots, and de Boissière realized that the novel he had been writing was no longer adequate to the historical situation in Trinidad. In particular, he shifted the focus of his writing from a critique of the middle class to a positive depiction of the revolutionary potential of the working class. The development of de Boissière's writing career, like the development of Caribbean literature as a whole, was then derailed by **World War II**, which led the British to institute strict suppression of the publication of any anticolonial materials in their empire. Meanwhile, the colonial society of Trinidad experienced strong upheavals, as the island was essentially occupied by American forces (at the request of the British) for the duration of the war.

After the war, de Boissière traveled to Chicago to study auto mechanics. In 1948, he immigrated to Australia and got work in a General Motors plant in Melbourne. This proletarian experience was crucial to his subsequent growth as a writer and to his ability to rewrite his original novel as *Crown Jewel*, a work that not only includes but in fact focuses on the Trinidadian labor unrest of 1937, during which it is set. That novel was eventually published in 1952, with the support of a radical Australian labor union. It was followed in 1956 by a sequel, *Rum and Coca-Cola*, which takes the story forward into World War II and the American occupation. A third novel, *No Saddles for Kangaroos* (1964), is based on de Boissière's Australian experience, focusing on the repressive practices of the Menzies regime of the 1950s, which roughly corresponded to the American phenomenon of McCarthyism. All of de Boissière's novels show a strongly leftist sympathy for the working class and for the attempts of workers to organize to resist oppression by their capitalist bosses. Written in a straightforward, highly accessible style, the books feature realistic characters who are highly individuated but nevertheless "typical" in the sense of the Marxist critic **Georg Lukács**—that is, they clearly derive their individual characteristics from their specific social and historical situations. Meanwhile, the plots move forward in a way that suggests the inexorable forward movement of history toward liberation for the working classes and the eventual achievement of Socialism.

Selected Bibliography: Gardiner, Allan. "Striking Images: Ralph De Boissière's Australian Socialist Realism." *Rereading Global Socialist Cultures after the Cold War.* Ed. Dubravka Juraga and M. Keith Booker. Westport, CT: Praeger, 2002; Ramchand, Kenneth. "An Interview with Ralph de Boissière: Back to *Kangaroos.*" *CRNLE Reviews Journal* 1 (1994): 7–32; Sander, Reinhard W. *The Trinidad Awakening: West In-*

dian Literature of the Nineteen-Thirties. Westport, CT: Greenwood, 1988; Sealy, Clifford. *"Crown Jewel: A Note on Ralph De Boissière." Voices* 2.3 (March 1973): 1–3.

M. Keith Booker

DEBORD, GUY (1931–1994). Born in Paris and raised in relative comfort in the south of France, Debord's life as a writer, cinematographer, political theorist, and—as he preferred to put it, quoting from Josef von Sternberg's *The Shanghai Gesture*—"doctor of nothing" began upon return to his native city in 1951. There he became a member of the Left Bank bohemia of the time, involving himself in the largely forgotten lettrist movement and its minor scandals. In 1952, with a small group of like-minded colleagues he founded the so-called Lettrist International which, over the next five years, metamorphosed from a postsurrealist formation into a politico-aesthetic avant-garde dedicated to a maximal program for the revolutionary transformation of both culture and society at large. This program would be advanced through the 1960s by Debord and the members of the Situationist International (1957–1972), an almost legendary group whose writings—disseminated through its eponymous journal—became widely read by student radicals in the years leading up to the convulsions of May 1968. Debord's *Society of the Spectacle* is a synopsis of that thought, a revision of the Western Marxism of **Georg Lukács** and of the critique of everyday life of **Henri Lefebvre**, updated for the mediatized "consumer society" of the postwar world. Debord's later work, written largely in the 1980s and early 1990s (just prior to his suicide in 1994), became increasingly bleaker in its social analyses and often retreated to melancholic reflections on the years of his dissolute youth as an idealized moment of total "negation."

Debord's political radicalism was, notably, inseparable from the radical form that his writing took: his texts, whether political theory, polemic, or personal elegy, were composed through a tissue of citations, unacknowledged borrowings, and plagiarisms. The situationists had called this technique *détournement,* and defined it as the "integration of present or past productions of the arts into a superior construction"; it has clear precedents in the work of Lautréamont as well as in the procedures of **Bertolt Brecht**, beyond its obvious debt to the collage strategies of Dada and surrealism. This method of working through appropriation found clear, if unavowed, echoes in the later theoretical writings of the Tel Quel group and became a staple of the cultural postmodernism of the 1980s.

Selected Bibliography: Debord, Guy. *Comments on the Society of the Spectacle.* Trans. Malcolm Imrie. London: Verso, 1990; Debord, Guy. *Panegyric.* Trans. James Brook. London: Verso, 1991; Debord, Guy. *The Society of the Spectacle.* Trans. Donald Nicholson-Smith. New York: Zone Books, 1994; Jappe, Anselm. *Guy Debord.* Trans. Donald Nicholson-Smith. Berkeley: U of California P, 1999; Kaufmann, Vincent. *Guy Debord.* Paris: Fayard, 2001; McDonough, Tom, ed. *Guy Debord and the Situationist International.* Cambridge, MA: MIT P, 2002.

Tom McDonough

DELANY, SAMUEL R. (1942–). A 2002 inductee into the Science Fiction Hall of Fame, Delany has published more than thirty books of **science fiction** (SF) and fantasy, scholarly criticism, and erotica. He is the first African American science fiction writer to win multiple Hugo and Nebula awards, the genre's highest honors, and he also won the Bill Whitehead Award for Lifetime Achievement in Lesbian and Gay Writing. As Jeffrey Allen Tucker says, Delany "has been a trailblazer for black SF writers who have followed," such as Octavia E. Butler, Steven Barnes, and Nalo Hopkinson. Delany's work has "engaged with the most vital social and political issues of his times: race and racism in America, gay liberation, feminism, the AIDS crisis and more" (Tucker 1), furthermore influencing a range of writers and thinkers such as **Fredric Jameson**, **Eve Kosofsky Sedgwick**, Umberto Eco, **Donna Haraway**, Henry Louis Gates, Charles Johnson, William Gibson, and Thomas Pynchon.

Born in Harlem, New York, into a middle-class family, Delany attended a private school, just off Park Avenue, with very different demographics than his Harlem neighborhood. The school's students were mostly white and mostly wealthy, and Delany's experience of negotiating the very different worlds of Harlem and the school would inform all of his subsequent work. Delany, a self-proclaimed Marxist, is intensely aware of social, economic, and ethnic differences; he argues that all art is political "because art is an expression of the very political practice of asking questions about the world" (qtd. in Tucker 29).

Delany began his career as a writer of SF with *The Jewels of Aptor* (1962), set on a post-holocaust earth. By the publication of *Babel-17* (1966), which won the Nebula, he had published several more novels and was beginning to make notable advances in sophistication. That novel was quickly followed by such works as *The Einstein Intersection* (1967) and *Nova* (1968), then eventually by *Dhalgren* (1975), *Triton* (1976), and *Stars in My Pocket Like Grains of Sand* (1984)—works that took Delany's writing (and the genre of SF) to an entirely new level of literary and conceptual sophistication. Carl Freedman, for example, calls *Stars in My Pocket* "the most intellectually ambitious work in the entire range of modern science fiction" (147). Meanwhile, Delany's series of Nevèrÿon novels brought new sophistication to the fantasy novel in the 1980s. His stories are collected in the volume *Aye, and Gomorrah: Stories* (2003).

Delany is particularly concerned with the concept of difference, in both the poststructuralist, linguistic sense and a more politically engaged social sense. Typically regarded by critics as a practitioner of **postmodernism**—particularly in his desire to decenter or displace racial, gender, and sexual norms, and his engaging of poststructuralist theory—Delany is arguably a writer just as—if not more—firmly rooted in literary **modernism**, making the cognitive estrangement that is typical of the best SF not only a part of the content of his books but a part of the experience of reading as well.

Selected Bibliography: Delany, Samuel R. *Jewel-Hinged Jaw: Notes on the Language of Science Fiction.* New York: Berkley, 1977; Delany, Samuel R. *The Motion of Light in Water.* 1988. New York: Kasak, 1993; Delany, Samuel R. "Racism and Science Fiction." *Dark Matter: A Century of Speculative Fiction from the African Diaspora.* Ed. Sheree R. Thomas. New York: Warner Books, 2000; Delany, Samuel R. *Silent Interviews: On Language, Race, Sex, Science Fiction, and Some Comics.* Hanover, NH: Wesleyan UP, 1994; Delany, Samuel R. *Starboard Wine: More Notes on the Language of Science Fiction.* Pleasantville, NY: Dragon P, 1984; Delany, Samuel R. *Times Square Red, Times Square Blue.* New York: New York UP, 1999; Freedman, Carl. *Critical Theory and Science Fiction.* Hanover, NH:

Wesleyan UP, 2000; Sallis, James, ed. *Ash of Stars: On the Writing of Samuel R. Delany*. Jackson: U of Mississippi P, 1996; Tucker, Jeffrey Allen. *A Sense of Wonder: Samuel R. Delany, Race, Identity, and Difference*. Hanover, NH: Wesleyan UP, 2004.

Sandy Rankin

DELEUZE, GILLES (1925–1995). French philosopher linked to such concepts as "becoming," "difference," the "event," the "virtual," and, with Félix Guattari, "nomadic thought" and "minor literature." Deleuze's work can be roughly grouped into three categories: single-author studies of other philosophers (Hume, Nietzsche, Spinoza, Kant, Bergson, Leibniz, Foucault); coauthored works with the French psychiatric analyst and activist Guattari (*Anti-Oedipus* [1972], *A Thousand Plateaus* [1980], *Kafka: Toward a Minor Literature* [1975], *What Is Philosophy?* [1991]); and writings on cinema and the visual (*Cinema 1* [1983], *Cinema 2* [1985], *Francis Bacon: The Logic of Sensation* [1981]). The coauthored works have been particularly influential in literary studies. Other works fall outside these categories, such as numerous essays on literature, including a book on Proust, and two seminal studies from 1968 and 1969: *Difference and Repetition* and *The Logic of Sense*. The latter works put forward a theory of difference, in which difference is not something derived from a fundamental notion of the same but is the fundamental unit from which similarity and identity can be thought at all.

Deleuze's engagement with and indebtedness to his philosophical predecessors is enormous. One of the strongest such links is to Spinoza, whose notion of all things partaking of a single substance (God is indissociable from nature, mind, body, and so on) informs much of Deleuze's thought and in particular his two books on Spinoza, *Expressionism in Philosophy* (1968) and *Practical Philosophy* (1970). This single substance is in some ways resonant with Leibniz's concept of the monad, and even in a heterodox sense with Plato's ideal form, though Deleuze uses this idea to overturn Plato's hierarchies. If one thinks of mind and body as two different ways of conceiving the same thing, then there is no longer a hierarchy of categories (mind over body, human over animal, man over woman) but rather a set of relations between forces and a positive transformative process of becoming, where the first and more traditionally favored term may become the second (becoming woman, becoming animal). This might seem at odds with a strong notion of difference, and in some sense it is, but this can be resolved if one thinks difference as an operation not so much between recognized oppositions (man versus woman) but between nonessential attributes (blue versus green in eye color, clothing, and so on).

The notion of becoming is something that Deleuze and Guattari outline in *A Thousand Plateaus*. This work also uses the model of the root or rhizome as opposed to the hierarchical logic of the tree. Such a model that emphasizes horizontal exchange anticipates contemporary discussions of globalization that move away from a nation-state model into a discussion of networks and zones. Deleuze and Guattari's concept of "deterritorialization," where a subject traces a real or imagined "line of flight" from a stable identity or locale, has been mobilized in an array of disciplines.

Deleuze's two-volume study of cinema has received considerable scholarly attention in recent years. Here, Deleuze traces a shift from cinema preoccupied with movement before **World War II** to a postwar cinema more focused on time and temporality. Deleuze reads individual films through a logic of difference where he is attuned to disjunctions between what is seen and what is heard, where, for example, a voice will rise and an image will recede. Deleuze's work has had considerable influence in the field of architecture.

Selected Bibliography: Boundas, Constantin, and Dorothea Olkowski, eds. *Gilles Deleuze and the Theatre of Philosophy.* London: Routledge, 1994; Flaxman, Gregory, ed. *The Brain Is the Screen: Deleuze and the Philosophy of Cinema.* Minneapolis: U of Minnesota P, 2000; Foucault, Michel. "Theatrum Philosophicum." *Language, Counter-Memory, Practice.* Trans. Donald F. Bouchard and Sherry Simon. Ithaca, NY: Cornell UP, 1977; Hardt, Michael. *Gilles Deleuze: An Apprenticeship in Philosophy.* Minneapolis: U of Minnesota P, 1993; Massumi, Brian. *A User's Guide to* Capitalism and Schizophrenia*: Deviations from Deleuze and Guattari.* Cambridge, MA: MIT P, 1992.

Eleanor Kaufman

DERRIDA, JACQUES (1930–). Born in Algiers, the son of French-speaking Jews, Derrida has characterized his cultural identity as divided and foreign: neither African nor European but also both; Jewish but nonobservant and Christian, insofar as he belongs to a Christian culture. His sense of nonidentity can be seen as one source for his insistence on difference, alterity, and the divided origin. He was expelled from school in Algiers in 1942 in accordance with anti-Semitic measures taken by the Vichy government. He returned to the public system in 1944–1945, when he began an intense reading of literature (Rousseau, Gide, Nietzsche, Valéry, Camus). In 1947, he began his philosophical studies, beginning with Bergson and Sartre but soon turning to Kierkegaard and Heidegger. He made his first trip to France in 1949 to study philosophy; he entered the Ecole normale supérieure in 1952. There he met **Louis Althusser** and attended lectures given by **Michel Foucault.** He wrote his thesis on the concept of genesis in Husserl under the direction of Jean Hyppolite.

Derrida's first major publication was a translation and introduction to Husserl's "Origin of Geometry" (1962). At the invitation of Althusser, he joined the faculty of the Ecole normale in 1964. In 1967, he published three books: *Of Grammatology, Writing and Difference,* and *Speech and Phenomena*—introducing the deconstruction of logocentrism, the principle that speech is the sign of self-presence and truth; and elaborating the concept of writing as the system of difference that accounts for meaning, truth, and the "real." Instead of thinking of existence on the basis of identity, self-presence, and the present, Derrida proposes in their stead otherness, difference, and absence as the impossible conditions for the possibility of experience. The critique of metaphysics, along with an often unclassifiable prose style, led to his early reception in literature departments in the United States, and in 1975, he began teaching part of the year at Yale. The predominance of **new criticism** in American universities facilitated the reception of Derrida's concepts of writing and the text, but it also led to the misconception that deconstruction simply represents the text's undermining of itself. This early phase passed, and greater attention has since been given to the ethical and affirmative nature of his thought, particularly his account of responsibility, singularity, and justice.

A steady stream of publications followed, including three more books in 1972: *Dissemination*, *Margins of Philosophy*, and *Positions*. That same year, he broke with the Tel Quel group, which included **Julia Kristeva**, because of its Maoism. Although he always aligned himself with the Left, he never joined the French Communist Party because of its Stalinist dogmatism. His silence on Marx's texts themselves reflects his preference for a style of thought that is phenomenological and transcendental, a style that does not foreclose questions about such topics as history, objectivity, theory, and science. Good politics, Derrida insists, never places limits on questioning, and his 1987 book *Of Spirit: Heidegger and the Question* represents a more explicit engagement with politics. However, in this and other recent works, including *The Force of Law* (1990), *The Other Heading* (1991), *Specters of Marx* (1994), and *Politics of Friendship* (1994), Derrida's resistance to anything resembling a program makes them a continuation of his earliest deconstructions of presence, historicity, and metaphysics.

Selected Bibliography: Beardsworth, Richard. *Derrida and the Political.* London: Routledge, 1996; Bennington, Geoffrey, and Jacques Derrida. *Jacques Derrida.* Chicago: U of Chicago P, 1991; Cohen, Tom, ed. *Jacques Derrida and the Humanities: A Critical Reader.* Cambridge: Cambridge UP, 2001; Gasché, Rodolphe. *Inventions of Difference: On Jacques Derrida.* Cambridge: Harvard UP, 1994; Sprinker, Michael, ed. *Ghostly Demarcations: A Symposium on Jacques Derrida's* Specters of Marx. London: Verso, 1999.

Joseph G. Kronick

DESAI, ANITA (1937–). Born to a German mother and an Indian father, Desai was raised in New Delhi, India. She grew up speaking German and Hindi, but embraced English as her literary language. Although Desai was raised in India and did most of her writing there, her mixed-race heritage and the ability to study India from a bird's-eye view led her to admit that "I feel about India as an Indian, but I suppose I think about it as an outsider" (Bliss 522). She deals specifically with the experiences of immigrants in two of her novels, Indians in Britain in *Bye-Bye, Blackbird* (1971) and German immigrants in India in *Baumgartner's Bombay* (1988).

Desai graduated with honors in English from the University of Delhi and has won many accolades, including the National Academy of Letters Award for *Fire on the Mountain* (1977) and the Guardian Prize for Children's Fiction for *The Village by the Sea* (1982). Desai's *Clear Light of Day* (1980) and *In Custody* (1984) were nominated for the Booker Prize of the United Kingdom. Desai has also served as a fellow of the Royal Society of Literature. The critical acclaim accorded to her work enabled Desai to win the Literary Lion Award in 1993, and she was named Helen Cam visiting fellow, Ashby fellow, and honorary fellow of the University of Cambridge. Desai has taught at Smith College, Girton College at Cambridge University, and Mount Holyoke College.

Desai has published twelve books of fiction and many essays, reviews, and articles. *Games at Twilight* (1978) is a collection of short stories; the rest of her books are novels. Desai says that the dominant theme of her works is "the terror of facing, single-handed, the ferocious assaults of existence" (Libert 47). Desai's works have won critical and literary acclaim in India and in the West. Although some critics are of the opinion that her ornate and lyrical prose obscures the characters in her novels, most of them commend the profoundly psychological depth of her fiction. As Judie Newman points out, "Without minimizing the real horrors of the past, Desai emphasizes the need not to be complicit with those forces that would erase historical truth, reducing events to myth, fantasy or silence" (45).

In her novels, Desai foregrounds powerful feminist trends in the third world and depicts the cultural and social transformations that India has undergone in its postcolonial phase. Most of Desai's works delve into the construction of the "third-world woman," who is in search of an identity other than the one imposed on her by the nationalist movements and literatures of postcolonial India. Desai's novels explore the constitutive elements of the postcolonial sense of Indian society, while critiquing the objectification of third-world women as the repositories of a precolonial cultural essence. As Jasbir Jain puts it, in Desai's work, "the themes are analyzed, the social and political elements are subtly camouflaged and subdued by dwelling on emotions and responses which are far more engrossing than the hard facts of reality" (1).

Selected Bibliography: Bliss, Corinne Demas. "Against the Current: A Conversation with Anita Desai." *Massachusetts Review* 29.3 (Fall 1988): 521–37; Choudhury, Bidulata. *Women and Society in the Novels of Anita Desai.* New Delhi: Creative Books, 1995; Jain, Jasbir. "Anita Desai." *Indian English Novelists.* Ed. Madhusudhan Prasad. New Delhi: Sterling Publishers, 1982. 23–50; Libert, Florence. "An Interview with Anita Desai." *World Literature Written in English* 30.1 (1990): 47–55; Newman, Judie. "History and Letters: Anita Desai's *Baumgartner's Bombay.*" *World Literature Written in English* 30.1 (1990): 37–46.

Nyla Ali Khan

DETECTIVE AND CRIME FICTION. Detective narratives can be traced back as far as Sophocles and, according to some, the Bible. However, critics often point to Arthur Conan Doyle and Edgar Allan Poe as the sources of what we now recognize as detective and crime fiction. From these sources, detective and crime stories branched out into at least two major streams: the whodunit and the police procedural. Each of these has continued to flourish: the whodunit from the distilled puzzle narratives of Agatha Christie to Mary Higgins Clark, and the procedurals from Erle Stanley Gardner's Perry Mason to Tony Hillerman's Jim Chee and the forensics squad of television's *C.S.I.* These streams have in turn given rise to a variety of subgenres. For instance, the American hard-boiled narrative, pioneered by writers like James M. Cain, **Dashiell Hammett**, Raymond Chandler, and the writers of *Black Mask* magazine, filtered Doyle's Holmes and Poe's August Dupin through the Western and adventure tale, contemporaneous mass-media tales of gangsters and cops, and an indigenous tradition of muckraking journalism. The historical whodunit joins the detective plot with nonfictional narrative, producing texts like Umberto Eco's *The Name of the Rose* (1980) and more postmodernized exemplars, such as Arturo Perez-Reverte's *The Club Dumas* (1993) and A. S. Byatt's *Possession* (1990).

Narratives of crime and detection have come to occupy an amazingly durable and versatile place in modern culture. These stories of social transgression have been disseminated across all major media—television, film, print, music—and around the globe. Not only are detective and crime tales central to contemporary cultural production, but from Bogota to Dubuque to Tokyo, they form a lingua franca of images, characters, plots, settings, and styles. Confronted by this plethora, literary critics have tended to adopt a defensive position, and much of the critical debate about detective fictions has revolved around their cultural status: are they literature or merely popular ephemera?

A broader view would recognize that detective narratives are central to many celebrated literary texts, from **William Faulkner**'s *Absalom, Absalom* (1936) to Pynchon's *The Crying of Lot 49* (1966). Meanwhile, popular detective narratives—including those by writers such as **Charles Dickens**, Dashiell Hammett, and Walter Mosley—have established a beachhead in university syllabi. Indeed, one way of reckoning the politics of detective and crime fiction is by focusing on the kind of cultural work these narratives enable, whether in Penguin Classics, prime-time television, or gangster rap. Alternatively, we can understand the politics of detective and crime narratives by focusing on their ideological messages. And, finally, plot itself (especially the strong causality and narrative closure of the mystery plot) provides another way of thinking about the politics of detective and mystery fiction.

Plot is of course essential to detective and crime narratives. In their strongest forms, these narratives are structured around enigmas that propel the reader forward. Strong detective plots generate ambiguity only to ruthlessly eliminate it, and though they may open with chaos and disruption, endings in strong detective plots put everything back in its right narrative order. Detectives are often surrogates for the readers of fiction, and in wringing coherence and meaning from disorder, they seem to enact the reader's similar desires. Yet taking their cue from the French critic **Roland Barthes**, recent poststructuralist critics see these features of the strong plot as simply reinforcing or "re-inscribing" readers into dominant ideologies and subjectivities rather than opening readers and texts up to alternative ways of seeing and understanding. Thus, for instance, while a queer or gay detective like Abigail Padgett's Blue Mc-Carron may unsettle readers' expectations, these effects will be quickly neutralized by a strong detective plot that obeys the imperative to eliminate and resolve ambiguities and contradictions.

The work of form in detective narrative may reflect its origins in middle-class Victorian society. Early detectives like Holmes or Sergeant Cuff of Wilkie Collins's *The Moonstone* (1868) played an important social role: they were called on to repair violations of middle-class social rules and roles. Typically, these violations centered on two pillars of the middle-class way of life—family and property. The detective's greatest tools were reason, organization, and his knowledge of class proprieties. Deploying these, he modeled bourgeois virtues even as he set about redeeming their lapses. American crime novels began with the same class themes of family and property, as in such novels as Cain's *The Postman Always Rings Twice* (1934), Hammett's *The Dain Curse* (1929), and Chandler's *The Big Sleep* (1939), where wandering daughters, unfaithful wives, and greedy heirs are the usual sources of crime and disruption. However, rather than vindicating middle-class ideology, the American crime novel ruthlessly exposes the corruption and hypocrisy it harbors and, ultimately, depends on. This critique is carried out under the auspices of an alternative ideology—individualism—exemplified by the lone detective. Thus, the endings of novels by writers like Hammett, Chandler, and Cain are typically saturated in either nihilism or cynicism. This critique of bourgeois ideology links early hard-boiled writers to film noir and to contemporary crime writers like James Crumley, Carl Hiassen, and James Ellroy. It also points to a smaller tradition of explicitly left-wing crime and detective narratives, beginning with such 1930s writers as Benjamin Appel, **Kenneth Fearing**, and Eric Ambler.

Detective and crime narratives have been used in so many different ways by so many different writers and consumed by so many different kinds of readers that the ideology of these narratives—conservative or critical—is probably impossible to determine. However, we can look at the ways in which writers have used the genre to stretch its forms, to explore its ideological legacies, and to draw readers into new cultural and social territory. Particularly important here is a new generation of writers, following in the footsteps of African American predecessors like **Chester Himes** and Rudolph Fisher, who extend the genre into new settings and characters. Writers like Sara Peretsky, Barbara Neely, Rudolfo Anaya, Michael Nava, and John Ridley, for instance, replace the typically white, middle-class detective with African American, Latino, working-class, queer, and feminist protagonists.

These writers have used the detective narrative to connect the genre to new readers; these new constituencies have in turn exerted pressure on classic detective and crime themes. Barbara Neely's Blanche White series inverts the classic "parlor" mystery to narrate events from the perspective of a female, African American domestic worker. In the process, Neely produces finely crafted whodunits but also social and philosophical commentaries on black-white and boss-employee relations. Likewise, through his chicano detective, Sonny Baca, Rudolfo Anaya rewrites the hard-boiled genre to recover the secret histories and social relations of the American Southwest. For these and other writers, the detective narrative provides an occasion for exploring social, cultural, and political issues. Whatever their ultimate political effects, these narratives are practicing a sophisticated cultural and literary politics. This same dynamic drives more global appropriations of the classic detective narrative by writers such as Henning Mankell (Sweden), Paco Ignacio Taibo II (Mexico), and Leonardo Padura Fuentes (Cuba).

Detective and crime fictions provide an important vehicle for cultural and social outsiders because they have become such an established and instantly recognizable genre of narratives. The cultural currency of this genre has provided in turn the opportunity for a whole genre of self-reflexive detective narratives—many associated with postmodernism—by writers such as Paul Auster, Pynchon, and Ishmael Reed. These narratives typically launch a frontal assault on the formal, thematic, and generic conventions of detective and crime fiction—strong plots, narrative closure, coherence, ratiocinative and hard-boiled detectives—as a way of critiquing conventional narrative representation itself. Rather than discrediting the genre, however, the deconstruction of the detective and crime narrative testifies to its continuing popularity and fecundity.

Selected Bibliography: Klein, Kathleen Gregory. *Diversity and Detective Fiction*. Bowling Green, OH: Bowling Green State U Popular P, 1999; Knight, Damon. *The Futurians*. New York: John Day, 1977; Mandel, Ernest. *Delightful Murder: A Social History of the Crime Story*. Minneapolis: U of Minnesota P, 1984; Porter, Dennis. *The Pursuit of Crime: Art and Ideology in Detective Fiction*. New Haven, CT: Yale UP, 1981; Priestman, Martin, ed. *The Cambridge Companion to Crime Fiction*. Cambridge: Cambridge

UP, 2003; Symons, Julian. *Bloody Murder: From the Detective Story to the Crime Novel.* New York: Viking, 1985; Winks, Robin, ed. *Detective Fiction: A Collection of Critical Essays.* Englewood Cliffs, NJ: Prentice-Hall, 1980.

Larry Hanley

DEVIL ON THE CROSS (*CAITAANI MUTHARABA-INI,* 1980) is the first of **Ngũgĩ wa Thiong'o**'s novels to have been written in Gikuyu, published in the author's English translation in 1982. In this sense, the novel is the embodiment of Ngũgĩ's belief that African writers should write in indigenous African languages and not in the European languages of their formal colonial rulers. It is also a powerful political novel, painting a disturbing picture of a postcolonial Kenya succumbing to the lures of capitalism, rejecting its independence struggle, and victimizing the same members of society whom colonialism oppressed. According to Ngũgĩ in his prison diary, *Detained* (1981), the novel was written on toilet paper in Kamiti Maximum Security Prison, where he was incarcerated without formal charges for most of 1978.

In addition to writing in Gikuyu, Ngũgĩ attempts in *Devil on the Cross* to interweave into the Western novel form aspects of the Gikuyu oral tradition. This story of modern Kenya is narrated by a gicaandi player—a traditional verbal artist who acts in Ngũgĩ's book as a social critic, even a "Prophet of Justice" (8). Drawing on these different aesthetic traditions, Ngũgĩ's novel incorporates fantastic symbolic events and realistic social commentary. The story follows the fortunes of Wariinga, representative of the victimization of Kenyan women after independence; she was impregnated as a school girl by a rich predator, fired by her boss in Nairobi because she will not sleep with him, abandoned by her boyfriend who falsely accuses her of infidelity, and evicted and threatened by her landlord. Her fortune changes when she is saved from suicide by a young man who gives her a card announcing the "Devil's Feast." On her way in Robin Mwaura's matatu (a kind of bus), she trades stories with the other passengers, who come from different classes of postcolonial Kenyan society. From her fellow passengers, she hears firsthand accounts of Kenyan colonial history and the role of women during the 1950s uprising of the land and freedom fighters (Mau Mau). In Limuru, she is terrified by an apparition of the devil and outraged by the proud revelations of the thieves and robbers—comprador bourgeoisie who compete to see who has been most successful in exploiting the Kenyan people in the interests of their foreign bosses. Eventually, Wariinga becomes engaged to one of her fellow passengers, the intellectual composer Gatuiria. Wariinga breaks gender barriers by going on to study mechanical engineering and to work as an auto mechanic, and (in a scene that can be taken as a call to violent revolt) takes revenge by shooting the "Rich Old Man from Ngarika," who had raped and impregnated her when she was young—and who turns out to be Gatuiria's father.

In his English translation of the book, Ngũgĩ crafts an English that incorporates both Gikuyu terminology and the biblical cadence he is well known for using in all of his novels. The multiple hybridities of *Devil on the Cross* make it one of Ngũgĩ's most complex considerations of the continued oppression of the workers and peasants by a capitalist bourgeoisie.

Selected Bibliography: Booker, M. Keith. *The African Novel in English.* Portsmouth, NH: Heinemann, 1998; Gikandi, Simon. *Ngugi wa Thiong'o.* New York: Cambridge UP, 2001; Jeyifo, Biodun.

Ngugi wa Thiong'o. London: Pluto, 1990; Killam, G. D. *An Introduction to the Writings of Ngugi*. London: Heinemann, 1980; Ngũgĩ wa Thiong'o. *Decolonising the Mind: The Politics of Language in African Literature*. London: James Currey, 1986; Ngũgĩ wa Thiong'o. *Detained: A Prison Diary*. London: Heinemann, 1981; Sicherman, Carol. *Ngugi wa Thiong'o: The Making of a Rebel*. London: Hans Zell, 1990.

Arlene (Amy) Elder

THE DEVILS (BESY, 1871). Also translated as *Demons* and *The Possessed*, **Dostoevsky**'s third major novel centers on a political conspiracy (modeled on an actual conspiracy of the day headed by Sergei Nechaev, 1847–1882). However, the book also explores, through its enigmatic hero, Nikolai Stavrogin, profound philosophical and religious questions.

The action takes place in a provincial town over the period of about a month. It begins and ends with Stepan Verkhovensky, an archetypical idealistic liberal of the 1840s. Although he had achieved a brief and modest reputation as a thinker in his heyday, Verkhovensky has spent the rest of his life in idleness as a hanger-on in the household of the wealthy Varvara Stavrogin. Stepan's son, Peter, has become a revolutionary (although he describes himself as "a rogue, not a socialist"), and at the beginning of the novel he returns from abroad. A masterful manipulator who is entirely without scruples, he quickly manages to impress or intimidate the local elite while covertly spreading unrest to destabilize their society. He also convinces a group of the town's freethinkers that he represents a vast organization of Russian revolutionary émigrés abroad and controls a network of revolutionary cells in Russia. He sets up one such group of five and convinces them to murder a sixth, Ivan Shatov, whose sympathy for the revolutionary cause has faded. The crime is quickly discovered, although not before a half dozen other townspeople meet violent death. Peter's father, appalled to see how the well-intentioned ideals of his Western-oriented generation have been transformed into cynical and brutal exploitation, ends with a tragicomic pilgrimage to discover the Russia he has ignored all his life.

The ideas of one of the town's radicals, Shigalyov, represent both a caricature of the utopian Socialism of the 1840s and a chilling forecast of totalitarian ideas of the twentieth century. His plan for an ideal social system began with the idea of unlimited freedom but has ended, he admits, with unlimited despotism. In his utopia, one-tenth of the population would enjoy unlimited power over the others who, having surrendered their freedom and individuality, would revert to a state of primal innocence, materially secure and happy in their slavery.

The novel's central figure is Nikolai Stavrogin, an enigmatic character of great charisma and will who has managed to inspire radically different ideas in his many admirers. Shatov has derived his ardent Russian religious nationalism from Stavrogin, while another "disciple," Kirillov, has developed an arch-individualism that leads him to commit suicide as a challenge to the power of God. Peter Verkhovensky also hopes to use Stavrogin as a figurehead for his movement. Stavrogin, however, has found nothing in which he can anchor himself among the various ideologies and identities he has taken on and ends by hanging himself.

As a political novel, *The Devils* fits partly within the tradition of Russian "antinihilist" novels of the 1860s and 1870s. Dostoevsky, however, does much more than caricature the ideas and behavior of Russia's radicals. His thesis, that the rejection of a God-centered worldview by the "fathers" of the 1840s has produced the nightmarish amorality of the human-centered views of "children" of the 1860s, adds to the novel's philosophical, psychological, and religious depth.

Selected Bibliography: Leatherbarrow, W. J., ed. *Dostoevsky's* The Devils: *A Critical Companion.* Evanston, IL: Northwestern UP, 1999.

Kenneth Lantz

DICK, PHILIP K(INDRED) (1928–1982) was an American novelist and short-story writer. A Chicago native, he spent most of his life in California, where much of his fiction is set. He was married five times and had three children but was unmarried at his death. He produced over forty novels and many dozens of stories; the great majority of his work, and practically all his best work, is science fiction.

Though Dick was only modestly successful during his lifetime, since his death, his reputation has skyrocketed. Many of his books, previously available only as cheap mass-market paperbacks, have been reprinted in a handsome uniform edition, and a number of his novels and stories have been made into films. He has been the subject of many books and articles, both popular and scholarly, and is frequently taught in college literature courses. The eminent Marxist critic **Fredric Jameson**, in an obituary, hailed Dick as "the Shakespeare of science fiction." Beyond science fiction, an increasing number of critics rank Dick as one of the most important and original American novelists during the second half of the twentieth century.

Dick is often described as an "ontological" writer—that is, one concerned with fundamental questions of being. One typical theme expressing this element of his work is the difficulty of determining whether a given set of circumstances represents "objective" reality or some sort of hallucination or some even more complex possibility; another is the difficulty of distinguishing between human beings and simulacra of them. But Dick nearly always interweaves such philosophical concerns with a darkly humorous and radically left-wing critique of American society. Unlike much science fiction, Dick's work is normally set on earth and in the near future; he stays "close to home" also in that he uses his wildest imaginings to estrange and criticize such mundane social realities as the increasing commercialization of life and the increasing power of governmental despotism. His protagonists tend to be decent, ordinary working people attempting to grapple with forces nearly always beyond their control and frequently beyond even their understanding.

As with any prolific and frequently discussed writer, Dick's readers do not always agree on which of his many works represent him at his best. Still, most of Dick's admirers—whether among professional critics or general readers—would probably say that any list of his finest novels should include the following: *The Man in the High Castle* (1962), probably his most famous work, an alternative-history novel in which the Axis has won the Second World War and divided the United States into German and Japanese sectors; *Martian Time-Slip* (1964), his finest novel with an extraterrestrial setting, in which the red planet provides the locale not for bug-eyed monsters but for schizophrenia, racism, commercial speculation, and political corruption; *Dr. Bloodmoney* (1965), an elaborately plotted work that ranks as the best novel yet written about life after nuclear holocaust; *Do Androids Dream of Electric Sheep?* (1968), probably Dick's most sustained meditation on the nature of humanity, known to many through Ridley Scott's film *Blade Runner* (1982), which is loosely based on Dick's novel; *Ubik* (1969), which many consider his single most brilliant performance, a hilarious and terrifying work in which the theme of multiple realities is handled with extraordinary elegance; and *A Scanner Darkly* (1977), Dick's longest novel and his own personal favorite, which offers a science-fictionalized version of the hippie drug culture of the 1960s.

Selected Bibliography: Mullen, R. D., et al., eds. *On Philip K. Dick.* Terre Haute, IN: SF-TH, 1992; Robinson, Kim Stanley. *The Novels of Philip K. Dick.* Ann Arbor: UMI Research P, 1984; Sutin, Lawrence. *Divine Invasions: A Life of Philip K. Dick.* New York: Harmony Books, 1989; Williams, Paul. *Only Apparently Real: The World of Philip K. Dick.* New York: Arbor House, 1986.

Carl Freedman

DICKENS, CHARLES (1812–1870). Born in the naval town of Portsmouth, Charles Dickens, the son of a naval clerk, was both the most popular and the most commercially successful novelist of the Victorian era. He was a highly inventive comic writer and caricaturist, as well as a powerful social commentator on all aspects of nineteenth-century culture, society, and politics.

Dickens was a writer of great inventiveness and creative energy, developing a sharply perceived, often satirical mode of observation based on his early writing experiences for London periodicals. Throughout his career as a novelist, Dickens would continue to edit journals and magazines, most famously *Household Words*, which contained published work by **Elizabeth Gaskell**, and, in 1845, *The Daily News*. He established himself as a successful novelist in the 1830s, writing initially under the pen name Boz, but dropping this when the three-volume edition of *Oliver Twist* was published (1838). In 1836, Dickens began the serial publication of his first novel, *The Pickwick Papers*, which drew on the picaresque novel tradition of the eighteenth century for its form. All Dickens's novels were first published in serial form through journals, and then subsequently reissued as novels. *The Pickwick Papers*, which satirized, among other things, local elections, was completed and issued in one volume in 1837, the year in which Victoria became queen and which also saw the beginning of the serial publication of *Oliver Twist*. This novel drew the public's attention to the conditions of the workhouse and the failures of the 1834 Poor Law, while *Nicholas Nickleby* (1839) exposed the appalling conditions in Yorkshire schools.

In the 1840s, Dickens consolidated his success, beginning with novels such as *Barnaby Rudge* (1841), a historical novel of the Gordon Riots of 1780, much indebted to Sir Walter Scott. Subsequent novels of the decade included *A Christmas Carol* (1843), *Martin Chuzzlewit* (1844), and *Dombey and Son* (1848). The two latter novels marked a transition in Dickens's writing, away from the earlier largely comic work to darker satires and critiques of society and patriarchy.

In 1849, Dickens began serial publication of *David Copperfield*, a novel largely acknowledged by critics as semiautobiographical. Completed in 1850, it was followed in 1852–1853 by *Bleak House*, Dickens's darkest satire yet, with its savage critique of the English legal system. In 1853, Dickens gave his first public readings in Birmingham with much public approbation, going on to give reading tours throughout Britain (and one in the United States, where he was greatly admired) almost to the end of his life. The 1850s also saw the publication of *Hard Times* (1854), unsuccessful at the time, but a novel whose sympathy for the working class drew the later admiration of Socialists such as **George Bernard Shaw**. *Little Dorrit* was published in 1857, followed in 1859 by *A Tale of Two Cities*—a novel of the **French Revolution** influenced by Thomas Carlyle. This novel, like *Barnaby Rudge*, shows a clear horror of mass political action by the working classes, complicating Dickens's sometime reputation as a champion of the working class. *Great Expectations*, a **bildungsroman** that became one of Dickens's most enduring works, appeared in 1860–1861; between 1864 and 1865, he wrote what was to be his last completed novel, *Our Mutual Friend*. His health failing, Dickens cut short a reading tour of North America in 1867. In 1870, he gave his farewell readings in London and began publishing *The Mystery of Edwin Drood*, which was incomplete at his death.

Selected Bibliography: Ackroyd, Peter. *Dickens.* London: Sinclair Stevenson, 1990; Miller, J. Hillis. *Charles Dickens: The World of His Novels.* Cambridge, MA: Harvard UP, 1958; Sanders, Andrew. *Charles Dickens.* Oxford: Oxford UP, 2003.

Julian Wolfreys

DICTIONARIES (ENGLISH). The descriptive culture of modern dictionaries has led to a formal insistence on impartiality. Earlier dictionaries, however, could reflect the political allegiances of their editors, as in Samuel Johnson's definition of *Tory* as "a cant word signifying a savage" in his *Dictionary* (1755). Later dictionaries, such as the *Oxford English Dictionary* (1st edition 1884–1928), stressed the status of the lexicographer as historian rather than critic. Political definition was, as a result, assimilated within historicist rather than personal ideologies, as in the densely detailed definition of *Tory* ("from 1689, the name of one of the two great parliamentary and political parties in England. . . . As a formal name, 'Tory' was superseded c 1830 by Conservative, merged after 1886 [when the Conservatives were joined by many who had previously belonged to the Liberal party]"). Nevertheless, political ideologies of various kinds can be manifest within the ostensible neutrality of many entries. Definitions within the first edition of the *OED* could reflect a culture of empire and imperialism, as in the original entry for *canoe*: "1. A kind of boat in use among uncivilized nations . . . used generally for any rude craft in which uncivilized people go upon the water; most savages use paddles instead of oars . . . 2. In civilized use: a small light sort of boat or skiff propelled by paddling." Embedded ideologies of race, gender, and class can likewise intervene. *White man* in *OED1* is defined as "a man of honourable character such as one associates with a European (as distinguished from a negro)," while the definition of *gent* exhibits unmistakable class bias ("a mark of low breeding . . . except as applied derisively to men of the vulgar and pretentious class who are supposed to use the word, and in tradesmen's notices"). *Petticoat* is still defined as "the characteristic or typical feminine garment; . . . the symbol of the female sex or character." The earlier dominance of male-orientated definition (*first-fruit*: "the first products of a man's work or endeavour"; *arson*: "The act of wilfully and maliciously setting fire to another man's house, ship, forest, or similar property") is being eradicated in the ongoing revisions of *OED Online* (2001–). Such shifts typify the currents of modern lexicographical practice in which, as in the *Encarta World English Dictionary* (London: Bloomsbury, 1999) an ever-increasing regard for neutrality aims to occlude bias in entry words and in accompanying definitions and citations. As other critics have warned (see Landau 234), this may run the danger of failing to represent linguistic reality in other ways. The labeling of words such as *madness* as "offensive" in *Encarta* has, for example, attracted considerable criticism and debate.

Selected Bibliography: Bejoint, Henri. *Modern Lexicography. An Introduction.* Oxford: Oxford UP, 2000; Landau, Sidney. *Dictionaries: The Art and Craft of English Lexicography.* 2nd ed. Cambridge: Cambridge UP, 2001; Mugglestone, Lynda, ed. *Hidden Histories: The Making of the Oxford English Dictionary.* New Haven, CT: Yale UP, 2005; Mugglestone, Lynda, ed. *Lexicography and the OED: Pioneers in the Untrodden Forest.* Oxford: Oxford UP, 2002.

Lynda C. Mugglestone

DICTIONARIES (FRENCH). Jean Nicot's *Thrésor de la langue françoise* (1606) is considered to be the first French dictionary. However, it was the *Dictionnaire de l'Académie française* (1694) that marked the passage of the French language to the rank of "langue classique." The eighteenth century was dominated by the *Dictionnaire de l'Académie française* (three editions) and the *Encyclopédie* of Diderot and D'Alembert (1753–1771), which was not intended to be a language dictionary. The nineteenth century has been dubbed "the century of dictionaries": more than eight hundred French dictionaries were published between 1800 and 1900. Various factors played a role in the development of French lexicography on such a large scale: the development of the school system; technological improvements of the printing press and a decline in book prices; and the rise of large publishing houses. French lexicography was also influenced by the new development of historical methods of investigation. The political imperative to teach French to all citizens—to create a national symbol shared by all—gave the final impetus to what would become a lucrative industry.

As early as 1790, the Revolutionaries declared that teaching French to the "new citizens" was a national priority, but political turmoil and the difficulty of finding qualified teachers rendered the task almost impossible. It was only in 1833 that François Guizot, minister of King Louis-Philippe, implemented what was to become a truly national schooling system, which would reach its full potential only in the 1880s. The French language occupied a central position in the new curriculum, triggering a fierce competition among lexicographers.

For three quarters of a century, the lucrative school market was dominated by F.J.M. Noël (1755–1841), who was, rather conveniently, general inspector of the Université de Paris. He co-opted a young grammarian, C. P. Chapsal (1788–1858), to write a textbook that would combine a grammar and a dictionary. In addition, the book was to offer "a moral lesson" through well-chosen quotations from great writers (mostly from the seventeenth century). The *Nouveau Dictionnaire de la langue française* was born in 1826 and was to enjoy a lasting success (21st edition in 1872):

from 1833, the government bought it in large quantities, and it was officially adopted by primary schools and military colleges.

In 1846, L.-N. Bescherelle (1802–1883) published his most important work, the *Dictionnaire national ou dictionnaire universel de la langue française.* The subtitle left no room for interpretation; the *Dictionnaire* was a "a monument to the glory of French language and literature." Aimed at secondary schools, the *Dictionnaire* offered an ideological portrait of the French language, a reflection of how France wished to see herself in the world. The French language was described as "elegant," "clear," "precise," "refined," "nuanced," and the "universal" language.

In the 1840s, Pierre Larousse (1817–1875) developed the idea of a "total" dictionary that would be an encyclopedia as well: *Le Grand Dictionnaire unversel du 19e siècle* (published in cheap monthly installments between 1866 and 1875). Larousse's objective was to spread the idea of a republican France, a dangerous task to pursue under the Second Empire. His treatment of the French language was very similar to that of Bescherelle and other lexicographers of the time; he treated it reverently, as a fundamental component of the French nation that transcended political regimes. The encyclopedic part of the *Grand Dictionnaire*, on the other hand, was highly political. Under a political regime that had reestablished censorship, Larousse celebrated the freedom of the press whenever he could do so, while Republicans sent into exile after Napoléon III's coup of December 1851 were celebrated in detailed biographical entries. The Third Republic embraced the militant lexicographer and his work, in particular the numerous grammar books he wrote for schoolchildren. Larousse became a household name, and a monument was dedicated to him in 1877, only two years after his death.

From 1841, Émile Littré (1801–1880) devoted most of his energy to what would become the *Dictionnaire historique de la langue française* (published 1863–1872). A disciple of Auguste Comte, Littré combined both positivism and a historical approach applied to language. The French language had historical roots that could be traced back to the thirteenth century, showing, once again, that the French nation had a permanence that outlived the changing political regimes. The *Dictionnaire historique* was an immediate success, in spite of its scholarly character. It dethroned the *Dictionnaire de l'Académie française* and remained the ultimate reference for almost a century (until the publication of *Le Robert*, in 1960).

Selected Bibliography: Baldinger, Kurt. *Introduction aux dictionnaires les plus importants pour l'histoire du français.* Paris: Klincksieck, 1974; Mollier, Jean-Yves. *Pierre Larousse et son temps.* Paris: Larousse, 1995; Pruvost, Jean. *Les Dictionnaires de langue française.* Paris: Honoré Champion, 2001; Rétif, André. *Pierre Larousse et son oeuvre.* Paris: Larousse, 1975; Rey, Alain. *Émile Littré. L'humaniste et les mots.* Paris: Gallimard, 1970.

Yannick Portebois

DING LING (1904–1986). This Chinese writer of stories, novels, and essays chronicled the evolving role of women in Republican China. Born Jiang Bingzhi in Linli county, Hunan, she was the daughter of a wantonly prosperous gentry family, but her father died when she was only four, leaving her mother to bring up Jiang Bingzhi and her newborn brother. After attending Shanghai's Common People's Girls School and Shanghai University, she moved to Beijing, where she met and married editor Hu Yepin and adopted the pen name Ding Ling.

In 1927, she published her first short story, "Meng Ke." "Miss Sophie's Diary"—her signature story about a depressed, manipulative, almost pathetic young female and her erotic fantasies—followed the next year. Critics like her friend **Shen Congwen** were aware that Ding Ling's writing constituted "something entirely new, something that surpassed the standard of the most recent generation and was setting a new direction." In 1928, she published her first collection of short stories, *In the Darkness.*

In 1931, Hu Yepin was executed by the nationalist Guomindang because of his activities as a member of the Chinese Communist Party (CCP). In 1932, Ding Ling herself joined the CCP and decided to cease writing about bourgeois themes like love and the conflict between love and revolution. Her novel *Flood* (1932), for example, broke new ground in the search for **socialist realism**; unfortunately, like her other works of book-length fiction, including her Stalin Prize–winning novel *The Sun Shines over the Sanggan* (1949), it would never be fully completed. Ding Ling's involvement with the CCP led, in May 1933, to her abduction by the nationalists, who held her captive until 1936, when she escaped and made her way to Yan'an with the help of CCP operatives. There, under pressure from the party, she renounced her earlier literary views to embrace socialist realism; in return, she was protected by Mao and promoted in the bureaucracy. Subsequent political problems haunted her to the very end of her days. After the Anti-Rightist Campaign of 1958, she lost her publishing privileges and went into exile (joining her husband) in the Great Northern Wasteland. During the Cultural Revolution (1966–1976), she was branded a traitor and spent five years in prison. Nevertheless, she remained loyal to the CCP until the end of her life.

Selected Bibliography: Alber, Charles J. *Embracing the Lie: Ding Ling and the Politics of Literature in the People's Republic of China.* Westport, CT: Praeger, 2004; Alber, Charles J. *Enduring the Revolution: Ding Ling and the Politics of Literature in Guomindang China.* Westport, CT: Praeger, 2002; Feuerwerker, Yi-tsi. *Ding Ling's Fiction: Ideology and Narrative in Modern Chinese Literature.* Cambridge, MA: Harvard UP, 1982; Goldman, Merle. *Literary Dissent in Communist China.* Cambridge, MA: Harvard UP, 1967; Goldman, Merle. *Sowing the Seeds of Democracy in China: Political Reform in the Deng Xiaoping Era.* Cambridge, MA: Harvard UP, 1994.

Charles J. Alber

DOCTOROW, EDGAR LAWRENCE (E. L.) (1931–). Resistant to political labeling, the author of *Billy Bathgate* (1989) is generally associated with the Left. Indeed, according to **Fredric Jameson**, he is "one of the few serious and innovative leftist novelists at work in the United States today" (21). Conservative critics have shown an appreciation for Doctorow's style but balk at his message, as when Hilton Kramer complains that Doctorow's *Ragtime* is a novel in which "bourgeois America is consigned to eternal damnation," and those critical of America are "elevated to sainthood" (79). Doctorow's novels and short stories examine social injustice in the United States, especially in regard to class and to a lesser extent **gender** and **race**. If

Doctorow ultimately finds the source of injustice in the operation of capital, he fails to offer any remedial social program. His work is more concerned with how the citizen reader identifies herself (or not) within the historical moment and with the radical **alienation**, under capitalism, of the individual human life from the destiny of the social being. Doctorow claims the novel should be about understanding power and its relation to history.

Though achieving commercial and critical success with his first novel *Welcome to Hard Times* (1960), his third and fourth novels, *The Book of Daniel* (1971) and *Ragtime* (1974), are often cited as his best sustained work. *Daniel*'s story is loosely drawn from the lives of the executed cold-war-espionage conspirators Julius and Ethel Rosenberg and their children, including the title character, who attempts to reconstruct his family's past (a metafictive act that ends up producing the novel itself, much like **Rushdie**'s *Midnight's Children*) in order to establish historical ground for his life. Though the novel looks skeptically at both the dogmatic Old Left and uncompromising ideologues of the 1960s New Left, the basic social critique of those movements is treated without irony.

Ragtime (1974), set in early-twentieth-century New York, is Doctorow's most contentious novel. It continues to develop one of his common themes, that of the corruption of family and community relations in the United States. The fortunes of three families of varying class and ethnicity are traced, each becoming intertwined with the others in a web of coincidence. While *Ragtime* utilizes many historical persons and events (J. P. Morgan, Henry Ford, **Emma Goldman,** the Lawrence textile strikes), the sometimes fictional fine details of these lives and events—and the **magical realism** of coincidence—suspend the reader somewhere between fiction and history. *Ragtime* is best understood as a social novel that answers Doctorow's own charge that novelists are being forced, by television and social science, to write only personal experience.

Critics have labeled Doctorow's novels as examples of **postmodernism** for their experimental form and unusual use of historical knowledge. *World's Fair* (1986) is almost self-consciously autobiographical. Others, such as *The Book of Daniel* and 2000's *City of God* (Doctorow's most thorough treatment of religion), use rapid point-of-view shifts and metafiction to construct their histories, while *Loon Lake* (1980) uses the technique of pastiche.

Selected Bibliography: Doctorow, E. L. *Reporting the Universe.* Cambridge, MA: Harvard UP, 2003; Harter, Carol C., and James R. Thompson. *E.L. Doctorow.* Boston: Twayne, 1990; Jameson, Fredric. *Postmodernism; or, The Cultural Logic of Late Capitalism.* Durham, NC: Duke UP, 1991; Kramer, Hilton. "Political Romance." *Commentary* 80 (October 1975): 76–80; Tokarczyk, Michelle M. *E.L. Doctorow's Skeptical Commitment.* New York: Peter Lang, 2000; Trenner, Richard, ed. *E.L. Doctorow: Essays and Conversations.* Princeton, NJ: Ontario Review P, 1983.

David Leaton

DON QUIJOTE (1605; 1615), an important classic of **Spanish literature** by **Miguel de Cervantes** (1547–1616). Often regarded as the world's first modern novel, *Don Quijote* was published in two parts. The first part, published in 1605 as *El ingenioso hidalgo Don Quijote de la Mancha*, is primarily episodic in structure. The second part, published in 1615 as *La segunda parte del ingenioso hidalgo Don Quijote de la Mancha*, shows more narrative cohesion. In 1614, while Cervantes was working on the second part of *Don Quijote*, a man named Alonso Fernández de Avellaneda published *El segundo tomo del Ingenioso Hidalgo don Quijote de la Mancha*, his own continuation of Cervantes's book. In response, Cervantes not only expedited the completion of his sequel but also used it in order to critique Avellaneda's effort. Both the first and second parts of *Don Quijote* creatively reflect other themes and events from Cervantes's life, such as his five-year captivity in Algiers under Turkish pirates.

Though *Don Quijote*'s biographical value may be significant, its literary, cultural, and social importance is enduring. *Don Quijote* is primarily a parody and critique of the romances of chivalry, such as *Amadís de Gaula*, that were popular throughout the sixteenth century. The plot of *Don Quijote* features the wanderings and adventures of a middle-aged man from La Mancha who, after voraciously reading scores of romances of chivalry, strives to emulate the image, words, and deeds of chivalric heroes. This man, eventually known as Don Quijote, gradually attains and invents a host of quasi-chivalric trappings, including a horse (Rocinante), a squire (Sancho Panza), and a lady (Dulcinea). In addition, *Don Quijote* artfully uses the language, style, and content of other literary genres (such as epic, pastoral, the novella, and picaresque) in order to examine a variety of issues related to life and literature, reality and fantasy, the art of narration, and many other themes. In effect, *Don Quijote* serves as a nuanced compendium of glimpses into a wide range of artistic, cultural, social, and political issues. Some of these issues appear regularly throughout the work, such as the role of honor and *limpieza de sangre* (purity of blood) within golden-age Spain's rigid caste system. Other issues, such as the career of Roque Guinart (a legendary Robin Hood figure) and Sancho's governorship of the island of Barataria, are featured in specific chapters.

The legacy of *Don Quijote* has been immense. During Cervantes's lifetime, several editions of the first part were printed in the original Spanish, and English and French translations were published. Since Cervantes's death, *Don Quijote* has been translated into more languages than any other work of fiction. A short list of writers significantly influenced by *Don Quijote* includes Borges, Defoe, **Dickens**, **Dostoevsky**, Fielding, **Flaubert**, **García Márquez**, Goya, **Joyce**, Melville, **Swift**, and **Tolstoy**.

Selected Bibliography: Dudley, Edward. *The Endless Text:* Don Quixote *and the Hermeneutics of Romance.* Albany: SUNY P, 1997; Higuera, Henry. *Eros and Empire: Politics and Christianity in* Don Quixote. Lanham, MD: Rowman & Littlefield, 1995; Maravall, José Antonio. *Utopia and Counterutopia in the "Quixote."* Trans. Robert W. Felkel. Detroit: Wayne State UP, 1991; Parr, James A. *Don Quixote: An Anatomy of Subversive Discourse.* Newark, DE: Juan de la Cuesta, 1988; Quint, David. *Cervantes's Novel of Modern Times: A New Reading of* Don Quijote. Princeton, NJ: Princeton UP, 2003.

R. John McCaw

DOS PASSOS, JOHN (1896–1970). One of the most important and formally innovative radical novelists of the 1920s and 1930s, Dos Passos is best known for his monumental *U.S.A.* **trilogy** (1930–1937) but over his lifetime authored over forty novels, plays, travelogues, and works of nonfiction, as well as scores of journalistic pieces. Dos Passos was born out of wedlock to a Virginia blue blood, Lucy Addison Sprigg, and a wealthy Portuguese immigrant lawyer, John Roderigo Dos Passos, who authored several pro-capitalist books. Memories of the author's unhappy "hotel childhood" and outsider status find their way into the Camera Eye sections of *U.S.A.* Dos Passos attended the Choate School and then Harvard University. Dos Passos saw the Great War at first hand as a participant in the Norton-Harjes Ambulance Service in 1917–1918. Ejected for disloyalty, he joined the army and was headed back to Europe when the armistice was declared. Dos Passos remained in France through May Day 1919, served in a military hospital, went AWOL and was discharged, traveled in Spain and the eastern Mediterranean, and settled in New York in the early 1920s. ("Settled" would never describe Dos Passos, however; all his life he was a peripatetic traveler.) *Rosinante to the Road Again* (1922) reflected Dos Passos's sympathies with Spanish anarchism. *One Man's Initiation—1917* (1920) and *Three Soldiers* (1921) drew upon his wartime experiences, as would *Nineteen-Nineteen*, the second volume of *U.S.A.*

Dos Passos was deeply involved in the cultural radicalism of the 1920s. **Ernest Hemingway**, Edmund Wilson, Gerald and Sara Murphy, F. Scott Fitzgerald, and *New Masses* editor **Mike Gold** were good friends for some years. Dos Passos's expressionist plays—including *The Garbage Man* (1925) and *Airways Inc.* (1928)—and his 1925 collage-style novel, *Manhattan Transfer*, manifested the influence of modernist experimentalism in combination with a growing critique of capitalist alienation and commodification of human relationships. The campaign to save the Italian anarchists Sacco and Vanzetti from execution moved Dos Passos to the Left, prompting him to interview the men on death row for his pamphlet *Facing the Chair* (1927) and subsequently to compose *U.S.A.*, consisting of *The Forty-Second Parallel* (1930), *Nineteen-Nineteen* (1932), and *The Big Money* (1936).

Dos Passos's most serious engagement with leftist politics occurred in the early 1930s. Part of a writers' delegation including **Theodore Dreiser**, Lester Cohen, and Samuel Ornitz, he reported on conditions among striking miners in Harlan County, Kentucky, in 1931. In 1932, he derided the Socialists as "near beer," supported CPUSA presidential and vice presidential candidates William Z. Foster and James W. Ford, and wrote in defense of the Scottsboro boys. In 1935, Dos Passos gave a speech entitled "The Writer as Technician" at the founding convention of the League of American Writers. By the mid-1930s, however, when the Popular Front was drawing increasing numbers of writers toward the CPUSA, Dos Passos was turning away from the Communist Left. His 1939 novel about the Spanish Civil War, *Adventures of a Young Man* (1939), is a chronicle of disillusionment, ending in its hero's death through Communist betrayal.

Dos Passos's subsequent writings limn a dramatic move to the Far Right and, for the most part, loss of literary power. The historical meditations in *The Ground We Stand On* (1941) testified to Dos Passos's rediscovery of the legacy of the founding fathers. *The Grand Design* (1949) attacked the New Deal. The autobiographical *Chosen Country* (1951) revisited the terrain of Dos Passos's childhood, this time in a somewhat forced affirmation of Americanism. *Most Likely to Succeed* (1954), a roman à clef focusing on Dos Passos's former friend John Howard Lawson, lampooned Hollywood leftists. *Midcentury* (1961) bitterly chronicled "the century's decline." Dos Passos became not just anti-leftist but anti-liberal, supporting Joseph McCarthy in the 1950s and Barry Goldwater in the 1960s.

To understand Dos Passos's dramatic political and literary reversal, some scholars have turned to psychoanalysis, arguing that Dos Passos's early radicalism was based in repressed anger toward his politically conservative father. His midlife rightward swing presumably reflected an eventual identification with the patriarchal authority he had once rejected. Others have proposed that Dos Passos's radicalism was always tinged with libertarian individualism and suspicion of collectivism; his later conservatism is seen as not entirely incompatible with his earlier radicalism. The voice of the Left heard intermittently in *One Man's Initiation, Three Soldiers*, and *Manhattan Transfer* is noted to be more anarchist than Communist. In *U.S.A.,* it is stressed that the I.W.W. member Fenian McCreary ("Mac") and the Left-liberal fellow traveler Mary French are much more positively portrayed than are the Communists Ben Compton (a neurotic Trotskyist) and Don Stevens (a cardboard Stalinist). Critics pursuing this consistency argument note the autobiographical Camera Eye's continual "peeling the onion of doubt" regarding leftist political commitment.

To comprehend fully Dos Passos's move to the Far Right, however, it is necessary to view critically his embrace of American nationalism over many decades. Although Dos Passos's writings of the 1920s and 1930s display sharp class polarities, and the Camera Eye famously declares, "all right we are two nations," it also evinces disappointment that "America our nation has been beaten by strangers . . . who have taken the clean words our fathers spoke and made them slimy and foul." Moreover, there is a distinctly nativist tinge even in Dos Passos's most leftist writings. With the possible exception of *Manhattan Transfer's* Congo Jake, characters of non–Anglo Saxon descent are portrayed in distasteful language; Sacco and Vanzetti, in *Facing the Chair*, are reconstituted as the true descendants of the Pilgrims. Such early manifestations of populist patriotism and nativism would be reinflected in Dos Passos's later work and thought.

Selected Bibliography: Landsberg, Melvin. *Dos Passos' Path to U.S.A.: A Critical Biography, 1912–1936.* Boulder, CO: Associated UP, 1972; Ludington, C. Townsend. *John Dos Passos: A Twentieth-Century Odyssey.* New York: E.P. Dutton, 1980; Rosen, Robert C. *John Dos Passos: Politics and the Writer.* Lincoln: U of Nebraska P, 1981; Smith, Jon. "John Dos Passos, Anglo-Saxon." *Modern Fiction Studies* 44 (Summer 1998): 282–305.

Barbara Foley

DOSTOEVSKY, FYODOR MIKHAILOVICH (1821–1881).

The son of a doctor, Dostoevsky completed studies at the Academy of Engineers in St. Petersburg and served briefly as a military engineer. His heart was always with literature, however, and in 1844 he resigned his commission to become a writer, achieving instant success with his first novel, *Poor Folk (Bednyye lyudi,* 1846). His humanitarian concerns and his passionate opposition to the institution of serfdom led him to become involved with a small group of radicals dedicated to promoting social justice. He was arrested in 1849, and held in solitary confinement for eight months. After being subjected to a mock execution, he was transported to Siberia, where he served four years at hard labor, followed by nearly six years of army service.

After his release, Dostoevsky returned to St. Petersburg at the end of 1859 and resumed his literary activities, establishing, with his brother, Mikhail, the monthly journals *Time* (*Vremia*, 1861–1864) and *Epoch* (*Epokha*, 1864–1865). Both attempted to maintain an independent policy among the contending groups within the Russian intelligentsia; their relationship with the radicals deteriorated, however, and *Epoch's* political stance moved distinctly to the Right.

Political issues figure prominently in Dostoevsky's *Winter Notes on Summer Impressions* (*Zimnie zametki o letnikh vpechatleniyakh*, 1863), a critique, in the form of travel notes, of European (chiefly Parisian) society. The ideals of the **French Revolution**, he argues, have led to fragmented societies that can be held together only by the power of law; Russia, by contrast, has preserved the principle of genuine Christian brotherhood that can ensure both social justice and individual freedom. *Notes from Underground* (*Zapiski iz podpolya*, 1864) dismisses the utopia envisioned by radical thinkers as an "antheap" in which humans may gain material security only at the price of their freedom.

Dostoevsky's first major novel, *Crime and Punishment* (*Prestupleniye i nakazaniye*, 1866), was a critical success, but a heavy burden of debt meant that he and his wife had to spend the period 1867–1870 abroad in order to escape debtor's prison. Here his views grew increasingly nationalistic and sharply critical of European influence on Russian institutions. Western Europe, he believed, lacked a solid spiritual foundation and was plagued by divisions—religious, intellectual, and political—that doomed it to eventual collapse. The two novels he wrote while abroad, *The Idiot* (*Idiot*, 1868) and **The Devils** (*Besy*, 1871), reflect some of his antipathy toward Europe and his hopes and fears for Russia.

After his return to Russia, he again gravitated toward journalism, taking the position of editor of a conservative weekly, *The Citizen* (*Grazhdanin*), through 1873 and early 1874. Here he produced a series of articles entitled "A Writer's Diary" ("Dnevnik pisatelya")—a title he revived a few years later for his own independent periodical, of which he was publisher, editor, and sole contributor. *A Writer's Diary* became enormously influential in its time and was read regularly by members of Russia's ruling circles. Monthly issues appeared through 1876 and 1877, when Dostoevsky suspended publication to write his final novel, *The Brothers Karamazov* (*Bratya Karamazovy*, 1879–1880); single issues were published in 1880 and 1881. The *Diary* provided Dostoevsky a forum to express his views on a broad range of topics, but its focus was his commentary on the current state of Russia. Dostoevsky's political stance was one of religious nationalism; the orthodoxy of Russia's peasant masses, he maintained, had preserved the genuine message and practice of Christianity that had been lost in the West. Although he admired European culture, he was suspicious of Western democracy and contemptuous of a constitutional monarchy. Russia should maintain its own "Russian socialism," in which an autocratic monarch, who shared the orthodoxy of his people, would act on the basis of popular consensus and respond to the needs of his subjects. Russia's mission, according to Dostoevsky, was to convey this message of brotherhood to a Europe that was living out its final days.

Selected Bibliography: Carter, Stephen K. *The Political and Social Thought of F.M. Dostoevsky.* New York: Garland, 1991; Frank, Joseph. *Dostoevsky.* 5 vols. Princeton: Princeton UP, 1976–2002.

Kenneth Lantz

DOUGLASS, FREDERICK (1818–1895). Born a slave in Maryland, Frederick Augustus Washington Bailey was to become one of the greatest African American abolitionists of the nineteenth century. Escaping from slavery in 1838, he became a personal favorite of the abolitionist leaders William Lloyd Garrison and Wendell Phillips. His first of three autobiographies—*Narrative of the Life of Frederick Douglass, an American Slave*—was published in 1845. (The second, *My Bondage and My Freedom*, appeared in 1855, and the third, *Life and Times of Frederick Douglass*, was published in 1881.) This first book testifies to his journey from slavery to freedom as Douglass dramatizes an important transformation within black consciousness: "you have seen how a man was made a slave; you shall see how a slave was made a man." Long neglected, this volume was reprinted by black-power activists and black-studies supporters in the twentieth century in their search for black heroes. Consequently, Douglass was canonized as the quintessential "self-made man" and black slave narrator, a position he still holds within African American studies today, as Black History Month is annually held in February, the month of his birth. Within his own lifetime, Douglass, however, remained uneasy with his representative status as exemplary "chattel" and with the parameters placed around his creativity by white philanthropists. As a sign of his rebellion, Douglass published in 1853 one of the earliest works of black fiction—a novella entitled *The Heroic Slave*, in which he exulted over the possibilities of his romantic imagination by presenting his protagonist, Madison Washington, as the ideal Byronic hero: "Hereditary bondmen! / Know ye not, he who would be free, themselves must strike the blow!" Douglass spent 1845–1847 in Europe, when he became both legally free and possessed of enough funds to launch his own newspaper, the *North Star* (later to become *Frederick Douglass's Paper* and later still, *Douglass's Monthly*). By the mid-1850s, Douglass was no longer interested in performing the role of outraged fugitive, a curiosity to audiences. He had acquired a reputation as an antislavery orator in his own right, he had established himself as a crusader for women's rights and for the suffering laborer as well as the bondman, and he had proven his capabilities as an author; he was later to distinguish himself as a statesman as consul-general to Haiti. Douglass laid the foundations for black literature as we know it today by his unflinching determination to resist oppression of all kinds (going well beyond the opposition to slavery) in his relentless pursuit for freedom. He espoused a radical politics of personal liberation but also a literary poetics that sought to secure African American independence of aesthetic expression.

Selected Bibliography: Andrews, William L., ed. *The Oxford Frederick Douglass Reader.* Oxford: Oxford UP, 1996; Gates, Henry Louis, Jr. *Figures in Black: Words, Signs, and the "Racial" Self.* New York: Oxford UP, 1987; Levine, Robert S. *Martin Delany, Frederick Douglass, and the Politics of Representative Identity.* Chapel Hill: North Carolina UP, 1997; Rice, Alan J., and Martin Crawford, eds. *Liberating Sojourn: Frederick Douglass and Transatlantic Reform.* Athens: U of Georgia P, 1999; Sundquist, Eric J., ed. *Frederick Douglass: New Literary and Historical Essays.* New York: Cambridge UP, 1990.

Celeste-Marie Bernier

DREISER, THEODORE (1871–1945), prolific American novelist, essayist, belletrist, social thinker, and public intellectual. From the 1890s until his death, he was as adroit at lauding the success ethic as he was in describing an exploited tenement population. His journalistic outrage at the working-class poverty of Progressive Era New York City, poured out in socialist *New York Call* pieces, was no bar to his eagerly seeking profits from mainstream popular magazines and anything he penned, from stories to plays to novels such as *Jennie Gerhardt* (1911). Some of his newest and most persuasive explicators find him long engaged in the "business" of writing realist fiction and thereby upholding the monied hegemony of the United States. Yet Dreiser, well before the 1921 founding of the **Communist Party** of the United States (CPUSA) and certainly in his "Red years" (1929–1945), was crusading in print for the underclass and welcomed to the CPUSA literary organ, ***New Masses***.

Such dualities have puzzled Dreiser scholars for generations. The intemperateness of his journalism, interviews, and assorted ephemera heightens the confusion inscribed in his key novels *Sister Carrie* (1900); *Jennie Gerhardt*; *An American Tragedy* (1925); and the Frank Cowperwood trilogy: *The Financier* (1912), *The Titan* (1914), and the posthumously published *The Stoic* (1947). Was he a wavering Socialist? An inconsistent capitalist? A subversive in disguise, even to himself?

One way to clarity is to question the way Dreiser has been periodically reinvented as an apologist for competitive individualism, a charge that his writings belie. His allegiance to the American upward-rise ethic is permeated with challenges and subversions. Contextualizing, say, *An American Tragedy* in terms of Dreiser's interest in the communist economic system can reveal a far more "proletarian" author than has hitherto been recognized; including his many pronouncements in leftist periodicals can only enhance this assessment. Examining the many documents, archival and otherwise, that attest to Dreiser's wariness about CP solutions may provide an understanding of his peculiarly American brand of radicalism.

Eric Homberger has found in many U.S. social protest writers of Dreiser's lengthy era an equivocal commitment to revolutionary change. Encoded in Dreiser's many writings is a leftist understanding of American class boundaries; a critique of nativist prejudice against "un-American workers," including within the labor movement itself; and a condemnation of the sexual exploitation of women in the workplace. Only by a thorough reading of the leftist Dreiser can we come to a better comprehension of the American one.

If there was any major lesson Dreiser learned from the thwarted attempts of his embittered blue-collar father and unrealistic servant mother to provide a large family with stability and economic well-being, it was the shameful constrictions of the lived experience of downward mobility. Unlike **Jack London** and the more privileged **Upton Sinclair**, Dreiser neither expected the working class to triumph nor offered socialist political narratives that foregrounded class struggle. Throughout his writer's life, Dreiser built on the "family narrative" played out by the hapless Dreiser family, for it was a model for key characters: the doomed Hurstwood, the exploited Jennie Gerhardt, the ambitiously unskilled Clyde Griffiths, the corporately absolute Frank Cowperwood.

Perhaps Dreiser's greatest virtue as a political thinker was his portrayal of how the American quantification of success as monetary gave "average" people a language in which to articulate far more than consumer longings: desires for love, for agency in the world, for the very spiritual essence. Enacting his own dialectic between the craving and transcending acquisitiveness, Dreiser was eloquent on the dangers of a commodifying culture that thrived on the widening gap between rich and poor.

As a storyteller, Dreiser's forte was the prescient sense of the power of money as an affective force in people's lives. He shows rather than tells how marginalized groups of hyphenated Americans are a microcosm of the larger society in which labor and capital are at odds, there is little escape from the economic tyranny of low-wage jobs, and the battles between corporate absolutism and industrial unionism are abstractions in the mental landscape of most breadwinning or homeless people. As his letters chastising luminaries such as American Federation of Labor president William Green or supporting the Left-led National Maritime Union on the Pacific Coast attest, Dreiser deplored the exclusionary politics of "Big Unionism" and the tendency of union hierarchies to profit from their members' dues.

Dreiser in modern readings was indisputably an "American" upward mobility author in that, like many American authors before and since, he was expert at marketing his impoverished ethnic boyhood in everything from retrospective memoirs to visits to the Soviet Union. He never wished to be considered an agitprop author and criticized those like **Mike Gold** for vitiating their own art by preaching the workers' revolution. He often explained away any contradictions he entertained between supporting radicalism and dwelling within a capitalist system and did so skillfully and repeatedly, as in his *Russian Diary* (1928). Yet for decades he was lauded by the Communist Party and its news organs for visiting Harlan County with **John Dos Passos** and *New Masses* artist William Gropper. Well past the Great Depression, he continued to be honored by the Soviets for what they saw as his class analyses in the major novels. One of his last letters, written in 1945, was a letter to William Z. Foster applying for membership in the Communist Party.

Dreiser was at his best as a political thinker when he immersed his writing in the reporter's trade he had so long practiced. His great strength was his belief in the power of certain individuals to surmount oppressive conditions and empower themselves in American society. Yet, always the observer, his fascination with all sorts and conditions of people did not extend to leftist or centrist ideologies, much less to passionate commitment to enabling an exploited social class to rise. If the American narrative that most concerned him was ultimately his own, that narrative was also a speaking chronicle of bourgeois strivings among the many disenfranchised who had neither access to radical theory nor an understanding of its power to inspire.

Selected Bibliography: Dowell, Richard. Introduction to *An Amateur Laborer* by Theodore Dreiser. Ed. Richard W. Dowell, James L. W. West III, and Neda Westlake. Philadelphia: U of Pennsylvania P, 1984; Dreiser, Theodore. *Dreiser's Russian Diary.* Ed. T. P. Riggio and James L. W. West III. Philadelphia: U of Pennsylvania P, 1996; Dreiser, Theodore. *Newspaper Days.* Ed. T. D. Nostwich. Philadelphia: U of Pennsylvania Press, 1992; Homberger, Eric. *American Writers and Radical Politics: Equivocal Commitments, 1900–39.* New York: St. Martin's P, 1989; Lingeman, Richard. *Theodore Dreiser.* 2 vols. New York: Putnam, 1990.

Laura Hapke

DU BOIS, W.E.B. (1868–1963). Du Bois's political career encompassed most of the major radical ideologies of the twentieth century: black nationalism, Marxism,

pan-Africanism, and anticolonialism. His body of political work reveals changes and vacillations endemic to the scope of his thought. Born just three years after emancipation, Du Bois's Ph.D. training in history at Harvard produced the first major study of the African slave trade in 1896. Culturally, the early Du Bois was strongly influenced by German idealism and nineteenth-century U.S. historian Alexander Crummell, a father of "contributionism"—a proto-Afrocentrism dedicated to revealing Africa's influence on world cultures. By 1900, Du Bois had thrown his support behind an emerging pan-Africanism, attending the first Pan-African Conference in London in 1900. These ideas and influences merged in his first famous work *The Souls of Black Folk* (1903). Du Bois argued that black Americans must enter the "kingdom of culture" and offered an essentialist and idealist interpretation of "double consciousness" more indebted to the dialectics of Hegel than **Marx**. Simultaneously, Du Bois began an interest in Socialism and international events, writing in support of the Indian National Congress and continuing his readings of Marx and Engels, which he had begun as a student in Berlin. In 1906, Du Bois published the essay "The Color Line Belts the World," which extended his famous trope from *The Souls of Black Folk* to encompass struggles of brown, black, and yellow people across the world.

From 1905 to 1910, Du Bois was a cofounder and general secretary of the Niagara Movement, dedicated to black civil rights and antilynching activism. In 1910, Du Bois became a member of the board of directors of the newly formed National Association for the Advancement of Colored People (NAACP) and editor of its journal, *Crisis*. From 1911 to 1912, Du Bois was a member of the U.S. Socialist Party. He abandoned it because American Socialists refused, in his view, to criticize white supremacy and racism in the U.S. labor movement. The outbreak of **World War I** jolted Du Bois's thinking on race, nationalism, Socialism, and colonialism. Though he supported U.S. entry into the war, in 1915 he published the essay "The African Roots of the War," criticizing capitalists for exploiting Asian and African labor and predicting a growing resistance to colonialism. Du Bois carried this view at the first, second, and third Pan-African congresses in 1919, 1921, and 1923. Simultaneously, the **Russian Revolution** forced him to think of black American labor as part of the international proletariat. In 1926, Du Bois traveled for six weeks in the Soviet Union. In 1928, he published the novel *Dark Princess*, an allegory of efforts by Indian, Japanese, and black radicals to carry out a Soviet-inspired revolution of colored peoples in the United States, India, and Berlin. The novel is a messianic romance synthesizing Du Bois's pan-Africanism, pan-Asianism, and interest in Soviet Comintern support during the fight for black national self-determination.

Dark Princess also anticipated Du Bois's efforts in his historical opus *Black Reconstruction* (1935) to describe racism as a byproduct of capitalism. The book anchored Du Bois's "color line" thesis in economic exploitation: race supremacy was one of the "wages of whiteness," an economic benefit that prevented white worker unity with workers of color. This influential thesis, the foundation of so-called whiteness studies in the contemporary academy, moved Du Bois closer to a historical-materialist paradigm. The beginnings of **World War II** tested this paradigm anew. In 1936, Du Bois visited Germany, the Soviet Union, China, and Japan. Japan's imperialist venturing in China was initially excused by Du Bois as preferable to a white colonial takeover of the country. Du Bois's lingering "racialism," a carryover from his Afro-

centric origins, informed what was arguably the worst political judgment of his career. By the end of the war, he had recanted; Du Bois proclaimed all imperialisms
evil and concentrated his attention on new anticolonial movements in Africa and
Asia. In 1945, he was coauthor, with the communist William Patterson, of *We Charge
Genocide*, a tract attacking white supremacist colonialism presented to the newly
formed United Nations; published the book *Color and Democracy: Colonies and Peace*;
and attended the Fifth Pan-African Congress in Manchester, organized by **George
Padmore** and **Kwame Nkrumah**. In 1947, Du Bois published *The World and Africa:
An Inquiry into the Part Which Africa Has Played in World History*. The book both
sustained and revised Du Bois's earlier "contributionist" arguments, perceiving
Africa's anticolonial struggles as the key to the liberation of the colored world.

China's Communist revolution was the greatest political influence on the last period of Du Bois's life. Du Bois predicted that not just Vietnam but the Caribbean
and Africa could follow China's example. Yet Du Bois's open endorsement of China's
revolution, and increasing support for U.S. Communists and Socialists under attack
by McCarthyism, caused his dismissal by the NAACP, his firing from Atlanta University, his arrest and indictment as an "unregistered foreign agent," and the denial
of his U.S. passport in 1952. During the same period, Du Bois became vice chairman of the Left Council on African Affairs, an anticolonial organization that included Communists; chaired the Peace Information Center devoted in part to nuclear
disarmament; and was a candidate for the U.S. senate in New York on the progressive American Labor Party ticket. Demonized at home, he was lionized abroad: in
1959 he received the Lenin Peace Prize and visited China one final time, where he
was hailed by **Mao**. In the late 1950s, he topped off his literary career with an impressive epic trilogy of historical novels, *The Black Flame* (1957–1961), which is unwavering in its Marxist vision of all African American history as the history of class
conflict. In 1961, Du Bois joined the U.S. **Communist Party**, and was invited by
President Kwame Nkrumah to travel to Ghana. He became a citizen of Ghana, where
he died on August 27, 1963, on the eve of the historic March on Washington.

Du Bois's lifelong radicalism, communist sympathy, and dedication to international liberation make his the most important black political life of the twentieth
century. Scholars are still charged with the difficult task of making coherent a political career that was mercurial, contradictory, and evolutionary.

Selected Bibliography: Du Bois, W.E.B. "The Color Line Belts the World." *Collier's Weekly*, 20 Oc-
tober 1906; Du Bois, W.E.B. *The Souls of Black Folk: Essays and Sketches*. 1903. London: Penguin, 1996;
Du Bois, W.E.B. *The World and Africa*. New York: International Publishers, 1946; Horne, Gerald. *Black
& Red: W.E.B. Du Bois and the Afro-American Response to the Cold War, 1944–1963*. Albany: SUNY P,
1986; Lewis, David Levering. *W.E.B. Du Bois: Biography of a Race*. New York: Henry Holt, 1993;
Marable, Manning. *W.E.B. Du Bois: Black Radical Democrat*. Boston: Twayne, 1986.

Bill V. Mullen

DURAS, MARGUERITE (1914–1996). Born in French Indochina, Duras was a
prodigious writer, dramatist, and filmmaker, whose career spanned over fifty years. She
became one of the most influential and fascinating cultural and intellectual figures in
postwar France. Her early, fairly conventional novels appeared during and just after

World War II, when she was a member of the French Communist Party. Expelled from the party in 1950, she published *The Sea Wall* (*Un Barrage contre le Pacifique*), a harsh neorealist tale of growing up in Indochina. With the blank, seemingly nonexpressive prose of *The Square* (*Le Square*, 1955) and *Moderato Cantabile* (1958), Duras became associated with the nouveau roman, although her themes of subversive female desire, pain, and alienation set her firmly apart. She achieved international fame with her screenplay for Alain Resnais's 1959 film *Hiroshima mon amour*, followed by her major long novels—all fragmentary, abstract, and non linear in style—including *The Ravishing of Lol Stein* (*Le Ravissement de Lol V. Stein*, 1964), *The Vice-Consul* (*Le Vice-consul*, 1965), and *L'Amante anglaise* (1967).

A member of the revolutionary action committee of students and writers at the Sorbonne during May 1968, Duras reached a kind of end point with *Destroy, She Said* (*Détruire dit-elle*, 1969) and *L'Amour* (1971), after which she turned almost exclusively to filmmaking. Films such as *Nathalie Granger* (1972), *India Song* (1975), and *The Lorry* (*Le Camion*, 1977) revealed her aim to destroy the conventional foundations of cinema. Her films became ever more minimalist and desynchonized, employing neutral "master-images," black screen, and her own voice-over. Upon her return to writing in 1980 with *L'Été 80* (*Summer*, 1980), a new set of thematics emerged, including explicit incestuous and sadomasochistic desire, selfhood, aging, collaboration, and the situation of the Jews with whom she increasingly identified. The sparse and poetic *The Malady of Death* (*La Maladie de la mort*, 1982) was a brilliant deconstruction of sexual difference and fantasy, and the autobiographical novel, *The Lover* (*L'Amant*, 1984*)*, winner of the Prix Goncourt and a global best-seller, transformed her into France's most widely translated living writer. Radically diverse works followed, including *The War: A Memoir* (*La Douleur*, 1985), based on her experiences in the Resistance in World War II, and *Blue Eyes, Black Hair* (*Les Yeux bleus cheveux noirs*, 1986), a brave study of an impossible love between a straight woman and a gay man, which reflected her own turbulent relationship with Yann Andréa, with whom she lived from 1980 until her death. By now a virtual icon of the Mitterrand Left, Duras also worked intensively in the media, particularly journalism.

Duras's absolutist artistic practice often operated in the reverse direction of her stated commitment to the "other" due to a compulsive rhetorical practice of appropriation, recuperation, and sublimation. In 1988, she suffered a nearly fatal coma yet still continued to write. Her final text, *No More* (*C'est tout*, 1995), which stages her own physical death, is one of her most searing and uncompromising works.

Selected Bibliography: Cohen, Susan D. *Women and Discourse in the Fiction of Marguerite Duras: Love, Legends, Language.* Oxford: Macmillan, 1993; Crowley, Martin. *Duras, Writing and the Ethical: Making the Broken Whole.* Oxford: Clarendon P, 2000; Hill, Leslie. *Marguerite Duras: Apocalyptic Desires.* London: Routledge, 1993; Williams, James S. *The Erotics of Passage: Pleasure, Politics, and Form in the Later Work of Marguerite Duras.* New York: St. Martin's, 1997.

James S. Williams

DYSTOPIAN LITERATURE. The word *dystopia* is a combination of the Latin root *dys-*: "bad" or "abnormal" and the Greek root *-topos*: "place." The term *anti-utopia* is also sometimes used. Dystopian literature therefore tells stories about bad places;

specifically, it is literature about possible future or near-future societies that will re-sult if current or hypothetical political, environmental, and technological trends are amplified by history into overarching principles of social organization. Usually dystopias are dominated by a sinister political elite, but the evils of dystopias are also sometimes attributed to ignorance, poverty, overpopulation, commercialism, or tech-nology run amuck.

Though the genre of dystopian literature has precedents dating back to such satir-ical works as **Swift**'s *Gulliver's Travels* (1726) and Voltaire's *Candide* (1759), the genre in its modern form was defined by three works: **Orwell**'s *Nineteen Eighty-Four* (1949), **Huxley**'s *Brave New World* (1932), and **Zamyatin**'s *We* (1924). Together these titles represent the most widely discussed **science fiction** novels of the twenti-eth century. All three exhibit the essential themes and motifs of the dystopian genre: a totalitarian state that uses technology, modern compartmentalized bureaucracy, total surveillance, and engineered sexual norms to control every aspect of people's lives. In the case of *Nineteen Eighty-Four*, the state even constructs the very "thought crimes" that lead individuals to their criminal dissensions. Each novel portrays the unsuccessful efforts of protagonists who struggle with the authority of the state, with the understanding that the protagonists' efforts transcend mere individualism and as-pire to nothing less than the struggle to maintain humanity itself. At this level, dystopian literature takes on the task and methods of **Menippean satire**, not only of-fering a warning of bad times to come, but advancing a diagnosis of the intellectual myths and the philosophical credulousness that make dehumanization possible. A host of dystopian works variously explore these problems, bringing with them vary-ing perspectives on the criteria of human nature and speculating on possible tech-nological and bureaucratic methods of social control. Drugs, poverty, lobotomy, consumerism, relentless propaganda, laissez-faire capitalism, micro-managed bureau-cracies, police states, psychological theory, book burning, ecological disaster, computer-generated false realities, psychopathic computers, runaway robots, forced immigrations—there are as many ways to dehumanize the human race as there are authors seeking to publish novels on the subject.

Some critics explain dystopian literature as a dialectic development of the utopian literary genre; others see the form as an outcome of Menippean satire. Both per-spectives are correct. Dystopian literature clearly represents a response to the claims advanced by utopian literature, while an examination of the distinctions between sat-ire and dystopian literature underscores their shared philosophical project. Both forms pursue the analysis of intellectual mythology through portraying the conflict, brutality, ignorance, intolerance, euphemism, and passivity that are the result of pos-itivism, scientism, and various modern orthodoxies; both forms are literary. Perhaps as an outgrowth of their metaphysical activity, Menippean satire and dystopian lit-erature explore the limits of idiosyncratic humor. Although the humor of literary dystopia is often manic and bizarre, it functions (as it does in satire) as a source of normalizing understanding through which dichotomies of right/wrong and good/evil are identified and established. Nevertheless, the humor of dystopia is usually dark and pessimistic, reflecting alarm, paranoia, confusion, and hysteria, while satire is often simply clever or funny. The key distinction, however, is in the way the two forms analyze intellectual mythology. Dystopian literature locates conceptual confusion in the future and portrays hypothetical institutions that illustrate the sociological ramifications of intellectual mythology and modern orthodoxy. While dystopian literature essays prognostication and prophecy, satire locates conceptual confusion and intellectual mythology in the present and provides a diagnosis—the emphasis is not on the possible future histories of individuals and societies, but on the specific forms of the philosophical credulousness, the conceptual confusion, and the misapprehensions of language that produce intellectual mythology.

A host of dystopian works can be approached through identifying the modernist myths they are attacking. In *That Hideous Strength* (1945), C. S. Lewis demonstrates that the psychology of the scientific corporate institution is the culprit. Lewis's scientific bureaucracy emerges where human identification is displaced by a system that divorces people from the core tradition of their own humanity. The hegemony of the scientific bureaucracy is rooted in an environment of fear, politicized science, and overwork, and the institution works to enhance these conditions. Lewis suggests that the university is the ideal context in which this dystopian corporate psychology can germinate and evolve. In the novel *Bend Sinister* (1947), **Vladimir Nabokov** identifies mechanistic ontological theory as the root of dystopia. The plot of *Bend Sinister* follows the movements of a philosophy professor who is pursued by a despot seeking an endorsement of his party's theory of human nature, which emphasizes the practical virtue of dumbing down the population to a consistent generalized level. In *A Clockwork Orange* (1962), Anthony Burgess perfectly realizes the generic dynamics of intellectual myth and dystopia. In this work, the myth is predicated on the absolute vindication of the inner child. Burgess portrays a society that assumes the realization of one's immediate desires is the one legitimate goal of all individuals. Where conflicts occur, torture and conditioning are the essential means through which social equilibrium can be identified and restored. Burgess's evil protagonist, who is himself the subject of torture and conditioning, ironically represents the novel's greatest advocate of such measures. Torture and conditioning is the direct and simple solution that appeals to the selfish and immature mind, and in this dystopia (as in many others), it is the selfish and immature mind, vindicated by the intellectual pretensions and Paleolithic symbology of the authoritarian state, that holds sway.

The dystopian genre has continued in subsequent decades to be an important element of science fiction. Of particular note in this regard is the work of the British science-fiction writer John Brunner, who produced a sequence of impressive dystopian satires that included *Stand on Zanzibar* (1968), *The Jagged Orbit* (1969), *The Sheep Look Up* (1972), and *The Shockwave Rider* (1975). In addition, writers with literary reputations outside the realm of science fiction—such as **Angela Carter**, P. D. James, Iain Banks, John Updike, T. C. Boyle, and **Margaret Atwood**—have also produced dystopian works.

Selected Bibliography: Booker, M. Keith. *Dystopian Literature: A Theory and Research Guide.* Westport, CT: Greenwood, 1994; Kaplan, Carter. *Critical Synoptics: Menippean Satire and the Analysis of Intellectual Mythology.* Madison: Fairleigh Dickinson UP, 2000; Kumar, Krishan. *Utopia and Anti-Utopia in Modern Times.* Oxford: Basil Blackwell, 1987; Moylan, Tom, and Raffaella Baccolini, eds. *Dark Horizons: Science Fiction and the Dystopian Imagination.* London: Routledge, 2003.

Carter Kaplan

◦ E ◦

EAGLETON, TERRY (1943–). A third-generation Irish Catholic immigrant with a working-class background, Eagleton is a renowned Marxist critic and theorist who was born in Salford, England, and educated at Trinity College Cambridge, where he studied with the Marxist cultural theorist **Raymond Williams**. He taught at Oxford University for over thirty years and has acquired a reputation for his eclectic but trenchant political approach to literary and cultural studies. He has also become known for popularizing Marxism and literary theory with such well-known primers as *Marxism and Literary Criticism* (1976, 2002) and *Literary Theory: An Introduction* (1983, 1996), the latter having sold nearly one million copies worldwide. In addition to his academic work, he has written fiction, plays, poetry, and memoirs.

Primers aside, Eagleton's most influential works of theory are *Criticism and Ideology: A Study in Marxist Literary Theory* (1976), *Walter Benjamin; or, Towards a Revolutionary Criticism* (1981), and *The Ideology of the Aesthetic* (1990). The first work attempts to fashion a "science of the text," drawing its inspiration from the fusion of Marxism and structuralism in the writings of **Louis Althusser** and **Pierre Macherey**. *Walter Benjamin* advocates a more practical and committed approach to literature, supplementing textual studies with cultural criticism, and taking its cue not only from **Walter Benjamin** but also from **Bertolt Brecht** and feminist criticism (the book is dedicated to the Norwegian feminist critic Toril Moi, with whom Eagleton had a ten-year relationship). *The Ideology of the Aesthetic*, finally, examines the political, social, and ethical issues raised by the category of the aesthetic, focusing primarily on German philosophy, and proceeding from Alexander Baumgarten and Immanuel Kant to Friedrich Nietzsche, Martin Heidegger, and **Theodor Adorno**.

More recently, Eagleton has criticized postmodern theory in *The Illusions of Postmodernism* (1996) and suggested new directions for cultural studies in the wake of the era of "high" theory in *After Theory* (2003). Drawing mainly on his occasional journalistic work, Eagleton has also assembled his polemical pieces on major modern and contemporary writers and critics in *Figures of Dissent: Critical Essays on Fish, Spivak, Zizek and Others* (2003). In addition, he has argued for the political and ethical relevance of tragic literature in *Sweet Violence: The Idea of the Tragic* (2003), touching on major theories and texts from the classical world to the present.

Selected Bibliography: Eagleton, Terry. *After Theory.* New York: Basic Books, 2003; Eagleton, Terry. *Criticism and Ideology: A Study in Marxist Literary Theory.* London: NLB, 1976; Eagleton, Terry. *Figures of Dissent: Critical Essays on Fish, Spivak, Zizek and Others.* London: Verso, 2003; Eagleton, Terry. *The Function of Criticism: From the Spectator to Post-Structuralism.* London: Verso, 1984; Eagleton, Terry. *The Idea of Culture.* Oxford: Blackwell, 2000; Eagleton, Terry. *The Ideology of the Aesthetic.* Oxford: Blackwell, 1990; Eagleton, Terry. *The Illusions of Postmodernism.* Oxford: Blackwell, 1996; Eagleton, Terry. *Literary Theory: An Introduction.* 1983. 2nd ed. Minneapolis: U of Minnesota P, 1996; Eagleton, Terry. *Marxism and Literary Criticism.* London: Routledge, 2002; Eagleton, Terry. *The Significance of Theory.* Oxford: Blackwell, 1989; Eagleton, Terry. *Walter Benjamin, or, Towards a Revolutionary Criticism.* London: Verso, 1981; Haslett, Moyra. "Terry Eagleton." *The Edinburgh Encyclopedia of Modern Criticism and Theory.* Ed. Julian Wolfreys. Edinburgh: Edinburgh UP, 2002; Regan, Stephen, ed. *The Eagleton Reader.* Oxford: Blackwell, 1998.

Mitchell R. Lewis

EASTER RISING (1916). On Easter Monday, April 24, 1916, Irish nationalists launched an armed insurrection aimed at establishing political freedom in Ireland. Long-standing discontent with British rule and the British decision to suspend the Home Rule Bill following their entrance into **World War I** in 1914 exacerbated anti-British sympathies. Temporarily putting aside ideological differences, the insurgents—including one thousand five hundred members of the largely pro-Catholic and Gaelic Irish Volunteers Force (IVF), a two-hundred-person contingent from the socialist James Connolly's Irish Citizen Army (ICA), and volunteers from both Cumann na mBan (League of Women) and Sinn Féin—seized several key targets in Dublin, most notably the General Post Office (GPO). The British military's response was brutally effective, and on April 29, Rising commander Padraig Pearse surrendered unconditionally. British officials imposed martial law, executed fifteen revolt leaders, and jailed over thirty-five hundred suspected nationalists across the country, turning a relatively unpopular and ineffective military campaign into a powerful myth of martyrdom that sped along the demise of direct British rule. Comments by Connelly and Pearse, themselves executed, suggest that the real object of the revolt was to create a "blood sacrifice" that would inspire Irish antipathy toward the British. On the other hand, despite the Catholic resonances of this sacrificial notion, much of the ideology of the rebellion was modern, modeled after events such as the **French Revolution**.

The literary connections of the Rising are inherent because many of its leaders came from the intellectual and artistic circles inspired by the Irish Renaissance, including the Gaelic scholar/poet Pearse, whose patriotic poem "Mother" was written while he awaited execution; the poet Thomas MacDonagh; and Joseph Plunkett, who coedited the *Irish Review* with MacDonagh. The Rising also inspired a number of memoirs, such as *Fighting Women* (1934) by Constance Markeivicz, the "Red Countess" who was an ICA commander, and eyewitness accounts of noncombatants, such as *The Insurrection of Dublin* (1916) by the poet James Stephens.

Almost every major Irish writer of the twentieth century responded to the Easter Rising, either in literary works, interviews, or personal correspondence, and often less than sympathetically. **William Butler Yeats**'s "The Rose Tree," "Sixteen Dead Men," and "Easter 1916" commemorate the executed leaders; however, the latter poem's oft-mentioned ambiguity about the necessity of political violence continues to cloud critical assessments of Yeats. **James Joyce**'s portrayal of the belligerent, xenophobic Citizen in the "Cyclops" chapter of *Ulysses* (1922) reveals his own conflicted thoughts about the tenor of Irish nationalism, and **Sean O'Casey**'s proletarian play *The Plough and the Stars* (1926) offers an appraisal of the Rising's leaders so vitriolic that it allegedly inspired a riot at its first production. Most recent treatments of the Rising have been conventional historical romances but notable politically conscious works include Roddy Doyle's mock historical novel *A Star Called Henry* (1999), which focuses on the class divisions among the insurgents, and Jamie O'Neill's investigation of the significance of homoerotic desire in his portrayal of Pearse and Roger Casement in *At Swim, Two Boys* (2001).

Selected Bibliography: Caulfield, Max. *The Easter Rebellion, Dublin 1916.* Dublin: Robert Rinehart, 1963; Coogan, Tim Pat. *1916: The Easter Rising.* Cassell: London, 2001; Kiberd, Declan. *Inventing Ireland: The Literature of the Modern Nation.* London: Jonathan Cape, 1995.

James Laughton

EASTERN AND CENTRAL EUROPEAN LITERATURE. The historically unstable political landscape of eastern and central Europe makes discussion of politically themed literature from the region both difficult and vitally important. Although the ethnic, linguistic, and cultural subdivisions in the region are traceable over time despite oft-shifting political boundaries, the definition of national political literatures is dicey work at best. The eighteenth and nineteenth centuries witnessed a continual competition among Prussia (later Germany), Austria (later Austria-Hungary), Russia, and the Ottoman Empire for political influence in the region. Only with the weakening and eventual collapse of Austria-Hungary and the Ottoman Empire in the late nineteenth and early twentieth century did most of the contemporary eastern and central European nation-states begin to emerge, although most have undergone numerous permutations to arrive at their current borders and political systems. As a result, the bulk of the political literature that is associated with the ethnic/national groups that comprise contemporary eastern and central Europe dates from roughly the mid-nineteenth century onward. Poland and Greece, nations with somewhat longer histories of political independence, are perhaps the most notable exceptions to this rule. [**Note:** Since **Yugoslav literature** and **German literature** are covered in other entries, eastern and central Europe is herein defined as the contemporary nations of Albania, Bulgaria, the Czech Republic, Greece, Hungary, Poland, Romania, and Slovakia. The Baltic states, Belarus, and Ukraine are covered within **Russian literature** because of Russian cultural dominance in those areas since the Napoleonic wars.]

Lóránt Czigány describes the early to mid-nineteenth century as the time during which the "distinctly Eastern European phenomenon" of the "National Poet" emerged. He states that "the poet became the mouthpiece of his community, giving moral sustenance and political guidance in verse." Because of the supremacy of "foreign" powers (i.e., Prussia, Austria-Hungary, Russia, and the Ottomans) in the region, literary language has always been deeply politicized. Greek and Polish writers who chose to use their ethnic/national vernacular rather than the language of their respective overlords were instrumental in fortifying the nationalist movements in those areas during the early nineteenth century, even when their subject matter was not explicitly political. For example, Adam Mickiewicz became an icon of Polish nationalism from the 1830s onward even though his masterpieces *Forefathers' Eve* (1823–1833) and *Pan Tadeusz* (1834) owe more to Slavic and Lithuanian folkloric traditions than to contemporary politics. Mickiewicz was personally active in the fight for liberation and died while organizing a Polish legion to fight against Russia in the Crimean War; nevertheless, the political dimension of his literary works remains more implicit than explicit. A similar sort of implied nationalism informed such Greek intellectuals as Adamantios Korais and Rhigas Pheraios, whose works in turn influenced groups—such as Philike Hetairia—that revolted against Ottoman rule in the early nineteenth century.

Other vernacular writers throughout Eastern Europe played roles in their nations' attempts at sovereignty, although after the widespread revolts of 1848, literary expressions of nationalist (and, increasingly, socialist) political themes generally became more overt. In the first half of the 1800s, such writers as Jan Kollár, Ľudovít Štúr, Pavel Šafárik, and František Palacký produced works heavily imbued with a Pan-Slavist spirit that opposed Austro-Hungarian cultural dominance, thereby spurring the so-called national revival among both Czechs and Slovaks. Sándor Petőfi acts as "National Poet" in Hungarian literature, especially in his involvement with the radical Fiatal Magyarország (Young Hungary) group. Despite being influenced as much by German philosophy and Hinduism as by Romanian traditions, Mihai Eminescu is widely recognized as the progenitor of modern Romanian literature, especially poetry. Ivan Vazov is considered the father of Bulgarian literature not just for his copious output in a variety of genres but for his active support for and participation in the extended period of Bulgarian liberation during the late nineteenth century.

The combined influence of **realism** and **naturalism** from both eastern (e.g., **Ivan Turgenev**) and western (e.g., **Émile Zola**) Europe was pronounced in the region's literature during the period 1870–1918. The Polish novelists Bolesław Prus, Stefan Żeromski, and Stefan Gałecki were all noteworthy for their socially conscious fiction during the period, although their political perspectives differed widely, ranging from Prus's Spencerian positivism through Gałecki's fervent Socialism. Gałecki remained among the most prominent political writers—along with Juliusz Kaden-Bandrowski and Leon Kurczkowski—of Poland's brief period of independence between **World War I** and **World War II**. Although Mór Jókai may have been the best-known Hungarian writer of the late nineteenth century, his work was only tangentially political. In contrast, Kálmán Mikszáth injected politics into Hungarian literature both through his journalism and through his satires of the Hungarian gentry. At the outset of the twentieth century, poet/journalist Endre Ady produced a voluminous body of work that frequently included scathing critiques of pre-WWI Hungarian society. The philosopher **Georg Lukács** was a contemporary of Ady, although it was not until after World War I that he achieved his greatest influence on **Marxist criticism**. The poet/journalist Jan Neruda and the novelist Karolina Světlá were among the leaders of the Czech writers known as the *Máj* generation, who blended Byronesque revolutionary romanticism with themes of social and political emancipation. The poets Svatopulk Čech and Viktor Dyk were among the most prominent politicized successors to the *Máj* generation. Concurrently, Slovak writers such as Josef Gregor-Tajovský and Božena Slančiková-Timrava used realistic fiction as a means of social commentary. Franz Kafka's literary career also began in the years just prior to World War I, though the prescient political dimension of his work was generally acknowledged only after the rise of totalitarianism in the 1930s. The comic playwright Ion Luca Caragiale and the essayist Titu Maiorescu—founder of the avant-garde *Junimea* circle—injected social and political themes into the predominantly romantic/lyric literary traditions of Romania.

Most of the contemporary nations of eastern and central Europe existed in some independent form between the world wars, but the politics of the region were far from stable during this time. The collapse of the Ottoman Empire and Austria-Hungary after World War I allowed Czechoslovakia, Hungary, Romania, Poland, Greece, and Albania to become sovereign nations within eight years of the end of World War I (Bulgaria had already become independent in 1908). The **Russian Revolution** and the grave economic problems in Weimar Germany contributed to the region becoming a political battleground among factions representing the old aristocracy (e.g., Ioannis Metaxas in Greece), democratic reformers (e.g., Tómaš Masaryk in Czechoslovakia), socialist and communist revolutionaries (e.g., Georgi Dimitrov in Bulgaria), and extreme nationalists who would later ally with the fascists (e.g., Miklós Horthy in Hungary). As a result, much of the politicized literature of the interwar period—though not necessarily that with the most lasting influence—cleaved along these same lines.

One of the most familiar—though perhaps most difficult to pigeonhole—political works of this time period is Jaroslav Hašek's novel *The Good Soldier Švejk*, a broad-ranging satire on pettiness, inhumanity, and incompetence in the Austrian military during World War I. Czech novelist and dramatist **Karel Čapek** produced a number of works of social criticism during the interwar period, including **dystopian** satires such as *R.U.R.* and *The War with the Newts*. Hungarian writers such as Zsigmond Móricz, László Németh, and Dezso Szabo were among the leaders of the *népi* (populist) movement, which was a prominent feature of Horthy regime literature. While not ideologically aligned with the Soviet proletarian writers, the *népi* writers believed the peasantry to be the embodiment of authentic Hungarian culture and produced works designed to improve their social status. Milo Urban and Josef Cíger Hronský both examined similar issues in a Slovak context, as Yordan Yovkov and Elin Pelin did in a Bulgarian one, and as Mihail Sadoveanu, Liviu Rebreanu, and Lucian Blaga did in Romania. While few of these writers were outspokenly political in their works in comparison with the American proletarian writers of the 1920s and 1930s or the writers of **Soviet socialist realism**, their examination of the changing nature of their respective cultures during this period of independence is inherently politicized by the history of the region. Noteworthy among the more explicitly politicized writers was the Czech Communist journalist Julius Fučík. His *Reportage: Written from the Gallows* is a posthumously published account of his political martyrdom at the hands of the Gestapo during the Nazi occupation of Czechoslovakia. This widely translated work almost immediately became a classic of pro-Communist propaganda in the vein of **John Reed**'s *Ten Days That Shook the World*.

After World War II, most of eastern and central Europe—Greece being the exception as a result of the Truman Doctrine—fell under the direct influence of the Soviet Union, which exerted a rigorous ideological control over literature. Until the "thaw" that followed **Stalin**'s death in 1953, socialist realism was the officially mandated literary form for most of eastern and central Europe. Even in cases such as Nicolae Ceauşescu's Romania or Enver Hoxha's Albania, where the Soviet influence was less direct or even rejected, substantial governmental constraint of literature was still present in most of the region. As a result, much of the most important post-WWII political literature was produced by writers living in exile. This is especially true of Eastern European Jews who had fled and/or survived the **Holocaust** (e.g., Polish novelist/memoirists **Elie Wiesel** and Jerzy Kosinski), as well as writers who faced punishment for their support for the revolutions in Hungary in 1956 (e.g., novelist Péter Halász, essayist György Pálóczi-Horvath, and other writers associated with the Hungarian émigré journal *Literary Gazette*) and Czechoslovakia in 1968 (e.g., novelists **Milan Kundera**, Arnošt Lustig, and Josef Škvorecký). To escape repressive regimes, a number of other prominent Eastern European literary intellectuals emigrated, including dramatist Sławomir Mrożek and poet **Czeslaw Milosz** (Poland); philosophers E. M. Cioran and Mircea Eliade (Romania); novelist Georgi Markov and literary theorists Tzvetan Todorov and **Julia Kristeva** (Bulgaria). The Greek writer Nikos Kazantzakis—an idiosyncratic "fellow traveler" who professed sympathies with Henri Bergson, **Vladimir Lenin**, and Benito Mussolini at various stages of his life—briefly attempted to enter Greek politics as a Socialist immediately after World War II but eventually went into exile when the monarchy was restored in 1947.

A number of notable writers flourished in Eastern Europe during the period of Communist control. As was the case in the Soviet Union, most did so by conforming to the ideological restrictions on style and content (e.g., Ali Adbihoxha in Albania, Vitězslav Nezval in Czechoslovakia, Marin Preda and Geo Bogza in Romania, Zoltán Zelk in Hungary). Others worked within the system by being—or at least seeming to be—generally apolitical in their work (e.g., Wisława Szymborska in Poland, Yordan Radichkov and Emiliyan Stanev in Bulgaria, and Ladislav Fuks in Czechoslovakia). Nevertheless, a number of dissident writers still gained large followings despite the fact that they were often allowed to publish only in clandestine form (*samizdat*) or in foreign countries (*tamizdat*). The latter group includes such writers as novelist Ismail Kadare (Albania); poet and dramatist **Václav Havel**, poet Dominik Tatarka, the intellectuals involved with the dissident Charter 77 movement, and novelists Bohumil Hrabal, Ivan Klíma, and Ludvík Vaculík (Czechoslovakia); poet Sándor Csoóri, fiction writer Tibor Déry, novelists Peter Esterházy and György Konrád, short-story writers Erzsébet Galgóczi and Miklós Mészöly, and essayist Miklós Haraszti (Hungary); poet/dramatist/essayist Tadeusz Rózewicz, and novelists Jerzy Andrzejewski, Jiří Gruša, Tadeusz Konwicki, and Andrzej Szczypiorski (Poland); poet Marin Sorescu, and novelists Eugen Barbu, Augustin Buzura, and Constantin Toiu (Romania).

The definition of political literature has changed substantially with the renewed independence of nations in eastern and central Europe in the wake of the **cold war**. With the monumental force of communist ideology removed as a source of either positive or negative inspiration, debates over literary aesthetic and stylistics no longer contain a necessarily implicit political dimension. Many of the aforementioned dissidents and exiles have continued to write, but many of them (Konrád, Kundera, Škvorecký) have shifted somewhat away from politics toward more philosophical themes or experiments with technique. Others remain engaged with politics but have broadened their scope from a contemporary scale to an epic one; for example, Esterházy's *Harmonia Caelestis* (2000) is a sweeping novel about the history of Hungary, and Stelian Tanase has undertaken a similar project examining his native Romania. The Greek novelist and short-story writer Vassilis Vassilikos continued to produce politically themed works, although none have had the impact of his 1966 novel *Z*. Havel has been the most directly political figure in the post-Communist era, having become president of the Republic in Czechoslovakia in 1989 and then the Czech Republic in 1993.

Selected Bibliography: Black, Karen, ed. *A Biobibliographical Handbook of Bulgarian Authors*. Trans. Predrag Matejic. Columbus, OH: Slavica, 1981; Czigány, Lóránt. *The Oxford History of Hungarian Literature: From the Earliest Times to the Present*. Oxford: Oxford UP, 1986; Elsie, Robert. *History of Albanian Literature*. New York: Columbia UP, 1995; Hosking, Geoffrey A., and Cushing, George F., eds. *Perspectives on Literature and Society in Eastern and Western Europe*. New York: St. Martin's, 1989; Milosz, Czeslaw. *The History of Polish Literature*. Berkeley: U of California P, 1983; Novák, Arne. *Czech Literature*. Trans. Peter Kussi. Ann Arbor: Michigan Slavic Publications, 1986; Petro, Peter. *A History of Slovak Literature*. Montreal: McGill-Queens UP, 1995; Steiner, Peter. *The Deserts of Bohemia: Czech Fiction and Its Social Context*. Ithaca, NY: Cornell UP, 2000.

Derek C. Maus

EASTMAN, MAX FORRESTER (1883–1969). Born into an abolitionist family in Canadaigua, in northern New York, Eastman attended Mercersburg Academy, Williams College, and later Columbia, where he studied philosophy with John Dewey before embarking on a controversial career as an American radical and editor. He arrived in Greenwich Village in 1907, then a hotbed of radical freethinking, where he joined his sister Crystal Eastman—a labor lawyer and suffragist—in campaigning for the vote. He became involved with *The Masses*, which he edited from 1912 until 1917, when he and other members of the collective were prosecuted under the Espionage Act for antiwar activities. A year later, Max and his sister started *The Liberator*, which advocated universal birth control and supported the complete independence of women. With the war at an end, the magazine campaigned against lynch law as a crime against human decency that caused hundreds of innocent deaths each year.

Eastman also had literary ambitions, and found the bohemian life of Greenwich Village full of poetic inspiration to his liking. He published several volumes of poems, as well as *Venture* (1927), a proletarian novel about the Red decade. His more lasting talents, however, were as a critic and translator. He produced some twenty-five works on a range of subjects, from questioning U.S. motives during **World War I** in

Understanding Germany: The Only Way to End War and Other Essays (1916) to attacks on state Communism in *Stalin's Russia and the Crisis in Socialism* (1940). His most thoughtful pieces, however, concerned aesthetics and literature—*The Enjoyment of Poetry* (1913), *The Literary Mind* (1931), *Artists in Uniform* (1934), as well as an autobiography, *Love and Revolution: My Journey through an Epoch* (1965). His essay "The Cult of Unintelligibility" (1929) was a controversial attack on modernism.

Though a critic of dialectical materialism, Eastman nevertheless worked on an edition, published in 1932, of **Karl Marx**'s *Capital*, which included *The Communist Manifesto* and other writings. He cherished his working relationship with **Leon Trotsky**, whom he met in Moscow in 1922, translating such works as *The History of the Russian Revolution* (1961) and *The Revolution Betrayed: What Is the Soviet Union and Where Is It Going* (1972). At the time of his death in 1969, Eastman was at work completing a translation of Trotsky's *Young Lenin*. Eastman also had a close relationship with the Jamaican poet **Claude McKay** and helped to publicize his poems.

With the onset of **World War II** and the rise of **Stalin**, Eastman's views on patriotism and nationalism shifted dramatically, particularly after the Moscow trials and the assassination of Trotsky. He eventually became convinced of the necessity for vigilance against communist infiltration in the United States and praised Joseph McCarthy. He lent his name—and reputation as an independent critic—to the founding editorial board of the right-wing *National Review*. The final years of his life were spent as a roving editor for *Reader's Digest*.

Selected Bibliography: Cantor, Milton. *Max Eastman*. New York: Twayne, 1970; Diggins, John Patrick. *The Rise and Fall of the American Left*. New York: Norton, 1992; O'Neill, William L. *The Last Romantic: A Life of Max Eastman*. New York: Oxford UP, 1978; Wetzsteon, Ross. *Republic of Dreams: Greenwich Village: The American Bohemia, 1910–1960*. New York: Simon and Schuster, 2001.

Josh Gosciak

ELIOT, GEORGE (1819–1880). Born Mary Anne Evans, the youngest daughter of a rural middle-class family, Eliot would grow up to become one of the most popular and critically acclaimed British novelists of the nineteenth century. She took the male pen name George Eliot in 1857 with the publication of her first novella, *Scenes of Clerical Life*. Prior to her career as a novelist, she worked as an editor and translator and came into contact with many radical figures of her time—arguably even **Karl Marx**—but was never radicalized herself, remaining a self-proclaimed conservative. Nevertheless, her editorial writings on religion, foreign policy, and social reform were often progressive in their orientation.

In her subsequent novels, Eliot would devote considerable efforts to depicting the lives of working-class characters and debating social reform. *Felix Holt, the Radical* (1866) is perhaps the most explicitly political example, featuring an election and a struggle between Tories and radicals (liberals). Though Eliot, through the figure of Felix Holt, seems to toy with radical politics in this novel, Holt is in fact more of a conservative than a radical, his "Address to Working Men" advocating restraint and gradual change.

Eliot took a conservative yet perhaps more complex position on the question of women as well. She rejected female separatism, including what she deemed feminine writing, and seemed to have unproblematically accepted the idea of male social dominance. Yet all her novels—from *The Mill on the Floss* (1860) to her great masterpiece *Middlemarch* (1871–1872) to *Daniel Deronda* (1874–1876)—feature female protagonists who are bound by and struggling against the confines and limitations of this dominance; such struggles, however, always end with self-censoring and further acceptance of patriarchy. Though Eliot was sympathetic to women's political campaigns in the areas of marriage, divorce, and property laws, she refrained from publicly participating in the incipient women's movement. The only cause that she publicly embraced and to which she contributed funds was women's education.

Internationally, Eliot's last novel, *Daniel Deronda*, had the greatest political impact. It was, among other things, a proto-Zionist novel that preceded the creation of the official Zionist movement by nearly twenty years. Though badly received in England, it made its way to Eastern European Jewish circles, where Daniel Deronda became a romantic prototype and a figure of identification for many young Jewish men. Here, too, Eliot's politics are a mixture of conservatism and progressiveness: she espouses a separatist solution for European Jews, a highly controversial position from which many Jews refrained, yet also boldly organizes the plot of a **bildungsroman** around a Jewish character, countering not only anti-Semitic conventions but the novelistic convention that precludes the hero from having a minority identity. A mild yet consistent voice against the explicit racism of British imperialist practices, in *Daniel Deronda* Eliot seems to critique its suppression of cultural and historical differences as well.

Selected Bibliography: Frederick, Karl R. *George Eliot: Voice of a Century*. New York: W.W. Norton, 1995; Haight, Gordon S. *George Eliot: A Biography*. New York: Oxford UP, 1968; Henry, Nancy. *George Eliot and the British Empire*. Cambridge: Cambridge UP, 2002; Paxton, Nancy L. *George Eliot and Herbert Spencer: Feminism, Evolutionism, and the Reconstruction of Gender*. Princeton, NJ: Princeton UP, 1991; Semmel, Bernard. *George Eliot and the Politics of National Inheritance*. New York: Oxford UP, 1994; Thomas, David Wayne. *Cultivating Victorians: Liberal Culture and the Aesthetic*. Philadelphia: U of Pennsylvania P, 2003.

Mikhal Dekel

ELIOT, T(HOMAS) S(TEARNS) (1888–1965). Arguably the most influential English-language poet of the twentieth century, Eliot was also an important dramatist, editor, and critic. Born in St. Louis, Missouri, Eliot was educated at Harvard, the Sorbonne, and Oxford. He immigrated to Europe in 1914, traveling in Germany and France before settling in England. From 1917 to 1925, Eliot worked at Lloyds Bank, dealing with the foreign monetary repercussions of **World War I** while writing poems and essays of increasing notoriety. He was a leading modernist; an associate of Bertrand Russell, John Maynard Keynes, **Virginia Woolf**, and **Ezra Pound**; an editor at the *Egoist*; and founding editor of the *Criterion* (1922–1939). From 1925, he was poetry editor at Faber, where he supported modernists as different as Pound, **W. H. Auden**, and Djuna Barnes.

Eliot's early poems—collected in *Prufrock and Other Observations* (1917), *Poems* (1919), and the posthumous *Inventions of the March Hare* (1996)—depict the bourgeois society of his New England and midwestern origins while betraying his fascination with the erotic vulgarity of mass culture, from blackface minstrelsy to prole-tarian scenes. His most celebrated poem, *The Waste Land* (1922), mixes social satire with a learned and paranoid elegy for Euro-American high culture, fragmenting under the pressures of finance capital, sexual freedom, and the rise of European na-tionalisms. In 1927, Eliot became a British subject and converted to Anglicanism, inaugurating the period in which his poems and essays, from *For Lancelot Andrewes* (1928) to *Four Quartets* (1935–1942), address the nature of European and Christian culture.

Eliot's thought centers on questions of order and tradition, combining an "im-personal" aesthetics with the authoritarian impulses of the French writer and politi-cian Charles Maurras. In 1928, Eliot described himself as "classical in literature, royalist in politics, and Anglo-Catholic in religion," echoing a 1913 description of Maurras as "classique, catholique, monarchique." Eliot has often been accused of making anti-Semitic statements, as in *After Strange Gods* (1930), where he asserts that society cannot tolerate many "free thinking Jews." Eliot objected that this remark was not racial but sociohistorical; but his defense (still repeated by some scholars) is undercut by prejudicial references to Jews in several poems. Eliot is thus often linked with Pound, **W. B. Yeats**, and **Wyndham Lewis** as a neofascist writer. Yet he was scathing about the populism and statism of fascist regimes, he accused Maurras of wrongly inciting political hatred, and he rejected the British Brownshirt—Oswald Mosley—as "puerile."

Eliot's dismissal of fascist politics reflects his characteristic interest in literature, di-vinity, and anthropology over questions of state policy. As a dramatist, he attempted to revive poetic drama, writing in verse. His late verse-dramas marry mannerist com-edy with theology, mirroring this tendency to subsume politics to culture. Despite the controversies that still surround his writings, Eliot's political legacy is, perhaps, best measured in terms of his quintessentially "high modernist" aestheticization of political life.

Selected Bibliography: Levenson, Michael, ed. "Does *The Waste Land* Have a Politics?" *Modern-ism/Modernity* 6.3 (1999): 1–13; Moody, David, ed. *Cambridge Companion to T. S. Eliot.* Cambridge: Cam-bridge UP, 1994; Ricks, Christopher. *T. S. Eliot and Prejudice.* Los Angeles: U of California P, 1988; Schuchard, Ronald. "Burbank with a Baedeker, Eliot with a Cigar: American Intellectuals, Anti-Semitism, and the Idea of Culture." *Modernism/Modernity* 10.1 (2003): 1–26.

Matthew Hart

ELLISON, RALPH (1913–1994). Author of *Invisible Man* (1952), Ellison had a complex relationship to the Left. *Invisible Man* is a key text of **cold war**–era U.S. **anticommunism**. Yet in the years 1937–1945, Ellison composed a significant body of Left-inflected fiction, journalism, and criticism, some of it manifesting a close ad-herence to **Communist Party** doctrine.

Born and raised in Oklahoma City, and thus cushioned from the worst manifes-tations of Jim Crow, Ellison lost his father at an early age but was strongly influenced by his mother, who insisted on educational rigor for her two children and supported various socialist causes. A talented trumpet player, Ellison studied music and litera-ture at Tuskegee Institute at a time when the court proceedings in nearby Scottsboro were attracting attention, as was the militant sharecropper organizing elsewhere in Alabama. Ellison left college after his junior year to earn money in New York and never returned. He met **Langston Hughes** and Alain Locke soon after arriving in New York in the summer of 1936; within a year, he had become acquainted with **Richard Wright**. Fiction writer, critic, and head of the Harlem Bureau of the *Daily Worker*, Wright would have an enormous influence, both literary and political, on the young Ellison.

Beginning work with the New York City branch of the **Federal Writers' Project** in 1938, Ellison soon started publishing the more than two dozen pieces of journalism and criticism that would appear over the next several years in the leftist press, especially *New Masses*. In pieces focusing on cultural issues, Ellison adopted an orthodox Marxist stance, castigating writers of the **Harlem Renaissance** for their lack of class analysis and praising both white and African American writers who linked antiracism with anticapitalism. Articles on political themes supported communist organizing among workers and the unemployed, and addressed international antifascist concerns. While Ellison would later fault the Communist Party for flip-flopping during **World War II** and selling out African Americans in the process, his wartime commentaries adhered quite closely to the CP line, advocating **Popular Front** unity up to September 1939, "Yanks Are Not Coming" isolationism until June 1941, and subsequently "Win the War" solidarity. In 1943, Ellison coedited—with communist activist and autobiographer Angelo Herndon—an African American leftist journal called *Negro Quarterly*, which sought to mediate between the Double-V campaign (Victory at Home and Victory Abroad) advocated in the black press and the Communists' less equivocal support for the Allied war effort.

In the late 1930s and early 1940s, Ellison wrote a number of proletarian short stories, many of them unpublished in his lifetime. While some treated Jim Crow violence, many of these skillfully crafted stories focused on the formation—however hesitant and incomplete—of militant multiracial class consciousness among whites and African Americans alike. Outstanding among these are "The Birthmark," "A Party Down at the Square," "The Black Ball," and "In a Strange Country." At this time, Ellison also drafted portions of a novel about a black worker called *Slick*, of which one brief segment appeared in *New Masses* as "Slick Gonna Learn." Growing recognition of these stories' importance in the novelist's oeuvre will significantly reshape Ellisonian scholarship and pedagogy.

As Wright's principal correspondent and confidant in the period following the publication of ***Native Son*** (1940), Ellison shared his mentor's distressed reaction to the negative response to the novel by some influential Communists, especially African Americans. The exchanges between Wright and Ellison about communist literary obtuseness fueled the younger writer's skepticism. Contrary to Ellison's post-*Invisible Man* assertions, however, he maintained a cordial relationship with a number of Communists into the late 1940s and continued to support aspects of their program. The drafts of *Invisible Man* reveal that only gradually did the novel become the familiar seamlessly constructed cold-war classic that would win the National Book Award in 1953.

While in the period preceding the publication of *Invisible Man* Ellison had significant literary relationships with Albert Murray, Shirley Jackson, and Stanley Edgar

Hyman, after 1952 Ellison entered the ranks of New York literary society, forming connections with a number of the **New York intellectuals**. Along with **James Baldwin**, he increasingly turned his back on the traditions of social protest and literary **naturalism** associated with Wright. Ellison also became identified as a staunch supporter of U.S. foreign policy, associating himself with the Congress for Cultural Freedom. Accepting an invitation to Lyndon Johnson's White House that other anti–Vietnam War writers, such as Robert Lowell, had turned down, Ellison declared that since the president did not tell him how to write his novels, he would not advise the president on how to run the country. In the late 1960s and 1970s, various writers and critics connected with the black arts movement criticized Ellison sharply for his assimilationism, Americanism, and inattention to the African roots of black culture. In the 1980s, however, Ellison regained much of his lost stature; vernacular theory and post-structuralist-influenced literary critics such as Houston Baker and Henry Louis Gates have praised Ellison as a riffer and signifier, while celebrants of cultural pluralism have hailed him as a multiculturalist *avant la lettre*.

After the publication of *Invisible Man*, Ellison was best known as an essayist. The pieces gathered in *Shadow and Act* (1964) and *Going to the Territory* (1986) displayed his talents as a commentator on a wide range of issues, from jazz to U.S. literary history. Starting in the 1950s, Ellison generated thousands of pages of what would be a never-published novel; some portion of these were lost in a fire in his upstate New York house. Several years after Ellison's death, John C. Callahan, literary executor of the Ellison estate, produced from these drafts a novel titled *Juneteenth* (1999), which is focused around the life of a reactionary Southern senator who is an African American passing for white. It is on his achievement as the author of *Invisible Man*, however, that Ellison's reputation principally rests.

Selected Bibliography: Foley, Barbara. "Ralph Ellison as Proletarian Journalist." *Science and Society* 62 (Winter 1998–99): 537–56; Foley, Barbara. "Reading Redness: Politics and Audience in Ralph Ellison's Proletarian Short Fiction." *Journal of Narrative Theory* 29 (Fall 1999): 323–39; Jackson, Lawrence. *Ralph Ellison: Emergence of Genius*. New York: John Wiley and Sons, 2002.

Barbara Foley

ENGLISH LITERATURE (MEDIEVAL). In the general prologue to his *Canterbury Tales*, Chaucer tells us that the Knight, the first pilgrim to be portrayed, "loved chivalrie, / Trouthe and honour, fredom and curteisie." These five terms describing the ideal predicates of a Christian knight offer us a working vocabulary of the politics of medieval English literature.

The most important of the five is *trouthe*. This word meant much more in late medieval England than it does today, where the sense of verifiability is uppermost in our technological culture. The most important medieval meaning of *trouthe* was "fidelity," especially fidelity to persons. Numerous works of Middle English literature incorporate and stress this meaning, most famously in the anonymous *Sir Gawain and the Green Knight* (ca. 1400). In all of these works, maintaining *trouthe* is the highest value to which an individual can subscribe. *Trouthe* is owed to one's superiors in the hierarchical stratification of society (reinforced everywhere by the church), beginning with God, devolving then to the king, and moving downward to one's most immediate, personal overlord, whether secular or ecclesiastical. Inversely, to break *trouthe*, or faith, with one's superior was to be guilty of the highest crime—treason.

The culture in which this understanding of *trouthe* prevailed was the culture of chivalry, or courtesy. Although these two terms are not interchangeable, they are practically inseparable in the literature and the politics of the period. Chivalry is the military context in which courtesy is practiced, and courtesy is the social practice that gives meaning to chivalry, which is otherwise barely disguised aggression on the smallest to the largest scale, from individuals to entire kingdoms. *Chivalry* derives from the word for "horse," and this derivation indicates the connection between landed wealth and military enterprise in the medieval world—to own a horse or, generally, the accoutrements of war required land and wealth. *Courtesy* derives from the word *court* and suggests the social habits of the court as codified by generations of practice, involving women as well as men. The practitioner of chivalry, or the knight, is ideally courteous and practices courtesy through his familiarity with the habits of the court to which he is related by his wealth and status. It goes without saying that this ideal was rarely achieved—there is even some question about Chaucer's Knight.

Honor is the personal, emotional, and ultimately subjective quality that unites truth, chivalry, and courtesy in the individual. Again, Sir Gawain is probably the most representative character in late medieval literature of this quality. He will do everything in his power to preserve his honor, and when it turns out that not everything is in his power and so he loses his honor, he is so profoundly ashamed that nothing whatsoever can console him. To be sure, he is a literary character representing an ideal that innumerable real, historical knights of the period repeatedly betrayed—for example, in 1388, in the Merciless Parliament, the lords appellant, as they were called, all but stripped their king, Richard II, of power when they condemned several members of his affinity to death. But to understand the literature and politics of the period, it is crucial for us to recognize that each side in this particular instance was convinced that the other was betraying the ideals of honor and *trouthe*. And so it went throughout the period.

If *honour* is the emotional and subjective quality that binds *trouthe*, *chivalrie*, and *curteisie* in the individual, *fredom* is the external manifestation of that quality. Here, we encounter even more difficult semantic change. In late medieval England, *fredom* meant much more than simply the absence of constraint (a privative definition); above all, it meant "generosity" or "largess." *Magnanimity* ("of great soul") probably comes the closest, if we understand magnanimity to include generosity, largess, and an element of display meant to suggest the opposite of miserliness and meanness (or *pusillanimity*, "of small soul"). Throughout the period, writers of all persuasions celebrate *fredom* as a paradigmatic quality of all who aspire to nobility. Again, it comes as no surprise that many failed to live up to this ideal, which, perhaps more than any other ideal, was more literary or fictional than anything else, especially when one considers that a common complaint against princes of the period—for example, of the Lords Appellant against Richard II—was that they were profligate with their wealth, squandering their nations' treasure.

This brief survey of the five predicates listed by Chaucer in his portrait of the Knight suggests valid if provisional generalities about the politics of literature in late medieval England. Throughout the period, the literature was written for, and to, those who controlled political power—the nobility. It was their political values that secular literature largely celebrated, even in works as religious and reformist as William Langland's *Piers Plowman*. (Sacred literature sometimes looked to these same values but subordinated them to spiritual values presumed to take precedence over them.) Secular writers like Chaucer and the *Gawain* poet clearly understood that they were writing for those who were privileged with political and economic power that they were hardly likely to relinquish (the church itself repeatedly failed to seize it from them). Circumspection was therefore needed and frequently practiced—as, for example, by Chaucer's contemporary John Gower, perhaps the most politic poet of the period. Ultimately, patronage and patriarchy defined both the literature and the politics of the period, as they would for centuries to come. Even so, we can see in the work of Chaucer and his contemporaries, who were increasingly attuned to the discrepancies between the ideal and the real, that there is, especially in the modes of allegory and satire, increasing representation of a more inclusive humanity more alive to the liberating potential of literature in political practice; barely seventy years after Chaucer's death, the printing press appeared in England and, with it, a nascent English literature that included not only knights but also women, tradespeople, children, the lay pious, bureaucrats, and politicians.

Selected Bibliography: Green, Richard Firth. *A Crisis of Truth: Literature and Law in Ricardian England*. Philadelphia: U of Pennsylvania P, 1999; Saul, Nigel. *Richard II*. New Haven, CT: Yale UP, 1997; Shoaf, R. Allen. *The Poem as Green Girdle: Commercium in* Sir Gawain and the Green Knight. Gainesville: UP of Florida, 1984; Strohm, Paul. *Social Chaucer*. Cambridge, MA: Harvard UP, 1989.

R. Allen Shoaf

ENGLISH LITERATURE (RENAISSANCE). Traditional sociohistorical and Marxist approaches to period study of culture have examined cultural responses to social change, and in this approach, the major cultural shifts in sixteenth- and seventeenth-century England can be seen to reflect the growing economic and social complexity of the period. In mid-sixteenth-century England, the only socially respectable verbal art was poetry; players were vagabonds, there was no domestic prose fiction, and there were no professional writers. By the end of the century, the situation had significantly changed; while poetry retained its status as a liberal art, generally free from commercial taint, theater and fiction were thriving industries, offering a new audience a different perspective.

Drawing on classical forms, poetry was learned in character, and it was therefore more integrated into, and more a bearer of, the dominant culture. The aesthetic values of Jonson's classically modeled verse and **Edmund Spenser**'s *Faerie Queene* implied social values—literary order was related to social order and hierarchy. The most popular poetic form of the age was the sonnet, and sonnet writing was regarded as the polish of a complete gentleman. Publication (i.e., making public) was usually through manuscript circulation, partly because going into print had commercial associations and therefore risked loss of status.

Theater, on the other hand, had no reservations about being commercial; from the time the first playhouse—the Theatre—was built in a London suburb (1576), theater was an entertainment business. But it was also a forum for social commentary, and its critical content changed over the period. In 1587, Marlowe's *Tamburlaine* offered a rhetorically magnificent assertion of individual worth in the face of inherited hierarchy, whereas in *Hamlet, King Lear,* and *Macbeth,* some fifteen to twenty years later, **Shakespeare** dealt more naturalistically with the social destruction wrought by rampant striving for personal advancement.

The most interesting manifestations of a changing social situation were developments in prose fiction, which grew along with the book trade. The content and perspective changed to accommodate a new readership, and the mode of address changed to meet new conditions of story distribution. Like theater, most fiction published in the last quarter of the sixteenth century was unashamedly entertainment. But whereas theater involved immediate contact with an audience, and poetry could sustain at least the image of personal contact, prose fiction was mediated; the author was separated from the audience by the physical book. Thus, oral forms were gradually dropped from the relationship that the author created with the audience/readership, and the text came to reflect the actual relationship, moving from what was in effect a spoken-narrative transcription to written text for a reader, from an oral to a literary style.

Prose fiction developed within a predominantly Protestant consciousness, in which reading the Bible and books of self-improvement was welcomed but reading for pleasure was a dubious activity. Thus, some justification or relabeling was required for fiction. Narratives, as Sir Philip Sidney stressed in his *Apology for Poetry,* presented a model of behavior:

> The poet never maketh any circles about your imagination, to conjure you to believe for true what he writes. He citeth not authorities of other histories, but even for his entry calleth the sweet Muses to inspire into him a good invention; in truth, not labouring to tell you what is or is not, but what should or should not be.

Sidney took his own prescription seriously, and in the revision of his *Arcadia,* he recast the framework of his original from witty comic situations to a model of "what should or should not be." Without losing any of the delight of adventure, he puts forward role models and examines the consequences of specific behavior. However strenuous the role of literature for Sidney, there were also many works of shallow moralizing, and the outstanding style model of the age, John Lyly's *Euphues: The Anatomy of Wyt* (1578), simply played with moral precepts. The form, rather than serious moral content, was what was demanded.

A change more profound but less obvious was the shift in the content of the fiction, as the material of daily life began to play a more important role. Unlike Geoffrey Fenton, whose *Certain Tragicall Discourses* (1567) imposed militant Protestant judgments on events that were given no detailed depiction, Sidney's concerns were drawn from a well-realized picture of material existence, which, even though the main characters are royal, would be recognizable from readers' own lives. From the 1580s, more of the narratives were populated by ordinary people. Robert Greene, the first professional writer in England, began to give characters of low station a central role in his narratives. The tales in *Perimedes the Blacke-Smith* (1588), for example, are related by an artisan couple at the end of their day's labors and contain problems that affect poor working people.

The most important, popularly successful, and frequently reprinted of such works is Greene's *Pandosto* (1588), which Shakespeare parodied in *The Winter's Tale*. The story allows two different perspectives. In one, the reader knows that the heroine, unbeknownst to herself, is a princess, and thus there is no social discrepancy in her elopement with a prince. In the other, the heroine has been raised and lives as a shepherd, and she judges the world from a shepherd's standpoint. Greene gives considerable space to her worry that romance across such a social gulf violates social order. She tells the prince that she could love him if he were a shepherd, but when he appears in shepherd's clothes to claim her love, she says:

> rich clothing make not princes: nor homely attire, beggars: shepherds are not called shepherds, because they wear hooks and bags, but that they are born poor, and live to keep sheep; so this attire hath not made Dorastus a shepherd, but to seem like a shepherd.

She understands events in an artisan perspective; he is playing pastoral whereas she is a real working shepherd. Even so, she makes the choice of individual love over the dictates of custom. Although Greene protects his propriety by the eventual uncovering of the heroine's royal birth, he not only articulates the experience of ordinary people but, through his construction of the heroine, validates an artisan perspective. This is a development of class consciousness: ordinary people can read their own viewpoint in the fiction, and the fiction confirms it.

The artisan perspective, although not as polished as it was in all of Greene's later works, appears in a number of other writers' works toward the end of the century. Emanuel Forde models his *Ornatus and Artesia* on Sidney's *Arcadia* but finds a different significance in events because they are viewed in terms of a different class reality. Sidney mocks the death of peasants in a rebellion in *Arcadia*, whereas Forde shows concern for the impositions suffered by the lower classes. In the fiction of Thomas Deloney, productive work has pride of place. The eponymous hero of *Jack of Newbury* (1597) tells the king who offers him a knighthood that he holds economic achievement and its assumed benefit to the community to be more important than the titles of honor.

In political terms, this development of a new class perspective was the most important change in the literature of the period. Not only could commoners see themselves in literature, but they could find their own values inscribed in it. Writers like Greene, with an orientation toward a new class of popular readers, helped the budding bourgeoisie become not just a class "of itself" but, in Marx's famous distinction, a class "for itself."

Selected Bibliography: Baugh, Albert C., ed. *A Literary History of England*. New York: Appleton-Century-Crofts, 1948; Bristol, Michael D. *Carnival and Theater: Plebeian Culture and the Structure of Authority in Renaissance England*. New York: Methuen, 1985; Margolies, David. *Novel and Society in Elizabethan England*. Totowa, NJ: Barnes and Noble, 1985; Sinfield, Alan. *Literature in Protestant England, 1560–1660*. Totowa, NJ: Barnes & Noble, 1983; Weimann, Robert. *Shakespeare and the Popu-*

lar Tradition in the Theater: Studies in the Social Dimension of Dramatic Form and Function. Ed. Robert Schwartz. Baltimore: Johns Hopkins UP, 1978.

David Margolies

ENGLISH LITERATURE (RESTORATION AND EIGHTEENTH CENTURY).

The period between 1660 and 1800 is crucial for the relationship between literature and politics because within it occurred the crucial precondition for that relationship—the conceptual separating out of both "literature" and "politics" as distinct categories. Of course, in one sense literate culture has always produced "political literature." But the significance of this conjunction for modern culture lies in the implicit tension between its two terms. For this tension to be felt, both categories had to be disembedded from the matrix of traditional experience, in which the dominance of religious, social, and rhetorical modes of understanding the world imbue all activities with a powerfully unifying family resemblance. The emergence of politics as an autonomous and self-standing realm of discourse and action is most often associated with the sixteenth-century writings of Niccolò Machiavelli, whose influence in the two centuries that follow is deep and pervasive. The Machiavellian idea of *realpolitik* found especially fertile ground in the English civil war and interregnum, in which the 1649 execution of the king was only the most dramatic evidence of a fundamental crisis in ideas of political authority.

The sovereignty of the monarch had been tacit knowledge; now it became a matter of explicit public debate. With the outbreak of civil war came an explosion of print, marking the historical moment to which the emergence of the "public sphere"—located by **Jürgen Habermas** in the early eighteenth century—might arguably be backdated. Andrew Marvell's "An Horatian Ode upon Cromwell's Return from Ireland" (1650) balances the maxim that might is right against more traditional views that right—divine, ancient, patrilineal, republican, natural—should be prior to and determinant of political power. Marvell also charges the old pastoral opposition between contemplation and action with a new urgency for both the statesman and the poet.

After the Restoration, public debate concerning the foundations of political authority continued unabated, and poetry was one of its most common media. John Dryden's *Absalom and Achitophel* (1681) is the most famous of the "poems on affairs of state" of this period, a subgenre whose coherence and appeal were enhanced by the publication of several collections of the same name between 1689 and 1716. Dryden's poem sets the standard for later ones in a number of ways, not least the self-consciousness with which poetry undertakes the subject of politics. This flowering of "political poetry" entails a compelling contradiction. As Habermas among others has argued, the coalescence of an idea of the privacy of "civil society" at this time is established in conjunction with a notion of the public "state," more focused than it had been, so as to create both a basic division and the conditions for its breaching. Habermas postulates the growth of the public sphere as a virtual institution within civil society that enables discourse in the private realm to reflect on state policy formulated in the public realm. In a related if more volatile fashion, "state poetry" addresses matters of public policy with a sense both of its entitlement to do so and of the growing divide between the private and the public, between poetry and politics. The severity of state laws regulating publication encouraged poets to avoid the risk of prosecution by writing not libel but "satire"—political critique that was purportedly free of personal reflection. The greatest products of the Augustan "age of satire"—**Jonathan Swift's** *Gulliver's Travels* (1726), Alexander Pope's *The Dunciad* (1728–1742)—evince the ambivalent instability of a motive both to be and not to be "political" in this sense of the term. More broadly, the era of England's greatest outpouring of political poetry is also the era in which the seeds are sown for the modern tendency to view political poetry as a contradiction in terms.

This autonomization of "politics" took place during the same period as the constitution of "literature" in its modern meaning as that which evokes an aesthetic response. Traditionally, rhetoric had defined most writing according to its designs—its persuasive and in this sense "political" effect—on its audience. The idea of the aesthetic coheres around not effect but affect, the feelings aroused by the representation of actions that are not actual or real but real-like. Dryden's *Essay of Dramatic Poesy* (1667) reminds contemporaries that the unities of time and place and their naive empiricism were no part of Aristotle's teaching, for which the proper pleasure of drama on the contrary requires a certain detachment, the awareness of illusion. In the *Spectator* papers (1712), Joseph Addison suggests that the imagination has its own standards of veracity, related to but divergent from those governing strictly empirical experience. Our disinterested response to literature is subtly but fundamentally different from our response to empirical reality and its irresistible physical, social, and political interestedness.

The writings of the third earl of Shaftesbury (1711, 1714) and others soon find in the dialectical relationship between author and reader a textual equivalent for the theatrical dialectic between staged action and spectatorial affect. Literary reflexivity—the mirroring of literary form and worldly content—announces not their inseparability but the detachment necessary for reciprocal reflection. If literature is "political," it is so on its own terms. In the preface to his edition of *The Plays of William Shakespeare* (1765), Samuel Johnson pursues the implications of detachment in the realm of aesthetic response into the territory of the problem of aesthetic judgment. Like others before him, Johnson had puzzled over the insight—a product of the quarrel of the ancients and moderns—that the "arts" and the "sciences" are radically distinct from each other, most evidently because only the latter are susceptible to positive—quantitative and material—standards of judgment. To make value judgments about literature, Johnson reasoned, we must discover and employ those quantitative measures that are suitable to the qualitative nature of the arts. The best works are those that pass the test of time, "length of duration and continuance of esteem." Shakespeare's perdurability enacts a historical purification process whereby the more personal, local, and politically motivated responses to his plays are winnowed out over time, leaving a detached residue of essential "pleasure" as testimony to his aesthetic value. By the end of the eighteenth century, the modern attitude toward the relationship between literature and politics had been established. The best literature is supposedly recognizable by its detachment from politics. Literature that proclaims its political aims and effects flies in the face of this cultural norm, occasionally to be accorded, for this act of defiance, the dubious award of artistic excellence.

In a more extended sense of the term, however, the conjunction of politics and literature is not frustrated but facilitated by the rise of aesthetic thinking, whose equivalent in novel theory is **realism**. One hallmark of the emergent genre of the novel is its reflexive capacity to evoke the real without laying claim to being the real. In the novel, "literary" detachment from the world signifies not apartness but the empirical distance required for authoritative sociolitical critique. The early novel— paradigmatically, Samuel Richardson's *Pamela* (1740) and Henry Fielding's *Joseph Andrews* (1742)—offered a crucial arena for the critique of both traditional ideologies of status hierarchy (birth equals worth) and emergent ideologies of class mobility (the career open to talents). The authority of the novel in this critical project depends entirely on its "literary" detachment from what it criticizes, the formal self-consciousness with which it proclaims and qualifies the truth of its content as not real but realistic, true to life as we tend to experience it.

Selected Bibliography: Edwards, Thomas R. *Imagination and Power: A Study of Poetry on Public Themes.* London: Chatto and Windus, 1971; Goldgar, Bertrand A. *Walpole and the Wits: The Relation of Politics to Literature, 1722–1742.* Lincoln: U of Nebraska P, 1976; Habermas, Jürgen. *The Structural Transformation of the Public Sphere: An Inquiry into a Category of Bourgeois Society.* Trans. Thomas Burger. Cambridge, MA: MIT P, 1989; Lord, George deF., et al., eds. *Poems on Affairs of State: Augustan Satirical Verse, 1660–1714.* 7 vols. New Haven: Yale UP, 1963–75; McKeon, Michael. *The Origins of the English Novel, 1600–1740.* Baltimore: Johns Hopkins UP, 1987; Williams, Raymond. *The Country and the City.* New York: Oxford UP, 1971.

Michael McKeon

ENGLISH STUDIES AND POLITICS. "Always historicize," the critical slogan with which **Fredric Jameson** begins *The Political Unconscious*, has been the theme of much of the best work in the politics of literature in the past thirty years or so. But, in addition to considering the politics of literary works, it is important to consider the institutional politics of criticism, theory, and pedagogy, and the various practices (including the teaching and theorizing of rhetoric and composition) that are grouped within the hybrid field of English. Although other institutions are also significant (publishers, foundations, government agencies such as the National Endowment for the Humanities), the institutional politics of the English profession are primarily the politics of colleges and universities, and of schools and schooling in general.

As presented in the national media, the most prominent political issue in universities appears to be the **culture wars**, in which the humanities—and especially English departments—are often presented as attacked bastions of the Left. The power of right-wing critics who have enlisted the support of wealthy foundations and prominent figures to demonize professors should not be underestimated. However, while the culture wars have received more attention, the labor practices within English departments (most of which are able to function only by exploiting the labor of ever-increasing numbers of part-time faculty) are more telling of the place of the English profession within the political economy of global capitalism.

Whatever the ideological disputes engaged in by professors of English, most professors are workers in a profession that is increasingly exploitative of the labor of those in its lower-tier, non-professional jobs. As the Coalition for the Academic Workforce noted in "A Collaborative Study of Undergraduate Faculty, Fall 1999," in that year, only 36.3 percent of the faculty in English departments were full-time and tenure tracked—in other words, were treated as full members of the profession—and in free-standing composition programs (writing programs outside English departments), this was true of only 14.6 percent of faculty. The division between **composition studies and literature** has itself been, historically, a class division within English studies; until very recently, almost all professionals in composition studies received markedly lower status than those in literary studies. At present, those who teach lower-level courses are still predominantly lower-status, part-time faculty—many of them graduate students at large, Ph.D.-granting institutions, and many more part-time, underpaid workers without benefits at the non-Ph.D.-granting institutions that predominate in the field nationwide.

While this entry focuses on English at the college and university level, it is also important to remember that the exclusion of lower levels of schooling from consideration can be misleading. Much of the awareness of institutional politics began with the 1960s, and if the movements of that decade taught us anything, it is that the exclusion of the less valued term in a definition is, consciously or unconsciously, a gesture of power. As **Richard Ohmann** notes in his tribute to Louis Kampf, reprinted in *The Politics of Knowledge* (2003), it was at the end of the 1960s, in works such as Kampf and Paul Lauter's *The Politics of Literature* (1972), that intellectuals relearned an astonishing basic truth: "*Teachers are workers; teaching is a job*" (45). No book did more to remind English professionals that their work was teaching as well as research, and that English professionals had alliances with colleagues who taught school as well as with those who wrote prestigious books than Ohmann's *English in America: A Radical View of the Profession* (1976), which codified many of the best insights of the radicalism that had helped redefine English studies. The legacy of the 1960s movements not only helped usher in black studies, women's studies, and other ethnic/cultural studies—as well as such comparative latecomers as gay and lesbian studies and working-class studies—but also introduced a critique of schooling and higher education, suggesting that both reproduced capitalist ideology, presenting America as a meritocracy even while teachers were engaged in a process of grading and sorting in which the children who came out on top were usually wealthy and white. As the 1960s waned, social reproduction theory was developed in works such as Ohmann's *English in America* and Samuel Bowles and Herbert Gintis's *Schooling in Capitalist America* (1976). And although not enough teachers of college English are aware of it, the study of the ways in which education, and especially literacy practices, tend to reproduce the inequalities of the social order has continued in works such as Patrick Finn's *Literacy with an Attitude*, which goes beyond the critique of social reproduction and stresses strategies for empowerment.

Since the 1960s, English has been increasingly friendly to critical discourses that challenge and critique the dominant social order, though the field has never been nearly so dominated by oppositional thinkers as its critics on the New Right have claimed. At the same time, English has continued to be part of a system of social

sorting based on class and race. To some extent, multiculturalism and radical liter-
ary theory constitute an ideological challenge, if we judge by the shrillness with which
English departments have been attacked by the Right for becoming dominated by
leftist faculty who have abandoned the traditions of the humanities in pursuit of obscure theoretical work and radical advocacy. This pattern dates from the 1980s, when
William Bennett, later secretary of education in the Reagan administration, wrote
"To Reclaim a Legacy: A Report on the Humanities in Higher Education" (1984).
The New Right's criticism of the humanities is rooted in the reaction against the
1960s, as is apparent in the title of Roger Kimball's book, *Tenured Radicals* (1990),
which notes with dismay that many of the radicals of the 1960s who protested against
the university are now ensconced within power as faculty at those same institutions.
But the end of the 1960s also signaled an increase in exploitative labor practices
within English, as the collapse of the job market for Ph.D.'s in the humanities coincided with the end of the Vietnam War—a period that also saw the rise of a new
kind of capitalism.

That new global capitalism had to scramble to maintain U.S. hegemony through
war and economy policy. On the one hand, it needed educated workers for an information society, and on the other, it began to export jobs abroad and cut back on
the policies that funded educational expansion so lavishly in the 1960s. Real wages
for most workers began to decline at the end of the Vietnam War, and U.S. society
saw a greater divide between the wealth of the top tier and those at the bottom, with
a shrinking middle-income group in between. Class division became more real as
class consciousness declined. As the legal implications of the Taft Hartley Act (1948)
worked themselves out, strikes and union organizing became more difficult, far fewer
workers in the United States belonged to unions, and working-class identity became
harder to maintain as working-class institutions declined. As Michael Zweig notes,
the working-class of late-twentieth-century America constituted a clear majority—
more than 60 percent of the population, if we define working-class jobs as those in
which the worker has little control over the conditions and pace of work—even
though the myth of America as a middle-class society was as strong as ever, and even
though many professionals—those who had greater control over working conditions—became increasingly proletarianized, until even physicians in some instances
sought to unionize, as they lost autonomy to health-care-maintenance organizations.

Changes in class relations in the United States have everything to do with the politics of English studies. English is a profession that, as Ohmann has argued in *The
Politics of Knowledge*, is undergoing the same dynamics that other professions are experiencing, as the identity of professional work is threatened by outsourcing and two-
tiered employment practices. It is ironic that some of the critics of English on both
the Right and Left assume that English is the home of a radicalism that is cut off
from effective social action. For members of the New Right such as Kimball, this
lack of political efficacy is a source of consolation; for others on the Left, the lack of
connection of university radicalism to anything resembling the social movements of
the 1960s is a source of lament. However, the exploitative labor practices of English
studies suggest that in many respects, English is a profession like others, which (whatever its claims about service to students and to society at large) is partly about the
maintenance of the privilege of professionals and of the privileges of top-tier work-

ers over lower-tier workers who are not given full professional status. Moreover, those exploitative practices suggest that it is not necessary for radicals in English to look with dismay at the lack of prospects for a large counter-hegemonic movement in global capitalist society; they need only to look at their own institutions, and many of them will find ways to connect to a movement for social justice. Building unions within academic institutions is not easy, and in some states it is legally impossible— but it was not easy in the 1930s, either.

One should not minimize the importance of cultural criticism, romanticize the labor movement, or discount the difficulties of building an academic labor move-ment with alliances between academics and other workers. However, it may well be that some of the most significant political struggles in English and other white-collar professions in the twenty-first century will be over work—clearly one of the trends at the beginning of the century. Graduate student unions are organizing across the United States—an encouraging sign, although unionization by itself is not the an-swer, especially given the obstacles to unionization faced by certain groups. Even more troubling is the way privileged academics have too often acted as *professionals*—with a narrow concern over their own specializations and self-interest—rather than *workers*—with a sense of solidarity shared with those in the lower tiers of the pro-fession. Essays by part-time faculty, such as Michael Dubson's edited collection *Ghosts in the Classroom*, recount too many cases in which full-time faculty undercut the in-terests of part-timers to protect their own turf, and the Yale graduate-student strike of 1995–1996, receiving national attention, was supported by few established Yale faculty in the humanities.

If English studies were to become truly radical, several changes would have to occur. One would be an increased sense of urgency and solidarity among those in the lower tier of the profession and the so-called tenured radicals, attitudes such as those expressed by Cary Nelson and Stephen Watt in *Academic Keywords: A Devil's Dictionary for Higher Education*, who note that the problem of part-time teaching is *the* central problem faced by the university; they excoriate professional organizations like the Modern Language Association (MLA) for long ignoring the problem. The MLA has since put forth more radical resolutions about part-time issues; hopefully, these will be accompanied by increased activism at many levels, for such activism is the other change that is needed. Activism can take many forms, including union ac-tivity, faculty senate resolutions, and public protests.

The holding of the first Campus Equity Week in the fall of 2001, where protests and forums led by part-time faculty activists were held at colleges and universities throughout the United States and Canada, may signal a new wave of activism on part-time issues. It would be unfortunate if social reproduction theory, which locates English studies as a profession destined to decline within a changing form of capi-talism, were to lead to a pessimism that does not embrace the need for such activism.

Selected Bibliography: Bennett, William. "'To Reclaim a Legacy': Text of Report on Humanities in Education. *Chronicle of Higher Education*, 28 November 1984, 16–21; Bowles, Samuel, and Herbert Gintis. *Schooling in Capitalist America: Education and the Contradictions of American Economic Life*. New York: Basic Books, 1976; Coalition for the Academic Workforce. *Who Is Teaching in U.S. College Class-rooms? A Collaborative Study of Undergraduate Faculty, Fall 1999*. American Historical Association Web-site. 21 March 2003 (http://www.theaha.org/caw); Dubson, Michael, ed. *Ghosts in the Classroom: Stories* of College Adjunct Faculty—And the Price We All Pay. Boston: Camel's Back Books, 2001; Finn, Patrick. *Literacy with an Attitude: Educating Working-Class Children in Their Own Self-Interest.* Albany: SUNY P, 1999; Jameson, Fredric. *The Political Unconscious: Narrative as a Socially Symbolic Act.* Ithaca, NY: Cornell UP, 1981; Kampf, Louis, and Paul Lauter, eds. *The Politics of Literature.* New York: Pantheon, 1972; Kimball, Roger. *Tenured Radicals: How Politics Has Corrupted Higher Education.* New York: HarperCollins, 1990; Nelson, Cary, and Stephen Watt. *Academic Keywords: A Devil's Dictionary for Higher Education.* New York: Routledge, 1999; Ohmann, Richard. *English in America: A Radical View of the Profession.* New York: Oxford UP, 1976; Ohmann, Richard. *Politics and Letters.* Middletown, CT: Wesleyan UP, 1988; Zweig, Michael. *The Working Class Majority: America's Best Kept Secret.* Ithaca, NY: Cornell UP, 2000.

Raymond A. Mazurek

ENVIRONMENTALISM. A social, political, and ethical movement arguing that human survival depends directly on the health of nonhuman nature and its interconnected parts; it seeks to protect and preserve the quality of the natural environment—soil, water, air, plants, animals, and microorganisms—by reducing harmful human activities and destructive land-use patterns, by preventing pollution, and by adopting legislation to safeguard natural resources. Although the tone of environmentalism often strikes an apocalyptic note—warning of potentially destructive and devastating consequences of human action—it ultimately maintains a philosophy of hope that we can save ourselves and the endangered natural world by shifting from anthropocentric ("human-centered") practices to those that are biocentric ("life-centered").

Environmentalism is a wide-ranging subject whose ideas reach back to ancient times, but it does not flow in a single, unbroken channel. Modern environmentalism has its roots in the **romanticism** of nineteenth-century America, which evoked in painting and writing a reverence for the beautiful, the primitive, and the sublime aspects of the natural world and gave rise to a cult of the wilderness. As early as the 1830s, George Catlin was arguing for a wilderness preserve, and by the 1840s, artists like Thomas Cole were warning of nature's doom in the shadow of America's advancing industrialism. The "nature writing" of American naturalists such as William Bartram, John Burroughs, and John Muir (founder of the Sierra Club) also played a major role in drawing attention to the environment. However, it is the work and thought of such writers as Ralph Waldo Emerson and **Henry David Thoreau** that are most often cited as the bedrock of environmentalism. Thoreau's passion for nature and distrust of society struck a chord with those seeking to protect the environment from an increasingly materialistic and urbanized world, and his statement—in the essay "Walking"—that "in Wildness is the preservation of the World" echoes in the environmental movement of today (613).

In 1864, science introduced the factual basis for rethinking the relationship between humans and the natural world. George Perkins Marsh's book *Man and Nature; or, Physical Geography as Modified by Human Action* provided the first historical record of the damage that human technology and society were having on the environment. The book examines the consequences of deforestation, soil erosion, and the draining of wetlands, and its conclusions anticipate the dust bowl of the 1930s and the loss of numerous plant and animal species. Two years later, Ernst Haeckel coined the term "ecology," which describes the interconnectedness of all organisms in a shared environment and provides the premise from which all subsequent environmental thinking proceeds. In 1948, Aldo Leopold's touchstone environmental work, *A Sand County Almanac,* added an ethical dimension to the idea of ecology with its suggestion that everything in the environment is interdependent, and that "a thing is right when it tends to preserve the integrity, stability, and beauty of the biotic community" (262). All subsequent environmental thinking follows from this premise.

Ecology, however, has been criticized by opponents because its conclusions challenge the continuous growth economy that dominates most developed, industrialized countries. Indeed, many of the ideas of environmentalism have been attacked as a threat to economic prosperity, especially by those who prefer a laissez-faire approach to free-market capitalism, as seen in the recent presidential administrations of Ronald Reagan, George H. W. Bush, and George W. Bush. Environmentalism has also been condemned for its more radical elements and tactics, like using vandalism and "ecosabotage" to disrupt logging and mining operations. In literature, evidence of such subversive elements dates back at least to the civil disobedience of Thoreau, as well as his implication, in *A Week on the Concord and Merrimack Rivers,* of using a crowbar against the Billerica Dam to save the fish in the river. Such radical expressions are also found in the twentieth century in the highly regarded work of Edward Abbey, whose acclaimed first book, *Desert Solitaire* (1968), describes the narrator following a government road crew, pulling up and discarding their survey stakes to prevent road construction through Arches National Monument. Abbey's controversial *The Monkey Wrench Gang* (1975) is a fictional account that describes several acts of ecosabotage by the main characters, including vandalizing billboards, destroying grading and logging equipment, and blowing up a dam. The exploits detailed in the book resemble, and possibly inspired, the tactics of more militant environmental groups like Greenpeace, Earth First! and the Earth Liberation Front. Numerous other literary works of this period were inspired by environmentalism as well, including Ernest Callenbach's widely read *Ecotopia* (1975), an account of a fictional utopian state founded on the twin principles of respect for the environment and respect for all individual human beings. Alternatively, dystopian works such as John Brunner's *The Sheep Look Up* (1972) were inspired by visions of ecological disaster.

Overwhelmingly, though, the environmental movement has been a social force that uses mainstream channels, such as organization and legislation, to facilitate a program for change in environmental social values. By the 1960s, large numbers of citizens were concerned enough about increasing water pollution, air pollution, and the chemical poisoning of the environment (frighteningly described in Rachel Carson's influential and best-selling *Silent Spring,* 1962) that they succeeded in making environmental issues a serious part of the political landscape. The U.S. Congress began responding by passing the Wilderness Act in 1964 and the Wild and Scenic Rivers Act in 1968. Then, in 1970, environmentalism crystallized into a worldwide movement with the first Earth Day on April 22, a watershed for environmental legislation. That same year, congress established the Environmental Protection Agency (EPA) and passed the Clean Air Act. Two years later, the Clean Water Act and the Endangered Species Act were passed. The first major international conference on environmental issues took place in Stockholm, Sweden, in 1972, sponsored by the United Nations. Since then, environmentalism has been an increasingly global movement, culminating with the meetings of the UN Conference on Environment and Development (the Earth Summits) throughout the 1990s and into the twenty-first century.

At the same time that environmentalism was becoming a global phenomenon, its values were penetrating a variety of cultural areas, not the least of which has been in the "greening" of college humanities programs. For example, ecocriticism blossomed in the early 1990s as an environmentally informed approach to literary studies. As a form of literary criticism, ecocriticism investigates the relationship between humans and the environment by exploring the ways in which texts represent the physical world, as well as addressing ethical questions raised by our interactions with nonhuman nature. Ecocriticism's offshoots include ecofeminism and the environmental justice movement, "emancipatory" schools that seek to empower disadvantaged groups and increase health and welfare by drawing attention to discriminatory environmental practices. As such, ecocriticism adds environmental concerns to the categories of gender, race, and cultural studies.

Selected Bibliography: Glotfelty, Cheryl, and Harold Fromm, eds. *The Ecocriticism Reader: Landmarks in Literary Ecology.* Athens: Georgia UP, 1996; Nash, Roderick. *Wilderness and the American Mind.* 3rd ed. New Haven, CT: Yale UP, 1982; Shabecoff, Philip. *A Fierce Green Fire: The American Environmental Movement.* New York: Farrar, Straus, and Giroux, 1993; Thoreau, Henry David. *Walden and Other Writings.* New York: Random House, 1981; Thoreau, Henry David. *The Writings of Henry David Thoreau.* Boston: Houghton Mifflin, 1906.

Brian Hardman

ENZENSBERGER, HANS MAGNUS (1929–) With his first publications as a poet and essayist (the two genres in which he has excelled) in the late 1950s and early 1960s, Enzensberger gained the sobriquet of Germany's "angry young man." He showed scant patience for national preoccupations, such as the division of the country, and basing his analysis on the ideas of the **Frankfurt School**, excoriated the mass media, dubbing them the "consciousness industry," which became the English title of a collection of essays on the subject. After giving lukewarm support to the Social Democratic Party (SPD) in the 1961 election, he joined in the student protests of that decade, declaring that the political system of the federal republic was "irreparable" and demanding that the French May 1968 be repeated in Germany. Moreover, he declared literature as irrelevant to the political struggle, instigating what became known as the "death of literature" debate. A period as visiting fellow at the Wesleyan University in Connecticut ended with his announcement of a move to Cuba.

A decade later, his much-vaunted support for Castro had waned. In 1978, he published the long poem *The Sinking of the Titanic* (*Der Untergang der Titanic*), which can be read as a farewell to Socialism. In the 1990s, he supported the Gulf War and lamented that the "autistic" behavior of young people could change any tram into the equivalent of Bosnia. In 2003, he was again supporting war and attacking left-wing prophets of doom. In recent decades, he has frequently shown scorn for intellectual and political elites.

Even if the above sounds like a typical, even banal, intellectual biography—moves to the Right with advancing years are common—it would be wrong to dismiss Enzensberger's work as in any way conventional. He has always consciously refused to be predictable, as the title of one essay collection—*Zigzag* (*Zickzack*, 1997)—shows. He refuses, as he mischievously stated in one interview, to be the "cloth to polish the world with." While this chameleon-like tendency has exasperated some critics, who point to inconsistencies, the rejection of ideology—visible from his earliest poems—has to be seen as typical of a generation whose youth was abused by national Socialism.

Another consistent feature in Enzensberger's writing is his carrying of an argument to (and sometimes beyond) its logical extreme. In his volume *Politics and Crime* (*Politik und Verbrechen,* 1964), which deals with such figures as Papa Doc Duvalier and Trujillo, he concludes that there is always a link between his two title subjects. Similarly, the vacuous nature of much television has led Enzensberger to the conclusion that it is a "nothing-medium." Whatever the nature of the arguments expressed, Enzensberger's essays are invariably provocative and stimulating in that they are the product of a fearsome intellect and of a major literary talent.

Selected Bibliography: Fischer, Gerhard, ed. *Debating Enzensberger: "Great Migration" and Civil War."* Tübingen: Stauffenburg, 1996; Siefken, Hinrich, and J. H. Reid, eds. *"Lektüre—ein anarchischer Akt":* *A Nottingham Symposium with Hans Magnus Enzensberger.* Nottingham: U of Nottingham, 1990.

Stuart Parkes

EPIC THEATER. Epic theater is the best known dramatic theory of **Bertolt Brecht**. It was conceived in the 1920s and developed both practically and theoretically until Brecht's death in 1956. The term literally means "narrative theater," and using the technique, Brecht sought to break the illusion of naturalist theater by contrasting dramatic action with epic narration in performance. Moments of high emotion, for example, were broken up by the entrance of narrators. Elsewhere banners may have announced the content or denouement of a scene, robbing it of its tension and encouraging the spectator to observe the process of the action on stage. Narrative devices prevented complete empathy and allowed the audience thinking room. The audience was perhaps the most important factor in the formulation of epic theater in that writing and performance practices were both predicated on the activation of the spectator. The stage was a site of questions, which were presented to the spectator for his or her consideration, hence the open ending of plays such as *The Good Person of Szechwan* or *The Threepenny Opera*. Epic theater, together with the *Lehrstück*, were also means through which Brecht sought to realize a political theater based on an active engagement with the aesthetics of representation. If one views the world, as Brecht did, as dialectical, one develops a historicized concept of human nature. If human beings are constituted by the ensemble of their social relations, as **Marx** maintained, then their "nature" will inevitably change along with their social context. This postulate is the center of political drama as Brecht understood it: by changing the world, one changes humanity. Consequently, Brecht sought strategies to problematize the easy consumption of character and situation in a bid to reveal their constructed nature. To this end, he developed the concept of *Verfremdung*, often translated in English as "alienation," though more appropriately translated as "estrangement" or "defamiliarization." This effect may be seen in all the epic plays. The generosity of the philanthropist Pierpont Mauler in *St. Joan of the Stockyards* is contrasted with his ruthlessness as a businessman; the boldness of Galileo's scientific revolution is tempered by his recantation before the Inquisition in *Life of Galileo*. Brecht called epic theater a "theater of the scientific age," an epithet that has often allied the form with coldness and intellectualism, a belief that the audience's role is that of a detached observer. This assertion ignores Brecht's more important contention that the theater should be used to educate *and* to entertain. It is thus difficult not to share in the emotion of the plays, such as when Grusha risks losing her surrogate child in *The Caucasian Chalk Circle* or when dumb Kattrin is murdered for alerting the city of Halle to an imminent attack from an enemy army in *Mother Courage and Her Children*. In contrast to the *Lehrstück*, Brecht described epic theater in 1930 as "minor pedagogy [. . .] a democratization of the theatre" because the actor/audience divide had not been breached. Today, the devices of epic theater have become commonplaces in much contemporary drama. Yet it is worth stressing that Brecht's conception of the form was intimately related to a political agenda of dialectical theater, in which the dynamic relationship between individual character and social formation took center stage.

Selected Bibliography: Brecht, Bertolt. *Brecht on Art and Politics*. Ed. Tom Kuhn and Steve Giles. London: Methuen, 2003; Brecht, Bertolt. *Brecht on Theatre: The Development of an Aesthetic*. Ed. and trans. John Willett. London: Methuen, 1964; Bryant-Bertail, Sarah. *Space and Time in Epic Theater: The Brechtian Legacy*. Jameson, Fredric. *Brecht and Method*. London: Verso, 1998.

David Barnett

○F○

FANON, FRANTZ (1925–1961). Fanon's work unravels the complex psychology of the victim of racism, the dispossessed, the colonized, as well as the decolonized. Born in Martinique, where his paternal ancestors were brought from Africa as slaves to work the sugar plantations, Fanon completed his high school education in the Antilles, joined the resistance against the pro-Nazi French government, and went to France to fight in the Free French army against the German occupation in 1943—even before he was twenty. When the war was over, he went to Lyon on a scholarship to study medicine, specializing in psychiatry. Fanon grew unhappy in France when he realized the extent of racism in French society and what it does to the black psyche; he wrote about the phenomena in *Black Skin, White Mask* (1952). After graduation, Fanon went to Algeria and chaired the department of psychiatry in a hospital. When the Algerian nationalist struggle began in 1954, he resigned from his job, joined the movement, and supported the National Liberation Front (FLN) by editing its newspaper. He died prematurely at the age of thirty-six of leukemia in Bethesda, Maryland, where he had come to seek treatment.

Black Skin, Fanon's first work, studies the effects of racism on its victims. The mind of the black man, Fanon argues, develops through a *process of accommodation and alienation*. The white society lures the African man with its promise of justice and equality. Deep inside, however, it treats him as a savage and an inferior. The African's high education or skill makes no difference in this equation. (It is pertinent to mention that some French patients refused to be treated by Fanon at Lyon.) Faced with racial contempt, the African is forced to assimilate, pretending to be white. Fanon calls this adjustment "accommodation" because "[f]or the black man there is only one destiny. And it is white" (228). The African's skin, on the other hand, constantly reminds him of his true identity, thus alienating him from himself.

Fanon, however, envisions a bright future for humanity, one of harmony between black and white, for neither has to remain a prisoner of the past. This integration can occur through a process of disalienation. In the concluding pages of *Black Skin*, Fanon makes a series of statements seemingly laden with sarcasm. In one, he writes, "I as a man of color do not have the right to seek ways of stamping down the pride of my former master." In another, he states, "There is no Negro mission; there is no white burden." But the sarcasm disappears when Fanon finally says, "I find myself suddenly in the world and I recognize that I have one right alone: that of demanding human behavior from the other." He was in earnest when he was renouncing the black man's vindictive tendencies. A remarkable power of Fanon is the ability to look forward to the future, unsaddled by the racial damage of the past.

But Fanon is more in tune with the present than any other time in *Black Skin*, even expressing some concern about attempts to look for the past glory of African civilization. Perhaps this is his way of viewing the **negritude** movement—which had greatly influenced him at one time—with some skepticism. Fanon reveals that he would be quite pleased to learn that a contact occurred between Africa and classical Greece, but he sees no value in such a discovery since it would not affect "the lives of eight-year-old children who labor in the cane fields of Martinique or Guadeloupe."

Fanon's optimism and pragmatism derive from his Marxism, and he is best regarded as a Marxist thinker. In the categories of race and class, he believes class to be the dominant one. *The Wretched of the Earth* (1963), the book Fanon wrote shortly before his death, makes this point clear. In it, Fanon examines the condition of African societies after decolonization, pointing out the deleterious role that the national bourgeoisie play in them. The national bourgeoisie, who are ideologically aligned with the departed colonial masters, are black, but they share the same class interests of the masters. The fact accounts for the failure of many African nations to realize their nationalist potential after independence. However, Fanon differs from Marx on one key point in *Wretched*. Marx sees little role for peasants and the urban *lumpenproletariat* in any coming revolution, which for him is preeminently a project of the working class. Perhaps because of the absence of an organized working class in African nations, Fanon credits peasants and the *lumpenproletariat* with strong activist potential there.

Fanon's other influential works are *A Dying Colonialism* (1959), a collection of essays on the Algerian revolution, and *Toward the African Revolution* (1964), a book of his essays published posthumously. Fanon remains an influential theorist in postcolonial studies. Works of authors who deal with the ills of postcolonial societies yield very well to his insights, especially those authors who have been directly impacted by his works, such as Ayi Kwei Armah, Sembène Ousmene, and **Ngũgĩ wa Thiong'o.** Fanon's ideas also apply well to works by non-African authors, for example, to those of **Salman Rushdie.** Rushdie's *The Moor's Last Sigh* is a novel that depicts postindependence India and how the nation's corrupt politicians and national bourgeoisie collude together to advance their self-interest, thus illustrating Fanon's findings, especially in *The Wretched of the Earth*. There are also many scholars who have effectively used Fanon in their theoretical works on postcolonial culture and societies, for example, Homi Bhabha, Benita Parry, **Edward Said**, and **Epifanio San Juan Jr.**

Selected Bibliography: Caute, David. *Frantz Fanon.* New York: Viking, 1970; Gibson, Nigel. *Fanon: The Postcolonial Imagination.* Malden, MA: Blackwell, 2003; Gibson, Nigel, ed. *Rethinking Fanon: The Continuing Dialogue.* Amherst, NY: Humanity Books, 1999; Gordon, Lewis. *Frantz Fanon and the Crisis of European Man.* Cambridge, MA: Blackwell, 1995; Gordon, Lewis, ed. *Fanon: A Critical Reader.* Cambridge, MA: Blackwell, 1996; Sekyi-Otu, Ato. *Fanon's Dialectic of Experience.* Cambridge, MA: Harvard UP, 1996.

Farhad B. Idris

FARRELL, JAMES T. (1904–1979), American author and essayist whose forty volumes of fiction, essays, and poetry applied sociological naturalism to the voluminously documented lives of a series of semiautobiographical protagonists. Born in Irish Chicago to a poor teamster, Farrell soaked up the excitements, cruelties, and dead ends of the street. Both his underlying belief that capitalism was "impermanent" and his attraction to the **Communist Party** from the early to mid-1930s inform his signature trilogy, *Studs Lonigan*: *Young Lonigan* (1934), *The Young Manhood of Studs Lonigan* (1934), and *Judgment Day* (1935).

Begun when he was a freshman at the University of Chicago, the trilogy scrupulously details life among the Irish American metropolitan lower middle classes: conversational rhythms, leisure and drinking habits, taboos, courtship (and misogyny) rituals, and sometimes guilty devotion to an all-powerful Catholic Church. At the same time, Farrell provides a vivid cross section of urban America from World War I through the Hoover years. In the trilogy, the petty-bourgeois Mary and Paddy Lonigan and their children, particularly son Studs, stake their identities on individualistic separation from the worker class. Victims of their own false consciousness as much as of their devastating economic losses in the early Depression years, they remain as rabidly antileftist as they began. While Farrell's trilogy may not strictly qualify as **proletarian fiction**, it is a powerful indictment of American spiritual emptiness.

Near the end of *Judgment Day*, Studs's bewildered father encounters a parade of May Day marchers optimistically chanting "white and Jew and gentile, we will build Socialism in America" and "Down with Imperialist War." However, Farrell, who had been a fellow traveler but not a party member, was by this time already disenchanted with both the Communist Party and the proletarian literary movement he had once supported. His fervent anti-Stalinism propeled him to Trotskyism by 1936, and his horror at the Moscow trials moved him still farther from leftist politics by the late 1930s. Farrell's impending break with Marxist authors and critics was also hastened by his 1936 book *A Note on Literary Criticism*, in which he criticized political propagandizing in the fiction of the intellectual left.

Among the **New York intellectuals** of the 1940s and 1950s, the literary-political realignments caused by the embrace of high modernism and the fallout from the cold war elevated "classic authors" like **Henry James** over Farrell and his naturalistic mentor, **Theodore Dreiser**. Thus, the very qualities for which *Studs Lonigan* had received praise became suspect, and Farrell's reputation, like that of Nelson Algren, **Jack Conroy**, and other committed social-protest writers, declined. Farrell continued to write, but his prolific output was often less noted than his volatile political transformations, including his pro–Vietnam War stance and his self-labeling as a "socialist for Nixon."

Farrell's legacy, both as a lifelong Socialist and as an American writer, is still under debate. But there is little doubt that, like **Mike Gold**, Conroy, and so many talented and near-forgotten social-content authors, he was both an interpreter and a victim of the proletarian moment. The Depression was his heyday; better economic times muted his voice.

Selected Bibliography: Conn, Peter. *Literature in America.* Cambridge: Cambridge UP, 1989; Douglas, Ann. Introduction to *Studs Lonigan: A Trilogy* by James T. Farrell. New York: Penguin, 2001; Farrell, James T. *A Note on Literary Criticism.* New York: Vanguard, 1936; Foley, Barbara. *Radical*

Representations: Politics and Form in U.S. Proletarian Fiction, 1929–1941. Durham, NC: Duke UP, 1993; Wald, Alan M. *James T. Farrell: The Revolutionary Socialist Years*. New York: New York UP, 1978.

Laura Hapke

FAST, HOWARD (1914–2003). In a career that stretched from the 1930s to the publication of his last novel in 2000, Howard Fast was one of the most prolific and popular authors of the American Left. Fast, the son of a New York factory worker, wrote numerous best-selling novels, many of which have remained in print over long periods of time. Many of his early works were historical novels about the American Revolution, including *Two Valleys* (1933), *Conceived in Liberty* (1939), *The Unvanquished* (1942), and *Citizen Tom Paine* (1943). In such novels, especially the latter two, Fast attempts to portray the radical origins of American democracy, envisioning the founding fathers as the direct forerunners of the radical leftists of the 1930s and 1940s. Fast continued his fictional re-creation of the American Revolutionary period in such later works as *April Morning* (1961), *The Crossing* (1971), *The Hessian* (1972), and *Seven Days in June* (1994). Fast also wrote historical novels set in other periods of the American past, including *The Last Frontier* (1941, dealing with the brutal and sometimes genocidal treatment of Native Americans by the U.S. government), *Freedom Road* (1944, a critique of racism set during Reconstruction), *The American* (1946, a fictional biography of John Peter Altgeld, the Illinois governor who pardoned three of the Haymarket anarchists), and *The Passion of Sacco and Vanzetti* (1953). His novels *Silas Timberman* (1954), *The Story of Lola Gregg* (1956), and *The Pledge* (1988) deal with the McCarthyite **anticommunism** of the late 1940s and 1950s.

Fast also wrote historical novels set in ancient times, most notably *Spartacus* (1951), focusing on a famous rebellion in which the gladiator Spartacus led a rebel army composed of slaves and other gladiators in a two-year war against the power of Rome, ending in 71 B.C.E. While ultimately unsuccessful, this rebellion would long stand as a source of inspiration for the Left, as when the communist rebels who nearly took control of the German government under the leadership of Rosa Luxemburg and Karl Liebknecht in 1919 referred to themselves as "Spartacists." Fast's novel, meanwhile, serves as an important marker of the history of leftist culture in America. The early history of the book, for example, serves as a reminder of the tribulations of the American Left during the McCarthyite repressions of the early cold-war years. *Spartacus*, as Fast explains in his introduction to the 1996 reissue of the book, was written soon after its author was released from prison for his refusal to cooperate with the House Un-American Activities Committee (HUAC) in their now notorious investigations of communist activity in the United States. Meanwhile, as Fast describes in his autobiography, *Being Red*, he had to overcome a number of obstacles while writing the book (286–300). For example, he (along with thousands of other American leftists) was denied a passport and was therefore unable to travel to Italy to research the book as he had hoped. Then, despite his established reputation as a successful writer, Fast found that he was unable to place the book with a commercial publisher due to the government-supported blacklist that made it virtually impossible for writers suspected of leftist sympathies to get into print in the United

States in the early 1950s. Not to be dissuaded, Fast published the book himself and managed to sell over forty thousand copies. Meanwhile, the official attempt to suppress Fast's work gradually diminished, partly because of a general lifting of the repressive atmosphere of the 1950s and partly because of Fast's own disavowal of the Communist Party in his 1957 book *The Naked God*. As a result, it became possible to make a film version of *Spartacus*, and the 1960 film of the same title, directed by Stanley Kubrick, became one of the classic works of American cinema.

In addition to his turn to self-publication, Fast evaded some of the blacklisting associated with the darkest period of the repressive anticommunism of the 1950s by turning to the writing of a series of excellent thrillers, written under the pseudonym E. V. Cunningham and featuring a Japanese American detective. Ultimately, he published more than twenty novels under that pseudonym, in addition to the more than forty he published under his own name. Winner of the 1954 Stalin Prize, Fast was a member of the **Communist Party** from 1943 to 1956.

Selected Bibliography: Booker, M. Keith. *The Modern American Novel of the Left: A Research Guide.* Westport, CT: Greenwood, 1999; Fast, Howard. *Being Red.* Boston: Houghton Mifflin, 1990; Macdonald, Andrew. *Howard Fast: A Critical Companion.* Westport, CT: Greenwood, 1996; Rideout, Walter B. *The Radical Novel in the United States, 1900–1954.* Cambridge: Harvard UP, 1956.

M. Keith Booker

FAULKNER, WILLIAM (1897–1962). Generally regarded as one of the greatest novelists in the United States—and the world—Faulkner was born and raised in North Mississippi, the area that he would eventually explore in most of his best fiction. Largely self-taught, he typically portrayed the life and history of his fictional Mississippi county, Yoknapatawpha, with dizzying and dazzling complexity, focusing on characters sorting out their lives amid the South's massive cultural transformations, as traditional culture gave way to modernization and industrialism.

After two mildly successful novels set outside Mississippi—*Soldier's Pay* (1926) and *Mosquitoes* (1927)—Faulkner began in the late 1920s writing almost exclusively about life in North Mississippi. His best work followed, including *Sartoris* (1929), *The Sound and the Fury* (1929), *As I Lay Dying* (1930), *Sanctuary* (1931), *Light in August* (1932), *Absalom, Absalom!* (1936), *The Unvanquished* (1938), *The Hamlet* (1940), and *Go Down, Moses* (1942).

A tragic gloom cloaks almost all of Faulkner's work from this period, with the grinding forces of history progressively transforming the heroic "tall men" of the Southern past into piddling moderns, people more concerned with achieving success than upholding honor and tradition. So dark, violent, and extreme was Faulkner's fiction, so peopled with the troubled if not the psychotic, that many contemporary critics, particularly from the Left, saw his work tending toward the savage, anticivilization roots of Fascism.

Faulkner was anything but a fascist, however dark his fiction. In fact, during the late 1930s, Faulkner was deeply worried about the rising power of Nazi Germany and fascist Italy. When war broke out, he tried to join the war effort, and when that failed, he ended up in Hollywood writing screenplays, several of which were constructed as wartime propaganda.

Faulkner's time in Hollywood was more significant to his career than generally ac-knowledged, for there he began to reassess his role as artist, driven by his concerns regarding totalitarianism's threat to American democracy. He wanted to be more "ar-ticulate in the national voice," and after the war, he wrote fiction that grappled more openly (and more didactically) with contemporary social issues, particularly issues of freedom and democracy. Important work from his late period include *Intruder in the Dust* (1948), *Requiem for a Nun* (1951), *A Fable* (1954), *The Town* (1958), and *The Mansion* (1959).

Championed by proponents of the **New Criticism** as a paragon of **modernism**, Faulkner found his critical reputation on the rise in the postwar period. After win-ning the 1949 Nobel Prize, Faulkner became a public persona, giving numerous in-terviews, talks, and speeches in which he voiced a staunch antiauthoritarianism and anticommunism. That antiauthoritarianism included resistance to federal interven-tion regarding Southern race practices and laws; Faulkner instead endorsed, as did most Southern liberals, a wary gradualism for improving the lot of African Ameri-cans in the South.

Faulkner's greatest writing, that from 1929 to 1942, was less overtly political than his later, more predictable fiction. Even so, that earlier work pulsates with social and political issues, particularly those surrounding the breakdown of traditional culture, even if those issues rarely take center stage. In his best work, Faulkner instead de-picted political matters messily entangled with the desires, needs, and fears of indi-viduals, affirming little other than individual integrity and honor in times when traditional ideals have lost cultural authority.

Selected Bibliography: Blotner, Joseph. *Faulkner: A Biography.* 2 vols. New York: Random House, 1974; Brooks, Cleanth. *William Faulkner: The Yoknapatawpha Country.* New Haven, CT: Yale UP, 1963; Gray, Richard. *The Life of William Faulkner: A Critical Biography.* Oxford: Blackwell, 1994; Minter, David. *William Faulkner: His Life and Work.* Baltimore: Johns Hopins UP, 1980; Schwartz, Lawrence. *Creating Faulkner's Reputation: The Politics of Modern Literary Criticism.* Knoxville: U of Tennessee P, 1988; Singal, Daniel. *William Faulkner: The Making of a Modernist.* Chapel Hill: U of North Carolina P, 1997; Williamson, Joel. *William Faulkner and Southern History.* New York: Oxford UP, 1993.

Robert H. Brinkmeyer Jr.

FEARING, KENNETH (1902–1961). An enigmatic figure both in life and on the page, Fearing defies the usual critical categories. Neither "high" nor "low," neither orthodox Marxist nor mandarin modernist, Fearing began to slide into obscurity be-fore his death in 1961 but has reemerged within the past ten years, as critics have begun to revise and expand our sense of the culture of American modernism and es-pecially the interwar Left.

After his childhood in Oak Park, Illinois, and subsequent (though uncompleted) undergraduate education at the University of Wisconsin, Fearing moved to New York in 1924. There he began to publish poems in small left-wing magazines such as *New Masses* and *Dynamo* while supporting himself by writing pulp fiction at a cent or less per word. This combination, though certainly a marriage of convenience, is fitting insofar as Fearing, more than any other poet of his generation, takes the formal qual-ities and thematic content of mass culture as a primary subject. Poet Kenneth Rexroth once stated that Fearing writes "like a taxi driver reading a billboard while fighting traffic"—a simile that neatly captures both the working-class sympathies that distance Fearing from the mandarin **modernism** of **T. S. Eliot** and his emphasis on the increasingly looming presence of the culture industries in everyday life. Mass cultural forms such as comic strips and movies become, in Fearing's work, both objects of satire and models of a sort for poems that are demotic and reflective of the fragmentary texture of a media-saturated modern landscape.

In political terms, Fearing's vision is too cynical and ironic to conform to the utopian **proletarian literature** of committed communist writers like **Mike Gold** or the democratic nationalism of the **Popular Front**. It is closer in spirit to **Theodor Adorno**'s and Max Horkheimer's 1940s-era critiques of the "culture industry," as evidenced by Fearing's most commercially successful work, *The Big Clock* (1946), a novel that depicts a world in which Big Media increasingly subsumes alternative thought and practices within its consensus-producing machinery. As the "taxi driver" comment suggests, however, Fearing diverges from the **Frankfurt School** insofar as he stops short of a wholesale condemnation of mass culture (and its consumers). Rita Barnard wittily captures this aspect of Fearing's work in calling him a "double agent": he at once wants to expose the ideological nature of capitalist cultural production and to explore the democratic potential bound up in the consumption of these products.

It is this doubleness that has made Fearing newly interesting to critics and readers eager to make connections between interwar modernism and postwar postmodernism; to enrich understandings of the artistic and intellectual diversity within the interwar Left; to consider the relationships between canonical modernist texts and extracanonical materials. For these reasons, Fearing is, despite his "minor" status within the received literary tradition, peculiarly and compellingly contemporary.

Selected Bibliography: Barnard, Rita. *The Great Depression and the Culture of Abundance: Kenneth Fearing, Nathanael West, and Mass Culture in the 1930s.* Cambridge: Cambridge UP, 1995; Halliday, Mark. "Damned Good Poet: Kenneth Fearing." *Michigan Quarterly Review* 40.2 (Spring 2001): 384–411; Santora, Patricia B. "The Life of Kenneth Flexner Fearing." *CLA Journal* 32 (March 1989): 309–22.

Jeff Allred

FEDERAL WRITERS' PROJECT (FWP), a New Deal–era program that was part of the most substantive governmental support for the arts in American history. It was established as one of four arts programs within the Works Progress Administration (WPA) in 1935 and supported roughly five thousand writers, researchers, and clerical workers on average throughout its tenure. Like all of the WPA projects, it was primarily an employment program, and the vast majority of its "writers" were hired on the basis of demonstrated financial need rather than literary achievement. Nonetheless, the project compiled a vast and diverse body of work, including travel guides, essays, oral histories, fiction, poetry, and collections of folklore. The most prominent project was the American Guide series, which featured travel guides to each of the forty-eight states. These guides, researched and written by workers at the various state offices, aimed to "introduce Americans to America," combining history, geography, ethnography, and economics into detailed cultural maps for auto tourists riding the era's proliferating network of U.S. highways. In addition to the guides, the project produced a volume of essays and imaginative literature—*American Stuff* (1938)—and compilations of oral history, such as *These Are Our Lives* (1939) and *Lay My Burden Down: A Folk History of Slavery* (1945).

As is typical in New Deal discourse, one sees through the lens of FWP writings a national unity-in-diversity; throughout the project, differences of race, ethnicity, region, and class are subsumed within a harmonious and unified America. Scholars have recently begun to emphasize, however, the tension between this romantic American nationalism and competing regional, ethnic, and racial nationalisms. Perhaps the most dramatic example is the ambivalent status of African Americans in the FWP, both as employees and as objects of study. Although Sterling A. Brown played an important role in the federal office as editor of Negro affairs, advocating against stereotypical representations of African Americans, only about 2 percent of FWP workers were black. As a result, African American perspectives were often absent from FWP publications or, when present, were often represented in the distorting light of the racism or provincialism of white writers and researchers at the local level.

However mild the FWP's ideological commitments seem from a contemporary perspective, the project nonetheless found itself under increasing attack from conservatives in the late 1930s. Representative Martin Dies, chair of the newly formed House Committee on Un-American Activities, questioned project head Henry Alsberg and others in 1939 regarding both the alleged presence of Communists throughout the organization and the alleged bent of FWP publications toward anti-American propaganda in a harbinger of McCarthy-era Red-baiting. These attacks, along with a broader shift in the government's emphasis away from relief and toward war mobilization, ushered in the beginning of the end of the project, which underwent a slow process of defunding, devolution, and eventual demise between 1939 and 1942.

Selected Bibliography: Hirsh, Jerrold. *Portrait of America: A Cultural History of the Federal Writers' Project.* Chapel Hill: U of North Carolina P, 2003; Mangione, Jerre. *The Dream and the Deal: The Federal Writers' Project, 1935–1943.* Philadelphia: U of Pennsylvania P, 1983; Penkower, Monty Noam. *The Federal Writers' Project: A Study in Government Patronage of the Arts.* Urbana: U of Illinois P, 1977.

Jeff Allred

FEMINIST CRITICISM AND THEORY. "Definitions belong to the definers, not the defined," thinks a character in **Toni Morrison**'s 1987 novel ***Beloved***, contemplating his identity as a slave. The idea that definition is a gesture of mastery and exclusion is a foundational principle of contemporary feminism, which of course makes it problematic to attempt a definition of feminist criticism and theory itself. Feminist criticism is plural and interdisciplinary, borrowing concepts and methods from a variety of critical schools. It is, however, possible to trace the history of feminist criticism and theory and to outline some of the major strands of feminist thought, briefly situating them in relation to other critical discourses, and trying to give some idea of the range of interpretive possibilities they have opened up.

Feminist criticism emerged as a distinct field of textual analysis in the 1960s, born of the enormously fertile political climate that spawned the civil rights and so-called "women's liberation" movements in the United States Political tumult also swirled through Europe at that time, as activists campaigned for nuclear disarmament and a resurgence of labor unions in Great Britain, and students struck amid an atmosphere of intellectual revolution on campuses in France. As women in both the United States and Western Europe began to realize that the leadership of these leftist political movements did not consider the eradication of sexism a political priority, they began to break away from male-dominated political organizations. They formed women's groups, calling for equality of opportunity in the workplace, reproductive rights, representation of women in government, and university courses in women's studies.

Early feminist criticism focused on identifying stereotypical images of women in canonical literature and in scholarship by men, on discerning the presumed innate differences between men's and women's writing, and on recovering a lost tradition of women writers. The first two of these aims were anticipated in perhaps the most important founding text of feminist criticism and theory in English, **Virginia Woolf**'s *A Room of One's Own* (1929). In classic literature, she noted, women are goddesses and heroines; in historical reality, they are "locked up, beaten and flung about the room" (44). And, she notes, when women attempt to write the "man's sentence," their writing clanks; they must instead emulate Jane Austen, who discovered a "perfectly natural, shapely sentence proper for her own use and never departed from it" (80).

Then in 1968, Mary Ellmann published *Thinking about Women*, which theorized the existence of distinct "masculine" and "feminine" modes of writing, the former crisp and authoritative, the latter sensuous and playful. Kate Millett's *Sexual Politics* (1970) traced the patriarchal distortions in representations of women in works by D. H. Lawrence, Henry Miller, and **Norman Mailer**. Both Millett and Ellmann imagined gender as socially constructed rather than biologically determined, and both contributed to the conceptualization of literature as an instrument of masculine power and a means of socializing readers into appropriate sex roles.

Several works of 1960s and 1970s feminist criticism focused on recovering the submerged history of women writers and advanced the argument that the canon of Western literature is male-dominated as a result of political rather than purely aesthetic considerations. Ellen Moers produced a study of female influence entitled *Literary Women* (1976), and Elaine Showalter wrote another study tracing a women's literary tradition, *A Literature of Their Own: British Women Novelists from Bronte to Lessing* (1977). But it was Sandra Gilbert and Susan Gubar's study of nineteenth-century British women writers, *The Madwoman in the Attic: The Woman Writer and the Nineteenth Century Literary Imagination* (1979), that was most influential in this line of inquiry. They adapted Harold Bloom's theory of the contentious and ambivalent masculine poetic tradition, "The Anxiety of Influence," suggesting that women writers of the nineteenth century had to contend not only with male predecessors, as did their male peers, but also with strictures against female authorship. Thus, they resorted to subversive narrative and poetic strategies, appearing to accept but actually rebelling against prescribed sex roles. Much of early feminist criticism had been criticized for taking literature as too nakedly a reflection of social reality, of having lost sight of the fictive qualities that differentiate it from sociological documents. Gilbert and Gubar instead read these writers against the grain, looking beneath the textual surface for hidden meanings. They have been criticized for reading all the texts they deal with as, however obscurely, documents of victimization. But they did lift feminist criticism in English to a level of intellectual sophistication it had not before reached.

In the late 1970s and 1980s, feminist criticism began to diversify. Lesbian and black feminist writers and scholars published articles pointing out that feminist criticism had committed some of the same errors as had the male tradition it sought to undermine; the newly minted women's literary history was also selective and ideological in its makeup. It falsely universalized the experience of straight, middle-class, white women, as if whatever might be said about them would also be true of lesbians, working-class women, and women of color. So a "new feminist criticism" proliferated. Feminist poet and theorist Adrienne Rich wrote an enormously influential essay entitled "Compulsory Heterosexuality and Lesbian Existence," arguing that women's sexual identities fall along a spectrum she calls the "lesbian continuum." What makes a lesbian, she argues, is not sexual behavior but the degree to which a woman is "woman-identified." Bonnie Zimmerman wrote "What Has Never Been: An Overview of Lesbian Feminist Literary Criticism," which sought to establish a tradition of lesbian writing, unveiling both lesbian content in literature by women and lesbianism as the true identity of supposed spinsters and recluses like Emily Dickinson.

Black feminist authors and critics such as Alice Walker, **Audre Lorde**, Barbara Smith, Susan Willis, and Deborah McDowell argued that black women suffer a double oppression, on racial and gender grounds (triple if they are also lesbian). Two very important essay collections from the early 1980s explored the relevance of race to feminist literary criticism. *This Bridge Called My Back: Writings by Radical Women of Color* (1981), edited by Cherrie Moraga and **Gloria Anzaldúa**, featured a number of (for that time) shockingly personal and formally heterogeneous essays. True to its title, it sought to "bridge" the deep divides that were fracturing feminism. *All the Women Are White, All the Blacks Are Men, But Some of Us Are Brave: Black Women's Studies* (1982) contained essays that proposed reading lists and syllabi as well as overall plans for launching the field of black women's studies. Both these volumes began to define a canon of literature by women of color and elaborated critical strategies to take account of that literature's aesthetic and political differences from literature by white men and women. Of course, these canon-creating endeavors ran into the same set of problems that all canons do; the more one specifies categories of "women of color" and "lesbian," the more one runs the risk of homogenizing these groups and defining them in essentialist terms. It has become quite clear that the meanings of identity categories such as "lesbian" and "black" or "African American" change with historical shifts in the construction of sexuality and race. Moreover, seeking to create a great tradition reestablishes the aesthetic concepts and individualistic values that have defined the dominant order the feminist critic seeks to displace.

Some feminists, committed to generating interpretations attentive to social and historical specificity and to the interrelations of gender with class and race, found in Marxism the resolute materialism they sought. For Marxists, culture is historically produced and reflects the social and especially the economic relations of its time. **Marxist criticism** provides a window on literature as a means by which prevailing ideologies, like those of capitalism and patriarchy, are reproduced. It also encourages a focus on the material conditions under which women's texts are produced. **Marxist-**

feminism has proven a rich approach that combines the advantages of Marxist theory with the special insights of feminism.

In parallel (and in dialogue) with these developments in Anglo-American feminist criticism and theory, French feminism, heavily influenced by structuralist and poststructuralist thinkers such as **Jacques Derrida** and Jacques Lacan, has charted its own more theoretically informed course. French feminists such as Hélène Cixous, **Julia Kristeva**, and Luce Irigaray have placed particular emphasis on the construction of subjectivity in language and on the ways in which women may use language differently from men. In recent decades, Anglo-American and French feminism have tended to merge, producing increasingly sophisticated theories of subjectivity and difference to attempt to resolve problems of canonicity and identity. Identity is thus always fragmented and discontinuous, constituted as it is by a matrix of subject positions that are frequently inconsistent with one another. Lacanian psychoanalysis, on which poststructuralist feminists also draw, posits a patriarchal symbolic order, within which "feminine" difference functions as a fissure or silence within identity and language, not directly expressible but manifest in the paradoxes of rational patriarchal discourse. Feminist practice in this conception involves discerning eruptions of the feminine within masculine (not necessarily male-authored) texts, and a search for a new feminine language and textual practice.

As many have observed, one problem with such conceptualizations of sexual identity is that they continue to confine feminist analysis within a universal male/female binary, obscuring the heterogeneity of gender as it is lived. The most recent feminist criticism and theory has allied itself with postmodernism's (especially in the work of **Michel Foucault**) focus on "local and subjugated knowledges." Feminists like **Donna Haraway** and Rosi Braidotti concentrate on what Linda Hutcheon calls the "ex-centric," which is to say discourses and knowledges marginalized within the Western tradition. In addition, they look forward to the emergence of "cyborg" or "nomadic" subjects who will exist in a world beyond binary gender. Along with such theorists as **Judith Butler**, Haraway and Braidotti unsettle the foundations of feminism as it has heretofore been practiced, calling into question the reality of the category of women and thus the female subject of feminist criticism and theory.

Selected Bibliography: Braidotti, Rosi. *Nomadic Subjects: Embodiment and Sexual Difference in Contemporary Feminist Theory.* New York: Columbia UP, 1994; Butler, Judith, and Joan W. Scott, eds. *Feminists Theorize the Political.* New York: Routledge, 1992; Eagleton, Mary. *Feminist Literary Theory: A Reader.* 2nd ed. Cambridge, MA: Blackwell, 1996; Ellmann, Mary. *Thinking about Women.* Reprint, London: Virago, 1979; Fuss, Diana. *Essentially Speaking: Feminism, Nature, and Difference.* London: Routledge, 1989; Gilbert, Sandra M., and Susan Gubar. *The Madwoman in the Attic: The Woman Writer and the Nineteenth Century Literary Imagination.* New Haven, CT: Yale UP, 1979; Greene, Gayle, and Coppelia Kahn, eds. *Making a Difference: Feminist Literary Criticism.* London: Methuen, 1985; Haraway, Donna J. "A Cyborg Manifesto: Science, Technology, and Socialist-Feminism in the Late Twentieth Century." 1985. Rev. *Simians, Cyborgs, and Women: The Reinvention of Nature.* New York: Routledge, 1991: 149–81; Hutcheon, Linda. *A Poetics of Postmodernism: History, Theory, Fiction.* New York: Routledge, 1988; Millett, Kate. *Sexual Politics.* London: Virago, 1977; Moers, Ellen. *Literary Women.* London: Women's P, 1978; Moi, Toril. *Sexual/Textual Politics.* London: Methuen, 1985; Moraga, Cherrie, and Gloria Anzaldúa, eds. *This Bridge Called My Back: Writings by Radical Women of Color.* Watertown, MA: Persephone P, 1981; Rich, Adrienne. "Compulsory Heterosexuality and Lesbian Existence." *Blood, Bread, and Poetry: Selected Prose, 1979–85.* New York: Norton, 1986. 23–75; Showalter, Elaine. *A Literature of Their Own: British Women Novelists from Bronte to Lessing.* Princeton, NJ: Princeton UP, 1977; Showalter, Elaine, ed. *The New Feminist Criticism: Essays on Women, Literature and Theory.* New York: Pantheon, 1985; Warhol, Robyn R., and Diane Price Herndl, eds. *Feminisms: An Anthology of Literary Theory and Criticism.* New Brunswick, NJ: Rutgers UP, 1991; Woolf, Virginia. *A Room of One's Own.* New York: Harcourt Brace, 1929; Zimmerman, Bonnie. "What Has Never Been: An Overview of Lesbian Feminist Criticism." *The New Feminist Criticism: Essays on Women, Literature and Theory.* Ed. Elaine Showalter. New York: Pantheon, 1985. 200–224.

Susan Marren

FERNÁNDEZ RETAMAR, ROBERTO (1930–). A leading public intellectual of revolutionary Cuba, the Havana-born Roberto Fernández Retamar is an award-winning poet and literary critic best known outside Latin American studies for his influential postcolonial essay "Caliban," published originally in 1971. The **Cuban Revolution** (1959) launched a vigorous cultural project that promoted literature and the arts at the continental level, but was increasingly intolerant of internal dissent. Such cultural projects included film festivals, art biennales, and literary prizes. Various cultural institutes were established, such as the Cuban film institute (ICAIC), the Wilfredo Lam art center, and the literature center Casa de las Américas. In 1965, Fernández Retamar became the editor of the journal of Casa de las Américas, and since 1986 has been the director of Casa. He also founded the Cuban Writers Union (1962) and the center of Estudios Martianos (1977), promoting the work of the nineteenth-century Cuban poet and revolutionary **José Martí**.

In "Caliban," Fernández Retamar traces the genealogy of **William Shakespeare**'s character Caliban from *The Tempest* (1611). An anagram for cannibal, this figure of the savage would appear repeatedly in the subsequent centuries in its negative form; Fernández Retamar would turn Caliban into a positive figure contesting colonialism. Forced to learn the language of his master (Prospero), Caliban also learns to curse. Caliban thus becomes the emblematic image of Latin American literatures, written in European languages but writing back at the metropolis. In this way, Fernández Retamar revised José Enrique Rodó's 1900 essay *Ariel*, which viewed this other character of *The Tempest* as a representative figure of the Latin American intellectual. The Caliban/cannibal figure has since become a central figure in postcolonial criticism to question the representations of the Americas. Another important critical work of Fernández Retamar is "Some Theoretical Problems of Spanish American Literature" (1975), in which he questions the uncritical use of Western theories such as structuralism. He also calls for the need to historicize literary criticism and to better understand the historical specificity of Latin America.

Fernández Retamar has published several collections of poems, including *Patrias* (1951), *Sí a la Revolución* (1958–1962), *Poeta en la Habana* (1980), and *Palabra de mi pueblo* (1981). His literary work has received national and international recognition, including the National Poetry Award (1952), the National Literary Award (1980), the Bulgarian 1989 International Poetry Prize Nikola Vaptsarov, and the Pérez Bonalde Poetry Prize in Argentina in 1990. In 1995, Fernández Retamar became professor emeritus of the Universidad de la Habana, where he studied philosophy and literature. He has also received honorary degrees from universities in Peru (1986), Bulgaria (1988), and Argentina (1993).

Suggested Bibliography: Achugar, Hugo. "Local/Global Latin Americanisms: 'Theoretical Babbling,' a propos of Roberto Fernández Retamar." *Interventions* 5.1 (2003): 125–41; Fernández Retamar, Roberto. *Caliban and Other Essays.* Trans. Edward Baker. Minneapolis: U of Minnesota P, 1989; Hulme, Peter, and William Sherman, eds. *The Tempest and Its Travels.* Philadelphia: U of Pennsylvania P, 2000; Lie, Nadia, and Theo D'haen, eds. *Constellation Caliban: Figurations and Character.* Amsterdam: Rodopi, 1977; Sklodowska, Elzbieta, and Ben Heller, eds. *Roberto Fernández Retamar y los estudios latinoamericanos.* Pittsburgh: Instituto Internacional de Literatura Iberoamericana, 2000.

Luis Fernando Restrepo

FOR WHOM THE BELL TOLLS (1940), **Ernest Hemingway**'s novel of the **Spanish Civil War**, tells the story of Robert Jordan, a volunteer who fights and dies for the Spanish republic, but by the end of the novel, the reader is more likely to be impressed with the moral ambiguity of the war than with the justice of the republican cause. Moral ambiguity is suggested, for example, by Hemingway's depiction of those on the other side as ordinary, sometimes decent human beings rather than demonic Fascists. The Fascists of the novel include Don Guillermo, who "was only a fascist to be a snob and to console himself that he must work for little. . . . He was a fascist, too, from the religiousness of his wife" (117). It turns out, furthermore, that not all the opponents of the republic are Fascists. Lieutenant Berrendo, for example, fights for the nationalists, but the reader learns that he is no Fascist but a Carlist in politics, "a very devout Catholic" (318), and a good man who takes no pleasure in the brutality of war. Maria, Robert Jordan's beloved for the three days of the novel, tells Jordan that her father was a republican but her mother was not. Her mother's last words were "Long live my husband who was Mayor of this village," because, explains Maria, "my mother was not a Republican and she would not say, '*Viva la República*,' but only *Viva* my father who lay there, on his face, by her feet" (351). Meanwhile, some of the republicans are morally compromised in the extreme. Pablo leads a village massacre and, as the novel ends, kills fellow guerillas, explaining, "They were not of our band" (456). André Marty is "one of France's great modern revolutionary figures" (417) and comes "from the Central Committee of the French Communist Party" (424), but he is also a killer, "crazy as a bedbug," a man with "a mania for shooting people" (418).

When Robert Jordan first volunteered to defend the Spanish republic, he felt he was part of "something that you could believe in wholly and completely and in which you felt an absolute brotherhood with the others who were engaged in it" (235). He was willing to put himself "under Communist discipline" because the Communists seemed to have the "soundest and sanest" plan to win the war (163), even though, as he told himself, "You're not a real Marxist and you know it. You believe in Liberty, Equality and Fraternity. You believe in Life, Liberty and the Pursuit of Happiness" (305). Ultimately Jordan is reduced to justifying the republican cause not on its own merits but only because "as long as we can hold them here we keep the fascists tied up. They can't attack any other country until they finish with us" (436). Hemingway's novel, however, leaves one wondering whether the defeat of the republicans would be measurably worse for the Spaniards than a republican victory, certain to ensure the triumph of Stalinist Communism.

Selected Bibliography: Hemingway, Ernest. *For Whom the Bell Tolls*. New York: Charles Scribner's Sons, 1940; Josephs, Allen. *For Whom the Bell Tolls: Ernest Hemingway's Undiscovered Country*. New York: Twayne, 1994; Martin, Robert A. "Hemingway's *For Whom the Bell Tolls*: Fact into Fiction." *Studies in American Fiction* 15.2 (Spring 1987): 219–25; Seaton, James. "Was Hemingway an Intellectual?" *The Hemingway Review* 10.1 (Fall 1990): 52–56.

James Seaton

FORTINI, FRANCO (1917–1994). Italian poet, literary critic, translator, and leftist intellectual. Born Franco Lattes in Florence, he attended university there, studying law and art history. His family was of modest means, and his Jewish father was persecuted and incarcerated by the Fascists. In 1938, the year of the Race Laws in Italy, he adopted the beginning of his mother's surname, and in 1939, he was baptized in the Waldensian Church, a decision he tied to his "Calvinistic" formation and "aesthetic religion" of choice. Fortini served in the Italian military until late 1943, when he fled to Switzerland and participated in the Partisan Republic of Valdossola (one of several small republics established by partisan groups in areas they won from Nazi-fascist forces during the fighting of 1943–1945). After the war, he returned to Italy; he belonged to the Italian Socialist Party from 1944 to 1957 and worked for two years on its newspaper, *Avanti!*

Fortini contributed to many political and cultural journals, his essays treating a number of topics, both political and literary. He was also a major literary translator; one notes especially his versions of Goethe's *Faust* and the complete lyric poetry of Brecht and Éluard. As a poet he came of age with *Foglio di via* (Expulsion Order, 1946), a lyrical, often choral, testimony, of the poet's inner turmoil during wartime, and *I destini generali* (General Destinies, 1956). In his collected poems, *Una volta per sempre* (Once and For All, 1978), one senses the constant presence of plaints and stifled cries, a chorus of "slaves." Against this background, the reader is directed to recognize political change in process, and to accept a vision of the future in which collective suffering will be redeemed.

Like his mentor, the Catholic socialist Giacomo Noventa, Fortini opposed the idealist philosophers and hermetic poets whose influence was predominant during the fascist era. He took from Noventa the notion of the "verb in the future tense" as a means to project in his poetic work a time to come of liberation, equality, and justice. A self-described Communist, Fortini was an early critic of **Stalin** and never joined the Italian Communist Party. He criticized the "politicians among the politicians," the hierarchies of the major parties, the intransigent public institutions, and the entrenched literati. If, for **Antonio Gramsci**, ideology was based on one's actual activity in the world more than on abstract models, Fortini was a deserving heir. At the forefront of ongoing debates in Italy over the "question of the intellectuals," he would be accused of moralism, rigorism, and asceticism. He was ever firm in his support of labor movements and political prisoners, and he was a beloved teacher and supporter of young poets.

Selected Bibliography: Berardinelli, Alfonso. *Franco Fortini*. Florence: Nuova Italia, 1973; Forgàcs,

David. "Franco Fortini." *Writers and Society in Contemporary Italy.* Ed. M. Caesar and P. Hainsworth. Leamington Spa: Berg, 1984. 84–116; Fortini, Franco. *Insistenze: cinquanta scritti 1976–1984.* Milan: Garzanti, 1985; Fortini, Franco. *Nuovi saggi italiani.* Milan: Garzanti, 1987; Fortini, Franco. *Saggi ed epigrammi.* Ed. Luca Lenzini. Milan: Mondadori, 2003; Lenzini, Luca. *Il poeta di nome Fortini: saggi e proposte di lettura.* Lecce: P. Manni, 1999; Luperini, Romano. *La lotta mentale. per un profilo di Franco Fortini.* Rome: Editori Riuniti, 1986; Peterson, Thomas E. *The Ethical Muse of Franco Fortini.* Gainesville: U of Florida P, 1997.

Thomas E. Peterson

FOUCAULT, MICHEL (1926–1984). It is perhaps understandable that Foucault is a thinker who defies classification because one of his most sustained projects was to reflect critically on systems of knowledge. He has been called a philosopher, a historian, a social analyst, and a critical theorist. His work has also been of major importance in understanding relationships between literature and politics. As persistent as he was in excavating the underpinnings of those historically particular, enabling, and limiting systems of knowledge that he called *epistemés*, he was no less concerned with power, especially the power (or politics) of ways of knowing and the power of institutions over people's lives. His life, especially after his death from AIDS in 1984, has become no less politicized than his thought.

On March 4, 1972, an important public conversation took place between Foucault and **Gilles Deleuze**, later published under the title "Intellectuals and Power." At the time of the interview, Foucault was perhaps best known as the author of critical studies of asylums, hospitals, and other controlling institutions. But the fame of what is still widely regarded as his greatest book—*The Order of Things* (first published in French in 1966)—was also very much in the air. Toward the end of that conversation, Foucault said,

> Isn't [the] difficulty of finding adequate forms of struggle a result of the fact that we continue to ignore the problem of power? After all, we had to wait until the nineteenth century before we began to understand the nature of exploitation, and to this day, we have yet to fully comprehend the nature of power. It may be that Marx and Freud cannot satisfy our desire for understanding this enigmatic thing which we call power, which is at once visible and invisible, present and hidden, ubiquitous.

It is entirely appropriate, therefore, that one of the three superb volumes in the uniform English translation of Foucault's work is entitled simply *Power*.

In one of his most important essays, "Nietzsche, Genealogy, and History," Foucault echoed Nietzsche's conviction (in "The Use and Abuse of History for Life") that definitive origins and outcomes in historical processes cannot be determined. Just as we cannot determine in advance how things will end, so too can we not recover their originary moment. History, therefore, must settle for what lies between, which Nietzsche called genealogy. Despite Foucault's advocacy of this important insight, some commentators on his work (Arnold Davidson, for example) have attempted to think of his work in terms of three supposedly successive stages: (1) his analysis of systems of knowledge, (2) modalities of power, and (3) the self's relation to itself. This scheme would locate his political thought only in his studies of repressive institutions, such as asylums and prisons, rather than seeing it also as permeating his studies in the archaeology of knowledge and his final work on the history of sexuality. In fact, Foucault is as much a genealogical thinker as Nietzsche.

Two of Foucault's most important concerns were how deeply reason can look within itself to understand its enabling and limiting ways of knowing and how far reason can look beyond itself to understand madness. Concerning this second matter, he wrote,

> We have yet to write the history of that other form of madness, by which men, in an act of sovereign reason, confine their neighbors, and communicate and recognize each other through the merciless language of non-madness; to define the moment of this conspiracy before it was permanently established in the realm of truth, before it was revived by the lyricism of protest. We must try to return, in history, to that zero point in the course of madness at which madness is an undifferentiated experience, a not yet divided experience of division itself.

These words still cut through from the concentration camps in Germany and California during World War II to the more recent systems of confinement in Iraq and Guantánamo Bay. His concern, obviously, is with the ways repressive reason justifies itself by concentrating on the efficiency of its methods instead of its right.

In *The Order of Things*, Foucault looked for ways of encountering the experience of order itself between the ordering codes of given cultures and the philosophical, transcendent systems for sorting things out. By examining the epistemés of sign, function, and conflict from the Renaissance through the Enlightenment to modern times, he was able to argue that one of these epistemés dominates each age, as perhaps the epistemé of economic conflict dominates our own. Running counter to this politics of the epistemé, however, is the fact that when new paradigms are needed, they are produced by processes of hybridization. (For example, the gene code is a concept produced by combining biological function—the gene—with the linguistic sign—the code.)

Foucault's thought has had a decided influence on many subsequent writers and theorists (**Edward Said**, for example), and on much of feminist, psychoanalytic, and critical theory. His work on the history of sexuality has been particularly influential in the emerging fields of gender studies and **gay and lesbian studies**, while his methodology of historical research and argument has had a great impact on literary studies, especially in the critical approach known as the **new historicism**.

Selected Bibliography: Foucault, Michel. *The Care of the Self.* (Vol. 3 of *The History of Sexuality.*) Trans. Robert Hurley. New York: Vintage-Random House, 1988; Foucault, Michel. *Discipline and Punish: The Birth of the Prison.* Trans. Alan Sheridan. New York: Vintage-Random House, 1979; Foucault, Michel. *The History of Sexuality, Volume I: An Introduction.* Trans. Robert Hurley. New York: Vintage-Random House, 1980; Foucault, Michel. *Language, Counter-Memory, Practice: Selected Essays and Interviews.* Ed. Donald F. Bouchard. Ithaca: Cornell UP, 1977; Foucault, Michel. *Madness and Civilization.* Trans. Richard Howard. New York: Random House, 1965; Foucault, Michel. *The Order of Things.* Trans. Alan Sheridan. New York: Pantheon, 1970; Foucault, Michel. *Power.* Ed. James D. Faubion. New York: Free P, 2000; Foucault, Michel. *The Use of Pleasure.* (Vol. 2 of *The History of Sexuality.*) Trans. Robert Hurley. New York: Vintage-Random House, 1986; Gutting, Gary, ed. *The Cambridge Companion to*

Foucault. Cambridge: Cambridge UP, 1994; Macey, David. *The Lives of Michel Foucault: A Biography.* New York: Vintage-Random House, 1993; Payne, Michael. *Reading Knowledge: An Introduction to Barthes, Foucault and Althusser.* Oxford: Blackwell, 1997.

Michael Payne

FOX, RALPH (1900–1936 or 1937). The most traveled of the leftist intellectuals of the 1920s and 1930s, Fox died fighting in the **Spanish Civil War** and became a myth. His death occurred during an attack on the village of Lopera on the Córdoba front on either December 28, 1936, or January 2, 1937; recent research suggests the former. John Cornford died in the same fighting on the same day, and a monument to both has recently been erected. Fox was assistant political commissar to No. 1 Company of the Twelfth Battalion, Fourteenth International Brigade. He left cover during heavy firing to organize a machine-gun position, which led to his death.

Fox joined the Communist Party of Great Britain (CPGB) in 1926. Born in Halifax, he gained a First in French at Oxford in 1922, and that year joined the Friends' Relief mission to Kazakhstan and southern USSR. His travel narrative *The People of the Steppes* (1925) shows that he was in Moscow in 1922 and had at that time a critical admiration for the revolution. From 1927, he reviewed books for the CPGB's *Sunday Worker*, and moved to the *Daily Worker* (London) when it began publication on January 1, 1930. His literary work develops a Marxist theory of the novel, climaxing in his outstanding achievement, *The Novel and the People* (1937).

In 1930–1931 Fox worked at the Marx-Engels-Lenin Institute in Moscow as English librarian, where he researched subsequent books. From 1933, the foundations were laid for an orthodox British Marxism. With Montagu Slater and Tom Wintringham, Fox founded *Left Review* in 1934. His daily column "A Worker's Notebook" began in the *Daily Worker* on October 21, 1935, and continued almost uninterrupted until April 11, 1936. In 1936 alone, Fox published *Genghis Khan, France Faces the Future,* and *The Novel and the People* (dated 1937). The memorial volume *Ralph Fox: A Writer in Arms* appeared quickly, in March 1937, and set the terms of the myth of the writer dying for a cause.

Fox interprets literature as a humanist contribution to the understanding of social relations, a position not consistent with his Stalinist political writings. In *Lenin: A Biography* (1933), **Lenin**'s admiration for **Tolstoy** is really Fox's (161–65), while his regard for the importance of women in the revolution becomes attached to **Stalin**. An account by Ann Brett-Jones (a niece) suggests that Fox married twice, once in Moscow and again in England, without divorcing—apparently to help his second wife get a visa to travel to Spain. There remains the question of why the CPGB would ask a man of thirty-six to fight in the front line in Spain when his writings had contributed so much to defining Communism in Britain.

Selected Bibliography: Brett-Jones, Ann. "Ralph Fox: A Man in His Time." *Bulletin of the Marx Memorial Library* 137 (Spring 2003): 27–41; Fox, Ralph. *The Novel and the People.* 1937. Intro. Jeremy Hawthorn. London: Lawrence and Wishart, 1979; Lehmann, John, T. A. Jackson, and C. Day Lewis, eds. *Ralph Fox: A Writer in Arms.* London: Lawrence and Wishart, 1937.

Alan Munton

FRANCOPHONE AFRICAN LITERATURE. *See* AFRICAN LITERATURE (FRANCOPHONE).

FRANCOPHONE CARIBBEAN LITERATURE. *See* CARIBBEAN LITERATURE (FRANCOPHONE).

FRANKENSTEIN; OR, THE MODERN PROMETHEUS **(1818).** Reissued with a new introduction in 1831, this story of an artificial man created and brought to life by scientist Victor Frankenstein has become one of the central narratives of modern Western culture, though it may now be better known through its various film adaptations than through the original novel. *Frankenstein* was the first novel of Mary Wollstonecraft Shelley, daughter of political radicals **Mary Wollstonecraft** and **William Godwin.** As such, it reworks key arguments of the post–**French Revolution** British literary debate. Engaged with the relationship between private life and the health of the state, it examines authority—domestic, political, and divine.

Dedicated to Godwin, author of *Political Justice* (1793), *Frankenstein* is an imaginative reply to his radical novel *Things as They Are; or, The Adventures of Caleb Williams* (1794), in which the hero is persecuted through the legal system for his curiosity concerning his powerful employer, Mr. Falkland. While Godwin explores the flawed nature of the legal and social system, however, Shelley implies that such unfairness is inevitable. *Frankenstein* is littered with ineffectual judges. She adds a metaphysical dimension to this problem by persistently referring to **Milton's** *Paradise Lost* (1667), a text engaged with issues of both civil and divine authority.

Frankenstein also reexamines the extent to which sensibility or personal feeling might be used to build a better political environment. Wollstonecraft had suggested that private morality was the basis for public virtue; Godwin had questioned whether the selfishness of family ties was socially destructive. In Shelley's novel, the family initially appears as a location for rational sensibility, where orphans, friends, or even servants can be included in the sentimental bond. Far from providing a stable foundation for public life, however, the family is depicted as a fractured unit, continually under threat from economic hardship, political tyranny, or personal betrayal. Moreover, at the crucial moments when the creature turns to the notion of family for support, he is rejected. Shelley's novel implies that the family is almost as marked by prejudice and irrationality as society's other institutions.

The novel explores the role education has in perpetuating this situation. In *A Vindication of the Rights of Woman* (1792), Mary Wollstonecraft had argued that women were educated to make alluring mistresses, then condemned by men for their irrationality and viciousness. The creature's situation parallels this. He is rejected by the De Laceys because of his appearance, and by his creator for his immorality, despite Victor's failure to educate him. Wollstonecraft had argued that the consequence of poor education was degradation, for master and slave. The creature suffers a similar fate. This is evident not only in the murders he commits but in his desire to dominate Frankenstein.

Often noted as the first **science fiction** novel, a contextual reading reveals that

Frankenstein is a work of immense complexity that uses both content and form to raise epistemological and hence political doubts.

Selected Bibliography: Baldick, Chris. *In Frankenstein's Shadow: Myth, Monstrosity, and Nineteenth-Century Writing.* Oxford: Clarendon P, 1990; Botting, Fred. *Making Monstrous*: Frankenstein, *Criticism, Theory.* Manchester: Manchester UP, 1991; Levine, George, and U. C. Knoepflmacher, eds. *The Endurance of Frankenstein: Essays on Mary Shelley's Novel.* Berkeley: U of California Press, 1982; *Frankenstein: Complete, Authoritative Text with Biographical, Historical, and Cultural Contexts, Critical History, and Essays from Contemporary Critical Perspectives.* Ed. Johanna M. Smith. Basingstoke: Macmillan, 2000.

Fiona Price

FRANKFURT SCHOOL. A group of leftist scholars associated with the Institute of Social Research in Frankfurt, Germany. Founded in 1923, the institute initially focused on issues of economics and politics, especially those involving the working class. Gradually the membership shifted to a largely Jewish group of intellectuals, whose interests encompassed more theoretical, cultural, and aesthetic topics. Under the directorship of Max Horkheimer, the institute pursued an interdisciplinary integration of social theory. When Hitler came to power in 1933, the institute was forced to abandon Germany, eventually relocating at Columbia University in New York. Wartime activities scattered the core group of the Frankfurt School, but in 1950 Horkheimer, along with **Theodor Adorno** and Felix Pollack, moved the institute back to Frankfurt; several members (Herbert Marcuse, Leo Löwenthal, Erich Fromm) remained in the United States. After Adorno's death in 1969, the mantle of leadership in the Frankfurt School passed to a second generation, whose most prominent representative was **Jürgen Habermas.**

Initial investigations of literature occurred on the fringes of the central theoretical concerns of the Frankfurt School. Löwenthal contributed a series of essays to the institute's journal, the *Zeitschrift für Sozialforschung* (Journal for Social Research), on literary topics, developing a sophisticated sociology of literature. His essay on Knut Hamsun in 1937 accurately predicted the author's fascist tendencies. **Walter Benjamin**'s essays dealing with engaged literature and with aura that has been lost in modern reproducible works of art were especially important for a rethinking of modern culture and its possibilities.

The essay "The Culture Industry" by Horkheimer and Adorno provided a contrasting view to Benjamin's portrayal of the emancipatory potentials of mass culture. Appearing in the volume *Dialectic of Enlightenment* (*Dialektik der Aufklärung,* 1947), written toward the end of **World War II**, it shows a pessimistic view of the modern world. Just as Fascism in Europe and Communism in the Soviet Union exemplify the tendency toward a totally administered society, so too culture in liberal democracy functions to eliminate critical reflection and genuine dissent. The products of culture, which are supposed to demonstrate creativity and individuality, have been reduced to a repetitive monotony that precludes authenticity and opposition. They have become commodities and, as such, are subject to a technological development that carefully controls the recipient's responses. The culture industry, in fostering an ideology of individuality while enforcing a reality of sameness, is thus the counterpart to the overtly oppressive political regimes in Europe.

After the war, Adorno became the chief spokesperson for the Frankfurt School. His preoccupation with literature increased, resulting in four volumes of occasional essays under the title *Notes to Literature* (*Noten zur Literatur,* 1973–1976). In these essays, and more theoretically in his final posthumously published work, *Aesthetic Theory* (*Ästhetische Theorie,* 1970), Adorno developed a defense of **modernism** as a progressive alternative to an administered world. Rejecting idealist aesthetics with its notion of an identity of subject and object, Adorno argues for a truth content in authentic art that relates negatively to its sociohistorical context. For him, the autonomous work of art, illustrated paradigmatically in the modernist works of **Samuel Beckett** and Arnold Schönberg, captures a utopian potential by gesturing, however obliquely, toward a world in which the deformities of a capitalist, bureaucratic culture are overcome.

Selected Bibliography: Adorno, Theodor W. *Aesthetic Theory.* Trans. Robert Hullot-Kentor. Minneapolis: U of Minnesota P, 1997; Adorno, Theodor W. *Notes to Literature.* Trans. Shierry Weber Nicholsen. New York: Columbia UP, 1991; Benjamin, Walter. *Illuminations.* New York: Harcourt, Brace & World, 1968; Horkheimer, Max, and Adorno, Theodor W. *Dialectic of Enlightenment: Philosophical Fragments.* Trans. Edmund Jephcott. Stanford, CA: Stanford UP, 2002; Jay, Martin. *The Dialectical Imagination: A History of the Frankfurt School and the Institute of Social Research, 1923–1950.* London: Heinemann, 1973; Löwenthal, Leo. *Literature and the Image of Man.* New Brunswick: Transaction Books, 1986; Wiggershaus, Rolf. *The Frankfurt School: Its History, Theories, and Political Significance.* Trans. Michael Robertson. Cambridge, MA: MIT P, 1994.

Robert C. Holub

FREEMAN, JOSEPH (1897–1965). Joseph Starobin called Freeman "probably the most talented intellectual" in the U.S. Communist Party. He earned this reputation with his introduction to the influential 1935 anthology *Proletarian Literature in the United States* and his 1936 autobiography, *An American Testament.* A refugee from Ukraine at age seven, Freeman went on to graduate from Columbia in 1919—after stateside military service during World War I—and to join Greenwich Village's thriving Bohemia. He served as the European correspondent for the *Chicago Tribune* in 1920 and became one of **Max Eastman**'s assistant editors at the *Liberator.* In 1921, Freeman joined the new Communist (Workers) Party, serving from 1925 to 1929 as a New York correspondent for the Soviet news service, TASS, and cofounding *New Masses* with Eastman and **Mike Gold** in 1926. Three books followed: *Dollar Diplomacy*, a muckraking collaboration with ACLU cofounder Scott Nearing; *Voices of October*, a co-written account of a trip to the USSR; and *The Soviet Worker*, a statistical study.

On assignment for TASS in Mexico in 1929, Freeman met and married Ione Robinson, an American painter and a Diego Rivera protégée. In 1934, he married another painter, Charmian von Wiegand, a protégée of painter Piet Mondrian. In that same year, Freeman joined Philip Rahv in launching **Partisan Review**, which published Freeman's most significant work as a literary theorist. Freeman bitterly broke with the Communists in the late 1930s, soon after the publication of *An Amer-*

ican Testament, which prompted party stalwarts to denounce Freeman as a "roman-tic" and an "enemy of the people" because the narrative did not praise **Stalin** enough and disparaged **Trotsky** only perfunctorily. Freeman went on to publish two more books, both novels: *Never Call Retreat* (1943), which depicts a young and reluctant Viennese Socialist in the years leading up to World War II, and *The Long Pursuit* (1947), the story of a European USO tour. *The Long Pursuit*—an exposé of mass-media crassness—draws on Freeman's work as a researcher for *Information Please*—then a popular radio quiz show.

During his last two decades, Freeman worked for public-relations pioneer Edward Bernays. In testimony in 1953 before the House Un-American Activities Commit-tee, Freeman identified himself to the committee as a "man out of politics." Through-out his post-party career, Freeman continually revised and retitled a never-published autobiographical narrative, usually cast as a novel. Unpublished efforts during this period also include screenplays and poems in traditional forms—especially sonnets.

Selected Bibliography: Aaron, Daniel. *Writers on the Left: Episodes in American Literary Communism.* New York: Harcourt, Brace and World, 1961; Beck, Kent. "The Odyssey of Joseph Freeman." *Historian* 38.1 (November 1974): 101–20; Bloom, James D. *Left Letters: The Culture Wars of Mike Gold and Joseph Freeman.* New York: Columbia UP, 1992; Gilbert, James. *Writers and Partisans: A History of Literary Radicalism in America.* 1968. New York: Columbia UP, 1992; McConnell, Gary Scott. "Joseph Freeman: A Personal Odyssey from Romance to Revolution." Diss. U of North Carolina, 1985; Robinson, Ione. *A Wall to Paint On.* New York: Dutton, 1946.

James D. Bloom

FRENCH LITERATURE. Literature in France has been closely associated with pol-itics since the Middle Ages. The twelfth-century epic *The Song of Roland* has a strong nationalistic tone to it; a little later, the part of Chrétien de Troyes' romance *Yvain* describing a group of virgins spinning in a tower can easily be read as a commentary on the plight of an under class. Within less than a century, Rutebeuf would vigor-ously satirize all classes of society and write especially against those guilty of bene-fiting from their position or of exploiting others. Much later, in the sixteenth century, Rabelais, with a mixture of satire, humor, and the grotesque, not only ridiculed the political, social, religious, and educational practices and systems of his day, but pleaded for their reform. Corneille, Racine, La Fontaine, and Molière in the follow-ing century all drew directly or indirectly on the same features, and satirical broad-sides against the establishment in all its forms continued in the eighteenth century, notably in the writings of Voltaire. Forced into exile and to publish anonymously, Voltaire, more than any other, used his pen to effect change. It was also during his lifetime that the political and social base for much literary inspiration began to grow. Servants, peasants, and the urban underclasses all became the subject of works by Marivaux, Beaumarchais, Diderot, Prévost, and Restif de la Bretonne. In the after-math of the French Revolution, with the gradual emergence of republicanism, the influence of Marxism, and the growth of journalism, it was hardly surprising that, to use **George Orwell**'s phrase, France witnessed "the invasion of literature by poli-tics." While not overtly engaged with any specific political project, **Honoré de Balzac**'s "Comedie humaine" and many of Victor Hugo's works revealed an increasing interconnection between art and politics. Still, the idea that art should remain pure, that, in Gustave Flaubert's phrase, a writer "had no right to express an opinion on anything," continued to be held by many. Nonetheless, literature as a vehicle for political ideas and subsequently as part of a political or ideological program would be a major phenomenon by the end of the nineteenth century.

What particularly brought literature and politics together in this more militant and even didactic way was the Dreyfus Affair. Captain Alfred Dreyfus, an Alsatian Jew accused in 1894 of having passed military secrets to the Prussians, was court-martialed and sentenced to life imprisonment on Devil's Island. Subsequently it was discovered that he had been wrongly accused, that the "evidence" was false and that the government had been withholding vital information at the trial. Dreyfus was subsequently acquitted, but the affair developed into a national debate between those—with **Émile Zola** as their foremost spokesman—who supported the rights of the individual and those who held that the state and in particular its key institutions (the church, the army, and the judiciary) should not be destabilized. But it also marked the moment when writers began to espouse political programs or voice political preferences in a more overt and vigorous way than before.

On the political left, imaginative writing took in particular the form of descriptions of working-class life. With *Germinie Lacerteux* (1864), the Goncourt brothers produced a fictionalized and sympathetic account of their own servant's humble existence but without suggesting how it might be changed. With novels like *The Dram Shop* (*L'Assommoir*, 1877) and *Germinal* (1885), Zola—however much he wanted to demonstrate his quasi-scientific and determinist theories about inherited characteristics—paved the way for much more militant writing. Of the former, in which he dealt with the problem of alcoholism among the working class, he wrote that he wanted not only to describe fully the conditions of this class but "to appeal for the enlightenment and education of the lower classes." With *Germinal* he went further, but notably could still not provide a positive solution or alternative to the plight of the exploited miners whose lives he described.

For writers of all political persuasions, this was a problem to be faced. While it was one thing to analyze and expose and perhaps therefore indirectly make a case for change or improvement, it was entirely another to describe how this could be achieved. Those on the Left were particularly challenged. Change for many writers of socialist and communist persuasion could only be achieved through revolution, and several looked to the Soviet Union for a model. As Jean-Richard Bloch pointed out in 1934, however, France had not undergone the kind of revolution that Russia had experienced in 1917. Nonetheless, writing that positively advocated ways in which society might be changed began to appear. Important in this development was Henri Barbusse and his novel *Under Fire* (*Le Feu*, 1916), depicting the appalling fighting conditions of **World War I**. Barbusse uses the squad of foot soldiers, of which he is part, as a symbolic representation of France's working class as a whole, but he also takes advantage of his role as omniscient author to preach, somewhat intrusively, the virtues of revolution and in particular of "equality." In a second war novel, *Clarté* (1919), this would be even more apparent, but Barbusse had become an important voice. He joined the French Communist Party (FCP), founded in 1920, and, through his periodical *Clarté*, provided a vital channel for information on the literary and cultural matters within the Soviet Union to be made known in France. By the end of the decade, however, when the FCP was becoming increasingly hard-line, Barbusse was deemed insufficiently orthodox and was heavily and publicly criticized. Not surprisingly, committed left-wing writers now championed communism and viewed the Soviet Union with open admiration. **Louis Aragon**, who was to become one of the FCP's dominant and most influential intellectuals, largely abandoned the innovative and experimental poetry he was producing as a surrealist to turn out simplistic verse in praise of the Soviet Union. At the same time in his novels *The Bells of Basel* (*Les Cloches de Bâle*, 1934) and "The Finest Districts" (*Les Beaux Quartiers*, 1936), he satirized the superficiality and corruption of bourgeois society but could never provide as an integral part of the fiction a revolutionary socialist alternative. He would not achieve this until he produced his four-volume apology for communism, *The Communists* (*Les Communistes*, 1949–1951), a work that now seems hopelessly dated. More successful was **Paul Nizan**, who had been a fellow pupil and close friend of **Jean-Paul Sartre** and **Simone de Beauvoir**. Nizan's militancy was already apparent in early essays, and in his first two novels—*Antoine Bloyé* (1933) and especially *The Trojan Horse* (*Le Cheval de Troie*, 1935)—he illustrates both the corrupting, stifling nature of bourgeois society and how through struggle it can be overcome. This was a period when left-wing political writing in France was dominated by **socialist realism** and by the idea that literature was not for entertainment but should educate its readers and shake them out of their complacency—a view that had much in common with **Bertolt Brecht**'s notion of "estrangement."

Although politics was central to a large amount of the imaginative writing produced during the years of the occupation in **World War II** (see, for example, the issues of *Poésie;* Vercors' *Put Out the Light* [*Le Silence de la mer*, 1942]; Sartre's *The Flies* [*Les Mouches*, 1942]; or Anouilh's *Antigone* [1944]), circumstances meant that literature written to an ideological or political program temporarily disappeared. But after the liberation, with the growing marginalization of the FCP and the development of the cold war, a new wave of influence spread from the Soviet Union. Works on all aspects of artistic, cultural, and intellectual issues by **Joseph Stalin**'s minister of culture, Zhdanov, were translated and imitated in France by Jean Kanapa and Laurent Casanova. Aragon and Paul Eluard produced poems full of admiration for the Soviet Union as a nation of peace and optimism. Socialist realism reappeared. André Stil and Pierre Courtade—with the trilogy "The First Blow" (*Le Premier Choc*, 1951–1953) and *Jimmy* (1951), respectively—wrote violently anti-Western and anti-American novels in which true enlightenment and real change is seen to be realizable only through an espousal of communism. Stalin and even Maurice Thorez, the first secretary of the FCP, are worshiped as heroes. With the novels *Beau Masque* (1954) and *325,000 francs* (1955), Roger Vailland explored capitalism and revolutionary activity, but by broadening his picture to include a study of the psychology of his characters, he successfully managed to avoid overschematization. But, especially after Khrushchev's 1956 denunciation of Stalin, a new sense that literature could not be produced to order and according to a formula or program—that it would always contain some nonreducible element to do with a writer's creative talent—was beginning to surface and became "officially" recognized at the major FCP conference held at Argenteuil in 1966.

For the first two-thirds of the twentieth century, French leftist literature tended to be programmatic, produced in opposition to the prevailing social and political climate—even when, temporarily, France had a radical or socialist government, as in 1924–1925 and 1936–1937. If there was less or indeed no need, therefore, for a similar politically driven literature of the Right, there were, nonetheless, writers—some of whom regularly upheld moderate conservative values in their work and others who went even further. By the late nineteenth and early twentieth centuries, for example, there was Maurice Barrès (1862–1923), a conservative republican who was already underlining the importance of "blood and soil" and of allegiance to one's region or country in works like *Colette Baudoche* (1909), and spelling out the dangers of attempting to break free from these formative influences in "Uprooted!" (*Les Déracinés*, 1896). Barrès's influence would be powerful, acknowledged by or traceable in the work of writers as disparate in other ways as **Malraux**, Mauriac, Camus, and Giono. This kind of intense patriotism would also become prominent again during the occupation. Writers such as Michel Mohrt, René Benjamin, and Pierre Benoit considered France's fate to be inevitable, if not even deserved. There is no better example than Benjamin's "That Tragic Spring" (*Le Printemps tragique*, 1940), in which a character roundly attacks French society of the previous twenty years for having completely abandoned its standards.

But such views were mild in comparison with those expressed by writers who openly admired the various fascist regimes to emerge in Europe during the interwar period. In some of his World War I poetry—*Interrogation* (1917), *Fond de Cantine* (1920)—Pierre Drieu la Rochelle, who became a self-acknowledged fascist in 1934, had already described the delights of virile man-to-man fighting with Germans. In *The Comedy of Charleroi and Other Stories* (*La Comédie de Charleroi*, 1934), the same delight is expressed along with a barely concealed homoerotic dimension, and in *Gilles* (1939), Drieu openly embraces the fascist campaign in Spain. A similar desire to be dominated—and by extension the view that France should submit willingly to Nazi power—is found in the work of Robert Brasillach, especially in "The Seven Colors" (*Les Sept Couleurs*, 1939). Brasillach was an anti-Semite—the anti-Semitism of the Right already manifest at the time of the Dreyfus Affair continued to be strong—as were Louis-Ferdinand Céline and Lucien Rebatet. But like many of the early writers at the other end of the political spectrum, their works—such as Rebatet's "The Rubble" (*Les Décombres*, 1942) and "The Two Standards" (*Les Deux Etendards*, 1952)—are limited to violent attacks on the corrupt society of previous years and do not, except perhaps by implication, advocate the implementation of an alternative political program.

For a while after the liberation, a nostalgic review of lost values and an attempt to reconstruct a picture of society based on them was developed by a group of writers known as the "Hussards," containing, among others, Roger Nimier, Jacques Laurent, and Thierry Maulnier. While again they did not propose any particular program for reform, the group was evidence of the strong and continuing tradition of writers and intellectuals sympathetic to the values of the Right.

With the socialist presidency of François Mitterrand, many felt that oppositional literature on the Left was no longer needed. Still, large political and social concerns—immigration, tourism, colonialization, poverty, terrorism, the status of women—continued to provide the subject matter of important works of imaginative writing of the late twentieth and early twenty-first centuries. Michel Tournier's *The Golden Droplet* (*La Goutte d'or*, 1985: immigration), Patrick Modiano's "Unknown Women" (*Des Inconnues*, 1999: the plight of women and threat of indoctrination), and Michel Houllebecq's *Platform* (*Plateforme*, 2001: sexual tourism and terrorism) are all testimony to this, and continue a tradition that had its roots in the distant past, but programmed political writing no longer appears to be either desirable or indeed necessary.

Selected Bibliography: Cryle, Peter M. *Thematics of Commitment: The Tower and the Plain.* Princeton, NJ: Princeton UP, 1984; Flower, J. E. *Writers and Politics in Modern France, (1909–1961).* London: Hodder and Stoughton, 1977; Flower, J. E. *Literature and the Left in France.* London: Macmillan, 1983; Hewitt, Nicholas. *Literature and the Right in Postwar France.* Washington, DC: Berg, 1996.

John E. Flower

FRENCH REVOLUTION. Traditionally seen as a key marker in the centuries-long transition from aristocratic to bourgeois rule in Europe, the French Revolution has also provided a model for many subsequent revolutionary movements, from the **Haitian Revolution** to the **Russian Revolution.** The dramatic change brought about by the French Revolution led to a thoroughgoing reorganization of the country's administration, finances, and legal system, consecrated by Napoleon Bonaparte, whose coup d'état in 1799 put an end to the republican stage of the revolution. As a revolutionary general, Bonaparte defended the republic against its outside enemies, and then took power to defend the nation against its own internal strife. To this day, France is a republic with a strong presidency, which both marks and seals the original wound, the point where the nation had splintered during the tumultuous days following the declaration of the First Republic by the National Convention (September 21, 1792), after which King Louis XVI was finally removed from the historical stage by the guillotine.

In recent times, historians have chipped away at the powerful myth of the French Revolution. First, Anglo-American historians, less inhibited perhaps by patriotic loyalties, started questioning some of the ruling assumptions that dominated the historiography of the French Revolution, from the conservative François Guizot during the Restoration, to the romantic liberal Jules Michelet, to the socialist Jean Jaurès. According to Alfred Cobban, one of the best-known figures of the revisionist trend in the Anglo-American world, the French Revolution had not been initiated by the bourgeoisie, which was feebly represented at the time due to the insufficient development of a capitalist economy in France. Nor was it a series of class revolts, as Georges Lefebvre asserted in his classic study *The Coming of the French Revolution* (1939). Similarly, in her convincing refutation of Lefebvre's thesis, Elizabeth Eisenstein pointed to the leading role of "men of letters" in the revolution.

From the French side, the most severe blow to the traditional myth of the French Revolution came from François Furet, who, abandoning his prior allegiance to the **Communist Party** after **World War II** and coming from the Annales school, mounted a full-scale attack on the theses of the Marxist historian Albert Soboul, who was from 1967 until his death in 1982 professor of the history of the French Revolution at the Sorbonne. Following in Cobban's steps, who had already argued that the French aristocracy at the time of the revolution was more bourgeois than feudal, Furet asserts in his important *Interpreting the French Revolution* (1978) that the peasant's opposition to the nobility was not anti-feudal but rather anti-bourgeois and anti-capitalist.

The period of the Jacobin Terror is probably the most sensitive and most intensely debated element in this process of historical reassessment. Although it was brief—the period of the terror covers the rule of the Committee of Public Safety from September 1793 to July 1974, when the Jacobins were finally rounded up and shot or executed—this episode of the revolution was the most violent and bloody. The guillotine in Paris and the provinces was functioning nonstop, and the victims, many of them innocent, were in the thousands. While no historian can ignore the terror, no consensus seems possible between Marxist historians, such as Soboul and Lefebvre, who tend to justify the terror as a historical necessity (a means to counteract the threat of civil and foreign wars), and those, like Furet and Pierre Chaunu, who repudiate it as a shameful episode in the history of the Revolution, and see in it a precursor of twentieth-century mass exterminations, from the Soviet Gulag to the excesses committed during the Chinese Cultural Revolution to the Pol Pot massacres.

More moderate historians, like Richard Cobb, find themselves stymied in their discussion of the terror by the absence of reliable sources. For instance, to this day, the exact number of victims produced by the terror is not known or agreed on. The archives of the Paris Commune, represented by the *sans-culottes*, the most radical faction of the Revolution, were housed in the Hotel de Ville, which was burned down during the Paris Commune of 1871. Many execution orders given by Robespierre and Saint-Just during that period were destroyed. Eyewitness reports are considered unreliable, or so embarrassing as to be passed in silence. Louis-Sébastien Mercier, the Girondin journalist and writer who gave an extensive account of the terror in his documentary book *Le Nouveau Paris* (1799), is regarded as an eccentric whose word cannot be trusted.

The revisionist historians, however, have not been able to have the last word or close the debate. Michel Vovelle, Soboul's successor as chair in the history of the French Revolution at the Sorbonne, has mounted a counter-attack from the Marxist side against the conservative, counterrevolutionary wing represented by Furet and Chaunu. These ideological battles were most vividly displayed during the recent bicentennial celebrations. The stakes have been raised by recent political developments, in which the very idea of the Revolution has taken a hard blow from the collapse of Communism and the rise of neoconservatism in many European countries, including France.

Nevertheless, the Revolution remains one of the crucial events in Western history and has spawned a rich legacy of literary works. Several histories of and commentaries on the Revolution are widely regarded as works of literature, including Michelet's seven-volume *History of the French Revolution* (1847–1853), Edmund Burke's horrified *Reflections on the Revolution in France* (1790), and Thomas Carlyle's *History of the French Revolution* (1837). The French Revolution has understandably inspired a great deal of French literature, such as **Honoré de Balzac**'s *Les Chouans* (1834), Victor Hugo's *Quatrevingt-treize* (1874), and Anatole France's *Les Dieux ont* *soif* (1911–1912). English literature has also responded to the French Revolution, which provided inspiration for the initial rise of English **romanticism** and for such works as **Charles Dickens**'s *A Tale of Two Cities* (1859). The Revolution has continued to inspire literary works more recently, from **Peter Weiss**'s *Marat/Sade* (1964) to Marge Piercy's *City of Darkness, City of Light* (1996).

Selected Bibliography: Chartier, Roger. *The Cultural Origins of the French Revolution.* Durham, NC: Duke UP, 1991; Cobban, Alfred. *The Social Interpretation of the French Revolution.* Cambridge: Cambridge UP, 1964; Higonnet, Patrice. *Goodness Beyond Virtue: Jacobins during the French Revolution.* Cambridge, MA: Harvard UP, 1998; Hunt, Lynn. *The Family Romance of the French Revolution.* Berkeley: U of California P, 1992; Lefebvre, Henri. *The French Revolution: From Its Origins to 1793.* Trans. Elizabeth Moss Evanson. New York: Columbia UP, 1962; Lefebvre, Henri. *The French Revolution: From 1793 to 1799.* Trans. John Hall Stewart and James Fruguglietti. New York: Columbia UP, 1964; Michelet, Jules. *History of the French Revolution.* Trans. Charles Cocks. Chicago: Chicago UP, 1967; Rudé, George. *The French Revolution.* New York: Grove, 1988; Woloch, Isser. *The New Regime: Transformations of the French Civic Order, 1789–1820s.* New York: W. W. Norton, 1994.

Alina Clej

FUENTES, CARLOS (1928–). The son of a Mexican diplomat, Fuentes was born in Panama City and grew up in various capital cities of the Western Hemisphere, including Washington, D.C. His cosmopolitan upbringing helps account for the sophisticated and erudite quality of much of his work, but Fuentes also inherited his father's intense nationalism, and his fiction and essays focus insistently on the history, character, and destiny of Mexico. In the 1960s, he was closely associated with the boom in Latin American literature, and like other members of this quasi-movement, he was a strong supporter of the **Cuban Revolution** in its early years. After he was attacked in 1966 by a group of Cuban writers for attending a PEN Club meeting in New York, Fuentes decided to keep his distance from Cuba, but in the international arena, he has maintained a consistently leftist and nationalist posture. In the 1980s, he was a strong defender of the Sandinista Revolution in Nicaragua, and he has been a frequent critic of U.S. foreign policy. On the domestic front, his record is more ambiguous. He played the role of both critic and friend to the undemocratic regimes of the PRI (Institutional Revolutionary Party), which ruled Mexico for approximately seventy years before finally being ousted from power in 2000. In the 1970s, Fuentes even served as Mexico's ambassador to France under President Luis Echeverría, a man responsible for extensive human-rights abuses in Mexico.

Fuentes has produced a vast oeuvre consisting of novels, short stories, essays, and plays, as well as a huge amount of journalism. As a fiction writer, Fuentes mixes modernist and postmodernist experimentation with a simultaneous commitment to realist representation and historical investigation. Two early novels, *Where the Air Is Clear* (*La región más transparente*, 1958) and *The Death of Artemio Cruz* (*La muerte de Artemio Cruz*, 1962), display a dazzling use of the modernist techniques of interior monologue, fragmented chronology, and shifting point of view. But these novels are also ambitious explorations of Mexico's historical trajectory in the first half of the twentieth century. In the way he confuses the distinction between history and fiction in *Terra Nostra* (1975), we can see Fuentes moving toward a postmodernist aesthetic. Yet the overarching vision of the history and development of Hispanic culture he expresses in *Terra Nostra* is very much at odds with the postmodernist suspicion of grand historical narratives. In his literary essays, Fuentes repeatedly argues for the social and political power of literature. In *La nueva novela hispanoamericana* (1969), he contends that a revolution in literary form can help bring about a revolution in society, while in *Geografía de la novela* (1993), he describes literature as a kind of equipment for living in a multicultural world. What has remained consistent is his faith in the redemptive power of literature, although it is worth noting that Fuentes tends to conceive of this redemption in cultural rather than explicitly political terms.

Selected Bibliography: Boldy, Steven. *The Narrative of Carlos Fuentes: Family, Text, Nation.* Durham: U of Durham, 2002; Grenier, Yvon. "Cambio de piel: disposiciones y posiciones políticas de Carlos Fuentes." *Foro Hispánico* 22 (2002): 121–35; Popovic Karic, Pol. *Carlos Fuentes: perspectivas críticas.* Mexico City: Siglo XXI, 2002; Van Delden, Maarten. *Carlos Fuentes, Mexico, and Modernity.* Nashville, TN: Vanderbilt UP, 1998.

Maarten van Delden

∘ G ∘

GAO XINGJIAN (1940–). Born in Ganzhou, Jiangxi Province, China, Gao was a compulsive writer by the time he was a teenager. At the time, under the postrevolutionary Chinese communist government (formed in 1949), literature was regarded as a tool of the revolution. By failing to contribute to this project, a writer risked punishment as an enemy of the state, so the teenage Gao wrote in secret. Graduating in 1962 with a major in French literature at the Beijing Foreign Languages Institute, he was assigned work as a translator and editor.

As documented in his largely autobiographical novel *One Man's Bible* (*Yige ren de shengjing*, 1999), written thirty years after the events, Gao was initiated into politics during the Cultural Revolution (1966–1976). He had protested against the violence of the Red Guards and found himself leading an opposition group of Red Guards. His activities came under investigation and he fled to a remote mountain village in Sichuan Province, resigned to living the life of a peasant. In the novel, Gao examines the trauma and dysfunction of a whole population that had been consigned to endless self-criticism by their political masters. The protagonist "you" of the present, now a French citizen, recalls a past in which the psychology and actions of "he" of that time is subjected to ruthless scrutiny.

When the Cultural Revolution ended, Gao returned to Beijing. His short fiction and essays began to appear in publications, but he was singled out for promoting "decadent" Western modernism. His *Xiandai xiaoshuo jiqiao chutan* (Preliminary Explorations into the Art of Modern Fiction, 1982) was banned, and his play *The Bus Stop* (*Chezhan*, 1983) was banned after several packed performances. He again fled Beijing and certain persecution until it was safe to return. His play *Wild Man* (*Yeren*, 1985) was staged, but his play *The Other Shore* (*Bi'an*, 1986) was banned at rehearsal.

Gao left China in late 1987, and by the end of the year, he had settled in Paris. Begun in China in 1982 and published in Taipei, his first novel, *Soul Mountain* (*Lingshan*, 1990) is based on his 1983 flight from Beijing. The critical and theoretical essays contained in his collection *No Isms* (1996) argue stridently against the intrusion of politics on literary and artistic creation. A large part of his major writings had been published in French, Swedish, and English when it was announced in October 2000 that he had won the Nobel Prize for Literature.

Selected Bibliography: Quah, Sy Ren. *Gao Xingjian and Transcultural Chinese Theatre.* Honolulu: U of Hawaii P, 2004; Tam, Kwok-kan, ed. *The Soul of Chaos: Critical Perspectives on Gao Xingjian.* Hong Kong: The Chinese UP, 2001; Zhao, Henry Y. H. *Towards a Modern Zen Theatre: Gao Xingjian and Chinese Theatre Experimentalism.* London: School of Oriental and African Studies, 2000.

Mabel Lee

GARCÍA LORCA, FEDERICO (1898–1936). The oldest son of an Andalusian landowner, Lorca became the most famous Spanish poet and playwright of the twentieth century. Athough he forswore political affiliations, Lorca was an outspoken critic of social injustice and a prominent supporter of the Second Spanish Republic. His implicit endorsement of the Left, together with his homosexuality, antagonized the Spanish Right. Lorca was murdered by a nationalist firing squad in the first month of the **Spanish Civil War.**

Born on the outskirts of Granada, Spain, Lorca grew up amid images and social conditions that influenced his work throughout his life. Initially drawn to music— he was a prodigious pianist—Lorca began writing in his teens. In 1919, he moved to Madrid, where he remained for most of his life, making regular visits to Granada. Throughout the 1920s, Lorca struggled to establish himself as a poet and playwright. Early works were critical failures. In 1922, Lorca collaborated with the Andalusian composer Manuel de Falla on a festival of gypsy "deep song" in Granada, an endeavor that helped inspire Lorca's first best-selling poetry collection, *Gypsy Ballads* (1928). He achieved his first theatrical success in 1927 with the premiere of *Mariana Pineda*, about a nineteenth-century Granadan rebel. The painter Salvador Dalí, with whom Lorca had become passionately involved, designed the sets.

By 1930, Lorca was known throughout Spain and gaining a growing readership abroad. With the start of the Second Spanish Republic in 1931, he and his fellow poets, known collectively as the "Generation of '27," came into their own. Thanks to his friendships with members of the republican government, Lorca was asked to direct a government-sponsored theater group, La Barraca. With the triumphant 1933 premiere of his first Andalusian tragedy, *Blood Wedding*, Lorca helped inaugurate a second golden age of Spanish theater. Two more Andalusian tragedies, *Yerma* (1933) and *The House of Bernarda Alba* (1936), followed, in addition to other plays and poetry collections. By 1934, the republican government had come under fierce attack from right-wing factions. Appalled by the political turmoil, Lorca signed petitions supporting the government, but unlike fellow poet Rafael Alberti, Lorca did not join the Communist Party—or any other party. His work remained essentially apolitical, although his unfinished *Play without a Title* (1934) alludes to the Asturian Revolution of 1934.

Lorca was in Granada in July 1936 when the Spanish Civil War began. On August 16, nationalist forces arrested him. On the night of August 18 or 19 (the precise date is unknown), he was driven to a hillside near the town of Viznar and shot. Although officials in the nationalist movement clearly sanctioned the killing, the government of Francisco Franco never accepted responsibility for it. In 1986, the government of Felipe González erected a monument on the site of Lorca's murder. The gesture bears witness to Lorca's stature as one of Spain's greatest writers.

Selected Bibliography: Gibson, Ian. *The Assassination of Federico García Lorca.* New York: Penguin, 1983; Gibson, Ian. *Federico García Lorca: A Life.* New York: Pantheon, 1989; Stainton, Leslie. *Lorca: A Dream of Life.* New York: Farrar, Straus and Giroux, 1999.

Leslie Stainton

GARCÍA MÁRQUEZ, GABRIEL (1928–). The best-known and most widely read Latin American author, 1982 Nobel Prize winner in Literature, and member of the boom generation that brought Latin American literature and **magical realism** to worldwide attention in the 1960s. García Márquez began his career as a journalist in his native Colombia. While fiction is the genre for which he is best known, he continues to focus on journalism—even buying a 50 percent interest in a Colombian newsweekly in 1998, for which he occasionally continues to report and edit—and he has recently published the first volume of his autobiography, *Living to Tell the Tale* (*Vivir parla contarla,* 2002).

García Márquez's breakout (and most widely read) novel is *One Hundred Years of Solitude* (*Cien años de soledad,* 1967), which went on to become the signature text of magical realism. The novel borrows liberally from accounts of early explorers, biblical tales, Latin American history, and Hispanic literature to reinvent the New World as Macondo—the fictional town where the novel takes place. The novel's play with structure and time, its links between fiction and reality, and its poetic language accompany its concerns with the traditional dominance of sex over love, the elites over the poor, and men over women.

The focus on Latin America as the foundation of the "boom texts" disguises both the distinct discomfort the works display toward Latin American reality and the way the texts rewrite it to be less marginalized and less a part of the third world. García Márquez's preoccupation with isolation, both of the individual (particularly in old age) and of Latin America, is a common thread in many of his novels, notably *No One Writes to the Colonel* (*El coronel no tiene quien le escriba,* 1961), *The Autumn of the Patriarch* (*El otoño del patriarca,* 1975), and *Chronicle of a Death Foretold* (*Crónica de una muerte anunciada,* 1981). His mythification of history and increasingly leftist perspective also become more prominent over the course of his career.

Love in the Time of Cholera (*El amor en los tiempos del cólera,* 1985) represents García Márquez's attempt to move beyond the strictures of the boom to the "post-boom"—the reigning Latin American literary movement after 1975. The new aesthetic tells intimate stories that have a deeper focus on a limited number of characters. For García Márquez, this becomes the story of two lovers trapped in an endless cycle on a riverboat. While the novel succeeds, it pays little attention to post-boom concerns of social justice and allowing the marginalized to speak over the elites who had monopolized Latin American fiction previously.

Suggested Bibliography: Shaw, Bradley A., and N. Vera-Godwin, eds. *Critical Perspectives on Gabriel García Márquez.* Lincoln: U of Nebraska P, 1986; Swanson, Philip. *The New Novel in Latin America: Politics and Popular Culture after the Boom.* Manchester: Manchester UP, 1995; Valdés, María Elena de, and Mario J. Valdés, eds. *Approaches to Teaching García Márquez's "One Hundred Years of Solitude."* New

York: Modern Language Association, 1990; Williams, Raymond Leslie. *Gabriel García Márquez*. Boston: Twayne, 1984.

Jason G. Summers

GASKELL, ELIZABETH (1810–1865). Elizabeth Cleghorn Stevenson was the daughter of one Unitarian minister and married another, becoming Elizabeth Gaskell in 1832. She is best known for her "social-problem" or "industrial" novels, *Mary Barton* (1848) and *North and South* (1855), which deal with contemporary class conflict in Manchester. Her domestic image as "Mrs. Gaskell" has drawn patronizing comment on her fitness to treat these issues, but her Unitarian milieu made her familiar with contemporary social theories. Her father, William Stevenson, published articles on "the political economist" in the 1820s, and her husband, William Gaskell, was minister of Cross Street Chapel, Manchester, a noted center of progressive ideas. William Gaskell's congregation included "enlightened" factory owners, who combined laissez-faire economics with "self-help" principles, embodied in such movements as the Mechanics' Institutes and sanitary reform. The Unitarians, however, were also active philanthropists, and from 1833, the Manchester Domestic Home Mission—cofounded by William—provided not only practical help for the poor but also firsthand, accurate information comparable to that in Engels's *Condition of the Working Classes in England* (1844, though not translated into English until 1892).

Elizabeth Gaskell's novels, inspired by the Unitarian imperative to "bear true witness," drew on this detailed knowledge to make a courageous intervention in the debate between the advocates of laissez-faire economics and those of humanitarian relief. Published in 1848, the year of the final Chartist petition, *Mary Barton* deals so vividly with working-class suffering that it was widely regarded as a pro-**Chartism** novel. *North and South* possibly responds to criticisms of *Mary Barton*'s one-sidedness by using a middle-class heroine to mediate between a "master" and one of his "hands," both sympathetically handled.

Gaskell's analysis of class relations is driven by horror at the distress produced by market forces and industrial confrontations, and invokes Christian principles of tolerance, understanding, and communication as prerequisites for social progress. Hotly debated at the time of publication, these novels were revalued in the 1950s by Marxist critics who praised their accurate representations of working-class life but disparaged their conciliatory politics. Since the 1980s, Gaskell's work has been reassessed by feminist critics who see Gaskell's refusal of oppositional struggle as a deliberate, and gendered, response to dehumanizing ideologies. Feminist recognition of intelligent gender politics in Gaskell's nonindustrial novels—*Cranford* (1853), *Ruth* (1853), *Sylvia's Lovers* (1863), and *Wives and Daughters* (1866)—is fast establishing Gaskell as a major Victorian novelist.

Selected Bibliography: Cazamian, Louis. *The Social Novel in England, 1830–1850*. 1903. Trans. Martin Fido, London: Routledge, 1973; Easson, Angus. *Elizabeth Gaskell*. London: Routledge, 1979; Gallagher, Catherine. *The Industrial Reform of English Fiction: Social Discourse and Narrative Form, 1832–1867*. Chicago: U of Chicago P, 1985; Harman, Barbara Leah. *The Feminine Political Novel in Victorian England*. Charlottesville: UP of Virginia, 1998; Kestner, Joseph. *Protest and Reform: The British Social Narrative by Women, 1827–1867*. London: Methuen, 1985; Stoneman, Patsy. *Elizabeth Gaskell*.

Hemel Hempstead: Harvester Wheatsheaf/Prentice Hall, 1987; Williams, Raymond. "The Industrial Novels: *Mary Barton* and *North and South*." *Culture and Society, 1780–1950*. London: Chatto & Windus, 1958.

Patsy Stoneman

GASTONIA MILL STRIKE. In the spring and summer of 1929, the communist-organized National Textile Workers Union led a strike at the Loray Mill in Gastonia, North Carolina. The striking workers gained some concessions, including a slightly reduced work week, but their efforts largely failed due to the violent efforts of the company, supported by the local police, to suppress the strike. This violence included a shoot-out in which the local police chief was killed, leading to the arrest and subsequent conviction of many of the strike leaders, who then fled to the Soviet Union. The Gastonia Mill Strike formed the basis for an entire family of works of **proletarian fiction**, including Mary Heaton Vorse's *Strike!* (1930), Sherwood Anderson's *Beyond Desire* (1932), **Fielding Burke**'s *Call Home the Heart* (1932), **Grace Lumpkin**'s *To Make My Bread* (1932), **Myra Page**'s *Gathering Storm* (1932), and William Rollins's *The Shadow Before* (1934).

Selected Bibliography: Beal, Fred E. *Proletarian Journey: New England, Gastonia, Moscow*. New York: Hillman-Curl, 1947; Cook, Sylvia Jenkins. "Gastonia: The Literary Reverberations of the Strike." *Southern Literary Journal* 7.1 (1974): 49–66; Draper, Theodore. "Gastonia Revisited." *Social Research* 38 (1971): 3–29; Hapke, Laura. *Daughters of the Great Depression: Women, Work, and Fiction in the American 1930s*. Athens: U of Georgia P, 1995; Sowinska, Suzanne. "Writing across the Color Line: White Women Writers and the 'Negro Question' in the Gastonia Novels." *Radical Revisions: Rereading 1930s Culture*. Ed. Bill Mullen and Sherry Lee Linkon. Urbana: U of Illinois P, 1996. 120–43; Urgo, Joseph R. "Proletarian Literature and Feminism: The Gastonia Novels and Feminist Protest." *The Minnesota Review* 24 (1984): 64–84; Weisbord, Vera Buch. *A Radical Life*. Bloomington: Indiana UP, 1977.

M. Keith Booker

GAY AND LESBIAN STUDIES. This branch of literary studies involves an expansion and extension of the concerns of **feminist criticism and theory** to include a broader and more fluid conception of gender identity and, in particular, to address the concerns of gay and lesbian readers and writers. As a result, gay and lesbian studies enables a broader approach to issues of **gender and literature** than can be encompassed through traditional feminism. Much like feminist critics, gay and lesbian critics have been concerned both with a critical analysis of the treatment of gay and lesbian characters in mainstream canonical literature and with the exploration of an alternative canon produced by gay and lesbian writers. However, proponents of gay and lesbian studies, such as **Gloria Anzaldúa**, have often been highly critical of Western feminist theorists, who purport to represent a "woman's" perspective yet one that is strictly heterosexual, and who meanwhile ignore issues such as race and class, which place different women in widely varying positions within patriarchal society.

Gay and lesbian studies has historically taken significant inspiration from the work of the French poststructuralist thinker **Michel Foucault**, whose *History of Sexuality* sequence is intended, among other things, to explore the historical foundations of homophobia and of the marginalization of homosexuals in Western society. The field began to congeal in the Western academy with the work of **Eve Kosofsky Sedgwick**, who used Foucault as a starting point for her investigations of the representation of male homosexuality in Western culture. Subsequent theorists, such as **Judith Butler**, have further employed the insights of poststructuralist theory to produce a highly flexible notion of gender identity as a socially situated performance rather than a fixed property of any specific individual.

Beginning in the late 1980s, the field of gay and lesbian studies has been enriched by the rise of "queer studies," or "queer theory," driven by a particularly militant and politically engaged group of critics and theorists who have sought to seize control of the traditionally derogatory notion of the "queer" as part of their larger project of challenging systems of symbolic representation by which individuals are defined and controlled. Queer theory builds on the insights of theorists such as Sedgwick and Butler to produce a version of literary and cultural criticism that is committed to a sweeping reassessment of all forms of Western culture, with an eye toward exposing the ways in which texts of various kinds employ subtle ideological messages designed to reinforce the normalization and regulation of sexual behavior. These messages contribute to the marginalization, or even demonization, of sexual dissidents, often in ways that reinforce the repression of other forms of dissidence as well.

Queer theorists aim is to destabilize cultural ideas of normality and to encourage a radically critical stance with regard to social norms and the cultural mechanisms through which those norms are enforced. By challenging these rigid structures of normalization, queer theorists seek to open a space in which individuals will be free to explore and define their own sexualities—and thereby challenge any number of other social limitations placed on individual identity as well. On the other hand, Foucault warned that sexuality has traditionally been more effective as a locus for the official administration of subjectivity than as a space in which official power can be challenged, and it is clearly the case that the emphasis on individuality in queer studies threatens to undermine its effectiveness as a rallying point for collective action, even as it seeks to invite a wide variety of individuals, with a wide variety of sexualities, to follow its banner.

Selected Bibliography: Abelove, Henry, Michele Aina Barale, and David M. Halperin, eds. *The Lesbian and Gay Studies Reader*. New York: Routledge, 1993; Butler, Judith. *Gender Trouble: Feminism and the Subversion of Identity*. New York: Routledge, 1990; Foucault, Michel. *The History of Sexuality*, Vol. 1, *An Introduction*. Trans. Robert Hurley. New York: Vintage-Random House, 1980; Jagose, Annamarie. *Queer Theory: An Introduction*. New York: New York UP, 1997; Sedgwick, Eve Kosofsky. *Between Men: English Literature and Male Homosocial Desire*. New York: Columbia UP, 1985; Sedgwick, Eve Kosofsky. *Epistemology of the Closet*. Berkeley: U of California P, 1990; Sedgwick, Eve Kosofsky. *Tendencies*. Durham, NC: Duke UP, 1993; Sullivan, Nikki. *A Critical Introduction to Queer Theory*. New York: New York UP, 2003; Zimmerman, Bonnie, and Toni A. H. McNaron, eds. *The New Lesbian Studies*. New York: Feminist P, 1996.

M. Keith Booker

GENDER AND LITERATURE. Perhaps the most striking development in the humanities of the past several decades has been the recognition that assumptions about gender structure human thought at every level. The universal ideals of Western culture—truth, rationality, the objectivity of knowledge and of values—mask hidden subjectivities and unexamined claims. When read against the grain, the most basic structures of language—as well as literary tropes, authorial voices, genres, and interpretations—reveal how entangled they are in the meshes of sex. Careful, nuanced reading for gender—far from reducing works of art to political tracts, as is often charged—lifts literary interpretaton from an unemotional, inanimate algebra to a revelation of richly hued human life.

With the advent of **feminist criticism and theory** in literary studies, reading and writing become an arena of political struggle, but not a struggle in which the outcome is known in advance. In addition, recent work in the field of **gay and lesbian studies** calls attention to the fact that the phenomenon of gender is far more complex than a simple opposition between the unproblematic poles of "masculine" and "feminine." So what do we mean when we say "gender?" First, it must be differentiated from "sex." Most feminists distinguish between corporeal sex, the realm of anatomical facts, and gender—the social expectations and behaviors that are considered culturally appropriate to men or to women, respectively. Gender is a feature of the social arena within which the body operates; there, men and women are unequally raised and disparately valued. The word *sex* comes from Latin, and simply means the biological categories male or female among humans or animals. *Gender*, too, comes from the Latin, where in one of its meanings it refers to the grammatical categorization of nouns and their modifiers in languages such as French and Spanish. Thus, sex is associated with anatomy and gender with symbols. But even within languages that do not assign gender to all nouns, such as English, the masculine is the universal and the feminine is particular, indicated by a suffix or some other distinguishing mark.

Amittai Aviram has offered two reasons that feminists focus on gender as a social construct distinct from biological sex. First, he argues, the purpose is to challenge the naturalized hierarchy characteristic of patriarchy: the devaluing of supposedly feminine gender attributes (passivity, nurturing, intuition, cooperativeness) and the overvaluing of supposedly masculine ones (competitive aggressiveness, rationality, physical strength). Second, Aviram claims that to recognize that gender is not natural removes the coercive force of it, so individuals of whatever sex can be as "feminine" or as "masculine" as they wish (343). When binary gender is no longer compulsory, the rich variegation of actual human lives can be recognized and valued.

However, not all feminists accept the commonsense notion that sex is altogether natural and gender altogether cultural. The rejection of this dichotomy can fall anywhere along the nature-culture spectrum: some feminists believe that gender wholly or in part arises from biological sex, and is therefore not a pure cultural construction, while others believe that biological sex (or even the human body itself) is not wholly free from constructedness. The sex-gender distinction is thus further complicated by a related conceptual opposition: essentialism-constructionism. Constructionism is the belief, expressed above, that "masculine" and "feminine" traits are not emanations of natural, universal essences of man and woman, but are social conventions. If gender is socially constructed, we could presumably construct it differently and free both women and men from a gender hierarchy. If instead we believe that femaleness and femininity, maleness and masculinity, are naturally connected, we are essentialists. Constructionism is appealing, obviously, because it weakens gender stereotypes by depriving them of a basis in unquestionable nature. But its emphasis on the multiplicity and contingency of collective identities tends to undermine group solidarity and therefore organized political effort.

How do we recognize masculinity and femininity, or even male and female, except through categories of perception that are themselves culturally constructed? If culture is so deeply enmeshed in gender, is it even possible to challenge the hierarchical gender system? Can we do so simply by learning to read the world differently? We are formed within the culture that has produced the gender system against which we struggle; can we stand aside from it in order to reimagine it? If we can, what shapes might we imagine gender taking that will be fairer to both men and women, more just and equitable? If we cannot, why bother with feminism?

Constructionism can seem to imply that we are wholly socially determined. Essentialism, on the other hand, has the advantage of offering people a sense of belonging to a group identity grounded in common experience. Many women, for instance, want comparable pay for comparable work and equal access to social and political power and authority but are nonetheless deeply attached to certain elements of their feminine gender, wanting to believe them natural attributes. To call the deeply felt emotions associated with mothering, for instance, a mere social fiction feels alienating and oppressive to many women (Aviram 345). And if there is no such absolutely distinct entity as "woman," on whose behalf do we agitate for women's rights? The problem with essentialism, however, is that it minimizes important differences among women, implying that race, for instance, is a less significant category of experience than gender.

The construction of gender is not, however, an entirely conscious process; we cannot autonomously will it into being. Becoming gendered is not simply a matter of enacting or refusing to enact what our culture teaches us. Gender is a fundamental element of subjectivity, and integrated subjects are not born as such, but formed via an unconscious developmental process. So even if one believes that gender is thoroughly constructed, this does not mean that it is also weightless, that it can easily be sloughed off and an alternative gender assumed.

To complicate this further, Diana Fuss has argued that the constructionism-essentialism opposition is itself a fiction. "To insist that essentialism is always and everywhere reactionary is, for the constructionist, to buy into essentialism in the very act of making the charge; it is to act as if essentialism has an essence" (Fuss 21). Neither constructionism nor essentialism, she suggests, is necessarily more liberating than its putative opposite. To conceive of sex as essence seems deterministic, but feminists have imagined myriad ingenious ways of dealing with anatomical limits (Aviram 344). And to a thoroughgoing constructionist, one's conception of freedom could only take shapes imaginable within the very culture that constructed one's gender to begin with.

Some theorists take up midpoint positions, however, on this issue of constructionism versus essentialism. Many assume a real but unspecified biological essence existing within a moderately constructionist framework. Others set aside the issue of whether members of social groups share essentially differentiating qualities and encourage, instead, elective affinities. Feminist historian of science Donna Haraway, for instance, advocates affinity politics; political theorist Iris Marion Young, interest-group pluralism. Some theorists consider how race, class, and gender intersect in the social construction of subjectivity (Hazel Carby, Valerie Smith, **Chandra Talpade Mohanty**, Barbara Smith).

Most feminists take for granted the existence of anatomical differences between men and women but insist that the conventions governing the behaviors of gendered individuals are cultural constructions unrelated to biological sex. But Judith Butler, perhaps feminism's most influential constructionist, questions that basic distinction, arguing that our gender performances so deeply affect our material bodies that even our perception of anatomical differences is culturally conditioned. Corporeal sex, in Butler's view, is "an ideal construct which is forcibly materialized through time. It is not a simple fact or static condition of a body, but a process whereby regulatory norms materialize 'sex' and achieve this materialization through a forcible reiteration of those norms" (*Bodies* 2). This is of course an extension of the postmodern tendency to understand reality as a linguistic construct, so that it is not possible to think or say anything about sex without imposing cultural norms, and not possible to use language without triggering its patriarchal structures of thought.

For Butler, therefore, not only is gender inauthentic but sex is, too. What appears to be the "mute facticity" of male and female bodies is instead constructed by our culturally constituted and culturally specific perceptions of otherwise heterogeneous phenomena. And "the category of sex imposes a duality and uniformity on bodies in order to maintain reproductive sexuality as a compulsory order" ("Contingent" 17). To liberate oneself from this violent "ordering and production of bodies," one must engage in ironic and subversive performances of one's gender, violating heterosexist gender norms. The object is, she says, to "deprive the naturalizing narratives of their protagonists, man and woman." Butler uses speech act theory to analyze gender, particularly the distinction between performative and constative utterances. She takes up the performative, the sort of speech act that does something rather than merely representing something; among performative utterances such as "I now pronounce you husband and wife" and "I thank you" she would place the statement "I am a woman (or man)." She explores the sense in which our reality in general is created through the speech acts that we perform every day. We enact that reality, incorporating it through our bodies, but it remains a social construction. So our performances are real in that they have real consequences for people, but they are also thoroughgoing constructions. Thus we cannot opt out of the performance of gender, but we can subvert its force through parodic gestures.

Often the word *gender* calls to mind women specifically, and in the early days of feminist criticism, most feminist scholars studied women's literature and images of women in male-authored texts, rarely treating literature by men as if it raised the issue of gender at all. To speak of gender thus highlights the way that the experiences and perspectives of women have been systematically erased, subsumed within a generic, universal masculinity. But more recent treatments of gender also spotlight men, pointing to differences between men and women as readers, writers, and characters, and between masculinity and femininity as social constructs and textual productions. Most interestingly, gender also raises the specter of difference within the categories men and women, masculine and feminine.

Difference has been conceptualized in two disparate ways within the field of feminist theory. Within Anglo-American feminist criticism, man and woman are conceived as unproblematic, self-evident categories. On the basis of that assumption, the Anglo-American critic imagines that social and psychological differences between men and women lead to discernible differences of genre and style in their writing. It makes sense, then, to consider men's and women's writing as separate traditions, identifiable through certain sex-specific stylistic traits or contents. These critics pay particular attention to locating instances of misogyny and revealing gender stereotypes in male-authored works. They discover sexism at higher discursive levels as well, noting biases in favor of the masculine in determining literary value and the consequent marginalizing of women's writing. Anglo-American feminist critics then theorize about how women's writing ought to be related to canonical literary traditions: should the canon be pluralized, or should there be multiple canons? While differences internal to the category "woman," such as race or class positioning or sexual orientation, are sometimes considered, the emphasis of this criticism remains on continuities rather than differences among women writers over time. Critics of Anglo-American feminism reject this tendency to universalize on the basis of women's experience, and suggest that feminist criticism should disrupt such humanist concepts rather than embrace them. As Catherine Belsey has argued, this is an effect of ideology: "within the existing ideology it *appears* obvious that people are autonomous individuals, possessed of subjectivity or consciousness which is the source of their beliefs and actions" (594–95, my emphasis).

But if subjectivity is instead constructed in language, identity becomes not a unified essence but a matrix of subject positions that may be inconsistent with one another. French feminism wholly embraces the view that subjectivity is constructed discursively. It is called "French" not because its practitioners are all or mostly from France but because it centers on the poststructuralist notion of difference, derived from the theories of Ferdinand de Saussure, **Jacques Derrida**, Jacques Lacan, and **Michel Foucault**. In this body of theory, difference is an internal and inevitable condition of identity, conceived as fragmented, unstable, and dispersed. Lacanian psychoanalysis posits a patriarchal symbolic order, within which feminine difference functions as a gap or silence within identity and language, not directly expressible but evident in the paradoxes of rational patriarchal discourse. Feminist practice in this conception involves discerning eruptions of the feminine within masculine (not necessarily male-authored) texts and searching for a new feminine language and textual practice.

As many have observed, one problem with these conceptualizations of difference is that they continue to confine feminist analysis within a universal male/female opposition, obscuring the heterogeneity of gender as it is lived. "To lay the emphasis on difference and the specificity of women (as of men) in the paradigm man/woman," says Stephen Heath, "is a gesture within the terms of the existing system, for which, precisely, women are different *from* men" (117, his emphasis). Within that system— what Hélène Cixous has called "patriarchal binary thought"—male and masculine are the norm, positive and superior, while female and feminine are aberrant, negative, and inferior. Even to extol the feminine is simply to accept and participate in the long tradition of labeling women's language as subjective, emotional, and impressionistic, in comparison with the authority and rationality associated with the masculine.

Do women write differently from men? One position, famously articulated by **Virginia Woolf** in *A Room of One's Own*, is that great minds must be "androgynous," must be "incandescent, unimpeded" by anger or any other "hardship or grievance." All such partialities, Woolf insists, must be consumed in the fire of composition. Joyce Carole Oates has famously aspired to an authorial voice that transcends material and political concerns "while being fueled by them." This view recalls **T. S. Eliot**'s stirring description of poetry as the working of a catalyst on the raw materials of a poet's emotion, resulting in the "extinction of personality." This ahistorical, aestheticizing view is obviously incompatible with the basic feminist insistence on the inescapably political nature of literature and criticism.

A contrary position, strangely, is also famously articulated in *A Room of One's Own*: the idea that women's writing is identifiably distinct from men's. Jane Austen, Woolf says, "looked at [the man's sentence] and laughed at it and devised a perfectly natural, shapely sentence proper for her own use and never departed from it" (80). And in an earlier review, Woolf praises Dorothy Richardson for having "invented . . . a sentence which we might call the psychological sentence of the feminine gender. It is of a more elastic fiber than the old, capable of stretching to the extreme, of suspending the frailest particles, of enveloping the vaguest shapes" ("Dorothy" 191). Heath has written a fascinating critique of the language Woolf uses to advance her theories in *A Room*, suggesting that the seeming contradiction between the notions of the "woman's sentence" and the "androgynous mind" recedes in importance when the patriarchalism of the language itself is seen clearly. Woolf's own images fail the test of androgyny, encoding the male as active and the female as passive, as when, for example, she says of the male and female portions of the mind of the artist that "some marriage of opposites has to be consummated," after which, "when his experience is over," the writer must "lie back and let his mind celebrate its nuptials in darkness" (Heath 113; *Room* 108).

Some feminist critics of more recent vintage than Woolf have suggested that women's writing tends to deploy image patterns different from those men would use. Ellen Moers, for instance, in her *Literary Women* (1977), says: "I find that the caged bird makes a metaphor that truly deserves the adjective female" (250). But only one who has never read Paul Laurence Dunbar's line "I know why the caged bird sings" can make such a statement—not because Dunbar is so unmistakably "male" but because the constrained condition Moers so beautifully describes in her treatment of that metaphor is simply not, biologically or culturally, distinctive to women. One runs immediately into the problem that differences among women (of race, class, region, sexual orientation) far outnumber similarities, and that authors' life situations do not leave obviously readable traces in their work.

Feminist critics following Moers are less likely to believe an author's biological sex is discernible in the text he or she produces. Instead, the text itself is spoken of as gendered: there are masculine and feminine modes of writing, with masculine texts embodying such features as linearity and authoritativeness, and feminine texts disrupting the rational in various ways. Usually it is held that any writer can employ either mode, and this has led to some surprising analyses, as when Mary Ellmann describes the prose style of feminist icon **Simone de Beauvoir** as masculine and that of **Norman Mailer**, notorious sexist, as feminine. **Julia Kristeva** allows for the possibility that some commonalities of theme and style may be characteristic of women's writing, but rejects the notion of a specifically female writing because she rejects the notion of fixed sexual identity altogether; she allows the political necessity of a category of women's writing, but refuses to define it too stringently.

Feminist theorists Peggy Kamuf and Mary Jacobus have rejected the premise behind the effort to discover a distinctively feminine type of writing, even when the ultimate purpose is to demonstrate its quality. To seek such a thing is to give way to biological determinism, they feel; instead, they suggest, feminist critics ought to ask not "is this a male- or female(-authored) text" but "how are masculinity and femininity produced in this text?" (Eagleton 285–86).

Kamuf criticizes Patricia Meyer Spacks for trying to determine what is distinctive about women's writing by reading works by women, suggesting that to do so "[reduces] the literary work to its signature," enabling only meaningless tautologies ("women's writing is writing signed by a woman") and illuminating neither the text itself nor the question of what difference a writer's gender might actually make. Furthermore, she writes, it is biological determinism precisely like that which is routinely, and rightly, identified as "antifeminist sexism." Instead, Kamuf argues, feminist criticism ought to recognize that within Western culture, women's works are classified separately from men's, and men's are universal: men are poets, women poetesses. An effective feminist practice must reject the fundamental assumptions of patriarchy, including the "cult of the individual and the temptation to explain artistic and intellectual productions as simple and direct expressions of individual experience." Feminist criticism ought to "point to the masks of truth with which phallocentrism hides its fictions," particularly the "mask of the proper name," laden as it is with the freight of our patriarchal heritage (Kamuf 286).

Jacobus also worries about what she sees as the naive preoccupation of Anglo-American feminist criticism with supposedly distinctively feminine experience: women's writing, the woman reader. She points to the "assumption of an unbroken continuity between 'life' and 'text'—a mimetic relation whereby women's writing, reading, or culture, instead of being produced, reflect a knowable reality" (108).

Jacobus is equally critical, however, of French feminism and its emphasis on "*l'écriture feminine*"—on woman as writing effect rather than origin. As she cleverly puts it, French feminism concerns itself not with "the sexuality of the text, but with the textuality of sex." Gender difference on this model is produced by the text, and the "feminine" is "to be located in the gaps, the absences, the unsayable or unrepresentable of discourse and representation." She points out, however, that French feminism's insistence that women must "write the body," that only the eruption of female desire can disrupt masculine discourse and challenge the "law of the father," seems inevitably to give rise to "biologistic images of milk or jouissance." If *l'écriture feminine* can only represent itself to our understanding through sex-specific images, Jacobus argues, the flaw in French feminism is not, as is often argued, essentialism. Instead, French feminists stumble into what Jacobus calls "representationalism"—another sort of oversimplification in which theorists cannot resist the urge to formulate representations of what has not yet been written, what has only been dimly imagined. That is, for Jacobus, neither Anglo-American feminism nor French feminism can tolerate the essential elusiveness and unrepresentability of the feminine within any language we can currently use (Jacobus 109).

In all of this complexity and uncertainty, there is one area in which the implications of gender for genre have been explored thoroughly: the special affinity of women for the novel. Forty years ago, Ian Watt argued that the genre developed a female readership made up of middle-class eighteenth-century women, literate and newly leisured, but that thesis has been questioned by Terry Lovell and Nancy Armstrong, among others. Lovell argues that this leisure has been overstated, that in fact these women were responsible for the "work of surplus consumption" and were also charged with producing "middle class gentility" (151). Moers and Woolf describe the advantages to women of that time in becoming writers: they could earn money, but also remain properly within the home. Negotiations with publishers could be handled by husbands, fathers, or brothers. Moreover, the novel seemed a particularly suitable genre for women; it was believed that writing novels was less intellectually rigorous than poetry, for instance, especially since it required no knowledge of the classics. And it was a more inviting form because it grew out of genres familiar and appropriate to women—diaries, letters, and journals—and it carried no long, forbidding history of male precursors (Eagleton 137–38).

Some critics believe that when women writers do employ traditionally male-dominated forms, it is revolutionary: they appropriate a public voice traditionally denied them. Sandra Gilbert and Susan Gubar have made such an argument with respect to women's use of the assertive "I" of the lyric, and Cora Kaplan has discussed the epic in similar terms. Marginal generic forms, on the other hand, are sometimes considered sites of resistance or liberation. In science fiction or fantasy, the current social order can be examined, and possible transformations of it imagined. Romance and detective fiction would seem to be less open to such critiques since in them, the prevailing social order is usually buttressed. Romance idealizes happy heterosexual union; the detective hero or heroine solves the mystery, catches the criminal, and restores peace to the village. The earliest generation of feminist critics had often rejected these genres, especially romance, for their retrograde gender politics, but later studies, such as Janice Radway's readership analysis and Rosalind Coward's psychoanalytic studies, attempt to understand the astonishingly broad appeal of such texts (Eagleton 140–42).

How can women speak and create within misogynist structures, including language itself, that define themselves by means of the devaluing and exclusion of the feminine? Is theory itself so masculine that a feminist position cannot be conceptualized? What happens to feminist argumentation when it is articulated through misogynist structures? If feminist political positions are asserted from a position of mastery, women risk co-optation by the very patriarchal values that silenced them to begin with. But if women attempt to speak the feminine, they risk trivialization or incomprehension—some critics would say, even self-destruction. The question becomes whether women can both work within the dominant, symbolic order and disrupt it at once.

The same sorts of questions have been asked about the effect of the sex of readers as of writers. Do men and women read differently? Is the gender of a reading a matter of the reader's identity (an essentialist view) or simply of the reader's position (a constructionist view)? In other words, does one read *as* a man or woman, or only *like* a man or woman? And if the gender of a reading is a matter of position rather than identity, does the reader's biological sex matter to her or his reading at all?

An early study of gender and reading was Judith Fetterley's *The Resisting Reader*, which in the empiricist spirit of Anglo-American feminism takes sexual identity for granted rather than seeing it as a problem. Nonetheless, it raises an interesting question, one that continues to intrigue feminist readers: what effect does it have on women readers of canonical American literature to encounter, again and again, texts that portray women as obstacles to men's freedom? Her answer was that the narrative strategies of such texts require women to undergo what she terms "immasculation," an alienating identification with a masculine point of view. To combat this, Fetterley argues, women must become "resisting readers." More than a decade later, law professor and feminist Patricia J. Williams explores a parallel question in *The Alchemy of Race and Rights*. What psychological and intellectual contortions are required, she asks, of the African American law student who, in a criminal law class, faces an exam question that presents a hypothetical laden with racial stereotypes like those of the innocent white victim and the menacing black male mugger? She, too, imagines that student bearing an extra burden, due to the supposedly transcendently neutral arena of the law harboring racism. The political necessity of what **Gayatri Chakravorty Spivak** has called "strategic essentialism" is obvious here: whether or not we can determine precisely what makes a law student black, or a student in an English class a woman, clearly an injustice is done to them in such situations, and those injustices cannot be redressed in the absence of an acknowledgment of the students as black or female.

The unfolding of the argument on the relation of gender to reading thus parallels that of the relation of gender to writing: concern with the sex-identified (male or female) author gives way to an interest in the textuality of sex (masculinity or femininity). Discussions like Fetterley's of the relevance of the sex of the reader thus evolve into a concern with reading positions—reading *like* rather than *as* a man or woman. Jonathan Culler, in the section entitled "Reading as a Woman" in *On Deconstruction*, lays out this change: it is necessary to separate the idea of "reading as" from that of "being" a man or woman. If, as Fetterley argues, women can read "as men," men can, similarly, read "as women." This suggestion has, however, been hotly opposed by many critics concerned that the specificity of women's experience of sexist oppression will become irrelevant, magically erased rather than redressed.

This debate of course mirrors one crucial aspect of the relation of gender to writing: the question of what continuity there is or may be between the reader's life and the text. Robert Scholes's conclusion is that women risk too much when they abandon concepts of authenticity and experience because they are theoretically untenable. What is needed, he suggests, is a more theoretically aware conceptualization of such politically indispensable ideas. One study that has provided such a conceptualization is Satya Mohanty's painstaking, politically responsible *Literary Theory and the Claims of History: Postmodernism, Objectivity, Multicultural Politics*, which advances a post-positivist realist position reconceiving "objectivity" as an "ethical achievement rather than a dream of transcendence" and, while embracing the theoretical rigor of post-modernism, stopping short of its most relativist implications. For Mohanty, that experience and identity are constructions does not deprive them of epistemic status and value. Instead, experience is "socially and 'theoretically' constructed, and it is precisely in this mediated way that it yields knowledge" (206).

Time and time again, feminist critics find themselves trapped between the demands of theoretical adequacy and political effectiveness. Presumably, most feminist literary critics work within academic institutions not immediately open to visionary feminist transformation. It is difficult to work actively for the leveling of patriarchal hierarchies while caught up in the struggle for tenure and promotion. Similarly, how does one challenge what to some feminists seem white, bourgeois, masculine critical standards while also having to meet them in order to publish? There is an obvious risk, too, in the glorification of marginalized discourses and genres, especially those (like hysteria or silence) that are traditionally associated with women. And to claim that mere changes in states of consciousness are revolutionary can drown out calls for necessary changes in political and economic systems. Both are salutary, but we must not mistake one for the other. In any case, it seems certain that an increasingly materially grounded, historically aware, and yet also theoretically sophisticated feminism is required.

Selected Bibliography: Aviram, Amittai F. "Gender Theory." *The Oxford Companion to Women's Writing in the United States.* Ed. Cathy N. Davidson and Linda Wagner-Martin. New York: Oxford UP, 1995; Belsey, Catherine. "Constructing the Subject, Deconstructing the Text." *Feminisms: An Anthology of Literary Theory and Criticism.* Robyn R. Warhol and Diane Price Herndl, eds. New Brunswick: Rutgers UP, 1991, 657–73; Belsey, Catherine. *Critical Practice.* London: Methuen, 1980. Butler, Judith. *Bodies That Matter: On the Discursive Limits of "Sex."* New York: Routledge, 1993; Butler, Judith. "Contingent Foundations: Feminism and the Question of 'Postmodernism.'" *Feminists Theorize the Political.* Ed. Judith Butler and Joan W. Scott. New York: Routledge, 1992; Butler, Judith. *Gender Trouble: Feminism and the Subversion of Identity.* New York: Routledge, 1990; Culler, Jonathan. *On Deconstruction: Theory and Criticism after Structuralism.* London: Routledge, 1983; Eagleton, Mary. *Feminist Literary Theory: A Reader.* 2nd ed. Cambridge, MA: Blackwell, 1996; Ellmann, Mary. *Thinking about Women.* London: Virago, 1979; Fetterley, Judith. *The Resisting Reader: A Feminist Approach to American Fiction.* Bloomington: Indiana UP, 1978. 101–53; Fuss, Diana. *Essentially Speaking: Feminism, Nature, and Difference.* London: Routledge, 1989; Heath, Stephen. *The Sexual Fix.* London: Macmillan, 1982; Jacobus, Mary. *Reading Woman: Essays in Feminist Criticism.* New York: Columbia UP, 1986; Kamuf, Peggy. "Writing Like a Woman." *Women and Language in Literature and Society.* Ed. Sally McConnell-Ginet et al. New York: Praeger, 1980; Kristeva, Julia. "Women's Time." Trans. Alice Jardine and Harry Blake. *Feminisms: An Anthology of Literary Theory and Criticism.* Ed. Robyn R. Warhol and Diane Price Herndl. New Brunswick, NJ: Rutgers UP, 1991. 860–77; Lovell, Terry. *Consuming Fiction.* London: Verso, 1987; Moers, Ellen. *Literary Women.* London: Women's P, 1978; Mohanty, Satya. *Literary Theory and the Claims of History: Postmodernism, Objectivity, Multicultural Politics.* Ithaca: Cornell UP, 1997; Moi, Toril. *Sexual/Textual Politics.* London: Methuen, 1985; Warhol, Robyn R., and Diane Price Herndl, eds. *Feminisms: An Anthology of Literary Theory and Criticism.* New Brunswick, NJ: Rutgers UP, 1991; Williams, Patricia J. *The Alchemy of Race and Rights.* Cambridge, MA: Harvard UP, 1991; Woolf, Virginia. "Dorothy Richardson." *Women and Writing.* Ed. Michele Barrett. New York: Harcourt, Brace, 1979; Woolf, Virginia. *A Room of One's Own.* New York: Harcourt, Brace, 1929.

Susan Marren

GENERAL STRIKE (1926). The only occasion in British history when the trade union movement has struck as a unit for more than a day in support of a particular body of workers. The strike began at 11:59 P.M. on May 3, 1926, when the Trades Union Congress (TUC) ordered one and a half million trade unionists, mainly in the transport and communication industries, to support approximately 800,000 coal miners who had been locked out for refusing to accept wage reductions and a worsening of their working conditions. The strike ended at noon on May 12, 1926, when the TUC called off the action in a meeting with Stanley Baldwin, the Conservative prime minister.

The dispute was the result of the confluence of several factors, most particularly the government's desire to force down wages, the TUC's attempt to prevent such an occurrence, and the peculiar conditions in the coal industry at the time. Wages had already fallen by 30 percent in the early 1920s, though up to 40 percent in some regions of the coal industry, and as Britain returned to the gold standard and free trade in 1925, Baldwin declared that wages would have to fall further. The TUC was beginning to oppose such developments in 1925 and decided to support the coal miners in their resistance to further wage reductions in the summer of 1925. Such support had not been forthcoming on April 1, 1921, when the coal miners first found their wages reduced. Indeed, on April 15 of that year, a day now known as Black Friday, the National Union of Railwaymen and the transport workers specifically refused to support the coal miners. When the TUC salvaged their conscience on July 31, 1925, Baldwin stepped in with a nine-month subsidy to stop the dispute; that day became known as Red Friday.

For the next nine months, the government prepared for threatened industrial action, although it hoped that the dispute would be settled by the Samuel Commission on the coal industry. However, this settlement did not occur, and the TUC gave its support to the miners. During this period, the railways practically came to a halt, the government turned Hyde Park into a food center, and there were riots and considerable civil unrest. There was also a propaganda war between the TUC (which published the *British Worker*) and the conservative government (which controlled the BBC and published the *British Gazette*, edited by Winston Churchill).

The strike was called off because the TUC began to fear that it would lose control of its members and also because it doubted its ability to defeat the government. It sought a settlement, the Samuel Memorandum, which would have reduced wages temporarily and closed inefficient mines. When the miners refused to accept this proposal, the TUC called off the strike, much to the chagrin of Communists and many other sectors of the trade-union movement. Since then, stories of the TUC's betrayal of the miners have dogged the history of events surrounding the General Strike. The strike has been the subject of a number of literary works, including Ellen Wilkinson's *Clash* (1929) and **C. Day Lewis**'s *Starting Point* (1937).

Selected Bibliography: Laybourn, Keith. *The General Strike: Day by Day*. Stroud, UK: Sutton, 1996; Laybourn, Keith. *The General Strike of 1926*. Manchester: Manchester UP, 1993; Morris, Margaret. *The General Strike*. London: Journeyman Press, 1976; Phillips, Gordon. *The General Strike: The Politics of Industrial Conflict*. London: Weidenfeld and Nicolson, 1976; Renshaw, Patrick. *The General Strike*. London: Eyre Methuen, 1975.

Keith Laybourn

GERMAN LITERATURE. The myth that German writers, the "*poètes et penseurs*" of Madame de Stael's influential phrase, were traditionally not concerned with the grubby business of politics has been remarkably long-lived. In the "literature quarrel" of 1990, West German critics, seeking to discredit writers who had made a career in the German Democratic Republic (GDR), argued for an end of what they termed *Gesinnungsliteratur* in both East and West Germany and demanded that literary practitioners return to purely aesthetic matters. Yet it had been by no means rare in the classical period for writers to take a passionate interest in political affairs, such as revolt and repression (**Goethe**'s *Egmont*), relations between the individual and state authority (Kleist's *The Prince of Homburg*), racial tolerance (Lessing's *Nathan the Wise*), or social rebellion (Schiller's *The Robbers*). Often circumstances meant poets had little choice but to be concerned with politics, as they had to come to terms with the absolutist ruler of their particular petty state. Their critiques of power came as a result from the outside.

What hampered more sophisticated interaction between *Geist* (mind or spirit) and *Macht* (power), however, was the absence of a fully functioning public sphere. Only with unification in 1871 did Germany acquire a capital city to compare with Paris or London, where cultural producers rubbed shoulders with political decision makers. The genre that flourished in the nineteenth century was the regionalist novella: Theodor Fontane (1819–1898), who chronicled the social and economic aftermath of unification, was Germany's first great social novelist.

The German-speaking lands were not forever thus fragmented. At the zenith of the Holy Roman Empire of the German Nation, the *Minnesinger* Walter von Vogelweide was drawn into the power struggle between the papacy and the emperor. Wolfram von Eschenbach endowed the legend of a sacral ruler with great poetic force in *Parzifal* and made a plea for religious tolerance in the more remarkable crusading epic *Willehalm*. The anonymous *Nibelungenlied* is a great poetic disquisition on political leadership, the futility of war, and the clash between religious conscience and political imperative. While the late Middle Ages and Reformation produced much satire, politics took a backward step in the seventeenth century. Baroque poets rarely acknowledged the significance of secular as opposed to metaphysical power, viewing all human activity *sub specie aeternitas*. In the "Trauerspsiele" (Tragedies), analyzed by **Walter Benjamin** in *The Origins of German Tragic Drama*, the legitimacy of absolutist rulers is not seriously questioned. Only Grimmelshausen, in a series of allegorical episodes in his picaresque account of the Thirty Years War, *Simplicius Simplicissimus* (1669–1676), glimpses a possiblity of a socially just earthly order. Yet while his novels would inspire both **Brecht** and **Grass**, Grimmelshausen's solution lay in transcendental religion rather than in a fairer social settlement.

After the eigtheenth-century Enlightenment, criticism of social organization, inequality, and economic injustice became possible. Plays such as Lessing's *Emilia Galotti* (1772), J.M.R. Lenz's *The House Tutor* (1774), and Schiller's *Intrigue and Love* (1784) brought class conflict between the aristocracy and the aspirant but disempowered bourgeoisie to the stage. The modern era of the political writer begins in the *Vormärz*, those two decades which precede the failed revolution of March 1848. While Heinrich Heine (1797–1856) mocked such writers as Karl Gutzkow and Ludwig Börne associated with "Das Junge Deutschland" in *Germany: A Winter's Tale* (1844), they set a valuable precedent for political commitment. Georg Büchner (1813–1837), who died in exile like Heine, was aesthetically and politically the most radical German playwright before Brecht. When it was performed fifty years after his

death, *Woyzeck* overwhelmed the emergent modernists with the immediacy of its fragmentary style and social message.

Gerhart Hauptmann (1862–1946), the leading German naturalist, elaborated one
of Heine's motifs in *The Weavers* (1892), based on the plight of the workers in the
Silesian textile industry in the 1840s. Hauptmann's account of their failed revolt
against poverty wages resonated in the newly industrialized *Kaiserreich*, where Bis-
marck's "Anti-Socialist Laws" had recently been repealed. In Hauptmann's wake, an
increasing number of writers attacked the authoritarian moral values and rigid social
structures of Wilhelmine Germany. Chief among these are Frank Wedekind in plays
such as *Spring Awakening* (1891, not performed until 1906), Hermann Hesse in
Beneath the Wheel (1906), and Heinrich Mann in *The Blue Angel/Small Town Tyrant*
(1905) and *The Man of Straw* (1918). Yet most German writers still welcomed the
outbreak of war in 1914, seeing military action as an opportunity to test the moral
fiber of the nation and assert—in **Thomas Mann**'s phrase—the superiority of Germanic *Kultur* over Western *Zivilisation*. Heinrich Mann conducted a bitter quarrel
with his younger brother, which he began with an essay on the French social novelist and champion of Dreyfus, **Émile Zola**, who was said to embody a literary practice based in social reality that was alien to the Germans. Thomas responded with a
work he realized had been overtaken by the times before he completed it but in which
he was determined to set out the intellectual case for Germanic values, *The Reflections of a Nonpolitical Man* (1918). Thomas Mann's subsequent career in the public
arena as an anti-Nazi and beleaguered defender of democracy during the Weimar Republic is all the more remarkable given these conservative beginnings.

The first republic on German soil lasted from 1918 to 1933 and was beset from
the Left, who wanted a Bolshevik Revolution as in Russia, and the Right, who never
accepted the legitimacy of the fledgling democratic order. In these highly ideological times, virtually all German writers engaged with politics. Ernst Jünger glorified
the military experience in the trenches of Flanders in *The Storm of Steel* (1920), which
made him a leading spokesman for the intellectual Right and proponent of a "conservative revolution." In a more populist vein, Hans Grimm gave the Nazis one of
their more memorable slogans with the title of his novel of colonial expansion, *Volk
ohne Raum* (1926). Gottfried Benn is the only poet of note who greeted the Nazis
coming to power, although like philospher Martin Heidegger, who also welcomed
them, he had become disaffected by the end of the 1930s. It was on the Left, however, that most significant literary activity took place during the interwar period. Kurt
Tucholsky's campaigning journalism in Germany was matched in Austria by Karl
Kraus, editor of *The Torch* and author of a satire on the mentalities responsible for
World War I, *The Last Days of Mankind* (1919). Ernst Toller, who was imprisoned
for his role in the short-lived Soviet Republic of Munich in 1918/1919, wrote a series of plays on revolutionary themes. There is no more incisive political drama from
the interwar period than *Italian Night* (1930) by Ödön von Horváth, who, next to
Marieluise Fleisser in Berlin, founded the critical folk play, which would be revived
by radical dramatists such as Franz Xaver Kroetz and Rainer Werner Fassbinder in
the 1960s. Bertolt Brecht, who collaborated with Fleisser, followed his youthful phase
of "shocking the bourgeoisie" with political dramas designed to enlighten audiences
by fostering an attitude of critical reflection. The "dark times" in which he wrote en-

tailed that all of life acquired a political dimension. Brecht's literary practice and moral example exercised great influence in both German states after 1945.

Critical writing became an increasingly dangerous business during the Hitler period. The Nazis murdered Erich Mühsam in 1934 and Karl von Ossietzky four years later. Their propaganda chief—Josef Goebbels, who had himself once written a novel—first courted illustrious cultural figures but ultimately set little store by their support. Most writers fled Germany in 1933, when the Nazis showed their contempt for works they deemed unpatriotic by burning them on public bonfires. "When they burn books, they will burn people next," Heine had presciently remarked a hundred years earlier. The Nazis' success signaled a defeat for political literature, but writers resisted Nazism more resolutely than other sectors of the population, even though they failed to prosper in exile and failed also through clandestine distribution channels to reach a wider public in Hitler's Germany. Those who did not succumb to suicidal despair, like Tucholsky in 1935 and Toller in 1940, continued the antifascist fight through journals and printing presses based in Prague or Amsterdam until the outbreak of war, from London and the United States thereafter. Some exiled writers, such as Alfred Döblin and Klaus Mann, donned the uniforms of the Nazis' enemies and entered the defeated country in the armies of the victorious Allies in 1945.

After **World War II**, writers once again enjoyed great prestige, as the battle for the hearts and minds and "reeducation" of surviving Germans began. Brecht, first equipping himself with an Austrian passport, was the most prestigious figure to return to the GDR, where exiled writers were at first more inclined to settle as the communist regime promised a complete break from the past, which was not obviously the case in the West. The history of the interaction between writers and "real existing socialism" in the GDR is, however, one of repeated disaffection, immigration to the West, or private withdrawal. Brecht died before direct confrontation with the regime became inevitable. Critics received summary justice in the early days: Erich Loest and Walter Kempowski were sent to jail. The year 1976, when the singer-songwriter Wolf Biermann, whose mother had died at Auschwitz and who had come East in 1953 to help build socialism, was stripped of his citizenship while on tour in West Germany, marked the point of no return. Yet what distinguished East German writers from dissidents in other Soviet-bloc states was their continued allegiance to an idea of socialism. **Heiner Müller**, **Christa Wolf**, Christoph Hein, and even Jurek Becker attacked the state in the name of a better, more socialist alternative; none wanted annexation by the West. When the GDR finally crumbled, state apparatchiks like Hermann Kant who had chaired the Writers' Union rightly found their integrity in tatters; the veteran **Stefan Heym**, on the other hand, who had been the regime's greatest critic up to 1989, became the former state's greatest defender. Yet so close was the association of writers with the discredited regime—even those who had been in opposition—that GDR dissidents were a spent force once the Berlin Wall was breached.

The first decade of the federal republic was less auspicious, as, by and large, writers felt they were making a new beginning and imitated foreign models—such as **Faulkner**, **Hemingway**, and Camus—rather than continuing the antifascist struggle. As the relationship between writers and the state was worked out in freedom, however, political writers ultimately enjoyed greater influence in the West. Hans Werner

Richter's Gruppe 47, which first met two years after the end of the war, developed over the following two decades into a forum for liberal-Left authors to try out their new work. It became associated with a set of values at odds with the conservative orthodoxy of the ruling Christian democrats under Konrad Adenauer. Richter's informal group never published a manifesto and had no official program but served as a forum for emerging writers, such as Heinrich Böll, Günter Grass, **Hans Magnus Enzensberger**, Martin Walser, Ingeborg Bachmann, and **Peter Weiss**, all of whose work made a direct political impact. Weiss's verse drama on the Frankfurt-Auschwitz trials, *The Investigation* (1965), brought the subject of the **Holocaust** to the attention of a new generation, as had Rolf Hochhuth's *The Representative* (1963); Böll's *The Lost Honour of Katharina Blum* (1974) was a political intervention on the media response to the excessive counter measures on the part of the state to the threat posed by the Red Army Faction (RAF, or Baader-Meinhof Group). These writers were more inclined, however, to invest their cultural capital in the production of polemical speeches and articles that often prompted national debate. They supported Willy Brandt's social democrats in the 1960s. Some, like the émigré poet Erich Fried, moved further to the Left after the formation of a Grand Coalition of the Social Democratic Party (SPD) and the Christian Democratic Union (CDU) in December 1966, aligning themselves with the radicals in the student movement in 1968 or the newly refounded Communist Party (DKP) after 1971. The greatest political novel produced in this period is Uwe Johnson's mournful epic *Anniversaries* (1970–1983), which takes no sides. Political activism continued into the 1980s as writers supported women's rights, disarmament, ecology, and antiracism. So far, under the new Berlin Republic, political literature has concerned itself with the recent past of the twentieth century; no new chapter has yet been opened.

Selected Bibliography: Bance, Alan, ed. *Weimar Germany: Writers and Politics.* Edinburgh: Scottish Academic P, 1982; Benn, Maurice B. *The Drama of Revolt: A Critical Study of Georg Büchner.* Cambridge: Cambridge UP, 1976; Cooke, Paul, and Andrew Plowman, eds. *German Writers and the Politics of Culture: Dealing with the Stasi.* Basingstoke: Palgrave, 2003; Dove, Richard. *A Biography of Ernst Toller: He Was a German.* London: Libris, 1990; Görner, Rüdiger, ed. *Politics in Literature.* Munich: Iudicium, 2004; Kane, Martin, ed. *Socialism and the Literary Imagination: Essays on East German Writers.* New York: Berg, 1991; Lawrie, Steven W. *Erich Fried: A Writer without a Country.* New York: Lang, 1996; McGowan, Moray, and Ricarda Schmidt, eds. *From High Priests to Desecrators: Contemporary Austrian Writers.* Sheffield: Sheffield Academic P, 1993; Parkes, Stuart, and John J. White, eds. *The Gruppe 47 Fifty Years On: A Re-appraisal of Its Literary and Political Significance.* Amsterdam: Rodopi, 1999; Reeves, Nigel. *Heinrich Heine: Poetry and Politics.* London: Libris, 1994; Reid, James H. *Heinrich Böll: A German for His Time.* Oxford: Wolff, 1988.

Julian Preece

GERMINAL (1885). Socialist novel by French Naturalist **Émile Zola**, one of the first works to feature protagonists from the working class. Its starkly accurate portrayal of the life of French miners under the Second Empire bears the mark of Zola's methodical research into subjects ranging from geology to political economics and Socialism. In preparing his project, Zola traveled in February 1884 to the site of a strike of twelve thousand miners at Anzin, where he visited workers in their homes and descended into a mine. Inspired by Hippolyte Taine's formula of "race, milieu, moment," Zola explores how the forces of heredity and environment converge to determine an individual's conduct. Equal parts documentary, *bildungsroman*, and **naturalism**, *Germinal* depicts Étienne Lantier's attempts to unionize miners in northern France. At the heart of the novel is the violent strike at the Montsou mine, a response to the company's cost-cutting measures. On the brink of starvation, the miners are forced back to work without having won any concessions, their already meager earnings diminished and their safety at work further jeopardized. The novel, initially published as a serial in the magazine *Gil Blas* (November 1884–February 1885), is the thirteenth in the twenty-volume *Rougon-Macquart* series. Although much of *Germinal* deals with the misery, exploitation, and despair of those who toiled in the mine shafts, the work ends on a note of optimism. Disillusioned by the bitter strike and a terrorist act by the Polish anarchist Souvarine that takes the life of the woman he loves, Lantier nonetheless resolves to continue his pro-union crusade in Paris in the hopes of creating a more just society. One of the strengths of the work is the fact that Zola, who was clearly sympathetic to the proletarian cause and convinced of the need to give the working class a voice, succeeded in conveying a balanced view of the bourgeois management figures who, like the miners, were victims of the capitalist system and struggling with personal tragedies. At times, the narration appears to be little more than an annotated list of facts and figures of the mining industry in mid-nineteenth-century France. Those facts, combined with Zola's genius for storytelling, come as an indictment of the social and political forces of the Second Empire. When critics denounced the novel as pornographic and excessively violent, Zola responded that he portrayed the miners and their milieu as they were. His goal, he explained, was to incite bourgeois outrage at the social injustices that he described in his narrative.

Zola's portrayal of the capitalist machine ruthlessly crushing the working class stands as a monument in French literature. Not only does he create an engaging study of miners interacting in claustrophobic tunnels and in violent clashes with police, but he captures the political fervor of the Second Empire, characterized by a mix of Socialism, capitalism, collectivism, and anarchism.

Selected Bibliography: Guillemin, Henri. Preface to *Germinal* by Émile Zola. Paris: Garnier Flammarion, 1968. 9–23; Reid, Donald. "Metaphor and Management: The Paternal in *Germinal*." *French Historical Studies* 17 (1992): 979–1000.

Kathy Comfort

GHOSH, AMITAV (1956–). One of the most established and best known Indian writers in English, Ghosh was born in Calcutta, India. Subsequent to graduating from the University of Delhi with a master's in sociology, Ghosh studied at Oxford, where he received his doctorate in social anthropology in 1982. An award-winning journalist, Ghosh has published novels that continue to gain critical attention in their attempt to establish the process of diasporic identity formation as one of perpetual struggle. His first novel, *The Circle of Reason* (1986), won the *Prix Medici Etranger*, one of France's most prestigious awards. Ghosh's second novel, *The Shadow Lines* (1988), won the Sahitya Akademi award, India's most renowned literary prize. Since then, he has published *In an Antique Land* (1993); *The Calcutta Chromosome* (1996), a science-fiction novel that won the Arthur C. Clark Award; and *The Glass Palace* (2000), which won the Grand Prize for Fiction. He writes for the *New Yorker*, the *New York Times*, and the *Observer*.

The ability of Ghosh's texts to draw on various cultural traditions (along with Ghosh's own diasporic subjectivity as an Indian who was raised in Bangladesh, Iran, and Sri Lanka, and has lived and worked in Egypt and the United States) corresponds well with the subjects of emigration, exile, and cultural displacement addressed in his work. In his novels, Ghosh presents the reader with a political vision that not only questions the ethnolinguistic and cultural divides created by the fiery resurgence of nationalist ideologies in postcolonial India, but interweaves that vision with the human stories he delineates in the novels. His novels are informed by his poignant awareness of the error of not attempting to transcend ethnolinguistic divides, caste and class barriers, and religious dogmas in postcolonial societies. He is critical of the purported historical and religious necessity to forge a unified nationalist identity.

In "The Diaspora in Indian Culture," Ghosh suggests that India does not create a sense of nationhood in her diasporas, partly because the dislocated people of India do not carry one language as other diasporic groups have done but, on the contrary, carry innumerable languages and religious cultures already rooted in "systematic diversity" (76). For Ghosh, Indian culture "has been constructed around the proliferation of differences" (77). Ghosh encourages a nationalist self-imagining and rewriting of history that incorporates profound cultural, religious, and linguistic differences into the text. His diasporic subjectivity and the subject matter of his fiction have led many critics to see him as a blossoming postcolonial writer.

Selected Bibliography: Bhatt, Indira, and Indira Nityanandan. *The Fiction of Amitav Ghosh*. New Delhi: Creative Books, 2001; Bose, Brinda, ed. *Amitav Ghosh: Critical Perspectives*. New Delhi: Pencraft International, 2003; Dhawan, R. K. *The Novels of Amitav Ghosh*. New Delhi: Prestige Books, 1999; Ghosh, Amitav. "The Diaspora in Indian Culture." *Public Culture* 2.1 (1989): 75–77.

Nyla Ali Khan

GIBBON, LEWIS GRASSIC (1901–1935). Son of working farmers in Aberdeenshire, Scotland, and christened James Leslie Mitchell, Gibbon took his mother's name for his Scottish fiction and wrote under his own name in English. He referred to himself as a Communist and was beginning to support Scottish nationalism before he died prematurely of peritonitis. He worked as a journalist before joining the army and traveling to the Middle East. After **World War I**, he experienced poverty and unemployment in London, then served in the Air Force until 1929. He settled as a full-time writer in Welwyn Garden City in England.

His major work is the trilogy of novels *Sunset Song* (1932), *Cloud Howe* (1933) and *Grey Granite* (1934), collectively published as *A Scots Quair* (1946). The first novel tells the story of a young woman, Chris Guthrie, growing up on a farm from the beginning of the twentieth century to the end of World War I. She marries and has a son, Ewan, but her husband and their farming friends are all killed in the war. The book ends with the funeral of their way of life: "*They died for a world that is past, these men, but they did not die for this that we seem to inherit.*" Instead of sentimental nostalgia, Gibbon projects the values of the older Scotland as a permanent sharp critique of mechanized modernity. In *Cloud Howe*, Chris is married to a minister and living in a small town, where her husband's visionary hope for a better future is finally frustrated and she is left alone once again. In *Grey Granite*, she has moved to the city and her son has grown up to become a communist activist, leading strikes and being brutalized by thuggish police. At the end, Gibbon opens a radical dialectic, returning Chris to the land of her youth and the image of regeneration inherent in the conservative cycle of seasons, while Ewan leads a socialist march across the border toward a future he believes he can help make better. Gibbon does not ironize or privilege either option. His sympathies are evidently with both Chris and the older Scotland she inhabits as well as Ewan's steely determination for a better future. The ending is a recognition of the necessity of the continuing struggle and elemental realities.

Gibbon's most memorable short stories, "Clay," "Smeddum," and "Greenden," were published in *Scottish Scene* (1934)—a book of stories, poems, essays, biographies, and "newsreels" (cuttings from newspapers of the day), which Gibbon coauthored with **Hugh MacDiarmid**. The book remains a sparkling, contradictory, and passionate document of its era, condemning the shortcomings of Scottish attempts at self-determination and castigating Ramsay MacDonald (the first Labourite British Prime Minister) as "the Wrecker," destroying hopes for real Socialism in Britain.

The short stories, like the trilogy of novels, achieve the radical development of a narrative prose idiom that represents the speech of the characters. Since Walter Scott, narrative prose in Scottish novels had traditionally been English while characters spoke Scots. Gibbon's achievement was to create a Scots prose, a brilliantly vivid depiction of what he calls "the speak of the place." As art, this writing is related to similar experiments in literature by **James Joyce** and **William Faulkner** and the modern movement's key characteristics of multiple perspectives and a relative sense of time.

Gibbon/Mitchell wrote seventeen books in the last seven years of his life. Of the novels in English, *Spartacus* (1933) is the most powerfully politicized, and *Stained Radiance* (1930) and *The Thirteenth Disciple* (1931) are revealingly autobiographical. *Gay Hunter* (1934) and *Three Go Back* (1932) are **science-fiction** novels of time travel and social critique. Gibbon was protofeminist, deeply concerned with the place of women in society, and fierce in his depiction of the brutalities of male dominance and the evils of militarism, class, competition, and war. His early death should not diminish our recognition of the major quality of his achievement.

Selected Bibliography: Campbell, Ian. *Lewis Grassic Gibbon.* Edinburgh: Scottish Academic P, 1985; Gifford, Douglas. *Neil Gunn and Lewis Grassic Gibbon.* Edinburgh: Oliver & Boyd, 1983; McCulloch, Margery Palmer, and Sarah M. Dunnigan, eds. *Lewis Grassic Gibbon: A Centenary Celebration.* Glasgow: Association for Scottish Literary Studies, 2003; Munro, Ian S. *Leslie Mitchell: Lewis Grassic Gibbon.* Edinburgh: Oliver & Boyd, 1966; Young, D. F. *Beyond the Sunset: A Study of James Leslie Mitchell.* Aberdeen: Impulse Books, 1973.

Alan Riach

GILBERT, KEVIN (1933–1993). Like that of many indigenous Australians of his generation, Kevin Gilbert's early life was one of severe deprivation and institutionalization. Descended from the Wiradjuri and Kamilaroi peoples of New South Wales, following the death of both parents, he was raised in a succession of welfare homes. In 1957, he was sentenced to life imprisonment for the murder of his wife. Prison, however, finally gave him the opportunity to learn to read and to develop knowledge of art and literature. In addition to painting and beginning to write the poetry for which he was to become best known, he wrote *The Cherry Pickers* (1968), a play about Aboriginal seasonal workers. Performed in 1971, when he had been released on parole, it was the first Aboriginal play to be staged.

Gilbert became active in a number of indigenous political movements during the 1970s, playing an important role in the establishment of the Aboriginal Tent Embassy in the Australian national capital of Canberra. He also published two polemical works arguing the need for land rights and recognition of Aboriginal prior occupation and ownership of Australia—*Because a White Man'll Never Do It* (1973) and *Aboriginal Sovereignty: Justice, the Law and the Land* (1993)—as well as one of the first collections of indigenous oral histories, *Living Black* (1977). As well as publishing several of his own collections of protest and other poems, including *People Are Legends* (1978), *The Blackside* (1990), and the posthumous *Black from the Edge* (1994), Gilbert also edited an important anthology of indigenous Australian poetry, *Inside Black Australia* (1988), to mark the bicentenary of the white invasion of Australia.

Selected Bibliography: McMillan, Pauline. "Kevin Gilbert and 'Living Black.'" *Journal of Australian Studies* 45 (June 1995): 1–14; Mudrooroo. *Writing from the Fringe: A Study of Modern Aboriginal Literature*. Melbourne, Victoria: Hyland House, 1990; Van Toorn, Penny. "Indigenous Texts and Narratives." *The Cambridge Companion to Australian Literature*. Ed. Elizabeth Webby. Cambridge: Cambridge UP, 2000. 19–49.

Elizabeth Webby

GINSBERG, IRWIN ALLEN (1926–1997). Although Allen Ginsberg's legendary October 13, 1955, Six Gallery (San Francisco) reading of the poem *Howl* was a moment of validation and unification for many of the Bay Area antiestablishment artists, the poet's eventual prominence gained its first major boost from the subsequent attempt by the San Francisco police to block the sale of *Howl and Other Poems* (1956) on a charge of obscenity. The trial that followed eventually gained international attention and began Ginsberg's long battle with censorship.

The poet spent most of the decade previous to the *Howl* reading in isolation, virtually unknown, patiently developing—with the help of fellow **beat** generation originals Jack Kerouac and William Burroughs, and established poet **William Carlos Williams**—his characteristic open, honest, spontaneous, here-and-now, experimental style of poetry. After the *Howl* reading, Ginsberg's celebrity rose steadily, eventually making him one of the most recognized poets of the twentieth century. Ginsberg used his celebrity status to forward his causes, giving hundreds of interviews, lectures, and readings, as well as lending his name to and helping organize numerous protests and movements, including the 1967 Gathering of the Tribes for a Human Be-In, the Chicago Festival of Life (across the street from the 1968 Democratic National Convention, and from which emerged the Chicago Seven trials), and the 1978 Rocky

Flats nuclear protests. In 1965, Ginsberg was deported from both Cuba and, shortly thereafter, Czechoslovakia (where he was crowned May king by students) for discussing homosexuality and government affairs with students and reporters.

Through his poetry and activism, Ginsberg tirelessly defended homosexuality, the use of certain drugs (LSD, marijuana, and psilocybin) to "expand the consciousness," and the need to end the military-industrial complex and its global campaign against street-level democracy. Along with *Howl*, key texts, all found in *Collected Poems* (1984), are *Planet News* (1968), which contains poems written from 1961–1963, including "Television Was a Baby Crawling Toward That Deathchamber"; *The Fall of America* (1973), which contains work from 1965–1971, including "Wichita Vortex Sutra" (often cited as his best politically motivated work); and *Plutonian Ode* (1982), which is notable for the title work and for "Birdbrain" and "Capitol Air."

The bulk of negative criticism on Ginsberg's literature comes from the Right-leaning critics, conservative Christians (frowning on his antiestablishment mysticism and eventual Buddhism, and condemning his homosexuality), and Establishment opinion makers (*Time*). Conservative cultural critic Norman Podhoretz—who had a long history of verbal warfare with Ginsberg, and who devotes a chapter to Ginsberg in his book *Ex-Friends* (1999)—claims that the poet is adept at pointing out the flaws of capitalism and Soviet-style Communism but has little to say toward concrete solutions. Ginsberg's ultimate legacy may be an unabashed willingness to shatter conventional thinking and writing in the most public way, not to create spectacle in a move complicit with consumer capital but instead to reintroduce the openness and honesty necessary for human community.

Selected Bibliography: Ball, Gordon. "Ginsberg and Revolution." *Selected Essays: West Georgia College International Conference on Representing Revolution 1989*. West Georgia International Conference, 1991: 137–50; Ginsberg, Allen, and David Carter, eds. *Spontaneous Mind: Selected Interviews 1958–1996*. New York: HarperCollins, 2001; Katz, Eliot. "Radical Eyes: Political Poetics and the Work of Allen Ginsberg." Unpublished Dissertation. Rutgers, May 2000; Schumacher, Michael. *Dharma Lion*. New York: St. Martin's, 1992.

David Leaton

GLADKOV, FYODOR VASILYEVICH (1883–1958).

Born into a poor peasant family in Saratov Province, arrested in 1906, imprisoned and exiled for his revolutionary activities, and member of the **Communist Party** from 1920, this former primary-school teacher was to become one of the most popular proletarian writers in the Soviet Union. He was to combine writing, teaching, and official posts, ultimately serving as director of the Gorky Literary Institute.

Gladkov's literary output included stories about convicts, exiles, and political prisoners, such as *Three in One Hut* (1905), *The Outcasts* (1908), and *The Old Secret Prison* (1926); tales about Russian village life, such as *The Abyss* (1917); autobiographical reflections, such as *The Fiery Steed* (1922) and the trilogy *Story of My Childhood* (1949), *The Outlaws*, and *Evil Days* (1954), the first two parts awarded Stalin Prizes; and three satirical sketches about party meddlers (1928–1930, republished as *A Little Trilogy*, 1936). The thematic influence of **Dostoevsky** and **Gorky** is discernible in many of his works.

Gladkov is best remembered for the novels *Cement* (1925) and *Energy* (1932–1938). The second concerns the construction of a massive hydroelectric power plant during the first Five-Year Plan. However, it is on *Cement*, "the first Soviet novel of the working class," that Gladkov's reputation rests. It is set at the end of the civil war and the beginning of the NEP (New Economic Policy). Gleb Chumalov, the hero, returns to find the local cement factory in a parlous state. He does not recognize his wife, Dasha. Emancipated, she now works for the party's women's section, having put their daughter in a children's home where the child subsequently dies. Gleb sets about rebuilding the factory along socialist lines, overcoming many obstacles. He cannot, however, fully come to terms with the changes in his wife, who eventually leaves him. This clash between the public and the personal is the major theme of the novel.

Gladkov willingly revised *Cement* for subsequent editions to be in line with the changing party line, especially with regard to the role of women. Enthusiastically received at home and abroad, *Cement* was admitted retrospectively into the pantheon of **socialist realism**, although it might more accurately be seen as the prototype of the Soviet industrial novel.

Selected Bibliography: Brown, Edward J. *Russian Literature since the Revolution.* London: Collier-Macmillan, 1969; Durfee, Thea Margaret. "*Cement* and *How the Steel Was Tempered*: Variations on the New Soviet Woman." *A Plot of Her Own: The Female Protagonist in Russian Literature.* Ed. Sona Stephan Hoisington. Evanston, IL: Northwestern UP, 1995. 89–101; Friedberg, Maurice. "New Editions of Soviet Belles-Lettres: A Study in Politics and Palimpsests." *American Slavic and East European Review* 8 (1954): 72–88; Mathewson, Rufus W., Jr. *The Positive Hero in Russian Literature.* Stanford, CA: Stanford UP, 1975. 205–9.

Frank Beardow

GLISSANT, EDOUARD (1928–). The work of the Martinican-born novelist, poet, and philosopher Edouard Glissant, in its formal variety, rhetorical mastery, and critical acumen, stands as the foremost attempt to illuminate the contradictions of the neocolonial culture of Martinique in the postwar period. Following on the work of his compatriots **Aimé Césaire** and **Frantz Fanon**, Glissant explores the ambiguities and contradictions of life in the postmodern French neocolony that is Martinique since 1945. Glissant first came to the attention of the French-speaking public when his novel *La Lézarde* won the Renaudot Prize in 1958. Over his entire career, Glissant has simultaneously worked in three literary genres: the novel, poetry, and cultural and philosophical criticism. His novels recover the history of Martinique from its discovery to the present, a history that, Glissant argues, has been systematically buried and actively repressed following the primary erasure of sociohistorical continuity in the Middle Passage of Africans to slavery in the New World. Novels such as *La Lézarde* and *The Fourth Century* (*Le Quatriéme Siécle*, 1964) undertake a protean reconstruction of this indigenous historical awareness, while *Malemort* (1974), in its Joycean obscurity, compels the reader who will unlock the secrets of its narrative to a mimetic identification with the multiple dimensions of the Martinican subject's postcolonial alienation. Glissant's poetry—beginning with his 1956 poem *The Indies* (*Les Indes*) and continuing through the collection *Le Sel noir; Le Sang rive; Boises*

(1983)—reveals the lyrical influence of the Guadeloupean poet Saint-John Perse, while refusing the latter's topical erasure of his colonial roots in favor of a critical historical awareness.

Though this concern for history and a characteristic literary voice distinguish the entirety of Glissant's production, in his critical-philosophical works, Glissant's oeuvre most clearly shows a division between two periods of production. Up to and including his masterpiece *Caribbean Discourse* (1981), Glissant undertook a critique of Martinican cultural alienation and French neocolonialism that implicitly adapted the Western Marxist model of **Georg Lukács's** *History and Class Consciousness* (1923) to the postcolonial sphere. Works such as *Soleil de la conscience* (1956), *L'Intention poétique* (1969), and *Caribbean Discourse* elaborate this immanent postcolonial cultural critique. In all their diversity, these texts seek to ground a class consciousness of the colonized in a total vision of neocolonial alienation that would further the drive for Martinican political and psychological independence from France. In later texts such as *Poetics of Relation* (1990) and *Traité du tout-monde* (1997), Glissant elaborates in contrast a postmodern vision that transcends the specificity of the ongoing Martinican dilemma to describe subjectivities of infinite and rhizomatic "relation" amid the increasingly globalized and transnational cultures of the late twentieth century. Though this second phase arguably dilutes the critical and polemical force of Glissant's earlier philosophical work, the entirety of his production demonstrates the immense force of a culturally, historically, and imaginatively informed poetics to encompass and illuminate the dilemmas of postcolonial transnational experience.

Selected Bibliography: Britton, Celia. *Edouard Glissant and Postcolonial Theory: Strategies of Language and Resistance.* Charlottesville: U of Virginia P, 1999; Dash, J. Michael. *Edouard Glissant.* New York: Cambridge UP, 1995; Glissant, Edouard. *Caribbean Discourse: Selected Essays.* Trans. J. Michael Dash. Charlottesville: UP of Virginia, 1989; Glissant, Edouard. *Poetics of Relation.* Trans. Betsy Wing. Ann Arbor: U of Michigan P, 1997; Glissant, Edouard. *Traité du tout-monde.* Paris: Gallimard, 1997.

Nick Nesbitt

GODWIN, WILLIAM (1756–1836). Usually acknowledged as the first systematic exponent of philosophical anarchism, Godwin also enjoyed a long career as a writer of fiction, children's literature, and history. Born in Wisbech, England, Godwin came from a line of Protestant nonconformist ministers, and trained for the ministry himself at Hoxton Academy in London. After losing his faith, he settled in London in 1783, where he made a precarious living as a political journalist, reviewer, and novelist. He rose to sudden fame in 1793 with the publication of *An Enquiry concerning Political Justice, and Its Influence on General Virtue and Happiness. Political Justice*, as the work came to be known, was an important contribution to the British pamphlet war that surrounded the outbreak of the **French Revolution**. Responding to the conservative criticisms of Edmund Burke, Godwin crystallized and extended existing critiques of aristocracy and monarchy, arguing ultimately that all government was immoral, as it controverted the human individual's essential and definitive right of private judgment. The work caused a sensation, and during the mid-1790s, Godwin was regarded as Britain's premier liberal intellectual. Godwin's fame was enhanced by his publication in 1794 of the novel *Things as They Are; or, The Adventures of*

Caleb Williams. Part detective novel, part psychological thriller, part damning critique of the British political, social, legal, and penal systems, *Caleb Williams* instantly achieved, and has deservedly retained, the status of a classic. It was, as Godwin admitted, an attempt to disseminate to a wider audience the political and moral ideas of *Political Justice*. In 1797, Godwin married the feminist philosopher and novelist **Mary Wollstonecraft**, with whom he had a daughter, Mary, later the author of the pioneering horror novel *Frankenstein*.

Although prolific in his literary output over the rest of his long life, Godwin never attained the fame of this early phase of his career. Godwin's life was also a continual struggle against poverty, and his choice of literary output usually reflected his financial needs. Among Godwin's important other writings are the novels *St. Leon* (1799) and *Fleetwood* (1805); his biography of Mary Wollstonecraft, *Memoirs of the Author of "A Vindication of the Rights of Woman"* (1798); and his *History of the Commonwealth of England* (1824–1828). Godwin's writings attract increasing scholarly interest, but most attention continues to be devoted to *Political Justice* and *Caleb Williams*. Godwin was undoubtedly an innovator in the detective novel and an important political theorist who took to its logical, if extreme, end the rationalism and belief in human perfectibility of liberal Enlightenment thought.

Selected Bibliography: Clemit, Pamela. *The Godwinian Novel: The Rational Fiction of Godwin, Brockden Brown, Mary Shelley.* Oxford: Oxford UP, 1993; Locke, Don. *A Fantasy of Reason: The Life and Thought of William Godwin.* London: Routledge & Kegan Paul, 1980; Marshall, Peter. *William Godwin.* New Haven, CT: Yale UP, 1984; Philp, Mark. *Godwin's Political Justice.* London: Duckworth, 1986; St. Clair, William. *The Godwins and the Shelleys: The Biography of a Family.* London: Faber & Faber, 1989.

Rowland Weston

GOETHE, JOHANN WOLFGANG VON (1749–1832). Born into the wealthy bourgeoisie of Frankfurt am Main, a prospering free city within what was then a huge patchwork of disconnected German-speaking principalities, Goethe was destined to become Germany's greatest poet and an icon of it's national unity. In addition, he was a novelist, playwright, and philosopher. Despite his hostility to more extreme forms of the movement, he was a central figure in European **romanticism**, as well as an important political figure who served as privy councillor and minister within the small state of Saxony-Weimar. He first attracted attention with his impassioned novel *The Sufferings of Young Werther* of 1774, a typical product of the Sturm und Drang (storm and stress) movement, in which social prejudice proves no less damaging to the hero than misfortune in love. In 1775, Goethe moved to Weimar, where he was put in charge of several important projects, including the local highways and silver mines. The frustrations that Goethe encountered when trying to implement social and managerial improvements may have persuaded him that it was only by cooperating with the aristocracy that he could wield lasting influence. In his creative works, poets are often thwarted in the face of hostile or indifferent patrons (*Torquato Tasso, Wilhelm Meister's Apprenticeship*); where revolutionary action is depicted, as in the plays *Götz von Berlichingen* and *Egmont*, it is, paradoxically, in support of the restoration of ancient—indeed feudal—procedures and values.

Goethe responded with acute dismay to the **French Revolution** and even denounced the relatively moderate July Revolution of 1830. Legitimate contemporary aspirations are mocked in many poems and epigrams, and Goethe appears to have favored muzzling the press and restricting the circulation of newspapers. In the second part of *Faust*, completed in 1831, the hero's supposedly humanitarian schemes bear little fruit and regularly rely on support from the devil. However, in some ways Goethe's influence was powerfully progressive and liberating. He did not share his compatriots' shallow nationalism and derided the inward-looking cult of the gothic revival and the false pietism typified by pseudomedieval painting. His attitude toward Napoleon was much less hostile than that of most Germans of his time; he was quick to recognize the benefits of cosmopolitanism and the enfranchisement of minorities. His poetry is emancipatory in its anticipation of Darwin and its ruthless condemnation of religious bigotry. In his scientific investigations, he insisted on an unbiased perspective and on unswerving scepticism toward received truths. Many of his literary works were ahead of their time and provoked uproar when they were performed or printed. This is true of his early poem "Prometheus" no less than of the final part of *Faust*, published posthumously in 1832. Throughout the nineteenth and twentieth centuries, Goethe has remained controversial, and many traditionalists find him uncomfortable. The National Socialists attempted to exploit his work for their purposes, using the notion of "Faustian man" as a representative of German self-assertion in propagandist contexts. The East German state made great efforts to portray him as a forerunner of their own brand of Socialism, citing carefully chosen lines in isolation. Goethe's political outlook was ultimately bound up with a deep and lasting nostalgia for the spirit of classical antiquity, and his recurrent expressions of gentle resignation stemmed from the knowledge that its ideals could never be implemented in a modern setting.

Selected Bibliography: Boyle, Nicholas. *Goethe: The Poet and the Age. Revolution and Renunciation, 1790–1803.* Oxford: Clarendon P, 2000; Brown, Jane K. *Goethe's "Faust": The German Tragedy.* Ithaca: Cornell UP, 1986; Grimm, Reinhold, and Jost Hermand, eds. *Our Faust? Roots and Ramifications of a Modern German Myth.* Madison: U of Wisconsin P, 1987; Rothe, Wolfgang. *Der politische Goethe: Dichter und Staatsdiener im deutschen Spätabsolutismus.* Göttingen: Vandenhoeck & Ruprecht, 1998; Witte, Bernd, Theo Buck, Hans-Dietrich Dahnke, and Regine Otto, eds. *Goethe-Handbuch.* 5 vols. Stuttgart: Metzler, 1996–1998.

Osman Durrani

GOGOL, NIKOLAI VASILIEVICH (1809–1852). Born in today's Ukraine, the brilliantly eccentric Gogol authored prose fiction and plays that led nineteenth-century leftist critics to anoint him "the father of Russian realism" for exposing the backwardness of Russian society and the corruption of Russian officialdom while engendering sympathy for the victimized "little man." In fact, Gogol was politically conservative, deeming the reigning tsarist political system a divinely ordained institution with no conceivable alternative. Hence, he did not expect his works to inspire social or political change but, at most, to spur the reformation of wayward individuals and unfeeling bureaucrats. Dedicating himself to writing after an abortive stint as a professor of world history at St. Petersburg University, Gogol spent much of his adult life in Western Europe, where his conservatism was enhanced by his increasing idealization of Russia's historical and spiritual destiny.

Notwithstanding this conservatism, Gogol satirized aspects of Russian life to socially and politically progressive, even subversive, effect. This effect is most palpable in his best-known play, *The Inspector General* (*Revizor*, 1836)—which Tsar Nikolai I surprisingly allowed to be staged despite its comedic exposure of bureaucratic corruption—and in his only novel, *Dead Souls* (*Mertvye dushi*, 1842). In this novel, Gogol implicitly condemns the immorality of serfdom by portraying a shady traveling businessman who schemes to purchase from rural landowners the names of dead serfs—termed souls—on whom, as property, the landowners are still paying taxes. Gogol wildly caricatures these owners, whose souls may truly be the dead ones, for their bottomless vacuity and greed. He also turned a satirical eye to the absurdity and inhumanity pervading urban existence in his stories set in St. Petersburg, especially "The Diary of a Madman" (*Zapiski sumashedshego*, 1835), "The Nose" (*Nos*, 1836), and "The Overcoat" (*Shinel*, 1842). These stories depict government functionaries resorting to ludicrous psychological strategies—including delusions of regal grandeur, acceptance of sheer irrationality, and submission to self-annihilating conformity—in an effort to cope with the unyielding impersonality of the bureaucracy enmeshing them.

In his final decade, Gogol lost the comic feel for grotesque imagery, extravagant digression, absurdist logic, and at times surreal plot lines that had given unique expression to his acute awareness of the banality, corruption, and dehumanization permeating Russian society. After this loss, Gogol published only nonfiction, primarily self-righteous homilies urging spiritual regeneration and obsequious tributes to ecclesiastical and secular authorities, which reform-minded critics derided as reactionary and obscurantist. Despite these humorless late writings, Gogol's earlier, satirical fiction opened an irrationalist vein in Russian literature that future authors, most notably **Fyodor Dostoevsky** and **Mikhail Bulgakov**, would mine to their own distinctive political and artistic ends.

Selected Bibliography: Annenkov, P. V. *The Extraordinary Decade: Literary Memoirs.* Trans. Irwin Titunik. Ann Arbor: U of Michigan P, 1968; Erlich, Victor. *Gogol.* New Haven, CT: Yale UP, 1969; Fanger, Donald. *The Creation of Nikolai Gogol.* Cambridge, MA: Harvard UP, 1979; Maguire, Robert A. *Exploring Gogol.* Stanford, CA: Stanford UP, 1994; Nabokov, Vladimir. *Nikolai Gogol.* Norfolk, CT: New Directions, 1944.

Elizabeth Cheresh Allen

GOLD, MICHAEL (1893–1967). The son of impoverished Jewish immigrant parents on Manhattan's Lower East Side, Gold would go on to become one of the leading figures in American leftist culture in the twentieth century. Born Itzok Granich, he changed his name during the Red Scare of 1919–1920 in an attempt to avoid the persecution that often focused on Jewish immigrants at that time. Inspired early on by anarchism and syndicalism, Gold would go on to become a committed Communist and a leading cultural activist in the **Communist Party**. Known for an acerbic style that often led to bitter conflicts with those of whom he was critical, Gold was nevertheless an influential activist whose editorial work on journals such as *New Masses* made him a central figure on the American Left, especially during the period from the founding of the journal in 1926 through the mid-1930s, when Gold's championing of **proletarian literature** did much to promote that phenomenon. Gold was also influential as a columnist for the *Daily Worker*, to which he contributed regularly from 1933 until his death. Many of his columns are reprinted in the volumes *Change the World!* (1936) and *The Hollow Men* (1941).

Gold has often been singled out by his critics as an example of dogmatic and doctrinaire cultural thought. However, though his writing style was unpolished, Gold's own literary production, informed by his strong political commitment and his own experiences with urban poverty and injustice, was not without merit. Early in his writing career, he was the author of a number of plays, three of which were performed by the Provincetown Players during the period from 1916 to 1920. Unquestionably, however, his most important literary work was the novel *Jews without Money* (1930), a semiautobiographical portrait of poverty among the Jewish immigrants on the East Side in the early part of the twentieth century. This novel became an early model for American proletarian writers and continues to gain critical attention and respect more than seventy years after its publication.

Selected Bibliography: Bloom, James D. *Left Letters: The Culture Wars of Mike Gold and Joseph Freeman*. New York: Columbia UP, 1992; Folsom, Michael Brewster. "The Education of Mike Gold." *Proletarian Writers of the Thirties*. Ed. David Madden. Carbondale: Southern Illinois UP, 1968. 222–51; Folsom, Michael Brewster. "The Pariah of American Letters." Introduction to *Mike Gold: A Literary Anthology*. Ed. Michael Brewster Folsom. New York: International Publishers, 1972. 7–20; Gold, Michael. *Change the World!* New York: International Publishers, 1936; Gold, Michael. *The Hollow Men*. New York: International Publishers, 1941; Pyros, John. *Mike Gold: Dean of American Proletarian Writers*. New York: Dramatika P, 1979.

M. Keith Booker

GOLDMAN, EMMA (1869–1940).

Born in what is now Lithuania to Jewish parents, Goldman immigrated to the United States in 1885. Under the early tutelage of Johann Most, Goldman quickly emerged as one of the most prominent spokespersons for individualistic anarchism, a role she retained until her death. Her conversion to anarchism (and deep distrust of governments) stemmed from her outrage at the execution of the Haymarket anarchists in 1887. Later study in Europe—including her exposure to Nietzsche and Freud as well as the modern drama (which she saw as a powerful conduit of revolutionary thought)—influenced her thinking and her writing. From 1906 until 1917, Goldman published *Mother Earth*, a magazine devoted to anarchism and avant-garde thinking. She supported the magazine through extensive lecturing on anarchists themes; her most popular, if controversial, lectures were on women's issues and the modern drama. From her lectures, Goldman published *Anarchism and Other Essays* (1911); five of the twelve essays in the book focus on women. She and her long-time compatriot Alexander Berkman were deported in 1919, allegedly for inciting resistance to conscription. After her escape from her Russian exile, Goldman sought to expose the abuses of the communist regime there in *My Disillusionment in Russia* (1922), but her efforts had little impact. To raise money, she published her autobiography, *Living My Life*, in 1931—arguably her most important work and one that garnered her widespread recognition by second-wave feminists. Goldman died in 1940, and her body was returned to the United States to be buried in Chicago near her early heroes, the Haymarket anarchists.

Goldman was a synthetic rather than creative thinker; her published essays are replete with references to those who influenced her: Peter Kropotkin, Freud, Nietzsche, and scores of others. Almost all of her lectures and essays attack what she saw as the primary enemies of individual thought and freedom: capitalism, government, and religion. Perhaps her most significant intellectual contributions involved her discussions of the modern drama and her iconoclastic view of women. Though heavily colored by her ideology, her popular lectures on drama—later forming *The Social Significance of the Modern Drama* (1914)—nonetheless introduced the works of **Ibsen**, Hauptman, **Shaw**, Galsworthy, **Yeats**, and Chekhov to thousands of Americans. An opponent of the contemporary woman's suffrage movement because of its elitism and focus on the ballot, Goldman advocated internal emancipation—freeing one's self from the constraints of society—as the key to a woman's personal development. A forceful speaker, Goldman outraged her listeners as often as she persuaded them. Thus, contemporary public reaction to her advocacy of free love often eclipsed her significant contributions in support of women's control of their reproductive rights. By the time of her last lecture tour in the United States in 1934, Goldman's anarchism was outdated. Today, her fame rests on her lived feminism rather than on her anarchist advocacy.

Selected Bibliography: Drinnon, Richard. *Rebel in Paradise: A Biography of Emma Goldman*. Chicago: U of Chicago P, 1961; Falk, Candace. *Love, Anarchy, and Emma Goldman*. New York: Holt, Rinehart, & Winston, 1984; Goldman, Emma. *Anarchism and Other Essays*. 1911. New York: Dover, 1969; Goldman, Emma. *Living My Life: An Autobiography of Emma Goldman*. 1931. Salt Lake City, UT: Peregrine Smith Book, 1982; Shulman, Alix Kates, ed. *Red Emma Speaks: An Emma Goldman Reader*. New York: Schocken, 1983; Solomon, Martha. *Emma Goldman*. Boston: G. K. Hall, 1987; Wexler, Alice. *Emma Goldman: An Intimate Life*. New York: Pantheon, 1984.

Martha Watson

GOLDMANN, LUCIEN (1913–1970). Born and raised in Rumania, Goldmann's intellectual trajectory brought him as a young man to Vienna, where he was first exposed to contemporary Marxist thought, and then to Paris. His education there interrupted by the German invasion of 1940, Goldmann would ultimately land in Switzerland, where he would complete a doctorate in philosophy with a dissertation on Kant. It was during these wartime years that he also discovered the writings of the young **Georg Lukács**, which, along with those of Hegel and **Marx**, would have a lifelong impact on his thought. After the liberation he returned to Paris and began an illustrious academic career at the Centre National de la Recherche Scientifique, where he published his pathbreaking study of Pascal and Racine, *The Hidden God* (1956); later he organized a center for the sociology of literature at the Free University of Brussels. While much of his work addressed the sociology of culture, both literary and philosophical, throughout his life, Goldmann concerned himself with political, ideological, and social questions as well.

Goldmann's work on literature cannot be understood apart from its specific historical context, namely the Stalinist dictates of **socialist realism** that formed the horizon for any orthodox Marxist analysis of culture in postwar France. Goldmann's "genetic structuralism" was a punctual response to this crude methodology and entailed two complementary postulates. First, the work was to be understood as a totality that was held together by its "signifying structure," which Goldmann defined as the entirety of the necessary relations between the various elements that constituted it (as, for example, between content and form); it is this structure that alone determined the nature, meaning, and necessity of each individual element in the literary narrative. Second, the signifying structure of the work was to be placed within broader structures of which it constituted a partial element: mental structures, the worldviews of social classes, and in the last instance the socioeconomic structure of a given historical period. Goldmann, that is, sought the relationship between a literary work and collective thought and social classes not—as socialist realism directed—in an identity of content but in what he called a "homology of structures." In *The Hidden God*, for example, Goldmann did not posit a link between the content of Racine's plays (Greek mythological dramas) and the content of the religious consciousness of the Jansenist *noblesse de robe*; only at the structural level did a homology appear, in their shared conception of the presence/absence of a hidden and spectatorial god. While this genetic structuralist method would be severely critiqued by later Althusserian Marxists, for whom the terms *totality* and *homology* were idealist anathemas, Goldmann's contribution to a non-Stalinist study of culture should be acknowledged.

Selected Bibliography: Cohen, Mitchell. *The Wager of Lucien Goldmann*. Princeton, NJ: Princeton UP, 1994; Goldmann, Lucien. *The Human Sciences and Philosophy*. Trans. Hayden V. White and Robert Anchor. London, 1964; Goldmann, Lucien. *Marxisme et sciences humaines*. Paris: NRF and Gallimard, 1970; Goldmann, Lucien. *Recherches dialectiques*. Paris: NRF and Gallimard, 1959; Goldmann, Lucien. *Structures mentales et création culturelle*. Paris: Anthropos, 1970; Williams, Raymond. "Literature and Sociology: In Memory of Lucien Goldmann." *New Left Review* 67 (May/June 1971): 3–18.

Tom McDonough

GORDIMER, NADINE (1923–).

South African writer of short stories, novels, and essays, and Nobel laureate in literature for 1991. With a searching intelligence and sustained artistry, her work has explored the shifts and turns of life in her country—in both the apartheid and the post-apartheid eras. Gordimer was born in the small mining town of Springs, to the east of Johannesburg; her father was an immigrant Jewish watchmaker and jeweler from Latvia, while her mother, also Jewish, came from England. There were divisions in the Gordimer household between her mother, rather colonial in her preoccupations, and her father, who was old-worldly and more absorbent of the racial attitudes of South Africa. Gordimer grew up in a nonreligious ethos, though she attended a convent school—fairly customary at the time for those seeking a superior education. She has described herself as a periodic truant whose physical energy and predilections found their natural outlet in the veld and on the mine dumps of Springs; her affiliation to the land and landscape of South Africa has been a feature of her life and writing ever since. When Gordimer was ten or eleven, her mother took her out of school on the pretext of a mysterious—and quite likely invented—heart ailment. This turned the young Gordimer, as she has said, into a mimic, performing for her elders in the domestic environment of her mother; she became a voracious reader (consuming the works of everyone from Pepys to Burton) and a budding writer. Her first stories were children's fables for a local Sunday paper; her first "adult" story, "Come Again Tomorrow," was published when she was fifteen. Gordimer attended only one year of university and then, after a period of indecision, committed herself to the life of a writer, gravitating toward Johannesburg, where she has lived ever since.

Inspired by the work of Eudora Welty and Katherine Mansfield, Gordimer soon realized that her local South African setting provided legitimate and appropriate material for her fiction—an important step away from the colonial mentality that defined only Europe as "real." It was fiction that led her to politics rather than the other way around; she was guided, as she put it, "by Kafka rather than Marx" ("A Bolter and the Invincible Summer," in *The Essential Gesture*). Her early short stories show these first explorations, often detailing the woes and ironies of relations between masters and servants, though a story such as "Is There Nowhere Else Where We Can Meet?" sets out archetypal Gordimer territory—unmarked border space where a young white woman and a black man exercise their mutual fears, needs, and entanglements. Through the 1950s and 1960s, though Gordimer always maintained a refreshing sense of the nonpolitical in people's lives, she was drawn to some of the demanding scenarios of the time—a young woman embarking on her first moment of political action ("The Smell of Death and Flowers") or a young black man, his ("Some Monday for Sure"). Her dominant mode was irony, and there was always an eye for the nonformulaic depths of experience, whether personal or political. In due course, a certain taut poetic quality entered in, as some of her stories, such as "A Lion on the Freeway," entertained a quasi-symbolic mode. Throughout, Gordimer's eye for detail has been matched by a sinuous and often sensuous linguistic precision and an intricate syntactic complexity.

Gordimer's early novels explored the contours of the "world of strangers" in South Africa, particularly the potential and limits of personal relations under the increasing strains and invasions of **apartheid**. *The Late Bourgeois World* (1966) responded to the political crises of the early 1960s, while *A Guest of Honour* (1971), set in an unnamed African country, surveyed the prospects and obligations of the committed white African. Gordimer's middle period, including her extraordinary trilogy of novels—*The Conservationist* (1974), *Burger's Daughter* (1979), and *July's People* (1981)—saw her at her greatest power, creating work that was at once artistically and conceptually profound. The first of these is a poetic and prophetic masterpiece envisioning an eventual transfer to black power in South Africa; the second is a probing and compassionate inspection, in the person of the daughter of a communist revolutionary, of the place of the white dissident in the wake of the Soweto Revolt; the third is an examination of the "morbid symptoms" of the interregnum in South Africa, when "the old is dying and the new cannot be born" (the epigraph to the novel is from **Antonio Gramsci**). These novels were succeeded by works such as *My*

Son's Story (1990) and *None to Accompany Me* (1994), set in South Africa's transition out of apartheid, and then by novels of the post-apartheid period proper—*The House Gun* (1998) and *The Pickup* (2001). The latter, in an almost prescient way to the attacks of September 11, 2001, left behind the South African setting to explore the world of Middle Eastern migrancy in its complex relations with the West.

Gordimer has always been a writer first and foremost whose objective is "the transformation of experience," yet she has also said that "art is on the side of the oppressed" and that the essential gesture of the writer is "a revolutionary gesture" ("The Essential Gesture," in *The Essential Gesture*). In her essays since the 1950s, she has borne witness to the travails of South Africa, exploring its complexities with a penetrating intelligence and abiding sense of accountability. That sense of accountability has been manifest throughout her life, whether in collaborating with black writers in her early years, working through the challenges from some of those same writers during the black consciousness era, or indicating her affiliation to the African National Congress before that was legal. Finding a balance between life and work, addressing questions of accountability not only in her fictional themes but in the forms of her writing, there has been a luminous clarity to her courage and commitment as both an artist and a person.

Selected Bibliography: Bazin, Nancy Topping, and Marilyn Dallman Seymour, eds. *Conversations with Nadine Gordimer.* Jackson: UP of Mississippi, 1990; Clingman, Stephen. *The Novels of Nadine Gordimer: History from the Inside.* 2nd ed. Amherst: U of Massachusetts P, 1992; Cooke, John. *The Novels of Nadine Gordimer: Private Lives/Public Landscapes.* Baton Rouge: Louisiana State UP, 1985; Ettin, Andrew Vogel. *Betrayals of the Body Politic: The Literary Commitments of Nadine Gordimer.* Charlottesville: U of Virginia P, 1993; Gordimer, Nadine. *The Essential Gesture: Writing Politics and Places.* Ed. Stephen Clingman. New York: Knopf, 1988; Gordimer, Nadine. "A Writer in South Africa." *London Magazine* (May 1965): 21–28; Head, Dominic. *Nadine Gordimer.* Cambridge: Cambridge UP, 1994; JanMohamed, Abdul R. *Manichean Aesthetics: The Politics of Literature in Colonial Africa.* Amherst: U of Massachusetts P, 1983; King, Bruce, ed. *The Later Fiction of Nadine Gordimer.* New York: St. Martin's, 1993; Newman, Judie, ed. *Nadine Gordimer's "Burger's Daughter": A Casebook.* Oxford: Oxford UP, 2003; Smith, Rowland, ed. *Critical Essays on Nadine Gordimer.* Boston: G. K. Hall, 1990.

Stephen Clingman

GORKY, MAXIM (1868–1936). After a difficult childhood and youth, chronicled in an autobiographical trilogy (*Childhood, Among People, My Universities*), Gorky achieved relatively rapid success once he embarked on a literary career. From the late 1890s until his death, he was renowned not just for his fiction—where he achieved success as a short-story writer, novelist, and playwright—but also for his memoirs and essays. He did not, however, confine his efforts to writing. Around the turn of the century, he emerged as the leading figure among the so-called "critical realists," writers who tended to follow the realistic tradition established by the great Russian writers of the nineteenth century while exposing the injustices and flaws in the society of their day. Gorky's extensive editing and publishing efforts at the time helped bring these works to the attention of the reading public, and his roles as editor and publisher were also important during the years surrounding the **Russian Revolution** of 1917 and, after an interval abroad, during the last years of his life. Finally, and not least important, Gorky was a political activist who worked for the Bolshevik cause before the revolution and who, despite some strong differences at times with the direction of the **Communist Party**, used his connections with the Soviet leaders to assist writers and other cultural figures under the harsh conditions that followed the revolution.

Born in the Volga city of Nizhny Novgorod as Alexei Maximovich Peshkov, he adopted the name M. Gorky (the Russian word for "bitter") in 1892, when he published his first story, "Makar Chudra." Like the first-person narrators in that and other tales, Gorky had spent time tramping through southern Russia—going to the Ukraine, the Crimea, and the Caucasus—gathering the impressions that he was later to use in his writing. In "Chelkash" (1894), the first of his stories to appear in a major journal, he develops the figure of the *bosiak*, or vagabond. These characters are not merely wanderers but people who have consciously broken with society, who have little sympathy with either the indecisiveness of Russia's educated elite or the passivity of the peasantry. In other works, such as "Creatures That Once Were Men" (1897) or "Twenty-six Men and a Girl" (1899), he focuses more on those who are near or at the bottom of the social order and who struggle, usually unsuccessfully, to find hope. A similar theme pervades his greatest play, *The Lower Depths* (1902), set in a lower-class lodging house, where the mood veers between the promise of a better life provided by the actions or words of a few characters and the sense of despair that pervades the everyday existence for most of the figures in the play.

For the most part in his dramatic works, Gorky focused on groups that were more privileged, attacking the failures of the intelligentsia and of Russia's merchant class. *Summerfolk* (1904) portrays a wide swath of society, including a writer who realizes that he has lost touch with the needs of his readers and a lawyer who has become quite comfortable in his corrupt surroundings. In *The Zykovs* (1912–1913), the father has created a profitable lumber business from which many benefit, but he is also ruthless toward those around him, most notably his own son. This theme of generational decline also appears frequently in Gorky's novels, beginning with *Foma Gordeev* (1899), in which the father of the eponymous hero had gone from working on a river barge to owning numerous vessels, while Foma himself lacks direction and ends up squandering his opportunities in life.

In his fiction, Gorky rarely attempted to portray those who were leading the struggle for a new social order. Interestingly, the two most notable exceptions were largely composed while he was in the United States, on a trip that had been planned to raise money and support for the Bolshevik cause. The play *Enemies* (1906) highlights the divide between factory workers and owners during a time of unrest. The men in the factory are all idealistic and hard working, while the upper classes range from merciless to weak, along with a very few who show genuine sympathy for the workers. In *Mother* (1906–1907), Gorky shows the development of a revolutionary consciousness on the part of a formerly naive woman who is roused to action by the arrest of her son on account of his political activities. But these descriptions of the proletariat are unusual for Gorky; even during the postrevolutionary years, he tended to return to the bourgeois elements that he had described earlier. Such is the case with *The Life of Klim Samgin* (1925–1936), a four-volume epic still unfinished at the time of Gorky's death. The novel chronicles the life and the entire era of its eponymous antihero, starting in the final decades of the nineteenth century and concluding with the 1917 revolution. One of Gorky's last and best plays, *Yegor Bulychev and Others* (1932), takes place in 1917, as the old order is collapsing and as Bulychev, a well-off merchant dying of cancer, questions the values by which he has lived.

Gorky's personal interest in politics seems to have begun during his teenage years in Kazan, where he had hoped to enter the university but instead worked at odd jobs and became connected with radical political circles. In 1898, just as he was becoming famous, he was arrested for his connections with a social democratic (the future Bolshevik) circle, and other run-ins with authorities over the next several years followed. A witness to the "Bloody Sunday" events that sparked the uprisings of 1905, he was again arrested, and in January 1906, he left Russia on a journey that carried him to the United States and then to exile on Capri, where he maintained regular contacts with **Lenin** and other Bolshevik leaders. An amnesty allowed Gorky to return to Russia seven years later. As the revolution approached and then occurred, he openly expressed opposition to some of the extreme policies of the Bolsheviks. Nonetheless, he was able to use his influence to assist writers and other cultural figures in the years immediately following the revolution, both materially and by initiating various publishing endeavors. In 1921, he again left Russia, ostensibly for health reasons, returning for visits beginning only in 1928 and then permanently in 1933. During his final years, he wrote numerous essays in support of the Soviet government, while at the same time, it appears, doing what he could to help some of those who were threatened by the onset of the Stalinist regime. While at first Gorky was said to have died of natural causes, the former head of the secret police and several others were later executed after being accused of murdering him.

In death as in life, Gorky has remained a controversial figure. The cause of his death remains open, with many believing that **Stalin** himself had a hand in it. Some see his late essays as making him an apologist for a brutal regime, while others take a more nuanced view of his role. Even his literary reputation has fluctuated, particularly in the former Soviet Union, where his writings are no longer accorded the supreme status they once held. Nevertheless, none question the genuine achievement of his best literary works—including *The Lower Depths*, a number of his short stories, and his autobiographical writings and memoirs—as well as the sincerity of the convictions that led him to write so tellingly about the life he witnessed in the Russia of his day.

Selected Bibliography: Barratt, Andrew, and Barry P. Scherr, eds. and trans. *Maksim Gorky: Selected Letters.* Oxford: Clarendon P, 1997; Borras, F. M. *Maxim Gorky the Writer: An Interpretation.* Oxford: Clarendon P, 1967; Levin, Dan. *Stormy Petrel: The Life and Work of Maxim Gorky.* New York: Appleton-Century, 1965; Scherr, Barry P. *Maxim Gorky.* Boston: G. K. Hall, 1988; Weil, Irwin. *Gorky: His Literary Development and Influence on Soviet Intellectual Life.* New York: Random House, 1966; Yedlin, Tovah. *Maxim Gorky: A Political Biography.* Westport, CT: Praeger, 1999.

Barry P. Scherr

GOTHIC LITERATURE. The formal origin of gothic literature is inextricably linked to the American and **French Revolution**s. Freighted with political meanings during this rebellious period, the term "gothic," as Richard Davenport-Hines points

out, was "synonymous with warlike barbarism, . . . the lust for domination and in-
veterate cruelty" (1) because of its association with the fifth-century Goths who
sacked Rome. As Fred Botting has evinced, however, the "gothic" label was also positively charged at this time, as it became a tribute to these same "northern, Germanic
nations whose fierce avowal of the values of freedom and democracy was . . .
[o]pposed to all forms of tyranny and slavery" (5).

It is within these oppositional contexts that constructed "gothic" as threatening to
some but liberating to others that the first gothic novel—Horace Walpole's *The Castle of Otranto* (1764)—was published. A British member of Parliament, Walpole in-
habited a gothic revivalist castle on his Strawberry Hill estate, which he credited with
inspiring *Otranto* because the stronghold's battlements, tower, and cloister had such
an eerie effect on him. This first "gothic story" introduced certain literary conventions—particularly supernatural contrivances that emphasize a haunted past—that
shaped the gothic novel for decades. Dealing primarily with the horrifying effects of
illegitimate claims to political power, which European audiences could relate to as
they began to rethink their relationship to oppressive monarchical and religious authorities, *Otranto*, in its indictment of Manfred, lord of the manor, ultimately critiques patriarchal institutions such as feudalism, aristocracy, and the church. Similar
criticism of corrupt European sites of power set in dark and decaying milieus are
found in Clara Reeve's *The Old English Baron* (1778), but it is especially evident in
Ann Radcliffe's *The Mysteries of Udolpho* (1794), which presents the archvillain, Mon-
toni, as a monstrously decadent Italian Catholic aristocrat who attempts to pilfer the
female protagonist's titled land.

Although Jane Austen would satirize the gothic novel's melodramatic qualities in
her *Northanger Abbey* (1818), these stories' excessive use of horrifying, supernatural
elements helped sell them to a reading public clamoring for sensational fiction as an
antidote to Enlightenment values espousing strict order, rationality, and logic. While
some of this literature devolved into popular "shilling shockers" (especially the penny
dreadfuls published by Minerva Press in the 1840s–1850s), novels like Matthew
Lewis's *The Monk* (1796), Charlotte Dacre's *Zofloya; or, The Moor* (1806), Mary Wollstonecraft Shelley's **Frankenstein** (1818), Charles Robert Maturin's *Melmoth the Wanderer* (1820), and Bram Stoker's *Dracula* (1897) would continue to portray the
haunting effects of sociocultural transgressions such as the abuse of political power,
the confinement of women, the hypocrisy of institutionalized religion, and the bias
against foreign, often racialized "others."

Across the Atlantic Ocean, gothic impulses had manifested themselves over a century earlier, when the Puritans in the 1630s brought with them from Europe a host
of burgeoning anxieties about institutional power, especially their disdain for the superficial "popery" of the Church of England. Obsessed with establishing a new sociopolitical order that would "purify" religious practices by eradicating the
materialistic trappings of ritualized worship, the Puritans ironically invoked a dark,
supernatural rhetoric (somewhat like the gothic) that did not liberate their followers
but scared the faithful into submission. At the end of the eighteenth century, Charles
Brockden Brown challenged the type of religious zealotry represented by the Puritans in what critics agree is the first American gothic novel—*Wieland; or, The Transformation* (1798). Resituating gothic stories away from a medieval European past and

toward a more immediate American present, Brown destabilizes status quo theological sensibilities by constructing the fanatical Theodore Wieland as a character haunted by a God he believes is ordering him to commit horrible atrocities against his own family. Building on *Wieland*'s wildly disturbing portrait of familial dysfunction, Edgar Allan Poe continued to examine the nightmarish world of domestic space in stories such as "Ligeia" (1838), "The Fall of the House of Usher" (1839), and "The Black Cat" (1843), in which cultural anxieties about gender politics and familial bloodlines take precedence over European-influenced fears about state and church. This developing emphasis on domestic horrors in the American gothic tradition is advanced in works such as Nathaniel Hawthorne's *The House of the Seven Gables* (1851), Henry James's *The Turn of the Screw* (1898), William Faulkner's *Absalom, Absalom!* (1936), Truman Capote's *Other Voices, Other Rooms* (1948), Stephen King's *The Shining* (1977), and Dorothy Allison's *Bastard Out of Carolina* (1992), which variously shatter idealized representations of "home" in excessively macabre and distressing ways.

Some of the clearest examples of domestic horror come from writing that Ellen Moers coined "female gothic" in her *Literary Women* (1976), which has its earliest roots in the literature of Radcliffe, Dacre, and Shelley. While this term has come to have multiple meanings, it still generally refers to gothic literature that explores female characters' entrapment by and (attempted) escape from paternalistic, patriarchal systems of power. While male writers have contributed to this type of writing, the most popular American examples have been written by women, such as Charlotte Perkins Gilman's "The Yellow Wallpaper" (1892) at the end of the nineteenth century; Flannery O'Connor's and Carson McCullers's short stories and novellas and Shirley Jackson's *The Haunting of Hill House* (1959) in the twentieth; and the stories of Joyce Carol Oates and Poppy Z. Brite into the twenty-first. Related to the American gothic's examination of sociopolitical gender inequities is its exploration of what Teresa A. Goddu refers to as the "Ghost of Race" (73), which continues to burden an American polity seemingly incapable of reconciling past (and present) transgressions against members of its nonwhite populace, especially those of African descent. Some of the best-known works by African American writers that explore the inherent spectrality of slavery's legacy include Harriet Jacobs's *Incidents in the Life of a Slave Girl* (1861), Charles Chesnutt's *The Marrow of Tradition* (1901), Jean Toomer's *Cane* (1923), **Richard Wright's** *Native Son* (1940), **Ralph Ellison**'s *Invisible Man* (1952), and **Toni Morrison**'s *Beloved* (1987).

As scholars continue to scrutinize gothic literature's political contexts, which emphasize sociocultural imbalances of power, they remain within the antiauthoritarian traditions embraced by pre-revolutionary Europe and North America that spawned this literature in the first place. Increasingly informed by psychoanalytic, queer, Marxist, feminist, and postcolonial approaches to the literary "dark" side, critics have not only applied these cultural theories to the works of both canonical authors and more contemporary writers such as Kathy Acker, Clive Barker, Angela Carter, Bret Easton Ellis, **Amitav Ghosh**, Anne Rice, and Louise Erdrich, but have also begun to look at the ways in which national narratives from Canada, Ireland, Japan, Russia, Scotland, and other countries have contributed to our understanding of the often frightening tensions between institutionalized hegemony and the desire for social parity.

Selected Bibliography: Botting, Fred. *Gothic.* London: Routledge, 1996; Davenport-Hines, Richard. *Gothic: Four Hundred Years of Excess, Horror, Evil and Ruin.* New York: North Point, 1998; DeLamotte, Eugenia. *Perils of the Night: A Feminist Study of Nineteenth-Century Gothic.* New York: Oxford UP, 1989; Fleenor, Juliann E., ed. *The Female Gothic.* Montreal: Eden, 1983; Goddu, Teresa A. *Gothic America: Narrative, History, and Nation.* New York: Columbia UP, 1997; Martin, Robert K., and Eric Savoy, eds. *American Gothic: New Interventions in a National Narrative.* Iowa City: U of Iowa P, 1998; Punter, David. *Gothic Pathologies: The Text, the Body, and the Law.* New York: St. Martin's, 1998.

Bruce G. Johnson

GOYTISOLO GAY, JUAN (1931–). Creative writer, cultural critic, and political activist, Goytisolo is one of the most contentious and celebrated writers of modern Spain. Born into a prosperous family of Basque descent, Goytisolo lost his mother in an air-raid attack on his native Barcelona during the **Spanish Civil War,** an event that fueled his hatred for the hypernationalistic, ultra-Catholic dictatorship of Francisco Franco. Goytisolo's early writings—from *The Young Assassins* (1954) and *Children of Chaos* (1955) to *La resaca* (1958) and *Island of Women* (1961)—largely adhere to social realist dictates of mimetic transparency and political engagement and center on the exposure and denunciation of the petty grandeur and abject misery of the technocratic capitalism of the Spanish state under Franco. Influenced by the existentially inflected Marxism of **Jean-Paul Sartre** and unwilling to submit to Francoist censorship, Goytisolo moved to Paris in the 1950s as a self-declared exile and came into contact with **Simone de Beauvoir,** Roland Barthes, and, most importantly, Jean Genet, whose influence Goytisolo has deemed crucial to his artistic and personal transformation. From his vantage point as insider-outsider, Goytisolo produced two highly critical, semidocumentary travelogues of rural Spain: *Campos de Níjar* (1959) and *La Chanca* (1962). By the late 1960s, his dissatisfaction with the formal limits of social realism and his growing disenchantment with the Soviet system and its Cuban satellite, which he once so admired, led him to adopt a more experimentalist mode of writing, adumbrated in *Marks of Identity* (1966) and realized in *Count Julian* (1970), which **Carlos Fuentes** described as "the most monumental questioning of Spain, its history and culture, ever written."

Count Julian consolidated Goytisolo's growing fascination with the Islamic heritage of Spain and, more generally, with marginalized and oppressed people the world over (especially Chechnians, Palestinians, Kurds, and Bosnians). *Juan the Landless* (1975), which grapples with exile and globalization, confirms Goytisolo's commitment to Islamic culture and closes, after a page in which Spanish is twisted and transformed, in Arabic. The assault on purist concepts of language and nation marks Goytisolo's later works, including *Makbara* (1980), in which a (trans)sexualized Angel rejects the oppressive uniformity of heaven, and *Landscapes after the Battle* (1982), in which third-world characters partly restyle a postcolonial Paris as Marrakech and Istanbul. Goytisolo's interest in difference and otherness also distinguishes his two-volume autobiography, *Forbidden Territory* (1985) and *Realms of Strife* (1986), in which grand notions of revolution and redemption fold in and out of personal reflections on family, friendship, work, and sex. Goytisolo's explicit, though ambivalent, relation to homosexuality takes a dramatic turn in *The Virtues of the Solitary*

Bird (1988), which brings Sufi mysticism to bear on the politics of HIV/AIDS. *Quarantine* (1991) deepens the author's reflections on death, while *The Marx Family Saga* (1993) addresses the dissolution of revolutionary projects. *State of Siege* (1995), set in a worn-torn Sarajevo; *The Garden of Secrets* (1997); and *A Cock-Eyed Comedy* (2000) reaffirm Goytisolo's commitment to the communitarian power of storytelling and to the struggle against racism, terrorism, xenophobia, and other varieties of intolerance.

Selected Bibliography: Black, Stanley. *Juan Goytisolo and the Poetics of Contagion: The Evolution of a Radical Aesthetics in the Later Novels*. Liverpool: Liverpool UP, 2001; Epps, Brad. *Significant Violence: Oppression and Resistance in the Narratives of Juan Goytisolo, 1970–1990*. Oxford: Oxford UP, 1996; Fuentes, Carlos. "Juan Goytisolo or the Novel as Exile." *Review of Contemporary Fiction* 4 (1984): 72–76; Labanyi, Jo. *Myth and History in the Contemporary Spanish Novel*. Cambridge: Cambridge UP, 1989; Levine, Linda Gould. Introduction to *Reivindicación del Conde don Julián*. Madrid: Cátedra, 1985. 25–44; Pope, Randolph. *Understanding Juan Goytisolo*. Columbia, SC: U of South Carolina P, 1995; Ugarte, Michael. *Trilogy of Treason: An Intertextual Study of Juan Goytisolo*. Columbia, MO: U of Missouri P, 1982.

Brad Epps

GRAMSCI, ANTONIO (1891–1937). While lingering near death in Italian Fascist prisons for the last decade of his short life, Gramsci produced a voluminous series of fragmentary reflections on Italian political and cultural history, the rise of Fascism, and Marxist theory. These notes—jotted down in more than thirty school exercise books and smuggled out of prison by his wife—would become what we now read as *The Prison Notebooks*. (It should be noted that their publication history in Italy was quite different from their appearance in English.) Despite the desperate and trying conditions of their production, Gramsci's prison writings would exercise a profound influence on leftist politics in Europe and significant if less deep and lasting effects on Anglo-American cultural criticism. While Gramsci's legacy within Marxist literary and cultural criticism remains unfinished, his body of work continues to challenge classic and later poststructuralist Marxist approaches to literature, culture, and politics.

Gramsci was born on the island of Sardinia, an impoverished and querulous outback of the modern nation of Italy. His father was a civil servant, imprisoned for six years by political opponents when Gramsci was seven. His mother was the daughter of moderately prosperous local landowners. As a child, Gramsci suffered from rickets, which inflicted both physical deformity and lifelong frailty and ill health. Despite limited educational opportunities in Sardinia, Gramsci proved to be a brilliant student and won a university scholarship to Turin. In this most industrialized and modernized of Italian cities, Gramsci, along with his brother, Gennaro, first came into contact with the Italian proletariat and radical politics. A mental and physical breakdown early in his college career forced Gramsci to drop out of the university in 1915. However, his interest in linguistics and philosophy as a student would later shape the planning and writing of *The Prison Notebooks*. After he recovered his health, Gramsci plunged into political activism, joining the PSI, or Italian Socialist Party, and writing and editing for Party newspapers like *Il Grido del Populi* and *Avanti*. Most significantly for his future, after **World War I**, Gramsci participated in a new journal, *Ordine Nuovo* (New Order), dedicated to teaching workers about the power of workers' councils, or soviets, and worker control of the means of production. His experience in the hotbed of proletarian rebellion and with the failure of the workers' council movement would shape two of Gramsci's most basic premises: that radical politics must engage with the everyday cultural world and consciousness of workers; and that, given the vastly more complicated political, cultural, and institutional landscape of modern capitalist society, the proletariat by itself could not achieve total revolutionary victory.

In 1921, in the wake of the **Russian Revolution**, Gramsci left the PSI to help form the Italian **Communist Party** (PCI). While visiting the Soviet Union to confer with his colleagues in the Comintern, Gramsci again suffered a physical breakdown. Recovering in a Russian sanitorium, he met his future wife, Julia Schucht. (The couple would have two children, Delio and Giuliano, though Gramsci's imprisonment would prevent him from ever seeing his younger son.) Gramsci had predicted the rise of Italian Fascism well before Mussolini's seizure of power in 1922. In 1926, he began work on his seminal essay, "The Southern Question," an extended and brilliant exploration of the relation between workers and peasants in Italy and of the conditions for political alliance between classes and class fractions in modern society. This work was cut short in November 1926 when, despite immunity guaranteed by his election as a Communist deputy to the Italian parliament in 1924, Gramsci was arrested and imprisoned by the Fascists. Gramsci was permitted to read and write in prison, although receiving books became more difficult the longer he was in prison. His deteriorating health, coupled with international pressure, resulted in his removal to a prison hospital in Formia, Italy, in 1933 and then to a Roman clinic in 1935. Gramsci's prison sentence was commuted and ended in April 1937. Late in that month, he suffered a cerebral hemorrhage and died on April 27, 1937.

The bulk of Gramsci's original plans for the notebooks focused on cultural analysis, including studies of comparative linguistics, Pirandello's theater, and serial novels and popular taste. In the traditional or classical Marxism **base and superstructure** model of society, culture is a byproduct of the forces and relations of production and belongs to the "superstructure," thrown up largely to justify and obscure the deeper realities of the economic "base." Books, paintings, music, and other cultural artifacts may sugarcoat dominant ideologies, but they reflect the class position of their creators and are finally reducible to the "deeper" realities of the capitalist mode of production. The critic's work consists, then, of uncovering a text's representation of capitalism, its class structures, and its contradictions. Gramsci condemned this reductive view of culture as passive reflection because he rejected the idea of any simple relations between base and superstructure. Castigating such approaches as "politico-economic romances" (*Gramsci Reader* 191) and "economic superstition" (*Gramsci Reader* 215), Gramsci instead saw culture as a central arena of the struggle for political and social power.

In Gramsci's notion of **hegemony**, nothing is guaranteed by economics or relations of production; instead, power and domination are the result of active, strenuous work by competing classes and class fractions. Control and domination are the contingent and partial effects of "a continuous process of formation and superseding of unstable equilibria between the interests of the fundamental groups [or classes] and those of the subordinate groups" (*Gramsci Reader* 206). Indeed, in modern liberal societies, class power is less about coercion and force than about the forging of an "intellectual and moral unity, posing all the questions around which the struggle rages" (*Gramsci Reader* 205). That is, securing the consent of the subordinate classes and fractions is essential to exercising power. "Every relationship of 'hegemony,'" Gramsci writes, "is necessarily an educational relationship" (*Gramsci Reader* 348). Those who hold and contest power engage in an ongoing battle to coach, persuade, and reform what Gramsci calls "common sense"—the contradictory, volatile, and complicated stuff of everyday consciousness.

Gramsci's more open and dynamic sense of social power profoundly recasts the central terms of classical Marxism. For instance, rather than merely cloaking class interests, **ideology** becomes an "intellectual-moral" tool for assembling and unifying the "historic bloc" of classes and class fractions necessary for hegemony. Ideology, Gramsci argues, should be studied as the "creation of concrete fantasy which acts on a . . . people to arouse and organize its collective will" (*Gramsci Reader* 239). Ideology is the glue that holds together a hegemonic bloc, and because they are the formulators and diffusers of ideas and fantasies, intellectuals become especially important in Gramsci's thought. He devotes many pages of *The Prison Notebooks* to analyzing their identity and role in ancient and modern Italy, including the differences between "traditional" and "organic" intellectuals, the relation between intellectuals and popular life, and the intellectual's role as the "organizer of masses of men" (*Gramsci Reader* 301).

Gramsci's understanding of culture is thus much more political than is that of classical Marxists: for him, texts and other cultural artifacts must be understood not simply as reflections of deeper realities but as polemics, as ongoing efforts to transform meanings and audiences in accordance with hegemonic (and counter-hegemonic) tendencies. In turn, according to Gramsci, it is no longer sufficient to understand the political meaning of an artifact as determined by the class position of its author or source. If hegemony is all about persuasion and the battle to secure consent, then the political significance of a cultural artifact lies in the role it plays within this process, whatever the class origin of particular artifacts or authors. The political significance of **Henry James**'s novels, for instance, cannot be wholly exhausted by locating James ideologically or socially, nor by simply using the novels to "read" capitalism. Rather, historically, James's novels take up positions within contemporary debates and contribute to particular versions of the "collective will." Nor do these original contexts fix James's work forever. As the **cold-war** revival of his oeuvre indicates, James's novels will be taken up in different ways, with new meanings, and toward new ends as they participate in new "formation[s] of a national-popular collective will" (*Gramsci Reader* 242). As the British cultural critic **Stuart Hall** describes this relational approach to cultural politics: "The meaning of a cultural symbol is given in part by the social field into which it is incorporated, the practices with which it articulates and is made to resonate. What matters is *not* the intrinsic or historically fixed objects of culture, but the state of play in cultural relations. . . . [W]hat counts is the class struggle in and over culture" ("Deconstructing" 235).

In the United States, the political dimensions of Gramsci's thought—his interest in national contexts, his anatomy of modern civil society, his notion of "hegemony," and his discussion of the party's role—would draw more attention than his thinking about culture. The cultural implications of Gramsci's writing would emerge much more prominently in Great Britain, especially in the work of the Birmingham Center for Contemporary Cultural Studies from the late 1970s through the 1980s. There, Gramsci enabled critics like Hall, Dick Hebdige, and Angela McRobbie to analyze culture, especially popular culture, as a site of play between containment and resistance. Following through on Gramsci's view of cultural artifacts as active elements of political struggle, the Birmingham School, as it was sometimes known, also emphasized the ways in which audiences use texts to make new meanings. A series of Gramscian-inspired projects in **cultural studies**—including *Resistance through Rituals: Youth Subcultures in Postwar Britain* (1976), *Learning to Labour* (1977) by Paul Willis, and *Working Class Culture: Studies in History and Theory* (1979)—culminated in the collectively authored *Policing the Crisis: Mugging, the State, and Law and Order* (1978), a study of race, class, and politics in contemporary Britain. After this, the Birmingham School began to focus more exclusively on popular culture, especially pop music, television, and cinema. The Birmingham School continued to produce groundbreaking work on race, gender, sexuality, and nationalism. But as class became less central to these efforts, so too did the influence of Gramsci's fuller understanding of the relations between capitalism, culture, and politics.

While certain of Gramsci's central concepts, particularly a highly metaphoric version of hegemony, migrated along with cultural studies to the United States, American critics have never fully addressed the Gramscian challenge to and within Western Marxism. The influence of **Georg Lukács**, **Theodor Adorno**, and **Louis Althusser** remains strong, and an approach to culture inflected by very different notions of ideology, textuality, and power continues to dominate, even if implicitly, the Marxist study of literature and culture.

Selected Bibliography: Boggs, Carl. *Gramsci's Marxism.* Ann Arbor: U of Michigan P, 1976; Clark, John, Charles Critcher, and Richard Johnson, eds. *Working Class Culture: Studies in History and Theory.* London: Hutchinson, 1979; Gramsci, Antonio. *An Antonio Gramsci Reader.* Ed. David Forgacs. New York: Schocken Books, 1988; Gramsci, Antonio. *Letters from Prison.* Ed. and trans. Lynne Lawner. New York: Farrar, Straus and Giroux, 1973; Gramsci, Antonio. *Prison Notebooks.* 2 vols. Ed. and trans. Joseph A. Buttigieg. New York: Columbia UP, 1992, 1996; Hall, Stuart. "Notes on Deconstructing 'The Popular.'" *People's History and Socialist Theory.* Ed. R. Samuel. London: Routledge and Kegan Paul, 1981. 227–40; Hall, Stuart, et al. *Critical Dialogues in Cultural Studies.* New York: Routledge, 1996; Hall, Stuart, et al. *Policing the Crisis: Mugging, the State, and Law and Order.* London: Macmillan, 1978; Ransome, Paul. *Antonio Gramsci: A New Introduction.* Hempstead, UK: Harvester Wheatsheaf, 1992.

Larry Hanley

THE GRAPES OF WRATH (1939). **John Steinbeck**'s popular and controversial masterpiece helped make the so-called Dust Bowl migration to California the quintessential popular image of the Great Depression. The story begins with the Joad family's eviction from their Oklahoma tenant farm, then follows them through a harrowing auto journey westward. Once in California, the Joads experience the brutal conditions for migrant workers in the fertile agricultural valleys, where great growing corporations harshly rule both the fields and the towns. By the end of the story, the family has greatly diminished, but its key members, Ma and son Tom, have gained a socioeconomic analysis of the forces acting on them.

The novel supplements the Joads' narrative by alternating it with discursive inter-chapters that explain their experience to readers and place it in a larger sociohistor-ical—and spiritual—context. Like so many novels of the 1930s, *The Grapes of Wrath* offers a sympathetic portrayal of worker suffering and exploitation from a leftist per-spective, yet it differs from most proletarian novels of the period by leaving out any reference to the organized Left or even to any specific union efforts (apparently re-flecting Steinbeck's disdain for formal political affiliations). Nevertheless, *The Grapes of Wrath* offers a remarkably powerful condemnation of the logic of private property and of the insatiable character of capital accumulation. Capitalism becomes a "mon-ster" that "has to have profits all the time," no matter the effect on humans, including those "children dying of pellagra because a profit cannot be taken from an orange." The destruction of crops in the midst of starvation and destitution had actually oc-curred during the Depression, a fact that seemed to expose the cruel logic of capi-talism. As Steinbeck declares famously: "There is a crime here that goes beyond denunciation." The novel also suggests that a (not necessarily violent) revolution is inevitable, in terms of both history and nature. Steinbeck thereby grafts a stagist Marxist understanding of the course of history onto an idiosyncratic, egalitarian Dar-winism. It is important to note, however, that this is not a biological determinism that defends hierarchies of power, as some critics have misapprehended; rather, evo-lution and revolution are intertwined.

The Grapes of Wrath is not only a condemnation of the superexploitation of sub-altern workers but offers a critique of bourgeois individualism and acquisitiveness that invites middle-class readers to join the poor workers in both labor solidarity and the spiritual experience of the "great big soul." The monster that would devour the Joads simultaneously alienates the middle and upper classes from the deep sense of community possible for the working class. Even the Okies must learn that their her-itage of rugged individualism and family autonomy will no longer be adequate to combat the combined power of the great growers and their servants in government. As Ma Joad notes, "'Use' ta be the family was fust. It ain't so now. It's anybody. Worse off we get, the more we got to do."

However, as recent critics have pointed out, the novel seems to imagine that this nascent collective is composed only of Anglo-Saxon whites. Excluded from the Joads' story (as they are from *In Dubious Battle* and *Of Mice and Men*) are the workers of Mexican and Filipino descent who had until the 1930s been a majority of the mi-grant workforce. Ironically, nonwhite workers had proved to be increasingly militant in their opposition to grower control, a key reason that they were being replaced in the fields by the less well-organized Okies. In this respect, *The Grapes of Wrath* seems to echo the popular mythology that westering Anglo-Saxon white "pioneers" uniquely define America. In fact, framing the dust bowl in terms of the pioneer myth was not unique to Steinbeck, and the misery of California agricultural workers was largely ig-nored by the mainstream press until whites became involved. The novel is, then, complicit to some extent in this racism. However, *The Grapes of Wrath* also seems to implicitly debunk white supremacism by demonstrating that economic vulnerability is a much more powerful determinate of group fate than race. The Joads' white skin means nothing to the growers, and the epithet "Okie" marks a quasi-racialization of their class position. The gas-station attendants who watch the Joads venture into the Mojave Desert on their journey west see them not as pioneers but as "gorillas" who are "so goddamn dumb they don't know it's dangerous." The politics of the novel must therefore be regarded as contradictory with respect to race.

The Grapes of Wrath passed almost instantly into American folklore and became even better known through John Ford's successful (but less politically radical) film adaptation in 1940. The novel has been taught and read widely ever since, and as a touchstone cultural intervention, it continues to produce controversy and debate across the political spectrum.

Selected Bibliography: Cunningham, Charles. "Rethinking the Politics of *The Grapes of Wrath*." *Cultural Logic* 5 (2002), http://eserver.org/clogic/2002/cunningham.html; Denning, Michael. *The Cultural Front: The Laboring of American Culture in the Twentieth Century.* New York: Verso, 1996; Heavilin, Barbara, ed. *The Critical Response to John Steinbeck's "The Grapes of Wrath"* Westport, CT: Greenwood, 2000; Mitchell, Don. *The Lie of the Land: Migrant Workers and the California Landscape.* Minneapolis: U of Minnesota P, 1996; Steinbeck, John. *Working Days: The Journals of "The Grapes of Wrath."* Ed. Robert DeMott. New York: Viking, 1989; Wyatt, David, ed. *New Essays on "The Grapes of Wrath."* Cambridge: Cambridge UP, 1990.

Charles Cunningham

GRASS, GÜNTER (1927–), politically committed German author, winner of the 1999 Nobel Prize for Literature. Grass first achieved national and international fame on the publication of *The Tin Drum* in 1959. His output of speeches, public letters, and press articles has been all but constant in volume since August 1961, when he called on **Anna Seghers** as chairwoman of the German Democratic Republic's Writers' Union to protest against the building of the Berlin Wall. As a political activist, he was most effective in two periods: the general elections of 1965 and 1969, when he campaigned on behalf of the ultimately victorious Social Democrats; and in 1989–1991, in what amounted to a one-man campaign against Helmut Kohl's path to reunifying the country. Grass was intent in the 1960s on not repeating what he regarded as the mistakes writers had made during the 1920s, when they either kept themselves out of politics altogether or rejected the imperiled and imperfect democracy of the Weimar Republic in favor of a more radical, utopian alternative. In 1965, Grass contradicted Kurt Tucholsky's cry "This is not my republic!" by embracing the Federal Republic with all its imperfections. In particular, he was inspired by the former anti-Nazi émigré Willy Brandt, who became chancellor in the watershed elections of 1969. In 1968 Grass argued his case for gradual Social Democratic reform with the radical students who wanted to overthrow the state rather than change it.

Grass insists that his literary writing—including political novels such as *Dog Years* (1963), *Local Anaesthetic* (1969), and *The Flounder* (1977)—is separate from his public role, in which he speaks as a citizen with a facility for expressing an opinion and access to the media rather than as a lyric "seer" privileged with superior insights. His fiction and poetry are often more pessimistic in outlook than his political speeches, although in speeches of the 1970s (on world hunger) and 1980s (on disarmament), he tended to the apocalyptic. Grass is preoccupied with the history of German writers and the public sphere. *The Plebeians Rehearse the Uprising* (1966), in which **Bertolt Brecht** takes center stage during the workers' uprising in East Berlin in June 1953, and *The Meeting in Telgte* (1979), a historical novella on the post war Gruppe 47 set three hundred years in the past at the end of the Thirty Years War, both conclude that writers can have little direct effect on events. Yet Grass's novels do often trigger debate on political issues, none more so than *Too Far Afield* (1995), which was savaged in the press for its critique of reunification. More recently, *Crabwalk* (2002) opened up discussion on commemorating German suffering in **World War II**. German society has changed immeasurably in the forty-five years Günter Grass has been writing. In particular, democratic thinking has become deeply embedded; Grass's contribution to this process has been, quite simply, immense.

Selected Bibliography: Brockmann, Stephen. *Literature and German Reunification.* Cambridge: Cambridge UP, 1999; Mason, Anne L. "The Artist and Politics in Günter Grass' *Aus dem Tagebuch einer Schnecke.*" *Germanic Review* 51 (1976): 105–20; Preece, Julian. *The Life and Work of Günter Grass: Literature, History, Politics.* 2nd ed. Basingstoke: Palgrave, 2004; Tudor, J. M. "Soups and Snails and Political Tales . . . Günter Grass and the Revisionist Debate in 'Was Erfurt außerdem bedeutet' and *Der Butt.*" *Oxford German Studies* 18 (1988): 132–50.

Julian Preece

GREENE, GRAHAM (1904–1991) was the founder of what might be termed the "intellectual thriller," a genre that possesses all of the narrative momentum and violent action of the popular espionage or suspense novel, but that deals seriously and continuously with questions of politics, sexual desire, guilt, and large existential concerns. After an interesting historical novel—*The Man Within* (1929)—which he wrote soon after leaving Oxford and finding work as a journalist, he discovered his true generic home with *Stamboul Train* (1932). He followed this critical and popular success with a string of noir productions throughout the 1930s, including *England Made Me* (1935), *A Gun for Sale* (1936), and *The Confidential Agent* (1939). These novels are characterized by protagonists who are in some way or other losers, but who, when under the shadow of danger and death, discover within themselves unexpected pockets of altruism and empathy; they also possess a distinct left-wing political cast, with the forces of international capitalism and incipient fascism often portrayed as the enemy.

The publication of *The Power and the Glory* (1940) inaugurates what is commonly thought of as the Catholic phase of Greene's career. However, while it is true that the protagonists of his novels of the 1940s and early 1950s are Catholics, Greene is more interested in their faith as an engine of excruciating moral choices than as a reliable road map to existence, and it is heresy and even blasphemy that drive the plots of *The Heart of the Matter* (1948) and *The End of the Affair* (1951).

From the mid-1950s on, Greene's heroes, when Catholic, are only of the long-lapsed variety, and indeed his novels are remarkable for centering on characters who begin their narratives already middle-aged, world-weary, and profoundly skeptical about the redemptive possibilities of romantic love. Beginning with *The Quiet American* (1955) and increasingly in *The Comedians* (1966) and *The Honorary Consul* (1973), the transient attractions of *eros* must be abandoned for the more difficult and dangerous satisfaction of *caritas* (charity), expressed as commitment to various (usually quixotic) causes of political liberation—in Vietnam, Haiti, and South America, respectively. These supposedly burnt-out protagonists are surprised by capacities they believed themselves immune to—in this case, a simmering hatred of injustice that, like a secular prompting of grace, inspires them to cast aside indifference and take up arms in defense of the helpless.

During the latter half of his career, Greene also produced comic novels such as *Our Man in Havana* (1958), in which the standard material of the espionage world is played for laughs. In addition, he wrote several plays, numerous essays, and two volumes of an autobiography, nearly all his novels have been turned into movies. Graham Greene, while eschewing modernist narrative experimentations, possessed a thoroughly modern allegiance toward the misfit over the good citizen, the life of exhilarating danger over that of domestic safety, and the tortured doubt over the comforting belief.

Selected Bibliography: Baldridge, Cates. *Graham Greene's Fictions: The Virtues of Extremity*. Columbia: U of Missouri P, 2000; Diemert, Brian. *Graham Greene's Thrillers and the 1930's*. Montreal: McGill-Queen's UP, 1996; O'Prey, Paul. *A Reader's Guide to Graham Greene*. New York: Thames and Hudson, 1988; Pendelton, Robert. *Graham Greene's Conradian Masterplot: The Arabesque of Influence*. New York: St. Martin's, 1996; Sharrock, Roger. *Saints, Sinners, and Comedians: The Novels of Graham Greene*. Notre Dame: U of Notre Dame P, 1984; Sherry, Norman. *The Life of Graham Greene*. Vol. 1, *1904–1939*. Vol. 2, *1940–1955*. New York: Penguin, 1989, 1995.

Cates Baldridge

GUILLÉN, NICOLÁS (1902–1989).

A career of some sixty years of poetic production has won Nicolás Guillén worldwide fame and a place of distinction among Spanish American poets of the twentieth century. On the strength of the perspicacity of his social and political insights, he was always in the vanguard of the Cuban revolutionary process. He gives philosophical breadth to an exceptional range of the facets of that process and, by doing so, ensures the universal relevance of his work, which has been translated into more than thirty languages. Love—as motivating force, as observed human aspiration in sometimes difficult social circumstances, or as experienced in its fulfillment or in its loss—is a powerful factor in his poetry. But whatever his subject might be, he writes with profound candor and tenacious passion, balanced with the wit, grace, lively communicativeness, and musicality that are such appealing traits of the Cuban people. He also writes with serene awareness of poetic achievement in the Hispanic and Western traditions, an awareness that facilitates his own fertile innovativeness.

This high level of accomplishment, which he extended to his essays and his journalism, earned him, by acclamation, recognition as Cuba's national poet. In addition, the Cuban government awarded him his country's highest honor, the José Martí National Order. Great appreciation of his achievement has been shown outside Cuba as well; honorary degrees were bestowed on him by several universities, including the University of Bordeaux and the University of the West Indies. Like **Pablo Neruda**, he was awarded the Lenin Peace Prize by the Soviet Union. Literary critics and fellow writers in many countries nominated him for the Nobel Prize for Literature.

Guillén was born in Camagüey, on July 10, 1902, seven weeks after the founding of the Republic of Cuba. In 1917, his father, who had served as a senator and as editor of a local newspaper, was killed by soldiers. It was inevitable that a poetry would emerge showing the depth of the passion deriving from the indignation caused by the early loss of his father, his own encounters and those of black people in general with racial prejudice, and the links between all this and the febrile national condition. The indignation would be heightened by his recognition of a Cuban heritage of uncompromising struggle against oppression and injustice, which began with slave rebellions and continued in the arduous quest for independence.

In his first book of poetry, *Motivos de son* (*Son Motifs*, 1930), Guillén brought the black sector of the population into the national picture by using images of their real lives and adapting the popular Cuban musical form, the *son*, for use in an innovative poetic way, as a vehicle to convey their privations and their aspirations. That he did this within the concept of patriotism manifested by predecessors such as the black heroes of the War of Independence, Antonio Maceo and Juan Gualberto Gómez, is made clear by themes he developed throughout his poetry. In his books up to *La paloma de vuelo popular* (*The Dove of Popular Flight*, 1958), he promoted social justice, sovereignty, and independence through revolutionary change. From *Tengo* (*I Have*, 1966) to his last book, *Sol de domingo* (*Sunday Sun*, 1982), he defends the revolution, saluting the changes it has brought.

Guillén also excelled as a love poet, and the depth of the passion in most of his love poems alerts us to the fact that love is the mainspring of his poetry: love for his ancestors and their fellow beings, who suffered the unspeakable atrocities of slavery and, subsequently, the deprivations caused by racial discrimination; love for the broader Cuban community, which suffered the brutality of colonialism and the humiliations and strictures of neocolonialism. He extends the sympathy internationally to other similar sufferers.

Guillén is acclaimed as his country's national poet not only because he deals with the salient aspects of Cuba's life but also because he reflects the essential character of his people. As with the long line of Cuban heroes—extending from the sixteenth-century leaders of and participants in slave revolts and continuing through the nineteenth-century agitators for independence, including Félix Varela and the heroes of the independence struggle, such as **José Martí** and Antonio Maceo—indignation is a pronounced and positive quality in Guillén. Indignation is at the root of the motivation to effect real change, to be uncompromising concerning the will to oppose colonialism, imperialism, and racism. The capacity for indignation is the twin of the capacity for love, and it underlies the strength and power of the imagery of Guillén's poetry and its connectedness with the poet's compatriots, among whom the spirit of the heroes is widely dispersed.

Selected Bibliography: Ellis, Keith. *Cuba's Nicolás Guillén: Poetry and Ideology.* Toronto: U of Toronto P, 1985; Williams, Lorna V. *Self and Society in the Poetry of Nicolás Guillén.* Baltimore: Johns Hopkins UP, 1982.

Keith Ellis